Accounting for Genocide

ACCOUNTING

FOR

GENOCIDE

National Responses and Jewish Victimization
during the Holocaust

Helen Fein

THE FREE PRESS
A Division of Macmillan Publishing Co., Inc.
NEW YORK

Collier Macmillan Publishers
LONDON

The Free Press
A Division of Macmillan Publishing Co., Inc.
866 Third Avenue, New York, N.Y. 10022

Collier Macmillan Canada, Ltd.

Library of Congress Catalog Card Number: 78-53085

Printed in the United States of America

printing number

1 2 3 4 5 6 7 8 9 10

Library of Congress Cataloging in Publication Data

Fein, Helen
  Accounting for genocide.

  Bibliography: p.
  Includes index.
  1. Holocaust, Jewish (1939-1945)   I. Title.
D810.J4F376   940.53'1503'924   78-53085
ISBN 0-02-910220-0

To the sewing-machine writer
and the other extinguished writers and readers,
poets and listeners,
parents and children.

Contents

Contents

PART TWO: THE VICTIMS' VIEW

List of Figures

List of Maps

List of Tables

Prologue

To the Sewing-machine Writer

How are we to confront the Holocaust? It was not only a secular event in history but an event challenging earlier notions of history as well, leading to the repudiation of the idea of human progress. The idea that humanity was in command of the forces of nature became suspect as our species began to kill itself off. While we learned, in discovering atomic energy, how to transform matter to energy, the Nazis demonstrated how readily we could destroy energy by converting spirits to matter.

Although one may be able to grasp the essence and entirety of the Holocaust only through art, there is no intrinsic reason to assume that what we do not yet understand cannot be understood by reason. Was the planned extermination of the Jews of Europe a unique experience of the Jewish people or a repetition on a wider scale of previous attempts at genocide? Can genocide itself be understood simply as an escalation of collective violence? Can the will to destroy the Jews of Nazi Germany be ascribed to the development of the German state, the character structure of Germans, the particular history of German relations with Jews, and/or the more general history and transformation of anti-Semitism in the Christian world? Is the destiny of the Jews of Europe best understood by focusing on the characteristics or responses of the victims, the victimizers, and/or the onlookers? How did the victims themselves apprehend and construct the experience?

To begin with, it seemed to me that to understand the implications of the Holocaust, one had to understand its success, which has too often been taken for granted. To think about the unthinkable productively, it is better to start out with the right questions than to give facile answers. I began this work with the assumption that Jewish victimization was a test case of the response of nations, the end product of a process testing human bonds within nations subject to German instigation or occupation. The appalling number of Jews murdered—by 1945, two out of every three Jews living in Europe in 1939 were dead—has diverted attention from the fact that in almost half (nine of twenty-two) of the states and regions occupied by or allied to Germany, fewer than half of the Jews counted there were killed.[1] The explication and testing of this hypothesis relating Jewish victimization to national response are the principal focus of this book (Chapters 3 to 6).

But the destruction of the European Jews cannot be understood if we view the states subject to German control or influence in isolation. They existed within a macrosystem of international power, drawn by attraction or coercion to Nazi Germany, whose dominion was opposed by the alliance of the United Kingdom, the United States, the Union of Soviet Socialist Republics, and others. First, we must understand the will of Germany to annihilate the Jews (Chapter 1).

Why were the potential counterforces against the will of Germany so passive? What accounts for the Allies' initial lack of interest in the denial of the rights of the Jews of Germany and their belated recognition of the enormity of the threat to the Jews of Europe? Even when the Allies recognized the ongoing extermination, they were unwilling to commit resources to thwart the German aim, overlooking or rejecting strategies that might have saved the lives of countless Jews and other victims incarcerated in the camps. Chapter 7 explores the causes and consequences of Allied policies.

Other actors within the macrosystem with potential for opposing or deterring the fulfillment of Nazi plans included the European neutrals and the Vatican. The evidence regarding differences between Roman Catholic and other Christian churches (in states where they were the dominant churches) and the consequences of actions not taken by Pope Pius XII are evaluated in Chapter 4. The significance of counterinstitutions to state power created by Christians and Jews is explored in Chapter 6. The response (or lack of response) of Jews in the West to the Jews in Europe is explored in Chapter 7.

Whereas Part One explains the structure of the social forces and contingencies that checked or facilitated the destruction of the Jews, Part Two explores the responses of Jews, drawn from first-person records in three communities of high victimization—Warsaw, the Netherlands, and Hungary—showing how they recognized, defined, and responded to threat. Rather than explore the uniqueness of individual experience, I use these sources—as some were consciously intended to be used—to reconstruct the collective social history of the community, to show the interaction between threat, defense, and ultimate defenselessness once Jews were isolated, regardless of whether the victims fled, fought, or offered no resistance. The institutional response of Jewish leaders to the German-imposed organs of social control over the Jewish community, known as *Judenrat,* is examined in Chapter 5, which attempts to unravel the implications of their response as cause or symptom of the powerlessness of Jews once they had been segregated.

This work, then, is an application of historical sociology, not a conventional history. I assume that readers are not turning here for an explanation of the development of the SS state, a recounting of the history of Nazi Germany and World War II, or a factive description of the actual organization of the death machine, all of which have been well documented previously. Readers not familiar with these matters will find sufficient references herein to fill in their background. There are other subjects not covered here: the concentration and extermination camps themselves, the Jewish armed resistance movement, the settlement of Jewish refugees who fled, the response of the Palestinian Jewish community and Zionist organizations, the postwar sanctions against war criminals implicated in the "Final Solution," and postwar reactions to the victims in Europe.

A word about my sources is due here. While I have acknowledged not only those individuals who helped me personally but also people whose work is reproduced, it is not sufficient to recognize only those who furnished answers and to ignore those who asked the questions I have tried to clarify. This study would have been impossible had there not been models of persistence and passion among the victims of the Holocaust itself. "Yidn: fahrschreibt! fahrschreibt!" ("Jews: record! record!") are alleged to be the last words of the Jewish historian Simon Dubnow before his murder in Latvia in 1941.[2] The movement to record began in 1940 in Warsaw, organized by Emmanuel Ringelblum. Also in Warsaw, Chaim Kaplan wrote in his unheated flat, separated by politics and sympathy from Ringelblum, but sharing the passion to confront the truth, the refusal to allay his fears by repressing insights, the refusal to be resigned or consoled. It is this Promethean will that unites the men and women, girls and boys, in ghetto, bunker, and garrets. When one reads their writings, one realizes that it is not their deaths alone that ought to elicit awe, but their rage and the relentless passion that compelled them to assert that their deaths were extraordinary events, events not to be taken for granted.

The demon to record, to cry out, to communicate possessed other Jews throughout Europe who did not have time or the materials with which to tell their story. Abba Kovner, Israeli poet and former resistance leader in Vilna, tells the story of one of these people.[3] In the Vilna ghetto, after a raid by Lithuanian police in which Jews were removed, soon to be murdered in the Ponary forest, he entered what he thought was a deserted room in an empty house. There sat a man pushing the treadle of a sewing machine, under whose empty needle was a piece of white paper, punctuated by the needle's incision of the pattern of stitch-holes.

"What are you doing here?" Kovner asked.

"I am writing the history of the ghetto," the man replied.

"You are writing the history of the ghetto on paper on a sewing machine without thread?"

"When the war is over," the man replied, "there will be time to pull through the thread."

I have tried to pull through the threads as best I can. Others may find a different pattern, and still others may note punctures that I have failed to see and complete the tale.

Acknowledgments

This research was initially supported by the City College of New York Department of Jewish Studies Research Foundation, with the material assistance of the Bergen-Belsen Association. I am grateful to both of them for this opportunity and to Irving Greenberg, former chairman of the Jewish Studies Department, for his confidence. The study was also encouraged by the interest shown by Yehuda Bauer, director of the Institute of Contemporary Jewry of the Hebrew University. Gathering data would not have been possible without the cooperation demonstrated by the staff of the Yad Vashem in Jerusalem and YIVO Institute in New York City. The American Jewish Committee also allowed me to use their library in New York City, which contains some singular sources.

I am indebted for information and ideas to the ready cooperation of many other scholars and survivors, including the following (listed alphabetically): Samuel Abrahamsen (Brooklyn College), Mordecai Altschuler (Hebrew University), Yehuda Bauer (Hebrew University), Randolph Braham (City College of New York), Bogdan Denitch (Columbia University), L. Dobroszycki (YIVO), Giuliana Donati (Centro di Documentazione Ebraica Contemporanea, Milan), Harriet Freidenreich (Temple University), Israel Gutman (Yad Vashem), Raul Hilberg (University of Vermont), Edward Homze (University of Nebraska), Louis de Jong (Director, Netherlands State Institute for War Documentation), Bronya Klibanski (Yad Vashem), Abba Kovner (Tel Aviv University), Schmuel Krakowski (Yad Vashem), Moshe Krauss (Jerusalem), Erich Kulka (Yad Vashem), Lloyd Lee (SUNY, New Paltz), Dov Levin (Hebrew University), Joseph Melkman (Jerusalem), Meier Michaelis (Hebrew University), Robert Paxton (Columbia University), Liliana Piccioto Fargion (Centro di Documentazione Ebraica Contemporanea, Milan), Norman Rich (Brown University), Jacob Robinson (YIVO–Yad Vashem), Herbert Rosenkrantz (Yad Vashem), Lydia Rotkirchen (Yad Vashem), Henry Sachs (YIVO–Yad Vashem), Israel Schirmann (Kibbutz Revadim), Isaiah Trunk (YIVO), Aharon Weiss (Haifa University), and Leni Yahil (Haifa University).

Research assistants whose abstracts have been indispensable, include Susan Hecker, Anna Kossman, Bernard Liebtag, Gertrude Miller, Dusica Seferagic, and Anne Weiss. Judith Bloom and Myra Sorin also helped to gather data, conducting the Polish sample study. For translating sources, I am indebted to Lena Alphonso-Karkala (for translations from the Finnish), Myra Sorin (for translations from the French), and Anne Weiss (for translations from the Italian).

Among my early readers, I am especially grateful to Joyce Freedman Apsel for her encouragement and keen criticism of the manuscript in its first stage. Isaiah Trunk and Leni Yahil generously offered their expert knowledge in their respective reviews of Chapters 5 and 6. Leni was especially helpful throughout this enterprise in exposing other points of view and sources that ought to be taken into account and helped in the last stages by her critical reading of the manuscript. Richard J. Fein (State University of New York, New Paltz) made a valued contribution to the style and clarity of this book. Rusty Kauffman (Widener College), Joel Pitt (State University of New York, New Paltz), and Suzanne Vromen (Bard College) aided me in clarifying the text by criticizing points in earlier versions of chapters. John Hammond (Hunter College) was helpful in advice on methodology of multiple regression analysis. From the beginning, Eleanor Thoben, who typed the manuscript, was consistently helpful and cooperative despite a constantly amended text.

Finally, I am grateful to the following authors, translators, editors, and publishers for permission to cite their works:

Mary Berg (Wattenberg). *Warsaw Ghetto: A Diary.* Edited by S. L. Schneiderman. Translated by Sylvia Glass and Norbert Guterman. © 1972 Norbert Guterman and Sylvia Glass. Reprinted by permission of A. A. Wynn, Inc.

Elie A. Cohen. *The Abyss: A Confession.* Translated by James Brockway. © 1973 W. W. Norton and Company, Inc. Original Dutch Edition by PARIS/MANTEAU, Amsterdam-Brussels, 1971. © 1971 Dr. E. A. Cohen. All rights reserved. Reprinted by permission of W. W. Norton and Company, Inc., and the Julian Bach Literary Agency, Inc.

Alexander Donat. *The Holocaust Kingdom: A Memoir.* © 1963, 1965 Alexander Donat. Reprinted by permission of Holt, Rinehart, and Winston, Publishers.

Eva Heyman. *The Diary of Eva Heyman.* Introduction and notes by Dr. Judah Marton. Translated by Moshe M. Kohn. © 1974 Yad Vashem. Reprinted by permission of Yad Vashem.

Jewish Publication Society of America. *The Torah: The Five Books of Moses.* © 1962 Jewish Publication Society of America. Reprinted by permission of the Jewish Publication Society of America.

Jewish Spectator. "Pope Pius XII and the Jews." Letter from Leon Bérard. Translated by Abraham G. Duker. *Jewish Spectator,* February 1964. © *Jewish Spectator.* Reprinted by permission of the *Jewish Spectator.*

de Jong, Louis. "The Netherlands and Auschwitz: Why Were the Reports of Mass Killings so Widely Disbelieved." In *Imposed Jewish Governing Bodies under Nazi Rule,* YIVO Colloquium, December 2-5, 1967. © 1972 YIVO Institute for Jewish Research. Reprinted by permission of YIVO.

Chaim A. Kaplan. *The Warsaw Diary of Chaim A. Kaplan.* Translated and edited by Abraham I. Katsch. © 1963, 1965, 1973 Abraham I. Katsch. Reprinted by permission of Macmillan Publishing Company, Inc., and (under the title, *The Scroll of Agony)* by Hamish Hamilton Ltd., London.

Jan Karski. *The Story of a Secret State.* © 1972 Jan Karski. Reprinted by permission of Houghton Mifflin Company.

Martin Lowenthal. *The Jews of Germany.* © 1970 Jewish Publication Society of America. Reprinted by permission of the Jewish Publication Society of America.

Philip Mechanicus. *Year of Fear.* Translated by Irene S. Gibbons. © 1968 Hawthorn Books. Reprinted by permission of Calder and Boyars, Ltd.

Joseph Michman. "The Controversial Stand of the Joodse Raad in the Netherlands: Lodewijk E. Visser's Struggle." *Yad Vashem Studies* X (1974). © 1974 Yad Vashem. Reprinted by permission of Yad Vashem.

Emmanuel Ringelblum. *Notes from the Warsaw Ghetto: The Journal of Emmanuel Ringelblum.* Edited and translated by Jacob Sloan. © 1958 Jacob Sloan. Used with permission of McGraw-Hill Book Company and Jacob Sloan.

Johan Snoek. *The Greybook: A Collection of Protests against Anti-Semitism and the Persecution of Jews Issued by Non-Roman Catholic Churches and Church Leaders during Hitler's Rule.* © 1968 Koninklijke Van Gorcum and Company, B.V. Reprinted by permission of Van Gorcum and Company.

Eli Wiesel. *Night.* Translated from the French by Sheila Rodway. © 1958 Les Éditions de Minuit, English translation © 1960 MacGibbon and Kee. Reprinted with the permission of Farrar, Straus, and Giroux, Inc., and Georges Borchardt, Inc.

David Wyman. "Why Auschwitz Was Never Bombed." *Commentary,* May 1978. © 1978 American Jewish Committee. Reprinted by permission of *Commentary.*

Michael Zylberberg. A Warsaw Diary. © 1969 Vallentine, Mitchell and Company, Ltd. Reprinted by permission of Vallentine, Mitchell and Company, Ltd.

PART ONE

A Macroscopic View

Twentieth-century Paths
to Genocide

In the beginning, there was no word. There was no word adequate to label and mentally assimilate the murder of two of three European Jews in states occupied by and/or allied to Nazi Germany in World War II. Although the West had been informed about the extermination plot and the camps since the summer of 1942, belief in their accomplishments and actuality had not spread among the public until after Allied soldiers, liberating the camps in 1945, themselves saw the survivors—skeletons of skin and bone with burning eyes—behind the barbed wire of the camps and filmed them.[1]

The survivors themselves had to assimilate the fact that their families were dead, communities where hundreds of thousands of Jews had lived for centuries were destroyed, and often there was no turning back. The few to return to homes in Poland risked lynching if they attempted to reclaim homes and shops.[2] With few exceptions, Jews seeking to reoccupy or get compensation for their homes and property were greeted with hostility throughout Europe.[3] Those who did not wish (or dare) to return to the nations in which they lived in 1939 were detained in Allied camps that included former concentration camps.

The experience was known as the "disaster," the "great catastrophe," before it became generally called (in Hebrew) *ha-shoah* ("the Holocaust"). The consummation of the victims in central and eastern Europe was almost total. No other people or any European nation suffered losses of this magnitude, throughout Europe, not overlooking drives to kill Serbs and Gypsies and German plans to decimate the Slavic nations. Raphael Lemkin coined the term "genocide" in 1944 to denote the attempt to destroy a nation or an ethnic group by depriving them of the ability to live and procreate or by killing them directly.[4] The definition includes not only direct, immediate extermination and indirect murder (through starving people) but also the slower extinction of distinct populations by preventing new conceptions while increasing mortality and the extinction of the culture distinguishing a people by the decimation of their intellectual leaders, prohibition of free cultural institutions and media, and suppression of literacy.

What was seen as novel and defined as a crime against humanity—rather than a war crime—at the International Military Tribunal at Nuremberg was the premeditated attempt to destroy a group permanently. However, only thirty years earlier, a *New York Times* headline read: YOUNG TURKS SAID TO HAVE DECLARED ANNIHILATION OF ARMENIANS (6 May 1915). Had such tribunals been instituted after World War I, the western Allies might have recalled the extermination of Armenians in Turkey in 1915, a genocide denounced in the United States and Great Britain in mass meetings and petitions. But the Armenians had not been awarded an opportunity for public judgment, and the promises (encouraged by all Allies) of an independent Armenia outside the Soviet Union were betrayed by the peace treaty of Lausanne in 1923. The lesson, Housepian points out, was appreciated by Hitler.[5] In a speech to his chief commanders before the September 1939 Polish invasion, he is said to have justified the annihilation of Polish civilians as a war aim by referring to his predecessors' success:

> Only thus shall we gain the living space [*Lebensraum*] which we need. Who, after all, speaks today of the annihilation of the Armenians?[6]

The slaughter of selected categories of Poles aroused persisting protests among army leaders, inducing Hitler to reconsider and to countermand earlier orders.[7] But the extermination of the Jews of Germany and Europe aroused no similar protest. One may ask how the Germans had been conditioned to expect and/or not to be alarmed by the subsequent disappearance and annihilation of the Jews. Was it solely propaganda and debate reiterating the notion of the "Jewish problem" during the preceding decades that made it possible to imagine annihilating the Jews? And similarly, one may ask, why were the Turks and other Muslim neighbors of the Armenians so ready to discriminate and slaughter them in 1915?

EXCLUDING THE VICTIMS: A PRECONDITION OF GENOCIDE

For over a millennium preceding their annihilation, both Jews and Armenians had been decreed by the dominant group that was to perpetrate the crime to be outside the sanctified universe of obligation—that circle of people with reciprocal obligations to protect each other whose bonds arose from their relation to a deity or sacred source of authority. Since the fifth century of the Christian Era (C.E.), the Jews—most of whom even prior to the Christian Era lived in dispersed Mediterranean communities—had survived in Europe dependent upon the toleration of Christian rulers. They had been collectively defined by the Roman Catholic Church as a people capable of the greatest crime in history, deicide, and their exile from their ancient homeland was commonly explained as God's punishment.[8] Having been defined as outside the European community—the Christian universe of obligation—since the state establishment of Christianity by the Roman Empire, there were always ready justifications for victimizing them. From the eleventh to the thirteenth centuries, they were slain by roaming Crusaders seeking accrual of spiritual credits by murdering the infidels. Between the twelfth and the fourteenth centuries, they were expelled from western and central Europe, fortuitously eliminating competitors against the rising bourgeoisie. From the Middle Ages to modern times, they were intermittently lynched after accusations of spurious crimes: poisoning of wells believed to cause the bubonic plague, killing Christian children to extract their blood for ritual purposes, and desecrating the host used in communion. Massacres were organized by their neighbors battling for their own independence in the Ukraine during the seventeenth and twentieth centuries. Pogroms—episodic massacres sometimes staged to appear spontaneous—were organized through the declining empire of the Russian Czar beginning in the late nineteenth century to deflect the potential for revolutionary unrest. Anti-Semitic "excesses" crossed ideological lines as marauding revolutionary and counter-revolutionary armies attacked eastern European Jews after World War I. It was natural for Jews to relate the Holocaust to this record of collective violence inspired by simple Jew-hatred, xenophobia, greed for economic spoliation, and theological and secular anti-Semitism.[9] Thus, many scholars focused on explaining why the Jews were now chosen as a target for total extermination, discussing the continuity or distinction of the new anti-Semitism that inspired the Holocaust with older species of anti-Semitism without discussing what function the extermination of the Jews of Europe served.[10]

The Armenians, like the Jews, lacked sovereignty or another state to defend them, although they were not as dispersed among the nations as were the Jews.* They had become subjects of the Ottomans after the successful conquest by the latter of west Asia during the sixteenth century. The Ottomans (known in the twentieth century as Turks) were Muslims and, as Muslims, defined non-Muslim "people of the book"—Christians and Jews—as *Dimmis* or tolerated infidels, whose lives were to be protected in exchange for their accommodation to civil discrimination, ritual subordination, powerlessness, and oppression:

> their evidence is not accepted against that of a Moslem in a Kadi's court; the
> Moslem murderer of a *Dimmi* does not suffer the death penalty; a *Dimmi* man

*According to legend, the Armenians have lived around Mount Ararat since 2350 B.C.E. and are descended from Haig, a scion of Noah. But scholars ascribe their origin to a migration of Indo-European peoples from Thrace during the twelfth or thirteenth centuries B.C.E. Between 600 B.C.E. and 428 C.E., the Armenian nation was a protectorate of Persia and Rome (excepting a brief period when a native dynasty was sovereign) until it was absorbed by the Parthian Empire in 428 C.E. The Armenians were the first state to establish Christianity (301 C.E.) and retained their autonomous Christian church, despite being later overrun by Arabs, Seljuks, Mongols, and Mamelukes prior to the Ottomans.

may not marry a Moslem woman, whereas a Moslem man may marry a *Dimmi* woman. . . . *Dimmis* . . . are forbidden to ride horses or to carry arms.[11]

Termed *rayah,* or sheep who might be fleeced, Christians and Jews were subjected to discriminatory taxes within the Empire. Armenians endured extra burdens, including the poll tax, military exemption tax, hospitality tax, and the *kishlak,* the obligation to board migratory Kurdish tribesmen in the winter, which frequently made the host prey to looting, rape, and other violations by the "guests."[12]

Turkish oppression against Christians began to be challenged both by the Armenians and by the great powers during the nineteenth century, leading Sultan Abdul Hamid to organize the Kurds into military regiments to loot and massacre Armenians in retaliation for their protests. The frequency and scale of these massacres escalated: an estimated 100,000 Armenians were killed between 1895 and 1909, the year of the Young Turks' coup.[13] Thus, it was natural for Armenians to relate the genocide of 1915 to the collective violence, subordination, and degradation they had endured within the Ottoman Empire.

But the political role played by the Armenians — a subordinated collectivity without civil rights but one organized for itself and able to challenge the center of authority — differed substantively from the role of German Jews who were most likely to view themselves as Germans "of the Jewish faith" and were assimilated in most of the major secular German parties. The definition of both groups as aliens did not arise from the roles played by the victims, but the roles open to the victims were socially restricted because of their original definition as aliens. It has been noted that both Jews and Armenians had performed similar economic functions (as did Greeks and other Christians within the Ottoman Empire), serving as "middleman minorities" who specialized in (and/or monopolized) commerce, finance, and the professions.[14] In fact, this was no longer true of Jews in Germany, but it was still true of Jews in parts of Eastern Europe.[15] Eliminating middleman minorities serves both to expropriate them and open up new positions. But attributing simple mercenary motives to the perpetrators of genocide is misleading; any class monopolizing political power can expropriate, despoil, and declassify a powerless group, for private property is finally dependent on the state that guarantees and enforces the rights of propertyholders. Thus, any monopoly enjoyed by a minority could have been redressed by the state without violence.

It was not the roles they played, but the very existence of the Armenians and Jews that was construed as alien. Both had been defined within recent memory similarly to pariahs outside the sanctified social order. Thus stigmatized, such groups are more readily redefined as strangers by the dominant group — strangers not because they were alien but because the dominant group was alienated from them by a traditional antipathy, Jew-hatred, or hatred of the infidel.[16]

CALCULATING GENOCIDE

Can we infer that genocide was simply the culmination of such earlier traditions of collective violence exemplified in nineteenth-century pogroms against Jews and Armenians? This would be in error. Focusing on persecution alone negates observation of the historical trend (since the eighteenth century) toward the emancipation of minority groups; the Jews, especially, were liberated from medieval statuses as they became citizens of the new triumphant nation-states. Genocide also differs from collective violence — deliberate injury or extraordinary punishments inflicted against people just because they are members of a collectivity (religious, ethnic, or racial group) — in that it is centrally planned and purposeful, and in that its intent is total. While collective violence often serves to put (or keep) a subjugated group in its place, genocide *eliminates* the group. Some commentators believe that they have explained genocide by referring to the victims as scapegoats who serve as substitute targets of aggression (without reflecting on the fact that the exercise of aggression often increases the need for further aggression rather than diminishing it) but such explanations fail to consider that the elimination of a group labeled as an enemy deprives the dominant group of a future scapegoat. What ends could a vanishing scapegoat serve?

To begin to grasp the origins of modern premeditated genocide,* we must first recognize it as organized state murder. To account for premeditated murder as would a jurist, we must consider how it may be motivated or appear as a rational choice to the perpetrator. Because the notion of a self-destroying society contradicts the classic rational notions of the

---

*Genocides not previously premeditated may be perpetrated by the dominant group reacting to a physical or political challenge to their domination by a previously subordinated class or tribe; such attempts, therefore, coincide with internal schisms and civil wars, as in Pakistan (1971) and Burundi (1972). The state, in these cases, is politically reconstructed by eliminating and/or terrorizing potential elites from the challenging group to insure that it may continue to serve as an instrument of the dominant group. Another type of genocide involves the physical elimination by the dominant group of an aboriginal tribe claimed to stand in the way of the state's expansion. This is illustrated in *Genocide in Paraguay* by Richard Arens (ed.) and others (Philadelphia: Temple University Press, 1976). V. N. Dadrian labels these types as "retributive genocide" and "utilitarian genocide" in contrast to "optimal genocide" — the latter exemplified by the extermination of the Armenians, Jews, and Gypsies; see the paper by Dadrian, "Genocide as a Function of Intergroup Conflict — A Paradigm in Macrosociology," presented at the annual meeting of the American Sociological Association, 1975. What is common to all these types is that the victims were previously excluded from the universe of obligation of the dominant group and stigmatized.

Premodern genocide and massacres that may be considered attempts at genocide can be related to the contemporary basis of social organization in societies where the nation-state was not the dominant form of social organization. Thus, in societies united by religious solidarity and in which both cities and states are subordinated to the hegemony of a church, the leaders of the reigning church may attempt to eliminate converts to another faith, as in religious wars between Catholics and Protestants. In communities based on tribal homogeneity, intertribal conflicts and warfare may lead toward extermination because the protagonists do not believe that their antagonists can be subdued or assimilated and, thus, cannot anticipate coexisting together within a more embracing community.

ends for which society is constructed, it is hard to conceive of genocide as "rational." The term is used herein completely neutrally, as "based on, or derived from reasoning," as Webster's puts it, without regard to how reasonable is the ideology that forms the gound of assumptions on which the murderer(s) draws to reason. To understand genocides as a class of calculated crimes, such crimes must be appreciated as goal-oriented acts from the point of view of their perpetrators: genocide is rationally instrumental to their ends, although psychopathic in terms of any universalistic ethic. This means that we must first concentrate on the goals of its perpetrators to understand why they define the problem as they do—the Jewish problem, the Armenian problem—implying that the object of their concern is the source of the problem. What ends does their murder serve?

I will attempt to show that modern premeditated genocide is a rational function of the choice by a ruling elite of a myth or "political formula" (as Mosca put it)[17] legitimating the existence of the state as the vehicle for the destiny of the dominant group, a group whose members share an underlying likeness from which the victim is excluded by definition. Such a formula requires a myth exalting the origins of the group and idealizing the idea of the people so that the "real" capacities of the group cannot be judged by its members' characteristics. This phenomenon has also been called "tribal nationalism" or "tribalism," "messianism," and includes forms of fascism.[18] It is most likely to be chosen by leaders of a state in which there is low underlying solidarity between major groups and a lack of correspondence between borders of the state and regions of settlement of the dominant nationality, and in which the state has suffered recent defeats or declines in territorial claims. The state's raison d'être as a competitor among other nation-states is in doubt. Since the old political formula that arose in the nineteenth century instigated the creation of new states, stirring people then to deny legitimacy to foreign authorities, a new political formula that rationalized the domination of the state by decreeing the creation of a mass master race was plausible.[19] While the liberal ideal of nineteenth-century nationalism justified removing authorities that were deemed illegitimate because they did not represent the people, the new formula justified eradicating peoples to fortify the state's legitimation, the national credo, or peoples' ideology. One way to excise elements that did not fit into this new nation was to assimilate them, another to expel them, and another to annihilate them. To be sure, the policy question is not always one of exclusive alternatives or unilateral choices, as flight is the potential victim's most common response when alarmed. Opportunities, costs, and sanctions are weighed by the perpetrators. But leaders could not have chosen annihilation (rejecting assimilation) had not the victims been previously defined as basically of a different species, outside of the common conscience, and beyond the universe of obligation; this was the precondition. Despite frequent accusations that the victims were clannish, unassimilable, or disloyal, the dominant group did not have the ability (in the Turkish case) or the desire (in the German case) to assimilate them. Within a context of national self-exaltation, the victims represented non-national creeds, universal religions with adherents among the state's former enemies. Armenians and Jews were also vulnerable because although both groups had international affiliations, neither had the protection of another nation-state that might deter aggression (as did Greek Christians within the Ottoman Empire).

But the perpetrators could not defend their annihilation before observers of other nations, for all nations knew that genocide, regardless of its labeling, was no less than mass murder. War reduced the deterrents against genocide for it obscured the visibility of such action and insured the perpetrators freedom from sanctions. It also enabled them to invent post facto justifications of the program, accusing the victim of aiding the enemy, betraying them, or causing the war. Such accusations served the perpetrators to rationalize their acts by the prevalent paradigm justifying collective violence: it was a just punishment (or reprisal) for a crime committed by the victim. But in both cases observed, the perpetrators knew they did not have to fear sanctions, only censure, having tested the ground by oppression and calculated violence against the victims for eight years in the German case and forty years in the Turkish case.

One can summarize the sequence of preconditions, intervening factors, and causes that lead toward genocide as follows:

1. The victims have previously been defined outside the universe of obligation of the dominant group. (This is a necessary but not sufficient condition for the third step.)

2. The rank of the state has been reduced by defeat in war and/or internal strife. (This is a predisposing condition toward a political or cultural crisis of national identity in which the third step becomes more likely to occur. The causes for such a decline are not predicted herein.)

3. An elite that adapts a new political formula to justify the nation's domination and/or expansion, idealizing the singular rights of the dominant group, rises to power. The means by which this elite captures power—a coup, democratic election, infiltration through parliamentary processes, or foreign intervention—are also not predicted herein. (Adoption of such a formula by a ruling elite is a necessary but not sufficient condition for premeditated genocide.)

4. The calculus of costs of exterminating the victim—a group excluded from the circle circumscribed by the political formula—changes as the perpetrators instigate or join a (temporarily) successful coalition at war against antagonists who have earlier protested and/or might conceivably be expected to protest persecution of the victim. This calculus changes for two reasons: the crime planned by the perpetrators becomes less visible and they no longer have to fear sanctions. The third and fourth conditions taken together constitute necessary and sufficient conditions or causes of

premeditated genocide. The following discussion on Turkish genocide and the German Holocaust will illustrate these factors; several of the subheads are numbered as to the particular condition they describe. Since the exclusion of the victim from the universe of obligation — exclusion of Jews from the Christian universe and exclusion of Armenians from the Islamic universe — has been previously demonstrated, it will not be reiterated. I will attempt to show the parallel developments of both cases (although, of course, not all of the background is parallel) and later relate the political formula adapted by Hitler that inspired the Holocaust to the drive to create a race "of pure blood," which accounted for murders of categories of Germans and the subsequent categorical extermination of the Gypsies in Germany. Discussion of the Holocaust in this chapter is restricted to Germany.

THE EXTERMINATION OF THE ARMENIANS

The majority of Armenians in 1914 inhabited western Asia between the Black and Caspian seas, divided between Persia and the Russian and Ottoman empires. According to the counts of Russia and Turkey, Russia contained almost two thirds of all Armenians in both countries in 1914, but if the figures of the Armenian Patriarch in Constantinople are accepted, more than half of the Armenians were in Turkey. Although figures vary on the ethnicity and religion of the population in the six Turkish vilayets in which Armenians were concentrated, it appears that Armenians constituted a minority there — from 27 to 39% — because of the Ottoman rulers' policy of resettling the Kurds in Armenian regions to serve as governing agents.[20]

Armenians (like Greek Christians and Jews) were organized as a separate community in a *millet*, headed by their Patriarch. The system enabled each group to govern its religious and social life as a corporate endogamous body, subordinated within the Empire to the oppressive rule of the dominant Ottom tribe. Legally barred from bearing arms (until 1911), and subjected to periodic violence and exploitation by their Kurdish chieftains, the Armenians were known as the *sadik millet*, or faithful community.[21]

All the non-Muslim monorities were powerless classes politically, excluded from serving in the government or army. Thus, some might have occasional influence over officials or achieve status by virtue of their special usefulness to the governing classes, but all lacked both civil rights and minority rights.

Although most Armenians were peasants and craftsmen, their distinct functions within the Empire were those of the middleman minority, similar to Greeks and Jews, and aroused similar prejudices among observers, such as Major General Harbord, who noted in his report of 16 October 1919 to the U.S. Congress investigating the justification for an American mandate over Turkey:

Notwithstanding his many estimable qualities, his culture, and his tenacity of race and religion, the Armenian generally does not endear himself to those of other races with whom he comes in contact. The Armenian stands among his neighbors very much as the Jew stands in Russia and Poland, having, as he does, the strong and preeminent ability of that race. He incurs the penalty which attaches among backward races to the banker, the middleman, and the creditor. Unjust as it may be, the sentiment regarding him is expressed by this saying current in the Near East: "The Armenian is never legally in the wrong; never morally in the right."[22]

Decline of the Ottoman Empire (2)

The Ottoman Empire began declining in its ability to rule and retain territory in the seventeenth century, two centuries before Nicholas I of Russia labeled it, in 1853, the "sick man" of Europe. The Ottoman governing class was unable to conceive of any way of transforming the Empire that would offer its many aspiring nationalities a credo to compete with that of national liberation of the nineteenth century. There was no basis of solidarity among its subjects to legitimate Ottoman domination. There was no notion of a common nationality among them, no representative mechanism, and no common bond of belief or language within the Empire, which stretched in the mid-seventeenth century from Persia to Hungary. The Ottomans had accepted Greek emancipation, the independence of Rumania and Serbia, and Bulgarian self-rule in the nineteenth century, and by 1908 had withdrawn from all of Europe except Salonica and Albania. The British had helped them to check the process in the nineteenth century, fearing Russian penetration of the straits. Britain viewed with alarm the Czar's expansion into Asia, and his declarations of concern for the Christian subjects of the Ottoman Empire, and rushed to defend the Ottomans in the Crimean war against Russia. But the Ottomans' oppression of their Christian subjects, which justified European intervention, obliged the Turks' allies to press them to institute reforms. To accommodate European demands (or to anticipate them), edicts and peace treaties were issued in 1839, 1856, 1863, and 1878 granting all subjects equal rights, opportunities, and justice under the law; but the promises were stillborn.[23]

Armenians developed a new collective consciousness in the latter half of the nineteenth century as western missions in the Armenian provinces inspired Armenian cultural, educational, and political self-organization. The latter included revolutionary groups, first founded by Armenian students abroad, who sought civil rights and communal autonomy. Some also envisioned a socialist society.[24] But the oppression of Armenians in the provinces was exacerbated. The dynamics of British pressure, Turkish persecution, and British nonresistance was explained in 1890 by the British Consul, Clifford Lloyd:

All the Christians asked for was protection, but this was the one thing the Government failed to provide. . . . The result is that this summer the valley has again been overrun by the Kurds, *who here, as elsewhere, openly declare that their action meets with the approval of the Turkish Government.* . . .

England's responsibility towards Armenia is attested by a triple bond of obligation. Together with France, she contracted through the Crimean War a special obligation towards all the Christian subjects of the Porte . . . the Crimean War convinced the Porte that the integrity and independence of the Ottoman Empire were absolutely essential to the balance of power in Europe. . . . The Porte . . . immediately fastened on the diplomatic advantage which the policy of the Crimean War had given it. . . .

From that day to this England has done nothing to fulfill her solemn obligation under that convention [of 1880]. And the Armenians, meanwhile, have been enduring the life of agony which the Consular Reports reveal.[25]

Armenian peasants began to collect arms so that when attacked, they would no longer be defenseless. As foreign attention turned away, Sultan Abdul Hamid retorted to critics by organizing the Hamidye, regiments of Kurdish tribesmen modeled after the Russian Cossacks who perpetrated massacres of the Armenians similar to the pogroms the Black Hundreds in Russia committed against the Jews during the same period. Nonviolent demonstrations to present petitions, provincial Armenian rebellions, and an occupation by young Armenian revolutionaries of the Ottoman Bank in 1896 (threatening to blow it up if their demands were not met) lent superficial credence to official allegations that the Armenians conspired with Russia and were seized upon by the government as provocations for massacre. While massacres of Armenians were rare in the first half of the nineteenth century, 10,000 were estimated slain at Sassoon in 1894 and a minimum of 100,000 were estimated to have been killed between 1895 and 1908 when the Sultan's despotism was ended.[26] During these massacres, the educated classes among the Armenians were special targets; Abraham Hartunian, an Armenian pastor, recorded his own experience of being stabbed, stripped, and stoned by a Kurd crying, "The infidel must die like a dog!" in 1895. After being left for dead, he was seized while hiding in a Turkish agha's home by soldiers who had his name on a death list.[27]

Thus, before World War I, Armenians were seen as a foreign ward that could be ravished periodically when her European great-aunts and -uncles were not looking. Some Armenians protested publicly in order to instigate foreign intervention and others organized self-defense groups. But great power protests only stirred resentment against the ward, instigating the warder's lust, which was never effectively sanctioned by her protectors.

Rise of the Young Turks and Pan-Turanianism (3)

The decline of the Empire provoked Turkish officers to challenge the government. The leaders of the "Young Turks," known as the Committee of

Union and Progress, or *Itahad,* were headed by a central committee, the *Jemiyet,* which in 1908 demanded and secured the Sultan's restoration of the 1876 constitution after two years of army mutinies. The party's slogan was "Freedom, Justice, Equality, Fraternity." Its victory was welcomed by Muslims, Christians, and Jews. Armenian revolutionary committees in exile cooperated with the *Itahad,* anticipating that Armenians would obtain civil rights and equal representation as it had promised. Because of Itahad's early promises, its role in authorizing the 1909 massacre against Armenians in Adana was not immediately apparent.[28] But early promises of rights and "Ottomanization," decentralization of administration, were forgotten as one faction became dominant in *Itahad* after 1911 when the political situation became more desperate.[29] No way seemed evident to the new men of power to retain the Empire and accept the demands of minorities that included the emerging pan-Arab movement, Maronite Christians, Greek Christians, Macedonians, Albanians, and Armenians. To justify their domination, they adopted a credo based on Pan-Turanianism, which alleged a prehistoric mythic unity among Turanian peoples based on racial origin to be implemented by "Turkification," instituting the Turkish language throughout, demanding Mohammedan ("read Turkish") supremacy and centralization of rule from Constantinople. [30] This implied a strategy of moving toward central Asia to unite the Turkish peoples stretching to China. But the Armenians were situated in their path in Anatolia.

The Young Turks who made the revolution "did not want only to save the state in its existing form . . . [but] wanted to revive it and make it a going concern in the modern world."[31] But the route of the Turks accelerated. Italy attacked Tripoli in 1911 and Austria-Hungary annexed Bosnia and Herzegovina. A coalition of Bulgaria, Serbia, and Greece attacked and defeated Turkey in the First Balkan War of 1912. However, Turkey regained some territory against a divided coalition in the Second Balkan War of 1913. Against this background, Djemal Pasha, appointed Governor of Constantinople by *Itahad* in 1913, explains why the original liberal vision of some of its founders was repudiated.

"Decentralisation of the Administration" meant administrative local autonomy in a single "Ottoman Empire" for the various parts inhabited by the different national elements. . . . But France coveted Syria, the English hoped to make themselves masters of Mesopotamia and the whole Arabian Peninsula, the Russians were only waiting for a favourable opportunity to seize the eastern provinces of Anatolia, the Bulgarians and Serbs wanted to carve up Macedonia, the Italians and Austrians wished to lay hands on Albania, and the Greeks hoped to incorporate the islands of the Archipelago in their kingdom. If all these regions had been created provinces on the principle of "political decentralisation," would those nations have had the slightest difficulty in swallowing them up one after the other? Would our decentralisation principle have stood the test of time any better than the decentralisation principle of Austria? . . .

Speaking for myself, I am primarily an Ottoman, but I do not forget that I am a Turk, and nothing can shake my belief that the Turkish race is the foundation-stone of the Ottoman Empire. . . . We appeal to all who wish to preserve the cause of Ottoman unity to realise their holy duty of encouraging the Turks, increasing their number, and giving them their place in the sun.[32]

Djemal Pasha tells us that all the minorities refused to accept this program. The Dashnagtzoutium, formerly an Armenian revolutionary organization, was the most favorably inclined, but insisted on continuing to exist as a public association, declining *Itahad's* bid to join the Committee and disband. *Itahad* not only could not assimilate the minorities on its terms, it was not able to monopolize control of the government and prevent a new Liberal Party from forming. It overcame its Turkish liberal opposition by a coup in January 1913, subjecting Turkey to a military dictatorship.[33]

Turkey Goes to War as Germany's Ally (4)

In 1913, Russia, responding to Armenian petitions, again proposed reforms to guarantee the Armenians' rights by instituting mixed police, judiciary, and local control over officials, to be supervised by foreign inspectors. After some modifications were made by Germany and Britain, Turkey signed an agreement with Russia on 8 February 1914. Djemal Pasha tells us that *Itahad* viewed this as the first step toward a Russian protectorate, and realized that the world war was an opportunity to liberate itself from such obligations.

Of course it was our one hope to free ourselves through the World War from all conventions, which meant so many attacks on our independence. . . .

This was our intention, and so the treaty dealing with the reforms for the vilayets inhabited by the Armenians, wrung out of us by our hereditary enemies (the Russians), had no further significance. This is not to say, however, that we had not the earnest intention of introducing reform in our country. On the contrary, we had determined on radical reform, as we were inspired by the conviction that otherwise we could not continue to exist.[34]

Djemal Pasha does not tell us that the radical reform was to eliminate the Armenian problem by eliminating the Armenians. Bryce, honorary author of the definitive official British report on the Armenian massacres (prepared by Arnold Toynbee), concluded:

It is evident that the war was merely an opportunity and not a cause — in fact, that the deportation scheme, and all that it involved, flowed inevitably from the general policy of the Young Turkish Government.[35]

Freedom from detection and obligation created the opportunity. Turkey's alliance with Germany diminished Allied influence and the observability of its policy by foreign diplomats, signifying the futility of British policy of the previous seventy years.

Turkey's initial thrust against Russia in the winter of 1915 was unsuccessful; it was pushed back from the Russian front bordering the Armenian vilayets by a Russian army including Russian Armenian units. However, the March setback of the English in the ill-fated Gallipoli campaign withdrew the threat of an invasion and increased the self-confidence of the Turkish leaders.[36] This insured the Turks' inviolability while implementing their plans for genocide.

BLAMING THE VICTIM AND ORGANIZING THE CRIME

As in most genocides, its planners attempted to project the blame onto the victim. The *Jemiyet* telegraphed governors of the vilayets on 28 February 1915:

> Periodic news arriving from Cairo recently indicates that Dashnagtzoutium [the Armenian Revolutionary Federation] is preparing a decisive attack upon the Jemiyet. . . .
>
> Jemiyet has decided to free the fatherland from the covetousness of this accursed race and to bear upon their shoulder the stigma that might malign the Ottoman history.
>
> Unable to forget the disgrace and bitterness of the past, filled with vengeful episodes, Jemiyet, hopeful about its future, has decided to exterminate all Armenians living in Turkey, without allowing a single one to remain alive and to this regard has given the Government extensive authority.[37]

There was never any doubt as to who the victims were; no need to require their registration as Jews were registered in Germany in 1935. Their identity was known to tax collectors, public officials, and neighbors. The campaign began with measures to strip them of the means to resist and to segregate them sexually. Armenians were ordered to hand in their weapons, and they usually hastened to find weapons to hand in even if they had to buy them, for fear that charges of noncooperation would be brought, used as evidence of disloyalty, and then employed to provoke violence against them. Armenian men in the army were segregated into special units ("labor battalions"), disarmed, and later slain. On the night of 24 April, some 1,000 prominent Armenians were arrested in the capital and secretly murdered, leaving the others numbed by terror.[38] The remaining males in each village were summoned by the town crier to report immediately, led out of town, and slain. Women, children, and a few infirm males previously exempted were then bidden by the crier to prepare themselves for deportation. They were driven into the desert by soldiers, staggering along until they dropped from drought, starvation, the lash, or their festering wounds. Women might elect or be selected to become wives of Muslims, thus gaining exemption but also requiring them to part with their children. The military was aided by surrounding Kurdish and Circassian tribesmen who looted and raped the women, kidnapping a few favorites and murdering many. For months, packs of bedraggled survivors wound through the deserts of western Asia until they fell or were slain. Toynbee, assessing all the evidence, estimated that two thirds of the 1,800,000 Armenians in the Ottoman Empire in 1914 were annihilated or deported to the desert.[39]

PUBLIC VISIBILITY OF THE ANNIHILATION INSTIGATES PROTESTS

The Turkish Minister of the Interior, Talaat Bey—whose correspondence authorizing the annihilation procedures was later discovered[40]—made no attempt to deny the government's responsibility for the extermination in conversations with American Ambassador Morgenthau.[41] But while he steadily refused any American requests to feed the survivors, the government anticipated occasions for foreign petitions, exempting most Armenians in the major cities where foreigners were concentrated—Constantinople and Smyrna—from expulsion. The only government with any potential means of sanctioning Turkey to stop its killing was Germany, but German officials made no general attempt to forbid the extermination of the Armenians (apart from local exceptions). Ambassador Morgenthau believed that the policy itself was instigated by Germans, but there is no evidence to corroborate this.[42]

German ambassadors denied and then tried to overlook the policy of their ally. They began to protest the massacres, first in an equivocating voice and later bluntly. The third German Ambassador, Count Wolf-Metternich, in December 1915 sought to get the Turkish government to issue a statement disassociating Germany from the Turks' crimes in order to repudiate allegations abroad that Germany had instigated them.[43] The Count wrote the German Chancellor on 7 December 1915:

> The rumour was spread about that the Germans desired to see Armenians massacred. I have employed extremely sharp language. Protests are useless, and the Turkish assertions that no further deportations will take place are worthless. . . . In order to have success in the Armenian Question we must instill into the Turkish Government the fear of consequences. If, for military reasons, we may not dare to act firmly, it is useless to protest any longer.[44]

Count Wolf-Metternich understood that the Armenian extermination was an end in itself to the ruling triumvirate and its party, as well as a portent of things to come. He wrote the Reich Chancellor in June 1916:

> I have discussed with Talaat Bey and Halil Bey the deportation of the Armenian

workers from the Amanus stretch, which deportation hampers the conduct of the war. These measures, I told the ministers, among other things, gave the impression as if the Turkish government were itself bent on losing the war. . . . But no one any longer has the power to control the many-headed hydra of the Committee, to control the chauvinism and the fanaticism . . . there is not much to gain any longer from the Armenians. The mob is therefore preparing for the moment when Greece, forced by the Entente, must turn against Turkey and her allies. Massacres of far greater scope will occur then. The victims are more numerous and the booty more enticing. Greekdom constitutes the cultural element of Turkey and it will be destroyed like the Armenian segment if outside influence will not put a stop to it. "Turkification" means to expel or kill everything non-Turkish.[45]

THE AFTERMATH AND SETTLING ACCOUNTS

To repel petitions, the Turkish government magnified its accusation that Turkey had been attacked by their victims. The victims' guilt was demonstrated by the few cases in which Armenians, having heard of the deportations of neighboring villages, defended themselves against the Turkish militia. Only in instances where the beleaguered defenders were ultimately saved by Allied forces (for example, the Russian Army at Van and the French Navy at Musa Dagh) did they avert annihilation. The government repeated the stab-in-the-back legend that Turks had been betrayed by Armenians conspiring with Russia, even later extrapolating evidence of Armenian reprisals in 1918 to account for the Turkish annihilation in 1915.

Djemal Pasha's account justifying the genocide,[46] like Talaat Bey's, reveals a definition of Armenians as the enemy simply because they were Armenians. Talaat Bey said in an interview in 1916 with the *Berliner Tageblatt:*

> We have been reproached for making no distinction between the innocent Armenians and the guilty; but that was utterly impossible, in view of the fact that *those who were innocent today might be guilty tomorrow* [italics in the original].[47]

In Germany, in 1921, Talaat Bey was assassinated by an Armenian who acted on behalf of the Armenian revolutionary federation. Dr. Johannes Lepsius, testifying for the assassin's defense, asserted that the Armenians had been defined as the prime enemy because of the Allies' rhetoric on their behalf during the previous century and their simultaneous refusal to protect them, thus further inflaming the Turks against the Armenians, while proving to them the powerlessness of the Armenians.

> In the game of chess between London and Petersburg the Armenian was the pawn, sometimes pushed forward, sometimes sacrificed. The humanitarian causes, "protection of Christians," were pretexts. When in 1895 Abdul Hamid was forced to sign the plan of reforms presented by England, Russia and France, he had already set in motion a number of Armenian massacres. Lord Salisbury an-

nounced that as far as England was concerned, the Armenian question had ceased to exist. Prince Lobanov indicated to the Sultan that he had nothing to worry about because Russia pays no attention to the execution of reforms. The Sultan drew his own conclusions.[48]

When the Young Turks attempted to establish their power with a new formula, annihilation of the Armenians became a rational means to fulfill their ideal. Superficially, this seemed to be an extension of the policy of Abdul Hamid, who periodically attempted to fortify Islamic unity and cement loyalties to the state by instigating Armenian massacres. But, Islamic traditionalism had assumed the continuous existence of the "People of the Book" while pan-Turanianism did not. It was a way of proving Turkish independence by eliminating a body perceived as foreign without incurring the costs that an attack against Greek Christians would have provoked. The calculus of the Young Turks proved correct, and the reliance of the Armenians on petitions to the Allies proved to be based on false trust. The Young Turks reestablished their domination after World War I, and the Allies abandoned promises of an autonomous Armenia or Armenian protectorate under an American mandate.

THE HOLOCAUST

Reverberations of German Defeat in World War I (2)

Germany, defeated by the Allies in World War I, resumed political existence as a republic after aborted revolutions and right-wing coups. The weakness of this republic, never formally overthrown even after Hitler's accession as chancellor, has been attributed to many causes: lack of a liberal tradition among the middle classes, lack of traditional legitimation, an authoritarian pattern of organization throughout German life, the insecurity among the middle classes generated by the catastrophic inflation of the early 1920s and the subsequent world depression, the inability of left-wing parties to work in concert, the accomodation of the middle-class parties, the opportunism of the conservative industrialists, and the onus of the Versailles Peace Treaty, which required Germany to assume war guilt and pay reparations. Although the reparations absorbed only 1.7% of Germany's budget between 1923 and 1929, less than half of the loans received from foreign governments, they were a symbol of German national subordination.[49] A. J. P. Taylor contends that it was the adherence of most German parties to the nationalists' goal of German supremacy that ultimately undermined the low potential for democracy: the antidemocratic parties could play the nationalist game better, as they were not inhibited by any respect for international commitments or internal democracy.[50] Hitler was an astute organizer and charismatic orator, but he was only one of many agitators demanding militant national action to redress German grievances. Many commentators agree that Hitler's popularity reflected how well he resonated popular moods — aspirations, resentment, and blame — and reiterated attacks on conventional targets, such as the Jews.[51] Germany's loss in World War I was never acknowledged as a defeat in either his oratory or his personal testament, *Mein Kampf,* written while imprisoned for his participation in the unsuccessful Munich putsch of 1923.[52] Instead, he attributed the loss to internal enemies, especially the Jews, who he claimed had stabbed Germany in the back.

Rise of the Nazi Party and Its Ideology (3)

Although the Socialist, Catholic Center, and Liberal parties obtained a parliamentary majority and formed the government in 1928, the Nazi party (the NSDAP) secured 12 seats in the Reichstag and 2.6% of the vote. They multiplied their representation ninefold after the Depression began, securing 107 seats in 1930. In 1932, they doubled their vote, winning 230 seats, thus becoming the strongest party in the Reichstag. Analyses of voting patterns show that the Nazis gained disproportionately from the lower middle classes, which had earlier been most likely to support the non-Catholic middle-class parties.[53]

President (and Field Marshal) von Hindenburg appointed Hitler chancellor on 30 January 1933, after Franz von Papen won support of the Ruhr industrialists for his appointment. Hitler was later named president after Hindenburg's death in 1934, fusing both offices and transforming the former parliamentary bureaucracy into a totalitarian state in which authority was legitimated by his charisma. Those not swayed by charisma were beaten up by his brown-shirted paramilitary (the SA). The Nazi goon squads magnified their own losses in order to sustain the fear of the Communist threat. The Nazis' exploitation of the burning of the Reichstag chambers, an arson that they attributed to a conspiracy involving German Communists despite the evidence that it was set independently by a Dutch Communist,[54] helped them to obtain more seats but not a majority (288 of 647) in the election of March 1933. The government invoked the emergency powers provided by the Weimar constitution not only to suppress all civil liberties but also to rule by decree. Its rule was confirmed by the Reichstag, which passed the Enabling Act granting Hitler this authority permanently. The Communist and Socialist parties were successively repressed and other parties dissolved themselves, so that the Nazi party was soon established as the only legal party. Taylor observes how Hitler's rule was consolidated by the rise of a new class personally loyal to him: "Hitler discovered a 'Hitler class,' his unshakeable resource in extremity. . . . The S.S.—the middle class of education but no property."[55]

The populist violence of Hitler's early street fighters, the SA, was replaced by the violence of the SS, a central internal security organization coordinating all the German states' police apparatus. Political prisoners were funneled into the vastly expanded concentration camps, from which they returned, if they returned, silenced, living testimonies to the cost of dissidence.

The ends that Hitler promised to achieve and the themes of his speeches that triggered most audience approval were not novel, but resonated German ideologies and popular notions fully developed fifty years before the beginning of World War II.[56] The German nationalist ideologies united romantic nationalism with anti-Semitism and modern racism. They assumed an underlying mythic identity or homogeneity among the German people, or *Volk,* based on "blood." The Jews were not *Volk,* but aliens to whom the Germans owed no obligation. This was explicit in the Nazi party program of 1920. While the Germans belonged to the Aryan race, whose supremacy over the Slav and nonwhite races they unhesitatingly asserted, the Jews, according to the Nazis, were nonhuman; bloodsuckers, lice, parasites, fleas, bacilli. The hidden agenda seems an obvious implication from the definition of the problem itself: these are organisms to be squashed or exterminated by chemical means. "The murderous design was made plain, for example, in a speech in May 1923 when he (Hitler) declared: 'The Jews are undoubtedly a race, but not human. They cannot be human in the sense of being an image of God, the Eternal. The Jews are an image of the devil. Jewry means the racial tuberculosis of the nations.' "[57]

The *Volk* had a messianic mission, entailing the destruction of other races and nation-states in the way of its achievement. This conception was expounded by pan-German ideologues in turn-of-the-century Vienna, where Hitler, by his own account, first became politically educated.[58] They were obsessed by envy of the Jews, of their cohesion and their claim to chosenness. The explanatory power of anti-Semitism was expanded by the diffusion of the fraudulent *Protocols of the Elders of Zion,* published by the Czar's secret police and spread by anti-Bolshevik émigrés to reactionary circles in Germany after World War I. The *Protocols* depicted a worldwide conspiracy, holding Jews responsible for Bolshevism.[59]

The metahistory of the *Volk* differed from the actual history of the Germans, for whose misfortunes actual Germans were not responsible. They had been betrayed, stabbed in the back, by the enemy within—the Jew. The *Volk* demanded not only equality with other nations—the right to defend their frontiers without restriction—but additional room to expand—*Lebensraum.* Other nationals of German blood (*Volksdeutsche*) who could be reclaimed resided from the Rhine to the Vistula. The nations that they inhabited would become incorporated into the Reich or colonized by it during the next decade. Natives of colonized nations belonging to the inferior Slavic race would be stripped of rights, reduced to subliteracy, exploited ruthlessly, and frequently subjected to collective violence.[60]

Paving the Road toward the "Final Solution" (4)

During the first five years of the Nazi regime, Germany prepared itself for European domination before intervening openly in 1938 in Czechoslovakia. It repudiated war reparations but attempted to show pacific intentions by signing a treaty respecting the Polish frontiers and professing diplomatic assurances to Western nations. The program to isolate the Jews by successively processing them in a functional sequence—first in order to expel them but later to annihilate them—was not rationalized until 1938, when it was tested in Vienna. In Germany itself, the regime wavered before initiating new steps, reacting to the consequences of earlier steps for the primary goals of that period, rearmament and economic autarchy. Jews were stripped of offices in the government and schools by local administrative actions beginning in 1933, and a boycott was instigated against Jewish enterprises that had been marked. But only in 1935 were Jews (as differentiated from non-Aryans) defined. They were classified by lineage, corresponding to the Nazi belief that Jews were a race, rather than a religious community, and new intermarriages and cohabitation were prohibited to prevent Jews from evading their fate by assimilation and to protect Aryans from being polluted by them. Identification mechanisms were perfected in 1938 with marked identification cards and passports preventing free movement within Germany and easy exodus from it. But exit requirements, foreign nations' immigration laws, Nazi regulations stripping the Jews of their wealth, and the hopes of some Jews that they could accomodate to the new regime deterred Jews from emigrating. From the 1933 peak of 37,000, annual Jewish emigration declined to 20,000 in 1938.[61] But in November 1938 their hopes were shattered as were the glass panes of Jewish enterprises in Germany.

Attempting to diminish the number of Jews on its soil, Germany reacted to an order by Poland revoking citizenship of Poles living abroad over five years—which was used to deprive about 50,000 Jews residing in Germany of the right to any state's protection—by physically expelling such Polish Jews over the border on 28 October 1938. Seventeen-year-old Hershl Grynzpan, then visiting Paris, was incensed to read his parents' report of the treatment they had endured after being ejected from Germany overnight despite having lived there for twenty-four years. Grynzpan responded by shooting Ernst vom Rath, a third secretary in the German embassy in Paris on 7 November 1938: the Ambassador, his intended target, was out. Allegedly reacting to this provocation, the Nazi party instigated a pogrom on 10 November 1938, burning nearly 300 synagogues, breaking windows and vandalizing Jewish shops and interning 30,000 male Jews in concentration camps. But *Kristallnacht,* the "night of the broken glass," was the SA's "final fling," as Hitler vowed.[62] Reichsmarschall Göring regretted the cost; damage for glass alone owed by insurance companies to German owners was estimated at 24 million marks. He solved the immediate problem by imposing a fine of one billion marks upon the Jews. Jewish policy was rapidly coordinated after this event and executed principally by the SS. With identification mechanisms accomplished, successive segregation measures inhibited the freedom of Jews to move and to communicate. The deprivation of liberty, the intensified drive to "Aryanize" economic enterprise, and the threat of further violence spurred Jews who still had businesses to liquidate them hastily and get out of Germany. By state decree, the Reichsvertretung der Juden in Deutschland, a nationwide Jewish voluntary association, became an organization coordinating all persons labeled as Jews; it was now the Reichsvereinigung. It informed the Jews of new government measures, fed the Gestapo the information they needed, and later assisted in the execution of such measures. Thus, Jews became collectively regulated by the co-optation rather than the elimination of Jewish leadership, although such leaders functioned within a control structure that insured their powerlessness. No ghettoization was instituted in Germany since the few remaining Jews had been completely segregated and isolated within the German sea before being compelled to wear the yellow star in September 1941, expediting the next task of the Gestapo — to seize them.

Although Germany sought to lessen the observability or perception of extermination in the old Reich, its organization, Raul Hilberg has pointed out, involved all agencies of the state: "The machinery of destruction, then, was structurally no different from organized German society as a whole: the difference was only one of function. The machinery of destruction *was* the organized community in one of its special roles."[63] With the modern social organization of bureaucracies, characterized by hierarchy and a high division of labor, the important killers are white-collar criminals who command the diverse staffs that must be mobilized. Bureaucracy is not in itself a cause of the choice of destructive ends, but it facilitates their accomplishment by routinizing the obedience of many agents, each trained to perform his role without questioning the ends of action. Max Weber foresaw society's becoming an "iron cage" in his classic analysis of modernity.[64] But he did not anticipate that the cage could become an elevator, descending mechanically to crush the members excluded from the universe of obligation. The passengers within shrank from observing the walls around them, denying or repressing their vision of former members being systematically extruded to the pit below, accustomed as they were to assigning direction to the Führer — the only operator.

When did the "Final Solution" begin? The answer depends on which phase of the transformation from conception to execution of the plan to annihilate the European Jews we focus upon. Its execution depended first on success of the plan of conquest.

It was established during the international trials at Nuremberg that the order to devise implementation of an annihilation plan all over Europe was transmitted orally from Hitler to Göring in the spring of 1941 and from Göring to Reinhard Heydrich, chief of the Reich Security Main Office (RSHA), on 31 July 1941. Heydrich was instructed to make "all necessary preparations . . . for bringing about a complete solution of the Jewish problem" — code words as usual.[65] Heydrich told Adolf Eichmann, his section chief on Jewish affairs, to make plans. Representatives of all major German bureaucracies and occupation authorities were informed of the blueprint for implementing the Final Solution at a conference at RSHA headquarters at Wannsee (a suburb of Berlin) on 20 January 1942, a meeting originally supposed to be held on 9 December 1941, but delayed because of United States entry into the war.[66] Orders to massacre Jews in the territory formerly occupied by the Soviet Union during the invasion were given by Hitler to the army High Command and the RSHA chief, who established the special SS mobile execution squads, the Einsatzgruppen, during the spring of 1941.[67] Between June 1941 and the spring of 1942, the SS discovered the superiority of prussic acid over carbon monoxide for mass gassing and built the extermination camps that enabled them to murder more Jews more efficiently than had been done before in mobile gas vans and carbon monoxide chambers.[68]

The date when the determination to annihilate the Jews crystallized in Hitler's mind cannot be proven. Before the war, the most radical goal of Germany — admitted without dissembling — was to expel the Jews from the country. Despite some German Jews' initial reluctance to leave (some leaders urged they not abandon their rights by flight) and the greater reluctance of other nations to accept them as immigrants, Germany would have succeeded, for by September 1941 over two of every three Jews in Germany in 1933 had fled.[69] But Germany's aggressive design vastly expanded the number of Jews in her domain: the Polish government-in-exile estimated there were 2,042,000 Jews in the German-occupied area in 1939.[70]

Scholars differ as to whether Hitler's decision to exterminate the Jews was latent from the beginning of his career or developed incrementally in response to the failure of previous plans to eliminate them — emigration, the Lublin reservation, and the Madagascar plan.[71] The proposal by German Foreign Office bureaucrats in 1940 to resettle the Jews in a ghetto within a police-state on Madagascar was not entirely original; Poland had proposed forced resettlement of its Jews there in 1937.[72] Christopher Browning, reviewing the Foreign Office and SS correspondence in 1940, concludes that Hitler selected extermination as the Final Solution sometime between the fall of 1940 and the spring of 1941 after it became evident the war against Britain would be prolonged, forestalling naval access to Madagascar. Contemplating the invasion of Russia, Hitler decided to slaughter the Jews in Soviet territory systematically.[73]

Others view the Madagascar Plan as a blind or way-station; in retrospect it appears both as a smokescreen and a strategic tactic to allow the German bureaucracies concerned to adjust by stages to their roles as white-collar executioners. Lucy Dawidowicz emphasizes that "the Final Solution had its origin in Hitler's mind," showing how his fantasy revealed in *Mein Kampf* (written in 1924) of gassing the Jews was related to their subsequent execution.[74] She infers that Göring and Himmler were told of Hitler's plans around 1936, a plausible happening considering Hitler's habit of freely verbalizing fantasies for extermination, but a disclosure that is not possible to corroborate.[75] There is no question as to "the purpose of a reservation that can be derived from the report—surely a sick joke—that Philipp Bouhler, the head of Hitler's private chancellery, was slated to become governor of the Madagascar reservation. Bouhler headed the so-called Euthanasia Program, the first mass murder by gassing; an experience that doubtless qualified him to run a reservation for Jews that would become truly their final destination."[76] Gideon Hausner, the Israeli prosecutor of Adolf Eichmann, also asserts that Reinhard Heydrich (RSHA head) was aware that extermination was to be the Final Solution by September 1939, based on his interpretation of Eichmann's pretrial police interrogation.[77]

Hitler publicly signified his intent in a speech to the Reichstag on 30 January 1939, masked characteristically by projecting onto the Jews his own aim of domination that would provoke war:

> And one thing I wish to say on this day which perhaps is memorable not only for us Germans: In my life I have often been a prophet, and most of the time I have been laughed at. . . . Today I want to be a prophet once more: If international-finance Jewry inside and outside of Europe should succeed once more in plunging nations into another world war, the consequence will not be the Bolshevization of the earth and thereby the victory of Jewry, but the annihilation [Vernichtung] of the Jewish race in Europe.[78]

Only nine days earlier, he had told the Czechoslovakian foreign minister that "we are going to destroy the Jews."[79] It appears that his closest associates were aware of his intent according to a memorandum reaching the British Foreign Office in November 1938. This recorded the message received by a British consul on leave who had gone to Germany to rescue a friend from the Dachau concentration camp and who had talked with a senior member of Hitler's chancellery in order to get him to intercede for his friend. The chancellery official had "made it clear that Germany intended to get rid of her Jews, either by emigration or if necessary by starving or killing them, since she would not risk having such a hostile minority in the country in the event of war." The official added that Germany "intended to expel or kill off the Jews in Poland, Hungary and the Ukraine when she took control of those countries."[80]

Although the Jews had been characterized by Hitler and Nazi ideologues as enemies of the new Germany before the war, Karl Schleunes stresses Hitler's paradoxical dependence upon the Jews earlier:

> It was the Jew who helped hold Hitler's system together—on the practical as well as the ideological level. . . . The continued search for a solution of the Jewish problem allowed Hitler to maintain ideological contact with elements of his movement for whom National Socialism had done very little.[81]

How then, one may ask, could one rid Germany of the Jews if they served as the mortar making the blocks of National Socialism cohere? One may infer that only when Germans were mobilized behind an external enemy could they live without an internal enemy. Once the war began, ideology and opportunities converged for Hitler, providing means to commit the crime while other options that might eliminate the Jews and deterrents to their annihilation vanished. But the war was not an instigator of their extermination but an enabling condition. SS Reichsführer Heinrich Himmler, speaking to assembled SS Major-Generals at Posen on 4 October 1943, justified the single-minded ideological motivation of the extermination of the Jews, discriminating them from other peoples whom they regarded as inferior:

> Our basic principle must be the absolute rule for the SS man: we must be honest, decent, loyal, and comradely to members of our own blood and to nobody else. What happens to a Russian, to a Czech does not interest me in the slightest. What the nations can offer in the way of good blood of our type, we will take, if necessary by kidnapping their children and raising them here with us. . . . Whether 10,000 Russian females fall down from exhaustion while digging an anti-tank ditch interests me only in so far as the anti-tank ditch for Germany is finished. We shall never be rough and heartless when it is not necessary, that is clear. We Germans, who are the only people in the world who have a decent attitude towards animals, will also assume a decent attitude towards these human animals. . . .
>
> I also want to talk to you, quite frankly, on a very grave matter. Among ourselves it should be mentioned quite frankly, and yet we will never speak of it publicly. . . .
>
> I mean the clearing out of the Jews, the extermination of the Jewish race. It's one of those things it is easy to talk about—"The Jewish race is being exterminated," says one party member, "that's quite clear, it's in our program—elimination of the Jews, and we're doing it, exterminating them." And then they come, 80 million worthy Germans, and each one has his decent Jew. Of course the others are vermin, but this one is an A-1 Jew. Not one of all those who talk this way has witnessed it, not one of them has been through it. Most of *you* must know what it means when 100 corpses are lying side by side, or 500 or 1,000. To have stuck it out and at the same time—apart from exceptions caused by human weakness—to have remained decent fellows, that is what has made us hard. This is a page of glory in our history which has never been written and is never to be written.[82]

To write this "page of glory" in history, war goals were not allowed to stand in the way. Skilled Jewish workers were killed and railroad cars diverted to bring the Final Solution into effect rather than to mobilize against the Allies, just as Armenian workers had been annihilated in Turkey during World War I, hindering Turkey's mobilization. The Final Solution became an end-in-itself, the only one attempted by Hitler that was virtually fulfilled in Central and Eastern Europe. Had Germany won, the Jews of North and South America were next on the list for gassing.[83]

PLAYING DEITY: CREATING A PURE RACE

Extermination of the Unfit

Reifying the *Volk* justified using the state to play deity, correcting the results of past breeding and exploiting new conceptions to transform the German people into a race "of pure blood," as Himmler put it.[84] The plan to kill people with physical or mental defects or diseases was implemented in 1939 simultaneously with the invasion of Poland. Hitler had observed in 1935 that if war came "such a program could be put into effect more smoothly and readily and in the general upheaval public opposition would be less likely."[85] On 1 September 1939, Hitler authorized Dr. Karl Brandt and Reichsleiter Philip Bouhler to authorize "certain physicians" to grant "incurable" persons a "mercy death."[86] In Nazi ideology, these were considered to be people unfit to breed, who served no function for the state. They included the mentally ill, deformed or retarded children, tuberculars, arteriosclerotic adults, and people of all ages held captive or institutionalized by the state.[87] This program, which led to the death of an estimated 275,000 German psychiatric patients alone, has mistakenly been called "euthanasia" when it was simple murder.[88] Supervised by psychiatrists, the program was justified by theories of eminent German psychiatrists writing from 1920 onward.[89] But the program did not serve only to eliminate Germans. It was also a prototype for future mass extermination. Jews, Poles, and Czechs in concentration camps interned as political prisoners, foreign workers in Germany who became unable to work, and Poles institutionalized in insane asylums also were killed. The same staff that developed the gas chambers for the special killing centers within Germany developed the massive installations at Auschwitz, and many members of the staff transferred to extermination camps.[90] The gassing of German children transported by the busload to special extermination centers was halted by Hitler's edict in response to protests by Germans and their widespread expressed revulsion and fears; however, he authorized murders to be continued by less visible means, such as the injection of poisons.[91] The gassing of German Jews was never stopped; few Germans felt any need to remark or protest their absence.

Expansion of the *Volk*

The fantasy of a pure race also inspired the *Lebensborn* ("well of life") program, first established by Heinrich Himmler within the SS in 1935 to enlarge and purify the Aryan race by selective mating from existing stock. During the war, maternity homes and clinics were established throughout Europe for women of diverse nationality whom SS officers had impregnated, thus fulfilling their duty (dictated by Himmler).[92] The pregnant women had to pass racial screening tests for admission (as the prospective fathers had done to become SS officers). The children of unmarried parents became the legal wards of Himmler and could not be claimed by their parents. Robert Kempner, chief U.S. prosecutor at Nuremberg (1946-1949), estimates that 50,000 to 100,000 children were born under *Lebensborn* auspices.[93] *Lebensborn* established homes in Germany, Austria, Czechoslovakia, the Netherlands, and Poland by taking over expropriated Jewish property and hospitals.[94] Further, children of suitable racial characteristics (screened in orphanages, schools, and special centers) in the Protectorate, Poland, and the occupied eastern territories were openly kidnapped, institutionalized, and later (if they passed all racial tests) adopted by German parents. Those not selected died in concentration camps. It is estimated that 200,000 children were snatched from Poland alone.

The kidnapping of Polish children also served the German drive to extinguish Poland as a nation through destruction of the intelligentsia, reducing the masses to subliteracy, lowering the rate of population growth (by raising the minimum marriage age, depressing the standard of living, penalizing out-of-wedlock births), physical resettlement, and racially stratifying the population to induce or coerce Poles classified (often arbitrarily) as of German blood to become "re-Germanized."[95] This plan for gradual cultural genocide — Poles might remain alive, but not as Poles — was supplemented by selective extermination of especially vulnerable groups: Polish workers in Germany who became incapacitated for some reason and those in mental institutions in Poland. An attempt (not successful, because of German opposition) was also made to exterminate tubercular Poles in institutions.[96]

While the ancient Pharaohs constructed pyramids triangulating to the heavens to symbolize their union with the immortals, Hitler's gas chambers produced pyramids of corpses whose ashes descended to the netherworld of Hell, symbolizing his kingdom over the dead. The living had to be annihilated for the sake of the new kingdom, the dominion of an ideal race, not yet existent. Hitler did not hesitate to authorize the sacrifice of Germans deemed imperfect in 1939. Nor did he hesitate in 1945 to order the destruction of basic resources affecting the food and energy supply of the German people whom he believed no longer deserved to live because they were unwilling to make the sacrifices he demanded.[97] It was never the real people but the ideal *Volk* that dictated any means necessary.

Extermination of the Gypsies

The Jews were not the only group in Germany stigmatized as alien, but they were the only stigmatized group of political significance whose elimination had been promised publicly by Hitler twenty years before it began. The Gypsies were also designated for destruction, although scarcely any publicity was devoted to the "Gypsy problem." We are indebted (except where otherwise stated) to Kenrick and Puxon for this documentation.[98]

Although Gypsies have not played a symbiotic role similar to that of the Jews—they cannot be labeled a "middleman minority"—they have been accused of crime and corruption since their entry into Europe, charged with assistance at the Crucifixion, unnatural copulation, cannibalism, necrophiliac activity, and spreading filth and disease. The first response of European states from the fifteenth to the eighteenth century was to expel them: 148 such laws were passed by German states alone between 1416 and 1774. Violence was commonly employed for enforcement and deterrence. As late as the nineteenth century, Gypsy hunts (like fox hunts) occurred in Denmark. Only after drives for expulsion and extermination had failed did states attempt to assimilate them, denying the right of Gypsies to live together, by encouraging settlement and criminalizing the nomads' life. By 1933 police in France, Baden, and Prussia already had files with fingerprinted identification of Gypsies there.

Gypsies were officially defined as non-Aryan by the Nuremberg laws of 1935, which also first defined Jews; both groups were forbidden to marry Germans. Gypsies were later labeled as asocials by the 1937 Laws against Crime, regardless of whether they had been charged with any unlawful acts. Two hundred Gypsy men were then selected by quota and incarcerated in Buchenwald concentration camp. By May 1938, SS Reichsführer Himmler established the Central Office for Fighting the Gypsy Menace, which defined the question as "a matter of race," discriminating pure Gypsies from part Gypsies as Jews were discriminated, and ordering their registration. In 1939, resettlement of Gypsies was put under Eichmann's jurisdiction along with that of the Jews. Gypsies were forbidden to move freely and were concentrated in encampments within Germany in 1939, later (1941) transformed into fenced ghettos, from which they would be seized for transport by the criminal police (aided by dogs) and dispatched to Auschwitz in February 1943. During May 1940, about 3,100 were sent to Jewish ghettos in the Government-General: others may have been added to Jewish transports from Berlin, Vienna, and Prague to Nisko, Poland (the site of an aborted reservation to which Jews were deported). These measures were taken against Gypsies who had no claim to exemption because of having an Aryan spouse or having been regularly employed for five years.

Some evaded the net at first. Despite a 1937 law excluding Gypsies from army service, many served in the armed forces until demobilized by special orders between 1940 and 1942. Gypsy children were also dismissed from schools beginning in March 1941. Thus, those who were nominally free and not yet concentrated were stripped systematically of the status of citizens and segregated. The legal status of Gypsies and Jews, determined irrevocably by the agreement between Justice Minister Thierack and SS Reichsführer Himmler on 18 September 1942, removing both groups from the jurisdiction of any German court, confirmed their fate. Thierack wrote, "I envisage transferring all criminal proceedings concerning [these people] to Himmler. I do this because I realize that the courts can only feebly contribute to the extermination of these people."[99]

The Citizenship Law of 1943 omitted any mention of Gypsies since they were not expected to exist much longer. Himmler decreed the transport of Gypsies to Auschwitz on 16 December 1942, but he did not authorize their extermination until 1944. Most died there and in other camps of starvation, diseases, and torture from abuse as live experimental subjects. By the end of the war, 15,000 of the 20,000 Gypsies who had been in Germany in 1939 had died.[100] Kenrick and Puxon make no estimate of those imprisoned Gypsies who endured sterilization and/or trauma leading to future debilitating diseases and breakdowns so their estimate of Gypsy victims is not comparable to my estimate of Jewish victims (see Table 3.1).

One explanation of Himmler's pause before the annihilation of the Gypsies was an early plan of his to spare two groups, the supposedly pure Sinti and the indigenous German Lalleri. But Martin Bormann, head of the Nazi Party Chancellery, objected on 3 December 1942:

> I have been informed that the treatment of the so called pure Gypsies is going to have new regulations. . . . Such a special treatment would mean a fundamental deviation from the simultaneous measures for fighting the Gypsy menace and would not be understood at all by the population and the lower leaders of the party. Also the Führer would not agree.[101]

Soon after (16 December), Himmler, when authorizing the transit of Gypsies to Auschwitz, exempted the two groups from the first police raids. He had co-opted representatives of these groups (as the SS had sought out Jewish elders), asking them to prepare lists of pure Sinti and Lalleri. But ultimately, these lists usually saved neither the named nor the namers: "Most of this activity proved a futile blind."[102]

CONCLUSION

The victims of twentieth-century premeditated genocide — the Jews, the Gypsies, the Armenians — were murdered in order to fulfill the state's design for a new order. That design arose from the political formulas adopted by the new elites that rose to power and transformed the state into a criminal instrument. Such ideologies radically denied their past national failures. Both Germany and the Ottoman Empire had suffered military defeats within the generation the new regime that authorized genocide came to power. Any elite seeking to capture the state needed a political formula to justify its rule, which addressed the critical question of the nation's existence. The right of a master race, the unique destiny of a chosen people, was such a formula. War was used in both cases (an opportunity anticipated and planned for by Germany but simply seized by Turkey after World War I began) to transform the nation to correspond to the ruling elite's formula by eliminating groups conceived of as alien, enemies by definition. Thus, victims are labeled as adversaries.

While the political formulas justifying the extinction of the targeted group were the tools of new leadership, in both cases the victims had earlier been decreed as outside the universe of obligation, by Koranic injunctions and by Christian theodicy, respectively. However, a church holding out the possibility of conversion to all must assume a common humanity, and therefore may not sanction unlimited violence. But a doctrine that assumes people do not belong to a common species knows no limits inhibiting the magnitude of permissible crime.

Can we apprehend other premeditated genocides? Paradoxically, at the beginning of such crimes are ideals, radical ideals actualized by organized movements or elites that were not checked. The last defense against actualization of such programs was sanctions from other nations. War between nations and internal war now (as then) diminishes the possibilities of observing and checking genocide; peace allows but does not in itself instigate allies to probe what may be considered "internal affairs." Those who seek to deter future genocide will have to look beyond preconceptions, for it has and will appear again masked by new ideologies that justify it among nations to whom racism is an abhorrent and/or stigmatized doctrine. Only by focusing on the identity of the victim and that of the perpetrator can we strip the mask of ideology and the accounting mechanisms used by perpetrators to disguise their responsibility.

The Calculus of Genocide

A Model and Method
to Understand National Differences
in Jewish Victimization

Why did the drive toward the "Final Solution" succeed so well in so many nations? The pyramids of corpses rose steeply in some nations, but victimization was limited or almost wholly averted in other nations. Despite widespread publicity after the Nuremberg trials regarding the six million Jews whom Adolf Eichmann estimated had been exterminated,[1] the success of the Final Solution has not seized many scholars' attention as a problem demanding explanation. It is not talked about conversationally or in scholarly orbits of discourse. Henry Friedlander has shown that, with a few notable exceptions, most modern historians and textbook writers on World War II have ignored the existence of a plan to exterminate the Jews, devoted scarcely any space to it, or mentioned it only parenthetically.[2] Similarly, anthropology, the most transhistorical social science, has totally ignored genocide as a distinctly human manifestation, as have most sociologists.[3]

The underlying reason for this neglect, Friedlander believes, was articulated by the German anti-Nazi historian Golo Mann, who admitted the crime but discussed it only in passing, as related to the SS, the police, or the concentration camps. Friedlander informs us that Mann admits

> the worst crimes were committed by units of the SS and SD. . . . Let us not describe and list those things. But let us not think either that inhuman cruelty is a specifically German characteristic. . . . The historian also does not like to speak of them. These are deeds and figures which the imagination cannot grasp, which the mind refuses to believe, however clearly they can be proved by reason.[4]

Such suppression among historians has facilitated the recent emergence of a revisionist school of pseudoscholarship alleging that the charge of the

mass murder of five to six million European Jews during World War II is a
fiction.[5]

PRIOR AGENDAS OF RESEARCHERS

Much significant research on the extermination of European Jewry was
prompted by the need to evaluate responsibility for it and account for its
underlying causes. This effort was inspired not only by the ordinary motives
instigating scholarship but by a collective need among Jews to grasp or impose a meaning upon the experience. The massive threat of extinction and
the specter of impotence were traumatic. The unspoken need of many was to
redeem the victims who had perished—to liberate them from the enforced
humiliation, degradation, and accommodation—and by redeeming belief in
their image, to redeem the image of our common humanity.

But needs prescribe a secret agenda of assumptions that limit findings,
for the evidence from which we draw our answers depends on our questions.
Many past questioners have labored under similar assumptions. First, there is
a paradigm of a closed system of perpetrator and victim—the Nazi versus the
Jew alone—in which the perpetrators are usually cast as acting and the victims as acted upon. Nations other than Germany, native institutions, and
other natives of occupied countries enter peripherally and generally receive
little sustained attention. Second, there is an evaluative preoccupation with
the culpability or innocence of the victim of involvement with the organization of destruction, on the implicit assumption that all Jews must be
blameless in order to be cast as victims and that the behavior of the victims
was a cause rather than a symptom of their victimization. The human need
to idealize victims so as to exonerate them has often obscured our vision of
the Holocaust. We often assume, too, that the isolation of the victim pursued
by the executioner was attributable to the executioner alone and was a normal situation. Thus, we overlook the interaction among potential murderers,
victims, accomplices, and bystanders that preceded the crime of genocide.
Only decades later did researchers begin to explore the question of the
culpability or responsibility of the bystanders.

GOALS OF THIS STUDY
AND GUIDING HYPOTHESES

Another agenda for research begins with the observation of sociologist
Everett Hughes that

the National Socialist Government of Germany carried out the most colossal piece
of "dirty work" in history on the Jews. The crucial problems concerning such an
occurrence are: (1) who are the people who actually carry out such work and (2)

what are the circumstances in which other "good" people allow them to do it. It seems probable that candidates for "dirty work" can be found in any society. What we need is better knowledge of the signs of their rise to power and better ways of keeping them out of power.[6]

My aim is to answer the second question, assuming the reader's awareness of the bureaucratic, military, and diplomatic apparatus mobilized by Germany to pursue an aggressive war successfully and to enlist allies. In order to explain the success of the Final Solution, one must explain how Jewish victims were dis-integrated from the social systems by which they were usually protected—defined, labeled, stripped, isolated, stored, and shipped. But to understand why Jews became victims, one must compare not only their varied experiences during the Holocaust but also the rights of citizenship Jews enjoyed before the war and the threats to those rights in states in which they endured more deaths and injuries during the Holocaust to the situation in those states in which Jews suffered less victimization. The most plausible unit of research is neither the perpetrator nor the victim but the community or nation-state subject to German instigation.

There is added theoretic reason to view Jewish victimization as a function of the response of the nation-state of which Jews were members if we view the modern nation-state as the perimeter of a compulsory universe of obligation. During previous research on the justification of collective violence,[7] I observed that the collective (or common) conscience is defined by the boundaries of the universe of obligation—that circle of persons toward whom obligations are owed, to whom the rules apply, and whose injuries call for expiation by the community. Within any polity, the dominant group defines the boundaries of the universe of obligation and sanctions violations legally. Injuries to or violations of rights of persons within the universe are offenses against the collective conscience that provoke the need for sanctions against the perpetrators in order to maintain the group's solidarity, as Durkheim first proposed in 1893.[8] Violations of (or collective violence against) those outside the boundaries do not provoke such a need; instead, such violence is likely to be explained as a just punishment for their offenses.[9] Thus, one would expect that resistance to legal and physical violence against the Jews as Jews would depend on their inclusion within the universe of obligation.

If we conceive of the German occupation (or alliance) as a test case of one social system seeking to incorporate others, the Germans had to change the boundaries of the universe of obligation of each nation in order to exclude Jews unless they had been previously excluded.

Let us assume that the nation-state's universe of obligation coincides with that of the dominant group in the polity. If Jews were included by the dominant group within the nation-state as members with equal rights, the likelihood of Jewish victimization should be negatively related to the intensity of solidarity among members of the state. The more solidary the nation, the fewer Jews would be victimized. The greater the solidarity within the occupied society, the more intense would be the sense of mutual obligation among members and the greater the need to protect one another if threatened by an enemy. One would expect the community to exercise social control to deter and punish informers and collaborators.

But if Jews were excluded by the dominant group from the universe of obligation — a condition one would expect to be associated with the success of anti-Semitism prior to World War II — there would be no incentive to protect them. Anti-Semitic movements, by their own definition, positively evaluate Jew-hatred and demand the disemancipation, legal discrimination, or expulsion of the Jews.[10] Viewing anti-Semitism on a continuum, one would thus expect that the more successful such movements were, the less resistance there would be to violations of rights of Jews and the greater would be Jewish victimization.

But what would we expect if national solidarity were low generally (regardless of the exclusion or inclusion of the Jews from the universe of obligation), if each person calculated his actions only on the basis of advancing his self-interest? The postinvasion situation can be understood as a prototypical example of an exchange between the powerful and the powerless. (For the satellite nations, one can substitute an exchange between the expansive donor and the dependent client.) Collaboration would then become a rational and statistically "normal" response to a normless situation. Accommodation and collaboration may be conceptually distinguished by whether compliance is exacted by force-threat or anticipation of force-threat, or is freely enlisted for mutually desired objectives or an exchange of values. Accommodation is an avoidance response to threat while collaboration is motivated by reward, incentive, or a desire to retain one's status as well as mutuality of goals. Expelling Jews — or any other class of persons — means redistributing their property, jobs, and statuses; helping to label, identify, and eliminate Jews ought, then, to lead to increasing one's share of the spoils and/or insuring one's own safety. Thus, the less solidarity there is, the more likely people would be to become detached from moral constraints. In an anomic condition — free from social regulation — people may respond without regard to the possibility of injuring others. In such a condition, they would be more likely to collaborate to eliminate a group targeted for destruction by the occupying power.

Despite the differing causes of compliance, the consequences of accommodation and of collaboration are the same. Given the existence of a prevailing generalized norm of obedience to authority, the norm of obedience, doing one's duty, playing one's role, inexorably leads to following orders, unless there is a collective definition of the ordering authority as illegitimate and a counternorm of resistance.[11] People accustomed to follow rules are easily organized to murder unless there is a collective redefinition of their obligation.

One might explain the victimization of Jews as a response to force-threat alone if the dominant response were accommodation and such accommodation could be accounted for by the intensity of German control alone. To test this, let us construct a complementary hypothesis: differences among nation-states in the percentage of Jews victimized are positively and regularly related to the intensity of German control. The greater the German control, the greater the native accommodation. The greater the accommodation, the more Jews became victims. Therefore, the greater the German control, the more Jews would become victims; conversely, the more Jewish victims there were, the greater was the German control. We should also expect the contrary: Where German control was less, there were fewer Jewish victims.

Three alternative explanations, restated below, categorically follow from these models. The critical hypotheses to be tested are italicized. Related implications that are not to be tested are summarized in parentheses.

1. *Solidarity Thesis:* Before the war, Jews were members of the nation-state, accepted within the universe of obligation by other natives. States differ, however, in the intensity of prewar solidarity uniting all citizens. Less solidary states were less likely to cohere and protect members under wartime stress. The intensity of solidarity explains the extent of native resistance against anti-Jewish discriminatory regulations. The less state cooperation there was, the fewer Jews became victims. Thus, *the more solidary was the nation-state before the war, the fewer Jewish victims there were.* It was also expected that the ability of natives opposed to the occupation to cohere under stress would be a function of how solidary they were earlier. Therefore, *the integration of the national resistance movement(s) during the war should be positively related to prewar solidarity.* One might also expect the intensity of resistance against German rule and extent of collaboration to be negatively related to solidarity.

2. *German Control Thesis:* Before the war, Jews were members of the nation-state, accepted within the universe of obligation by other natives. During the war, states were subjected to different stresses that paralleled their loss of autonomy and the formal assimilation of the state by Germany. The more direct the German control, the greater was German oppression, leading to disintegration of the nation-state and consequent erosion of solidarity. This lowered the probability of altruistic and cohesive behavior, a prerequisite of resistance, and led to societal breakdown and deregulation of mass behavior, producing typical anomic and opportunistic behavior expressed as accommodation to or collaboration with the Germans. *Jewish victimization is positively related to the lack of resistance and the extent of state cooperation and native collaboration. The more direct the German control, the less resistance and greater cooperation there were, and the more Jewish victims.*

3. *Value-consensus Thesis:* The extent to which Jews were included within a common universe of obligation by other citizens before the war varied. Their acceptance as members of the nation-state with equal rights

was inversely related to the achieved success of anti-Semitic movements. The extent of states' resistance to or cooperation with German-instigated or -imposed anti-Jewish policies during World War II was a function of the extent of value consensus between Germany and occupied states, satellites, and colonies. State authorities' policies reflected the maximal earlier success of anti-Semitic movements. *The more successful were prewar anti-Semitic movements, the more Jewish victims there were.* One might also expect that any value consensus leading to cooperation with the enemy against the enemy's enemy would inhibit effective resistance against the enemy. Therefore, one would expect that the more natives cooperated with Germany in expelling or exterminating the Jews, the less effective was national resistance against Germany.

DATA AND METHODS OF ANALYSIS

Data to test these hypotheses were derived from official postwar documentation of losses, primary documents — memoirs, diaries, and articles by participants — secondary monographs and histories, documentations on resistance movements, prewar political history, native responses to occupation, press surveys, internal political strife, and war crimes trials.[12] All research in English and major works in other languages that had not been translated were reviewed. Comparative data on national development for political indices were extracted chiefly from Banks.[13] Statistical handbooks of population were used with some alterations to insure that comparable units were estimated at the same point of time. Specific sources for each nation are enumerated in the notes to Table 3-1.

Methodologically, various sociological modes of knowing were used: inductive, historical analysis based on comparison of all known cases, a *verstehen* approach (taking the point of view of the victim), reconstructing the programing of Jews toward their destruction from their own writings, and statistical analysis, employing cross-tabulation and regression analyses. Substantively, the findings complement each other. Where regression was employed, non-interval-level variables were transformed into "dummy" variables — yes-or-no answers to primary questions — as recommended by Boyle, thus allowing us to trace the contribution of the presence or absence of an attribute or phenomenon.[14] For example: When ranking states on collaboration (after all evidence of indicators of collaboration was collected) to differentiate, within each German control class, high and low collaborators (the former coded one, the latter zero), one would ask, "Was state collaboration in discriminating against Jews higher in Hungary than in Denmark?" and so on.

All rankings were made by the writer. Since most such judgments are akin to those constantly made by historians and historical sociologists in evaluating their data, one should examine their validity with the same skepticism or credibility that characterizes one's approach to other historically reconstructed facts and inferences of patterns. To avoid making false inferences based on omissions or obscure points in leading works, I consulted with leading historians and specialists on particular countries who have written about this era, posing specific questions regarding omissions and/or ambiguities in the published research. Prior to analysis, the codebook and coded sheets for each national unit were submitted to the Division of Holocaust Studies of the Hebrew University's Institute for Contemporary Jewry for review and criticism.

DEFINITIONS AND INDICES OF VARIABLES

The first objective necessity was to establish a reliable measure of Jewish victimization and of the national units under study. Very different figures are sometimes presented because of the differences between prewar nation-states, administrative units during the war, and postwar borders of such states. In order to establish a separate measure of victimization, a consistent, exclusive basis of designation of units or "cases" was needed that was related to the prewar nation-state as closely as possible but would separate parts of states that experienced different types or lengths of German control. Generally, all states existent in September 1941 in continental Europe that were allied with or occupied by Germany (except the Soviet Union and Luxembourg) were taken as cases with the following additions. In Greece, split in 1941 between the German and Italian zones of occupation, Salonica — occupied in 1941 — and Athens (the city with the greatest number of Jews in the other zone) — occupied in 1943 — were discriminated. Since Greece is the one nation for which we have a measure of victimization for each city and town, and these vary widely, this was a plausible discrimination. Poland, broken up by Germany into ten administrative units, was counted as one unit (corresponding to the nation existing in September 1939) since all units were within the region of highest control, the zone of extermination. We have little reason to believe there was a substantive difference in victimization in different regions. The Protectorate of Bohemia-Moravia and Austria, both incorporated into the Reich, were counted as separate cases. The three Baltic states that were incorporated in the USSR in 1940 were also counted as separate cases, as they had been independent nations before the Molotov-Ribbentrop pact.

The Soviet Union itself was excluded from the study because of the difficulty of finding reliable estimates of the Jewish population at the time of the invasion, the number of Jewish refugees who had fled to the interior, and the Jewish population at liberation. Luxembourg was excluded because of the paucity of sources. Albania, Monte Carlo, and other ministates were excluded because of lack of a prewar established Jewish community that could be traced and/or lack of sources.

The Jewish population enumerated as the base population was the number registered or estimated as of June 1941 (or the date of occupation, if later) within the wartime borders of the state or region observed.

Jewish victims are defined as the sum of all persons killed, subjected to potentially fatal trauma, and dying by their own hand (to avoid potentially fatal trauma) because they were socially labeled or recognized as Jews. These include all Jews shot, gassed, or murdered by other techniques as Jews, others interned in extermination camps[15] or slave labor camps, and Jews killed through starvation, diseases of malnutrition, ghetto epidemics arising as a consequence of the occupier's policies, and related suicides. Jewish victimization is measured by the percentage Jewish victims constituted of all Jews (ranked by decile classes). Whenever possible, actual numbers based on racial registrations, government records, or transport lists were used for the computation of victims. When these were lacking—as in the zone of extermination—the deficit method, or the difference between Jews alive in 1941 and recorded in 1945, was used, deducting estimated combat deaths of Jews in the military, civilian casualties from Allied bombardment, and partisan casualties from Jewish victims.

Jewish evaders are constituted by deducting Jewish victims and Jews exempted from deportation from the total number of Jews registered: 100% − % victims − % exemptees = % evaders. Exemptees might include Christians of Jewish origin classified as Jews by racial codes and/or Jews with a Christian spouse. Where figures on exemptees were not available, these were estimated from prewar figures on intermarriage. Evaders were estimated as an alternate negative measure of victims in order to assess whether there were substantive differences between both rankings that could be attributed to differing proportions of exemptees in different Jewish communities. There were no substantive differences between these orders. The rankings of victims and evaders are inversely correlated almost perfectly ($r = - .993$). Evaders rather than victims are discussed whenever this is more plausible contextually. Evaders are ranked within 5 percent intervals (1 = 0 − 5% evaders; 20 = 95 − 100% evaders).

The intensity of German control was indexed for German access to direct means of control over Jews (arms zone) and for control over all natives (Nazi zone). Three Nazi zones were condensed from the five arms zones discriminated (see Table 2-1) and ranked on a Guttman-type scale, discriminating to what extent states possessed the bases of autonomy and were incorporated within or by the German state.[16] The limits upon German control over Jews and the protection of rights of all natives depended upon the state's independence and freedom from SS domination (the ultimate stage of Nazi control). The SS (including the Gestapo) was the functional agency with broadest responsibility for internal security, political repression, and extermination of the Jews. For analytical purposes, we focus on the three Nazi zones rather than the five arms zones.

The physical distribution of modes of German control over European states during World War II is shown in Map 2-1.

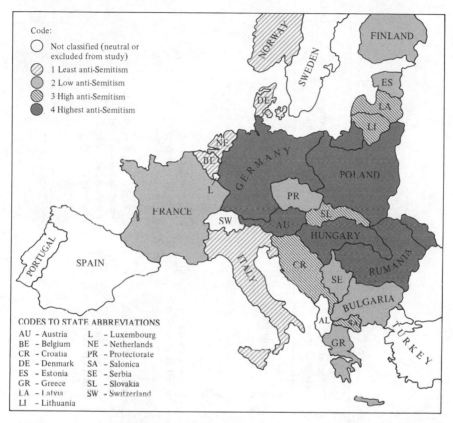

Code:

- ○ Not classified (neutral or excluded from study)
- ◐ 1 Least anti-Semitism
- ◑ 2 Low anti-Semitism
- ◍ 3 High anti-Semitism
- ● 4 Highest anti-Semitism

CODES TO STATE ABBREVIATIONS

AU – Austria	L – Luxembourg
BE – Belgium	NE – Netherlands
CR – Croatia	PR – Protectorate
DE – Denmark	SA – Salonica
ES – Estonia	SE – Serbia
GR – Greece	SL – Slovakia
LA – Latvia	SW – Switzerland
LI – Lithuania	

MAP 2-1. Intensity of German Control over European States at Time Deportation of Jews or Direct Physical Extermination Began

Note: Dates indicate the beginning of deportation or extermination; dates in parentheses indicate a less general, or localized, deportation or massacre; asterisks identify states in which direct extermination took place.

One may ask how these zones relate to the prewar states. States in the colonial zone (I) are states or quasi-states in Weber's terms—organizations claiming command of all native police power within the state.[17] None had governments-in-exile as did all states in the command zone (II). The latter states retained their prewar territorial integrity and were administered by the prewar bureaucracy (later often replaced by native collaborators) under German military commanders, or *Reichskommissars*. No plans were implemented to incorporate them into the Reich. The SS zone (III) includes the

TABLE 2-1. Bases and Attributes of German Control in Different Zones during World War II

I–III: Nazi Zone *1–5: Arms Zone*	*State's Political Status and Organization*	*Observable Attributes of German Power*	*Attributes Observed in Each Arms Zone:*			
			b	*c*	*d*	*e*
1. Colonial						
1. Instigation –Bulgaria, Croatia, Finland, Rumania, Slovakia	Ally or self-governing satellite	a. Diplomatic persuasion	0	0	0	0
2. Manipulation –France, Hungary 1944	Colony or neutral with self-government	b. Occupation or threat of take-over by German troops	+	0	0	0
II. Command						
3. Command –Belgium, Denmark 1943, Salonica 1941,	Defeated enemy with no responsible government but has prewar bureaucracy	c. Right to authorize deportations and right to command native bureaucracy	+	+	0	0

TABLE 2-1. (Cont.)

I–III: Nazi Zone 1–5: Arms Zone	State's Political Status and Organization	Observable Attributes of German Power	Attributes Observed in Each Arms Zone:			
			b	c	d	e
Athens 1943, Italy 1943, The Netherlands, Norway						
III. SS						
4. Domination —Germany, Austria, Protectorate	Greater German Reich	d. Ability to execute commands through German bureaucracy predominantly and high, constant, and early Gestapo sanctions against infractions	+	+	+	0
5. Extermination —Estonia, Latvia, Lithuania, Poland, Serbia	Defeated enemy; no responsible government nor prewar bureaucracy	e. German toleration of visible extermination of Jews by Germans or natives	+	+	+	+

NOTE: In cases of states whose relation to Germany changed — Italy, Hungary, Denmark, Greece — the state or region is classed by its last political status during the war or the status that it enjoyed when deportations began.

41

Greater German Reich, Serbia, and the incorporated occupied lands of the East. The Germans intended to depopulate, degrade, and restratify the population of the latter, destroying the native intelligentsia while they colonized these lands.[18] In the SS zone outside the Reich, there was little inhibition about shooting or flogging natives or capturing them for involuntary servitude in the Reich. The death penalty was affixed to numerous regulations, including aid to the Jews. Generally, the radius of terror expands as one goes from the colonial zone to the SS zone, but there are exceptions provoked by greater internal resistance in some countries than in others. Armed resistance was more likely to instigate German retaliation—usually as collective punishment or terror—than nonviolent resistance or nonresistance.

National solidarity may be conceived of as the attraction drawing citizens to identify with each other within a common national universe of obligation. This is an intuitive concept and perception of how community and nation are integrated but not an operational definition. Eckstein, studying democracy in Norway, found such solidarity exhibited by the Norwegians' sense of "we-ness" and highly developed reciprocal obligations toward each other stemming from identification of all with the community.[19] But bonds, obligations, and trust are not readily observed for a multinational comparison. One might postulate that national solidarity would parallel a nation's successful, continuous, nonviolent political experience with inclusive and representative government as an autonomous entity relative to the underlying sources of segmental cleavage, as it seems to do in Norway. Therefore, solidarity was defined as a function of the strength of inclusive bonds created by successful nonviolent national experience in proportion to the number of sources of segmental cleavage: $S = E_{nv}:C_n$. Each term of this equation was first ranked separately for all states. The first term, E_{nv}, was indexed by evaluating the length of representative government up to 1938 as a proportion of all the years since the nation's emergence (or resurrection) as an independent state, the stability of that government, and the presence or absence of regression in representation in the interwar years. Each component of this index was defined operationally by time-series political data collected by Banks.[20] Lines of segmental cleavage existent between 1930 and 1938 include major political parties organized on a particularistic (religious, ethnic, or regional) base,[21] popular radical right movements not competing in elections that threatened the state, and facist and communist parties gathering more than 12% of the vote in a general election and/or similar movement banned from electoral competition. The initial rank of each nation and a brief description of each class are shown in Table 2-2. One may observe how highly related rank is to the actual age of nation-states as autonomous entities: all states that emerged in the interwar period except Finland and those arising from the earlier breakdown of the Ottoman Empire fell in the lowest rank, while all arising before 1815 were ranked higher. The solidarity rank was later bisected in the regression analysis, so that more solidary states (1, 2, or 3) were compared with less solidary states (0).

TABLE 2-2.   Characteristics of Political Experience and Contemporary Partisan Cleavages in European States in the 1930s, Ranked by Solidarity

Rank	Characteristics of National-Experience to 1938	Nation-States (year of modern origin as an autonomous state)
3	Highly representative and stable for the great majority of years without interwar regression with no segmental cleavage	Norway (1905), Denmark (pre-1815)
2	Highly representative and stable, no interwar regression but party structure or significant regional movement based on segmenting cleavage	Belgium (1830), Netherlands (pre-1815)
1	Highly representative but less stable, threat of interwar regression, intense partisan cleavage associated with civil violence	France (pre-1815), Finland (1919)
0 = less than 1	Highly representative and stable for majority of years with many reinforcing sources of segmental cleavage	Czechoslovakia (1918)
	Neither representative nor stable for the majority of years and regression in interwar years and intense partisan cleavage and/or segmental ethnic/ regional cleavage	Austria (1918), Bulgaria (1878), Estonia (1919), Germany (1865), Greece (1830), Hungary (1919), Italy (1861), Latvia (1919), Lithuania (1919), Poland (1919), Rumania (1859), Yugoslavia (1919)

Anti-Semitism was also indexed on a Guttman-type scale (later bisected) of its progress from 1930 to 1936 on a natural history trajectory (later discussed) from the appearance of any movement to the institutionalization of its goals through legislation. Component factors include the breadth or strength of the constituency of the anti-Semitic party,[22] escalation from propaganda to symbolic attacks to mass violence, immediacy and consistency of the state's response to anti-Jewish attacks, and its success, registered by de facto or de jure state incorporation of goals of anti-Semitic movements or parties.[23] Table 2-3 shows the characteristics of each rank and the rankings of states in existence in 1941 by the success of the anti-Semitic movement or parties in that state or region in 1936. In most cases, all the states in each class exhibit all signs enumerated, but there are a few cases where a state exhibits one indication of a more developed anti-Semitic movement but not another, as in Croatia, where prewar attacks against Jews were not recorded. Map 2-2 shows the geographic distribution of political anti-Semitism in Europe by 1936.

Cooperation and resistance were assessed by actions of national

TABLE 2-3. Success of Anti-Semitic Movements up to 1936 in States Occupied by and/or Allied with Germany during the Holocaust

Success of Anti-Semitic Movement by 1936	States	Most Important Anti-Semitic Movements and/or Parties	Sources (see Bibliography for full reference)
4 Highest—governing party incorporates movement's goals enacting discriminatory legislation and/or judicial, legislative, or diplomatic attempt to deprive Jews of citizenship	Rumania	Iron Guard, National Christian Party	Vago, 1974, Sylvain, Starr
	Hungary	Party of Hungarian Life, Arrow Cross	Vago, 1974, Nagy-Talavera
	Austria	Fatherland Front	Fraenkel, AJYB
	Germany	Nazi Party (NSDAP)	Hilberg
	Poland	Sanacja; Endecja	Wynot, Johnpoll
3 High—major party or movement avows anti-semitic or exclusive nationalist goals and de facto quotas, state discrimination, and/or slow police response to physical attacks against Jews alleged	Croatia	Ustase, Catholic Action	AJC, Freidenreich, Hoetl, Yugoslavia, Embassy Rotkirchen, 1968
	Slovakia	Slovak People's Party	AJYB, UJE, Molho, Stavrianos
	Salonica	EEE	
	Latvia	Perkonkrust	Royal Institute, AJYB
	Lithuania	Iron Wolf	Royal Institute, Baltramaitis, AJYB

TABLE 2–3. (Cont.)

Success of Anti-Semitic Movement by 1936	States	Most Important Anti-Semitic Movements and/or Parties	Sources (see Bibliography for full reference)
2 Intermediate—Party or movement avows anti-Semitic or exclusive national goals: threatens coup, challenges public order, and/or instigates symbolic attacks on synagogues or prominent Jews—government commitment to preserve the civil rights of Jews expressed	Bulgaria	Ratnitsi	Chary, AJYB
	Finland	Lapua Party, IKL	Upton
	France	Action Française	Weber
	Athens	EEE	AJYB, UJE, Stavrianos
	Serbia	Zbor	AJYB, Freidenreich
	Protectorate	German students and anti-German movement	AJYB
	Estonia	Front Soldiers League	Royal Institute, UJE
1 Low—Minor anti-Semitic party obtaining 12% or less of the vote (when on ballot) whose acts are restricted to constitutional means (verbal propaganda only) with government commitment to preserve civil rights of Jews	Belgium	Rex Party, DINASO, VNV	AJYB, Clough, Hilaire, Yahil
	Denmark	Danish Nazi Party (DSNAP)	
	Italy	Farinacci faction of Fascists	Fonari
	Netherlands	Dutch Nazi Party (NSB)	Warmbrunn
	Norway	Nasjonal Samling	Hayes

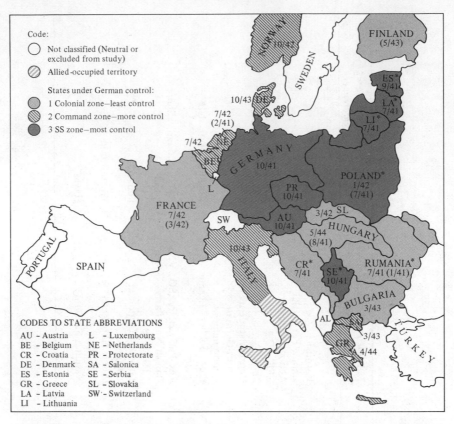

MAP 2–2. Development of Political Anti-Semitism up to 1936 in European States Occupied by and/or Allied with Germany during the Holocaust.

Note: Borders shown are as in 1941.

authorities and counterauthorities: the state, church, and resistance movements. State cooperation was observed from state officials' participation in extermination, agreements negotiated, regulations enacted, and consistency of enforcement of measures to define, segregate, concentrate, and/or deport Jews. Popular collaboration was indicated by whether natives were organized to kill Jews directly or to identify them.

Since the church is the institution claiming the monopoly of moral sanctions, the acts of its leaders should be sources of public definition of the situation and emergent norms in time of crisis. The resistance of the dominant church—the church or sect of the majority—was indexed by the public or private categorical protest by its highest prelate(s) on *behalf of all Jews* expressed in order to prevent deportation during the first six months of deportation or before half had been seized. The presence or absence of earlier church protest against anti-Jewish discrimination was also scored. The orientation of the major resistance movement(s) was ranked by the extent of public identification with Jews: were they accepted as members, was the major movement(s) publicly identified as against their discrimination by propaganda of word or deed, and did the movement mobilize its resources to help Jews evade deportation or notify them of impending raids? Those states in which the major movement identified publicly with Jews and/or mobilized to help them were later ranked as positive. Where one division of a movement identified publicly with Jews and another division identified against them and justified anti-Jewish violence—as in Poland—the movement was not ranked as having a positive slant toward Jews. Where there were two or more unintegrated or rival movements with different records and one had a greater constituency or controlled a larger liberated region (as in Yugoslavia and Greece), the record of the stronger movement was classified.

During the course of research, I identified what is later referred to as a Jewish social defense movement that was most developed in regions where there were significant percentages of evaders. These were movements intended to prevent deportations by instigating domestic or foreign pressure and/or aiding Jews *categorically* to avoid seizure and deportations by public warning, locating hideouts, guiding them in escapes, providing false papers and financial aid, and by other means that helped evaders without increasing the probability of other Jews' being caught. (This emphasis on categorical need distinguishes such movements from national and international efforts to aid special elites among Jews such as physicists, rabbis, Nobel Prize winners, young Zionist pioneers.) I am including movements using conventional political means—threat, exchange, and appeal—and movements creating counterinstitutions to render the official institutions powerless. The former could work in the colonial zone only, in which Germany needed the states' agreement and police power to deport its Jews.

Such movements were first ranked by their scope or maximum number of potential beneficiaries—that is, the percentage of Jews alive and free within the areas in which recorded testimonies indicate they operated. This yielded a crude interval scale (4 = 75 100%; the movement was established throughout the region where three-fourths or more of the nation's Jews lived before deportations began there). This may have discriminated against states in which such movements have been less well documented and Jews were more dispersed or social defense less centralized. Later, social defense movements were reranked (and scored herein) on the basis of immediacy (percent of Jews alive and free in that state when any recorded social defense movement began operations).[24]

All Jewish social defense movements required the cooperation of Christians to succeed: some were initiated by Christians, others by Jews, and still others arose from an organization in which both were integrated. The movement is defined by its objective. Discussion of Jewish social defense—that is, resistance movements seeking to save Jews—ought not to be confused with previous discussions of Jewish resistance — armed resistance in ghettos or forests — or with Jewish participation in national resistance movements.

Virtually all activities of such social defense movements were nonviolent, although not inspired by a philosophy of nonviolence. No attempt has been made to evaluate Jewish armed resistance in the ghettos as it relates to Jewish victimization, as it is not plausible to expect (from theory or experience) that armed resistance and confrontation would increase the chance for evasion, which was the most general strategy of social defense movements in occupied nations.

All variables indexed are listed below. Some were devised to test hypotheses either implicit in previous controversies on the history of the Holocaust or superficially plausible. Those previously discussed are indicated with an asterisk. The original base of ranking is given here: later, the rankings of some were transformed to sum subclasses of a variable and/or to transform non-interval-level variables to dummy variables suitable for correlation and regression analysis. The basis for ranking all variables not discussed in this chapter and subsequent transformations of variables are indicated in the codebook (Appendix A).

Prewar demographic characteristics of Jews: size of Jewish population (after occupation and/or termination or emigration); maximal visibility (percent of population in city with largest number of Jews); relative size (percent constituted of total population); strangers (percent of Jews within nations' borders not possessing citizenship); strangers' visibility (ranked by whether inside or outside prewar borders); spread of Jews (total number of cities within which two-thirds of Jews lived at most recent census date); concentration index (for Jewish populations over 100,000 spread in more than one city, concentration index = spread/size).

Prewar characteristics of nation-state (or region that is unit of analysis): state age (since 1830); dominant church (Roman Catholic or non–Roman Catholic); solidarity;* success of anti-Semitic movement by 1936.*

German control and time contingencies: arms zone,* Nazi zone,* duration (number of months state was in zone in which threat of deportation began), task time (duration/size), preparation time (number of months in zone in which threat began preceding deportation or direct extermination attempt), warning time or degree of awareness of goal of extermination: no warning = 0; rumor = 1; official information (BBC broadcast of June–July 1942) = 2; authoritative definition of the situation (Allied declaration of 17 December 1942, labeling extermination of Jews as a crime) = 3.

Native government's response: satellite obligations (ranking of rewards received by satellites from Germany based on the assumption that obligations correspond to rewards); satellite collaboration (ranking 0 to 2 = none to high); official collaboration (ranking 0 to 2); police cooperation (ranking 0 to 2); rank of state cooperation (ranking among all states in the same control zone only upon all measures applicable to all states in zone, rank 0 to 2);

popular collaboration (visibility of organized movements to apprehend Jews [1] and/or kill Jews directly [2]).

Jewish response as reactors and innovators: Jewish isolation (number of stages of processing undergone before deportation threat [0-5]); *Judenrat* (presence or absence of imposed Jewish administrative agent(s) responsible to German authority); Jewish control agent (presence of *Judenrat* or other Jewish agent responsible to government bureau or police); Jewish cooperation during deportations ranked [0], [1], [2]; none or some Jewish representatives' pleas for aid [0], [1].

Native authorities' response to occupation, discrimination against, and deportation of Jews: resistance integration (interval ranks corresponding to length of time before principal resistance organizations' integration, [0-4]; national unity, 0-2 (none [0], integration [1] and maintenance of counter-authority from occupation to liberation [2]); dominant church's protest against deportation;* dominant church's protest against discrimination;* movement identification;* Jewish social defense movement.*

Facilities and opportunities: open exits (product of probability of successful evasion of ghetto, border, and foreign doorkeepers multiplied by attraction of bordering neutral nations offering sanctuary to evaders); it should be noted that, although this is the most mathematically sophisticated scale and most objectifiable, it is probably least reliable because it is compounded of indices based on multiple assumptions, some of which cannot be corroborated, such as the vigilance of certain foreign doorkeepers (border guards, internal security agents) in instances where policy was not explicit or actual practices diverged from the stated policy. (The formula for this is shown in Appendix A.) Havens indicates the probability of hiding in temporarily viable internal sanctuaries and is computed by summing the probabilities of finding one or another sanctuary; sanctuaries include free zones, those liberated by partisans, and regions nominally controlled by foreign states or churches in which persons are immune from search and seizure.

3

The Bonds That Hold,
The Bonds That Break

Causes of National Differences
in Jewish Victimization

Why did so many Jews become victims? Where were they most likely to become victims? In this chapter, we will focus on the leading questions implicit in the hypotheses so far advanced and survey other explanations that are superficially plausible. To enable the reader to grasp the logic of findings, I shall indicate approximately how closely the factors in question are related to Jewish victimization in terms understandable to most persons.* Statistical analyses and the matrix of zero-order correlation supporting them are in Appendix B.

EXPLANATIONS FOUND WANTING

One might ask: *Does the proportion of Jews who became victims vary among the different zones of German control? Does the intensity of German control alone account for differences in the likelihood of becoming a victim?*

*The extent of linear relation is indicated by the Pearson product-moment correlation. The product-moment correlation varies from 0 to +1 or −1. If outcome B were completely predictable by factor A preceding it, B increasing as A enlarges, B and A should be perfectly correlated ($r = 1.0$). If B regularly became smaller as A grew larger (or vice versa), A and B would be inversely or negatively related ($r = -1.0$). One might infer in these cases that A causes B, although other inferences are also possible. A common factor may account for both A and B simultaneously, for example. In the social world, few correlations are perfect. For a convention, I will say that two variables are very highly related if the correlation between them is over .80, highly related if it is .65 to .79, related if it is .40 to .64, and weakly related if under .40. If a negative relation is not specified, it is assumed they are positively related.

How was the extent of Jews' losses related to their prewar distribution? What other aspects of German control or contingencies could explain it? Table 3-1 shows the numbers, distribution, and characteristics of Jews and the rank of Jewish victims and evaders in each state or region in all zones. The numbers and relative proportions of Jewish victims and evaders in different states are illustrated visually in Map 3-1. It is immediately apparent (Table 3-1, Col. B) that almost two out of three Jews in continental Europe outside the Soviet Union (apart from Jews in Luxembourg, the few states excluded, and the neutrals) lived in the SS zone, and the overwhelming majority of them in the zone of extermination: 53% were in Poland alone. Apart from Yugoslavia, all the states in this zone were in the region designated for future German *Lebensraum,* and their inhabitants' interests and right to life, liberty, and property were decreed to be disposable. Fewer than 6% lived in the com-

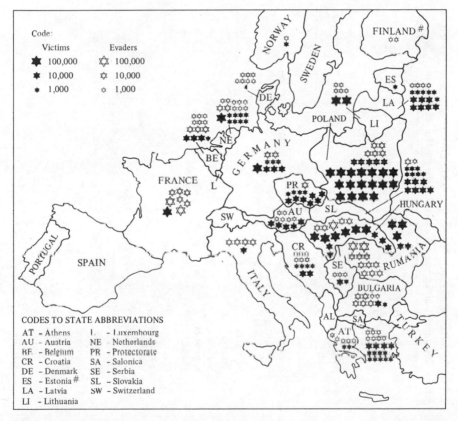

MAP 3-1. Jewish Victims and Evaders in European States during the Holocaust*

*Excluding the Soviet Union, part of Poland ceded to the Soviet Union (1945), Luxembourg, and other smaller states not included in this study.

TABLE 3-1. Characteristics of Jewish Population and Jewish Victims and Evaders in European States, by Zone of German Control during the Holocaust*

Nazi Zone Arms Zone	Jewish Population, 1941		Prewar Jewish Population		Rank	
	Size (in 100,000s) A	As % of all Jews in Table B	Maximum Visibility (% highest city) C	% Nation's Populace D	Jewish Victims (Max. = Rank × 10%) E	Jewish Evaders (Max. = Rank × 5%) F
I. Colonial	[19.74]	[31.3]				
1. Zone of instigation Subtotal	(7.99)	(12.7)				
Bulgaria	.63	1.0	10	.7	2	16
Croatia	.30	.5	5	.4	8	4
Finland	.02	.0†	1	.1	1	20
Rumania	6.15	9.8	12	3.6	6	8
Slovakia	.89	1.4	11	3.4	9	2
2. Zone of manipulation Subtotal	(11.75)	(18.6)				
France	3.50	5.5	6	.8	3	14
Hungary	8.25	13.1	16	5.6	8	4
II. Command	[3.44]	[5.5]				
3. Zone of command Subtotal	(3.44)	(5.4)				
Belgium	.67	1.1	18	.8	5	9

TABLE 3–1. (Cont.)

Denmark	.08	.1	1	.2	1	18
Greece	(.72)	(1.1)	23	1.0	8	4
Athens	.04	.1	1	1.0	3	13
Salonica	.56	.9	23	1.0	9	1
Italy	.55	.9	1	.1	2	16
Netherlands	1.40	2.2	8	1.6	8	3
Norway	.02	.0†	1	.1	5	11
III. SS	[39.84]	[63.2]				
4. Zone of domination						
Subtotal	(3.09)	(4.9)				
Austria	.56	.9	9	.8	9	1
Germany	1.64	2.6	4	.3	9	1
Protectorate	.89	1.4	4	1.2	9	1
5. Zone of extermination						
Subtotal	(36.75)	(58.3)				
Estonia	.01	.0†	2	.1	10	1
Latvia	.80	1.3	11	4.1	10	1
Lithuania	2.30	3.6	27	9.4	10	1
Poland	33.50	53.2	30	9.5	10	1
Serbia	.14	.2	3	.3	8	4
Total	63.02	100.0				

*Includes all states in continental Europe occupied by or allied with Germany except the Soviet Union, Luxembourg, and other smaller states not included in this study.

†Less than .05%.

53

Jewish population in 1941 was taken from the actual number of persons enumerated in racial registrations in Bulgaria, Slovakia, Hungary, Belgium, Italy, the Netherlands, Austria, Germany, and the Protectorate, as reported in the sources cited below for each nation. Prewar census figures for 1939–1940 or estimates based on community registers were available for Croatia, Rumania, Greece, and Serbia. The *Encyclopedia Judaica* estimate of Jewish population in Norway and Finland was accepted, as was Leni Yahil's estimate of the Jews of Denmark, based on both prewar studies and conforming to the aggregate of victims and refugees (reported by Yahil in *The Rescue of Danish Jewry: Test of a Democracy* [Philadelphia: Jewish Publication Society of America, 1969]). Dov Levin of the Hebrew University's Institute of Contemporary Jewry was able to estimate the probable number of Jews resident in the Baltic states after Soviet deportations preceding the German invasion of June 1941; his estimate is consistent with German sources for this period. The estimate for France is my own, based on the reported figures for the French census of 1941 in both zones, for which discrepant figures have been cited by Xosa Szajkowski in *Analytical Franco-Jewish Gazetteer* (New York: Frydmann, 1966), Michel Roblin in *Les Juifs de Paris* (Paris: Picardetcie, 1952), and J. Billig in *Le Commissariat Général aux Questions Juives*, II (Paris: Éditions du Centre, 1958). My estimate is based on a total of 320,000 persons recorded (spouses and minors recorded on the registrant's form) and 30,000 Jews probably already interned by November 1941. A precise account of this calculation is available upon request.

The percent that Jews constitute of the population in the city with the greatest number of Jews (maximum visibility) was taken from the *American Jewish Yearbook, 1941–42* (New York: American Jewish Committee, 1942), except in instances where the national sources cited enumerated more current figures. The nation's population within wartime borders was extracted from the *Statistical Yearbook of the League of Nations, 1941–42* (Geneva, 1943), except for Poland, where both the Jewish population and total population cited are as of 1 September 1939, as estimated by Poland's government-in-exile in the *Concise Statistical Yearbook of Poland, September 1939–June 1941* (London, 1941).

The decile rank of victims was computed from actual figures recorded of persons transported plus those dying indirectly that are cited in the works following, except for states in the "zone of extermination" where calculations were usually based on the demographic deficit between Jewish population recorded as alive in June 1941 and after liberation in 1945. Dov Levin's estimate of victims was accepted for the Baltic states: this is consistent with all recorded lists for survivors in particular cities in that region—however, no national registration was then taken there since Jews had been annihilated in the countryside in 1941. In computing the percentage of victims, it has been assumed that there would have been zero population growth among Jews during the war: that is, the number of natural deaths would be equaled by the number of births. For the Reich itself, this assumption was not tenable because of the age structure of the population. Therefore, the number of Jewish victims in Germany, Austria, and the Protectorate of Bohemia-Moravia was divided by the sum of victims plus exemptees plus Jews in hiding, excluding those cited officially as having died "natural" deaths outside any camp. This raises the percentage of victims about 5% but it did not change the decile rank in any case, so it made no difference in the analysis. Following are the sources for the victimization estimate for each state:

Belgium—Israel Schirman, "La Politique Allemande à l'Égard des Juifs en Belgique, 1940–44" Ph.D. dissertation, Université Libre de Bruxelles, 1970–1971).

Bulgaria—See Frederick Barry Chary's *The Bulgarian Jews and the Final Solution, 1940–1944* (Pittsburgh: University of Pittsburgh Press, 1972).

Croatia—See the explanation for Yugoslavia.

Finland—The Finnish magazine *Uusi Maailma* on 23 October 1964 published the names of eight non-Finnish Jews who had taken refuge in Finland but were deported during the war. See Chapter 3, note 1.

France—See France's Service d'Information des Crimes de Guerre, *La Persécution Raciale* (Paris, c. 1947), and Lucien Steinberg's *Les Authorités Allemandes en France* (Paris: Census, 1966).

Greece—See Michael Molho's *In Memoriam: Hommage aux Victimes Juives des Nazis en Grèce*, 2d ed., rev. by Joseph Nehama (Salonica: Communauté Isráelite de Thessalonique, 1973), and L. S. Stavrianos, "The Jews in Greece," *Journal of Central European Affairs* VII (October 1948), 265–269. Molho's figures (p. 326) on 1940 population and deportees needed some revision to be consistent with the numbers cited in the text itself: Molho particularly failed to account for the out-migration from Salonica and the in-migration of Jews to Athens in 1943.

Hungary—See the World Jewish Congress figures reprinted in Randolph L. Braham's *The Destruction of Hungarian Jewry: A Documentary Account* (New York: World Federation of Hungarian Jews, 1963) and E. Laszlo's "Hungary's Jewry: A Demographic Overview, 1918-1945," *Hungarian-Jewish Studies* II (1969), 137-182. WJC figures were adjusted to deduct Jewish laborers forcibly deported to the Soviet Union after the war, accepting the estimate of Eugene Duschinsky, cited in "Hungary," *Jews in the Soviet Satellites*, by Peter Meyer et al. (Syracuse: Syracuse University Press, 1953).

Italy—See Renzo de Felice, *Storia degli Ebrei Italiani sotto il Fascismo*, 3d ed. (Turin: Einaudi, 1972). For more recent research findings (not yet published) on Jewish victims and population in occupied Italy in 1943 I am indebted to Dr. Giuliana Donati and Dr. Liliana Picciotto Fargion of the Centro di Documentazione Ebraica Contemporanea in Milan. Their data alter the numbers involved but not the rank of Jewish victims calculated from de Felice.

Netherlands—All figures used were based on correspondence with Professor Louis de Jong, Director of the Netherlands State Institute of War Documentation.

Norway—Figures on deportees and other Jewish wartime deaths are based on Norwegian government lists found in Yad Vashem archives; I am indebted to Samuel Abrahamsen, chairman of the Judaic Studies Department of Brooklyn College, for giving me a copy of these lists.

The German Reich:

Austria—See Herbert Rosenkranz, "The Anschluss and the Tragedy of Austrian Jewry, 1938 1945," in *The Jews of Austria: Essays on Their Life, History, and Destruction*, ed. Josef Fraenkel (London: Valentine, Mitchell, 1967).

Germany—See Bruno Blau's "German Jewry's Fate in Figures," *Wiener Library Bulletin* VI:3-4 (August 1952), 25, and "The Last Days of German Jewry in the Third Reich," *YIVO Annual of Jewish Social Science* VIII (1953), 197-204.

Protectorate of Bohemia-Moravia—See Peter Meyer, "Czechoslovakia," in Meyer et al., *Jews in the Soviet Satellites*.

Rumania—See "Rumania," *Encyclopedia Judaica*, XIV, and Julius S. Fisher, *Transnistria: the Forgotten Cemetery* (South Brunswick: Yoseloff, 1968).

The following estimates are based on the demographic deficit:

Poland—My estimate for Poland is based on a systematic sample study supervised by Judy Bloom. Assistants indexed every sixth name and prewar residence of the registrant, collating cards for 1,680 names listed on pages randomly selected from the *Register of Jewish Survivors*, II: *List of Jews in Poland* (Jerusalem: Jewish Agency for Palestine, 1945) and the *Surviving Jews in Warsaw as of June 5th, 1945* (New York: World Jewish Congress, n.d.) (not included in the former register). These registers list 60,248 names. L. Dobroszycki (YIVO) helped me locate place names not found on maps and street names in Warsaw. It was found that 86% of the registrants sampled recorded prewar addresses in that part of Poland occupied in September 1939. The total number of Jewish registrations in Poland after the war (60,248) was multiplied by the percentage of the sample citing residence before the war in Poland (86%) in order to estimate the number of Jews alive in postwar Poland in 1945 who had resided there in 1939, assuming the sample to be representative of the population. This estimated number of Jews recorded alive there in 1945 was divided by the number of Jews who lived there in 1939, as estimated by the Polish government-in-exile, *Statistical Yearbook*, after deducting from the prewar estimate those Jews believed to have fled to the USSR or enlisted in the Polish Army. See P. Glickson, "Jewish Population in the Polish People's Republic, 1944-1972" (address presented to the Sixth World Congress of Jewish Studies, Jerusalem, 1973). From this calculation, it was found that only 2.5% of the Jewish population of 1939 was alive and registered in Poland in 1945. No basis has been found for estimating Jewish survivors in that part of Poland invaded in June 1941 and later ceded to the USSR.

Yugoslavia—Survivors were enumerated in Croatia and Serbia from lists of voluntary registrants gathered by the Union of Jewish Communities in 1946 and forwarded to the International Tracing Service in Arolsen, West Germany; the ITS forwarded copies of these lists to me. The prewar population is based on the addition of figures for each city and town in Croatia and Serbia for 1940 as reported in *Spomenica, 1919-1969* (Belgrade: Savez Jevrejskih Opstina Jugoslavije, 1969), an official publication of the Union; I am indebted to Mile Weiss, president of the Association of Yugoslav Jews in the United States, for this source. Harriet Freidenreich (Temple University) independently categorized the region in which each Jewish community was located during the war, enabling me to recheck my earlier estimate. Both computations led to the finding that 18% of the number of Jews registered in Serbia in 1940 were registered in 1946 and 17% of the 1940 number in Croatia were also registered in 1946. There are two reasons to expect that the actual percentage of Jews victimized as Jews should be no more than 80% (or below) if the demographic deficit is 82%. First, some of the deficit must be attributed to war losses and partisan casualties. Second, the large difference between the number recorded on the 1946 list (I counted 10,997 while the ITS cited 11,002) and the 14,000 subsequently reported by the community in 1947 (see the *Encyclopedia Judaica*, XVI) indicate that this was not a comprehensive registration. It must be recalled that prewar registration was legally mandated, the community having been granted the right to tax by the government, while postwar registration was voluntary.

------

mand zone but almost one-third (almost two million Jews) lived in the colonial zone.

The range of victims (col. E) in the colonial zone—from .5 to 85%—reflects the fact that deportation was an option requiring state authorization and state police power. Denmark and Italy—German-occupied states that were formerly in the colonial zone—produced no victims earlier because they never authorized deportations. Finland also never made an agreement to deport its Jews: five Jewish prisoners of non-Finnish nationality were handed over by a pro-Nazi police chief to German police on a ship bound for Germany before the cabinet became aware of this arrangement and deterred further extraditions.[1] Other states in the colonial zone — Bulgaria, France, and Rumania—failed to fulfill commitments they had made to pass or execute regulations authorizing the deportation of Jewish nationals. No reprisal was taken against any state in this zone just for its refusal or failure to deport its Jews.

Although there is a similar range in the rank of victims in the command zone, states in this zone did not have the choice of whether to deport their Jews. Deportations occurred despite the official refusal of police collaboration in Denmark and Belgium and despite evidence of unofficial noncooperation in Italy and Athens.

Among states in the SS zone there is a narrower range of victims. Focusing on Jewish evaders (col. F) rather than on victims, we find that fewer than one in 20 Jews actually evaded becoming a victim in all these states except Serbia. Jewish victimization is lower in all countries of the Reich than in other states within the SS zone (except Serbia) because some categories of half-Jews and Jews married to Christians were exempted from deportation in the Reich, but none labeled as Jews were exempted in these other states of the SS zone. Within the Reich, the Germans were inhibited from destroying those tied by blood to other Germans to whom they owed obligations, thus decreasing the percentage of Jewish victims. But Jews not bonded by kinship did not have any greater chance of evading incarceration there than in Poland.

There is a wide range of variation among states in the same zone at the time of deportation, except in the SS zone. The rank of victims is not explained any better by relating it to any single quantitative aspect of German control alone: the duration of German occupation, task time (duration in proportion to the number of victims), or preparation time (see Table B-1, Appendix B). Jewish victimization is positively related (but not highly) to the duration of occupation and very weakly related to the amount of German preparation time; there is a negative but weak relationship with task time.[2]

One contingency alone, the timing of threat, is highly related to the rank of victims. (Warning time is indexed by the degree of official [public] confirmation that reporting for collection/resettlement/deportation led toward the murder of the Jews. This information was spread by Allied news and warnings [see Figure 3-1], which confirmed rumors.) Comparing averages (means), the more warning time there was, the fewer victims there were. But there is great variation except in the states with least warning time. How do warning time and German control account for the rank of victims? Figure 3-1 shows the bearing of both on Jewish victimization.

The Jews of states within the SS zone had least warning time. But although we can expect lack of warning time to lead to high victimization, we find that ample warning time alone does not prevent high victimization, as in the cases of Salonica and Hungary. So neither German control nor German control and warning time together can explain the magnitude of Jewish victimization.

German control and initiation of deportations in Greece were postponed because most of Greece was in the occupational zone of Italy until 1943. The Italian-occupied section of prewar Croatia along the Dalmatian coast also provided a haven for Jews fleeing from deportation although Italy did not intervene to halt the ongoing extermination in Croatia.[3] However, the Italian military occupiers of southern Greece and the Maritime Alps in France prevented German troops and French police (in France) from arresting Jews there.[4] More Jews who flocked to the Italian zone in France could have been saved in 1943 if General Eisenhower, the Supreme Allied Commander, had not prematurely announced Italy's defection (without informing the Italians), thus triggering the German invasion of Italy and Italian-occupied areas. The hasty retreat of the Italian military prevented execution of plans of Delasem, an Italian Jewish refugee welfare organization, which had obtained cooperation of the Badoglio government in transporting the Jews from Italian-occupied France to the liberated zones in North Africa where they would have been immune to seizure.[5]

Holding warning time constant, Jews had a much greater chance—ranging from 4 to 25 times—of being caught in some states than in others. If we compare states within the SS zone in which extermination began in 1941, the actual ratio of percentages of Jews surviving in Serbia and Poland is 6.8:1 and the ratio of percentages of real evaders estimated is 25:1 despite the fact that a German expert on the scene declared Serbia the " 'only country in which Jewish question and Gypsy question [were] solved' " fully two years before the last ghetto was cleared in Poland.[6] Among occupied states in

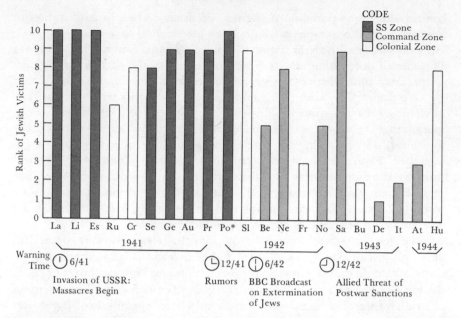

FIGURE 3–1.   Jewish Victims in European States by Nazi Zone and Maximum Warning Time before Deportations†

At–Athens	De–Denmark	Ge–Germany	No–Norway	Pr–Protectorate
Au–Austria	Es–Estonia	Hu–Hungary	La–Latvia	Ru–Rumania
Be–Belgium	Fi–Finland	It–Italy	Li–Lithuania	Sa–Salonica
Bu–Bulgaria	Fr–France	Ne–Netherlands	Po–Poland	Se–Serbia
Cr–Croatia				Sl–Slovakia

*Direct extermination began in Poland at the time of the invasion of the Soviet Union, as Jews in Soviet-occupied Poland were massacred by the Einsatzgruppen. Deportations from the Warthe-land (German-annexed territory of western Poland) began in December 1941, and deportations from the General-Government began in February 1942. As our victimization and prewar population estimates for Poland are based largely upon the territory of the General-Government, warning time is ranked herein on its experience.

†Includes all states in continental Europe occupied by or allied with Germany except the Soviet Union and Luxembourg (and other smaller states not included in this study), and Finland, where no general deportations occurred.

which deportations began in 1942, the ratio of percent of Norwegian to Dutch evaders was 3.6: 1. Comparing states and regions in which deportations commenced in 1943, the ratio of percent of evaders in Denmark compared to Salonica was 19: 1. Thus, neither German control nor warning time alone, nor both together, adequately explain the range of Jewish victimization.

   But may characteristics of Jewish settlement—their concentration and dispersion—in themselves account for the greater victimization of Jews in some nations than in others?

   One might expect that the more visible were Jews—the larger the percent they constitute in the city with most Jews and in the nation—the more victims there were, since the more readily would they be apprehended. Jewish victimization is positively related to Jews' visibility—the percent Jews constituted of the highest city—and Jews' relative size—the percent they compose of the nation—but this may be explained by how strongly related anti-Semitism is to Jews' visibility, relative size, and victimization. The relative size and visibility of Jews in prewar Europe is shown in Map 3-2. This will be discussed later.

One might expect that the more Jews (the absolute number) there were, the greater would be the proportion of victims, since Jews residing in distinct Jewish populations would be more visible, more readily apprehended if visible, and a more naked target for deportation. The size of the Jewish popula-

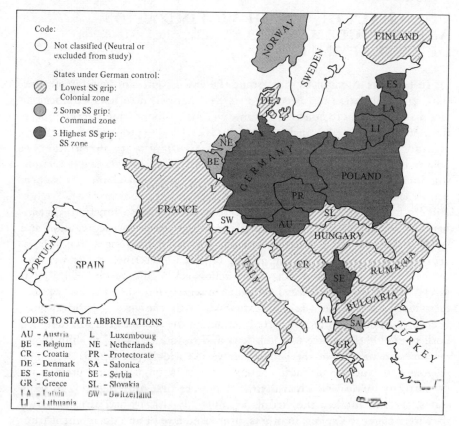

MAP 3-2. Relative Size and Visibility of Prewar Jewish Population in European States Occupied by and/or Allied with Germany during the Holocaust

Note: background code pattern in each state indicates the *relative size* of the prewar Jewish population as a percentage of the total population; where a distinctive circle of another code pattern is shown, this indicates *visibility*—the percent Jews constituted of the population of the city in which the greatest number of Jews lived; not coded are the states excluded from this study.

tion is weakly related to their rank of victims, accounting for little variation in victimization. It is not that Jews in large Jewish populations were not likely targets, we shall see later, but that small Jewish populations were so readily destroyed in certain milieus.

One might expect that the more Jews were dispersed throughout the nation, the fewer victims there would be. But, in actuality, this was not related as expected.[7]

Thus, no demographic attributes of Jewish population or settlement alone explain why some nations were more likely to produce more victims: the meaning and implications of any physical fact in social life depends on its social interpretation.

THE CHAIN OF JEWISH VICTIMIZATION AND THE GERMAN STRATEGY OF ENTRAPMENT

In previous attempts to understand the extensiveness of Jewish victimization, much attention has been paid to what happened to Jews who became victims rather than to *how* they became victims. Hilberg analyzed the process first: from "definition" (including registration) to "expropriation" to "concentration" (usually equated with ghettoization) prior to deportation.[8] I believe it is useful to label the second stage "stripping" to denote its function: this included stripping Jews of social roles, rights, and claims for respect within society as well as stripping them of material goods and legal rights. Hilberg failed to observe that concentration included two functions that inherently coincided with ghettoization but might preface it: segregation and isolation. Segregation ordinances banning Jews from mingling with non-Jews, communicating with them, and moving outside a prescribed radius were enforceable only if the stigmata of the yellow star could be successfully enforced. Therefore, states are classified as unsegregated when the star was not introduced or its use was not extended, with the order withdrawn or widespread nonobservance reported. Although the star insignia was designed both to enable the police to catch Jews and to induce others to shun them, responses to wearers of the yellow star varied widely (see pp. 61–62). The responses to, and the ultimate consequences of, stigmatization were not anticipated by many Jews when these orders were first promulgated. In some states, the star marked the victims whom many citizens had already shown they were eager to exploit; in others, it aroused awe of and detachment from the wearers; and in other states, it prompted ridicule. The generality of nonobservance was corroborated by German reports of officials' refusal to enforce star wearing and to punish Jews' nonconformity. In virtually all cases, only if segregation succeeded could isolation be introduced by requiring Jews to reside in designated dwellings, whether clustered or scattered.

Instigation and Some Responses to the Yellow Star

It may have been the Propaganda Ministry that first thought up the idea of forcing all Jews to wear a yellow star on their clothing. . . . The marking was intended to hinder any . . . assistance to Jews who were being harassed. We wanted Germans to feel embarrassed, to feel afraid of having any contact with Jews. — Adolf Eichmann, *Life,* 28 November 1960.

Hungary

Some of the prominent members of the community came to see my father — who had highly placed connections in the Hungarian police — to ask him what he thought of the situation. My father did not consider it so grim — but perhaps he did not want to dishearten the others or rub salt in their wounds: "The yellow star? Oh well, what of it? You don't die of it." — Eli Wiesel, *Night,* p. 22.

Bulgaria

Furthermore, the RSHA [SS agency charged with implementing deportations] statement continued, application of the order regarding stars and house signs was something less than complete for Jews not covered by the new exceptions. There were not enough stars to go around because power rationing at the manufacturing plants delayed their output. Only 20 percent of the quota was fulfilled. Jews who had stars did not bother to wear them or took them off when they saw the laxity of enforcement. Others who did wear them received so much sympathy from their Bulgarian neighbors that they wore them proudly. Some Jews even disregarded the regulation stars of the commissariat and devised their own, which contained pictures of the king and queen. The Germans in Sofia took a dim view of this "arrogant behavior" and attributed it to the indifference of the populace. — Frederick B. Chary, *The Bulgarian Jews and the Final Solution, 1940–1944,* pp. 57–58.

France

Q. "Did you see in camp [French concentration camp at Drancy] non-Jews who were arrested because they showed sympathy with the Jews?"

A. "Yes I did. Yes — I do remember non-Jewish groups arrested on the 8th June, 1942 . . . the day on which the yellow badges were introduced for Jews in France . . . mostly young people. . . . They had tried to demonstrate their support for the Jews and to ridicule this measure of wearing the yellow badge. They went out into the streets and wore paper made imitation yellow badges, with ridiculous inscriptions such as: 'Negro,' 'A man from the Papuan Islands.' They even put these yellow badges on dogs, and promenaded in the streets with these dogs — to kill the measure, as it were, by ridicule. These people were arrested, brought to Drancy — about thirty of them — and they lived like us. There (*sic*) were also made to wear a special yellow badge, with an inscription, 'Jew lover.' These people, then, on the 1st September, 1942, were liberated." — Testimony of George Wellers at the trial of Adolf Eichmann (from official Israeli transcript), session 32, 5 September 1961.

Poland

People are fined for wearing a dirty or wrinkled arm band. A lawyer covered his arm band with his briefcase. They put his fur coat on him backwards and commanded him to walk the streets that way—The madwoman of Marszalkowska Street is loose again. She beats Jews with a stone she wears in her glove.—Emmanuel Ringelblum, *Notes from the Warsaw Ghetto*, p. 18.

Figure 3-2 shows how the extent of earlier isolation imposed upon the Jews in different states and regions conditioned their later probability of victimization. States in which Jews had been defined, registered, and stripped produced almost four times as many victims as states in which they had never been officially defined (.37: .1). But the greatest gap is between states in which Jews had been successfully segregated and isolated and those in which the majority were neither segregated successfully nor isolated. Ghettoization added relatively little to the toll once Jews were isolated.

Isolation enabled police forces to overcome the desperate and futile efforts of evasion within the ghettos, signified by building bunkers and secret walls. Once the ghetto or zone of segregated housing was sealed, police could seize the quota desired by a dragnet strategy without specifying the individual victim. Wherever Jews were not previously segregated, raids by local police failed to catch a majority, even with maximal local police cooperation and minimal apprehension on the part of the Jews.

The favored method of German authorities was to induce Jews to report by themselves for "resettlement," in response to notices sent them by their local police or Jewish control agency. The only trouble was that the method seldom worked outside the Reich, unless men had earlier been interned in labor camps.[9] Even in the Reich, notice was abandoned as the potential victims ceased to appear; they were then summoned and seized in one step by the policeman in the doorway.[10] In the command zone, failure was almost immediate. In Belgium, the callup system was replaced by roundups as early as 22 July 1942. The situation was similar in the Netherlands, where the German Foreign Office representative wrote in 13 August 1942:

After the Jews had found us out and got to know, what is behind the deportation and labor service in the East, they no more report for the weekly shipments. Of 2000 Jews called up for this week only about 400 showed up. In their homes the called up Jews cannot any longer be found.[11]

This mass attempt at evasion occurred in the Netherlands without any previously established Jewish social defense movement.

The method of next resort is the roundup, or residential raid: this is most inefficient in an unsegregated population. The probable percent that will be captured (mathematically) after the first raid should parallel the percent Jews constitute of the population if they are not segregated, must be individually identified, and seek to flee. When persons are not clustered together, the ratio of police power to the potential victim must be much

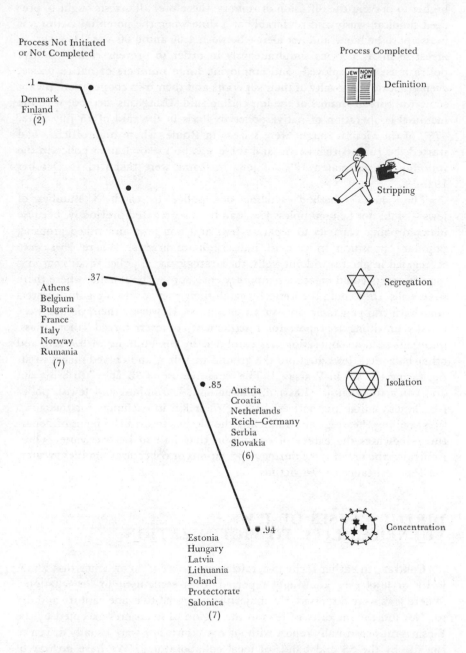

Process Not Initiated
or Not Completed

Process Completed

Definition

.1

Denmark
Finland
(2)

Stripping

.37

Athens
Belgium
Bulgaria
France
Italy
Norway
Rumania
(7)

Segregation

● .85   Austria
Croatia
Netherlands
Reich–Germany
Serbia
Slovakia
(6)

Isolation

● .94

Estonia
Hungary
Latvia
Lithuania
Poland
Protectorate
Salonica
(7)

Concentration

FIGURE 3–2. Probability* of Victimization by Stages of Isolation Experienced during the Holocaust

*Probability = mean rank of victims in each group ÷ maximal rank of victims (10).

higher to prevent the diffusion of rumors: therefore, all arrests ought to proceed simultaneously and preferably at a time when the potential victim was most apt to be home and not alert—between 4:00 and 6:00 A.M. However, to arrest so many persons simultaneously in order to prevent rumors, native police must be employed, and employing large numbers of native police, even granting the loyalty of their superiors and their own cooperation, means some will spread rumors of the impending raid. Using this method, with the maximal cooperation of native police in Paris in the raid of 15 July 1942, 47% of the victims sought were seized: in Rome, where high officials had started the rumors themselves and there was no use of Italian police in the roundup, an estimated 10% of Jews in Rome were taken in 16 October 1943.[12]

The "quota" method—sending out police to catch X number of Jews—could not be used unless Jews had been segregated previously, because it taxed police capacity to separate Jews and non-Jews and risked arousing popular opposition in case of indiscriminate arrests. Where Jews were segregated in ghettos without walls, the strategic use of police squads cordoning off streets could create a temporary enclosure without exits: where there were walls, they could theoretically catch their prey, as do big-game hunters who have trapped their prey in an enclosure. However, their victims were usually unwilling to report for resettlement, or even forced labor; mass, unorganized noncooperation was exhibited by the building of bunkers and other hideouts—Jews dug into the ground in Vilna, and carved niches in attics facing the sky in Warsaw.[13] The extensive use of "beaters" to bring out and catch the victims—Latvian, Lithuanian, Ukrainian, and Jewish police (the latter, unlike the natives, beating their kin in exchange for their own lives) pulling, beating, and funneling the victims toward the point of departure—indicates the extent of opposition that had to be overcome. Thus, ironically, the use of force during deportations or collections signifies greater, not less, resistance of the victims.

DIRECT CAUSES OF JEWS' VULNERABILITY TO VICTIMIZATION

Contrary to earlier facile generalizations, there is no evidence that a majority of Jews ever knowingly reported for resettlement or "evacuation." Where Jews were dispersed, the majority attempted to evade capture and did so. Nor did the majority of Jews in the region of massacres executed by the Einsatzgruppen usually report without coercion; they were usually driven to the site by the SS and bands of local collaborators.[14] We have no way of discerning how many among the victims attempted to evade capture only to be apprehended, how many were aware of the threat but made no attempt to evade capture because of isolation and despair, and how many were unaware of the threat or denied others' recognition. The cases where many Jews were caught without initially isolating them are explained by the prior segregation of the sexes introduced by forced labor drafts, leaving behind vulnerable groups of the population—the aged, the ill, the mad, children, and mothers— already segregated and all dependent on public assistance. These people were usually nonresistant because they lacked the ability to get away or to defend themselves in any manner. More compliant Jewish populations are generally characterized by atypical sex-age distributions weighted by the aged and/or children and their mothers. This was especially true of Germany and Austria as a consequence of the earlier drive to expel the Jews. The majority of Jews emigrating included more of the younger people and men. Half of the Austrian deportees were over 60 (although previously this age stratum had composed only one-fifth of the Jewish community) and two out of three were women.[15] Successful segregation of the Jews is the most important proximate cause or intervening condition producing high victimization. The chain of causes of Jewish victimization is shown in Figure 3-3.

Figure 3-3 illustrates that were we to inquire which single cause best predicts the likelihood of more Jews' becoming victims, it would be the success of prewar anti-Semitic movements by 1936, which best explains high state cooperation in segregating and isolating the Jews, making successful defense or evasion less possible. Later, we shall show how the cooperation of natives with anti-Jewish discrimination and their defense of Jews against deportation are inversely related to each other and how both are linked to Jews' isolation and chances of victimization.

The most important direct cause of Jewish segregation was the extent of native officials' cooperation in promulgation and enforcement of anti-Jewish

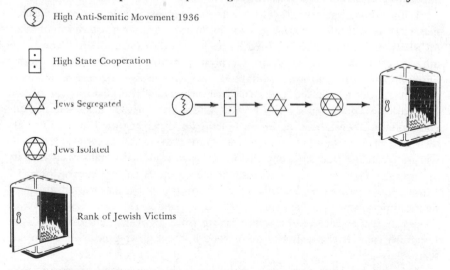

High Anti-Semitic Movement 1936

High State Cooperation

Jews Segregated

Jews Isolated

Rank of Jewish Victims

FIGURE 3-3.   The Chain of Jewish Victimization

ordinances. Throughout western Europe, the Reich, and most satellites, Jewish population registries were established by the state. In eastern Europe, the borders of the Jewish ghettos were ordinarily guarded by the native police, and direct identification of potential evaders was made by ordinary police as well as organized local collaborators. Such collaborators, organized in "police battalions," participated extensively in killing of Jews directly in the Baltic states and the Ukraine. Other collaborators did not kill firsthand but were organized to detect Jews in hiding, and many acted on their own initiative to blackmail Jewish evaders. State cooperation facilitated segregation regardless of its causes. The more efficient, and almost foolproof, method of Jewish identification was devised not in the Reich, but in the Netherlands, by a prewar Dutch civil servant who traveled to Berlin with his superior's permission to display his innovation to the Gestapo: "The Gestapo had pronounced his identity card even more difficult to reproduce than its German counterpart."[16]

State cooperation was a function of countervailing (or reinforcing) pressure from Germany against internal resistance or nonresistance. If there was a high internal value consensus that getting rid of the Jews was a social good and/or consensual agreement that the "Jewish problem" was produced by the Jews, there was usually low or no resistance. Such a state was Slovakia, which gave away its Jews, Eichmann recalled (1970), like someone "throwing away sour beer."[17] Since the success of the anti-Semitic movement by 1936 was a sign of such a value consensus, it is not surprising that one finds its success was historically the leading underlying cause of Jewish victimization and the factor (among all prewar characteristics of the nation-state) most highly correlated with the rank of victims.

Where there was no anti-Jewish value consensus, the degree of resistance needed to counteract German strategy and the resistance mustered depended on whether the state had retained its prewar authority, and what line those authorities took in response to German pressure. Within the SS zone, autonomous native authority collapsed, was overthrown, or was successively contracted by accommodation. In Czechoslovakia, the government of the Protectorate appointed by the prewar Czech authorities incrementally accommodated by establishing an authoritarian Czech regime that adapted its own anti-Semitic legislative code and eventually urged accommodation to German rule so publicly that the Czech government-in-exile disowned its authority.[18] Occupied states outside the SS zone with less successful anti-Semitic movements were least likely to accommodate if there was an independent, functioning prewar state authority (Denmark) and less likely to cooperate if they received clear leadership from a government-in-exile (as in Belgium) than if the native bureaucracy had no clear guidance, as in the Netherlands.[19]

But the state is not the only social authority recognized by people. We may ask, *How do responses of leaders account for native resistance to col-*

laboration and the organization of defense of the Jews? Where both state and church refused to sanction discrimination—as in Denmark—internal resistance was highest. Where the state or native administrative bureaucracy began to cooperate, church resistance was critical in inhibiting obedience to authority, legitimating subversion and/or checking collaboration directly. Church protest proved to be the single element present in every instance in which state collaboration was arrested—as in Bulgaria, France, and Rumania. Church protest was absent in virtually all cases in which state cooperation was not arrested. Church protest was also the intervening variable most highly related to the immediacy of social defense movements that enabled Jews successfully to evade deportation.[20] The majority of Jews evaded deportation in every state occupied by or allied with Germany in which the head of the dominant church spoke out *publicly* against deportation before or as soon as it began. How the church operated to legitimate government policies and could delegitimate them and instigate noncooperation and resistance is illustrated in detail in Chapter 4. Church resistance operated in two ways. Within the colonial zone, from which Germany could deport Jews only if an agreement was concluded with state authorities and if native police power was mobilized to collect them, church threats and protest operated directly to check government readiness to collaborate. The greater the church resistance, the fewer Jews became victims. Resistance ranged from an appeal to the head of state (in Rumania), publication of the protest to church members (in parts of France), to publication and exhortation in Bulgaria, including an implicit threat of withdrawal of loyalties.

By contrast, states in the colonial zone with high Jewish victimization are states in which the dominant church was actively antagonistic toward Jews and/or failed to protest deprivation of their rights and liberties before the majority of them were held captive in the state's concentration camps. For example, In Hungary, the Primate had intervened constantly for baptized Jews but refused a Budapest Jewish leaders' request to appeal to the Regent on 23 June 1944. A week later he prepared to publish an address (but ceased on government request) in which he did not so much condemn the deportations as wash his hands of responsibility.

Within the command zone, church protest had no effect on deterring deportation initiated by the Germans, but it could deter collaboration and instigate cooperation with movements of social defense of the Jews. Early church antidiscrimination protests and later protests against deportations are positively related to the resistance movement's positive slant toward Jews (as one would expect) and also more positively related to the immediacy of establishment of social defense movements to evade later deportation. However, such resistance movements were either nonexistent or had little influence over the government of the satellites and France, whereas the national churches in these states were political actors that could directly influence government policy.

Among the occupied states, resistance movements' identification and mobilization on behalf of hunted Jews was strategically more important than church protest. Relying on appeals or official promises in this zone could increase Jews' vulnerability by reducing their apprehension.

The resistance movements of Denmark and Belgium themselves mobilized extensive networks and financial aid to enable Jews to flee (described in Chapter 6). The resistance movement in Norway employed its existing networks to help Jews reach Sweden.[21] The Jews of Athens were sheltered in the countryside and welcomed into liberated areas by the left-wing resistance movement (EAM) in Greece, where one guerrilla band was led by Rabbi Moses Pesah.[22] Yugoslavian Jews also participated actively in Tito's movement of national liberation and found a haven in the regions it liberated.[23] Independent Jewish leadership that was not co-opted into *Judenräte* or other Jewish control organizations played a significant role in some states in preventing Jews from becoming segregated.

Table 3-2 shows the relative contribution of the immediacy of social defense and lack of segregation in increasing an evader's chance and checking victimization. Defense has maximum impact when victims are unsegregated and they were unsegregated in virtually all cases in which a defense

TABLE 3-2. Jewish Evaders and Victims in European States during the Holocaust by Immediacy of Defense and Prior Segregation of Jews*

Jews' Condition before Deportation/ Extermination Attempt	Mean Rank of Evaders (1 = to 5% . . . 20 = 95–100%)	States or Units in Each Category and Rank of Victims	Mean Rank of Victims (deciles)
SEGREGATED (states are ranked by highest to lowest defense against discrimination and deportation):			
Early church protest + late Jewish social defense movement + resistance identification	3	Netherlands (8)	8
Late church protest + none or very late Jewish social defense movement + resistance identification	1	Salonica (9)	9
No church protest + none or very late Jewish social defense movement + no positive resistance identification	1.4	Slovakia (9), Hungary (8), Austria (9), Germany (9), Protectorate (9), Estonia (10), Latvia (10), Lithuania (10), Poland (10)	9.3

Jews' Condition before Deportation/ Extermination Attempt	Mean Rank of Evaders (1 = to 5% ... 20 = 95 100%)	States or Units in Each Category and Rank of Victims	Mean Rank of Victims (deciles)
UNSEGREGATED (states are ranked as above):			
Early church protest + early Jewish social defense movement + resistance identification	14.6	Athens (3), Belgium (5), Bulgaria (2), Denmark (1), Italy (2)	2.6
—with highest warning time	16	Athens (3), Bulgaria (2), Denmark (1), Italy (2)	2.0
—with some warning time	9	Belgium	5
Later church protest + early Jewish social defense movement + resistance identification	11.0	France (3), Norway (5), Rumania (6)	4.7
—with some warning time	12.5	France (3), Norway (5)	4.0
—with least warning time	8	Rumania	6
No church protest + none or very late Jewish social defense movement + resistance identification			
—with least warning time	4.0	Serbia	8

*Croatia and Finland have been omitted from this table because of lack of data on Croatia and the fact that no general deportations occurred in Finland. This table also excludes the Soviet Union, all states neither occupied by nor allied with Germany (Allies and neutrals), Luxembourg, and other smaller states not included in this study.

movement arose, since the factors checking segregation reflect an underlying disposition toward resistance later manifested as defense.[24] Although the lack of segregation enhanced a potential victim's opportunity to escape a particular raid, one's chances of escaping many raids decline successively in a geometric ratio as raids multiply if one relies on chance alone. The evader is the person who has escaped the first raid, and the second and third (and so on), successively. To do so requires active aid on the part of neighbors and other citizens to help evade the police and find escape routes, and to supply prolonged sustenance and shelter—services organized by social defense movements.

Among the states in which Jews had not been successfully segregated and a defense movement was created early, the later the threat, the lower was the percent of victims seized. Warning time diminished chances of becoming a victim when the preconditions for any defense were present: then, it inhibited state cooperation, altered German strategy, incited more immediate defense, and sharpened awareness among Jews of the potentiality of victimization.

Different solutions were discovered in each situation, but the organization of a social defense movement depended first on the clarity and unanimity with which social authorities said no. Only when such a movement existed could the physical potentialities provided by geography be exploited. The earlier it was organized, the more Jews were saved.

The difference between the rank of Jewish evaders of Denmark and Norway, both of whom were offered refuge in Sweden, illustrates this well. It was not the fortuitous proximity of the Swedish coast that explains the immediate rescue of 94% of Denmark's Jewry but the Danes' unity of will, which led to immediate organization of a defense movement. It was easier to reach Sweden from Norway because escape routes had been earlier established over the adjacent border (which could not be sealed) while the hazardous sea route by which the Jews escaped from Denmark had not been devised before the Danes organized the rescue of their Jews. But only 57% of Norwegian Jews escaped, the exodus (of which we have scant documentation from Norwegian sources) beginning apparently after the raid by Quisling's police imprisoning male Jews over 16 without warning in October 1942. The consensus of state and social authority against discrimination in Denmark, as contrasted to the dissensus in Norway under Quisling's rule, explains the readiness of the Danes to mobilize so swiftly to prevent the seizure of the Jews and the availability of the Danish police to help the Jews circumvent German police while the Norwegian police rounded them up.

Similarly, no evidence exists that organized social defense movements (or, indeed, any movements) are a simple reflection of preexisting attitudes although a positive predisposition toward the object of the movement may be a prerequisite for its success. The absence of anti-Semitism need not instigate sympathy for Jews, especially if identification implies risk-taking. Nor are unexpressed feelings always translated into spontaneous actions—movements do not erupt spontaneously from the unorganized concurrence of sympathies. There is no way we can infer how widely unexpressed sentiments are shared. Although it has been noted that public sympathy was often directly or symbolically expressed toward star-bearers in Paris, Belgium, and Amsterdam, yet it was also expressed in Berlin, albeit more surreptitiously.[25] Conversely, signs of personal aversion for Jews were shown by members of the Norwegian resistance, as well as by Dutch citizens who were later active in forming the first nationwide social defense movement for people in hiding.[26] The motivation to resist and to aid the victim may spring from duty toward ones' fellow citizens, aversion toward the conqueror, or loyalty to national and religious ideals and may coexist with social distance and even antipathy toward particular victims.

Furthermore, mass collective action reflecting popular sympathies is unlikely to be effective unless there are leadership cadres that survive repression. The Amsterdam strike of 1941 was easily squashed, as were other mass nonviolent actions (such as in Prague in 1939) by authoritarian governments.[27] Organizationally, the church can provide an ideal basis for a defense movement because its audience spans all social classes, its ministers are situated throughout the state, it has access to elites, and resources for hiding, and it serves a legitimating function.

One may ask, *How does prewar anti-Semitism explain the extent of both Jewish victimization and church protest?*

Table 3–3 shows that states with more successful anti-Semitic movements by 1936 (or movements in power) produced almost twice as many victims (8.8: 4.7) as states with less successful movements. The church was more apt to protest against early anti-Jewish discrimination in less anti-Semitic states. There was little or very belated church protest against deportation among high anti-Semitic states and no initial protests against anti-Jewish discrimination, but all churches in the less anti-Semitic states outside the SS zone protested deportations promptly.

There are several possible explanations as to why church protest against deportations was less likely in states in which anti-Semitic movements were successful before 1936. The policies clerics espouse may represent those held by their flock or their estimation of risk may be tempered by the milieu. But, since in no case where there was a high anti-Semitic movement by 1936 did church leaders then protest, the simplest explanation for their silence is lack of identification with the Jews. Although it is plausible that the earlier development of anti-Semitism might have inhibited church leaders during the Holocaust, it was the silence of those same church leaders that made the growth and daring of those movements possible. Franklin Littell has reached this conclusion regarding Germany where no church—including the dissenting Confessing Church, which refused to submit to the authority of a nazified Protestant state church—protested the denial of citizenship and consequent persecution of the Jews.[28] Although the Nazi movement was blatantly anticlerical, in other states the major anti-Semitic movement was proclerical, led by priests before the war and/or vocally supported by church leaders as in Rumania, Hungary, Slovakia, Poland, and Austria. The consequences of church resistance or nonresistance during the Holocaust and differences among churches are further discussed in Chapter 4.

Deviant cases—such as Rumania and the Netherlands—confirm that the linkage between anti-Semitism and victimization is produced by state cooperation, segregation, and late defense. These are instances in which internal resistance deterred or failed to impede the pressure to segregate the Jews, despite the success of anti-Semitism in Rumania and its lack of success in the Netherlands. Independent Jewish leadership that was not co-opted into *Judenräte* or other Jewish control organizations played a significant role in

TABLE 3–3. Jewish Victims in European States* during the Holocaust by Success of Anti-Semitic Movements up to 1936 and Church Protest†

Success of Anti-Semitic Movement by 1936 and Victims	Nazi Zone	Church Protest against Discrimination	Deportation	Dominant Religion	Mean Rank of Victims
MOST SUCCESSFUL					8.8
Highest:					
Rumania: V = 6††	I	—	+	Rumanian Orthodox	
Hungary: V = 8	I	—	—	Roman Catholic	
Austria: V = 9	III	—	—	Roman Catholic	
Germany: V = 9	III	—	—	Protestant	
Poland: V = 10	III	—	—	Roman Catholic	
High:					
Croatia: V = 8	I	—	—	Roman Catholic	
Slovakia: V = 9	I	—	+	Roman Catholic	
Salonica: V = 9	II	—	—	Greek Orthodox	
Latvia: V = 10	III	—	—	Lutheran	
Lithuania: V = 10	III	—	—	Roman Catholic	
LESS SUCCESSFUL					4.7
Some:					
Bulgaria: V = 2	I	+	+	Bulgarian Orthodox	
Finland: V = 1	I	—	—	Lutheran	
France: V = 3	I	—	+	Roman Catholic	
Athens: V = 3	II	—	+	Greek Orthodox	

TABLE 3-3. (Cont.)

Success of Anti-Semitic Movement by 1936 and Victims	Nazi Zone	Church Protest against		Dominant Religion	Mean Rank of Victims
		Discrimination	Deportation		
LESS SUCCESSFUL					
Some: (cont.)					
Serbia: V = 8	III	—	—	Serbian Orthodox	
Protectorate: V = 9	III	—	—	Protestant	
Estonia: V = 10	III	—	—	Lutheran	
Low:					
Belgium: V = 5	II	+	+	Roman Catholic	
Denmark: V = 1	II	+	+	Lutheran	
Italy: V = 2	II	+	+	Roman Catholic	
Netherlands: V = 8	II	+	+	Protestant	
Norway: V = 5	II	—	+	Lutheran	

*Includes all states in continental Europe occupied by or allied with Germany except the Soviet Union, Luxembourg, and other smaller states not included in this study.

†Where one church represents the dominant religion, the protests of the hierarchy of that church are analyzed under "Church Protest." Where followers of the dominant religion are divided among several churches, the largest of these is analyzed, although the church of the minority (if unified) may claim more members than the leading church of the dominant religion, as did the Roman Catholic Church in the Netherlands and in Germany. Protests include private communications to the governing authority or head of state on behalf of all Jews categorically delivered before the first six months of deportation and/or before half the Jews are deported (whichever is earliest). Note that no general deportation took place in Finland.

††Rank of victims.

deterrence in Rumania.[29] In the Netherlands, political anti-Semitism was openly expressed by only a small, politically uninfluential minority before the war while in Rumania anti-Semitism was rife among parties and Jew-hatred was taken for granted. Yet, less than one out of every four Jews from the Netherlands was alive in 1945 and over half the Jews of Rumania were saved (including those returned from Rumanian concentration camps). Since most of the Rumanian Jews killed were killed by Rumanians, this is an instance not of noncooperation but of very high cooperation that was arrested. The Rumanians were unwilling to wait for the Germans to begin liquidating their Jews; the government, which later refused to execute its deportation agreement with Germany, itself initiated the slaughter of Jews in the ex-Rumanian provinces of Bessarabia and Bukovina (recovered with the assault on the Soviet Union) and opened its own concentration camps and expelled Jews to Transnistria, where they could die of cold, and famine — the only means of inducing death not available was gas. But, initially, the Dutch administration was also highly cooperative with Germany. However, Jews were segregated effectively in the Netherlands despite the mass protest exemplified in the Amsterdam general strike in 1941, yet not segregated throughout Rumania. Legislation that defined and compelled registration of Jews throughout Rumania was not enforced in 1940 and 1941.

The German administration in the Netherlands systematically introduced registration to define, strip, segregate, and isolate the Jews. Dutch officials (who perfected the identity card marking Jews) cooperated so well in general that the head of the state institute of war documentation, Louis De Jong, told a Dutch television audience that "from 1940 to 1945 there was no scourge from which the Dutch received bloodier wounds than this execrable identity card — the invention of an over-zealous civil servant, himself not a Nazi."[30]

Within the Netherlands, the churches were neither united nor vocal on taking a position against discrimination. In October 1940 the Dutch Reformed Church (the major Protestant denomination) protested discrimination against Jewish civil servants to the Reichskommissar, but it did not inform its congregations of this action. It also later deferred to a German request not to read from the pulpit its protest against the deportation of the Jews. The Amsterdam Jewish Council followed the government's lead in accommodating to German decrees. Jews were progressively detached from Dutch institutions with hardly any dissent, excepting that of university students and professors. No leadership was exerted upon the prewar bureaucracy by either the Dutch Reformed Church or the government-in-exile to deter as prompt implementation of German regulations in wartime as they had ordered for Dutch regulations in peacetime. These church leaders relied on petitions alone, not going beyond the law to create a defense movement for people in hiding until the spring of 1943, when Dutchmen themselves were threatened with deportation for forced labor. By that time, less than half of the Dutch Jews were free.

In Rumania, Jewish resistance was instituted by Jewish leaders themselves, who campaigned against the yellow star (knowing this would signify the cue for massacring Jews), petitioned church leaders, party leaders, notables, and the Queen to protest deportation, and appealed directly to the head of state to release Jews in Rumanian prisons and camps and repatriate those exiled in Transnistria. But Jewish leaders pleaded almost everywhere, except in those states where there was no time to appeal or where they had previously learned it was futile. However, these leaders went beyond petition, lobbying among other Rumanian political parties to exploit the illusion that their influence among the western Allies through international Jewish organizations could be used to aid Rumania to retain her autonomy.

As German defeat became more probable, Rumanian leaders began considering leaving the Axis alliance. Deporting its Jews could be interpreted as a sign of continuing cooperation with Germany. Lavi (who has documented the activities of these leaders) believes that Premier Antonescu was moved to reverse his policy by the internal growth of opposition, "evinced by even such traditional anti-Semites as former political leaders, the Church and the Court," as well as by his desire to extricate Rumania from the German alliance.[31] The Rumanian Metropolitan's assumption of obligation toward the Jews was exhibited after the war by the performance of a ritual of atonement, kissing the bloodstains of Jews murdered in 1941 in Jassy, and leading a procession of Rumanians to the Jewish cemetery where he met the Chief Rabbi, to whom he publicly appealed for forgiveness.[32] The Germans never understood the motives of the Premier's refusal, the involved Foreign Office and SS representatives each blaming the other.[33]

DETERMINANTS OF THE TIMING OF THREAT AGAINST THE JEWS

Returning to our first question—how do we explain variations in the magnitude of Jewish victimization?—we find only one contingency of threat that is related to the extent of victimization, once we take anti-Semitism into account. Table 3-4, which relates warning time and the prewar success of the anti-Semitic movements directly to Jewish victims, shows that among states with less successful movements, the more warning time there was, the fewer victims there were. There is no substantive difference among states with successful anti-Semitic movements, regardless of whether deportations began in 1941 or 1944.

Among states in which the authorities resisted anti-Jewish discrimination that were wholly occupied and directly governed by the Germans only after August 1943—Denmark, southern Greece, and Italy—no attempt was made to initiate the yellow badge, or to institute gradual discrimination and stripping of the Jews, or to put out anti-Jewish propaganda for fear of threatening

TABLE 3-4. Jewish Victims in European States by Success of Anti-Semitic Movements up to 1936 and Warning Time during the Holocaust*

Success of Prewar Anti-Semitic Movement, 1930–1936	WARNING TIME			
	0: June 1941–Dec. 1941	1: 1 Jan.–24 June 1942	2: 25 June–16 Dec. 1942	3: After 17 Dec. 1942
High	Croatia 8			Hungary 8
	Rumania 6			Salonica 9
	Austria 9			
	Germany 9	Slovakia 9		
	Latvia 10			
	Lithuania 10			
	Poland 10			
	Mean 8.9			Mean 8.5
Low	Protectorate 9		France† 3	Bulgaria 2
	Estonia 10		Belgium 5	Denmark 1
	Serbia 8		Netherlands 8	Athens 3
	Mean 9.0		Norway 5	Italy 2
			Mean 5.3	Mean 2.0

*Finland is omitted since the Finnish government made no deportation agreement; hence, there was no threat of deportations. This table also excludes the USSR, Luxembourg, other smaller states excluded from this study, and all states neither occupied by nor allied with Germany (Allies and neutrals).

†Some 6,138 Jews incarcerated earlier in French camps were transported to Auschwitz in May 1942: these included 1,000 Jews sentenced in reprisal for an attack on German military personnel in Paris in December 1941 and 5,138 stateless Jews held in the French camp in Drancy (NG-3571, NG-4954, NG-5109 found in United States Military Tribunal "Documents: Staff Evidence Analysis" [see Bibliography]). Mass raids to seize Jews who were free (although lacking French nationality) began in July 1942.

them prematurely. Surprise raids or baited traps (handing out of free Passover matzoh at the synagogue in Athens) were planned to catch them. The demoralization among Germans made it more likely that knowledgeable Germans who were opposed to the extermination of Jews would try to subvert such raids by tipping off Jews and/or native leaders (as in Rome and Copenhagen), and German officers would look the other way to avoid catching Jews in flight (Denmark).

Satellite governments that hoped to retain their national identity in the postwar world, such as Bulgaria and Rumania, had an incentive to turn away from collaboration once it was clear that the Allies had defined the murder of the Jews as a crime demanding postwar retribution (17 December 1942) and more probable that Germany would be defeated. This increased their willingness to break agreements with Germany once native opposition developed. The recognition of extermination also impelled sympathetic officials to make a stronger effort to cancel them (Bulgaria) or subvert them in the occupied states (Denmark, southern Greece, Italy) by informing Jews of the authorities' plans.

But the will to resist and obligation to disobey, even if it meant taking risks (which, in fact, were always lower when resistance was universal within a group or community), was a function of earlier understanding of what right and whose rules defined the situation. Where the church had legitimated anti-Semitism earlier, as in Hungary, warning time made little difference.

But the warning time available to these states was not a matter of chance alone but depended on how they had used time for their own ends if they had the discretionary opportunity to delay deportations. The length of warning time afforded each state depended not only on German intentions and means of control but upon how a state availed itself of the initial opportunities to accommodate to German power through a colonial status, and whether a state that accepted such status resisted discrimination against the Jews. Initially, Bulgaria gained more warning time than Serbia by accepting a German alliance. Within Yugoslavia, internal political opposition to a non-aggression pact with Germany led Hitler to anticipate he could not rely upon the cooperation of the Yugoslavs and to invade Serbia and establish the independent state of Croatia (which turned out to be very cooperative as it had its own domestic extermination plan, described in Chapter 4). Norway's government refused to accept a similar offer of self-government in exchange for neutrality as Denmark had accepted and was fully occupied in 1940, governed by a Reichskommissar directly responsible to Hitler. If they were offered and accepted a colonial status, the less anti-Semitic states earned warning time for their Jewish community by resistance to German-instigated requests for anti-Jewish discrimination, while most of the more anti-Semitic states lost no time in responding to requests for deportation, reducing warning time.

As warning time was extended in the low anti-Semitic states, the potential victims in these nations were less vulnerable, for many processes previously discussed were altered. Warning time was like a developing fluid: if overextended, potential victims who introjected the vision of vanished victims themselves quickly disappeared, just as when film is overexposed the latent image does not emerge. Most often, states stretching warning time were those that resisted cooperating in deportations earlier and/or were occupied latest. But the opportunity for increasing warning time depended first on a state's autonomy or freedom from direct German control in 1941.

We can observe this clearly by noting how warning time among the less anti-Semitic states is inversely related to their status in 1941. If they were in the SS zone in 1941, extermination/deportation began that year in all cases. If they were occupied by 1941 but outside the SS zone (mainly western Europe), Germany initiated deportations in 1942 (except for Salonica). Deportations that began among the less anti-Semitic states in 1943 were in those states that were in the colonial zone in 1941 but had resisted or procrastinated longer and/or had only been subjected to complete military occupation by Germany in 1943 (Denmark, Italy, and Athens).

Because of anticipated resistance, Germany made no attempt to organize deportations from Italy and Denmark when the former was allied to Germany and the latter was neutral. Although the Danish government had not resisted German military occupation and exploitation and adhered to the Anti-Comintern Pact, it never agreed to restrict Jews' civil rights when the nation was self-governing (before Germany assumed greater civil authority in November 1942); nor would officials authorize such measures under occupation. The threat to Italian and Danish Jews was deferred until Italy was invaded in September 1943 and Denmark put under a state of military emergency in August 1943. German reactions were instigated by Italian defection from the Axis and Danish sabotage and strikes. But the German occupational authorities did not expect to obtain state cooperation in these cases and did not trust native police (with good reason) to aid them in rounding up Jews.

The most significant aspect of German control relative to the Jews was the directness of SS control in 1941 (shown in Map 3–3). The RSHA determined priorities and its agents, along with other divisions of the SS, executed them or instigated their implementation. Ideological priorities dictated extermination first by any means available in the zone where SS control was most naked—the SS zone. Direct extermination outside the Reich and deportation to Baltic and Polish ghettos and extermination camps from the Reich began in 1941. Next, in 1942, the RSHA initiated plans to deport Jews from the other occupied states without self-government except in Greece, where German military authorities were temporarily stalled by the Italian zone of occupation. In the colonial zone SS control was limited to instigation, as there was no SS or other German police power on which to draw and no authority to initiate deportations without state agreement. These states had the greatest opportunity to delay.

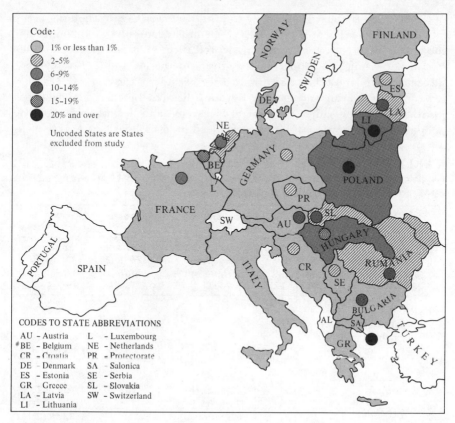

MAP 3-3. SS Grip over European States in September 1941

Therefore, if we take a state's political status in 1941 as a given, a clearer conception emerges of warning time as a function of interaction between the opportunity to delay (an inverse function of SS control in 1941) and the predisposition to resist (an inverse function of the earlier success of anti-Semitic movements). States that had more successful anti-Semitic movements or regimes before the war were not disposed to delay, regardless of opportunities.[34]

UNDERLYING CAUSES OF NATIONAL DIFFERENCES IN JEWISH VICTIMIZATION

Separating the factors producing warning time enables us to compare the impact of the directness of the SS grip in 1941—the critical element of German control that determined warning time, means available, and use of terror—and solidarity on Jewish victimization, holding prewar anti-Semitism constant, as in Table 3-4.

Were more solidary states likely to produce fewer victims, holding other factors constant? There is little basis for comparison once we take into account how different opportunities presented themselves and the earlier success of anti-Semitism. Proportionately more of the less solidary states were subjected to the most direct SS grip in 1941 because of the thrust of German expansion in central and eastern Europe, dictated by their ideology that justified exploiting, imposing a racial hierarchy, and decimating the Slavic peoples. The proportion of victims produced in less solidary states is best ex-

TABLE 3–5. Jewish Victims in European States during the Holocaust by Success of Anti-Semitic Movements up to 1936, SS Grip over State in 1941, and Prewar National Solidarity*

| By SSGRIP 41 | SUCCESS OF ANTI-SEMITIC MOVEMENT, 1936 | | | |
| | High | | Low | |
	Mean Rank of Victims of States in Category	States in Category (Rank of Victims)	Mean Rank of Victims of States in Category	States in Category (Rank of Victims)
(0) Colonial zone	7.8		2.0	
More solidary states	—		1.7	France (3) Denmark (1) Finland (1)
Less solidary states	7.8	Croatia (8) Hungary (8) Rumania (6) Slovakia (9)	2.3	Athens (3) Bulgaria (2) Italy (2)
(1) Command zone	9.0		6.0	
More solidary states	—		6.0	Belgium (5) Netherlands (8) Norway (5)
Less solidary states	9.0	Salonica (9)	—	
(2) SS zone	9.6		9.0	
More solidary states	—		—	
Less solidary states	9.6	Austria (9) Germany (9) Latvia (10) Lithuania (10) Poland (10)	9.0	Estonia (10) Protectorate (9) Serbia (8)

*Includes all states in continental Europe occupied by or allied with Germany except the Soviet Union, Luxembourg, and other smaller states not included in this study.

plained by the SS grip in 1941 and by the high proportion of anti-Semitic states among them.

Table 3–5 shows that with least SS control, high anti-Semitic states produced almost four times as many victims proportionately (7.8: 2) than did less anti-Semitic states: comparing their averages, when most free, the high anti-Semitic states produced 58% more victims ([7.8 − 2.0] × 10%). Among the less anti-Semitic states, the rank of victims climbed steeply as SS control intensified. Figure 3–4 shows the lines projected by regression equations, the mathematical formulas that best estimated the rank of victims in high and low anti-Semitic states separately.[35] The reader may observe that the line representing high anti-Semitic states also rises as SS control becomes greater, but the rise is less steep. Increases in the directness of SS control produced less of an increment in victims in those states because they had already

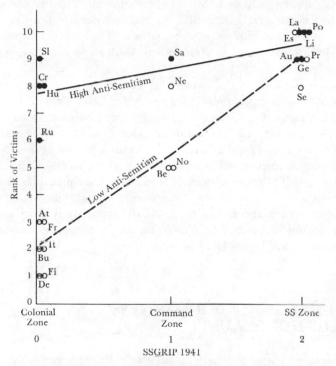

FIGURE 3–4. **Jewish Victimization Graphed as a Function of Prewar Anti-Semitism and SS Grip over the State in 1941**

● Actual rank of state in this class with successful prewar anti-Semitic movement.

○ Actual rank of state in this class with less successful prewar anti-Semitic movement.

At–Athens	De–Denmark	Ge–Germany	No–Norway	Pr–Protectorate
Au–Austria	Es–Estonia	Hu–Hungary	La–Latvia	Ru–Rumania
Be–Belgium	Fi–Finland	It–Italy	Li–Lithuania	Sa–Salonica
Bu–Bulgaria	Fr–France	Ne–Netherlands	Po–Poland	Se–Serbia
Cr–Croatia				Sl–Slovakia

reached four-fifths of the maximum level with virtually no SS control, transforming an average of 78% of their Jewish population into victims.

Thus, one finds that two causes alone — prewar anti-Semitism and SS control in 1941 — account for virtually all (86%) of the variation in Jewish victimization (see Table B-4, Appendix B). From the equations of the lines depicted on Figure 3-4, one can estimate the difference between the expected mean rank of victims in each state and the actual rank — this is easily observable in Figure 3-4 by noting the distance of each state from the line. Two states alone deviate from the expected ranks by more than 13% — the Netherlands and Rumania. Why the outcomes in these states deviate from what we would expect has been discussed in terms of intervening processes that mediated the likelihood of Jews becoming victims; although state cooperation was high in both cases, segregation was accomplished in the Netherlands but not achieved throughout Rumania. Finally, the greater autonomy of Rumania made it possible to foment internal pressures that instigated the state not to implement deportations. The exceptional role of independent Jewish leadership in Rumania in instigating such pressures was also noted.

Most of the variation in the intervening processes can also be accounted for by prewar anti-Semitism and the SS grip in 1941 (see Table B-4, Appendix B). But the forces disposing people to organize to check victimization are not simply the opposite of forces facilitating victimization. It was found that state age (see Table B-4) was also related to church protest against deportation and the immediacy of defense, even after taking anti-Semitism and SS grip into account. Churches were more likely to protest promptly in nations that had been autonomous longer. They were also more likely to have protested against earlier anti-Jewish discrimination. Similarly, social defense movements sprung up sooner in older nations. Tentative explanations of these phenomena will be explored later.

ANTI-SEMITISM AND READINESS FOR THE HOLOCAUST

The extent of Jewish victimization can best be understood by first accounting for the level of prewar anti-Semitism, which predisposed states to high cooperation with the drive to exterminate the Jews regardless of their degree of freedom. Among less anti-Semitic states, the rank of victims increased sharply as a function of the intensity of the SS grip over the state in 1941. Within those states where such control was almost total, victimization was almost total. Most differences among such states within the SS zone are eliminated once one takes into account the percent of Jews exempted. Jews bonded by kinship or conversion of Gentiles were exempted in the expanded Reich (Germany, Austria, and the Protectorate) and Serbia, but not in the Baltic states and Poland.

Clearly, when we evaluate the initial explanations, the most satisfactory one was the Value-Consensus Thesis. But the directness of initial German control did contribute heavily toward Jewish victimization among less anti-Semitic states by increasing the probability of state cooperation, facilitating isolation and inhibiting possibilities for defense and evasion. However, we would predict from the difference contributed by high anti-Semitism alone in the most autonomous states (58%) that had the majority of states in the SS zone (where deportations and extermination began in 1941) been accorded maximal autonomy as German satellites, most of them would have cooperated freely in exterminating the Jews, producing a high percentage of victims. Thus, the outcome among the highly anti-Semitic states of central and eastern Europe in which 87% of Jews (outside the Soviet Union) in German-occupied and allied Europe (see Table 3-1) were concentrated would have been similar, had these states been more autonomous.

National solidarity alone is not sufficient to predict how societies would respond under stress toward the Jews. Though all the high anti-Semitic states were less solidary, some of the less solidary states were low in anti-Semitism. We can predict their response from their disposition to resist discrimination against the Jews. Although the solidarity index was related to national cohesion under stress, as expected (length of time from formation to integration of major resistance movements), resistance movements' willingness to identify with Jews reflected not national unity but their earlier orientation toward the Jews. If the Jews were seen as the enemy within, the enemy's enemy could be one's ally, if only to do the dirty work of eliminating them.

The index of earlier success of the anti-Semitic movements tells us, in effect, how prevalent or dominating was the prewar cognition of the Jew as the enemy. To examine the predictive value of the warning symptoms observed and the dynamics of anti-Semitism in ethnic conflict, it is necessary to note two aspects of the index: the terminal date of 1936, and the discrimination between the second and third level of the scale separating them in the correlation analysis when the scale was bisected. (Those on the third and fourth steps were coded high [1]; those on the first and second steps were coded not high [zero] or low).

Had such a scale been constructed for August 1939 (immediately prior to the invasion of Poland) on these criteria, placement would be very different. The scale was developed to mark stages of movements developed from a mass base, viewing such movements on a political trajectory from entry in the political arena to legitimation. But previous success of movements alone could not explain the institutionalization of anti-Semitic legislation in Europe between 1937 and 1940, which also reflected the foreign policy orientation of states toward Germany. During that period, nations that had earlier guaranteed the Jews complete civil equality—Bulgaria, Yugoslavia, Italy, and the successor states of Czechoslovakia—adopted codes of anti-Semitic legislation discriminating against Jews categorically. However, only in Slovakia did this correspond with prewar demands by a major party. Mussolini spontaneously adopted a comprehensive program of anti-Jewish discrimination in 1938 (without any pressure from Hitler) to balance the fascist state's internal structure with its international commitments; since "international Jewry" was perceived to be inevitably anti-German, it was the enemy of his ally. But the program generated opposition from King, Pope, and the political opposition; most observers agree that it had no significant backing among elites or among the mass of Italians.[36]

ANTI-SEMITISM AND THE DEVELOPMENT OF THE NATION-STATE

Discriminating among states before 1936 enables us to discriminate among states in which there was a constituency to legitimate such legislation if imposed from above.

Such a constituency was mobilized in Europe after 1880 by modern anti-Semitic movements in central and eastern Europe in states with a history of primitive collective violence against Jews—pogroms, blood libels, and like group accusations. However, discrimination against Jews also appeared in new nations (Latvia and Lithuania) that had no history before 1919 of anti-Semitism as a modern political movement because they had no pre-statehood political experience of modern movements competing against each other. But there were other states whose populations exhibited, in the nineteenth century, signs of Jew-hatred—lynchings, pogroms, or rioting against Jews—that did not produce indigenous, modern anti-Semitic movements (Bulgaria, the Protectorate of Bohemia-Moravia). Some states, however, without such a history developed modern anti-Semitic and exclusive nationalist movements. This showed the need for further analysis of how associational and communal forms of anti-Semitism agitation and violence were related to the development of the nation-state.

All the highest ranking anti-Semitic states—Austria, Germany, Hungary, Poland, and Rumania—are in central and eastern Europe, had a late start as modern states, and developed modern, popular anti-Semitic movements between 1890 and 1914 (as did France), exhibiting in earlier centuries a history of popular susceptibility to group libels against Jews. Communal violence—seldom arising spontaneously without leadership—was more likely to be organized among people not yet politically mobilized by the nation-state. When organized, such populations could be transformed into audiences for new movements by reinforcing learned negative imagery of the Jew with ideologies claiming that Jews were responsible for contemporary problems. The paradigm of blame-casting paralleled that of earlier anti-Semitic theology which tutored the troubled to cast out the devil within. Now demagogues harangued their audiences to despoil, declass, expel the Jews. Both revolutionary parties of the right and counterrevolutionary parties found Jew-hatred a useful tool in these nations.

States initially classed on the third level (later aggregated as high on anti-Semitism) did not exist as states before World War I but were regions of nascent exclusive nationalism as was Poland (an older subjugated nation reborn as an entity after World War I), that had been subordinated to dominant nationalities. These nations managed after the Russian Revolution to achieve independence or later defected in response to the threat and opportunity posed by Germany before World War II.

How did such previously subordinated nationalities become carrier groups for anti-Semitic and/or exclusive nationalist movements regardless of their previous history of collective violence? Initially, all these nationalist movements professed democratic ideologies, and respect for the rights of minorities in accord with the treaties guaranteeing those rights imposed by the victors of World War I at Versailles. Regardless of whether such previously subordinated ethnic groups achieved or did not achieve independence after World War I, ethnic competition was intensified in the interwar years, reinforced by the new states' opportunity structure that increased self-conscious group comparison, inducing envy of dominant collectivities or other minorities that had traditionally played critical roles within the nation-state. The new nations' prospective elites perceived visibly dissimilar internal minorities sharing ethnicity of hostile neighboring states and/or playing the roles of the middleman minority.[37] Poles, Germans, and Jews were suspect. The state was seen by such groups as the vehicle to transform the political economy, which could oust the strangers who had illegitimately infiltrated or usurped positions they now wanted for themselves.

Within Salonica, Greek refugees from Turkey sought to label the Jews who had lived there before their expulsion as enemies.[38] Within the federated states of Czechoslovakia and Yugoslavia, the subordinated minorities' demands were basically directed against the dominant group, perceived to have an undue proportion of positions in the state bureaucracies, schools, and army. Resentment of the dominant role played by Czechs and Serbs was exacerbated by the similar religious schism between Slovaks and Czechs and Croats and Serbs — Roman Catholic versus other Christian — which reinforced hostility between communities. Jews did not play a salient political role in either state, but were identified with the dominant nationality politically.

Anti-Semitism was an ideal tactic for radical challengers, because it was simple, popular, and could be used to mobilize movement cadres to foment aggression. Where a tradition of collective violence against Jews did not exist, there was a tradition of collective accusation. Jews had been identified by Christian churches as criminals — deicides, child murderers, well poisoners — for almost two millennia and were often visibly different, speaking the language of the enemy (the dominant nationality or a previous ruling nation) in their homes. Anti-Semitism was also an economic means of arousing a constituency because of the empiric powerlessness of the Jews in political competition between ethnic groups, and the visible role that Jews often played as a middleman minority. Rather than serving as a catharsis for class conflict within a collectivity, as Blalock proposes,[39] anti-Semitism was a functional tactic to raise tension within a collectivity against a substitute target for combat with another collectivity. (In Germany, of course, it served as a trigger to mobilize Germans against others after German dissidents were suppressed but the Nazis' well-advertised animus against the Jews was not deflected by external aggression.) However, demands raised by radical groups among Croat and Slovak nationalists were often resisted by the party leadership (as similar demands were resisted by the governments of the Baltic states, Rumania, and Hungary), because leaders realized that those raising such demands aimed to replace them and make a revolution, a fascist social revolution. Similarly, anti-Semitism was a functional ideology for radical right challengers throughout Europe because the Jews were the only pan-European people who were culturally and politically visible, except for Germans.

Contrasting with the high anti-Semitic states, the lower ranking states include all the older states in Europe (established by 1830), homogeneous newer states with small ethnic minorities (Italy, Norway, Finland, and Estonia) and the severed, formerly dominant collectivities in the post–World War I federated states of Yugoslavia and Czechoslovakia. There was also Bulgaria, a successful multiethnic state with one numerical and politically dominant nationality. Bulgarian leaders (including 16 former premiers and cabinet ministers) reiterated a normative myth of Bulgarian anti-anti-Semitism in 1937 by repudiating anti-Semitism in a publication compiled by a Jewish journalist.[40]

The difference between states with less and more successful anti-Semitic movements gives us a clue to interpret the finding that state age is positively related to early church protest against anti-Jewish discrimination, church protest against deportation of Jews and the immediacy of social defense against deportation, and helps account for these responses, even after taking anti-Semitism and early SS control into account. How can one explain the impact of state age on leaders' disposition to defend the Jews?

Two complementary lines of reasoning are plausible. The emancipation of the Jews in Europe generally accompanied the consolidation of the modern nation-state because, Salo Baron asserts, the grant of citizenship to all and annulment of special statuses was a logical need of those states.[41] If Jews also became integrated following their inclusion — assuming the presence of other conditions mediating integration—the degree of integration should be positively related to the state's age. One then might argue that the better Jews were integrated (viewing state age as a surrogate standing for integration), the less likely were anti-Semitic movements to secure acceptance, and the more likely were other citizens to identify with and defend the Jews. But authorities had other compelling political reasons to defend them. The state's accession to demands for disemancipation of the Jews would signify the destruction of the nation-state's constituent assumptions. An attack upon the Jews was an attack upon the integrity of the nation: it was best realized and defined as that in Denmark (see pp. 114–115, 144–146), the oldest of the most solidary states. To protect the nation, one must also protect the Jews. This implication supports Hannah Arendt's thesis that the rights of the Jews in Europe depended on the maintenance of the nation-state: Arendt, of course, refers to the republican nation-states arising after the French Revolution.[42]

One would also anticipate that the longer the state had endured, the more it would be identified with the nation. Put more simply, the longer the state had lasted as an independent entity, the more likely were leaders to share a common identity and bond together against outsiders, explaining the extent of internal cooperation versus collaboration when invaded, instigated, or manipulated by foreign powers. Thus, Rumanians were more apt to realize that their past and future united them—as Rumanians—than were Hungarians; this may account for the success of Rumania in forging a united path under simultaneous German and Allied pressures as contrasted with the disintegration of Hungarian leadership in 1944, a contrast remarked upon by Nagy-Talavera.[43]

The identity of state and nation is also more common among the older states because they usually arose from a common nationality and/or religion. Viewing the states in our study as members of the state system existent in 1937, three out of every five that had achieved autonomy before 1918 (including all occupied states of western Europe and Greece) were marked by one dominant tongue and one religion to which the overwhelming majority of the population nominally belonged, whereas only three out of 10 states formed after 1918 had one dominant religion and language (see Table 3–6).

The course of German expansion overran the states most susceptible to internal breakdown. Those not slated for German colonization were offered the chance to collaborate. Thus, states within the SS zone (excepting Germany) exhibit many similar characteristics because of inner ethnic conflict and late political development. They are the successor states arising from the breakup of the Russian and Austro-Hungarian empires after World War I. During the interwar period, they showed low cohesion and high partisan polarization. Many also had sizeable ethnic collectivities seeking autonomy or union with a larger power of similar ethnicity. Most of these states had successful anti-Semitic movements before 1936.

TABLE 3–6.   Population Homogeneity* by State Age in 1937 of European States†

	LIKENESS AMONG MEMBERS OF STATE	
State Age in 1937	Alike	Less Alike
Established before 1918	Bulgaria (1878)	Belgium (1830)
	Denmark (pre-1815)	Germany (1865)
	France (pre-1815)	Netherlands (pre-1815)
	Greece (1830)	Rumania (1859)
	Italy (1861)	
	Norway (1905)	
Established 1918–1919	Austria (1918)	Czechoslovakia (1918)
	Estonia (1919)	Hungary (1919)
	Finland (1919)	Latvia (1919)
		Lithuania (1919)
		Poland (1919)
		Yugoslavia (1919)

*States are classified as alike (homogeneous) if three-fourths of the population are estimated to share the same religion (counting claimed membership of all Protestant churches together) and speak the same language, less alike (heterogeneous) if less than three-fourths share these characteristics. Prewar estimates of religious adherence are taken from Johan M. Snoek, *The Greybook: A Collection of Protests against Anti-Semitism and the Persecution of Jews Issued by Non-Roman Catholic Churches and Church Leaders during Hitler's Rule* (The Hague: Van Gorcum, 1969), 302–306. Estimates of linguistic diversity are taken from Stanley Lieberson, Guy Dalto, and Mary Ellen Johnston, "The Course of Mother-Tongue Diversity in Nations," *American Journal of Sociology* LXXXI, no. 1 (July 1975): 36–38 (table 1).

†Includes all states in continental Europe occupied by or allied with Germany except the Soviet Union, Luxembourg, and other smaller states not included in this study.

The most notorious of these anti-Semitic movements — excluding those of Germany and Austria — by 1936 was that of Poland. Parties of the Polish government camp then espoused anti-Semitism openly; annual anti-Jewish riots were organized in the universities to segregate or expel Jewish students; terror and boycotts were instigated against Jews in the countryside; and the government officially campaigned to get world sanction for involuntary emigration of Jews in order to solve Poland's "Jewish problem."[44]

ANTI-SEMITISM AND PATTERNS OF JEWISH SETTLEMENT AND STATUS

Differences between the distribution of Jews in more and less anti-Semitic states are also associated with the divergent courses of national development. High anti-Semitic states generally had substantively larger and more visible Jewish populations than the less anti-Semitic states, fortifying the general perception in prewar Europe that the cause of the Jewish problem was the

Jews. The median percent Jews constituted of the population was almost ten times larger in high anti-Semitic states than in low ones (4.85%: 0.5%) and median visibility (in the city with the most Jews) was almost five times (11.5%: 2.5%) higher in high than in low states. However, neither the perception nor the salience of the Jews was a simple function of their size, as their unfortunate history in Germany alone testifies.[45] Jews were no less visible in Sofia than in Vienna, but not stigmatized in Sofia as they were in Vienna. One of the factors distinguishing Bulgaria from the state of Austria-Hungary was that the role of the middleman in Bulgaria was most often performed by Greeks and Armenians rather than by Jews.

Both belated national emergence and the historic role of the Jew in economic development critically discriminate the higher anti-Semitic (usually younger, less economically developed, and more heterogeneous) states from the less anti-Semitic (generally older, more developed, and homogeneous) states. I suspect (but did not amass data to test the thesis) that a comparative analysis of the entry, growth, and migration of Jewish population and the rise of native social classes in Europe would show that Jews had played a more significant role as a middleman minority in the recent past in the more anti-Semitic states. Capitalism had developed earlier in the less anti-Semitic states by indigenous classes that restricted Jews from competing with the native bourgeoisie (Italy), expelled and readmitted them after the transformation of the economy (Belgium and France), first integrated them in the guise of Christians (such as the Marrano merchants of the Netherlands), or first admitted them in the twentieth century after modern social strata had emerged (Norway and Finland). Immanuel Wallerstein argues that the Jews were expelled from the core states of Europe (all of which are ranked as less anti-Semitic herein, although all the less anti-Semitic states are not core states) between the end of the thirteenth and the fifteenth century because of the greater political influence of the native bourgeoisie there and these states' need for greater ethnic homogeneity.[46] By contrast, the nobles and landowners of the eastern European periphery preferred that the Jews perform mercantile functions because they were a nonindigenous minority without a potential political base to whom the nobles were not socially bonded. It is consistent with his argument to observe that in the nineteenth century all the anti-Semitic states where Jews had performed such a role were in the periphery or semiperiphery. When they achieved statehood in the late nineteenth and twentieth centuries, it was the emergent educated class seeking to fulfill its own claims that demanded the state restrict the Jews, just as the bourgeoisie had done in the core states about five hundred years earlier.

Middlemen minorities are more liable to be ousted because they are from the start excluded from the universe of obligation and because the role they play motivates competitors to improve their own condition by getting rid of them. Wallerstein, discussing the expulsions from the thirteenth to fifteenth century C.E., notes that "the Jews were an easy target for their competitors because an ideological cause could be made of them."[47] By the twentieth century the ideological grounds had evolved, and the audience enlarged, but the target, the paradigm, and the instigators were similar. But the goal of most anti-Semitic movements before 1936 in eastern Europe was to restrict the Jews occupationally, employing quotas and/or de facto state discrimination, not to expel or exterminate them. Given a structural condition of blocked mobility—such as occurred during the depression of the 1930s—Jew-hatred was an opportune ideology. This is not to say that Hitler chose to annihilate the Jews for crass economic reasons: had such reasons motivated him, their subordination rather than extermination would have been sufficient.

IMPLICATIONS

These findings show that vulnerability to genocide is a function of the integration of the social system and the insulation of nation-states within the international system. Both institutional and personal behavior under unusual stress can be explained by the same propositions with which we explain everyday behavior. The response to the attempt to exterminate the Jews during World War II demonstrates that both identification with and disassociation from the victims were normal responses in different states. German instigation and organization of extermination usually succeeded because of the lack of counterauthorities resisting their plans, not because of their repression of such resistance.

We see again how accommodation to authority in the absence of counterauthorities offering models for resistance leads to victimization of the socially designated target. Similarly, Milgram found that the norm of obedience introjected by his subjects led most of them to inflict pain consistently on designated "learners" (actually experimental accomplices) in the laboratory when models defying the experimenter were lacking, despite the absence of any constraint or threat by the experimenter and despite the visible anxiety and anguish that this cost the subject.[48] Milgram also found that increasing the visibility of the learner diminished the likelihood that the subject would inflict the maximum electric shock upon him, thus decreasing the mean summit of shock inflicted. The routinization of the death machine and distancing of processing from killing sites functioned to allow the Germans to exploit the social-psychological mechanisms that Milgram observed could minimize the probability of disobedience. But it was never necessary to coerce anyone to do the "dirty work";[49] there were always enough recruits in communities in which getting rid of the Jews was an objective agreed on publicly before the war.

Among populations with a strong anti-Semitic tradition or movement, there was little need for distancing. Extermination camps' odors wafted into the Polish countryside, yet guards could be recruited and killers enlisted. Natives of Germany, Austria, Poland, Estonia, Latvia, and Lithuania actively participated in murdering the Jews of these states. The availability of native collaborators, later organized into "police battalions" in the Baltic states, enabled the Germans to convert these areas into warehouses for direct extermination, without need either to dull the killers' sensibility by removing and gassing the victims, as was done in the Reich and Poland. Instances are recorded in which the Jews collectively escaped ghettos in such environments by setting fire to them and fleeing to the forests, but the majority were hunted down and murdered by local peasants.[50]

Jewish response in such states was usually a function of their previous isolation and sensed powerlessness; this is discussed further in Chapter 5. Popular demonstrations of violence (and mass murder) reinforced direct German terror and produced isolation. Their isolation — physical and moral — directly increased the chances of becoming victims. Ghettoization reinforced but did not cause isolation: initially, ghettoization often prompted more interaction between Jews and other natives.

Natives gained new apartments, shops, household goods, and clothing during expulsions of Jews to ghettos and continued to barter with them. The ghetto was a veritable bargain basement in a debased social order. Peasants and merchants trading foodstuffs to hungry people on legal rations insufficient to sustain life — as in Warsaw — were well rewarded. As the ghettos were destroyed, more opportunities for private enterprise arose: Jews attempting to evade social definition as Jews outside the ghetto were easy marks for blackmailers who often exploited and then betrayed Jewish evaders.

Jewish victimization can be adequately accounted for only be relating it to the success of prewar anti-Semitism among European nations. The success of anti-Semitism made probable future political accommodation and the lack of church or resistance movements' opposition. The war provided a cover for Germany to impose Hitler's fantasy of exterminating the Jews. The planners correctly anticipated that they would not be checked. The lack of resistance and efficiency of the operation made it possible to go on to the next group that the Reich declared unwanted — the Gypsies.

The Gypsies, being socially invisible and unintegrated, had fewer ties to other citizens than did the Jews. No church spoke out in their defense nor did they create any defense movements — their sole mode of evasion was flight. This was effective in most nations in the colonial zone, except Croatia, which launched its own "Final Solution" against Gypsies and Orthodox Serbs, converting and massacring the latter (sometimes consecutively) in huge numbers (see Chapter 4). Again, they were unhindered by resistance from the dominant Roman Catholic Church, which consistently legitimated the Ustase regime.

The actions of social authorities — church leadership especially — did not merely reflect but defined the situation, instigating actors to avert or stop deportations in the colonial zone, and to inhibit collaboration and subvert raids in the command zone. We do not know whether either private appeals or public protest would have had any direct effect in the SS zone where there was least warning time. But news of church condemnation—however conveyed—might have at least impeded the efficiency of the operation by demoralizing the chain of accomplices. Now we know how many of Hitler's orders were averted, subverted, or contermanded—extermination of tubercular Poles, mass deportation of the Dutch, catching the Jews of Denmark, burning of Paris, destruction of Germany.[51] The order to exterminate the Jews was not checked because it was already taken for granted that getting rid of the Jews was a legitimate objective. Those who did not agree had learned to perceive that the "Jewish problem" was caused by the Jews (and hence would disappear if they did) and inhibited redefinition of the situation to avoid dissonant perceptions and avoid costs of involvement.

To this point, the research has implied a closed system by focusing exclusively on states within Germany's orbit. One cause not yet taken into account, when treating states in the German orbit as a closed system, was the absence of countervailing sanctions or threat of sanctions from the Allies before 1944 to check extermination directly or indirectly by arousing greater resistance among German satellites; the causes of this reluctance are discussed in Chapter 7.

Just as the Allies generally ignored the victimization of the Jews, the imperial powers and most Third World nations have generally ignored the victims of more recent genocides—Burundi, Bangladesh, and Paraguay, and tribal massacres in Nigeria, Rwanda, and Uganda. It is not by chance that these most often occur among newer nations. The dynamics of tribalism, like those of anti-Semitic agitation, are inexorably related to national development and ethnic conflicts. New nationalisms instigate new and previously suppressed groups to contest for power. They try to obtain a monopoly or quota of property and status through the state, using status-group politics, leading some to exploit exclusivist rallying cries and ideologies. Each contender is more likely to stress past grievances and persecutions rather than the aim of excluding and exploiting other groups.

There has been little change in the international system to make it more likely that nations will employ any sanctions against perpetrators of genocide, against their internal minorities. The toll of victims depends on the possibilities opened by the parameters of these situations (whether the attempt occurs within nations, between nations, or in a mixed situation), group location, bordering nation's policies, and access to flight. Experience suggests that flight is the best alternative unless the group is physically and strategically able to deter their enemy. If we take the encapsulation of minorities within the nation-state as a given condition, the implication of the Holocaust is that the life and liberties of minorities depend primarily upon whether the dominant group includes them within its universe of obligation; these are the bonds that hold or the bonds that break.

The Keepers of the Keys

Responses of Christian Churches to the Threat against the Jews

Scarcely two decades after World War II, a great controversy was ignited by a historically based drama, Rolf Hochhuth's *The Deputy*.[1] Hochhuth charged that Pope Pius XII had failed publicly to protest the extermination of the Jews during the war and that his silence was motivated by the church's self-interest. If we ignore Hochhuth's unsupported conjectures of motive, we find massive evidence of the Pope's knowledge of the extermination and of his failure to notify the world and publicly oppose the annihilation of the Jews.[2] Critics have charged that the Vatican helped to legitimate Hitler's regime by its haste in concluding the Concordat of 1933 and that the Catholic bishops of Germany and Austria facilitated the Nazi consolidation of power without limits by their continuous celebration of the state and by their encouragement of Catholics to obey the state unconditionally.[3] Others have charged that even after the war the Vatican identified with the perpetrators of war crimes rather than with their victims, basing their claim on evidence of specially organized Vatican aid that enabled war criminals to escape Europe rather than stand trial for their role in the extermination of the Jews and/or the extermination of Orthodox Serbs in Croatia.[4]

The controversy (as it unfolded) failed to answer some basic questions raised or implied by defenders of Pius XII. Did leaders of dominant Roman Catholic churches protest promptly the deportation and preliminary discrimination of the Jews as often (or any less often) than did leaders of other Christian churches in states where they were dominant? How can these differences be explained? If Roman Catholic churches were less likely to react vigilantly and swiftly to halt deportations, were there sanctions not taken by Pius XII that might have deterred priests from cooperating with anti-Jewish measures authorized by government leaders of Catholic nations? And, finally, what were the grounds for church protest, and what differences among churches were exemplified by their protests? These questions, of course, do not subsume the historic question of the Christian origins of Jew-hatred[5] but inquire into how the actual behavior of the churches as social organizations was related to the life chances of Jews in extreme peril.

FINDINGS ON ROMAN CATHOLIC AND OTHER CHRISTIAN CHURCHES

There is an inverse but weak association between early protest by churches against deportation and Roman Catholicism as the dominant religion and a negative association with public protest against deportation. High prelates of Roman Catholic churches were less likely to speak out publicly against deportations than were the hierarchs of other dominant Christian churches. At first it would seem that this response might be accounted for by the association between Roman Catholicism and high anti-Semitism. Roman Catholic churches were more likely to be located in highly anti-Semitic societies. Conversely, a greater proportion of high anti-Semitic states were dominantly Roman Catholic. Table 4-1 compares church protest in Roman Catholic and non-Catholic states, controlling for the success of the prewar anti-Semitic movement by 1936 and the intensity of German control at the time deportations were initiated. Looking at the top part of the table, one may observe that in states with low prewar anti-Semitism, the highest clergy of all Roman Catholic churches protested publicly or privately (usually privately), whereas in states with more successful prewar anti-Semitic movements, none of the Roman Catholic church heads protested deportations categorically before half of the Jewish population was deported or directly exterminated. However, the leaders of the Lithuanian Catholic Church congratulated Hitler for liberating Lithuania and forbade priests to aid Jews in August 1941 at the peak of their extermination.[6] But where another Christian church was dominant, in states where anti-Semitic movements had been highly successful earlier, half of these churches protested. In dominantly non–Roman Catholic states, where such movements had gained less support before the war, the majority of church heads protested categorically but a minority did not protest. The ambiguous relationship between prewar anti-Semitism and early church protest in non–Roman Catholic states suggests a confounding variable—German control—which is made explicit in the bottom half of Table 4-1. The minority of non-Catholic churches in states with low prewar anti-Semitism that abstained from protest were located in the SS zone at the time extermination or deportations began. Within this region, there was little reason to expect a response to protest and more reason to fear reprisals or repression. Outside the SS zone, no German sanctions have been reported against clergy for protest alone. No churches protested in the SS zone. There was no difference in the likelihood of protest between Roman Catholic and other churches in the occupied states of the command zone lacking self-government; anti-Semitism was low prior to the war in all of the Catholic states in this zone and in all but one of the non-Catholic states and regions. In the colonial zone, in which Germany could not initiate any deportation without state agreement and state police power, the majority of Roman Catholic churches in dominant Roman Catholic states did not protest state collaboration, but both the Orthodox state churches in predominantly Orthodox Catholic states (formerly under Ottoman domination) did, including patriarchs of the Orthodox church of Rumania, the first nation in Europe to begin independently to butcher its own Jews.[7] Theodor Lavi has commented upon the significance of the expressed change of heart by the high clergy of the Rumanian Orthodox Church, many of whom had publicly avowed Jew-hatred before the war and had been open partisans of the anti-Semitic radical movement, the Iron Guard.[8]

Table 4-2 sums up the differences in the response of churches and Jewish victimization between Roman Catholic and non-Catholic states in the colonial zone, in which Germany relied almost wholly on native police forces to do the dirty work. On the average, Roman Catholic states in this zone produced over twice as many victims proportionately as did non-Catholic states.

The majority of Jews were saved from death in all three non–Roman Catholic states in this zone: Bulgaria, Rumania, and Finland—over 99% were saved in Finland. Bulgaria and Rumania did make agreements to deport the Jews but refused to implement them, in effect exempting prewar Jewish citizens. Similarly, the Vichy regime of France retracted its commitment to extend the deportations to Jews who had been naturalized in the interwar years. No reprisal was taken against any of these states for refusing to deport Jews or failing to follow through on its commitment.

Why were dominant non–Roman Catholic state churches in the colonial zone more likely to protest collaboration by their government than were dominant Roman Catholic churches? Their response may be accounted for by the greater disposition on the part of authorities in the older nations to resist anti-Jewish discrimination as well as by the fact that anti-Semitism had been less successful in other states. Three of the four predominantly Roman Catholic states in this zone did not exist as nation-states before World War I; two of them—Croatia and Slovakia—were created in response to Hitler's invitation. Acting as guardians of the state, church hierarchs who protested in the older nations often expressed their belief that collaboration in the crime against the Jews denied the honor and integrity of the state. By contrast, collaboration in the younger nations—especially in Croatia and Slovakia—could be viewed as repayment for the opportunities offered to them (including their existence). For these reasons, their leaders continued collaborating even after German defeat became imminent.

TABLE 4-1. Early Church Protest against Jewish Deportation by Dominant Religion, Prewar Anti-Semitism,* and German Control in European States during the Holocaust†

Protest against Deportations by	DOMINANT RELIGION					
	Roman Catholic			Non-Roman Catholic		
	No Protest	Protest	Total States	No Protest	Protest	Total States
Success of anti-Semitic movement by 1936						
High	6 Hungary Austria Poland Croatia Slovakia Lithuania	—	6	2 Germany Latvia	2 Rumania Salonica	4
Low	—	3 France Belgium Italy	3	3 Serbia Protectorate Estonia	5 Bulgaria Athens Denmark Netherlands Norway	8
Total	6	3	9	5	7	12

TABLE 4-1. (Cont.)

Protest against Deportations by / German control at time of extermination/deportation	DOMINANT RELIGION					
	Roman Catholic			Non-Roman Catholic		
	No Protest	Protest	Total States	No Protest	Protest	Total States
III. SS zone	Austria Poland Lithuania — 3	—	3	Latvia **Germany** Serbia Protectorate Estonia — 5	—	5
II. Command zone	—	Belgium Italy	2	—	Netherlands Norway **Denmark** **Salonica** Athens — 5	5
I. Colonial zone	**Hungary** **Croatia** **Slovakia** — 3	France	4	—	**Rumania** Bulgaria — 2	2
Total	6	3	9	5	7	12

*Boldface indicates high anti-Semitic states.

†Includes all states in continental Europe occupied by or allied with Germany except the Soviet Union, Luxembourg, and other smaller states not included in this study.

One may also observe how different were the heritages of states with dominant Roman Catholic and Orthodox Catholic churches: most of the former arose from the breakup of Austria-Hungary, the nexus in which political anti-Semitism first developed, while the latter states arose from the disintegration of the Ottoman Empire. Although Jews and Christians as non-Muslims were subordinated at all times by the Ottomans, anti-Semitism did not achieve political significance in the Ottomans' domain when they were sovereign. It is likely that the development of anti-Semitism is associated with different culture areas because of variations in social structure. Austria-Hungary was a more fertile breeding-ground for anti-Semitism (as were Poland and Russia) because of the distinctive role Jews had once played as a middleman minority. As aliens they were invited to play that role because of the backward social structure of these areas, associated with their retarded national development and their consequent recent origin as nation-states. To be sure, the Balkan states emerging from the Ottoman Empire also had a backward social structure, but the role of middleman minority had been played by many groups in the Empire—Armenian, Greek, Syrian Christians, and Jews—so that Jews were less apt to be a focus of envy and resentment except in Rumania, where they did play that role.

Regardless of how one explains the fact that dominant Roman Catholic

TABLE 4-2. Early Church Protest and Jewish Victimization by Dominant Religion of States in the Colonial Zone during the Holocaust

Dominant Religion	Early Protest by Head of Church against Discrimination	Deportation	Jewish Population in 1941 (to nearest thousand)*	Rank of Victims
Roman Catholic				
Croatia†	—	—	30	8
France	—	+	350	3
Hungary	—	—	825	8
Slovakia	—	—	89	9
Total			1,294	
All States: mean rank of Victims				7.0
Other Christian				
Finland	—	DNA	2	1
Bulgaria	+	+	63	2
Rumania	—	+	615	6
Total			680	
All States: mean rank of Victims				3.0

*For sources on Jewish population and victimization see the notes to Table 3-1 (p. 54*f*).
†Boldface indicates high anti-Semitic states.
DNA–does not apply; there were no general deportations in Finland.

churches in the colonial zone were less likely to protest deportations than were other dominant churches in German-allied states, their failure to protest at a time when protest might have been a deterrent cannot be denied. Nor can the influence of the Roman Catholic Church in these states be denied, for clerics were the backbone of the anti-Semitic movements catapulted to power in Slovakia and Croatia in 1938 and 1941, and the Roman Catholic Church in Hungary had approved anti-Jewish legislation until these laws began discriminating against Christians of Jewish origin.

Because states in the colonial zone were free to deport or not to deport and the church played a leading role in legitimating the state, I shall first focus on the responses of dominant Roman Catholic churches in the colonial zone, showing their role in the three instances in which collaboration was unimpeded and the one Catholic state in which it was checked—France. To discriminate the role of the Vatican from that of the native hierarchy, I will examine how the threat against the Jews presented itself in each of the Roman Catholic states in the colonial zone, the response of the high clergy, and pressure upon them from the Papacy.

COLONIAL ZONE STATES

Slovakia

The first German-established satellite and the first state to make an agreement with Germany to deport its Jews was Slovakia. It was severed from Czechoslovakia after Munich with the ready cooperation of the radical wing of the Slovak People's Party, which had represented the union of clericalism and ethnic nationalism since its establishment by Father Andreas Hlinka in 1905. Party ideologues had consistently defined Jews as outsiders, economic and cultural enemies. The anti-Jewish motif was rearticulated by the radical wing and youth movement of the party in the thirties as they stirred up anti-Jewish street demonstrations and published anti-Semitic manifestoes, agitating for Slovak autonomy after the claims of the Czech German nationalists were granted at Munich.[9] The Parliament of the virtually autonomous federated state of Slovakia declared its independence in March 1939, after Hitler bid its leaders to do so.

A month after the state's establishment (April 1938) the Slovak government defined a Jew, in accordance with the Catholic anti-Semitic tradition, as one who practiced Judaism and/or was of Jewish birth and was not converted, thus exempting Catholics of Jewish birth or ancestry. A new definition including all Jews by "race," irrespective of religion, and a comprehensive code of anti-Jewish legislation were passed by the government in 1941. Opposition to the discrimination of Catholics of Jewish ancestry reflected the antagonism between clerical and radical anti-Semites, the latter quickly adapting Nazi ideology, which necessitated the more inclusive definition. This internal conflict was the source of most intragovernmental and church protests in 1942; the church claimed its right to protect Catholics from the fate to be meted out to Jews.

By the end of 1941, Jews had been effectively defined, registered, stripped of most wordly goods, segregated, and isolated in labor camps and countryside encampments after their expulsion from Bratislava. A special government bureau was established to superintend a government-appointed Jewish Council that, following the arrest of its first director in 1941, faithfully executed government orders during the period in which the majority of Jews were deported.[10]

Deportations began on 26 March 1942, after an agreement was signed with the German Foreign Office specifying that deportations would be stopped if they evoked internal opposition—"that is, no measures were to be taken that would antagonize the churches to such an extent as to threaten Slovakia's internal stability."[11] The Slovak government agreed to pay a fee to Germany for the expenses of deportation: 500 reichsmarks per capita.

A collective appeal to cancel deportations by the rabbis of Slovakia to Father Tiso, the head of state, in March 1942 was filed away.[12] By October 1942, two out of every three Slovakian Jews had been deported.

The Vatican's objections, like those of the Slovakian church, initially focused on the status of Catholics classified as Jews.[13] But Friedlander observes that the Vatican's diplomatic service in Rome and Bratislava clarified the meaning of "resettlement," indicating its appreciation of German intent.

> As early as February 1942, the Apostolic Nuncio in Slovakia had declared to Msgr. Vojtech Tuka, the Prime Minister, that "it is incorrect to believe that the Jews are being sent to Poland to work; in reality they are being exterminated there."[14]

Father Tiso answered the Vatican's appeals diplomatically rather than by filing them, as he had the rabbis' protest. The Slovak government denied the Nuncio's information on the fate of the deported, by repeating that the Jews were to be resettled to work for Germany. The attempts of Monsignor Burzio, the Apostolic Delegate, to instigate resistance within the Slovak Roman Catholic Church were notably unsuccessful. Although the bishops in April 1942 authorized publication in Catholic periodicals (documents do not make clear who read these journals) of a declaration asserting that Jews were also human beings, they said nothing about deportations. Not one of the priests acting as representatives to the Slovak Parliament voted against the body's post hoc authorization of the deportations on 15 May 1942.

Nor did anyone else vote No. Nevertheless, continued diplomatic protests, at last including a direct appeal to halt the deportations presented to the Slovakian representative to the Vatican in June 1942 in the name of the Pope, impelled Prime Minister Tuka to seek German reassurances on the fate of the deported Jews in order to exculpate himself.[15] Tuka's expressed need provoked SS Captain Wisliceny, the representative of the Reich Main Security Office in Bratislava, to request his superior in Berlin (Eichmann) to send a Slovakian delegation to inspect the living conditions of the deported Slovakian Jews. Eichmann naturally refused, since there were hardly any living Slovakian Jews to inspect. By 1943, the Germans' refusal, the eyewitness testimony of Jews who had fled from Poland to Slovakia, which corroborated the Vatican reports of extermination (received directly from the World Jewish Congress), similar Polish reports relayed by the BBC, and the changing tide of the war after Stalingrad impelled the Slovakian bishops to decry publicly the deportation of Jews in a pastoral letter read from the pulpits on 22 March 1943. The message, one informant states, was read in Latin, perhaps to render it incomprehensible.[16] But the German minister in Bratislava reported that many priests refused to read it or interjected their own comments negating its contents. Clerical opposition to the message was so strong that the Slovak church did not publish it with the official seal.[17] The Slovak government's demand for confirmation of the conditions of the deportees in 1943, instigated by persistent Vatican protest, led the German Foreign Minister to instruct his representative in Slovakia to put no "official" pressure on the government to begin further deportations in July 1943, in accord with their original agreement.[18] By that date, only one of every three Slovakian Jews was still alive in Slovakia. Deportations were not resumed until after the repression of the Slovak uprising in September 1944.

Despite its evidenced desire to curtail Slovakia's collaboration in delivering its Jews for deportation, the Vatican at no time threatened any sanctions for defiance of its wishes by the priests running the state. Nor did the Pope ever define cooperation in delivering Jews to the Germans as a sin or an act not permissible for a Catholic clergyman. Thus, when the Vatican representative in Bratislava, Monsignor Burzio, appealed to the "Catholic-Christian conscience" of Prime Minister Tuka, citing the massacre and extermination in Lublin and the Ukraine, Tuka replied

> that for him there existed a higher authority in this matter, to wit, his confessor. The latter had asked him if he could take upon his conscience the responsibility for the deportation of the Jews as a thing done for the good of his people. When Tuka replied in the affirmative, the confessor, he said, had not opposed the actions involved.[19]

The cessation of deportations in July 1943 was a belated response to Vatican appeals. However, the failure of the Vatican to employ sanctions to forbid the deportations from Slovakia drew questions from the British minister. Responding to such questions, Monsignor Tardini, a Vatican spokesman, noted (for his colleagues' eyes): "The misfortune is that the President of Slovakia is a priest. That the Holy See cannot bring Hitler in line all can understand. But that [the Pope] cannot curb a priest, who can understand that?"[20]

Croatia

Croatia's independence derived from Hitler's offer of sovereignty (reserving Germany's right to station troops there) in April 1941 to Anton Pavelic, the head of an exclusivist Catholic-Croat terrorist movement, the Ustase. The Ustase, established in 1919 and banned in Yugoslavia, had been financed in exile by Italy since 1929. The Ustase were held responsible for the assassination of King Alexander of Yugoslavia in Marseilles in 1934, an act intended to break up Yugoslavia. Hitler's offer to Pavelic followed the refusal of Vladko Macek, head of the Croatian Peasant Party—the leading prewar party in Croatia—to accept office and autonomy as Hitler's client.[21] Hitler had assented to Croatia's falling within the Italian zone of influence—an Italian army occupied its coast, and the Duke of Spoleto, a member of the Italian royal house, was persuaded to accept its throne, symbolizing the relationship—but Pavelic sought greater identification with Germany, even announcing in June 1941 that the Croats were not Slavs but descendants of the Goths, a Germanic people. However, Croatia was not simply a puppet state, despite the avidity with which it furthered German goals by slaughtering Jews and Gypsies. The policy that it pursued, initially of forced conversion and genocide of the Orthodox Serb minority—later a puppet Croatian Orthodox Church was established—was not instigated but tolerated by Germany. Rich tells us that the German officials there,

> concerned with the preservation of security and order, were dismayed by the effects of these policies. [The German military attaché] protested regularly against the ruthless persecution of the Serbs and other minority groups. . . . Hitler, however, not only condoned but actively encouraged the Croatian government's racial policies.[22]

Hitler ordered that Germany respect the treaty of May 1941 guaranteeing nonintervention in Croat internal affairs, despite the urgent military threat posed for the Germans by the growth of guerrilla insurgency in Yugoslavia, aggravated by the Ustase policies.

The literature of Croatia as an independent state (1941–1945) is sparse; most expatriated nationalist Croatian scholars would apparently prefer to forget or deprecate the bloody record of that state. Yugoslavian scholars are not apt to revive ethnic nationalism except in documenting fascist crimes during the war. The Tito government's trial of Archbishop Stepinac, the highest Roman Catholic prelate, for his support of the Ustase state enabled the Archbishop's sympathizers to exploit anti-Communist antipathy to the regime in the West after the war and to disregard the substantive evidence against him. Without denying the political functions of the postwar trials, one finds that nonpartisan sources agree that mass genocide was authorized by the state of Croatia. They concur that the state instigated, planned, and executed massacres against the Serbian Orthodox minority that made the Serbs more willing to accept conversion to Roman Catholicism, and that the Catholic clergy approved, led, or failed to denounce these massacres.[23] The Croats' collective hatred of the Orthodox Serbs was explicit in folk sayings such as "Serbs to the willows [hang the Serbs]." Their anti-Semitism was less openly expressed, for the Jews, unlike the Serbs, had not presented any political challenge to them in prewar Yugoslavia.

By June 1941, signs on public establishments read, NO SERBS, JEWS, NOMADS, AND DOGS ALLOWED.[24] The Serbs, unlike Jews and Gypsies, were sometimes offered the chance to become acceptable citizens by conversion. But only the Roman Catholic, Muslim, and German Evangelic faiths were recognized; the Roman Catholic Church had the exclusive right to convert; and the means of salvation offered were sometimes a hoax. Serbs awaiting the priest were at times locked in Roman Catholic churches and the churches set afire, as Jews had been set afire in synagogues in Poland. Many Serbs and Jews fled to the adjacent Italian zones, wherein Italian commanders gave them protection. Others joined the partisans fighting in the mountains. Thousands of Jews had fled from Croatian cities, leaving behind those unable to fight or flee—women, children, the elderly, and the ill. These people were interned in Croatian concentration camps whose officers made no provisions for feeding them. The few remaining Jewish community officials negotiated with Ustase officials in order to obtain the right to feed these helpless Jews, thus obtaining temporary stays of execution.[25] The small proportion of inmates who had survived these camps by November 1942 were deported to Auschwitz.

Archbishop Stepinac interceded consistently to protect Catholics of Jewish parentage (converts) and Jews with Catholic spouses or close relatives from discrimination and incarceration.[26] Rabbi Freiberger, Chief Rabbi of Zagreb, also relied on the protection of the Archbishop and appealed to Pope Pius XII, on behalf of Jews still alive in Croatia, acknowledging the need for his protection with attestations of gratitude.[27] Charles Stekel, the last rabbi of Osijek (Croatia) tells us that Dr. Freiberger was deported to Auschwitz in May 1943 despite assurances from the Archbishop, who repeatedly told him to remain in Zagreb.[28]

The Archbishop first publicly denounced racial dogma in a sermon on 14 March 1943, in which he affirmed the worth of the hunting peoples of Africa, and on 25 October 1943 he boldly asserted from the pulpit that "one cannot efface from the earth Gypsies or Jews because one considers them inferior races."[29] But both Gypsies and Jews had virtually been effaced from Croatia by that time. Indeed, Archbishop Stepinac had played a supporting role in the unfolding genocide by celebrating Pavelic's return and he continued to support the Ustase regime and defend the record of Croatia to the Vatican in 1943. The Archbishop's public stance of protest in that year may have been prompted by his desire to satisfy Vatican inquiries for information that would be useful to repudiate "Serbo-Orthodox propaganda"—allegations of persecution. Archbishop Stepinac in a note to Cardinal Maglione, the Vatican Secretary of State, on 24 May 1943 denied charges that the state of Croatia had committed any crimes—although he admitted that "irresponsible" persons might have done so in 1941 in the name of the state—and praised the many actions of the government of Croatia to rectify past evils (such as abolishing abortion and pornography), which, he said, had been committed in the past by Jews and Orthodox Serbs.[30]

Similarly, the spirit of the new state was acclaimed in Catholic publications. Priests participated in all aspects of political life, including extermination squads; the Franciscans were especially noted for their leadership. Paris tells us that nearly half of the twenty-two Croatian extermination camps were headed by priests.

More confirmation of the Vatican's early information regarding the events in Croatia is provided by Branko Bokun's diary. Bokun, a young official in the Yugoslavian Foreign Office, was delegated in August 1941 to appeal directly to the Vatican to stop the slaughter in Croatia. He brought a portfolio of evidence with him, including a copy of the speech by Mike Budak, Minister of Religion of Croatia, on 22 July 1941, promising three million bullets for non-Catholics. Bokun was admitted to the office of Monsignor Montini (subsequently Pope Paul VI), then a deputy to the Secretary of State, with whom he left his portfolio. Shortly thereafter he was told by Montini's secretary that the Croatian Ambassador had "explained that the atrocities described in your file are the work of the Communists, but maliciously attributed to the Catholics."[31] The secretary explained that nothing more could (meaning "would") be done.

News about Croatia came to the Vatican through many independent sources—its own Papal Legate, Italian army chaplains and soldiers stationed in Croatia, the official Yugoslav representatives to the Holy See, and Orthodox clergy representatives outside Croatia, as well as the Croatian Catholic bishops. Cardinal Maglione acknowledged the complaint of 23 December 1942 presented by the Embassy of Italy to the Vatican but rebutted its charges, affirming that

the Apostolic Visitator, to whom the Secretariat of State showed the note of the Embassy of Italy, was unable to conceal some surprise on reading what is stated without any reservation, that is, that the attitude of the [Croatian] clergy is certainly one of the most dangerous elements in the situation in Croatia. . . . both the Croatian episcopate and clergy respect the lawful authorities and collaborate effectively in the work of internal pacification: and that, in fact, the clergy, both secular and regular, supports and defends the central government, although it cannot always approve its attitudes.[32]

Such charges and reports to the Vatican about the means taken to propagate the faith did not diminish pride in the new, self-righteously Catholic state, exhibited in the honors accorded to visiting Ustase delegations and the state's official representative in Rome.[33]

The Apostolic Visitator in Zagreb, Abbot Marcone, pursued inquiries initiated in Rome by Italians and American Jews regarding the whereabouts of particular Croatian Jews but got no answers from Croatian ministers. Marcone reported that he attempted to delay the deportation of almost 5,000 Jews, which began in November 1942, and was told categorically by Croatian Chief of Police Kvaternik that the Jews would be shipped to Germany, where, the minister continued, two million Jews had been killed already—Kvaternik did not dissemble as the Slovakian ministers had done.[34] Nevertheless, the Vatican made no attempt to forbid the deportation. However, the great majority of the 24,000 Jews killed, virtually all the 28,500 Gypsies slain, and all the Serbs—around 570,000—who were slaughtered were murdered in Croatia—killed directly by knife or hatchet or by torture, rape, epidemics, and starvation while in Croatian camps. These facts are ignored in the Vatican's report of its activities during that period.[35]

Despite all these sources of information, Ustase representatives at the Vatican were occasionally questioned but never officially reprimanded. Falconi observes that

> simulated attack, patient listening, generous surrender: these were the three stages characteristic of every audience granted to the Ustase representatives by the heads of the Secretariat of State.[36]

Pope Pius XII never accused or simulated an attack on the behavior of the Ustase.

> The most astonishing fact of all is Pius XII's behavior—it is not only incomprehensible but quite unacceptable—is that he should have avoided even mentioning the constant massacres perpetrated in Croatia, either to the Poglavnik [Pavelic] or to the various Ustase representatives who managed to approach him. Judging by the Pope's words, Croatia was an exemplary, not to say idyllic, kingdom, with which the Holy See was impatient to establish long-lasting and official relations so as to weld modern developments on to the history of its glorious past: it was not the country where hundreds of thousands of Orthodox were being slaughtered for religious and racial reasons, where Jews and Gypsies were bloodily pursued.[37]

Thus, we cannot assess what the effects of any Vatican sanctions might have been upon the Ustase, for there were no sanctions. The state's chief leaders fled Yugoslavia in 1945 with Vatican aid.

OLDER NATIONS

Hungary

Hungary, as an Axis ally, was a completely autonomous, self-governing country until its invasion by Germany in March 1944. The government's commitment to Germany was based on a calculation of benefits received or expected from Germany, costs extracted for these benefits, and threats anticipated from Germany, the United States, Britain, and the U.S.S.R. Hungary had received portions of Rumania, Czechoslovakia, and Yugoslavia, much of which had previously been taken away from Hungary by the Trianon Treaty ending World War I, which the party in power had never accepted. Between 1941 and 1944, Hungary's policy zigzagged, directed by ministries of "pro-German" politicians and "reluctant collaborators," as Hilberg put it.[38] The last of the latter before the German invasion was Nicholas Kallay (March 1942–March 1944), who describes in his memoirs how he effectively used anti-Semitic rhetoric to mask his goal of protecting the Jews from both deportation and domestic discrimination.[39]

Although before March 1944 the Regent had rejected requests from the German Foreign Office to deport the Jews, the status of the Jews had begun declining in Hungary a quarter century earlier. The Regent, Admiral Horthy, came to power as a leader of the counterrevolution of 1920, which was accompanied by three years of pogroms known as the "White Terror." Horthy represented the Magyar gentry, or landed classes, known as the "Magyar Nation," who had until that time coexisted in a tolerant symbiosis with the Jews, the group that had originally filled the role of the absent bourgeoisie in Hungary. The Communist regime of Bela Kun in 1919 threatened the control of the Magyar gentry. Opponents of the revolution were divided into two camps: the Vienna group, headed by Count Stephen Bethlen, of traditional, authoritarian beliefs; and the Szeged group, identified with Gyula Gombos (Premier from 1932 to 1936), a radical rightist movement espousing national socialism. The latter exploited the visibility of a disproportionate number of Jews and converts of Jewish origin in the revolutionary regime's leadership to raise the rallying cry of a new counterrevolutionary ideology, the Szeged Idea. Both groups were responsible for the White Terror, implemented throughout the country by the officer corps and secret nationalist societies such as the Association of Awakening Hungarians and the Association of Hungarian National Defense (M.O.V.E.), headed by Gombos.

The government began stripping Jews of civil equality with the passage of the first numerus clausus act in 1920, limiting the entry of Jewish students to the university. Jews were also excluded from posts in the official bureaucracies, police, and schools between 1920 and 1938. However, the first comprehensive code defining Jews by racial ancestry was passed in 1938. Further discriminatory legislation expropriating Jewish-owned lands was passed in 1942.

Although in 1944 Hungarian Jews were still unsegregated, in 1941 the alien police agency expelled about 15,000 to 20,000 non-Hungarian-born Jews from Transylvania (Hungary's easternmost part, yielded to Rumania in 1919 and reannexed in 1940). These people were driven across the border to Poland, where they were massacred. News of a general extermination came with the return of some escapees of this group and from Polish Jews fleeing into Hungary. The intentions of the generals were clear: General Heszlenyi had requested German aid on 21 July 1942 to deport "about 100,000 Jews" who had entered Hungary illegally (a significantly larger estimate than others). Eichmann refused, anticipating that he would be able to catch all the Jews of Hungary in his net if he waited.[40]

Jews in Hungary were nominally free until 1944, except for men up to the age of 48, who were compelled to serve in labor brigades as a compulsory alternative to military service. Because of the punitive conditions and sometimes torture imposed by their commanders, they ran a high risk of death. Testimonies tell of commanders who sent men out in wintertime clad in summer clothing, employed Jews as human minesweepers, and organized shooting and torture parties against Jews. The army was responsible for the fact that 25,456 of the 37,200 Jews sent to Russia in 1941 were killed, wounded, or missing and for the massacre of about 3,300 Serbs and Jews in the Ujvidek area (formerly Yugoslavia) in 1941 in a supposed anti-partisan reprisal.[41]

The swing toward the radical right was a popular movement. Nagy-Talavera evaluates the popular vote in 1939, estimating that acknowledged native fascist parties won 45% of the total votes cast, and 41.7% in the industrial zone of Budapest, formerly called the "Red Belt." There they emerged as the strongest single party, consistently gaining as the Social Democrats' vote diminished.[42] The army, whose officer class was often active in radical right movements, was frequently of Swabian (ethnic German) origin, and an unreliable instrument of the Regent, of dubious loyalty. The Social Democrats, Workers Party (Communist), Smallholders and Peasants Party alone defended civil equality for the Jews, but their constituency was dwindling. Both the dominant Roman Catholic Church and the Lutheran Church had approved the 1938 Jew Law, seeking only to exempt converted Jews from its coverage.

Only against this background can we understand the consequences of the German invasion of 19 March 1944, authorized by Hitler to ward off Hungary's defection from the Axis alliance. The Regent agreed under pressure to appoint a pro-German cabinet, not to resist the entry of German soldiers, and to supply 100,000 Jews for *labor* in German aircraft factories. The Hungarian Under-Secretaries for Jewish Affairs, Laszlo Endre and

Laszlo Baky, *requested* the deportation of the Jews (after having authorized ghettoization), and the Council of Ministers approved the request on 20 April 1944. Eichmann recalled this period in an interview given to a journalist in Argentina before his capture:

> It was clear to me that I, as a German, could not demand the Jews from the Hungarians. We had had too much trouble with that in Denmark. So I left the entire matter to the Hungarian authorities. Dr. Endre, who became one of the best friends I have had in my life, put out the necessary regulations, and Baky and his Hungarian gendarmerie carried them out. Once these two secretaries gave their orders, the Ministry of the Interior had to sign them.[43]

Without full Hungarian cooperation and the Hungarian gendarmerie of 20,000 men, Veesenmeyer, the German Ambassador, testified after the war, the deportations would not have been possible.[44] Eichmann's force in Hungary constituted only eight SS officers and 40 enlisted men. The Hungarian collaborators would not publicly recognize the destiny to which they committed the Jews, issuing apologia such as the following:

> No one intends the extermination, annihilation or torture of the Jews. . . . Nobody intends to rid the world entirely of the Jew: we merely wish to save our race from their noxious influence. I think that all of us . . . will be very happy when at last the unfortunate people of Ahasueras finds, far from our borders, a home somewhere on the globe where it can establish a state of its own.[45]

Similarly, they held masses to celebrate the final departure from Hungary of the "sons of Ahasueras."

No adequate account has been written of the activities of the Roman Catholic Church during this period. However, Jëno Levai has collected documentation from Hungarian sources of Vatican diplomatic activities and the responses of the Hungarian church, headed by Cardinal Serenedi.[46] These documents were supplemented by others I found in the files of the American War Refugee Board (WRB), which had initiated a propaganda campaign to deter Hungarian cooperation in the deportations.

Before the deportations were stopped, Cardinal Serenedi had intervened continuously for baptized Jews but refused the request of Budapest Jewish leaders on 23 June 1944, that he appeal to the Regent to stop the deportation of the Jews. After previous attempts at negotiation through the Allies and domestic appeals to the ruling fascist clique had proved futile (lacking clerical or other base of internal support), Budapest Jews began to rely on instigating diplomatic intervention by Allies and neutrals—Sweden, Spain, Switzerland—who also provided them with papers of protection.[47] The Vatican's Nuncio cooperated with other neutrals in this endeavor.

But the Cardinal was pressed by one of his bishops and by the Apostolic Nuncio in Budapest to take a public stand. Therefore, on 30 June, he prepared to publish an address in which he did not condemn the deportations so much as wash his hands of responsibility. Even then, he desisted from publicizing the letter at the government's request. Not until 16 July—after the deportation order had been cancelled—did Serenedi authorize a reading of this address from the pulpit. The message was clearly intended to exonerate the church; there was not a single mention of the Jews as victims. After a comprehensive justification of the bishops' right to protest and citation of crimes of the Allies against the Hungarian people (bombings), he alluded to the unnamed victims of the unspeakable deed as "some of our Hungarian fellow-countrymen, including people bound to us by the ties of the same holy faith . . . our fellow-countrymen and fellow Catholics."

The Cardinal solemnly declared that the church's patient intercessions with the government (primarily to protect Catholics of Jewish ancestry) had failed, and thus "we solemnly renounce all responsibility."[48]

The Vatican's Nuncio in Budapest, Monsignor Rotta, in 1944 responded to the series of steps that always prefaced the deportation and destruction of the Jews by issuing the same type of appeal that had proved futile in Bratislava in 1942. Through March and April he consistently stressed the right of Christians to be exempt from the regulations that applied to Jews. After 17 May, Hungarian officials received word via Monsignor Rotta that *"he was directed* [by Pius XII] *to intervene on behalf of the Jews."*[49] But the Hungarian ministers denied complicity in mass-murder by asserting that Jews were being deported merely for labor. There is no evidence that the Nuncio used the Auschwitz Protocol, an eyewitness description of Auschwitz obtained in April 1944 from two escaped Jews, to refute these claims,[50] although he was fully aware (as was Cardinal Serenedi, who had also received the report) that the assertion was based on a lie.[51]

What more could be expected of the Vatican? The American government, the Archbishop of Canterbury, and Jewish leaders had called upon the Pope in 1942, to no avail, asking him to censure publicly the deportations and to label them as murder. The War Refugee Board had begun urging the Apostolic Delegate in Washington to appeal to the Holy See to protect the Jews of Hungary and Rumania on 24 March 1944. Once isolation of the Jews began, the Board initiated a request to the Pope on 26 May 1944 (through the State Department's Vatican representative, Harold Tittman) asking him to appeal to the Hungarian authorities and people, threatening "ecclesiastical sanctions." The Pope continued the policy of restricting himself to diplomatic means, appealing personally to the Regent to stop the deportations in a telegram on 25 June.[52] Horthy convened a meeting of the Crown Council the next day, according to Levai, calling on "the members of the government to put an end to the cruelties of the deportation." But the Pope's message implied no sanction: "When the Pope's intervention was not proclaimed 'urbi et orbi' [to the city—that is, Rome—and the world] and Hitler thereby branded as a murderer, the Germans were content to instruct their representative in Hungary, Veesenmeyer, to prevent Horthy . . . from complying with the Pope's wishes."[53]

Nevertheless, the Regent ordered the deportations stopped on 6 July 1944, citing the Pope's intervention and appeals of other neutrals and the Allies. Attempts to overthrow his regime and deport the Jews of Budapest — the only category remaining — were foiled in August. War Refugee Board records contain significant proof of the time lapses in the Pope's responses and his failure to respond after July 1944. The records also reveal the promptness of response of the Apostolic Delegates in Washington (Monsignor Cicognani) and in Ankara (Monsignor Angelo Roncalli, later to become Pope John), showing that time lapses could not be attributed to poor communications.[54] Between 26 April and 25 June 1944, 371,427 Hungarian Jews were deported, and others died or committed suicide in camps and ghettos in Hungary. Subsequent appeals to the Vatican by the director of the War Refugee Board, John Pehle, asking the Pope publicly to broadcast appeals to clergy and laity to conceal Jews (after the Arrow Cross coup of 16 October 1944) failed to elicit a response.[55] As in the case of Croatia, the policy of ignoring non-German Catholics' responsibility for massacres of Jews was pursued.

To assess the role of the Roman Catholic Church in Hungary, we must discriminate between the Vatican and the Hungarian hierarchy. The Hungarian Roman Catholic Church's role in making the Holocaust possible did not begin in 1944 but in 1919. Since the church provided no normative sanctions against anti-Semitism in Hungary, approving its unfolding until it threatened Catholics, the pro-German ministers that the Regent picked for the postoccupation cabinet had no reason to expect any significant resistance to the deportations from the church. Although eyewitness sources of information on the extermination of the Jews were many and had been received by the Vatican, no representative of the Vatican ever publicly told Catholics that they must not cooperate because Germany was killing Jews systematically and totally, and killing Jews was a sin. This enabled the government ministers working with Eichmann to deny that they knew about Auschwitz. The Pope refrained from any warning to Catholics; he appealed to the Regent privately in his own name two months after the War Refugee Board had asked him to employ the threat of ecclesiastical sanctions, three weeks after Rome was liberated. Thus, the Pope abstained from employing the only sanction he had that was unique by refusing to define the extermination of Jews publicly as a moral, rather than a political, issue.

France

Among predominantly Roman Catholic states in the colonial zone, the best instance of how the church legitimated the government and could apply the brakes to stop the destruction process is France. France had experienced a large influx of foreign Jews between world wars I and II. By 1940 foreign-born Jews constituted over half of the estimated 350,000 Jews in France. Their numbers and visible differences and the traditional hostility of the French rightists to the Jews, exacerbated by the rightists' identification of the 1936 antifascist regime of Leon Blum as a government of Jews, led to a revival of xenophobic anti-Semitism. By 1940, at least 6,000 Jews were incarcerated in detention camps and work camps for foreigners.[56]

The Vichy government, endowed by the National Assembly with complete authority to revise the constitution and govern, embarked on a new program repudiating guarantees of civic equality. No opposition was shown by the French Catholic Church to the spate of discriminatory legislation promulgated by Vichy in 1940 and 1941, which excluded French Jews as well as foreign-born Jews from government offices and the professions. The regime was sufficiently alert to potential objections to acting upon the program that Action Française had called for during the preceding four decades (disapproved by the Vatican but approved widely by French prelates) to ask its Ambassador to the Vatican, Leon Bérard, to determine whether the Vatican would repudiate anti-Jewish discrimination. Bérard's letter to Pétain enables us to understand how the Catholic Church reconciled its theoretic antiracialism (which repudiated stigmatizing Jews by blood as that violated the right of Jews to convert to Catholicism and be accepted as Catholics) and its toleration of discrimination against Jews with no grounds to disclaim being labeled as Jews.

Vatican City
September 2, 1941

Monsieur le Maréchal [Pétain]:

In your letter of August 7, 1941, you requested certain information as to the problems and difficulties which could arise from the Roman Catholic point of view in connection with the measures your government has taken with respect to the Jews. I had the honor of sending you a first reply in which I stated that at the Vatican I have never been told anything which—from the standpoint of the Holy See—implied criticism and disapproval of the legislative and administrative acts in question. . . .

The subject is complex. . . .

On July 29, 1938, in a speech addressed to students of the College of Propaganda, Pius XI said: "We forget that the human species, the whole human species is one single, grand, universal, human race. At any rate, we cannot deny that in this universal race there is place for special races, . . ." . . .

However, the teachings of the Church on racial theories do not necessarily mean that it condemns any particular measure of any state against the so-called Jewish race. . . .

The Church recognizes that among the distinctive features of the Israelitic community there are particular, not racial but ethnical, qualities. The Church has always clearly seen this fact and has always reckoned with it. History tells us that the Church often protected Jews against the violence and injustice of their persecutors and that at the same time it has consigned them to the ghettos. . . . While proscribing any policy of oppression towards the Jews, Saint Thomas recommends nevertheless to take measures designed to limit their action in society and to check their influence. It would be unreasonable, in a Christian state, to permit them to exercise the functions of government and thus to submit the Catholics to their authority. Consequently it is *legitimate to bar them from public functions, legitimate also to admit but a fixed proportion of them to the universities* (numerus clausus) *and to the liberal professions.* . . .

As I was told by an authorized spokesman at the Vatican: we shall not in the least be reprimanded for this statute on the Jews.[57]

The information that "we shall not in the least be reprimanded for this statute on the Jews" was used by the Commissariat Général aux Questions Juives, the government agency responsible for implementing the statute, in a press release on 13 October 1941:

According to certain prejudiced rumors, the Vatican is said to have made reservations concerning the measures taken by the French government with respect to the Jews.

We are in a position to oppose a most formal denial to these allegations; from information obtained at the most authorized sources it results that nothing in the legislation designed to protect France from the Jewish influence is opposed to the doctrine of the Church.[58]

Vatican correspondence reveals that Ambassador Bérard had consulted with officials of the Vatican's Secretariat of State, Monsignor Tardini and Monsignor Montini.[59]

Was such legislation, consistently enforced in the unoccupied as well as the occupied zone in 1940–1941, a response to German orders? Robert Paxton, a foremost authority on Vichy France, states: "I have been unable to turn up any direct German order for French anti-Masonic, anti-Semitic, or other legislation during the most active period of Vichy legislation in 1940."[60] Only after the first deportations of foreign and stateless Jews seized by French police from the unoccupied zone in July 1942 did the French Catholic Church's Assembly of Cardinals and Archbishops enter a formal protest. This was read by Cardinal Gerlier, the only cardinal in the unoccupied zone, but by no higher prelates in the occupied zone. Four other cardinals and archbishops spoke out from the pulpit in this region. However, Cardinal Gerlier (as well as several other French bishops) still recognized a "Jewish problem," but now he proclaimed that "the Jews are men, the Jews are women. All is not permitted against them."[61]

When only 150 Jews were seized in Bordeaux, causing the RSHA to cancel a train on duty, Eichmann "uttered the threat that he might even drop France as an evacuation land."[62] Because the Jews were instrumental to Vichy as a medium of barter with the Germans—like wampum, gold, or potatoes—in order to obtain a place in the "New Order," Premier Laval sought to cooperate with the new SS chief, Karl Albrecht Oberg, by devising legislation to make more Jews legally eligible for deportation through denaturalization of those who had acquired French citizenship most recently. Although Laval signed the law, he drew back from promulgating it after the official representative of the French cardinals protested, also conveying the Pope's opposition.[63] Since the church was by then (August 1943) the leading institutional mainstay of the regime, still urging loyalty, pushing the church into opposition could not be risked.

Laval told SS Lieutenant Colonel Rothke that Pétain's signature was necessary, and that Pétain would not sign: the SS representative believed that he had been tricked.[64] Unable to command French police power to seize French Jews, the SS sought the cooperation of the Wehrmacht in vain; the Military Commander, General Karl H. von Stulpnagel, was active in the anti-Hitler plot of 1944 and refused the help of the army to round up Jews.[65] Not until 14 April 1944 did SS Colonel Knochen give up and order all SS forces to seize any Jews they could find, exempting only those living in "bona fide" mixed marriages contracted before July 1940.[66]

Although the French police continued to seize foreign Jews and the French Milice — a paramilitary collaborationist organization — as well as German forces massacred Jews on several occasions, regardless of their nationality, some allege, as George Wellers testified at the Eichmann trial, that Vichy police "enabled many Jews to escape and deliberately sabotaged these round-ups."[67] We have no way of corroborating such testimony. Several regional officials made similar claims about their behavior and relationship to Pierre Laval, claims that would serve to exculpate them also from punishment as collaborators.[68] Jews seeking cover were aided in southern France by an elaborate Jewish-Christian defense movement that provided false papers, guidance in reaching Spain, and placement of Jewish children in homes of natives not threatened with deportation.[69] The defense movement unfolded most fully in the region where the Catholic prelates had protested, often aided by priests enjoying the protection of the bishops who spoke out. Many Jews were hidden by Protestant communities — whose leaders had consistently opposed discrimination — with the complete knowledge and aid of the whole community.[70]

The church's veto, which led to the French government's limitation of the class of Jews legally deportable, the widespread network for flight and hiding, the paucity of German police manpower due to the noncooperation of the Military Commander with the SS, and the physical dispersion of Jews themselves limited Jewish victims in France to about 29%, or about 93,000 of the 350,000 Jews in France in 1940, despite the avid cooperation of Vichy between 1940 and 1944. Had there been an earlier consensus on French obligation to protect the Jews, as there was in Denmark, these Jews, most of whom were seized by French police and/or earlier interned in French prisons and camps, might be alive. The French Roman Catholic Church's willingness to tolerate earlier discrimination denied such an obligation.

PROTESTS AGAINST DISCRIMINATION
OR DEPORTATION OF JEWS

Protests recorded during the war may indicate the sources of bonds uniting Christian and Jew as protestors felt compelled to explain the grounds motivating church identification with the Jews. These texts do not tell us how church resistance against Jewish deportation succeeded but indicate what instigated priest and preacher to resist. The grounds of protest can be located along a radius of social distance from the protestor, from the most intimate to more abstract bonds. Jews might be viewed as members of a common religious family, citizens within a nation-state, or simply members of humanity. Those churches affirming the closest identification also reiterated the more abstract bases for defense of the Jews, but those indicating only more abstract grounds sometimes denied identification within a common religious Judeo-Christian family. Churches that did not affirm that Jews and Christians were members of a common religious family but opposed the deportations on other grounds were apt to allege neutrality toward the Jews or defend them against previous collective accusations, both the Nazi charges and earlier theologically grounded charges. The churches that based their protest primarily on denial of the state's rights to deprive human beings of life and liberty—a violation of natural law without any particular identification with Jews—were those that denied the justification for racial anti-Semitism; but they had justified anti-Jewish discrimination (if Jews were not classified on racial grounds) and reaffirmed earlier collective accusations against the Jews on religious grounds. The churches that affirmed closer identification with Jews had more consistently attacked anti-Jewish discrimination earlier, and both worshippers and clergy were mobilized immediately at the time Jews were threatened.

The church responding most immediately in the state responding most immediately was the Lutheran Church of Denmark. Bishop Fuglsang-Damgaard of Copenhagen expressed the kinship of Christians and Jews as the first premise of his declaration of 2 October 1943:

> Wherever persecutions are undertaken for racial or religious reasons against the Jews, it is the duty of the Christian Church to raise a protest against it for the following reasons:
>
> 1.   Because we shall never be able to forget that the Lord of the Church, Jesus Christ, was born in Bethlehem, of the Virgin Mary into Israel, the people of His possession, according to the promise of God. The history of the Jewish people up to the birth of Christ includes the preparation for the salvation which God has prepared in Christ for all men. This is also expressed in the fact that the Old Testament is a part of our Bible.[71]

The idea that Jews and Christians were people related by sacred history, members of a common religious community but different communions, was not new to the Danes; the Bishop had expressed this in 1938 in denouncing the persecution of Jews in Germany after Kristallnacht. He instructed his pastors then to pray for the Jews and "to protect our people against the poisonous pestilence of anti-Semitism, hatred of the Jews and persecution of the Jews. Our Lord and Saviour Jesus Christ was David's Son after the flesh, and those who love Him cannot hate His people."[72]

Lutheran theologians had agreed at a conference at the University of Copenhagen in December 1941 to protest publicly should any discrimination begin, despite the absence of any threat at that time. German officials understood from the start that the Danish government would not tolerate such discrimination. Church gazettes still denounced Jew-hatred during the war and Bishop Fuglsang-Damgaard spoke out publicly against racial hatred in January 1943. Because it had earlier reached consensus, the church was completely prepared to protest in September 1943, and its members were ready to proceed from dissent to resistance immediately after they were informed of the threat of deportations. No distinction was made in their protests regarding Christians of Jewish origin. (Such appeals usually negated any categorical protest for Jews as Jews by implying that deprivation of Jews' rights could be tolerated if only the proper victims were selected, excluding Christians labeled as Jews. These appeals also gave the authorities concessions to dispense to exchange for the silence of potential resistors.)

The most common defense of the Jews put equal stress on national obligations and rights and religious values. This was exemplified best in Bulgaria, Greece, and Norway, where protests repudiated the doctrine that the Jews differed fundamentally from Christians by blood but recognized that they might collectively have sinned in the past or might be guilty of current crimes. Stefan, Metropolitan of Sofia, the Bulgarian Patriarch who had been outspoken against anti-Jewish discrimination since 1941, when discrimination was first introduced, explained in a sermon on 9 September 1942 that only God had any right to punish the Jews.

> God had punished the Jews for the crucifixion of Jesus in that He had expelled them from their country and had not given them a country of their own. And thus, God had determined the destiny of the Jews.
>
> However, men had no right to exercise cruelty toward the Jews and to persecute them. Especially Christians ought to see their brothers in Jews who had accepted the Christian religion and to support them in every possible way.
>
> He stressed several times in his sermon that truly it is in God's hands to punish twice and three times, but it is forbidden for Christians to do such a thing.[73]

When reports about the deportation of the foreign Macedonian Jews in territories annexed by Bulgaria in March 1943 began to circulate in Sofia, the Metropolitan immediately responded to a request from the head of the Jewish community by going to the King's palace to remonstrate with him and refused to leave until he had been seen. Stefan intervened again in May 1943

when the Jews of Sofia were once more threatened. The Holy Synod of
Bishops protested to the Prime Minister and other key cabinet ministers,
reiterating the special role of the church in regard to the state and its opposition to any racial discrimination against Jews.

> The idea of passing a Law for the Protection of the Nation which would annul
> dangers to our people and our state, on which the national, spiritual and moral
> units of the Bulgarian people is founded, was accepted by our Holy Orthodox
> Church which is the eternal guardian of the destiny of the Bulgarian people, and
> which knows better than others, from bitter historical experience, what it would
> mean to our people to be divided by false religious, national and economic
> teaching, and to be exploited by any minority. . . .
>
> The Law for the Protection of the Nation was created with the express purpose
> of limiting the Jewish minority; the main concept of the law is based on racialism.
> At that time the Holy Synod informed the Government that the principle of
> racialism cannot be justified from the point of view of the Christian doctrine, be-
> ing contrary to the fundamental message of the Christian Church, in which all
> who believe in Jesus Christ are men and women of equal worth. "There is neither
> Jew nor Greek, there is neither bond nor free, there is neither male nor female: for
> ye are all one in Christ Jesus" (Gal. 3, 28).[74]

(Paradoxically, the sentence "There is neither Jew nor Greek . . . " is
used in virtually all these protests to indicate the equality of all people rather
than all believers in Christ, as it meant in context, negating categorical
discrimination against Jews.)

The Norwegian Lutheran Church, the most threatened of all state
churches in occupied Europe (it had accepted disestablishment rather than
pledge loyalty to Quisling), the only church whose Chief Bishop had been interned in a concentration camp, nevertheless addressed a protest to Quisling
(along with the other churches) on 11 November 1942 against confiscation of
the property of Jews and arrest of Jewish men in October. After Jewish
women whose husbands had been caught earlier were seized with their
children during a surprise raid on the night of 25–26 November 1942 and
shipped to Auschwitz via Germany, the ministers read this protest from the
pulpit beginning within the next fortnight. Although the protest by the
church had no direct effect on Quisling, it may have alerted those Jews not
yet seized to the danger and instigated the Norwegian resistance movement
to aid them; over half succeeded in fleeing to Sweden, escaping the raids of
October and November and other hunts. The Norwegian bishops' letter of
protest echoed the theological position of the Danish church but stressed the
national rights of the Jews and the constitutional rights of the national
church, guardedly implying that the church had the duty to disobey while
avowing obedience in conformity with Luther's position and the political
reality.

> Paragraph 2 of the Constitution states that the Evangelical Lutheran religion will
> remain the religion of the State. That is to say, the State cannot enact any law or
> decree which is in conflict with the Christian faith or the Church's Confession.

When now we appeal to the authorities in this matter we do so because of the deepest dictates of conscience. To remain silent about this legalized injustice against the Jews would render ourselves co-guilty in this injustice. If we are to be true to God's Word and to the Church's Confession we must speak out. . . .

One cannot dismiss the Church with a charge that it is mixing into politics. The apostles courageously spoke to the authorities of their day and said: "We ought to obey God rather than men." Acts 5, 29. Luther says: "The Church does not interfere in worldly matters when it warns the authority to be obedient to the highest authority, which is God." . . .

We have mentioned it before, but re-emphasize it now in closing: This appeal of ours has nothing to do with politics. Before worldly authority we maintain that obedience in all temporal matters which God's Word demands.[75]

The authority of the church was again opposed to that of the state; the church resisted as it had resisted Quisling's attempt to subvert Christianity. Similarly, the teachers and other voluntary associations had resisted the Quisling government's drive for fascist coordination of schools and free institutions.

The most secular protest was that of Archbishop Damaskinos of Athens, who protested to the German Foreign Office and to the Greek Prime Minister against the deportation of the Jews of Salonica. The Greek protestors, including school and university rectors and representatives of business and professional associations, continually stressed the innocence of Greek Jews while acknowledging that Jews of other nations might have given the Germans reason for recrimination. The petition of Greek leaders of 24 March 1943 noted:

We must add that the above mentioned Jews have never acted against our interests, even in the smallest matters; on the contrary, they have always felt a sense of responsibility towards the Greek majority. Most of them belong to the poorer classes. It should be noted that Greek Jews have quite a different mentality to that of the Jews living in Germany and have no knowledge whatsoever of the language of Poland where they are being sent to live.

In addition to the above facts, we wish to add that during the long course of our history, ever since the era of Alexander the Great and his descendants, and through all the centuries of Greek Orthodoxy down to the present time, our relations with the Jewish people have always been harmonious. We believe therefore that, in your high office as ruler of our country during the present war, you will not hesitate to accept our present request and decide, even if provisionally, to suspend the expulsion of Greek Jews from Greece until the Jewish question can be examined in the light of a special and detailed investigation.

Our present request is based upon the recent historical fact, that during the surrender of Salonika and, later, that of the whole of Greece, among the clauses of the protocol, the following is included: "The Occupation forces promise to protect the life, the honour and the properties of the population." Certainly this clause implies, that no persecution would be made against Greek subjects, on the account of religion and race, and that consequently the theory relating to racial or religious discrimination would not be applied in Greece.[76]

Similarly, in their letter to the Greek Prime Minister, they distinguished Greek Jews from other Jews.

> We are well aware of the deep opposition between the new Germany and the Jews, nor do we intend to defend or criticize international Jewry and its activities in the sphere of the political and financial problems of the world.
> We are only interested in and concerned with, the lives of 60,000 fellow-citizens.[77]

This petition is manifestly designed to appeal to an authority rather than to arouse a constituency or warn that authority. Perhaps the writers believed they had a better chance of protecting their own Jews if they distinguished them from "international Jewry." But the church in Athens did not limit itself to legal appeal. The Archbishop later freely gave baptism papers to Jews in flight, arranged for aid to them in hiding, and authorized messages to the priests and people of Athens prescribing aid to the Jews when the dragnet occurred there.[78]

The protest of the French assembly of cardinals and archbishops on 22 July 1942 displayed a more abstract identification with the victims—"in the name of humanity and Christian principles"—perhaps because the first victims were for the most part foreigners, Jews who could not be defended as Frenchmen. The assembly declared to Marshal Pétain:

> Profoundly moved by what is reported to us of the massive arrests of the Jews carried out last week and of the harsh treatment which has been inflicted upon them, notably at the Winter Sports Stadium, we can not stifle the cry of our conscience.
> It is in the name of humanity and of Christian principles that our voice is raised in protest in favor of the imprescribable rights of human beings. It is also an anguished call to mercy for the immense sufferings, especially those which befall so many mothers and children.
> We ask . . . that you please take account of this in order that the requirements of justice and the rights of charity be respected.[79]

But the church's loyalty to the government was still reiterated. The church attempted both to set limits to the Vichy regime's participation so that it could continue to support the regime in good conscience and to set limits to the disorder it would countenance (subversion of the deportations) so that it did not encourage rebellion against Vichy.

IMPLICATIONS IN HISTORICAL PERSPECTIVE

Despite differences in the neutralization or denial of the collective guilt of the Jews and the intensity of bonds between the victim and the protestors, all the church leaders who protested affirmed by their actions their role as guardians of the state, a state whose fate and history were linked to the nation or collectivity whose conscience the church represented. The Jews, they affirmed, were part of that nation and could not be eliminated without a stigma to the honor of the state. To some, the Jews were possible future Christians; to others, the Christians were former Jews. Both positions negate racialism as a doctrine. But without some positive identification with Jews, alive and present, philosophical repudiation of the Nazi racial dogma alone did not deny a basis for discrimination against Jews; it simply justified discrimination on the basis of the current religious affirmation (or lack of Christian affirmation) of Jews. Thus, Pius XI's repudiation in 1937 (in his encyclical, "Mit Brenender Sorge") of the racial dogma of "blood" as the basis for segregating humanity into different species did not enjoin Catholics or church leaders to defend Jews against the segregation that facilitated their extermination or, later, their deportation. Falconi notes that the encyclical contained only one reference to Jews—as deicides—and failed to condemn the persecution either of Jews or of evangelical sects, censuring only "certain currents" within the Nazi ideology. He observes that "the one reproach made by Pius XI (and with all due respect) against the Nazi leaders, the one reason why the encyclical was written at all, was that the Concordat had been violated."[80]

Pius XI's own public identification with the Jews in 1937—"we are all Jews"—was evidently not premeditated and had not been publicized.[81] This reluctance publicly to affirm identification with the Jews may have been related to the church's earlier "teaching of contempt" toward the Jews; however, the "teaching of contempt" was not limited to the Roman Catholic Church.[82] But the Roman Catholic Church made little effort to undo the negative imagery with which its believers were indoctrinated before World War II, while the Scandinavian Lutheran churches (especially in Denmark) worked to deny the vilification of the Jews by Martin Luther. Even some churches that protested, such as the Calvinist Dutch Reformed Church and the Bulgarian Orthodox Church, expressed negative imagery.[83] However, within these societies the churches had not reinforced their theoretic hostility toward the Jews by sanctioning civil discrimination (as had the Roman Catholic Church in eastern and central Europe through the twentieth century and in France and Italy during the nineteenth century) and did not identify the Jews as enemies of clerical authority.

Where Jews had been positively integrated into the nation-state and secular anti-Semitic movements had not achieved a wide constituency, Roman Catholic Church leaders and priests usually spoke up and/or aided the defense of the Jews at the time of their greatest need, as in Belgium, the Netherlands (where Catholics are a minority), and France. But in Italy, Pope Pius XII lagged behind village priests, never speaking out publicly when Italian Jews were deported (although a threat of a public protest to the German Ambassador was noted),[84] and the bishops lagged behind the priests as the hierarchy had lagged behind earlier in response to anti-Jewish

discrimination introduced in 1938.[85] Some priests used their offices to direct
parishioners to aid the Jews, implying the Pope's authorization.[86] The mass
noncooperation of Italians with the German occupiers and their readiness to
strike in 1943–1944 make one suspect that the trains to Auschwitz from Italy
could have been halted (by strikes or sabotage) had the fate of their cargo at
its terminus been broadcast to partisans and workers. But this would not occur as Pius XII—who had consistently refused publicly to confirm (and denounce) the extermination of the Jews—feared the breakdown of authority
and specter of postwar communism, which political strikes signified to him.[87]

By contrast, all Roman Catholic states in eastern Europe had highly successful anti-Semitic movements before the war (although there was no occasion for mass testing of the anti-Semitic position in Croatia), often encouraged by the Catholic hierarchy. Such leadership cooperated in exterminating the Jews in every state, regardless of the extent of warning time
available, the state's relation to Germany, and degree of authority. Given the
instigation and these states' readiness to collaborate (and, in the case of the
Ustase, initiation of their own Holocaust of Orthodox Serbs in Croatia), only
a clear, public papal declaration on behalf of Jews as Jews, bluntly categoriz-
ing cooperation with their murder (and that of Serbs and Gypsies) as a violation of the Sixth Commandment, an intolerable act for a Catholic, a sin subject to sanctions, might have elicited prompt obedience on the part of those
who were intentionally culpable and/or deterred those unwittingly engaged
in their murder. In 1942 the Vatican's experience in Slovakia, using
"diplomatic" methods, testified to how unresponsive Catholic priests were to
influence alone. But Pius XII persistently refused to exploit the only sanction
available and unique to the Roman Catholic Church, regardless of how free
he was personally and how free Catholics were in instigating or executing
those murders, as he had failed to sanction Adolf Hitler, a Roman Catholic
in good standing. For these reasons, the official elaboration by Vatican
spokesmen of the many papal appeals, showing how ineffectual most were,
evades the problem of explaining the failure of Pius XII to use the sanctions
under his control alone in order to deter murder, rather than to proclaim
empathy with the victims.[88] As Falconi put it:

> The challenge was not only one of speaking out so as to fulfill a duty towards his
> office, but of speaking out as a duty to Christianity and mankind. His refusal to
> speak out played into the hands of evil as this grew bolder and fiercer and became
> more provocative. Silence amounted to complicity with iniquity. And this supreme
> omission was not redeemed by multiple acts of charity (always and inevitably in-
> adequate) towards the victims (which incidentally meant little more than making
> other people's donations available).[89]

The Judenräte *and*
Other Jewish Control Agents

The responsibility of the German co-opted or imposed Jewish leaders who headed or served on *Judenräte* for the victimization of other Jews has been the theme of acrimonious debate since World War II, spurred by the charges of Hannah Arendt.[1] Some critics were incensed by the diversion of attention from the responsibility of the Germans; others confused the problems of intention and consequences of lines of action in assessing *Judenräte* leaders' culpability; others confounded the objective question of causality with the ethical one of responsibility; and some categorically denied the right of the living to judge any victims. Still others, notably Jacob Robinson, have concentrated on refuting Arendt's many factual errors.[2]

The subject advanced significantly from invective toward analysis with a colloquium on "Imposed Jewish Governing Bodies under Nazi Rule" sponsored by the YIVO Institute of Jewish Research in 1967. But the great leap forward in availability of data amenable to reanalysis was the publication of Isaiah Trunk's *Judenrat* (1972), a massive, meticulously researched compilation and comparative analysis of the origin, functions, strategy, mechanisms, and dynamics of the Jewish councils in eastern Europe under Nazi occupation.[3]

Trunk concluded that *Judenrat* leaders did, in fact, cooperate with German authorities—if they remained alive in office—but distinguished their *collaboration d'État* from ideologically motivated collaboration, a distinction evolved by Stanley Hoffman (1968) to account for the collaboration of the government of France during the war.[4] Trunk's research did not address the

121

question of whether the performances of *Judenräte* leaders were related to the magnitude of Jews' victimization.

Trunk, however, insisted that *Judenräte* were Jewish, rather than German, institutions, despite their origins in the German bureaucracy of the SS. The *Judenräte* were hastily organized by the head of the Security Police, Reinhardt Heydrich, two weeks after the invasion of Poland in a conference in Berlin. The memorandum on their establishment read:

Berlin, 21 September 1939

The Chief of the Security Police
. . .
Special Delivery Letter

To *The Chiefs of all detail groups . . . of the Security Police.*

Concerning: The Jewish problem in the occupied zone.

I refer to the conference held in Berlin today, and again point out that the *planned joint measures* (i.e., the ultimate goal) are to be kept *strictly secret.*

Distinction must be made between

1. the ultimate goal (which requires a prolonged period of time) and
2. the sectors leading to fulfillment of the ultimate goal (each of which will be carried out in a short term). . . .

The first prerequisite for the ultimate goal is first of all, the concentration of the Jews from the country to the larger cities. . . . On principle, all Jewish communities *under 500 heads* are to be dissolved and to be transferred to the nearest concentration center. . . .

1. In each Jewish community, a Council of Jewish Elders is to be set up which, as far as possible, is to be composed of the remaining influential personalities and rabbis. The Council is to be composed of 24 male Jews (depending on the size of the Jewish community).

It is to be made *fully responsible* (in the literal sense of the word) for the exact execution according to terms of all instructions released or yet to be released.

2. In case of sabotage of such instructions, the Councils are to be warned of severest measures.
3. The Jewish Councils are to take an improvised census of the Jews of their area, possibly divided into generations. . . .
4. The Councils of Elders are to be made acquainted with the time and date of the evacuation.[5]

THE ARENDT HYPOTHESIS REVIEWED

To prove or disprove Arendt's contention, one must abstract her assertions and conclusions, separating the evaluative characterization from the implicit hypotheses.

Without Jewish help in administrative and police work—the final rounding up of Jews in Berlin was, as I have mentioned, done entirely by Jewish police—there would have been either complete chaos or an impossibly severe drain on German manpower. Hence the establishing of Quisling governments in occupied territories was always accompanied by the organization of a central Jewish office, and, as we shall see later, where the Nazis did not succeed in setting up a puppet government, they also failed to enlist the cooperation of the Jews. But whereas the members of the Quisling governments were usually taken from the opposition parties, the members of the Jewish Councils were as a rule the locally recognized Jewish leaders, to whom the Nazis gave enormous powers—until they, too, were deported. . . .

Wherever Jews lived, there were recognized Jewish leaders, and this leadership, almost without exception, cooperated in one way or another, for one reason or another, with the Nazis. *The whole truth was that if the Jewish people had really been unorganized and leaderless, there would have been chaos and plenty of misery but the total number of victims would hardly have been between four and a half and six million people.*[6]

Hence, Arendt asserted:

1. Native leaders who cooperated with the occupying Germans in governing their nations were not representative of prewar governments or national communities.
2. But Jewish leaders who cooperated were representative of the Jewish community.
3. If native leaders did not cooperate to establish puppet governments, Jewish leaders did not cooperate.
4. Wherever Jews lived, they were organized with recognized leaders.
5. Jewish leaders cooperated with the Germans in almost all times and places.
6. The extent of Jewish leaders' cooperation accounts for the extensiveness of Jewish victimization.

The initial argument is manifestly contradictory in that the third and fifth theses have contrary implications. Furthermore, the parallelism between the establishment of a *Judenrat* (under a Central Jewish Office) and "Quisling governments" is the reverse of the relation implied in the first two theses. Hitler generally preferred to keep in office prewar leaders representing major parties rather than rely on native fascist ideologues with little prewar backing who made demands for recognition of their nation's sovereignty. He refused to back an Iron Guard rebellion in Rumania (1941), rejected support for an Arrow Cross coup in Hungary until 1944 when the Regent announced Hungary was defecting to the Allies, repudiated the claim to self-government of the Baltic states, and rejected offers of Dutch and Belgian fascists to head governments in their nations.[7] Similarly, the Reich Security Main Office instructed its forces to co-opt, whenever possible, elected or appointed Jewish leaders from community councils or prestigious individuals who would enjoy greater personal authority initially than less well known figures.[8] A *Judenrat* was not always established in states with "Quisling governments"; neither Quisling's Norway nor Mussolini's Republic of Salo had a *Judenrat*.

Judenräte were established in states with functioning prewar bureaucracies (the Netherlands) and without any native government (Poland).

The entire phenomenon of cooperation — whether accommodation or collaboration — cannot be understood by assuming it was restricted to Quisling governments. There are at least as many examples of governments and bureaucracies appointed before 1941 by conventional means that cooperated as there are of governments achieving office by direct German military intervention that collaborated. In Czechoslovakia, France, the Netherlands, and Hungary there were governments or bureaucracies appointed by the prewar head of state, cabinet, or legislature that fully cooperated for an extended period.[9] Accommodation was a general phenomenon in occupied Europe among natives, local officials, and prewar bureaucracies, differing qualitatively only in the values sacrificed. Even occupied nations most resistant to anti-Jewish discrimination — Denmark and Belgium — initially acceded to German exploitation of their economy (and Denmark agreed to coordinate its foreign policy with that of Germany) to assure their people's survival and avoid destruction of native industry and resources.[10]

Disregarding the more general question of accommodation to German authority, we may still test Arendt's fifth and sixth theses; I am restating them for greater clarity as follows:

Judenräte leaders were representative of the Jewish community. This was indicated by their previous appointment or election to prewar leadership positions. Jewish victimization is a function of the degree of accommodation of *Judenräte* leaders. One would expect not only that the rank of Jewish victims — how many fell prey — is positively related to how well Jewish leaders cooperated but also that the degree of accommodation must account for the rank of Jewish victims. These may be coincident or parallel phenomena, symptoms of the same or related underlying causes.

Our aim here is to test this hypothesis. To begin to understand *Judenräte*, one must define what they were and for what ends they were instituted by the Germans. What concerns us first is what their functions were as organizations. This is not the same as the problem of weighing the culpability of individual *Judenräte* leaders or *Judenräte* leaders as a class. This is not to say that the analyst can or ought to be value-free or that analysis does not serve evaluative functions, but that one must first answer the outstanding question of the objective function of *Judenräte*.

DEFINITIONS, ORIGINS, AND FUNCTIONS

A *Judenrat* may be defined generically as an administrative body of Jews imposed by and responsible to German authority for the enforcement of German regulations over Jews in German-occupied states and regions. *Judenräte* were neither representative (answerable to or legitimated by the Jewish community) nor mediating organizations, but were organizations for collective control to which all Jews were subject without recourse to civil authority. Although the term *Judenrat* has been used interchangeably with "Jewish Council," I am using the German term to denote only German-imposed bodies, distinguishing these from other Jewish councils established in states allied with Germany and in France by these governments and usually responsible to their native governments. When I refer to "Jewish control organizations," these include Jewish councils as well as *Judenräte*. "Jewish control agents" include all Jewish control organizations, Jewish police, and similar bodies (*ordnen*), which were not always subordinated to the *Judenräte*. Weiss too, has analyzed how *Judenräte* and police were integrated: integration under a common executive, police subordination to a *Judenrat*, dual and competing power structures, or domination by the police with subversion of the power of the *Judenrat*.[11]

Few studies of *Judenräte* are comparative and sources vary in their focus.[12] Our knowledge of origins of *Judenräte* begins with the memorandum of Security Police chief Reinhardt Heydrich on 21 September 1939, previously quoted.[13] Whether Heydrich was then aware of "the ultimate goal" toward which Jews were being organized or whether it had been programmatically formulated yet is open to question. Gideon Hausner, the Israeli prosecutor of Adolf Eichmann (Heydrich's subordinate and a participant in the Berlin conference cited) asserts that Eichmann acknowledged during pretrial interrogation (later recanted) that this memorandum revealed that the goal of the Final Solution—extermination—was known to initiates in 1939.[14]

Functions for which *Judenräte* were immediately responsible included taking censuses of all Jews, arranging the evacuation of Jews from the country to the concentration centers (major urban ghettos), maintaining supplies, rehousing them, and preventing sabotage of instructions. Thus, *Judenräte* from the beginning were intended to be social control organizations to process Jews toward "the ultimate goal," facilities for which were not yet evolved in 1939. The SS bureaucrats designated to deal with Jews and other enemies evolved the plan to control Jews corporatively through their successful experience in the Reich, where they had converted the previously voluntary Reichsvertretung der Juden in Deutschland into a compulsory association in 1938, changing its name to the Reichsvereinigung der Juden, and found that it facilitated their aims. Jews individually had been legally disestablished, segregated, and completely without rights since 1935; the Reichsvereinigung and the similar Jewish communal organization in Vienna expedited their forced emigration. The SS overcame competitors to achieve supremacy over the "Jewish question" by rationalizing functions of all other agencies regarding the Jews.[15] The incorporation of all Jews as subjects of *Judenräte*, permitting control of them as a collectivity, was another sign of rationalization.

While the *Judenräte* were never representative, they did offer members and workers the illusion of Jewish autarchy and security within a legal order, an illusion expressly manipulated to reinforce Jews' dependency and lack of apprehension of the ultimate goal. This lack of apprehension served German strategic needs to eliminate the Jews in an orderly sequence. After the initial wave of terror in Poland and organized massacres in the territory occupied after June 1941, ghettoization and community organization appeared to Jews to offer them a chance for coexistence. Regardless of the extent of terror, Jews in all German-occupied states before 1943 were progressively defined, stripped, and segregated. After Jews were registered and stripped of jobs, property, and income, a "welfare" class was created, needing public assistance to survive. The *Judenrat* was employed to dispense such assistance, sometimes being endowed with funds confiscated from the Jewish community (thus legitimating their confiscation) and/or granted the power to tax Jews directly.

The functions that *Judenräte* were asked to perform were incremental, beginning with traditional welfare services and civil functions that municipalities had previously performed in the ghetto and abandoned. These gradually expanded to making selections, initially for forced labor, later for candidates for "resettlement," who were transported to extermination and labor camps. The exemptions given initially to certain groups — often workers or *Judenrat* employees — facilitated the *Judenrat*'s role as an instrument of exploitation and created a divisive class structure within the ghettos. The *Judenrat* was perceived as offering extensive opportunities, in terms of both immediate employment and later class privileges — exemptions, stamps protecting classes of Jews from deportation — that divided the community.[16] The "adjustment" of *Judenrat* officials themselves — advanced by German authorities who eliminated or replaced less responsive leaders — to relying on German authorities made them more dependent on them, often leading to illusions that they had a special relationship with their particular overlord, anticipating that he would protect them. This adjustment and the profusion of orders from German authorities lent an illusion of order, reliability, and legality to the *Judenräte*, inhibiting the Jews from initiating a social defense movement before there was any threat of deportation. In order to build a movement, one must subvert orders and invent novel and usually illegal resources for resistance. One must incur costs and take risks on behalf of the collectivity without immediate personal gain. The competitive incentive structure led the best informed and cleverest to judge that the most rational thing to do was work within the system, protecting themselves and their kin. If threat is conceived of as an individual risk rather than a collective threat, individual rather than collective means of coping with it are devised. The message is internally read: "They will kill some Jews — but I will not be among them."

JUDENRÄTE AND JEWISH ISOLATION

Judenräte were instituted in every state occupied and ruled directly by Germany before 1943 except Norway. Since there was more than one body in many states, this study focuses on the council in the capitol (usually the central Jewish council in states administered as one unit) except in states split by the Germans. Since Salonica and Athens were discriminated in all analyses, the *Judenrat* of each is also discriminated, referring to both cities after German occupation. In Poland, dismembered by Germany, seven *Judenräte* were selected from the ghettos of the largest city in each major German administrative district: Sosnowiec (Eastern Upper Silesia), Lodz (Wartheland), Warsaw (General-Government), Lvov or Lemberg (Distrikt Galizien), Rowne (Reichskommissariat Ukraine), Bialystok (Bezirk Bialystok), and Vilna (Reichskommissariat Ostland). Except for Rowne and Lvov (lying in the 1941 path of the Einsatzgruppen, or mobile execution units), ample evidence has been documented by Trunk and others on these *Judenräte* and their respective ghettos. Besides Trunk and Weiss (1974), diverse sources have been relied upon for nations outside eastern Europe.[17]

Since we have found that Jewish isolation was the most highly linked intervening variable leading directly to Jewish victimization, our first question is how the institutionalization of Jewish control agents was related to Jewish segregation. The indicator of segregation was the enforced wearing of compulsory star badges or armbands by Jews. The imposition of the yellow star, serving as sign and stigma, always preceded the isolation of Jews in marked houses and/or their concentration in walled camps or ghettos. Table 5-1 shows that *Judenräte* were more likely to exist in states in which Jews had been segregated than were other Jewish control organizations. Jews were not segregated in the few occupied states in which no Jewish control organization was instituted—Italy, Denmark, and Norway. The Germans' decision not to establish *Judenräte* in these cases can be attributed to tactical reasons: their apprehension of popular disapproval, the desire to lower apprehension among Jews, and the small size of the Jewish population to be seized. Table 5-2 shows that segregation was always associated with high victimization regardless of when the threat of deportation arose. But if Jews were not segregated, their chances of becoming victims declined when they had more warning time (a function of other factors discussed in Chapter 3).

Taking segregation as a given, did the extent of cooperation of Jewish control agents (including Jewish police) increase the percentage of Jewish victims caught? All Jewish control agents in German-occupied and German-allied states were ranked on their cooperation during deportations. Actions reported that enlarged the probability of Jews following German orders, regardless of whether the actor himself was motivated by a wish to avoid reprisals (accommodation) or to obtain other rewards (collaboration), were

TABLE 5-1. Segregation of Jewish Population Prior to Deportation/ Extermination Threat by Type of Jewish Control Organization in European States* during the Holocaust

Type of Jewish Control Organization	JEWISH SEGREGATION PRECEDING DEPORTATION				
	Segregated	Number in Category	Not Successfully Segregated	Number in Category	Total
Judenrat		(9)		(3)	12
	Salonica		Belgium		
	Netherlands		Athens		
	Austria		Serbia		
	Germany				
	Protectorate				
	Estonia				
	Latvia				
	Lithuania				
	Poland				
Other Jewish control organization		(2)		(3)	5
	Slovakia		France		
	Hungary		Bulgaria		
			Rumania		
No Jewish control organization		(0)		(3)	3
			Italy		
			Denmark		
			Norway		

*Excluding the USSR, Luxembourg, Croatia, Finland, and all states neither occupied by nor allied with Germany (Allies and neutrals).

classified as cooperation. "Low" cooperation usually denoted passing on German or government orders to report for resettlement, by putting up wall posters or sending out individual notices to a class of persons whose names had been selected by the authorities. "High" cooperation denoted use of police power to seize selected victims (regardless of the mode of selection) and/or of agents of the Jewish Council (or Jewish police) to make selections. Since the *Judenrat* and/or Jewish police in every one of the ghettos in Poland chosen for analysis showed high cooperation, Poland is evaluated as one unit in Tables 5-1 and 5-2 and in Figure 5-1. It is ranked high on Jewish cooperation.

Figure 5-1 shows the most direct paths leading to Jewish victimization and the paths toward cooperation of Jewish control agents. The paths that best account for each phenomenon are shown by solid double lines with arrows indicating the direction of causality implied. The bottom line of Figure 5-1 reiterates the chain of Jewish destruction (Chapter 3), showing how the

TABLE 5-2. Jewish Victims by Prior Segregation and Warning Time before Deportation/Extermination Threat in European States* during the Holocaust .

Preceding Degree of Jewish Isolation	TIME DEPORTATION THREAT BEGAN		
	Before Dec. 1941	Dec. 1941– 17 Dec. 1942	After 17 Dec. 1942
Segregated	9.6†	8.5	8.5
States in each category	Austria = 9†† Germany = 9 Protec- torate = 9 Estonia = 10 Latvia = 10 Lithuania – 10 Poland = 10	Netherlands = 8 Slovakia = 9	Salonica = 9 Hungary = 8
Not successfully segregated or not segregated	7.0	4.75	2.0
States in each category	Rumania = 6 Serbia = 8	Belgium = 5 France = 3 Norway = 5	Italy = 2 Athens = 3 Bulgaria = 2 Denmark = 1

*Excluding the USSR, Luxembourg, Croatia, Finland, and all states neither occupied by nor allied with Germany (Allies and neutrals).

†Mean (average) decile rank of Jewish victims in all states and regions in particular category.

††Decile rank of Jewish victims in each state or region.

prewar success of anti-Semitism best accounts for the rank of Jewish victims. The prewar legitimation of anti-Semitism is most highly related to coopera-tion to segregate the Jews, leading to their isolation and entrapment. Isola-tion, developing principally from official cooperation (which often also leads to other citizens' collaboration) accounts for twice the variance in Jewish vic-tims as does high cooperation of Jewish control agents (84%: 42%). (See also Figure B-1 in Appendix B.)

Whether a *Judenrat* was established in the first place depended on whether a state was German-occupied and on the occupier's choice of tactics. High cooperation of Jewish agents (including Jewish police as well as *Judenrat* officials) during deportations is a direct function of whether Jews were segregated. Thus, segregation of the Jews accounts for both their vulnerabil-ity to victimization and the likelihood of Jewish control agents showing high cooperation during raids. Both are effects of a common underlying cause.

Comparing the effect of high cooperation on victimization in states in which Jews were segregated from the native population before their seizure,

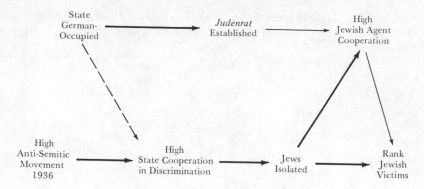

FIGURE 5-1. Jewish Victimization and Cooperation of Jewish Agents during Deportations

Note: Arrows indicate the direction of causality inferred from the findings (e.g., if $A \rightarrow B$, A accounts for B). Bold lines between two states indicate that the preceding state better accounts for the following state than any other preceding phenomenon. Narrow lines indicate that the two states (A and B) are positively related but that another variable (connected to the phenomenon accounted for by bold lines) better accounts for B. A dashed line between A and B indicates that they are either independent of each other or very weakly related.

one finds there is no difference in the mean rank of victims between communities in which Jewish control agents actively participated in the selection or collection of victims and those in which they played a passive role (tabulation not shown). High cooperation was obtained from Jewish control agents in virtually all instances where Jews had been segregated and isolated. Among the few exceptions were instances in which the Germans did not ask Jewish leaders to play any role in selections, as in Hungary in 1944. No pressure was put upon leaders of Hungary's Jewish councils to make selections because there were no selections: tactically, it was too late in the war to deport communities by stages. The only Jews exempted in provincial communities were those few selected by Rudolph Kastner in Budapest, chosen for a projected exchange or ransom with the SS. Local Jewish leaders later testified that they had not been informed about this exchange; nor were they informed by Kastner of the goal of the resettlement.[18] One may relate the lack of Jewish resistance in Hungary's provinces outside Budapest to provincial Jewish leaders' failure to recognize the threat. This in turn can be related to the conditions accepted by Kastner and his colleagues on the Budapest Rescue Committee in order to bargain with the SS, which meant that the Budapest leaders could not organize direct or indirect resistance to the deportations as they did in late June when Budapest Jewry was threatened.[19] Given the lack of organized resistance on the part of Jews in Hungary's provinces, high cooperation by Jewish control agents was not needed to round up the majority of Jews. One cannot infer from this case that high cooperation *was* not more likely to produce high victimization than low cooperation or noncooperation, given segregation, but one can conclude that the extent of Jewish agents' cooperation *at the point of seizure* does not account for any difference in the magnitude of victimization.

But perhaps we have tested the wrong question because Arendt made the wrong inference. Were Jewish councils themselves causal agents in segregating the Jews or agents imposed after segregation was an accomplished fact? In most cases, such councils were imposed in states in which the Jews had already been isolated by the native population, shunned, and/or singled out as targets of attack. Massacres in the Baltic states began before German rule was even consolidated or Jews were counted or any *Judenräte* were established. SS General Jeckeln declared at his trial in 1946 that he had no idea how many Jews were murdered in Latvia between 1941 and 1944 because the Latvians had killed so many before his arrival.[20] Similarly, German sources estimate that by 2 July 1941, when the Germans occupied the capital of Lithuania, Lithuanian anti-Soviet partisans, encouraged by the Germans, had themselves killed 5,000 Jews.[21] Within the Reich, Jews had been completely isolated politically since 1933, legally denied citizens' rights in 1935, and constant prey of the Gestapo from 1938 on. Within Poland, Jews became more isolated after 1935 — despite militant resistance to segregation and deprivation of their civil rights — once the leading political bloc pledged to strip them of citizenship and to expel some of them to solve the "Jewish question" there.[22] The situation is similar among Axis allies with high victimization where Jews councils were usually responsible to the state. Jews had been officially discriminated against in Hungary since 1919 and isolated in Slovakia since its formation in 1938. The identification of the Jews — a functional prerequisite for stripping and segregating them — was performed by the state, not by the *Judenrat* or other Jewish councils in the Reich, Protectorate, Netherlands, Belgium (although the task was later delegated to the *Judenrat* there), France, and all the German satellites and allies (except Hungary), which compiled such registries for enforcing their own codes of anti-Jewish legislation.

Observers have often inferred that *Judenräte* and high Jewish cooperation were causally related to high victimization because of the difficulty of discriminating among coexisting processes arising from the fortuitous conjunction of high anti-Semitism in the region of initial German expansion, the occupied East (where most of the *Judenräte* existed), which was intended to serve as German *Lebensraum*. State and popular cooperation was more likely in states such as these, with highly developed anti-Semitic movements by 1936, whose goals were incorporated by major political parties and/or the state itself. The abandonment by native leaders and the lack of identification with the Jews by church leaders and the national resistance movement (where there was a resistance movement in 1941) reinforced Jews' sense of powerlessness and dependency upon the occupiers in these nations. George Lichtheim has correctly observed, "Against this background, the question of whether the Jews might have done more to save themselves falls into place as a problem of the second order."[23]

German strategy to deport the Jews depended upon the state's sovereignty and the state's willingness to cooperate; the choice of tactics took into account the Jews' recognition of German plans, other natives' bonds to Jewish citizens and sojourners, and their toleration of discrimination. Thus, the likelihood of native resistance was one of the factors inhibiting the establishment of a *Judenrat*. Jewish leaders' response usually mirrored native leaders' response. Where a *Judenrat* was established and the state did not cooperate or resistance movements openly identified with the Jews, integrating them and denouncing discrimination, *Judenrat* accommodation was less likely. In the two cases where the *Judenrat* was subverted from its intended function — Belgium and Athens — there was a well established resistance movement identifying with the Jews, and local authorities made clear their resistance to enforcing discriminatory legislation. The different responses of the Belgian and Dutch governments-in-exile (previously discussed) and earlier development of the Belgian resistance movement rendered the Belgian AJB useless, while the Dutch Joodse Raad became an effective tool for fully segregating the Jews, who had been registered and stripped of government jobs by the state bureaucracy.

Although *Judenräte* accommodation to earlier German regulations can be understood as a symptom of their powerlessness, this does not deny that they could also serve to intensify Jews' isolation and inhibit the possibility of establishing a social defense movement. Besides co-opting leadership cadres through *Judenrat* employment and diverting Jews from perceiving threat, an accommodating *Judenrat* could diminish other natives' identification with Jews and their willingness to take risks to help those who apparently were not helping themselves. Two instances are well documented of accommodating *Judenräte* that facilitated the segregation of the Jews who had been identified and stripped with the aid of government officials. These are the Netherlands and Salonica.[24] Evidence does exist from the protests of the dominant church and resistance organizations in Amsterdam and Salonica — signs usually linked with an effective social-defense movement — that such movements could have been created there earlier had Jews not been segregated. The evidence from Poland, the Reich, and the Baltic states implies no possibilities for successful movements in those states.

Jewish survivors of this period in Amsterdam and Salonica relate their own and other citizens' wrath at *Judenrat* policies, holding their leaders culpable. In Salonica, Rabbi Koretz, the *Judenrat* chairman, barely avoided being attacked by congregants in his synagogue in March 1943, after deportations had begun, when he told them how much better life would be in Cracow (where they were to be resettled) and counseled resignation from the pulpit.[25] Rabbi Koretz's leadership facilitated the physical entrapment of the Jews and inhibited their early perception of threat and the formation of a social defense movement with allies in the Greek resistance who offered aid.[26] In Amsterdam, by contrast, there had been early signs of a mass basis for social defense, but mass resistance as well as Jewish self-defense groups were squashed after the strike of February 1941 with the cooperation of the *Judenrat,* which asked strikers to return to work. The Jews became progressively isolated and atomized in the 17 months after this before deportations began.

All observed instances of effective Jewish social defense movements instigated by Jews show that the authority of Jewish control agents over Jews was never established, as in France and Rumania, subverted, as in Athens and Belgium, or disestablished, as in Warsaw between July and August 1942, where public confidence in *Judenrat* authority (weak to begin with) was shaken by the suicide of Adam Czerniakow, chief *Judenrat* leader, at the beginning of mass deportations. Jewish control agents' authority was further shattered by the attempted assassination of the Jewish police chief who had assisted the Germans, on 20 August 1942, and of his replacement on 29 October 1942. But Jews' mobilization for physical resistance or social defense was not successful unless they could attract allies. Although Jews mobilized for armed resistance in Warsaw in 1943, the Polish resistance offered only token aid — 50 pistols (out of an estimated 6,000 in their possession) — and refused to instigate any public demonstration of sympathy.[27] Native assistance scarcely ever occurred unless Jews appealed or organized to aid themselves, although an active posture among Jews was not in itself a sufficient condition to prompt positive action by other natives.

MECHANISMS OF CONTROL OVER *JUDENRÄTE*

The dynamics of *Judenrat* leaders' accommodation and the social control mechanisms that explain how the *Judenräte* became a tool, in most cases regardless of the motives of its initial leaders, can be inferred from Tables 5-3 and 5-4. Because of the inadequacy of available data, we cannot fully analyze the other Jewish councils. Since these were under different stresses from those that the *Judenräte* experienced, they are excluded from Tables 5-3 and 5-4. Table 5-3 shows the continuity between prewar *kehillah* (community organization) or national Jewish association leaders or chief rabbis, on the one hand, and the leaders of the *Judenräte,* and on the other, and the latter's response to German demands for cooperation during mass deportations to extermination camps.

Throughout Europe, over two-thirds (11 of 15) of the first *Judenräte* leaders were co-opted from prewar positions. Co-optation of first-rank leadership was less common in Poland than in the West. Many prewar leaders had fled. Others were reluctant — because of fear as well as principle — to work with the Germans in any manner. Several communities (in-

TABLE 5–3. Response to Deportations of First *Judenräte* Heads by Mode of Selection of Leaders in German-occupied States* during the Holocaust

Response to German Demands during Deportations or Earlier	GERMAN-APPOINTED			Elected by Jewish Representatives	Total
	Prior Head of Prewar Council, Jewish Organization, or Chief Rabbi	Member of Prewar Council	Service Not Known		
Resistance or noncooperation observed	2 Warsaw Athens		2 Lvov Rowne	1 Kovno	5
Resistance alleged by Germans: previous cooperation shown	2 Protectorate Belgium				2
Nonresistant but no role in selection due to previous removal or actual replacement	2 Salonica Bialystok			1 Vilna	3
Cooperation	3 Austria Germany Netherlands	2 Lodz Sosnowiec			5
Total	9	2	2	2	15

*Although *Judenräte* were established in Estonia, Latvia, and Serbia, they are omitted from this table because of lack of any information (or of reliable information) on the formation of such organizations in these countries. States omitted from this study, such as the USSR and Luxembourg, not governed and occupied by Germany, and occupied states in which a *Judenrat* was not established are also not included in this table.

cluding Vilna and Kovno) chose *Judenrat* leaders either through election by assemblies of the whole or of all political parties or through lot to avoid selection of a German puppet.[28] These findings parallel those of Weiss, who traced the prewar careers of 279 heads of *Judenräte* in the General-Government and Eastern Upper Silesia and found that only 22% of the 128 leaders of the first *Judenräte* had been heads or members of the prewar community councils but that 68% (including the forementioned) had been active in Jewish political or communal activities in some way; the remainder were businessmen and professionals.[29]

Two significant processes occurred at the beginning that are not numerically noteworthy: self-selection by volunteering one's services in a situation where others had refused to serve and "negative selection," as Philip Friedman put it, the rejection of service by more resistant leaders and per-

TABLE 5–4. Destinies of First *Judenräte* Heads by Response to German Demands in German-occupied States* during the Holocaust

	RESPONSE TO GERMAN DEMANDS DURING DEPORTATION		
Tenure in Office and Modes of Termination†	Resistance Observed or Alleged	No Resistance Known	Total
(1) Deadly endings,† reprisals, or death threats	5	1	6
Killed or incarcerated by Germans	Protectorate Belgium†† Lvov	Vilna	
Suicide	Warsaw Rowne		
(2) Other endings: Escaped	1 Athens	2	3
Replaced without any reprisal		Salonica Bialystok	
(3) Not replaced	1 Kovno	5 Austria Germany Netherlands Lodz Sosnowiec	6
Total	7	8	15

*See the footnote to Table 5-3 for exclusions.

†These do not include deaths of *Judenrat* heads who were sent to extermination camps later upon the total annihilation of the ghetto.

††Rabbi Ullman, first head of the Association des Juifs de Belgique, was later freed by the German military commander after the Queen and Cardinal van Rocy petitioned for his release (see p. 156).

sonalities. Later, the more defiant individuals would be weeded out, as was reported in Poland, in the Netherlands, and in occupied France.[30]

Table 5-3 also shows that a third of the first leaders cooperated fully with German demands and a third did not fully cooperate. Comparing *Judenrat* heads in Poland and Lithuania (Kovno) to those in the Reich and other occupied states, it is clear that there was greater resistance among the eastern Jewish leaders despite the terror prevalent there. Half of them (four out of eight) rejected German demands overtly, whereas only one out of seven other *Judenrat* leaders subverted German demands to organize the community.

How did the life chances of noncooperators compare to those of cooperators? Table 5-4 shows that five of the seven leaders who resisted (or were accused of resistance) were killed, incarcerated, or committed suicide. By contrast, five of the eight compliant leaders were never removed; three of them survived the war because of their protected status in the Theresienstadt camp. The noncooperators who sacrificed their lives included three of the seven first leaders of *Judenräte* in the Polish ghettos surveyed. Another Polish leader was killed in a massacre of the first Vilna *Judenrat*. Councils of the *Judenräte* of Vilna and Lodz were massacred by the Gestapo shortly after the occupation, insuring the submissiveness of their replacements. Councilmen were apt to have a shorter life than other Jews: one fourth of them were shot prior to general deportation raids, according to Trunk's survey.[31] Suicide among councilmen was more frequent than resignation as a way out.

To establish how representative this was, I scanned histories of all communities in Poland with 1931 (or estimated 1941) Jewish populations of over 20,000; data on the destinies of the first *Judenrat* heads was found in Trunk and/or the *Encyclopedia Judaica* for 15 of them. Seven leaders (of those 15) were killed during early deportations, two others committed suicide, one was incarcerated, three were replaced without any reprisal noted, and only two were never replaced. Of the 10 who were killed, committed suicide, or were incarcerated, five were observed to have refused cooperation in deportations. Similarly, Weiss found that of 142 "first-round" *Judenrat* leaders (excluding the few who died natural deaths in office), 60 (42.3%) were replaced by the Germans either because they did not fill their positions properly or expressly refused to select victims; resigned because they refused to cooperate; or committed suicide. Weiss estimates that an additional 45 (30.8%) attempted to subvert German decrees in some manner, such as by warning the community of planned raids. He classifies 21 (14.3%) unqualifiedly as "yes-men." The murders of their predecessors helped to elicit greater cooperation from the "second-round" leaders. Weiss classified only 14% of 100 successors (deleting one who died from typhus) as refusing to fulfill their roles properly or rejecting participation in selection: these were all killed or committed suicide. Weiss categorizes 61% of the successors as fulfilling German demands consistently.[32]

A picture emerges of *Judenrat* evolution in Poland. There was a continuing selection of the most fit—those who most fit the occupier's needs. The initial terror was not enough to induce the kind of cooperation the Germans demanded from the majority. About half of the first *Judenräte* leaders did not adequately fulfill their assigned roles and were eliminated: about three-fourths of those expressly refused to cooperate in the selection of victims, usually inciting the German authorities to kill them, if they had not chosen to take their own lives, or increasing their chance of becoming victims of later selections by yielding their position. Outside Poland, the majority of *Judenrat* leaders were compliant, but half of the original leaders (three of six) co-opted were alleged to have later resisted (or subverted) selections, (if we omit one who was never tested because he was replaced).

The memories of the many who rejected accommodation, often at the cost of their lives, have been obscured historically because they did not live long enough to create records or legends. Most leaders of the first *Judenrat* in the 15 Polish ghettos scanned who were killed for resistance do not even receive individual entries in the *Encyclopedia Judaica*. They are not distinguished among the almost three million Polish Jews killed during the German occupation. The perception of *Judenrat* leaders' general readiness to cooperate during deportations is itself a function of the fact that the minority who cooperated most survived longest, acquiring the prerequisites for historical visibility—records, recollections, idolators, allies, and enemies.

The cost of arousing suspicion of noncooperation varied. Reprisals for resignation or protest depended not only on German readiness to use force (far greater in the occupied East than on the West) but also upon the possibility of evasion and/or escape, which depended on local assistance. The first leader of the Athens *Judenrat* informed Jews of the Germans' intentions, burned the files, and successfully arranged his own (and others') escape with the aid of the Greek Archbishop Damaskinos and the EAM resistance organization. The head of the Belgium *Judenrat*, the Association des Juifs de Belgique (AJB), Rabbi Ullman, had not been responsible for the burning of *Judenrat* files by Jewish partisans in July 1942, which impeded the AJB from continuing to send out deportation notices, but he was accused of resistance and was incarcerated with other members of the AJB board. However, he was released after the petition of the chief Roman Catholic cleric, Cardinal van Roey, and the Queen to the German commander.

Even in the West, if local leadership pursued anti-Semitic policies, protest might provoke death. Thus, two leaders of the two divisions of the French Jewish Council, the Union Général des Israelites Français (UGIF), André Bauer and Raul Lambert, were deported to extermination camps in 1943 upon the request of officials of the French government's Commission Général des Questions Juives, to which UGIF was responsible.[33]

EMERGENT TYPES OF LEADERSHIP

One can readily observe characteristic differences in the role conceptions and ideologies accounting for their actions between those *Judenrat* leaders who passively accommodated and those who actively collaborated. Some saw themselves as "suffering servants" who never personally profited from their status. Adam Czerniakow, for example, believed it was his obligation to allay the Jews' misfortune by saving those who could be saved, taking on himself the bitter task of mediating with the Germans.[34] But there was no way to mediate, since mediation presumes that both parties have bases of power. Instead, there was incremental adaptation. Maintaining this role depended on one's avoiding the recognition that the Germans' intention was not just to oppress and exploit Jews but to annihilate them. When Czerniakow could no longer maintain this illusion, he committed suicide.

A similar position was that of Leo Baeck, chairman of the Reichsvereinigung der Juden in Deutschland, which assisted in deportations by sending out Jewish orderlies to bring in the sick and disabled. Baeck also refused to disseminate news of extermination at Auschwitz while he was interned in Theresienstadt; he had been cognizant of similar reports earlier but hoped they were rumors or "the illusion of a diseased imagination."[35] Both Czerniakow and Baeck had rejected visas that would have enabled them to save themselves.

David Cohen of the Dutch Joodse Raad made the case for the pragmatists, adjusting to reality by seeking to soften German orders in correspondence with his former friend and critic Dr. L. E. Visser, the Jewish president of the supreme court of the Netherlands. (Dr. Visser realized this accommodation led down the slippery slope of full cooperation: this is recorded in Chapter 10, pp. 271–272.) Cohen maintained that

> we live in an occupied country where the occupier has his own way. We, for our part, can only try to obtain some concessions on certain points which would not be granted without our intervention.[36]

Those leaders who signified by initially volunteering—Chaim Rumkowski of Lodz and Moshe Merin, who headed the *Judenrat* of all of East Silesia—that they aspired to the role were more than accommodating and, therefore, were never replaced. They are the archtype of what Bloom called the "ghetto dictators,"[37] identifying with their German masters concretely by emulation shown in their mode of domination, demanding sycophancy and deference and displaying sometimes flagrant delusions of messianic selection. They ruled over their councils and populations autocratically, repressed smuggling to achieve total control, and stilled their political opponents within the ghetto by deportation. As resistant leaders were liquidated, accommodating leaders who could not command personal authority were often replaced by genuine collaborators such as, in Vilna, Jacob Gens, the police chief who rose to the top and was entrusted to seize Jews of neighboring villages for deportation. These collaborators, who achieved extended power by exchanging their role in selections for continued German preference, even handed over Jewish partisans to the Germans for execution, although Gens had verbally professed sympathy for the resistance. By contrast, some *Judenräte* leaders tolerated, overlooked, or aided the ghetto fighters, despite the opposition of most Jews within the ghetto to sabotage or overt armed acts that might provoke collective reprisals.[38] The risk of aiding resistance was escalated by the known placement of Gestapo spies and informers in the councils or staffs of virtually all *Judenräte*.

STRATEGY AND TACTICS
AS IDEOLOGY AND ACCOUNTS

In Poland, unlike western Europe, it was impossible to deny reports of Jewish extermination after July 1942 on the ground that they could not be verified. All ghetto dictators acknowledged them, directly or indirectly, after this date. Such leaders used two complementary ideological lines to justify their policies. The prime exponent of "rescue through work"—enabling Jews to live by exploiting them for the benefit of the German war machine—was Chaim Rumkowski, who developed Lodz into a mammoth workshop of factories, producing wargoods worth 19 million reichsmarks in 1942.[39] This position was based on the assumption that the Germans' principal aim was exploitation, that they were killing the Jews because they were "useless eaters" as they had killed defective children, mentally ill adults (beginning in 1939), and disabled foreign workers in Germany. Although the Lodz ghetto was an important asset to the German war machine, the remaining 76,701 Jews of Lodz were transported to Auschwitz in August 1944.

Jacob Gens of Vilna also used this line. Trunk cites a speech of his in January 1943 to work foremen. "It is urgent that we make changes to increase the output of the workers and thus enhance the justification for our existence." He also notes that "In the Vilna Geto-yedies, there often appeared such slogans as, Jewish woman, remember, work saves blood."[40] Gens also justified the sacrifice of the minority for the sake of the majority before it was apparent that it was the majority that was being sacrificed for the sake of the minority. He is recalled to have said, on 27 October 1942:

> I could have told them that I do not wish to smear my hands and send my police to do the filthy work, but I said, "Yes, it is my duty to foul my hands." After five million have been slaughtered, it is our duty to save the strong and the young and not let sentiment overcome us.[41]

In the Lodz ghetto, Rumkowski used the same argument to justify sacrificing the young to save the rest:

> I was given an order yesterday evening to deport some 20,000 Jews out of the ghetto [I was told that] if I refused, "We shall do it ourselves." . . . We all, myself and my closest associates, have come to the conclusion that despite the horrible responsibility, we have to accept the evil order. I have to perform this bloody operation myself; I simply must cut off the limbs to save the body! I have to take away the children, because otherwise others will also be taken.[42]

The assumption that there is some ethical justification for complicity in killing others who have ceased to be economically productive is without any support in Jewish law or tradition. Gen's role was explicitly condemned by the rabbis of Vilna, who referred to the dictum of Maimonides: "If pagans should tell them [the Jews], 'Give us one of yours and we shall kill him, otherwise we shall kill all of you,' they all should be killed and not a single Jewish soul should be delivered."[43] However, different rabbis took a contrary position as to the applicability of this injunction.[44]

Maimonides' dictum is sociologically sound from the viewpoint of the preservation of group solidarity. That any community could protect itself by the sacrifice of guiltless members is itself a fascist notion. It betrays a reified image of the community overarching the bonds pledging people to mutual protection and ignoring the fact that once the solidarity of the community is betrayed by its leaders, facilitating the extermination of members of that community, their association becomes inherently a state of war of all against all.

A final test of the functions of the *Judenrat* is the legitimacy credited to it at the time, and subsequently by ghetto dwellers and survivors. Although revulsion has been attenuated by memory, at the time most Jews living under it detested its role.[45] Virtually all sources from the Polish ghettos surveyed show that the *Judenräte* did not inspire awe, trust, or respect and were able to establish their authority over the ghettos only by force. Force was used more judiciously in some ghettos than in others; Lodz, for example, was virtually a totalitarian state within a state. Ghetto dwellers often did not report for work or pay taxes demanded by the *Judenrat* voluntarily, and strikes as well as noncooperation were reported in several ghettos. In the West, *Judenrat* functions were less inclusive and tended not to affect the lives of Jews totally. Alienation, disaffection, and anger toward the policies of the Jewish councils were reported in Salonica, Belgium, the Netherlands, and northern France.

The German strategy of using representatives of the victims for the preliminary processing of the whole collectivity was extended to other groups. Kenrick and Puxon report that the Reich Security Main Office appointed nine representatives of two tribes of German Gypsies whom SS Reichsführer Himmler wished to save from the extermination intended for all other Gypsies. These "so-called *pure* Sinti and Lalleri" were asked "to make lists of those to be saved."[46]

How well did they cooperate?

> Only three of the nine "spokesmen" had compiled the lists by January 11th, 1943 — Gregor Lehmann, Karl Weiss and one other. Heinrich Steinberg refused to write a list because his wife and son were already in concentration camps. Gregor Lehmann had travelled to annexed Moravska-Ostrava to seek out Lalleri. Survivors claim that he took bribes from persons who wanted to be put on the lists. . . . Most of this activity proved a futile blind. When the police came to collect the Gypsies at Magdeburg and at a camp near Neubrandenburg they took away everyone. This undoubtedly happened elsewhere.[47]

Just as the Germans found Jewish collaborators inside and outside the *Judenräte* to finger Jews and spy for them in virtually every nation they occupied,[48] so they found Gypsy collaborators as well.

> Apart from Germany and Austria, Poland was the only country where the German authorities appeared to have tried to deal with representatives of the Gypsies (as with those of the Jews). Although Janusz I Kwiek, who had been elected King of the Polish Gypsies, was arrested early in the war, there were some dealings between the German authorities and Rudolf Kwiek, his rival: In a letter written as early as 1941 he offered to point out the hiding places of Polish Gypsies in exchange for safe conduct passes for sixteen members of his family, expressing his wish to be of service to the German cause.[49]

CONCLUSION

The principal intervening factor accounting for the extensiveness of Jewish victimization during the Holocaust was the isolation of the Jews, which was not attributable to German control alone but is best accounted for by state cooperation to segregate Jews that was not checked by native resistance. State cooperation is principally accounted for by the degree of legitimation of anti-Semitic movements by 1936. German control, the choice of tactics, and the time the state was occupied account for the establishment of *Judenräte*, social control organizations designed to further isolate the Jews and facilitate their annihilation. Most *Judenräte* developed in milieus in which Jews were already segregated or politically isolated. *Judenrat* accommodation does not generally account for the Jews' isolation, but Jewish isolation accounts for Jewish leaders' accommodation. Resistance and noncooperation were common among the initial leadership of *Judenräte* but the leadership was continually sifted to adopt the tool for its intended purpose. The sifting mechanisms include self-selection, negative selection, physical liquidation of or suicide by the nonaccommodating, and replacement of less by more adaptable collaborators. Jewish leaders who adapted by accommodating or actively collaborating during deportations had different conceptions of their role and developed appropriate ideologies to justify their activities. The reasons that the symptom—use of Jewish control agents, often themselves threatened with death, as instruments of organization—has been mistaken for the cause are considered.

A RESEARCH NOTE

We can never probe questions that elicit resistance if inquiry is inhibited by fear of agitating others' shame, arousing reproach, and reviving negative self-identifications and defensive countermyths. Perhaps the fatal deterrent to previous research on *Judenräte* was not only the lack of evidence but the unconscious expectation that if we did not find all victims to be heroes or martyrs, we would be debasing their image. This expectation is based on the primitive paradigm that to be a victim one must be both innocent of all accusations, and uninvolved with the system that processed victims. Many earlier Holocaust researchers have had an unacknowledged bias either to evaluate the victims' behavior by singular normative standards, not related to how people in general behave under given stresses, or to deny any evidence of human corruptibility by selective aggregation of cases, idealizing the noble and rationalizing the ignoble. Both biases are pernicious for analysis, judgment, or evaluating the implications of given tactical policies for the future.

Because of these factors, many matters of general interest of which *Judenräte* provide illustrations have been ignored. These include the development of leadership types related to initial basis of council representation; responses to totalitarian rule as exemplified in ghettos combining political and economic power; civilian-military (*Judenrat* versus police) conflicts and the emergent authority structures; characteristics of political organization in relatively totalitarian and free ghettos; *Judenrat* policies, class structures of the ghettos, and the distribution of life chances; and the social psychology of mass resistance and accommodation as a function of the authority structure within the ghetto. Researchers focusing on disasters may see the *Judenräte* phenomenon and the collective behavior of ghetto dwellers as an example of how social organization conditions reactions to collective threats (see also Chapter 8 of this volume). Researchers of ideology may attempt to relate responses to such competitive social structures to the class status and prewar ideological positions held by ghetto dwellers. Those who go beyond questions of guilt and innocence in order to extract insights (and frame hypotheses) may reveal more to us about how "normal" is behavior in "extraordinary" situations and how extraordinary or pathological is behavior in normal situations than we wished to know.

Forging the Bonds That Hold

Social Defense Movements against the State in Denmark, Belgium, and Bulgaria

In this chapter, we will examine how social defense movements were mobilized to avert or help Jews to evade deportation. We focus on movements in three countries exemplifying different pressures, opportunities, and strategic responses: Denmark, Belgium, and Bulgaria.

Bulgaria differs from Denmark and Belgium in that states in the colonial zone had the freedom to deport or not to deport Jews. The Germans had no independent police power there, as they did in the occupied states, and Jews could avoid deportation if the state refused to allow it. In states under Nazi occupation Jews, to survive, had to become socially invisible. They either fled, tried to pass as Gentiles, or went into hiding to evade recognition and capture. Defense movements in these contexts were based on avoidance tactics—organized evasion—rather than confrontation. In Denmark, for example, the movement warned Jews in advance of the impending German raid and then arranged their evacuation to neutral Sweden, which guaranteed them sanctuary. To do this, they had to establish new and illegal sea lines of transport and communication. Within Belgium, the Comité de Défense des Juifs undermined German plans by impeding the deportation of Jews, attempting to prevent their detection by placing children in Christian orphanages and foster homes, and assisting adult Jews to pass as Aryans by providing them with false papers and material aid. But in Bulgaria, deportations were actually stopped by political means after the first deportations of non-Bulgarian Jews in the newly annexed territories of Thrace and Macedonia (parts of Greece and Yugoslavia before the war) bordering old Bulgaria. Thus, individual Jews were helped to escape or evade the German net in Denmark and Belgium, but native Jews were categorically bypassed—

exempted from deportation—by the government of Bulgaria despite their earlier passage of discriminatory legislation and grant of legal sanction for deportations.

Notwithstanding these different opportunities and responses, in the three cases we will examine the preconditions of defense were similar: social authorities with an organized constituency or power base—the dominant church, the resistance movement, and democratic political parties in each nation—had to censure the deportations. We will examine the relations between the organizers of the movement and the potential victims and between the organizers and domestic elites. How did the movement begin and spread? Was it formally or informally organized, a short-term or continuing venture? How did it establish its authority and prevent collaborators from subverting its goal? The means of social control—moral authority, economic sanctions, and violent coercion—will also be discussed. Who paid the price to save the Jews? The question of the cost of operations and how the movement exploited the resources and social networks of preexisting organizations will be probed. And, of course, we will examine the strategy and tactics they chose that were adapted to their particular problem and opportunities.

DENMARK

Denmark[1] consented to a German demand for military occupation on 9 April 1940, accepting assurances that its sovereignty and civil liberties would be respected in exchange for economic collaboration that facilitated German military objectives. The Danish parliamentary system still operated under an all-party government (formed to cope with the new conditions), and Danish citizens and refugees in Denmark (including German Jews) could be tried only by Danish courts. The German ethnic minority, specially privileged in most German satellites, had no privileges in Denmark, and was told by German authorities to cease anti-Danish agitation.[2] Thus, Denmark was actually a neutral occupied by Germany, which tolerated its self-governing colonial status until November 1942.

Three preconditions of cooperation were emphasized by the Danish government: no toleration of any discrimination against the Jews, maintenance of neutrality toward the Axis, and refusal to send a regular Danish army to fight on the eastern front. The German political and military administration, initially headed by non-Nazis with little interest in the Nazification of free Danish institutions, acceded to these conditions, which were also well understood by the German Foreign Office. The Undersecretary of State, Martin Luther, deferred any plans for deportation of Jews from Denmark (and Norway) when formulating general plans for the Final Solution at the first general conference of the RSHA at Wannsee (Berlin) on 20 January 1942, because of the difficulties that he anticipated in Scandinavia.[3]

But German political pressure on the anti-Communist front increased, instigating the Danish government to intern Danish Communists (in violation of the Danish constitution), prohibit any Communist activity, outlaw the Communist Party, and in November 1941 assent to the Anti-Comintern Pact. This accommodation provoked popular demonstrations in Copenhagen against the government, and Denmark's Ambassador to Britain joined the Free Danish Council in London, signaling the beginning of some counterauthority.[4] Yet the resistance did not win affirmation from most Danes until 1943, when a majority of respondents to a survey of public attitudes toward sabotage accepted the need for illegal action and the Freedom Council was formed within Denmark. Most reports indicate a general reluctance to sanction such activities until the raid on the Jews in October 1943.[5]

Despite the cooperation elicited from the Danish government, Hitler was dissatisfied by its freedom and the unresponsiveness of the German administration there to Nazi imperatives. He therefore replaced both political and military representatives in Denmark in order to achieve greater control and stimulate real collaboration. Dr. Werner Best was appointed General Plenipotentiary in November 1942. The independence of Denmark was demonstrated by parliamentary elections in March 1943, which again showed the lack of support for the Danish Nazi Party (NDSAP). Along with the fascist Bondepartiet, the DNSAP got only 3% of the vote, a decline from the 5% they obtained together in the 1939 elections. Similarly, monthly enrollment of new members, which had peaked in 1940, declined progressively thereafter, dropping most sharply in 1943.[6]

Resistance activity in Denmark rose in 1943, culminating in a dock workers' strike in August standing out amidst a wave of strikes, riots, and sabotage throughout Denmark. These prompted the Foreign Office to recall Dr. Best to Berlin, where Foreign Minister Ribbentrop instructed him to issue an ultimatum to the Danish government. It was expected that this would be rejected, justifying the Germans' assumption of unimpeded military command. Best acted as directed, the Danish government resigned on 29 August 1943, and German authorities proclaimed a state of emergency in Denmark.

The precondition for raids against the Jews was the state of emergency provoked by Danish resistance, annuling Danish self-government. Paradoxically, Jews had been protected for a year past the time deportations began in other occupied western nations by the Danish officials' accommodation as well as by their resistance; but accommodation no longer proved feasible because of both internal pressure and German demands for greater collaboration. The precondition for the defense of the Jews was consensus among both the Danish authorities and the Freedom Council, the source of counterauthority. "On this point," Yahil states, "there was no divergence between the attitudes of Danish officialdom and of the underground movement. There was not the slightest disagreement with the view that the rights and lives of the Jews had to be protected."[7]

To the Danes, it was not a question of altruism or benevolent paternalism toward a minority but of self-defense. Yahil observes that

> what is significant here is that for the Danes *national consciousness and democratic consciousness are one and the same.* . . . Equality, freedom, the rights assured to every Dane, and the duties incumbent upon him as laid down in the constitution are valid for all citizens without exception, and all citizens constitute a mutual guarantee to one another that these principles will be maintained. . . . The struggle of the Danish people for its national existence during the occupation therefore included the struggle for the equal rights of the Jews.[8]

The relation between the integrity of Danish democracy and defense of the rights of the Jews was articulated by Hal Koch, a young theologian at the University of Copenhagen, who gave a series of public lectures in 1940 that revived the democratic youth movement. Koch's aim was to boost Danish morale by renewing belief in the democratic principles underlying Danish society and political life rather than to contribute to the underground resistance movement. Yahil notes that the tie between those principles and defense of the Jews "was most clearly related in an article by Hal Koch . . . on the occasion of the New Year in January 1942" dealing with relations between Denmark and Germany and the promises of 9 April 1940. If Germany betrayed its promise by initiating anti-Jewish policies in Denmark, it would be evidence of betrayal of those principles.

> Certainly [Koch says] this is a question of right and justice for the Jews, but in addition — and this is something fundamental — justice and freedom in Danish life are at stake. . . . We should not forget that our country's fate will be decided not by the war in the outside world but by the extent to which we are able to maintain truth, justice, and freedom by being ready to pay the price.[9]

The Danish consensus was a product not simply of the absence of Jew-hatred but also of the acceptance of the positive obligations of Christians toward Jews. The critical role of the Danish national Lutheran Church in denouncing anti-Semitism and expounding such obligations is elaborated in Chapter 4. The consistent friendship demonstrated by the King toward the Jewish community — immortalized by the spurious legend that he donned or threatened to wear the yellow star (a device never imposed in Denmark) — exemplifies this consensus.

The deportation of the Jews was instigated by Werner Best, who played a curious double game, taking steps to subvert execution of the order despite the fact that he himself had suggested it to SS Reichsführer Himmler. His suggestion and his demand for SS police battalions to carry it out were motivated, Yahil believes, by the need to further his own flagging career and obtain an independent source of power against the German army in Denmark, which opposed him and refused to carry out the deportations.[10] Best told G. F. Duckwitz, a German shipping official in Copenhagen, on 11 September 1943, about the impending plans for arrest of the Jews. Duckwitz tried to dissuade Best from the fulfillment of these plans and flew to Berlin and later to Sweden to instigate Swedish intervention. When Best told him that the raids would be executed on the night of 1–2 October, Duckwitz secretly informed the leaders of the Danish Social Democratic Party.

Rumors of impending action against the Jews had circulated among the Jewish community since the lists of the Jewish community were seized by German police on 31 August and 17 September when the Chief Rabbi and the chairman of the synagogue had been arrested by the Germans and were interned in Denmark. But Jewish leaders, always relying on the protection of the authorities, made no arrangements for a warning system and no plans to distribute information and give assistance to Jews in need or without the necessary contacts in Denmark. Both the Bishop of Copenhagen and the Director-General of the Danish Foreign Ministry, Nils Svenningsen, had gone to Best to verify these rumors and been reassured by Best, who "declared that persecution of the Jews in Denmark would take place only over [my] dead body."[11] They related these assurances to the chairman of the Jewish community, Henriques. When the Social Democratic leader Hans Hedtoft conveyed Duckwitz's warning to Henriques, his first response was to repudiate the messenger's character and source:

> When the Dane had finished, the Jewish leader spoke only two words, "You're lying." It took a long time to convince Henriques of the truth. The president repeated despairingly that he just could not understand how it could be true; after all, he had just returned from a visit to Svenningsen, who had assured him that nothing could happen.[12]

The next day, 29 September, Rabbi Melchior publicly warned the Jews assembled for the morning services before the eve of the Jewish New Year to flee or hide. He told them that no services would be held this New Year. The board of the Jewish community made plans to arrange for legal protection of the community's property and affairs in their absence but no plans to warn Jews except by word of mouth. Warnings were systematically spread by the Social Democrats, priests, politicians, journalists, members of manufacturers' associations, and others to all the Jews they knew. Leaders of Hechalutz (young Zionist pioneers preparing for settlement in Palestine) sent a courier to their members. The diffusion of warnings was the first stage of social defense.

Henriques again relied on diplomatic appeal. As might be expected, after the government was made aware of the deportation order, the King formally protested to Best, unaware that he had instigated it. Yahil implies that the Danish higher civil servants were inclining toward accommodation when they realized that their resistance had been overridden. They refused Henriques's appeal on 29 September to resign in protest and considered offering the Germans a ransom to save the Danish Jews, a remedy rejected by Henriques. Yahil observes, "It is strange to note how at the twelfth hour the Danish authorities, of all people, seized upon proposals typical of the lifesaving efforts made by the Jews in various episodes of persecution and pogrom."[13] Perhaps the civil servants were deterred from accommodating not only by Henriques's protest but by the new counterauthority issuing from the Freedom Council in September 1943, which called for noncooperation with the deportations and direct aid to the Jews by every Dane, and promised future prosecution of collaborators.

The raid was carried out on 1–2 October 1943, as planned, using only Gestapo troops, who were instructed not to force the door if there was no response when they rang the doorbell. This restriction was designed to appease the Danes, who were not expected to cooperate. Two hundred Jews were caught that night in Copenhagen (and 84 elsewhere), including some 30 people in a Jewish old age home next door to the synagogue, whose existence had evidently not been known to the Danes warning Jews and had been ignored by the Jewish leaders. Ultimately, the number seized reached 475, or 6.2% of the 7,695 Jews (and members of families including Jews) affected by the raid. These 7,695 are the sum of the Jews seized in Denmark plus successful and unsuccessful evaders (the latter had died or were captured in flight); included among evaders are the spouses and offspring of mixed marriages who were not covered by the deportation order but feared apprehension by the Germans and/or wanted to remain with their families. The victims caught in Denmark were sent to Theresienstadt—a transport camp rather than an extermination camp—and all remained there, unlike the Jews deported from any other nation. They were protected by the constant inquiry and intercession of Danish officials, and their health was maintained by packages sent monthly by other Danes, often strangers. When we add the 30 Jews who are estimated to have died during transport to Sweden and another 30 who committed suicide to the 51 Danish Jews who died in Theresienstadt (41 of whom were over 60), we find that a total of 111 Jews died as a direct or indirect result of the German action. This represents 1.4% of all the Jews in the state, a smaller proportion than in any nation fully occupied by Germany.[14]

What happened to the Jews after the night of the Copenhagen raid has been well publicized. Yet the fact that the flight of the Jews to Sweden was hastily arranged has sometimes been mistaken for a sign of haphazard organization or lack of organization instead of an indication of the exceptional social cohesion and organizability of the Danes. The desperate situation of the Jews was publicized all over Denmark (despite press censorship) because of the bishops' protest, circulated immediately to ministers of all Danish churches and read from the pulpits on 3 October 1943. Besides the pastors, "at least forty" organizations protested; indeed, Yahil states, "There was scarcely an organized body which did not express its profound indignation to the German authorities."[15] These were followed by protests from all five of the principal political parties. But protest had no effect upon German policy makers and could not ward off physical threats of capture.

The Jews had relied on personal associations and many spontaneous offers of individuals to find immediate hiding places on the night of 1 October, without making further plans. They could not know that Sweden had offered them sanctuary. While the Swedish government hastened to make diplomatic inquiries and appeals to Germany, the Danish Freedom Council encouraged domestic Swedish protest. Nils Bohr, the atomic physicist (who had also fled, as he was listed as a Jew), pressed appeals to government officials, finally petitioning the Swedish King to announce the offer after Swedish diplomatic appeals to Germany had proved futile. Bohr's appeal to the King was successful; the invitation was broadcast over Swedish radio on 3 October. The Danish defense movement that arose to save the Jews agreed on the imperative need to get them into Sweden—a decision instigated by the Freedom Council—in order to evade the Nazi net. But there was no established route to Sweden (such as existed through adjacent Norway), the trip was hazardous and every day spent in Denmark multiplied the possibilities of capture.

The exodus to Sweden required enlisting fishermen for the perilous trip, financing their requested fee (commensurate to their risk), finding Jews in hiding (youths combed the woods to find the most isolated of them), recruiting hiding places, couriers, and Danish police cover, and supporting these with intelligence operations to protect them from German police. The actual coordination of arrangements for sailing and for hiding the Jews was undertaken by groups near the departure sites, at Lyngby, Humlebaek, Elsinore, and Helsingnor. These were neighbors, not necessarily active in the resistance, united by mutual interest and trust. Few Jews played leading roles in the rescue networks, most being occupied with their own flight.[16]

Within Copenhagen, rescue rings were based on preexisting organizations, as was the underground resistance: there were teachers' rings, a priest's ring, a journalist's ring, and doctors' rings. Professionals employed the resources of the organizations to which they belonged as a cover, while completely diverting their function to total mobilization for flight. The early consensus among Danes on protection of the Jews led them simultaneously to reject the routinization of time allotment in daily life. Hospital staffs held conferences daily to delegate duties in conveying their charges to the fishing boats waiting at the coast, and transported them in ambulances. Students closed down Copenhagen University and secondary schools so that they were available for retrieving Jews who had hidden in the country in order to transport them to the ports. There was also much unorganized collective helpfulness reported: the ready cooperation of anonymous strangers in giving keys to Jews and boarding them without payment rather than exploit the situation. This was a collective social movement, simultaneously spontaneous and structured. Unlike most social movements in opposition, it was tolerated or supported by Danish officials (at different levels). Danish ministers broadcast warnings to their parishioners not to cooperate with the Germans in any way. The Danish police down the line served the escape networks rather than the German authorities.

Before the regular escape routes were coordinated by the rescue organizations, the fee—from 1,000 to 10,000 kroner per person ($50 to $500)—was set by the demands of the few fishermen willing to risk loss of their boats, and only wealthier Jews were able to afford the flight. This was later reduced to 500 kroner ($25) per person evacuated. The rescue organizations drew upon funds of employers' and manufacturers' associations, other Danish organizations, and spontaneous donations. Funds were later supplemented by the Board of Trustees of the Jewish community (then in Sweden), which guaranteed collateral for a loan of 750,000 kroner ($37,500) from Danish banks, later repaid by the community after the war. Passengers who were relatively affluent were asked to pay more than their fare to cover costs for the less affluent.[17] The chairman of the Jewish community gave several hundred thousand kroner. Although the total cannot be established with certainty because of the number of private arrangements and the inability—and inadvisability— of keeping records during this period (substantial sums were often given to unknown couriers without receipt), Yahil estimates that rescue organizations spent about 12 million kroner, equivalent to $600,000.[18]

Subsequently, the Jews who had reached Sweden earlier were specially solicited by the Danish-Swedish Refugee Service (growing out of the cooperation between a Jewish Agency emissary to Sweden, Adler-Rudel, the Swedish Jewish community, and the Danish resistance) and transmitted promissory notes on their blocked accounts in Denmark, thus contributing altogether about eight million kroner (or two-thirds the cost of their own rescue) to the rescue operation, which also aided members of the Danish resistance and Allied pilots downed in Denmark.[19]

The solidarity of Danish resistance evidently caused many German officials to overlook the operation, or subvert fulfilling their usual roles, lessening the risk of the voyage over the North Sea. Not only G. F. Duckwitz but many others subverted the German operation by consciously or unwittingly failing to see or denying the unfolding of a grand conspiracy. Some even disabled the German response capacity, such as the commander who grounded the German Coast Guard vessels patrolling the ports for repairs so that apprehension of the illegal fishing vessels was delegated to the Danes. We do not know whether these officers failed to play their accustomed roles because they feared increasing their social and moral isolation from the Danes, because they feared provoking disturbances that they could not quell thus exposing their impotence, or because the Danish context enabled them to act out beliefs opposing Nazi persecution that they might have suppressed elsewhere.[20]

While the stunning success of the Danes was due to their consensus, their organization, and their mutual trust, they did not count on consensus alone to protect the operation. As everywhere in Europe, there were German-organized Danish collaborators (the *Hilfspolizei,* or auxiliary police), blackmarketers and petty criminals exploiting Jews, and informers posing hazards. Although their numbers were proportionately far less than in other occupied nations, even a handful of collaborators posed a risk when the price of being caught could be death. To deter betrayals, social control over collaborators was exercised. Yahil notes:

> It was impossible to hide the rescue operation of thousands of people from the eyes and ears of the population. . . . Here too there was a certain element of security in the general nature of the activity; a local resident, even if he were inclined to be pro-German, would certainly hesitate to call down upon himself the wrath of the overwhelming majority of the population who supported the rescue operation. This would seem to explain the fact that there were so few informers. Gersfelt tells of "three stages of warning" in such cases: first, informers would be sent a funeral wreath; if this did not help, they were sent a card on which was drawn a cross of the type engraved on tombstones; then they were sent a tiny model of a coffin.[21]

The final sanction, a watery grave, was later changed to imprisonment in Sweden when the Swedes agreed to incarcerate informers. This attentiveness to all sources of trouble paid off: less than 2% of the fleeing Jews were caught in flight.

Just as the organization and resources developed for transfer of Jews to Sweden evolved into a permanent ferry service for the resistance, conveying messages back to the Danes, the tie between helper and helped was not just a one-way transfer of assistance but a shared experience that transformed the lives of both parties. Aage Bertelsen, a leader of the Lyngby group, recalls their state of exaltation.

> I remember particularly one night late in October. We were walking along the beach after having sent the last boat off to the ship. . . . For fourteen days in succession we had shared the same experience, but nevertheless the finished embarkation filled our souls each time with this peculiar, almost too intense feeling of happiness, which seemed to me to be entirely different from all other emotional experiences. I was walking beside Dr. Strandbygaard. Suddenly she said, "Isn't this strange? Don't you think so? A very strange feeling! It's almost like experiencing again the overwhelming love of one's youth."
>
> My wife participated only once in an embarkation. Bound as she was night and day by the hard toil of the "office" in Lyngby, she allowed herself only this one evening toward the end of October to accompany me to Smidstrup. . . . But the whole atmosphere of the beach up there rested like a blessing on the relief work, and on the rooms in Buddinge Lane. . . . We agreed that no matter what might happen to us we could not have done without that period.
>
> "No, because it's like this," said Gerda very quietly, "it's as if we never realized before what it means to live."[22]

Soon after that, Bertelsen fled to Sweden when the activities of his group were exposed to the German police by a Danish Nazi posing as a member of the resistance needing passage to Sweden. Gerda Bertelsen was arrested by the Gestapo but was released after five weeks, largely because of the activity of a family friend who posed as a Gestapo agent offering to hunt throughout

Denmark for her husband. Thanks to this, we have the opportunity to share their exaltation. But at least two Danes lost their lives in the rescue operation.

The experience of acting outside the law in liberating the Jews also liberated the Danes from their previous respect for authority and fear of provoking reprisals. Sabotage, work stoppages, and other mass actions mounted in late 1943 and 1944, instigating the Germans to respond with anonymous assassinations in reprisal in 1944 and executions of saboteurs. The general strike of June 1944 in Copenhagen led the Germans to cut off all services there. The resistance then terminated the strike, but renewed it again on the eve of liberation in April 1945. The added warning time afforded the Jews by the initial accommodation of the Danish government with the Germans enabled the Danes to realize the threat posed by Germany toward the Jews, while the experience of protecting the Jews by organizing their exodus enabled the Freedom Council to command a counterauthority to that of the state. This gave the resistance the support of the great majority and inhibited any tendency among officials and leaders to defend collaboration with Germans. Nevertheless, the Freedom Council authorized 350 executions, indicating that even in the most solidary nations counterauthorities cannot combat the state without using violence as a sanction.[23]

BELGIUM

Belgium fought against the German invasion of May 1940 longer than any other lowlands nation, but finally capitulated on 27 May, with the government fleeing to England. Hitler had no clear plans for the future of Belgium, although an influential Nazi theorist rationalized restoring the "Westland" as a German border, placing Belgium and three provinces of northern France under a single military commander, and annexing to a Prussian province three districts granted to Belgium after World War I.[24] By chance, the goals of the Belgian government-in-exile paralleled those of Belgium's military commander, General Baron Alexander von Falkenhausen.

> Falkenhausen had a more cosmopolitan background than many of his military colleagues. . . . Like many Prussian officers he had far-ranging intellectual interests, he was a student of philosophy, a devotee of the novels of Stendhal, and an admirer of the teachings of Lao-Tzu. There can be no doubt of his loathing for the Nazi regime, and his appointment appears to have been due in large measure to the fact that he was the nephew of Germany's military commander in Belgium in the later stages of the First World War. During his own four years as military governor, he did what he could to prevent the introduction of the worst aspects of Nazi rule in Belgium. In 1944 he was implicated in the July 20 plot to assassinate Hitler and was thrown into a concentration camp.[25]

Falkenhausen tried to diminish Nazi intervention in Belgium by centralizing control over his administration and demonstrating his ability to prevent disorder and exploit Belgium economically. The government-in-exile sought to preserve Belgium's political integrity and prevent its material destruction by exercising firm control over officials and elites in Belgium through a few representatives there, including Cardinal van Roey.[26] Thus, both were willing to cooperate economically, but the pressure of other German agencies, especially the Gestapo and Security Police, and the provocation of Belgian collaborators instigating resistance counteraction ultimately proved such an accommodation unstable.

Two main nuclei of collaborators were encouraged in Belgium: the Rexists, an ideological native fascist movement that never obtained more than 10% of the vote in a Belgian election and whose support had dropped by 1939, and various Flemish movements aiming to achieve Flanders's autonomy (briefly asserted by a collaborationist schism during World War I). The support of the latter movements was concentrated in Antwerp, in which the majority of the Jewish population was concentrated. Since the goals of these movements were in conflict, encouragement of collaborators served to raise aspirations that their German mentors would not fulfill.

The Jewish population of Belgium could be said to be especially vulnerable, if vulnerability was a simple function of visibility and differentiation from other Belgians. It had more than doubled since 1921 because of Belgium's openness toward refugees: over 90% of the estimated 90,000 Jews in 1939 were not of Belgian citizenship, often neither French- nor Flemish-speaking.[27] Many fled to France during the invasion but most of these, finding themselves destitute, returned. Ultimately, 66,707 Jews were registered in Belgium, of whom only 4,125 (6.2%) were of Belgian nationality.[28] The majority of Jews (55,000) lived in Antwerp (Flanders), where they constituted 17% of the population in 1940 and had a visible and vibrant Yiddish-speaking culture.

Despite General Falkenhausen's disinterest in discriminating against Jews, there is no evidence that he subverted any German orders regarding implementation of the Final Solution. The German order requiring Jews to register, stripping them of businesses and posts, and segregating them proceeded on the same time schedule as in France (excepting, of course, for the many anti-Jewish laws that the French government spontaneously introduced). The yellow star ordinance tagging them for the police and deportation orders was initiated at the same time in Belgium, France, and the Netherlands. Although all preliminary measures against the Jews were initiated by military personnel, the influence of the RSHA (Eichmann's force) became dominant in 1942 and was not curbed in Belgium (or elsewhere) by the army. The German strategy of installing a *Judenrat,* the Association des Juifs de Belgique (AJB), was the same in Belgium as elsewhere throughout occupied Europe. Gestapo reprisals against the resistance were similar. German techniques of press control, propaganda, and the organization of collaborators also paralleled those in other occupied countries.

Where Belgium differed from the Netherlands (which also had a government-in-exile) and from France and Norway was in the response of civil servants, supported by the firm position of the government-in-exile against confirming any regulation contrary to The Hague convention.

A registration order defining a Jew was initiated by the military commander on 28 October 1940. But the secretaries-general of the Belgian ministries (the highest native officials) refused to issue the order on their authority, citing constitutional reasons, and the Germans issued the order directly to the Conference of Burgomasters. Some burgomasters (as in Antwerp) collaborated fully and others (as in Brussels) were accused of bad faith. But only 42,652 of those persons required to report (those over 15) declared themselves Jews, leading German authorities to estimate a maximum of 52,182 Jews in Belgium.[29] Measures to identify Jewish businesses and to strip Jews of property were difficult to execute. The Belgian government-in-exile declared all such transfers illegal, warning that new owners not only would not enjoy future legal protection but could be indicted. Hilberg has noted that "banks were slow in reporting Jewish accounts" and that the "president of the Brussels Stock Exchange, van Dessel, refused to accept the papers [for sale of shares owned by Jews] in the absence of the Jewish owners." A German official of the Economic Ministry under the military commander noted in December 1942 that "the Belgian public . . . exhibited an 'aversion' to the acquisition of Jewish real property from the *Militarbefehlshaber* [military commander]."[30] Similarly, ordinances to exclude Jewish university professors elicited protest from the University of Brussels. The Bar Association publicly protested an ordinance to exclude Jewish lawyers and refused to publish new lists of members.

The secretaries-general refused to execute the military commander's ordinance requiring Jews to wear the yellow star in May 1942, causing the commander to assign the order to the AJB, which also refused. Finally, the Military Command itself distributed the stars, except in Antwerp, where the municipality, eager as usual to cooperate, not only distributed them but stamped the identification cards of Jews with a "J."

The AJB was headed by Rabbi S. Ullman, former military chaplain, who had been approached by the German administration because two more prominent rabbis had fled the country. After consultation with Cardinal van Roey, Ullman accepted the charge. Initiated and supervised by the SS Security Police, the AJB's supposed function was to provide for the education of Jewish children, give public assistance to Jews in need, and arrange the "emigration" of Jews. Its first task in April 1942 was to make a new registration of Jews. This turned out to be lower than the October 1940 count, indicating greater reluctance among Jews to enlist and/or noncooperation among the AJB's local committees executing the task. An estimated total of 40,212 persons were listed.[31]

While Jews were stripped of status, they were not segregated effectively in Belgium, although legally restricted to four cities—Antwerp, Brussels, Liège, and Charleroi—within which the great majority of Jews of Belgium already resided. Ordinary Jews, those not engaged in professions or holding government posts, became subject to German physical controls by regulations ordering them to register for forced labor for the Organization Todt: those who registered and responded to the German summons to report were shipped to northern France, where they worked and lived in special camps from which they were eventually seized, dispatched to French or Belgian concentration camps, and ultimately sent to Auschwitz.

The threat to the greatest number of Jews in Belgium began with the start of deportations in the West in July 1942. The AJB dispatched young messengers personally to deliver orders from the military commander to report for forced labor under threat of arrest and deportation to a concentration camp for those who failed to report. An official assurance that it was a work order, not a measure of deportation, was enclosed.[32] However, Rabbi Ullman petitioned the Cardinal and the Queen to appeal to the military commander for the exemption of Belgian Jews, which both did. General von Falkenhausen's exemption so reassured many Belgian Jews, they were discovered in their own homes in September 1943, when the German Security Police began making raids without warning.

Representatives of the Armée Belge des Partisans reacted swiftly in order to deter further AJB cooperation, setting fire to the card file of registered Jews at AJB offices on 31 July 1942. "When this proved insufficient, the *Armée* executed Holzinger," the AJB official in charge of callups of Jews; he was shot on the streets of Brussels after being asked to identify himself.[33] Warnings by the resistance were effective enough so that Jews soon stopped reporting and went into hiding, according to a German Foreign Office spokesman. Jews had also stopped reporting in the Netherlands at this point; yet almost 80% of Dutch Jews had been transported to concentration and extermination camps by the date of liberation, whereas 53% of the 66,707 Jews recorded in Belgium (according to records of the Ministry of Health) evaded deportation. How can this be explained?

Not only had the resistance of the Belgian administration impeded the segregation of Jews, preventing their ready seizure, and inhibited collaboration; the Jews themselves, under the aegis of the popular front resistance movement, the Front de Indépendance (FI), began in June 1942 to form a social defense movement, the Comité de Défense des Juifs (CDJ), not relying solely on petition and appeals. Although the CDJ was founded by Jewish Communists and Socialist Zionist activists, its leadership included Jewish notables of bourgeois background, prewar Jewish officials, and a well-known Catholic journalist of the left. Steinberg reports that it represented all elements in Jewish life except the Bund, which feared cooperation with the Communists.[34]

The AJB was effectively disabled by the CDJ despite the increase of German threats. The Security Police's overseer of the AJB admitted the aim of the deportation to AJB leaders in September and had Rabbi Ullman and five other members arrested, threatening them with deportation or internment in a concentration camp if they did not become more cooperative. Nevertheless, they were liberated within a few days after Queen Elizabeth and Cardinal van Roey appealed to the military commander on their behalf.[35] Rabbi Ullman resigned as head of AJB after his release. The CDJ infiltrated the AJB by co-opting a member of its board, placing workers in AJB offices so as to get the names of Jews in need of help and later visiting them; at the same time, they diminished the authority of the AJB in the Jewish community by widespread publicity.

How the CDJ functioned to alert potential victims is made clear by the diary of Anne Somerhausen, the American-born wife of a Belgian Socialist parliamentary deputy, regarding a Jewish secretary she was hiding.

August 8, 1942.

I have spent twenty-four hours dreading that Mlle. V. would take her own life. But she has now come to her senses and gone away in comparative calm. A man came to fetch her big trunks yesterday. He told a gruesome tale of Jews shipped in hermetically sealed cars to Berlin, killed with poison gas on the way, and thrown into a canal on arrival. It is a ridiculous story, of course. Who would believe these fantastic tales about gassing people? I thundered at the man for telling this outrageous nonsense to a frightened woman like Mlle. V. It took a long time to quiet her. She talked incessantly about death, death. Now she is gone. I do not know her new address: I didn't want to know it, lest I be quizzed about her by the Gestapo.[36]

The CDJ worked through local committees, with the national organization directly controlling its functional divisions: welfare assistance for adults and children (including child placement), a financial section, a section that obtained and fabricated false papers, and a press and propaganda section. The last of these, which first circulated the rumors inducing Jews not to report, published papers in French, Dutch, and Yiddish and also circulated the resistance press of the FI. Determined to provide authentic information on the fate of the deportees (despite the fact that reports on the fate of the Polish Jews had already been broadcast by the BBC in July 1942), the CDJ commissioned Victor Martin, who as a university student had written a dissertation on German folklore, to visit his German teachers and continue eastward. Martin reached Auschwitz and was informed by foreign workers how victims were gassed and corpses burned there. Although delayed by a brief arrest by German police (who suspected him of industrial sabotage), he returned to Belgium on 15 May 1943. His report was published in two resistance papers of the CDJ and FI, *Le Flambeau* and *Indépendance,* and transmitted to London.[37] The FI published its information in a stern appeal to its readers:

Having lost all hope of obtaining a victory in the country which would permit them to oppress the Belgian patriots, the Rexist and Flemish bands redouble their efforts to accomplish, like dirty stoolpigeons, their criminal work [which is] so agreeable to their masters, the Nazis. By all means, they search to procure the addresses of Belgians who out of patriotism refuse to go to work for the enemy in Germany [i.e., evade the German-imposed labor draft], and of Jews who hide in order to avoid deportation. . . . Belgians, let us show our understanding and sympathy with these friends, Belgian noncooperators and Jews, who struggle with us. Let us stand together against the criminal plots of Rex and of V.N.V. in the pay of the Germans. For the Jews, deportation means death under the most atrocious conditions. . . . TO INFORM AGAINST A JEW IS TO MURDER HIM (HER)! . . . Belgians, without distinction of race, philosophic and political beliefs, let us unite to prevent such crimes. . . . DEATH TO THE TRAITORS AND THE INFORMERS! LONG LIVE INDEPENDENT BELGIUM![38]

Their appeal was edged with warning: collaborators were also well organized, and at least 100,000 Belgians belonged to collaborationist organizations. A virtual war between collaborators and the resistance was ignited by resistance assassinations of collaborationist officials and a prominent journalist, beginning in December 1942. Although Cardinal van Roey would not sanction armed resistance, he was moved to excommunicate the leader of the Rex Party, Leon Degrelle, in 1943 after he assaulted a priest who denied him communion because he was dressed in a German uniform.

If the Germans could promise collaborators material rewards and the spoils of office, the resistance could deliver reprisals, countering incentives with punishment. One Belgian perhaps overstated its effectiveness:

There was not a single potential Quisling, not a single weak character, who did not reconsider ten times before he dared commit an act of treachery or antisemitism. They knew of the seeing eye, the listening air—that somewhere in the dark there was the patriot who watched. Somewhere in the shadows, not far from him, was a witness to his deed, a member of the underground tribunal—a reporter from *La Libre Belgique*, or *Vrij*, who would tomorrow see to it that full retribution followed, a patriotic justice which knew of no mercy for traitors.[39]

The activity of the CDJ was predominantly nonviolent. Its most impressive achievement was to save the lives of 3,000 of the estimated 4,000 Jewish children saved in Belgium. These children were placed in private homes and institutions, disguised as Aryan Belgians.[40] They were recruited by special "assistants" from their mothers, who were not informed of the children's whereabouts for fear that they would visit the children and expose them and their temporary guardians to reprisals. A circle of "godmothers" themselves constituted the link between the home, the child, and the CDJ, representing the parents and guaranteeing the children's return to them. The CDJ was generously assisted by the official Belgian child-care organizations for public assistance and all the resources of the Catholic Church. Madame Yvonne Nèvejen, Director-General of l'Oeuvre Nationale de l'Enfance, ar-

ranged the placement of Jewish children in institutions and Cardinal van
Roey authorized this action, explicitly proscribing efforts to convert them.
The Cardinal also acted "to temper the pro-Nazi zeal of a certain number of
people who called themselves believing Catholics, including the Burgomaster
of Greater Antwerp."[41]

Official Belgian government departments and banks (including the
German-instigated welfare organization, le Secours d'Hiver) again came to
the aid of the CDJ by supplying material assistance and ration stamps to Jews.
The total receipts of the CDJ between 15 September 1942 and 15 October
1944 exceeded 48 million francs (equivalent to $2,117, 863), 51% of which
sum was directly paid for by the budgets of the Finance Minister and
Madame Nèvejen. An additional 11.4 million francs (24%) had been
pledged by the international Jewish relief organization, the Joint Distribution
Committee, and the cash advanced by Belgian banks in francs, so that three-
fourths of the funding of the CDJ came directly from Belgian banks, including government accounts. Only 6% was covered by CDJ's own collections
and reimbursement by parents who could afford to pay for child
placement.[42]

As its base broadened and the resistance in Belgium became more daring, CDJ also became more innovative. In Brussels, a cell of resistants within
the postal service intercepted denunciations to the Gestapo, and the CDJ
organized a service to warn those Jews living incognito who were
betrayed — among the estimated 25,000 in hiding — before the mail was
delivered. The CDJ also infiltrated the detention camp in which deportees
were held for later transport by cattlecar to the extermination camps. On 19
April 1943 (the day of the Warsaw ghetto revolt), a squad of Jewish partisans
attacked a deportation train, stopped it, opened the doors, and gave 50
francs each to the prisoners who jumped off. Ultimately, 108 persons
escaped, 75 others were recaptured, and another 21 were shot.[43]

But the success of the CDJ rested most not on such actions but on the immediacy of its establishment, its integration of all elements in the Jewish community, and the positive cooperation of authorities of the state, church, and
resistance. Steinberg lists 357 active members and 126 communes that
cooperated in one way or another with the CDJ.[44] Had not the threat been
immediately construed as a collective threat and organization been extant to
transform good will to cooperation, it seems unlikely that over half the Jews
of Belgium and almost the same proportion of non-Belgian Jews would have
survived the war.

Like other resistants in Belgium, the founders of the CDJ paid a higher
price than the population they defended. Six of the eight constituting
members of CDJ were deported to German camps; only two of them survived.
Similarly, Olga Wormser-Migot found that three out of every four resistants
in the whole general resistance movement were deported, only one of whom
ever returned.[45]

BULGARIA

Bulgaria had become progressively dependent upon Germany during the 1930s and benefited from Germany's adjudication of Balkan borders by acquiring territory from Rumania, Greece, and Yugoslavia, fulfilling Bulgaria's old claims to Macedonia. The prewar Bulgarian state was authoritarian, with an often interrupted tradition of party competition. By 1940, King Boris led the governing faction, which relied on manipulated elections to the Subranie (Parliament) for a pretense of consent. However, except for a significant Communist Party, driven underground during the war, the state was stable; there were no popular fascist movements or contenders for power waiting in the wings, as in Rumania and Hungary.

In March 1941 the government acceded to the stationing of 600,000 German troops in Bulgaria. The troops had no occupational duties and did not claim any right to intervene in Bulgarians' self-government. Although Bulgaria did make the gesture of declaring war against Britain and the United States, no pressure was put upon it to join the war against the Soviet Union or to sever diplomatic relationships.

The government showed its respect for Germany by pushing anti-Semitic legislation through the Parliament in January 1941, known as the Law for the Defense of the Nation. This law defined Jews on racial grounds, registered them, stripped them of positions and rights, expropriated their property, allowed for suspension of free travel, residential control, and future segregation. Members of the Ratnitsi, a prewar anti-Semitic movement, were appointed to key administrative posts; they included Minister of the Interior Gabrovski and, later, the Commissar of Jewish Affairs (Belev).

Despite its commitment to Germany and its chosen policy of collaboration, no Jews from prewar Bulgaria were deported, but 11,393 (96%) of the Jews from formerly Yugoslav and Greek territory were deported.[16] Thus, 18% of Jews within the expanded territory of the Bulgarian state became victims and 82% evaded victimization. The causes of Bulgaria's policy have aroused much postwar discussion, but no explanation of why collaboration was stopped is possible without examining how it was stopped.

Opposition to the Law for the Defense of the Nation was widespread, coming from the Bulgarian Orthodox Church and professional associations of lawyers, writers, and doctors. The Jewish community of Bulgaria was an old, established Sephardic community, still enjoying much collective autonomy as a heritage of the millet system established under Turkish rule, dominant in Bulgaria until 1878. Numbering less than 1% of the total population, Jews constituted between 4% and 5% of the urban population and 10% of the population of Sofia during the twentieth century. They were a small minority among the 20% minorities composed of Bulgaria's population and were less visible in trade and commerce than Greeks, Turks, and Armenians—thus not likely to be seen as competitors. For these reasons, the racist anti-Semitism promulgated in Vienna, Berlin, and Budapest had not taken hold among the educated middle classes of Bulgaria at the turn of the century, although there were some prominent Bulgarians oriented to the German intellectual and political orbit who openly espoused the new anti-Semitism in the thirties. Among the Bulgarian intelligentsia,

> the myth of the absence of anti-Semitism grew up. Although this was not strictly true, the myth became as important as the fact, for a large section of the Bulgarian intelligentsia became committed to fighting the growth (or, as they preferred to think of it, the appearance) of anti-Semitism in their country. In 1937, a Jewish journalist, Buko Piti, published a book of statements of some one hundred and fifty leaders of Bulgarian society denouncing anti-Semitism and proclaiming the reasons for its absence in Bulgaria.[47]

The Execution of the Law for the Defense of the Nation was lax. In August 1942, the law was amended to compel unemployed Jews in Sofia to leave on 1 September, to seize Jews' private property, and to distribute identity cards to them. Simultaneously, wearing the Jewish star (previously required only of Jews drafted into labor brigades) was required of all Jews. But the decree could not be enforced. Metropolitan Stefan of Sofia protested against it publicly; to be sure, his concern was also directed toward freeing Christians of Jewish birth of such a stigma. German diplomats complained that Jews would not wear the stars and that the population supported them. Finally, in October 1942, the Bulgarian government stopped producing the stars, claiming a shortage of the electric power needed to manufacture them. By November 1942, it seemed to Walter Schellenberg, chief of foreign intelligence for the RSHA, that the Bulgarian government had gone as far as it could against the Jews: indeed, the authorities "had overstepped the limit of what, in their opinion, was bearable."[48] Schellenberg cited the cordial relations between the royal family and particular Jews and the slackness of government enforcement of existing legislation. Chary believes that Schellenberg's sources included members of Bulgarian extreme right groups seeking German support to stage a coup d'état.[49] However, the German Foreign Minister, Beckerle, had a different view; that same month he obtained a written expression of interest from the Bulgarian Minister of Foreign Affairs in pursuing arrangements for deportations. One of the ever ready experts of the RSHA, Dannecker, was dispatched from Paris to Sofia.

To deter opposition, the ministers concluding the agreement to deport the Jews negotiated covertly to lessen its visibility, did not publish it, and specified in that agreement only Jews to whom the Bulgarian leaders had no ties, those from the newly acquired territories. This was done incrementally by asking the Parliament (generally a government rubber stamp) to delegate the execution of the Law for the Defense of the Nation to the cabinet (June 1942). The cabinet delegated its execution to the Jewish Commissariat (created in August 1942), whose representatives directly supervised the existing Jewish consistories in each community. The Commissariat, whose staff rose rapidly from 13 in October 1942 to 160 in January 1943, arranged the agreement with the RSHA representatives in February 1943, and it was then approved by the cabinet in March 1943, legally authorizing the deportation of up to 20,000 Jews "inhabiting the recently liberated territories." The Commissar knew from his own census that there were fewer than 12,000 Jews in these territories, meaning that 8,000 would have to be selected from old Bulgaria, almost one out of six Bulgarian Jews.

The decree was never published in the official gazette. The Commissariat contacted the civil and military rulers of the new territories (all from old Bulgaria) to notify them and make arrangements for the Jews' impending arrest by army and local police troops, who cordoned off the towns' Jewish quarters on the dawn of the specified days. Local representatives of the Commissariat all over Bulgaria prepared lists of Jews to be deported from old Bulgaria; selections were supposed to include Jews "who were 'rich, prominent, and generally well known' . . . leaders among the Jews, defenders of the Jewish spirit in the local community, or supporters of anti-government ideas or feelings."[50]

The arrests in Thrace and Macedonia were carried out with the full cooperation of Bulgarian officials, who concealed their orders so well that local Jews were completely unaware until their homes were surrounded by soldiers in the early dawn of 4–10 March 1943. However, Bulgarians employed in the central office of the Commissariat and local officials in Kiustendil, aware of the Commissariat's plans, tipped off Jews in Sofia (where very few were selected) and in Kiustendil (a medium-sized city of old Bulgaria whose entire Jewish community was scheduled to be deported) to the impending arrests. On the advice of the district governor, several Jews in Kiustendil raised money to bribe government officials, and a delegation of five Bulgarian friends, including some officials, agreed to go to Sofia on their behalf. Only two went; the others were detained by local Ratnitsi-inspired violence. "Kiustendil in the crisis did not really demonstrate solid support for or against the Jews, but was rather a microcosm of the forces and doubts at work in the entire country."[51] Iako Baruh, an official of an illegal Zionist group in Bulgaria representing the Jewish Agency, independently called upon government and opposition figures, employing personal contacts from university days and influence garnered from previous favors to such ministers. Baruh visited Dimitur Peshev, a representative from the first Kiustendil district who served as vice president of the Parliament, to inform him of the threat against the Jews. Peshev confirmed the information and demanded that Minister of the Interior Gabrovski annul the deportation order. Gabrovski assessed the opposition (swelled by other parliamentary delegates contacted by Peshev) and contacted Prime Minister Filov, who agreed to postponement of any action against Jews from old Bulgaria (not specified in the agreement) and telegraphed Commissariat representatives five hours before the action was to begin, calling off the raids.

But the message did not arrive in Plovdiv on time, and police began arresting Jews on 10 March, inciting another prominent citizen to petition the government. Bishop Kiril of Plovdiv (later Patriarch of Bulgaria) also wired the king "threatening a campaign of civil disobedience, including personally lying down on the railroad tracks before the deportation trains, if the planned operation was carried out.[52]

Peshev raised a motion of protest in Parliament against the government's anti-Jewish policy, objecting to any deportation of Jews, and was joined by 42 of the 160 delegates to the Parliament. The government demonstrated its strength by making the vote a test of confidence; the government faction voted unanimously to support the policy, but only 58% voted to censure Peshev. This was a suppressed rebellion symptomatic of widespread disapproval among the Bulgarian governing elite, including right-wing and left-wing opposition leaders. The chief Metropolitan, Stefan, protested most categorically (as did the bishops collectively), expressing his censure publicly to his congregation as well as to the King.

The government persisted in defending its policy. It initiated an anti-Semitic campaign in the press, which dwelled on the fact that two of the assassins of government and right-wing figures in Sofia were Jews associated with the Fatherland Front and similar partisan movements attempting to overthrow the government. King Boris, after negotiations with the German Foreign Ministry, approved a plan to expel the Jews from Sofia to the countryside, which the pro-Nazi ministers hoped would lead incrementally to their deportation, although Boris still refused to authorize further deportations.

When the Jews of Sofia received expulsion orders on 21 May 1943, telling them to leave the capital within three days, they reacted in desperation, convinced that the order meant deportation. Peasants who scurried to the Jewish quarter to purchase their household goods cheaply helped to convince them of this. Jewish leaders of the Consistory and other notables pleaded through all their contacts with church and court to annul the order. However, Stefan was apparently most impressed by Daniel Tsion, a rabbi disdained by the Jewish community for his interest in Dunovism, an occult Christian sect native to Bulgaria.[53] Tsion distributed a cyclostyled copy of a message warning against persecution that he believed was transmitted by God. Other functionaries at court were also impressed by Tsion's proclamation. The leaders of the Jewish Consistory disowned Tsion's action and pensioned him off.

Besides the protest of church leaders and figures within the court, Bulgarian leaders of democratic parties in exile and the underground Communist Party broadcast protests against the Jewish expulsion, urging non-cooperation. Ordinary Jews became impatient as the time of departure grew nearer. A crowd of Jews gathered outside the central synagogue on 24 May, the day of Saint Cyril (an important Bulgarian national holiday), were led to demonstrate at the palace by members of the Fatherland Front; however, they soon were blocked by armed police and Commissariat agents, who stopped them and arrested the younger men.[54]

The Jews expelled from Sofia were sent to country towns, where they were usually boarded among the local Jewish community but not threatened with deportation. The King responded to other German requests negatively, informing German Foreign Minister Ribbentrop that Jews were needed for road construction. The German Foreign Office acknowledged its defeat: it had no means to force or persuade Bulgaria to deport its Jews. Beckerle, the German Minister to Bulgaria, reported to the Foreign Office on 7 June 1943 that "direct pressure just didn't work. The Bulgarians had been living with peoples like the Armenians, Greeks, and Gypsies for so long that they simply could not appreciate the Jewish problem."[55]

What accounts for Boris's decision? His reputation has been enhanced by his sudden death in August 1943, attributed by the western press to the Germans, although there is insufficient evidence to support this charge. Chary reviews the role of King Boris, arguing against the popular legend that he saved the Jews. He concludes that the King's response was at all times a function of pressures put upon him. His reversal, Chary insists, was not attributable to popular attitudes alone.

> The relative lack of anti-Semitism among the Bulgarian peasants and the active objections from large segments of Bulgarian ruling society contributed to the prevention of deportations . . . [but] only through the channeling of popular discontent into political pressure could the political change required to eliminate deportations occur. . . . The degree of effectiveness of popular opinion depended upon the organization and influence of that opinion. Stefan and Peshev, protesting on behalf of the Jews, were more effective than a parish priest or a local official. The Holy Synod and a large section of the Subranie protesting on behalf of the Jews were more effective than Stefan and Peshev alone.[56]

According to Chary, it was not the opposition that sought to overturn the government (such as the Communist-dominated Fatherland Front) but opposition within the government, whose support was needed, that was most influential.[57] Nissan Oren, an authority on the Bulgarian Communist Party of this period, reviews the question of "The Bulgarian Exception: A Reassessment of the Salvation of the Jewish Community" (1968) and reaches a similar conclusion.[58]

However, the influence of the opposition and domestic elites need not be weighed as antithetical factors, but may be complementary. The consistent position of the church, the intelligentsia, the democratic party leaders, and the Communist Party showed that there was no taken-for-granted ideological base of anti-Semitism to exploit to legitimate the deportations. The government could collaborate only by diminishing the visibility of action against the Jews sufficiently to impede the mobilization of resistance. However, once actual physical threats to government authority were offered by the Communists, one may suspect that the King became more sensitive to the threat of delegitimation by domestic elites. This caused him to withdraw from confrontation over the Jews. Protestors against the deportation in March persisted in their opposition in May 1943, signaling their withdrawal of support. Since it became increasingly clear in 1943 that the war would be ended by a German defeat, Germany could no longer reward or threaten Bulgaria. Boris' decision to collaborate no further was a rational response to domestic pressures: he had to save the Jews to save his regime and preserve the integrity of Bulgaria. After the death of Boris and the westward march of the Red Army, the new government of Bulgaria was increasingly reluctant to collaborate with Germany, diminishing the volume of anti-Jewish propaganda. Responding to a request by Ira Hirschmann, American delegate of the War Refugee Board, the government annulled the Law for the Defense of the Nation (and other anti-Jewish legislation) on 31 August 1944, as the German Embassy staff fled Sofia.[59] A new democratic government of the old parties was formed on 2 September. Bulgaria declared war against Germany. It later negotiated an armistice with the Red Army representing the USSR, which declared war on Bulgaria on 5 September, a day before the Fatherland Front instigated a popular rising and seized power within three days, encountering little resistance.

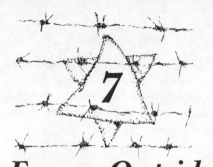

Forces Outside
the German Orbit

The Role of the Allied Governments,
the American and British
Jewish Communities,
and the European Neutrals

To this point, we have focused on nation-states drawn into the Nazi orbit voluntarily or involuntarily and have shown how the degree of German control and domestic forces affected the extent of state cooperation, resistance among authorities, and movement against deportations. We have assumed that the state is a rational actor and that its decision to deport or resist deportation of Jews can usually be explained by a rational weighing of interests as well as values. But the factors taken into account by states in the colonial zone and by Germany itself[1] included pressures by or expectations of sanctions and rewards from the Allies. The opportunities for evasion afforded Jews directly and indirectly also depended on the Allies' policies and those of the neutrals within Europe, in the midst of war.

In this chapter, we shall directly inquire what the Allies did to prevent, check, or counter the processes culminating in mass murder of Jews, from the initial discrimination against German Jews in 1933 to the incineration of the Jews of Europe. Were means available that were not used? Viewing states as rational actors, how do we explain their response? How was relevant information received by Allied countries diffused to or concealed from the public? What evidence is there of the primacy of rescue of Jews or prevention of their murder as a policy goal? And how do we explain the unity or disunity of the Jewish community of the United States and Great Britain when confronted by this challenge? What objectives, anxieties, and ideologies conditioned their responses? (Because of Soviet Jews' lack of freedom to organize on their

165

own behalf during this period, we will ask this question only regarding the American and British Jewish communities.)

Focusing on the neutrals, how do we explain the policies toward admission of Jews as refugees? What diplomatic actions were taken to inhibit deportation of or discrimination against Jews?

THE ALLIES

The United States

We begin with the problem of the organizational incapacity and unreadiness among nation-states to protect members of other nation-states. Since obligations are defined legally in the modern world finally by the nation-state, if a class of people are excluded by the nation-state, they are in an unprotected social void unless recertified by other nation-states as members, Arendt observes.

> The calamity of the rightless is . . . not that they are not equal before the law, but no law exists for them: not that they are oppressed but that nobody wants even to oppress them. Only in the last stage of a rather lengthy process is their right to live threatened: only if they remain perfectly superfluous, if nobody can be found to "claim" them, may their lives be in danger. Even the Nazis started their extermination of Jews by first depriving them of all legal status (the status of second-class citizenship) and cutting them off from the world of the living by herding them into ghettoes and concentration camps: and before they set the gas chambers into motion they had carefully tested the ground and found out to their satisfaction that no country would claim these people.[2]

The lack of will on the part of the United States between 1933 and 1945 to redress the loss of rights, status, and citizenship of German Jews and to deter or check the later annihilation of European Jews has been amply documented by researchers since 1968.[3] Despite certain differences in focus and audience, all present a similar picture of American administrative refusal to incur any costs on behalf of European Jewry.

What could have been done?

Two possibilities were open during the prewar period. The first was to assist the exodus of Jews between 1933 and 1940 by opening up American immigration and exploiting American influence to secure havens for refuge in other countries. Second, the United States could have imposed sanctions against Germany to censure past discrimination and discourage further oppression.

To sum up the dreary tale, the Roosevelt administration refused to aid Jewish and other refugees by attempting to amend U.S. immigration laws (based on national origins quotas since 1924). Furthermore, between 1933 and 1943 the State Department undermined fulfillment of the law by failing to approve enough visa applicants to fill the quota for Germany (despite the surplus of applicants) and repeatedly opposed allowing refugees into the United States or its territories by exploiting loopholes in the law. Proponents of rescue, such as Secretary of the Interior Harold Ickes, who wanted to admit any number who had escaped to the Virgin Islands, from which they could enter the United States without formal barrier, encountered unremitting opposition from the State Department. Confronted with a conflict between these advocates and the State Department or members of Congress, Roosevelt unhesitatingly supported the opponents of rescue.

To divert attention from the American policy of noncommitment, the President convened multinational refugee conferences (Evian in 1938, Bermuda in 1943), instigated the establishment of the powerless Intergovernmental Committee on Refugees, and initiated inquiries and diplomatic probes on the possibility of resettling Jews in undeveloped areas of Latin America, the Philippines, and Africa. Palestine, advocated by the Zionists, was rejected because of British opposition. Both nations rejected the possibility of taking in substantial numbers of Jews who sought to flee Germany. America's unwillingness to alter its own immigration policy justified to other nations at Evian in 1938 the closing of their doors; interested and disinterested spectators alike saw the Evian Conference as an exercise in Anglo-American collaborative hypocrisy.

The Nazis exploited their perception of the West's indifference to justify their own Jewish policy; the *Danziger Vorposten* observed after the conference:

> We can see that one likes to pity the Jews as long as one can use this pity for a wicked agitation against Germany, but that no state is prepared to fight the cultural disgrace of central Europe by accepting a few thousand Jews. Thus the conference serves to justify Germany's policy against Jewry.[4]

During 1938 and 1939, the Nazis calculated that expulsion was one way to rid the Third Reich of its Jews; it would serve several of their interests to exploit prospective refugees by seizing their property and obtaining foreign exchange by giving credits on the value of the confiscated goods to the nations of refuge with which they could purchase German imports. Such an agreement had previously been made with the Jewish Agency, enabling German Jewish immigrants to draw upon blocked accounts in Germany upon their arrival in Palestine. This arrangement—the Haavara agreement—aroused much controversy and indignation among Jewish leadership, Zionist and non-Zionist, especially among the American Jewish leaders who had been sponsoring a boycott of German goods since 1933. When, in 1939, the German government proposed an exchange plan of Jewish refugees with "International Jewry," using the United States and Great Britain as intermediaries for this fictitious corporate organism, these objections were reiterated by both Jewish leaders and the governments involved, each motivated by different sources of apprehension. Both correctly perceived it as ransom. Jews were to be completely stripped of their wealth and an exit tax of $250 per person (or $1,000 per family) was demanded. Unlike exchanges in classic economic theory, the price did not go down because of lack of demand for the commodity marketed; it escalated. Jewish leaders feared becoming commercial agents for a criminal regime (not realizing the immensity of the crime it intended), and the costs of rescue if Germany plowed through eastern Europe and began auctioning off the Jews of Poland. American officials feared that this would be a precedent for the mass marketing of unwanted peoples and dreaded the effects on America's world trade of guaranteeing a German export market based on blocked Jewish currency.

The Inter-Governmental Committee on Refugees (IGC) played at responding in 1939 to the Schacht proposal for refugee exchange. In retrospect, it appears that both sides were playing. The Germans knew that the West would not buy Jews who were pauperized. In 1938, they had unofficially tested such an offer at Evian through a prominent Viennese Jew manifestly representing the Jewish community and found there were no takers.[5] Hjalmar Schacht was dismissed as president of the Reichsbank by Hitler on 20 January 1939. Jewish policy was then coordinated by the Nazi radicals, who preferred to intern rather than exploit Jews.

The problem in the United States and Great Britain was not inadequate resources in relation to the numbers pleading for escape but a lack of commitment to lifesaving. The aim of American (and British) foreign policy before 1939 was to avoid war with Germany. The United States always maintained a correct, respectful, diplomatic posture toward Germany, rejecting economic sanctions such as blocking currency or cutting off trade or economic exchanges to save prospective refugees, as well as avoiding any diplomatic sanctions. Since 1933, Hitler's victims had been written off as casualties of the revolution that diplomatic observers recognized was occurring after his accession to power. They wishfully believed that "excesses" against the Jews—street violence, Gestapo raids by night, sending home the ashes of those recently deported to camps—would disappear as the revolution rid the country of its internal opponents and enemies as well as the Jews.

No protest was ever made against the practice of stripping the German Jews of jobs in 1933 or of citizenship rights in 1935. Only after Kristallnacht in 1938 did the Roosevelt administration imply a rebuke against Germany by calling the American Ambassador to Berlin home "for consultation." Again on this occasion, Roosevelt refused either to cut off trade with Germany or to propose new immigration laws. American protests were restricted to notes concerning American Jews in Germany.

Official denial, disbelief, and dispassion were the prelude to later resignation. In order to maintain such detachment later, it was necessary to obscure the visibility of the crime being committed. Thus, the State Department in August 1942 refused to relay reports to Rabbi Stephen S. Wise, president of the American Jewish Congress, from Gerhard Riegner, the World Jewish Congress representative in Switzerland, regarding the plan for the Final Solution, claiming that they were not sufficiently documented. Furthermore, it informed its Swiss representative not to accept any more messages of that type from Riegner. But, Friedman charges, "Wise not only knew about the death camps in the summer of 1942, . . . , but actively collaborated with the [State] department in keeping verified accounts of mass murder from the public" for three months.[6] Wise had received the same report from the World Jewish Congress representative in London, M. P. Sidney Silverman, and had confirmed it through Undersecretary of State Sumner Welles on 28 August 1942. Yet Wise agreed to Welles's request not to disclose it publicly until the department corroborated it through other sources. However, Yehuda Bauer has noted, the report essentially was substantiated by the first-hand reports of mass extermination in Poland collected by the Jewish Socialist Party of Poland (the Bund), transmitted by the Polish government-in-exile to London, and broadcast on the BBC two months earlier.[7] Bauer concludes, "It is somewhat difficult to put all the blame for complacency on British or American statesmen . . . when Jewish leaders made no visible attempt to put pressure on their governments for any active policy of rescue. The Jewish leadership could hardly plead lack of knowledge."[8]

The Allies refused publicly to acknowledge German crimes against Jews as Jews in their declaration on war crimes in January 1942: "General Sikorski, who served as the president of the St. James Palace Conference [on War Crimes] replied [to the protests of the World Jewish Congress] that the declaration had purposely omitted any specific reference to anti-Jewish crimes because the Jews were considered nationals of their respective states."[9] But the reports of systematic extermination could no longer be denied, prompting the Unites States and other Allies to recognize publicly on 17 December 1942 that the extermination of the Jews was a crime whose perpetrators "shall not escape retribution."[10] But this was forgotten by November 1943 (see p. 174). No immediate sanctions were announced that might have deterred execution of the crime.

At the beginning of 1943, the majority of Rumanian and Hungarian Jews—the two largest Jewish communities in Europe outside the Soviet Union and Poland—had not been deported. About one of every four Rumanian Jews had been massacred in 1941 and about the same proportion either driven into exile in Transnistria without sustenance or interned in Rumanian concentration camps; two-thirds perished before the war's end from starvation, cold, and torture.[11] Inducing Rumania to liberate these Jews and transmitting aid to them through a neutral could have saved up to 100,000 lives.

By 1943, Rumania was turning toward the orbit of the Allies. In 1942

Premier Antonescu, anticipating a German defeat, entertained the possibility of exploring a separate peace with the West. Although in July 1942 he concluded an agreement with the RSHA to deport the Jews from old Rumania, the plan was never implemented. Simultaneously, disengagement was being investigated by J. Maniu, leader of the National Peasant Party, who maintained contact with the British Near East command. Antonescu dragged out the investigation of such illegal activities to prevent Maniu's exposure. Alexandre Cretzianu, former head of the Ministry of Foreign Affairs, acted as Maniu's representative and was sent to Ankara in 1943 as Rumanian Ambassador by Antonescu, who was fully cognizant of his objectives. Maniu, Lavi points out, was one of the leaders who maintained contact with Jewish leaders and intervened with the dictator on their behalf.[12] Vago shows how Jewish leaders exploited the illusion of international Jewry's influence over the western Allies with Maniu and other allies in order to obtain their support[13]

In 1943, the Rumanian regime switched course, attempting to exploit the Jews by confiscatory taxes and expropriation and offering to allow 70,000 to 80,000 to emigrate in exchange for foreign currency. This plan, confirmed by leaders of the Emergency Committee to Save the Jewish People, was never carried out because of American delays attributable both to the State Department and to initial repudiation of the exchange by Stephen S. Wise, who opposed the leadership and strategy of the Emergency Committee. Wise used his personal influence against the campaign to raise money to ransom Jews in the Rumanian concentration camps of Transnistria by stating publicly that the offer was unconfirmed (untrue) and that the cost was too high.[14]

To the Rumanians, the Jews had become a utility to be bought and sold. When German victory seemed certain, they could be treated as an object and exterminated as an end in itself. When German victory was uncertain, the use-value of existing Jews outweighed the intrinsic value of dead Jews, and the opportunity of negotiations might be explored.

The State Department's role in preventing rescue and inhibiting public recognition of the Holocaust by neglecting opportunities, bureaucratic legalism (such as demanding recommendation letters from a refugee's local police agency, which might be the Gestapo), and simple prevarication was well known among rescue advocates but was not exposed until Secretary of the Treasury Henry D. Morgenthau, Jr., became aware of this conspiracy in December 1943, and supervised preparation of a personal report to the President, originally entitled "Report to the Secretary on the Acquiescence of this Government in the Murder of the Jews."[15] Only in January 1944, when Roosevelt was confronted with proof of the State Department's subversion, did he establish the War Refugee Board, which agency was granted authority to forestall "Nazi plans to exterminate all the Jews." In 1944 the United States authorized use of the threat of sanctions against the collaborating satellites, notifying foreign representatives of susceptible belligerents that still had Jewish populations (Hungary, Rumania, and Bulgaria) that they would be held responsible for their acts.

Ira Hirschmann, the American WRB representative in Ankara, arranged a meeting there with Alexandre Cretzianu in March 1944 and asked him to (1) immediately disband the Rumanian concentration camps in Transnistria, (2) expedite passage and exit visas for 5,000 children through the port of Constanca to Palestine, and (3) end all persecution and repression against minorities in Rumania. Hirschmann affirms in his memoir that nothing was promised in exchange but the good will of the United States and personal visas for the Cretzianus. One week after this request was made, the camp was disbanded. He also reports that the children had been sent to Constanca: WRB records show ships sailed from there to Istanbul with over 5,000 Rumanian Jews of all ages during July–August 1944. Hirschmann recalls:

> Before he left, Cretzianu had said something which, while it caused a twinge of conscience, strongly reinforced my belief in unhesitant, affirmative action. He said: "If this means so much to you in the United States, why didn't you come sooner? You could have saved more lives."[16]

The most inviting target for deportations were the 825,000 Jews of Hungary, whose safety, the WRB realized, was immediately threatened once German troops marched into Hungary in March 1944 without any Hungarian resistance and with a newly appointed pro-German Hungarian cabinet eager to assist them. The War Refugee Board attempted to deter deportations from Hungary by threats of postwar punishment of collaborators, appeals relayed to the populace by short-wave radio to hide Jews and record collaborators; the WRB tried to intensify threat and appeal by increasing visibility of any action, pleading with the International Red Cross to increase its observers in Hungary and with the Pope to broadcast his opposition and the threat of ecclesiastical sanctions; they did not elicit his cooperation in this (see Chapter 4).

Deportations were halted by 9 July 1944 by order of the Regent, responding to foreign protest and a private appeal from the Pope. But 435,402 Jews had been deported between 15 May and 9 July 1944. The Regent thwarted a coup by the radical right in July, a coup realized in October. However, by June 1944, it appeared that the Allies' effort to deter extermination in Hungary by the threat of future sanctions was ineffective. The question that has never been answered satisfactorily is why all the Allies rejected the most direct means suggested of preventing the extermination of the Jews of Hungary—bombing the rail lines leading to Auschwitz and/or the crematoria themselves.

Eyewitness reports and drawings of the Auschwitz facilities provided by two Slovakian Jews who escaped had reached the War Refugee Board representative in Switzerland, Roswell McClelland, in June 1944, and a summary was sent to Washington.[17] The complete text was first released by the

WRB in a 60-page report in November 1944. Erich Kulka relates the progress of the Auschwitz Protocol, concluding that the WRB, "by its half-hearted and protracted handling of the Protocols . . . allowed the Nazis in Birkenau to send several hundred thousand more people to their death."[18] According to War Refugee Board records, proposals to bomb Auschwitz were rejected by Assistant Secretary of War John J. McCloy *three times*. John Pehle, director of the War Refugee Board, first requested the bombing of Auschwitz gas chambers on 8 November 1944, having earlier made it clear that he was uncertain about the legitimacy of this request.[19] While requests came from the Polish and Czechoslovak governments-in-exile and a few Jewish groups, there was no united pressure from major American Jewish organizations, most of which were silent on this matter. Indeed, Leon Kubowitzki, head of the Rescue Department of the World Jewish Congress, advised against the bombing, suggesting instead that the Soviets and Polish underground mount an armed attack on Auschwitz—fearing the potential anti-Allied propaganda that bombing might provoke.

> The destruction of the death installations cannot be done by bombing from the air, as the first victims would be the Jews who are gathered in these camps, and such a bombing would be a welcome pretext for the Germans to assert that their Jewish victims have been massacred not by their killers, but by the Allied bombing.[20]

McCloy's stress on the technical lack of feasibility of bombing Auschwitz was a cover-up for a decision reached by the War Department in January 1944 not to employ any armed forces to rescue the European Jews, for the Air Force had no problem bombing that area; David Wyman tells us:

> From March 1944 on, the Allies controlled the skies of Europe. Official U.S. Air Force historians have stated that "by 1 April 1944 the GAF [German Air Force] was a defeated force." Allied air power had "wrecked Hitler's fighter [plane] force by the spring of 1944. After this . . . U.S. bombers were never deterred from bombing a target because of probable losses. . . ."
>
> On Sunday, August 20, late in the morning, 127 Flying Fortresses, escorted by 100 Mustang fighters, dropped 1,336 500-pound high-explosive bombs on the factory areas of Auschwitz, *less than five miles* to the east of the gas chambers. Conditions that day were nearly ideal for accurate visual bombing. . . . Available figures, which are incomplete . . . indicate that 100,000 Jews were gassed at Auschwitz in the weeks after the August 20, 1944, air raid on the camp's industrial sector. If the date is set back to July 7, the time of the first attack on Blechhammer, the number increases by some 50,000. . . . Much more significant, though, than attempts to calculate particular numbers is the fact that no one could tell during the summer of 1944 how many hundreds of thousands more would die at Auschwitz before the Nazis ceased their mass murder. . . . From July through November 1944, more than 2,800 bombers struck Blechhammer and other targets close to Auschwitz. The industrial area of Auschwitz itself was hit twice. Yet the War Department persisted in rejecting each new request to bomb the death camp on the basis of its initial, perfunctory judgement that the proposals were "imprac-

ticable" because they would require "diversion of considerable air support." That the terrible plight of the Jews did not merit any active response remains a source of wonder, and a lesson, even today.[21]

The other Allies agreed to divert no resources to save the Jews in Auschwitz. Kulka relates that Vishinsky himself, speaking for the Russian Foreign Ministry, rejected Kubowitzki's suggestion made to the WRB, that a special military operation be mounted to liberate Auschwitz.[22] Vago documents Britain's rejection of Chaim Weizmann's plea to bomb Birkenau (a component of Auschwitz) on the ground that the Air Command did not possess accurate maps: "In other words, the Foreign Office was not sufficiently interested in the topic to keep track of the camps or to note the failure of British Intelligence in this matter."[23]

The increased public awareness stemming from the WRB's publication of the Auschwitz Protocols incited demands by Jewish groups for a warning to Germans to abstain from exterminating prisoners still alive in Auschwitz and other camps.[24] This led to a public warning from the Supreme Allied Commander, General Eisenhower, addressed to Germans; significantly, references to Jews were deleted in the final version, which directs them to ignore "any order from whatever source" to injure prisoners in concentration camps and forced labor battalions "without regard to their nationality or religious faith." Other means used by the WRB to prevent further exterminations were appeals to the Soviet Union to safeguard the liberated Jews and indirect diplomatic approaches to Germany to deter the SS from killing their prisoners.

Strategies of Denial and Defense

The special character of German policy toward Jews had been denied since 1933, usually by tagging the victims with the universalistic label of "political refugee." Whereas being a political refugee, an opponent of the regime, was an earned or achieved status, being a Jew, under the Nuremberg laws, was ascribed by ancestry. President Roosevelt helped create the impression that there was something voluntary about the Jews' plight. The President, in fact, refused to recognize a particular Jewish problem, never mentioning Jewish victims until 1944. This denial was facilitated by Jewish groups which publicly recognized only infractions of "human" rights: they rejected special pleas for Jews as Jews because they believed that this would validate Hitler's charge that the Jews were united in a world conspiracy. How this blurred perception is shown in Feingold's description of Roosevelt's encounter with an American official negotiating with Hjalmar Schacht in 1939 for the emigration of 150,000 Jews from the Reich.

> Among the first questions asked by Roosevelt, when Rublee visited the White House in early February [1939] to present his final report, concerned the reason for limiting the agreement to Jewish refugees. It took some doing to convince the President that Berlin only recognized a Jewish problem and refused to negotiate on anything else.[25]

Wyman, who has shown how Jewish organizations concurred in labeling Jews political refugees, upon the advice of their Christian allies, does not recognize that this tactic of deemphasizing Jewish identity had unanticipated negative consequences.[26] When Jewish organizations in 1938 failed to back the Wagner bill, which would have admitted 20,000 German refugee children outside the quota, one of the arguments deterring potential sympathizers was that this would encourage the breakdown of nuclear families. They did not acknowledge that the crisis of German Jewish families (aggravated by the internment of 30,000 Jewish men in concentration camps after the pogrom of Kristallnacht) was a crisis of survival; such a realization might have convinced professional welfare advocates that the rules made to fit the ordinary range of families' domestic problems were not applicable. Similarly, the failure to stress that Jews as Jews had been defined officially as the enemy of the new Germany produced the paradox that Jewish refugees from the expanded Third Reich were denied entry by the State Department, which classed them among potential spies, untrustworthy because of their German nationality. Keeping potential German agents out was a persuasive argument to justify bureaucrats' keeping the victims out by withholding papers and by stalling admission procedures on visa applications indefinitely through security checks. Even after the Allies publicly acknowledged the extermination of the European Jews (in their declaration of 17 December 1942), they failed to recognize Jews among the victims specified in the Moscow Declaration of 1943, which threatened war criminals with postwar judgment "by the peoples whom they have outraged." "The Emergency Committee [to Save the Jewish People of Europe] quickly pointed to the dangers of such a 'fatal oversight' and argued that it would suggest to Nazi authorities 'that the United Nations are indifferent to Hitler's proclaimed intention to proceed with the extermination of the entire Jewish people of Europe.' " And the American Jewish Congress excoriated the indifference of the Allies, observing that "even 'Cretan peasants' had deserved mention as victims, but not Jews," reminding Roosevelt that "the Germans are half convinced that it is relatively safe to murder Jews."[27]

The victims' Jewish identity, although not acknowledged publicly until March 1944 was recognized earlier by the American administration through its establishment of refugee quotas. In 1940 the President recommended limiting Jews to 10% of the projected number of refugees to be resettled in Alaska — a plan he quickly vetoed when opposition developed. Even as late as 1944, he was concerned to avoid placing "undue proportions" of Jews in a temporary detention camp in Oswego (the first of its kind) for refugees without visas.[28]

Although rescue from German-occupied countries was not generally possible, the United States might have attempted to improve the status of the Jews interned in camps and ghettos by declaring them prisoners of war, a strategy called for in 1943 by the Emergency Committee to Save the Jewish

People of Europe. Redefining their status would have made these Jews subjects of international law, and Allied cooperation might have persuaded the International Red Cross to press attempts to inspect the camps before 1944 (when they were allowed into Auschwitz, Theresienstadt, and Rumanian and Croatian camps). The IRC had a legal claim to protect prisoners-of-war; it had no mandate to oversee the conditions of detention of incarcerated civilians. If their status were changed, it might have restored the inmates' right to existence by making them visible. Visibility of the victims' suffering did provoke the delegates of the International Red Cross (originally reluctant observers), who witnessed in October 1944 the forced marches of Hungarian Jews to the Austrian border to grant (with other neutrals) certificates of protection to 15,000 marchers. Within Budapest, the IRC protected Jewish children formally awaiting transit visas in special childrens' houses. The Swiss Consul also gave protective papers and housing to at least 15,000 Hungarian Jews; these papers multiplied as copies were printed by Zionist youths, helping added tens of thousands.[29]

Lives were also saved by the War Refugee Board, not as a result of direct sanctions to prevent deportation but through redefining the status of Jews by conferring papers, certificates of immigrant status, or foreign protection.

The most ingenious and dedicated exploiter of lifesaving through documentation was Raoul Wallenberg, a Swedish Legation attaché in Budapest working with the WRB. Wallenberg extended Swedish diplomatic protection to 20,000 Hungarian Jews and leased apartment houses for them in Budapest. Although he lacked arms and had no special diplomatic sanctions to inveigh against Germany to uphold the authority behind such recertification, he defended the status he had bestowed upon his clients to the point of physically interposing his own body when the German police came to the quarter to round up Jews for deportation, following (by auto) six of his "clients" on a train heading to Auschwitz and intercepting the train before it reached the border. (Little is known of the extent of his ingenuity as Wallenberg disappeared while in Soviet custody in January 1945.)[30]

The American State Department not only did not assist the recertification of the victims through deviant means but repudiated such means used by others. The Department even rejected the War Refugee Board's request to transmit a message to certain Latin American governments (through Switzerland as an intermediary) in 1944, imploring them to validate suspected fraudulent Latin American visas of Jews then interned in a German camp in Vittel, France. After several internal skirmishes between the WRB and the State Department, the message was transmitted, but too much time had been lost: 240 of the interned Jews had already been shipped to Auschwitz.[31]

Explanations of U.S. Policy toward Rescue

All sources agree on the widespread opposition to the admission of refugees before the war and the general public approval of the exclusionary function of the 1924 quota system. Wyman stresses that congressional opposition merely reflected the public attitude.[32] Xenophobia (often masking blatant anti-Semitism) was first justified by the Depression and a decade of high unemployment; keeping refugees out later was legitimated during wartime as self-protection against potential Nazi agents. Although anti-Semitism was usually muted in public halls, it was a widespread and growing phenomenon. The physical violence against German Jews during Kristallnacht (November 1938) evoked denunciations from American notables, church leaders, and major newspaper editors but their revulsion was not politically channeled. There was growing aversion and hostility toward Jews on the part of the American public during the war, a significant minority among them blaming the victims.[33]

How did American Jews respond to this situation? Feingold examines the divisions within the American Jewish community at the time on tactics of appeal and methods of rescue—public boycott or private petition, mass demonstration or elite representation, Zionism as a goal or as one of a number of means of rescue. These account superficially for the inability of that community ever to present a single demand with solidary backing. Breckinridge Long, the Assistant Secretary of State, who created the major procedural barriers to refugees seeking to enter the United States, saw that clearly:

> Before he surrendered his strategic position in January 1944 he confided in his diary that "the Jewish organizations are all divided amid controversies . . . there is no cohesion nor any sympathetic collaboration—rather rivalry, jealousy and antagonism."[34]

Feingold traces the splits on strategy and tactics, initially represented in the 1930s by the division between the American Jewish Committee and the American Jewish Congress, to the cleavage between Jews of different social classes, eras of immigration, ethnic and religious backgrounds. "Uptown" and "downtown" Jews had arrived at different times from different milieus and maintained distinctive life styles and relations to the non-Jewish community that rationalized their choice of different tactics of self-defense. The American Jewish Committee (emblematic of the style of uptown Jews) was founded in 1906 by the prosperous mercantile and professional scions of German Jewish immigrants, most of whom first arrived in the United States in the middle of the nineteenth century. The Committee operated upon the traditional model of appeals by influential men to other influential men—political notables and government leaders. The American Jewish Congress grew out of the movement among American Jews between 1915 and 1920 to send their own delegation to the Versailles peace conference to press for Jewish minority rights in Europe and Zionist demands: 350,000 (or one of every 10) American Jews voted for a convention to elect those delegates.[35] The American Jewish Congress, headed from the beginning by Rabbi

Stephen S. Wise, opposed the leadership, ideology, and mode of operation of the American Jewish Committee and attempted to create a more embracing participatory organization that could claim to represent all American Jews, the majority of whom are descendants of the great Jewish migration from eastern Europe after 1881. Both the Committee and the Congress are competing defense or "community-relations" organizations that attempt to protect the rights of Jews throughout the world as well as in the United States.[36]

During the 1930s, the need for collective defense produced a double bind among many Jews. The rise of anti-Semitism caused some American Jews to inhibit the assertion of claims on their own behalf as they internalized denigrating stereotypes of the Jews and tried to belie these accusations by their own accommodating behavior. German Jews, confronted by charges of the new Chancellor, Adolf Hitler, that worldwide Jewry was the enemy of Germany, initially sought to reaffirm their loyalty in order to defend themselves. Thus, the Centralverein, the leading defense organization of German Jews, rejected protests by foreign Jews and declared themselves against the boycott of Germany organized by foreign Jews in reaction to the initial discrimination and violence against Jews in Germany after Hitler's ascent to power. Such German Jews attempted both to confirm their identity as Germans and to appease the new regime, hoping discrimination would diminish and aiming to avoid reprisals.[37] Rabbi Wise ignored their advice—sometimes communicated under duress—to remain silent; the American Jewish Committee heeded it.[38]

While the American Jewish Congress sponsored rallies and public protests in the 1930s, the American Jewish Committee opposed any open condemnation of German policy, and made no effort to lobby to change the immigration quotas limiting the admission of Jewish refugees; nor did it press the Roosevelt administration to condemn discrimination and (by 1935) the legal disestablishment of German Jews as citizens. Frederick Lazin attributes the Committee's lack of response primarily to its members' estimate of their self-interest, fear that publicity generated by protest would arouse anti-Semitism in America; it was not oriented to Jews as a collectivity beyond national barriers.[39] But Naomi Cohen, author of the officially sponsored history of the American Jewish Committee, simply attributes the Committee's inaction to its failure to understand the difference between the Nazis and earlier persecutors.[40]

Although most Christians associated with committee members in such organizations as the National Conference on Christians and Jews advised Jews against making any distinctive protest as Jews for fear of arousing anti-Semitism, a significantly placed observer, Secretary of the Interior Harold L. Ickes, saw their protective stance itself as arousing contempt. He recalls a prewar conversation with Supreme Court Justice Louis D. Brandeis:

I spoke to him of the cowardice on the part of the rich Jews of America. I said that

I would like to get two or three hundred of them together in a room and tell them that they couldn't hope to save their money by meekly accepting whatever humiliations others chose to impose upon them. . . .

Justice Brandeis agreed with me completely. He said that there was a certain type of rich Jew who was a coward. According to him, these are German Jews, and he spoke of them with the same contempt that I feel for them.[41]

The cleavage in style and strategy between the American Jewish Committee and the American Jewish Congress had preceded the Nazi threat. Each class employed the strategies appropriate to the social position of its constituents. Thus, the elite opted for an Americanized appeal to the authorities by, as Sachar puts it, the *schtadtlan* (intercessors): "the well-groomed interview, the dignified letter, the restrained memorandum."[42] By contrast, the Congress exploited the democratic mechanisms of the mass meeting, petition, and boycott, in which mass rather than class counts. For example, the Congress endorsed the worldwide Jewish boycott of German goods in 1933 but the Committee refused to support it.

It is easy to scorn the genteel Americanized *schtadtlan* in retrospect by noting how the Committee's strategy functioned to secure its status, how it was based on the illusion that it was indeed composed of influential men, and how it provided a negative model of Jewish identity by demanding that Jews be less visible as Jews in order to be "effective." However, the Committee had been effective during the Taft and Wilson administrations in arousing American support for Jewish rights in eastern Europe. After 1933, it reiterated the rationale of its earlier memorandums justifying American protest against discrimination, showing how American tradition, ideals, and interests were in accord with the defense of human rights everywhere.

Similarly, the Congress appealed in the name of America, just as Jews in Germany and Hungary affirmed their national loyalty by holding out the standard of German or Hungarian ideals—symbolically waving the flag—when they appealed for mercy. The leadership of both the Congress and the Committee justified their objectives and choice of tactics by reference to American ideals; both groups implicitly accepting the "melting pot" model as the framework of justification. Thus both groups denied the legitimacy of particularistic identification of interests. Jews had become believers in the "cult of gratitude," as Melvin Tumin put it in 1964. His characterization of the Jews of that decade also fits the behavior of American Jews during the 1930s. He charges that the Jew "instead of asking that America accept him as he is and treat him as an equal in his full self-proclaimed identity . . . is, in effect, asking that his separateness shall be forgotten and ignored."[43]

Relying solely on normative appeals in the name of America and human rights, both Congress and Committee took for granted their powerlessness as petitioners, looking to Roosevelt as their patron, a benevolent one who was sometimes misled by underlings. Even after World War II, Stephen S. Wise eulogized Roosevelt, disassociating him from any responsibility for actions of the U.S. State Department.[44] Despite the Jewish voters' solid support for Roosevelt, such support was never used as a resource for bargaining.[45] Nor is there evidence that Jewish congressmen, a few of whom held influential committee chairmanships, ever worked in consort or understood the opposition to rescue.

One such congressman, Emanuel Celler, a fervid Democrat and supporter of Roosevelt with over forty years' service in the House of Representatives, recalls his sense of futility at the time, especially marked in memory by a correspondence with the President instigated by the frantic appeal of a Brooklyn rabbi. Roosevelt answered Celler's letter, detailing the ineffectual diplomatic appeals the United States had already made to Premier Laval to change France's policy and attempting to extenuate American policy by stating, "Unfortunately we have to face the disagreeable fact that most of the damage has already been done." The letter is dated 21 October 1942. Representative Celler was then confronted with the problem of relaying the administration's rationales for inaction to the rabbi.

> I tried to tell this to the old rabbi. I tried to tell him, too, that I was convinced that these officials of the State and Treasury Department wanted to do something. I believed this. But the rabbi kept interrupting, striking his cane on the floor of the office. "If six million cattle had been slaughtered," he cried, "there would have been greater interest. A way would have been found." . . .
>
> I dreamed about him that night. The old rabbi stood on a rock in the ocean, and hordes of people fought through the water to get to that rock. And the people turned into cattle and back again to people. I was on shore, held by a rope which somebody was pulling back.[46]

Celler never found out who was pulling the rope but woke up to discover that Palestine was the solution. The dream also deferred the possibility of seeking a new political stance for his constituents, within or without the Democratic Party; it cost nothing to oppose the British Empire from Brooklyn or Washington. The Jewish community's commitment to Roosevelt had foreclosed the possibility of an autonomous leadership electing alternate strategies, either bargaining within or threatening to withdraw from the New Deal coalition. Apparently, the possibilities of symbolic or mass civil disobedience were not even considered, although A. Philip Randolph's threat of a march by blacks on Washington in 1941 had caused the President to issue a decree against discrimination in employment.

It cannot be claimed that the leadership of American Jewish organizations was not informed by the end of 1942. But they still did not act. A socialist Zionist editor, Hayim Greenberg, assessed their mental state on 12 February 1943 (originally in a Yiddish paper):

> The time has come, perhaps, when the few Jewish communities remaining in the world which are still free to make their voices heard and to pray in public should

proclaim a day of fasting and prayer for American Jews. . . .

The murder of two million Jews . . . with the most inhuman methods of torture and degradation which sadistic fantasy has ever devised, still has not sufficiently impressed those among us who have donned the [hats] of Jewish guardianship, those who have assumed responsibility for Jewish interests, so that they could sit down around one table and look into each other's eyes and together try to do something to rescue at least one percent of the doomed millions. . . .

Never before in our history have we displayed such shamefully "strong" nerves as we do now in the days of our greatest catastrophe. We have become so dulled that we have even lost the capacity for madness and—may God not punish me for my words—the fact that in recent months Jews have not produced a substantial number of mentally deranged persons is hardly a symptom of health. . . .

I only know this, that we are all—all five million of us, with all our organizations and committees and leaders—politically and morally bankrupt. And I refuse to understand how and why all of us here have fallen to such a state of shameful degradation.[47]

By 1943, a more militant leadership had emerged from Palestinian and American Jews affiliated with the revisionist Zionists (Irgun Zvai Leumi), which had organized the Emergency Committee to Save the Jewish People of Europe. It achieved some success by public advertisement and secured "the nominal support of thirty-three senators, 109 representatives, fourteen current governors, fourteen ambassadors, sixty mayors of important American cities, 400 rabbis . . . twice that number in Christian ministers, 500 university presidents and professors, . . . and even several members of Roosevelt's cabinet."[48] They were repudiated as "opportunists" by Wise's American Jewish Conference for offering initiatives and commanding public attention without deferring to the hitherto recognized Jewish leadership.[49] But that leadership had forsworn strategies that might embarrass the administration. Instead of serving as Jewish representatives to the President, Jewish leaders had become the President's representatives to the Jews, reversing roles. When confronted with contrary obligations, Wise had resolved a role conflict by suppressing Jewish claims in order to reduce pressure on the administration. Friedman observes that Wise was well aware of the role he was playing.

> He wrote to Felix Frankfurter on September 16, 1942, "I don't know whether I am getting to be a *Hofjude* [court Jew], but I find that a good part of my work is to explain to my fellow Jews why our Government cannot do all the things asked or expected of it."[50]

Friedman shows how Wise had suppressed his earlier militant rhetoric and publicly counseled Jewish leaders in 1939 not to support the Wagner bill. The bill failed because of the efforts of opponents of refugees and also because of the administration's failure to back it. Jewish leaders responded to the warnings of professional refugee advocates drawn from the white Anglo-Saxon Protestant community who feared that any new proposal not only could not pass but might provoke congressional attacks on all immigrants, cutting down the present quotas. Their acceptance of such advice made it impossible for Jews to mobilize political support from their allies, who saw that the Jews would not turn out their own constituency.

The American Jewish community, like its leadership, was generally taken in by its own reified image of Roosevelt as a humanitarian, which kept it from pressing him to act humanely. The community was solidary not in its ability to mobilize members in its own behalf but only in its illusive dependence on the President. This version of the premodern client-patron relationship may have been the only political option for Jews within feudal society, but it had become dysfunctional in coalition politics.

One need not attribute the Jewish response to Roosevelt simply to the unwitting perseverance of a historical pattern of dependency upon patrons. The Jews' image of Roosevelt was intensely positive because he was seen as the enemy of their enemies, who berated him for supposedly identifying with the Jews. Their response exemplifies the human need to "balance" positive and negative sentiments in relations so that they are symmetrical, leading to the truism that "my enemy's enemy must be my friend."[51] Anti-Semites representing the elite and the mass castigated the President publicly and privately by labeling his regime a "Jew Deal": the pejorative epithets thrust on Eleanor and Franklin for their alleged fondness for Jews and blacks were circulated avidly among the WASP social elite from which Roosevelt originated.[52] The State Department was staffed largely by members of this elite and believed to be restricted to them, a belief no doubt reinforced when the American Minister to Lithuania made a public anti-Semitic address in Minneapolis in 1940.[53] Jewish attacks on the State Department encouraged its resistance to admitting Jewish refugees, rationalized and disguised as measures to keep out potential enemy agents. Roosevelt's sensitivity to rejection by the WASP elite may have reinforced his political calculation that agreeing to Jewish appeals arousing congressional and departmental opposition was not prudent.

The President was confronted with a readily resolvable role conflict: on one side was a small but strategically situated ally that escalated rhetoric but would never employ any sanctions, while on the other was a consensus of elite, ideological, and interest groups and political managers speaking in the name of the mass, all of whom wanted to check any measures that might open the gates to more refugees. Roosevelt yielded without demurral to the party that threatened sanctions for nonperformance as role theory predicts an actor will do when the other party—in this case, the Jews—offers no threat of penalty.[54]

Only when confronted with evidence of the State Department's subversion through suppression of information (as distinguished from bureaucratic evasion of rescue) by Henry Morgenthau, Jr., in December 1943, did Roosevelt withdraw some authority from the State Department. The Morgenthau memorandum was presented at a time when Jewish protest against Nazi extermination was rising among the public, demanding intervention instantly. Given the fact that immigration to the United States was practically fore-closed by 1943, the risks of a commitment were much less than they had been in 1938 while the risks attached to a public repudiation of rescue by support-ing the State Department were higher. By 1943, the calculus of political costs and payoffs had altered, but at all times Roosevelt behaved as a rational political actor, maximizing payoffs and minimizing costs. Edelman proposes that given a fundamental dissensus between constituencies on the ends the law ought to serve, the least costly mode of resolution is to substitute symbolic reassurance for commitment: Roosevelt achieved this admirably, having discerned how easily the Jews could be satisfied.[55]

Great Britain

British policy toward Jewish refugees before World War II seems to have been moved more by its fear of the international implications of Jewish im-migration than by domestic pressures similar to those within the United States. Before the war, although the British government had no quota system such as the American, aliens had to demonstrate means of support. The government accepted the assurances of the Council for German Jewry, which represented the organized Jewish community, guaranteeing the support of Jewish refugees whom they certified.[56] By contrast, the State Department refused to accept financial guarantees from non-kin of prospective refugees. Between 1933 and 1939, about 40,000 Jews from Germany found refuge in Great Britain, or eight per 10,000 population, a slightly higher proportion than were admitted to the United States.[57]

After the Anschluss in 1938, the British reacted swiftly to facilitate the entry of Jewish children from the expanded Reich, but began to help financ-ing the resettlement of refugees only in December 1939.[58] It appears that Bri-tain's hesitation to accept costs and encourage Jewish emigration grew out of both its own financial problems and its fear that Hitler would set a precedent by successfully expelling the German Jews, which would encourage Poland and Rumania similarly to solve their "Jewish problem." (Poland had been trying to force Jewish emigration since 1937 and openly threatened to use compulsion in 1939.)[59] Imperial and domestic resistance to the immigration of Jews underlay the government's unresponsiveness to American pressure to open new areas for settlement by Jews. Although cabinet members were sen-sitive to criticism by the American administration, in other nations within the Commonwealth there was real resistance to any influx of Jews that the Colonial Office could not overcome by fiat. Within Britain, the developing fascist movement may have stiffened resistance, reinforced by the perception, as Sir Samuel Hoare put it, that Jewish representatives themselves were "averse from allowing very large numbers of Jews to enter this coun-try . . . since they are afraid of an anti-Jewish agitation in this country."[60]

Jewish representatives were unwilling to move from the strategy of petition and appeal by elites to political threat and alliance with the left despite the fact that their perception of threat was clearer than that of their American counterparts. An influential delegation of the Council for German Jewry in December 1938 bluntly informed Lord Winterton, chairman of the nonfunctioning Inter-Governmental Committee on Refugees, that "it was convinced by recent information it had received that Jews remaining in Germany were in immediate peril of physical destruction."[61] This warning was paralleled by that of a member of Hitler's Chancellery in 1938 to a British consul in Germany (see Chapter 1, p. 24).

But Lord Winterton responded with no sense of urgency to the immediate plight of the German Jews. He refused to even pretend to answer a frantic appeal from the Berlin Jewish community in 1939, which had been ordered by the Gestapo to list 100 Jews daily who would be incarcerated in concentration camps unless they could leave Germany within two weeks. Like other bureaucrats who reject clients who overtax their organization's capacities, he refused to allow the Gestapo to determine how and when the IGC would define the problem.[62]

While Britain eased barriers to Jews fleeing there, it raised them against Jews fleeing to Palestine, the nation that had absorbed more Jewish refugees than any other between 1933 and 1939. The British policy toward Jewish refugees in Palestine was conditioned by their decision in 1939 to preserve the existing Arab-Jewish ethnic ratio there. Pressure was put on Balkan governments, especially Rumania, where Jews fleeing from German-occupied territory gathered to disembark illegally for Palestine, to avert such departures. British documents show the consistency of Britain's attempts to repress such flights, including confiscation of ships transporting illegal immigrants and deportation of illegal entrants to Mauritius. Ruth Kluger, a recruiter for the illegal emigration known as "Aliyah Bet," sponsored illicitly by the Haganah, the underground Jewish self-defense force of Palestine, relates in her memoir how this policy affected thousands, leading to the deaths of 481 Jews during 1940.[63] The sinking of the *Salvador,* an unseaworthy vessel that Turkey, under British pressure, refused to allow to anchor in its harbor, led to the drowning of 231 persons. The *Patria,* a ship holding 1,800 illegal Jewish emigrants, transferred by the British authorities for transport to Mauritius, was sunk off the coast of Haifa by the Haganah in a miscalculated attempt to disable the vessel; 250 of its passengers were drowned.[64]

Some may perceive the British policy toward Europe's Jews before and during the war as schizoid. Although the British were well informed of German brutality during the prewar years, it was taken for granted that anti-Semitism was intrinsic to Nazism "and must be accepted as such. As long as the majority of the German people supported Nazism and as long as Nazi anti-Semitism was legislative and non-violent, then Britain had no right or obligation to interfere."[65] The goal of European peace through appeasement

was widely shared from right to left. The British press explicitly and consistently covered German anti-Jewish measures, constantly expressing censure
of anti-Jewish persecution but never relating this to Britain's immigration
policy.[66]

No public protest against German anti-Jewish policies was issued until
after the outbreak of the war, when Britain issued a "Command
Paper . . . concerning the Treatment of German Nationals in Germany."[67]
Britishers received news of extermination through their press, the BBC, and
the Polish government-in-exile's exposés promptly beginning in June 1942.
By 14 July 1942, they were informed in the press that the Germans had
discovered new uses for a poison gas known as Zyklon B.

Yet, even during the war, British spokesmen opposed facilitating Jewish
flight from the Balkans and central Europe, where it might have been possible to do so. In March 1943, Anthony Eden cautioned Cordell Hull at Bermuda—according to Harry Hopkins—about facilitating the exodus from
Bulgaria of Jews threatened with deportation because, "if we do that, then
the Jews of the world will be wanting us to make similar offers in Poland and
Germany."[68] After Joel Brand, dispatched to Istanbul to pass on the offer of
SS Reichsführer Himmler to trade a million Jews for 10,000 trucks for Germany's use on the eastern front in 1944, had been interned by the British in
Cairo in 1944, an anonymous Englishman whom Brand believed was Lord
Moyne responded to this offer similarly: "But Mr. Brand, what shall I do
with those million Jews? Where shall I put them?"[69] This was not their only
reason for rejecting the plan, but it was viewed with alarm. However, standing orders to the British Passport Control Office in Istanbul during the war
were that Jews who had fled from German-occupied territory were to be
given visas to Palestine (provided they passed the British security check) and
deducted from the unfulfilled quota.[70]

One might argue that the British policy was a rational one, explicable in
terms of the imperial class's interest (well represented in Churchill's cabinet)
in maintaining the Empire: hence, the need to pacify the Arabs to prevent
their desertion to the Axis cause and to preserve the loyalty of Indian
Muslims to prevent their coalition with the Hindu-majority Indian National
Congress, in order to maintain a hold over India. However, Reuben Ainsztein argues that British policy was explicable in terms of their prewar
perception of the Jewish problem aggravated by the growth of protofascist
movements in Britain and the prewar belief that adapting to German
demands was the price of peace.[71] He cites evidence from conversations between Ben-Gurion and Lord Moyne of the British Foreign Office in 1941 that
Lord Moyne anticipated there would be at least six million Jews displaced
after the war and believed that the Jews could be resettled in a state in
eastern Europe—maybe East Prussia, which the victorious Allies could compel Germany to vacate—but the British ruling class gradually accepted the
fact "that the Germans were solving the Jewish problem for them" with the

same stoicism with which that class accepted the Irish famine in 1848 and recurrent Indian famines.[72] This is a provocative hypothesis but proof or disproof demands kinds of evidence not yet brought forth.

How was the government's policy related to British public opinion, party divisions, and the role of the British Jewish community? Ernest Hearst shows that there was consistently more positive identification with the Jews among the Labour Party and Liberals, but they were easily deflected by the bureaucratic shuffles of cabinet and Foreign Office representatives who responded to their inquiries in Parliament by showing why they could not do what they never had any intention of doing.[73] Little public empathy was shown in Britain before the disclosure in 1942 of the extermination of the Jews. Protest and calls for action were mobilized as dramatic performances, as they were in the United States. Calls for action were usually spearheaded by religious leaders, notably the archbishops of Canterbury and York and the Roman Catholic Archbishop. Little public leadership was exhibited by the British Jewish community, whose leaders were like those of the American Jewish communities, evidently adherents of the "cult of gratitude." When the House of Commons responded by standing up in silence to Anthony Eden's condemnation of the extermination of two million Jews in 1942, Mr. De Rothschild thanked them. When the *Jewish Chronicle* noted with disappointment Eden's failure to offer Jews any sanctuary, it did so "without wishing to appear 'ungracious.' "[74]

Unlike the American administration's response, which could be interpreted as an accurate reflection of public opinion, British response did not reflect British public opinion.

> There is no evidence to suggest that the abandonment of the doomed was, on the conscious level, motivated by any detectable antisemitic bias. On the contrary, contemporary researches record a strong preference for opening the country to the persecuted. A British Institute of Public Opinion Poll [of March 1943] revealed that a vast majority would have supported action to assist refugees. Asked whether "the British Government should or should not help any refugees who can get away?" no less than 78 per cent opted for such help.[75]

This is a significant finding, raising more questions as to the failure of the British Jews to mobilize the influence of their allies to change the direction of public policy.

The Soviet Union

The Soviet Union's activities before its invasion in 1941 and between 1941 and 1945 have seldom been assessed without bias. It is known that the Soviet Union contributed to the rescue of Jews from German domination in three ways, despite the fact that its intentions were to achieve other ends.

First, the Soviet Union allowed the entry of some Jews from the portion of

Poland and the Baltic states ceded to the U.S.S.R. by the Molotov-Ribbentrop pact of 1939 and deported many others without their consent for political reasons before the German invasion. P. Glikson notes that estimates of Jewish deportees and refugees range between 150,000 and 500,000; of these, he believes that 200,000 to 250,000 were of Polish nationality before the war. Since we have no way of verifying the numbers who died in Stalin's prisons and labor camps and those who did not return, a more exact estimate cannot be corroborated. He estimates that the maximum number of Jews returning to Poland after the war who were repatriated from the Soviet Union "did not exceed 175,000."[76] This estimate, of course, does not include Jews returning to that part of Poland incorporated in the U.S.S.R. and the Baltic states, also incorporated.

Second, a large number—possibly a majority—of Jewish citizens of the Soviet Union living before the war in territories later occupied by the German invaders were evacuated to the interior because of their occupational and urban distribution. Solomon Schwarz, who tendentiously denies this while citing the evidence for it, concludes that "As a result, the percentage of the evacuated who were Jews seems to have been more than proportionate to the number of Jews in the Ukraine's urban, let alone total, population."[77] Sources on the prewar and postwar populations of particular cities and German records confirming the number killed also show that large numbers had escaped.[78] Schwarz and others have held the USSR responsible for the innocence of the Jewish population in Soviet areas regarding German intentions toward Jews, citing the suppression of news of German treatment of Jews between 1939 and 1941. However, the signs of widespread flight by Jews before the German advance do not indicate that denial of threat was either universal or the majority reaction among Jews.

Third, the Soviet Union's policy toward encouraging partisan activity and its use of Jewish partisans directly affected the life chances of able young Jews in the Soviet territory.[79] The partisan had to be mobile in the forest: potential Jewish partisan cadres were torn between their wish to defend their people in the ghetto and their desire to fight the Germans, which could be done effectively only by leaving the ghetto. The Jewish partisans could not blend into the countryside as Christians could; nor could they leave their wives and children behind in good conscience. Some attempted to resolve this dilemma by establishing family camps, limiting their military flexibility. To evaluate partisans' policies and behavior toward Jews, Bar-On's discrimination between "anti-semitism from above" (legitimated or authorized by leadership) and "anti-semitism from below" is helpful. Although he does not reach a definitive conclusion as to the former because of lack of sufficient evidence, he cites cause for concluding that de facto evidence of an officially sanctioned double-standard was exhibited in the systematic replacement of Jewish commanders—Soviet sources indicate there were 92 of them originally—by non-Jews when the Jewish detachments were integrated into mixed units in

1943; in the demand for exceptional feats of courage to test Jewish recruits before accepting them as partisans; and in the judgment of conflicts between Jews and the local population when Jews punished collaborators among them who had helped to kill the Jews. The wide latitude necessarily allowed partisan commanders could mask many instances of hostility despite the absence of anti-Semitism in Soviet ideology of the period. The close dependence of Jewish partisans on their non-Jewish brothers-in-arms (who often did not mask anti-Semitic sentiments) produced many occasions for betrayal.

Bar-On concludes that there was general (but not universal) anti-Semitism from below.

> It is a proved fact that dozens and perhaps hundreds of Jewish partisans and their families were murdered by non-Jewish partisans, generally by a treacherous bullet in the back, in circumstances that enabled the murderers to deny without difficulty either the deed itself or its deliberate intention. In many cases murder was accompanied by robbery, rape and savage manhandling.[80]

Nevertheless, organized killing of Jewish partisans and other Jews in the forest was not authorized by the Soviet movement as it was authorized by the commander of the Polish Home Army and the right-wing underground defense forces in Poland.[81]

Recently, much more information on Jewish partisans and revolts in ghettos and death camps has become known to the English reader through the publication of Reuben Ainsztein's massive work *Jewish Resistance in Nazi-Occupied Eastern Europe.* Because Ainsztein's primary purpose was to disprove the myth of Jewish nonresistance to their extermination and to Nazi power in general, much space is devoted to documenting that Jews were prominent in the early leadership of the partisan movement and participated disproportionately to their percentage of the population (which can be confirmed for Lithuania only). This is a plausible finding, but Ainsztein's preoccupation deters him from seriously evaluating the questions that preoccupied potential Jewish partisans. Resistance for what? Survival for whom, at whose expense? What costs were intrinsic to the partisans' role, and which were incurred because of the disinterest of other partisans in the Jews' survival? There is little systematic evaluation of how the other partisan units helped or hindered the Jews' defense of their family camps in the forest, created by the evacuation of women and children from several villages. Nor is there any objective assessment of the magnitude and legitimation of discrimination and exploitation of Jews qua Jews. Ainsztein's qualification of his own observations lamely denies popular anti-Semitism without refuting evidence others have interpreted as indications of this sentiment.[82] He fails also to evaluate the political and strategic motives guiding Soviet policy and to relate these both to the immediate purpose of partisan warfare and to the Soviet's ideological goal of dissolving the Nazi-alleged nexus of "Judeo-Bolshevism" in the minds of the subject population of eastern Europe that was to be incorporated in the zone of Russian domination. If we asked, "To what extent did the Jews, as compared with other Soviet nationalities, actively participate in defense of the Soviet Union?" and "How did Soviet strategy exploit the extreme situation of Jewish encirclement to recruit candidates for high-risk services when the native population in many regions was unwilling to enlist for them?" we would learn more.

Another question not yet addressed is the interest or disinterest of Soviet military strategists in liberating Jews remaining in ghettos in 1944 as a factor in determining their military tactics. This question pertains particularly to Lodz, whose last 60,000 Jews were transported in August 1944, and Budapest, in which tens of thousands of Jews were estimated to have been massacred between the Arrow Cross coup of October 1944 and liberation in January 1945. War Refugee Board records reveal an attempt to deter extermination of Jews in camps and ghettos by direct and indirect warning of the Germans in late 1944 and direct American diplomatic intervention with the Soviet Union requesting them to do the same, but they do not show a Soviet response.

While there is yet no evidence bearing on the causes of the lack of Soviet interest in rescuing the Jews, the Soviet Union was more willing to identify rhetorically with the Jews collectively than were Britain and the United States at the beginning of the war. In 1942, to enlist western sympathies, the Jewish Anti-Fascist Committee was created in Moscow. That this was simply a rhetorical and opportunistic use of Jews rather than a commitment to recognize their collective identity was shown by the Soviet Union's murder of the first two nominees for leadership of that organization in December 1941 — Victor Ehrlich and Henryk Alter, leaders of the Polish Jewish Socialist Bund. Their error apparently was to propose sponsorship of the Anti-Fascist committee by Jews of all the Allied nations, which would have prevented effective Soviet control.[83] (The recruitment patterns of other committee members and reason for their murder and imprisonment and the final liquidation of the committee in 1948 are described by Leonard Schapiro.)[84] But the existence of the Jewish Anti-Fascist Committee always depended on whether it fit in with the needs of the Soviet Union. Redlich shows how the Soviet Union's willingness to identify with Jews publicly was limited to international audiences.[85] The Soviets did not publicly identify the special character of Nazi extermination of the Jews in internal media during the war, overlooked popular manifestations of anti-Semitism, which increased during this period, and failed to acknowledge the contributions of Soviet Jews to the war efforts (derogated popularly) in order to reinforce unity based on its ideology of a battle of all Slavs against the Germans. Nevertheless, both Redlich and Schapiro believe that the Anti-Fascist Committee had positive functions for Soviet Jewry, increasing their self-consciousness and self-esteem, moving noted Soviet Jews to become concerned with the others, and enabling them to establish contacts with worldwide Jewish organizations.

Soviet rejection of particularistic Jewish claims (both as victims and as citizens) in the name of a universalistic credo functioned—as did the exaltation of nationalism and the "cult of gratitude" in the West—to diminish the possibility of Jews maintaining their collective identity. Y. Gilboa shows the plight of Soviet Jewry through a more comprehensive analysis of Jews' place and identity in the Soviet Union during those years.[86] The Soviet strategy was similar to that of the United States and Britain in is indifference to Jewish survival. Saving the Jewish population was not a war goal: saving valuable categories of Soviet citizens was and great numbers of Jews survived because they were evacuated with government aid at the onset of the war or later fled to forests defended by Soviet partisans.[87] No concern was shown for the Jews at any time (to our present knowledge) in war strategy and tactics. The extent of rhetorical commitment to or concern for the Jews depended both upon the cost of rhetoric and resources committed and the symbolic value of identification with the audience addressed. Where positive identification was not costly for the United States, Britain, or the Soviet Union and was of potential benefit, it was employed; when it threatened the imperial or domestic order of domination (for Britain or the Soviet Union), it was not employed.

THE NEUTRALS

Spain, Sweden, and Switzerland

Neutrals whose policies made a significant impact include Switzerland, Sweden, and Spain. (The role of the Vatican is discussed in Chapter 4.) The neutrality of Spain, Sweden, and Switzerland during World War II was a tactical stance, as was Denmark's critical commitment to the Anti-Comintern Pact and accommodation to Germany, not guaranteeing them any German commitment in the future. Germany's plans in event of victory were to incorporate Sweden and Switzerland in the Third Reich and to overthrow France in order that a more pro-German clique could seize power.[88] No German pressure was exerted on these governments, to institute anti-Jewish discrimination during the war. Neutrality was an expedient cover for both sides to protect present needs, irrespective of ideology and sympathies, giving the neutrals a wide latitude in the range of actions they could take toward Jewish refugees and initiate diplomatically in capitals where they were represented.

The neutral that most exploited its position to help Jews of other nationalities was Sweden despite its restriction of prewar immigration (in the manner of the other Scandinavian nations and of Great Britain) to Jews who could prove means of support.[89] Once German intentions to exterminate the Jews became clear, Swedish officials generally used all diplomatic means available to help the victims. The Swedish Ambassador to Berlin, acting as a protective power representing the Netherlands, inquired into the deaths of Dutch Jews at Mauthausen in 1941 — all deaths reportedly occurred on the same day — and requested permission to visit the camp. Ironically, this only led the Germans to stop sending out death certificates to the murdered Jews' relatives. When the 1,800 Jews of neighboring Norway and 8,000 Jews of Denmark were threatened with deportation in 1942 and 1943, respectively, Sweden guaranteed sanctuary to all Jews who crossed their border and supported them in Sweden.[90] When deportations began in Hungary in 1944, the King of Sweden protested to the Regent of Hungary and employed the prestige of the Swedish government (also a protective power for Hungary abroad) to mask the mission of the Swede, Raoul Wallenberg, acting as an agent of the U.S. War Refugee Board.

This is not to say that any Swedish protest employed other than diplomatic means. Although a Swedish diplomat, Baron von Otter, had conversed in the summer of 1942 with SS Lieutenant Kurt Gerstein — an anti-Nazi German who had joined the SS and been delegated to deliver the poison gas used to kill Jews at Auschwitz-Birkenau — and reported his tale to Stockholm, the Swedish government did not release the news.[91] However, we know that the Allies had already received similar reports.

The motivation of Sweden's stance has seldom been assessed. Leni Yahil suggests their initiative to protect other Scandinavians later in the war arose "from the desire to lay proper foundations for renewed cooperation after the war."[92] One of the undisputed instances of their help, confused because of differing accounts of Sweden's agents, is the story of how the Swedish Minister of Foreign Affairs arranged the transfer of 2,700 non-Scandinavian Jews and about 5,000 other prisoners from concentration camps (released after Scandinavian prisoners were transported to Sweden) through the aegis of Dr. Felix Kersten, Himmler's masseur, who acted secretly as an agent of the Swedish government. Kersten also cooperated with representatives of the World Jewish Congress to get Himmler to issue an order safeguarding Jews in concentration camps and allowing food and medicine to be imported there. Kersten's role was not represented in the memoir first describing the operation by Count Folke Bernadotte, the Swedish diplomat, who accompanied the first buses of Scandinavian prisoners as a representative of the Swedish Red Cross.[93]

By contrast to Sweden, which accepted Jewish refugees openly and intervened diplomatically with some initiative, Spain tolerated Jewish refugees who escaped over the Pyrenees but intervened at a very late stage to save Jews holding Spanish nationality in Greece and protested the deportations from Hungary in 1944 only after other neutrals had protested. Although Jews entering Spain illegally were interned by the police, as were other foreign nationals without papers, no instances were recorded of Jews being repatriated by Spain to nations under German occupation.[94] Haim Avni concludes "that

Spain was open, in practice if not in theory, for the illegal rescue of Jews during the entire second half of the war."[95] Despite Spain's exaggerated postwar claims, it was reluctant to protect actively those descendants of Sephardic Jews expelled in the fifteenth century in Salonica who were still holding Spanish nationality in 1943.[96] This led to the Germans interning all Jews with Spanish nationality caught in Salonica (and in 1944 in Athens) in the Bergen-Belsen concentration camp before they were repatriated. Spain sought guarantees that they could reemigrate out of Spain and assurances of their financial sustenance from the American Jewish Joint Distribution Committee, and maintained a numerical ceiling on their influx, forbidding entry until earlier entrants had emigrated.[97] Thus, Jews were constantly discriminated from other Spanish nationals in occupied Europe. Aggregative estimates of the Spanish nationals among the Jews of Greece run from 600 to 750, of whom 38 probably perished in German camps.[98]

The neutral nation in Europe most hostile to Jewish refugees was the state in the most attractive geographic position to the greatest number of persons in flight. Alfred Haesler has documented with great clarity the mobilization of the Swiss government to exclude Jews from 1938 to 1944.[99] This effort began when Switzerland categorically insisted in 1938 that the passports of German Jews be distinctively marked, leading to the "J" stamp stigmatizing German Jews at every door of entry. Illegal refugees were ordered expelled without appeal after the war began. Later, they were refused any opportunity to communicate with persons on Swiss soil before being literally kicked back over the border. Yet the number of legal refugees mounted and the number of others attempting to evade Swiss border guards also increased. On 13 August 1942, a month after the beginning of deportations to extermination camps from the Netherlands, Belgium, and France, the Chief of Police "issues orders that all civilian refugees be turned back at the border. These orders are enforced to the letter."[100] Public criticism by some churchmen, refugee advocates, and the press that these regulations violated the Swiss tradition of asylum and consigned Jews turned away to death instigated a debate in the Swiss Federal Council on 22–23 September 1942, in which all major parties in the government camp backed the government. At the end of the debate, Federal Councilor Eduard von Steiger, head of the Justice and Police Department, rebutted critics of the government's position:

> When, then, the captain of this lifeboat must choose whom he shall embark and for whom he wishes to reserve the space and supplies that are still available, while thousands have the same right and while he should and would like to help thousands and thousands, he faces the great spiritual torment of choosing whom he shall and shall not take aboard. . . .
>
> It was proper to mention Sweden. . . . [But] it is not at all the same thing whether I admit people from my neighbor nation with which until a few decades ago I was united in a single state or whether I have to perform the task that now faces us.

There is no differentiation of nations or of any races whatever in our operation; but there are certain psychological postulates that are not always the same in the people's readiness to accept refugees. At this point I repeat: If we must come to the point of carrying out what the old Bernese and other cantons, but principally the Bernese, put into practice when they took the Huguenots from Geneva—that is, saying "Let us distribute the people among families—then I should like to see the degree of willingness, gentlemen, if I issue that appeal![101]

Responding to the criticism, the Federal Police maintained a virtually open border in September before the debate but on 26 September new instructions that "refugees for racial reasons alone . . . are not political refugees" were approved by the Federal Council and the police were instructed that "French Jews are to be turned back without exception because they are in no danger in their own country."[102]

Barbed wire was stretched across the border in October 1942 while government censorship tried to protect the Swiss from unpleasant eyewitness reports of extermination in the East, although the reports from Britain and France couldn't be suppressed. Well known conservatives joined with the Fatherland Front in November 1942 to declare the refugees a national peril, alien to the Swiss in culture and religion; one must keep them out to prevent the emergence of a "Jewish question."[103]

Refugees awarded legal status were placed in work, internment, and punishment camps unless they could be individually placed, which was not often the case for Jews. They were often treated in Swiss camps with antiseptic discipline, if not hostility. Haesler estimates that Switzerland, which held about 7,100 refugees at the start of the war in September 1939, and sheltered more than 115,000 refugees on 8 May 1945, gave sanctuary to 28,512 Jews among the 295,381 refugees finding shelter there at any time during the war.[104] This is the largest number finding refuge in a single state of Europe during the war.[105] There is no way to estimate how many Jews were turned away at the border. Although police reports cited by Haesler add up to 9,751 persons excluded from August 1942 through 1945 and Jews were officially defined as nonpolitical refugees in order that they should be excluded, reports of Swiss officials complaining about the number of persons attempting to infiltrate from August to December 1942 indicate that the figures cited are far too low.[106]

Swiss policy was altered on paper in 1944 after Germany's defeat became certain. By November 1944, Dr. Rothmund, the same police official who had demanded that German Jews' passports be stamped with a "J" in 1938 and who had ordered that Jews be turned back physically in 1942, ordered protests of deportation of the Jews to German authorities in Berlin. Haesler reports that on 6 February 1945 "the Federal Council intercedes with the German government against the mass slaughter of the Jews."[107] Switzerland prepared itself to face a brave new postwar world.

CONCLUSION

Between 1933 and 1939, the Jews of Germany (and of the expanded German Reich) were progressively stripped of the rights of citizens within view of the whole world without any attempt by Germany at concealment. The Allies did not protest Germany's repudiation of the rights of the Jews, preferring to regard it as an "internal affair." As rational actors, the United States and Great Britain were trying to reduce the risk of a new world war. Britain led the nations of Europe in attempting to appease the new Germany. The Allies' disinterest in provoking conflict with Germany over the rights of the Jews was reinforced by the lack of domestic pressure on the Jews' behalf. Domestic anti-Semitism and xenophobia, aggravated by worldwide unemployment, was not countered by any unified collective movement by Jews in the United States and Britain to defend the interests of European Jewry. These nations were unwilling to incur any of the costs involved in taking in German Jews and/or finding new homelands for the Jews whom Germany tried to expel prior to 1938. This reluctance on the part of other nations was used by Germany to justify her desire to get rid of the Jews. It seemed as if Germany was successful in convincing the community of nations that the cause of the "Jewish problem" was the Jews and that increasing the number of Jews in any nation would cause a similar "problem" to arise.

The inability of the American Jewish leadership to act in concert and press demands to protect European Jews by political means contributed to the disinterest of the American administration in Jewish rights. This failure of Jewish leaders has been attributed to many causes, but the most fundamental was their own internalization of anti-Semitic accusations and their need to prove their loyalty by showing that they were Americans first—and last. A similar phenomenon characterizes the initial reaction of German Jews to Hitler's reign.

Allied policy during World War II showed persisting indifference to the ongoing extermination of European Jewry, notwithstanding rhetorical denunciations from December 1942 onward, threatening postwar punishment for war crimes. However, domestic pressure instigated President Roosevelt to appoint the War Refugee Board in 1944 to deter further deportation of Jews. However, until 1944 there was continuous rejection of opportunities to rescue Jews through the European neutrals, Axis allies, and north African ports, and of diplomatic means to deter deportation and extermination through threats and incentives to Germany and its allies. Throughout the war, the use of physical force to disable the machinery of destruction was rejected by the Allies. Even in 1944, the Allies refused to bomb the rail lines leading to the extermination camps and Auschwitz itself.

Official strategies of denial of the identity of the victims (first incarcerated, then incinerated) and stigmatization of Jews reinforced their in-

visibility and the lack of public recognition of their extermination. But the
U.S. State Department also resorted to blatant suppression of news sources
and delayed public disclosure of the "Final Solution" in 1942.

The rejection of Jewish claims by Great Britain and the Soviet Union was
also rationalized by these states' national interest as empires, seeking to maintain or fortify their grip over other states. The British sought to maintain
their grip over India and the Mideast; Muslim loyalties, which might have
been undermined by free Jewish emigration to Palestine, were needed to
secure their objective. The Soviet Union needed to consolidate the empire in
eastern Europe acquired through prewar and postwar diplomacy and conquest during World War II. Their future reign encompassed a heterogeneous
region in which one common theme was the raw anti-Semitism prevalent
among dominant groups. However, the U.S.S.R., unlike the other Allies,
publicly identified with the Jews when it served their purpose, exploiting
Jewish leadership in guerrilla warfare and in public relations activities, while
at other times deporting Jewish leaders to Siberia and murdering them in
Moscow.

The policy of the major European neutrals—Spain, Sweden, and Switzerland—toward granting Jews havens in their countries differed. Sweden
granted sanctuary to the Jews of Denmark and Norway and publicized its
open door. Spain did not discriminate against Jews who entered illegally but
did not offer sanctuary. Switzerland consistently returned Jews to Germany
and German-occupied states and in 1942 erected barbed wire around its
border. Despite such a policy, it is estimated that Switzerland took in a
greater number of Jews than did Sweden, although less than 10% of the
refugees finding sanctuary in Switzerland were Jews. It seemed that these
states' readiness to aid Jews was inversely related to the number of Jews who
could have gained access to such sanctuary: the greater the number of Jews
who could have benefited from such sanctuary, the less willing they were to
accept them. Diverse motives have been attributed to these states. Swiss officials who had collaborated with Germany before the war in anti-Jewish
discrimination continued such collaboration. Vocal anti-Semitism was
espoused by major Swiss parties. Sweden's position may have been moved by
its conceived ties to other Scandinavian states. Besides providing a haven for
Scandinavian Jews, Sweden negotiated the early release of incarcerated Jews
from German concentration camps in 1945. Sweden also intervened
diplomatically to protect other Jews throughout Europe with less success.
Spain's position is less well known, but it seemed determined not to become
implicated with the Final Solution, despite previous cooperation with Germany and the ideological affinity between Spanish fascism and Nazism.

PART TWO

The Victims' View

Defining the Situation

Some Historical Paradigms

By September 1941, nine out of every ten Europeans living on the continent outside Russia inhabited states occupied by Germany, allied with Germany, or occupied by Germany's allies. The swift defeat of Poland in 1939, the occupation of western Europe in 1940 and of the Balkans in the spring of 1941, and the invasion of the Soviet Union in June 1941 were clear indications of Germany's achievement and its potential permanent domination of Europe. Postwar myths of resistance enable us to ignore the fact that native populations in most of the occupied countries had resigned themselves to German occupation by the fall of 1941.[1] Early manifestations of mass disaffection and nonviolent resistance in the Protectorate and the Netherlands had been easily crushed. Most resistance movements were neither integrated nor involved in any public actions and would not draw visible mass support in their native lands until 1944. Urban rebellion in occupied Europe occurred only as German defeat became imminent.

Although postwar chroniclers have shown that Jews were overrepresented in early resistance cadres and aggressive actions, most Jews, like other natives, conformed to the regulations of the occupiers, and those of western Europe were reassured to find that they were not immediately discriminated against by the occupiers.[2] To understand the fates they encountered later, one must explain first how Jews were programed toward destruction by isolating them progressively, thus constricting later opportunities for evasion. We will focus herein on understanding these processes, showing how Jews perceived the situation at the beginning and how they responded to state-instigated terror and coercion clothed in edicts designed to prepare them for ready victimization. How were they seen by native leaders, authorities, and the public? Did these latter identify with them or detach themselves and turn away? What taken-for-granted assumptions conditioned the way Jews and Christians defined the situation?

We will explore the accounts of experiences of Jews in Warsaw, the Netherlands, and Hungary through first-person documents—diaries, memoirs, and reports (using contemporaneously written sources whenever possible)—in order to reconstruct the transformations involved in victimization from the victims' view. These are all high-victimization states; in Warsaw, over 97% of Jews were killed or incarcerated in extermination and concentration camps, and in Hungary and the Netherlands almost 80% became victims. However, these states represent a variety of political settings in terms of degree of German wartime control and prewar experiences of Jews. Demographically, the cities studied range in numbers of Jews from 10,000 in Marmaroszeged (Hungary) to over 100,000 in Amsterdam and 500,000 in the Warsaw ghetto. Before the war, Jews constituted 9% of the population of Amsterdam, 28% of Warsaw, and 39% of Szeged (Marmaroszeged). The time span of the destruction process in these communities also varied radically. Whereas isolation spanned 33 months in Warsaw, only 2 months elapsed in the Hungarian provincial towns and cities between the time German troops entered Hungary and the start of deportations in 1944.

Because of the different aspects of these situations and characteristic prewar differences among Jewish communities, we may infer that what similarity we find in processes and tactics of control in varying contexts accounts for their isolation. But how they reacted to official labeling and discrimination might also have an effect upon their isolation. To understand how such Jews responded to these experiences and constructed a "definition of the situation," we must appreciate how they individually observed and internalized the views, feelings, and recognitions of Christian neighbors, colleagues, and citizens toward and about them and how they drew upon their collective experiences and resources (and resourcefulness).[3]

What definitions of the situation were available to Jews who were being discriminated against and segregated by official policy? What goals could they impute to the occupiers and/or their own governments (if they were citizens of the satellite states and other states allied to Germany) in 1941? To answer these questions, we will sketch alternate definitions of the situation and paradigms of responses, without assuming that one definition necessarily precludes partial acceptance of another by the same person. We do assume that people act meaningfully in terms of their assumptions and are constrained by the rational implications of those assumptions to follow certain strategies and avoid others, even though some persons may be less able than others to express why they are acting in a given manner. The rationality of unconscious defense mechanisms assists the calculating ego by compensating for its shortcomings and indicating other defenses. What we seek to discover is what their expectations were of the occupation (inherent in their definition of the situation) and how they could cope with such expectations. What past experiences could serve as models for such definitions?

THE CLASSIC PARADIGMS OF THREATS

Historically, the Jewish people have experienced a wide range of threats during their evolution from statehood (preceding the Christian era) to a semiautonomous colony of other empires to dispersed national communities in diaspora, their status preceding World War II. European Jews shared these memories, embedded in diverse interpretations of the Jewish tradition, although they were divided by distinctive national traditions within Sephardic and Ashkenazic ethnic communities; distinctive life styles corresponded to their social class and their integration within or separation from national communities. Regardless of whether they were internationally known bankers or locally familiar rag pickers, observant pietists or radical atheists, practicing Jews or newly baptized Christians, Yiddish-speaking peddlers or Ladino-speaking fishermen, members of Parliament or stateless migrants, all were defined as Jews by the Germans if they had at least three Jewish grandparents. The shared memories and myths of Jewish experience might suggest paradigms to guide them in defining the situation that confronted them in 1941. Like other conquered peoples, they had to recognize that their occupiers were the new masters. But masters may be oppressors, masters may be exploiters, or masters may be enemies.

The new masters might be *oppressors*, who might deprive Jews of achieved rights and statuses so as to reward other groups or classes more numerous or powerful. Punishment of the Jews might be a means of controlling other classes, either to preserve their obedience by the example of punishment following nonconformity or to deflect and canalize resentment against their own oppression or exploitation to the Jews. Discrimination and terrorization of the Jews have served both ends.

In antiquity, when Jewish communities had been collectively oppressed for their resistance to foreign customs distasteful to them but signifying loyalty to their imperial overlords, their oppressors' persistence — and Jewish zealots' leadership, instigating Jewish masses — provoked rebellion in 168 B.C.E. against the Seleucid Empire (commemorated by Chanukah) and the disastrous war against Rome in 66–70 C.E. (commemorated by Tisha B'Av, the day of the fall of the Temple). But in the diaspora, revolt against the state by a minority within the state — and usually a disarmed minority — was not viable; and community spokesmen, councils, and Jewish notables usually promised political conformity in exchange for religious and communal autonomy or toleration.

When Jews have been treated with collective punishment for their disbelief in Christ as the Messiah and offered the chance of escaping it by alleging such a belief, some have grasped and others rejected the opportunity. While we have many examples of individuals and communities threatened with extermination that chose the path of martyrdom, such as that of the Jews of York (England) who immolated themselves in 1190 C.E., there were large numbers of Jews during the Spanish Inquisition who converted, many nominally (known as Marranos), and were absolved from sin by the rabbinic authorities. We may have forgotten how many chose apostasy because rabbis and other pious chroniclers were more likely to commemorate those who fulfilled the injunction to santify the name of God ("Kiddush ha-shem") and thus chose martyrdom. However, regardless of how many chose each path, the path of conversion as a method of allaying oppression existed only because the church, then dominant, maintained that Jews ought to and could cease to be Jews. During the Holocaust, all previous experiences of op-pression were finally irrelevant, for nothing Jews could do or avow could undo the fact that to the Nazis they were defined as Jews by some ineffable and ineradicable racial essence. However, the unconscious belief (common to Christians and Jews) that good behavior could deter oppression caused some leaders to urge conformity to regulations serving to segregate and isolate the Jews. Their belief that their masters were new oppressors justified their in-junction: Be obedient.

The new masters might be *exploiters*, seeking to acquire as much of the Jews' worldly goods as possible and/or to transform them into a servile class. Although oppressors in one historical era have become exploiters in another, exploiters have also become oppressors and enemies. But without the basis of primordial obligation, or trust between weaker and stronger, and in the absence of countervailing power that the exploited can invoke, this is an unstable relationship, for the stronger can always seize the possessions of the weaker party. Nevertheless, gift-giving and bribery have been a classic and sometimes successful strategy for coping with exploiters throughout recorded time. The Bible is replete with examples of conquered nations paying tribute to their conquerors, indicating not only that they were willing to pay for pro-tection against them but that by such means they indicated their respect and deference. Alvin Gouldner observes that when both parties accept the "norm of reciprocity," the gift acts as a "starting mechanism" for mutual interac-tion.[4]

Marvin Lowenthal, reviewing in 1936 the history of the Jews of Germany, shows how forced securities were instituted after the First Crusade.[5] As the nobility became dependent on *Hof-Juden* (court Jews) to perform the varied financial and executive roles enabling them to maintain their rule, the nobility allowed the Jewish community opportunities for survival by paying indemnities to atone for their alleged crimes.

At the peak of the money-lending trade and before commerce had dwindled to peddling, the wealth of the Jews was huge. However, it is significant that research mainly learns of it through taxes, extortions and forced loans inflicted on its owners. It may have been "easy come"; but what with threats, imprisonment, and thumbscrews, it was hardly "easy go." A fine imposed on the Jews of Cologne in 1170 netted the archbishop 4200 silver marks. The archbishop of Magdeburg did better, in 1261, by extorting from its rich Jews 100,000 marks ransom. Duke

Vladislav I of Bohemia, about 1124, did better yet when he extracted 3000 pounds of silver and 100 pounds of gold for the release of a single Jew.[6]

However, this was not a stable institution guaranteeing security, as Lowenthal shows by recapitulating the massacres from the First through the Fifth Crusades. Besides these, there were other massacres incited by the charge that Jews caused the plague, by citing crimes of individual Jews, and by allegations of collective crimes, such as the apocryphal murder of Christian children for blood for Passover matzohs—and similar accusations of culpability for non-events made real by the medieval belief in malevolent magic. Allegations of crime usually precede collective violence against the accused, which such allegations serve to justify or account for. While noblemen might promise Jews security in exchange for their gold, other debtors found it cheaper to murder Jews and confiscate the booty. Nobles themselves often agreed to overlook massacres if they were compensated or indemnified for the loss of "their" Jews. The Jews had been turned from a source of commodities to a commodity themselves. Lacking obligation, contracts based on free exchange would not be honored, Emile Durkheim told us.[7] Hubert Blalock observes that "middlemen minorities"—distinct ethnic groups acting as intermediaries in trade, finance, and land management between nobles and peasants—are especially vulnerable to attack from elite and masses in times of depression, turmoil, or stress.[8] The medieval history of the Jews illustrates this phenomenon. Lowenthal relates how in the fourteenth century the hostility of the exploited classes was displaced against the Jews by the emergent middle classes, represented by the guilds, with the cooperation of clergy, nobility, and local governments. The usual charge was that Jews had caused the bubonic plague by poisoning the wells, but

> contemporaries were as aware of the true forces at work as any later historian. The Strasbourg chronicler knew that, although they were accused of poisoning wells, "money was likewise the poison which killed the Jews . . . if they had been poor and if the nobility had not been in their debt, they would not have been burned." The chronicler of the Peter's Kloster is even more explicit. Regarding the wells he writes, "I do not know if what they say is true," and then continues, "but I rather believe that the real grounds [for the Judenbrande Jew-burnings] was the huge, indeed immeasurable, amount of money which barons and soldiers, townsmen and countryfolk, were obligated to pay the Jews." Archbishop Gerlach, secure in his 100 marks annual tribute, was not fooled by the tale of poisoned wells, which he expressly declared to be unproved. "The Jews had a multitude of debtors, . . . in order to avoid paying them, the debtors put them out of the way—for a dead dog no longer howls."[9]

Assuming that the German motive was lust for gain, *Judenräte* of Poland during the Holocaust attempted to appease their local German masters by accumulating storehouses of watches, jewelry, furs, and other luxury goods. *Judenräte* leaders attempted to demonstrate the economic potential of their ghettos to prove that they could be exploited for the German war effort.[10] For

Jews who believed that exploitation was the German objective, the injunction was: Come laden with gifts! Produce! Work! These strategies failed consistently with the Germans.

Whereas during medieval and modern times Jews have often played the role of "middleman minority," the Jewish people entered history as a nation created by a landless tribe escaping enslavement in Egypt. But the Torah frankly tells us that the Jews did not aspire toward freedom but had accommodated themselves to exploitation and oppression. Their exodus was incited not by the noncooperation or rebellion of the slaves—a "mixed multitude," presumably of diverse loyalties and origins and of little cohesion—but by the actions of Moses, a Hebrew's son found in the bullrushes and reared as a royal scion. Moses' violent reaction to the sight of oppression can be understood in terms of his own lack of deference: he was a member of the ruling class. The Israelite foremen were incensed by Moses' claims made in their name because these pleas intensified their people's oppression by provoking Pharaoh's reprisals, as in the case following.[11]

> Afterward Moses and Aaron went and said to Pharaoh, "Thus says the Lord, the God of Israel: Let My people go that they may celebrate a festival for Me in the wilderness." But Pharaoh said, "Who is the Lord that I should heed Him and let Israel go? I do not know the Lord, nor will I let Israel go." . . .
> . . . The king of Egypt said to them, "Moses and Aaron, why do you distract the people from their tasks? Get to your labors!" And Pharaoh continued, "The people of the land are already so numerous, and you would have them cease from their labors!"
> That same day Pharaoh charged the taskmasters and foremen of the people, saying, "You shall no longer provide the people with straw for making bricks as heretofore; let them go and gather straw for themselves. But impose upon them the same quota of bricks as they have been making heretofore; do not reduce it." . . . (Exodus 5:1-8).
> Then the Israelite foremen came to Pharaoh and cried: "Why do you deal thus with your servants? No straw is issued to your servants, yet they demand of us: Make bricks! Thus your servants are being beaten, when the fault is with your own people." He replied, "You are shirkers, shirkers! That is why you say, 'Let us go and sacrifice to the Lord.' Be off now to your work! No straw shall be issued to you, but you must produce your quota of bricks!"
> Now the foremen of the Israelites found themselves in trouble because of the order, "You must not reduce your daily quantity of bricks." As they left Pharaoh's presence, they came upon Moses and Aaron standing in their path, and they said to them, "May the Lord look upon you and punish you for making us objectionable to Pharaoh and his courtiers—putting a sword in their hands to slay us!" (Exodus 5:16-21).

Moses' leadership would have been futile had not there occurred simultaneously a succession of disasters that culminated when "in the middle of the night the Lord struck down all the first-born in the land of Egypt, from the first-born of Pharaoh who sat on the throne to the first-born of the captive who was in the dungeon, and all the first-born of the cattle" (Exodus 12:30). Pharaoh had become convinced that these events were signs of symbolic retribution by the God of Moses and he could no longer defend his empire by resisting Moses' claims after this slaughter.

> And Pharaoh arose in the night, with all his courtiers and all the Egyptians—because there was a loud cry in Egypt; for there was no house where there was not someone dead. He summoned Moses and Aaron in the night and said, "Up, depart from among my people, you and the Israelites with you! Go, worship the Lord as you said! Take also your flocks and your herds, as you said, and be gone! And may you bring a blessing upon me also!"
>
> The Egyptians urged the people on, to make them leave in haste, for they said, "We shall all be dead" (Exodus 12:31–33).

Moses' self-conceived obligation to lead this alien, despised, and lowly multitude (despite the fact that he had been nurtured and accepted as an Egyptian and had married the daughter of a Midianite priest), the series of events themselves, and the adventitious escape route created by the parting of the Reed (often translated Red) Sea were attributed neither to the leadership of Moses nor to the determination of the Israelites but to the God of Israel, whose liberating power the Passover Haggadah commemorates annually. However, there is an intimation of collective violence (added on to the earlier slaughter) as the Israelites "had done Moses' bidding and borrowed from the Egyptians objects of silver and gold, and clothing": since the Egyptians were terrified of them by that point, "they let them have their request; thus they stripped the Egyptians" (Exodus 12:35–36).

So the children of Israel gathered their spoils, organized their cattle, baked their unleavened bread, and departed from Egypt. But when they were out of danger, wandering in the desert, the Israelites

> grumbled against Moses and Aaron. The Israelites said to them, "If only we had died by the hand of the Lord in the land of Egypt, when we sat by the fleshpots, when we ate our fill of bread! For you have brought us out into this wilderness to starve this whole congregation to death" (Exodus 16:1–3).
>
> From the wilderness of Sin the whole Israelite community continued by stages as the Lord commanded. They encamped at Rephidim, and there was no water for the people to drink. The people quarreled with Moses. "Give us water to drink," they said; and Moses replied to them, "Why do you quarrel with me? Why do you try the Lord?" But the people thirsted there for water; and the people grumbled against Moses and said, "Why did you bring us up from Egypt, to kill us and our children and livestock with thirst?" Moses cried out to the Lord, saying, "What shall I do with this people? A little more of this and they will stone me!" (Exodus 17:1–5).
>
> The riffraff in their midst felt a gluttonous craving; and the Israelites, moreover, wept and said, "If only we had meat to eat! We remember the fish that

we used to eat free in Egypt, the cucumbers, the melons, the leeks, the onions, and the garlic. Now our gullets are shrivelled. There is nothing at all! Nothing but this manna to look to!" (Numbers 11:4–6).

The Jews even threatened to desert the invisible God whom Moses claimed had given him authority over them. They were still slaves internally, incapable of revolt and not welded into a collectivity until they accepted contractual submission to the Covenant that incorporated the Ten Commandments.

Slaves find security in a rudimentary social contract: their masters are obligated to feed them in order to preserve their investment. Jews who anticipated German subjugation might rationally expect that enslavement might enhance their security because slavery is usually a self-maintaining institution with interdependent bonds of interest and obligation. Thus, there might be a symbiosis: the need of the German occupiers to manage the mass of Jews would require Jewish bosses, who would be able to protect the slaves who served as the masters' means of production. But the exploiter in Egypt had first turned oppressor before becoming an enemy, decreeing the end of the Jewish people gradually through killing newborn males, a policy that failed because of the noncooperation of Jewish midwives. Yet, that intent was forgotten as the escaped Israelites wandering in the Sinai looked back with nostalgia to their life in the delta, Goshen, where they had been regularly provided with a varied and savory diet.

Enemies, in contrast to exploiters and oppressors, have sought to destroy the Jewish people — not just to debase, oppress, and exploit them. A classic myth of Jews' victory over an enemy (believed to be of dubious historicity) stands out — the Book of Esther.[12] Set in a Persian kingdom, the story relates the calculating political intrigue of Mordecai, exploiting the sexual wiles of his well-tutored niece Esther, consort of the King, who first passed herself off as a non-Jew so as to be chosen for the royal harem. The King is depicted as indifferent rather than antagonistic to his Jewish subjects, accepting uncritically his minister Haman's interpretation that their refusal to bow down to him is a political act. Thus misled, the King authorizes the decree for their extermination. Esther and Mordecai undo Haman's influence by capturing the ear of the King, whose memory is fortuitously refreshed with the tale of Mordecai's previous loyalty, tipping him off to an earlier attempted palace coup. They induce the King to reverse the decree, hanging its author, Haman, on the gallows erected for Mordecai and the Jews. The order is not only countermanded, the Jews are given permission to defend themselves and plunder their enemies, indicating a social base for ethnic conflict within the Empire. Their revenge over Haman is celebrated gleefully every year (perhaps serving as a catharsis for all the occasions on which Jews have, in fact, been exterminated) in an annual night of collective amnesia. But, in fact, political appeal to a benevolent ruler alone seldom has guaranteed such reversal, unless the ruler had ulterior reasons for saving the Jews.

MODERN RESPONSES BY JEWS
TO COLLECTIVE VIOLENCE

Both in the ancient and the modern world, flight rather than appeal or self-defense has been the most often used and best means for beleaguered peoples to evade their enemies, especially when the enemy was the state itself. Because the pogroms in Russia from 1881 to 1917 were instigated to deflect social unrest of the oppressed against the more powerful classes onto the Jews, the scale of victims rose from two digits to four digits as the Czar's Empire declined. Whereas between 1881 to 1884 scores may have lost their lives in each incident, pogroms after the Russian Revolution that were waged by White and Red Army units "reached their climax in the massacre at Proskurov on February 15, 1919, when 1,700 Jews were done to death within a few hours."[13] An estimated 60,000 Jews were slaughtered during this period. Although self-defense units were formed among Jewish youth in 1904, they were prepared to deal with bands of pogromists, not army divisions.

The dominant response to violence by the Jewish masses was emigration, primarily to the United States. Between 1881 and 1914, almost 2.5 million Jews entered the United States: most of them came from Russia, followed by Jews from Austria-Hungary and Rumania, also propelled by violence and oppression. There was a progressive decline in the proportion of world Jewry inhabiting eastern Europe. While three out of every four Jews alive in 1880 had lived in eastern Europe and 3.5% then were spread through North and South America, less than half lived in eastern Europe in 1933 (46%) and almost one out of three (30%) lived in the new world.[14]

The ascent of Hitler and the formal disestablishment of German Jewry in 1935 provoked a similar flight, hastened by the fear of internment in concentration camps and the brutal pressure of the SS, increasing in 1938.

About seven out of every 10 Jews living in Germany in 1933 had left by October 1941 when emigration was forbidden. The same proportion of Austrian Jews fled between the time Hitler marched into Vienna, March 1938, and October 1941, exploiting all means — legal and illegal — available. A study of those remaining in Worms in October 1941 indicated that the overwhelming majority "had specific emigration plans and had applied for visas"; almost all applied to the United States, which rigidly restricted such immigrants (see Chapter 7).[15] Three fourths of the minuscule Jewish community of Estonia — the only Baltic Jewish community afforded an extended period for flight between the time the nation was threatened and the time it was fully occupied — are estimated to have fled to the interior of the Soviet Union in 1941.

Besides flight, there are few means for an oppressed class, surrounded by a hostile population, to evade annihilation by an enemy when that enemy is the state itself, endowed with armies, police, courts, and officials throughout its territory. The ability to evade identification alone depends not only on the size and visibility of the victims but on the identification of the majority or dominant group with them. The fact that only 19% of the Armenians were estimated to have survived the Turkish genocide of 1915 testifies to how readily large and concentrated numbers of people, once identified and isolated, can be murdered without any mechanical means of extermination such as the Germans devised.[16]

Both among the Jews during World War II and among the Armenians, during World War I, open rebellion—armed, defensive confrontation with the enemy—occurred only when there was no way out for flight and the cornered victims were convinced that submission meant collective death. This awareness opened up the freedom to decide which path to pursue and what price the enemy would pay for their murder. If the class of victims still believes that their enemy is an oppressor who employs violence either as example or threat in order to discipline them to submission, they must conclude that rebellion is irrational because it can only increase one's own risk of dying and the community's costs by provoking the oppressor's retaliation. The oppressed know from past experience that the masters punish individual rebellion with reprisals (often deadly) against both the individual and the group, employing collective punishment in which either an arbitrary number or the whole group are held responsible for the deeds of one member. Therefore, a premature or spontaneous act of rebellion is likely not to incite other acts but to extinguish the wish to rebel by proving that defense provokes fatal retaliation. If one defines the enemy as an oppressor, one should seek to reduce risks by avoiding disobedience and conforming to the rules, and to allay threat by propitiary behavior. But if one defines the masters as enemies, determined to kill, if one is trapped and can no longer evade a confrontation, the injunction is not to be obedient but to be cunning or daring. However, successful rebellion demands preliminary organization (not models of individual risk-taking), which is contingent upon a collective redefinition of the situation. Such a redefinition generated changes in the social organization and mobilization of resources in Warsaw that prepared the Jews to rebel in 1943. Previous adaptations of Jews to oppression and exploitation prolonged the time they needed to redefine the situation.

The Warsaw Ghetto

Nothing can be gleaned of the intensity of life and death — both so telescoped in time and space — in the largest Jewish community in Europe during the Holocaust without drawing upon the observations of those victims who knew that they might not overcome their enemies but refused to suppress their recognition of what they were undergoing or deny their lack of hope while they resisted being overcome by despair and anguish. The principal works from which we shall draw are *Notes from the Warsaw Ghetto: The Journal of Emmanuel Ringelblum, The Warsaw Diary of Chaim A. Kaplan,* Mary Berg's *Warsaw Ghetto: A Diary,* and the diary of the chairman of the *Judenrat,* Adam Czerniakow.[1] Other first-person documents used include Tuvia Borzykowski's *Between Tumbling Walls,* Alexander Donat's *The Holocaust Kingdom: A Memoir,* Bernard Goldstein's *The Stars Bear Witness,* Jan Karski's *Story of a Secret State,* Vladka Meed's *On Both Sides of the Wall,* Emmanuel Ringelblum's *Polish-Jewish Relations during the Second World War,* Halina Szwambaum's "Four Letters from Warsaw Ghetto," and Michael Zylberberg's *A Warsaw Diary, 1936–1943.*[2]

The immediacy of their perception varies, as these works were written at different distances from the events described. The diaries of Chaim Kaplan, Mary Berg, and Adam Czerniakow, the letters of Halina Szwambaum, and Ringelblum's notes (which he intended to elaborate and explicate for a history) were written at the time of the events recorded. The impressions of Jan Karski and Michael Zylberberg were written after they occurred but during the war, as was Ringelblum's treatise on *Polish-Jewish Relations.* The memoirs of Tuvia Borzykowski, Alexander Donat, Bernard Goldstein, and Vladka Meed were written from five to twenty-five years after the events recorded.

What part did each play? Ringelblum (1900-1944), an outstanding social historian of Polish Jewry and a Labor Zionist, also headed the Jewish self-aid organization based on tenants' committees. He exemplified the ideal of praxis, using his research to try to change as well as record history. He gathered source data for a future social history of the ghetto through trained informants linked in the network known as "Oneg Shabbat" ("Sabbath celebrants"—a code name of a convivial gathering). These data also provided sources for newsletters to Warsaw Jewry and the first reports to the West on the annihilation of the Jews of Poland. Ringelblum's often elliptical notes were jottings for a never completed work rather than a personal memoir.

Chaim Kaplan (1880-1942) was a teacher of Hebrew involved in the modern Hebrew literary revival. He had made his living as an independent schoolmaster in Warsaw. Kaplan's self-image is revealed in his diary in his scorn of the pretension of institutions and ideology and the frequent reiteration of his commitment to the ideals of the prophets: "I am the grandson of Isaiah the prophet, and I am at one with my ancestor in that bloodshed is abhorrent to me, in any form whatsoever." Although Kaplan was committed to Zionism and to Jewish self-help, he repeatedly exhibits contempt for Zionist officers and Jewish welfare officials (including Ringelblum), although he at first admired the network of mutual aid organized throughout the ghetto.

Both Ringelblum and Kaplan were men committed to universal social ideals, including both the preservation of the Jewish people and the introduction of new forms of community and expression. Both could also be considered free men in a unique way: they had chosen to return to or remain in occupied Warsaw, rejecting opportunities for flight. Ringelblum was in Geneva at a World Zionist Congress in September 1939; while other participants from Poland fled to the West, Ringelblum returned. Kaplan refused an exit visa to Palestine in 1941.

Adam Czerniakow (1880-1942) was a member of the educated class, politically outside the Zionist and religious camps. Before the war, he had been a member of the government-appointed Executive Council of the Jewish community and earlier an elected member of the Warsaw Municipal Council. Soon after Warsaw was occupied, he petitioned the (Polish) Mayor to be recognized as head of the Jewish community; later, he was appointed (by the SS) head of the *Judenrat*.[3] He committed suicide on the eve of mass deportations in July 1942, when he realized that the scope of the action meant mass extermination.

Mary Berg was unique among our witnesses; she was exempted from the threat of deportation and extermination by the Germans because her mother was an American citizen. The rights of Jews who were enemy nationals (to the Reich) were respected by the German Foreign Office until mid-1943 whereas Jews who were nationals of occupied nations had no rights. Mary, 15 years old in 1939, was the daughter of a prosperous Lodz art dealer who came to Warsaw in 1940 to escape the terror of Lodz. The family endured the tightening vise of terror in Warsaw until Mrs. Berg overcame her fear of registration with the German police and realized that their only opportunity lay in claiming special privilege as foreign nationals. They were removed from the ghetto by the German authorities before the deportations, temporarily interned, and later transported to Lisbon and freed in a wartime exchange.

Five witnesses were related to the Jewish underground in different roles. Jan Karski was the pseudonym of a Polish emissary from the Civil Directorate who entered the ghetto in the fall of 1942, and relayed a message from Jewish leaders to the Polish government-in-exile describing their state of enslavement and pleading for help. Tuvia Borzykowski was a member of the Zionist socialist youth organization, Dror. He fought in the ghetto revolt, escaped through the sewers with the aid of a Polish sewer worker from the PPR (Socialist Party), and also fought in the 1944 Warsaw uprising. Bernard Goldstein was a prewar leader of the Jewish Socialist Bund, active in the ghetto revolt, who also escaped and fought in the Warsaw uprising. Halina Szwambaum, a 22-year-old woman, died in the ghetto revolt, fighting alongside her lover. Vladka Meed was a courier for the Council for Aid to People in Hiding, which provided Jews in Warsaw hiding "on the Aryan side" with stipends received from Jewish aid organizations abroad through the Polish government-in-exile.

Michael Zylberberg was a Hebrew schoolmaster in Warsaw, as was Chaim Kaplan. Alexander Donat, the publisher of a Warsaw newspaper before the war, was captured with his wife during the ghetto revolt. He and his wife survived extermination and slave labor camps and their son survived the war in hiding; so did Borzykowski, Goldstein, and Meed, passing as Aryan Poles. Chaim Kaplan, Emmanuel Ringelblum, and Halina Szwambaum were among the 98 out of every 100 Warsaw Jews killed in Poland between 1939 and 1945.[4]

Individuals' deaths are ordinarily assimilated without trauma by the Jewish community living within its conceptions of God and history. But history is merely an abstraction arising from the fact that communities do span generations of existence in space and time. Such continuity maintains their members' sense of meaningful order in the universe. The history of the Jewish community of Warsaw during World War II is one of radical discontinuity, defying previous assumptions. It may be usefully divided into five periods, during which the properties of the community—density, composition, space, and numbers—metamorphosized rapidly as the community expanded and contracted. The members' sense of time and order in the universe was radically transformed during this time of antiorder.

At first, the war was one of devastation against all Poles. The populace of Warsaw was exposed to civilian bombardment for three weeks before the city's surrender. Between the occupation of Warsaw on 1 October 1939, and the closing of the ghetto in November 1940, the Jewish community (the largest in Europe) was inundated with Jewish refugees from other Polish cities and towns, who fled their homes to avoid the occupiers or were expelled by the Germans from the region of Poland incorporated in the Reich and made *judenrein* [free of Jews] rapidly. Over 150,000 Jews, or "one-third of all the ghetto inmates," had fled to Warsaw by mid-1941.[5] This increase in the dependent population and the elimination of customary occupations and opportunities in trade because of the occupier's discriminatory regulations produced a new social order. People rapidly fell to the bottom and some rose to the top within the Jewish community. Physically, they were compressed into run-down, stifling tenements with 68,000 persons per square kilometer by the time the ghetto was closed. The function of the first phase, noted by discriminatory regulations and marking of Jews, was the *segregation* of the Jews.

Between the closing of the ghetto and the first mass deportation raids on 22 July 1942, the Jews were wholly isolated, and concentrated behind the wall as the *social selection* of tens of thousands of the first victims began. They were decimated by starvation, disease, and enforced labor — the latter masked torture, starvation, and fatal accidents and led to epidemics. The causes of such deaths were a deliberate consequence of German policy. German regulations allowed Jews rations of "less than 10% of the minimum calorie requirements necessary to sustain human life" and produced an average of 7.2 persons per room within the ghetto, thus fostering the spread of disease.[6] Trunk records show that about 85,000 persons of a total Jewish population of over 500,000 — or more than one out of six — died between September 1939 and July 1942, *excluding* unrecorded deaths such as those of refugees and beggars on the streets. Most of these occurred after May 1941. Trunk concludes:

> One may reasonably infer that even had the Germans not "resettled" the Jews from the ghettoes for the purpose of mass killing, they would in any case have died at a "slow" death rate in five or six years. But the Germans were impatient. They could not wait.[7]

During this period, there were no deportations to extermination camps. The social selection of the victims was a function of the class order within the ghetto, rendering the powerless more vulnerable to selection for labor by the *Judenrat* and direct death by virtue of their helplessness, impoverishment, and homelessness.

Then came the time of contraction through *annihilation*. From 22 July 1942 to 11 September 1942, the overwhelming majority of Jews of Warsaw were exterminated. The Jewish population dropped from perhaps 390,000 to about 70,000: 310,322 Jews were transported to the extermination camps and 5,961 to 7,654 were shot within the ghetto. (The former is General Stroop's figure; the latter, the estimate of the Polish government, not including the 1,620 Jews officially recorded as shot in June.)[8] We have few written records during this period as all diarists were either in hiding or in transit to the camps. Ringelblum and Kaplan testify that the overwhelming majority of these victims were seized or pulled out by the Jewish police and the SS, despite their attempts to evade capture. Ringelblum has estimated that in response to the Germans' offer of three kilograms of bread to those who reported voluntarily, at least 20,000 volunteered of about 320,000 seized or shot — or one in 16 — among a population in which there was mass starvation.[9]

The fourth phase, September 1942 to April 1943, marked the *reorganization* of the Jewish community in readiness for battle. The authority of the *Judenrat* was destroyed, and combat organizations were formed by the survivors of the ghetto. The preparation for revolt began as a new consciousness emerged; survivors questioned old assumptions, asking themselves why they had not resisted collectively earlier. Despite the fact that their social organization by the Germans was more oppressive and control more pervasive — the Jews were virtual slaves of factory managers, segregated in barracks adjacent to their workplaces that were isolated from other workplaces — Jews felt more free to take risks because they abandoned their old assumptions and now recognized they shared a common fate. Just as they were stripped of illusions, they were stripped of bonds to kin as most family members had been slaughtered. New forms of community and temporary coupling — instigated more by despair than passion — became common. The communes sustaining the combat organizations emerging from the earlier *kibbutzim* — urban communes and training farms for emigration of young pioneers to Palestine — were the most significant of the new forms.

The fifth phase, that of the *rebellion* and its aftermath, is recorded in many later memoirs but will be described here only briefly, and only as a political phenomenon — in terms of the relations between Jews and Poles and the extent of the Polish leadership's identification with and against the Jews. Readers may wish to turn to the accounts cited and other accounts of this period for further documentation.

THE OCCUPATION AND INTRODUCTION OF GERMAN VIOLENCE

During the first days of the German occupation, Kaplan was impressed by the behavior and demeanor of the German troops. The Jews and other Poles were relieved by the Germans' efficient distribution of bread, in the beginning without discrimination. On the next day Kaplan heard rumors that the German Supreme Commander "has let it be known that he wants no difficulties set in the way of the Jews," but Jews were pushed aside on line.[10]

Almost immediately (2 October 1939), Kaplan was faced with homelessness. He and other tenants were expelled from their apartments by German soldiers: "They did not permit them to take even a shoelace out of their apartments: they did not permit them to don even an overcoat."[11] The Kaplans' Christian maid, who was allowed to remain, was raped. Sexual relations with Poles were not proscribed by the Nuremberg laws as were relations with Jewish women. The maid helped Kaplan recover his hidden copper box with his fortune of 600 zloty (about $120) by passing it out through the window. His wife almost fainted with the excitement of their good fortune. Yet they could not reoccupy their flat for an additional month; their return was "not to homes but to stables. Everything is broken and destroyed, stolen and plundered . . . even the electric fixtures were removed, and brooms were stolen. In short we have been cleaned out."[12]

Street robbery by German soldiers and Poles of German descent was common in streets and shops, but such behavior was generally ascribed to private venality among soldiers. Within two weeks, a succession of ordinances stripping the Jews of all property and civil rights was promulgated. On 10 October Jews were caught in the streets for forced labor, on 12 October their bank accounts were blocked, and on 16 October the Polish Mayor announced that all except the Jews would be entitled to public assistance. The ghetto ordinance was first published in November 1939, but the ghetto itself was not closed until November 1940.

Adam Czerniakow, vice president of the Jewish Advisory Council of Warsaw, had volunteered to Warsaw's Polish Mayor to represent the Jews of Warsaw after the chairman had fled. When later appointed by the Gestapo commander to head the *Judenrat,* he co-opted leaders of all Jewish parties, demanding that they share this responsibility. One of these leaders, Shmuel Zygelbojm of the Bund, instigated the *Judenrat* to resist issuing the order for a closed ghetto. Instead, they agreed to simply inform Jews of such an order. Zygelbojm later addressed a crowd milling around the *Judenrat* building, urging them not to leave their homes until removed by force. The Bund Central Committee, anticipating a Gestapo reprisal, smuggled Zygelbojm out of Poland. He fled to London, where he was appointed a member of the London Polish government-in-exile.[13]

Kaplan knew nothing of this but expressed relief on 7 November that a Jewish delegation had succeeded in easing the law. He immediately suspected to what use the *Judenrat* would be put eventually when news of a census was published on 25 October 1939:

> Yesterday we heard over the London radio that the Jews of Vienna have received an order to be ready to leave their native city and migrate to the Lublin district of Poland. This means: Prepare yourselves for total destruction.
>
> Another sign that bodes ill: Today, notices informed the Jewish population of Warsaw that next Saturday (October 29) there will be a census of the Jewish inhabitants. The *Judenrat* under the leadership of Engineer Czerniakow is required

to carry it out. Our hearts tell us of evil—some catastrophe for the Jews of Warsaw lies in this census. Otherwise there would be no need for it.[14]

Kaplan recognized that the Germans intended to destroy the Jews for ideological reasons, but their real motives were masked by accusations of blackmarketeering, of agitation, and of being socially useless or parasitical.

> Our tragedy is not in the humane or cruel actions of individuals but in the plan in general, which shows no pity toward the Jews. We are certain that this census is being taken for the purpose of expelling "nonproductive elements." And there are a great many of us now. No one knows whose lot will be drawn and therefore sorrow is on every face. We are caught in a net, doomed to destruction.[15]

He suspected a general plan but the worst objective that he could imagine was expulsion—what can be more dreadful than homelessness, being reduced to beggary as were the tens of thousands of dispossessed Jews wandering into Warsaw? Yet he assumes (26 October 1939) that "our existence as a people will not be destroyed. Individuals will be destroyed, but the Jewish community will live on."[16] Therefore, some would become victims of the oppressor. Kaplan knew that because he was a private schoolmaster and, hence, unemployed he was vulnerable. But he survived, possessing some savings, friends, an apartment, and—perhaps most important—a mission to record the testing and trial of Warsaw Jewry.

The Jews of Warsaw were first confronted with the problem of subsistence and survival, and only secondarily with violence. Violence might be exercised for profit (threats used for extortion or direct robbery) or for play. Violence for profit was widespread but not unique to the Nazis: Kaplan recognized it as an endemic byproduct of occupation. Soon there were some Jews who bought back the stolen goods (4 November 1939) from the Germans.

What Jews feared more than robbery was becoming a victim of violence for play, exemplified by the SS men who alighted from a car and began whipping Jews indiscriminately or who compelled clean and respected persons such as a bearded, black-frocked Chassid—member of a Jewish sect widespread in eastern Europe—or a correct, well-dressed lawyer, or a respectable matron to perform rituals of abasement.

> Eyewitnesses tell that even officers and high military officials are not ashamed to chase after an old Jew with scissors in their hands to cut off his beard. When they start chasing a bearded Jew, an uproar starts in the street, and the passersby and tradesmen flee (October 20, 1939).[17]

Soon the Chassidim quit wearing their distinctive garb. Everyone wore his oldest clothes to escape being distinguished. But the pathology sanctioned by the Nazis demanded degradation, the pollution of the clean by the unclean; the acting out of infantile excremental and sadistic fantasies was an end in itself. Kaplan observed on 16 December 1939:

> The beast within the Nazi is whole, completely healthy—it attacks and preys upon

others: but the man within him is pathologically ill. . . . People who may be trusted told me today of incidents of sadism towards Jews which only a sick mind would be capable of originating.

In Lodz some Jewish girls were seized for forced labor. Women are not given hard work, but instead perform various services, generally in homes. These girls were compelled to clean a latrine — to remove the excrement and clean it. But they received no utensils. To their question: "With what?" the Nazis replied: "With your blouses." The girls removed their blouses and cleaned the excrement with them. When the job was done they received their reward: the Nazis wrapped their faces in the blouses, filthy with the remains of excrement, and laughed uproariously.[18]

On 16 February 1940 he noted:

I know an intelligent, highly educated woman who, before going outside, always puts a scrub rag into her purse as a precaution in case of trouble, but she has no certainty that the Nazis won't order her to do the work with her blouse or her dress in any case. This is the face of Nazism unmasked.[19]

To be sure, there were mixed instances of violence for profit and play. Mary Berg recorded on 10 January 1941:

Last night we went through several hours of mortal terror. At about 11:00 P.M. a group of Nazi gendarmes broke into the room where our house committee was holding a meeting. The Nazis searched the men, took away whatever money they found, and then ordered the women to strip, hoping to find concealed diamonds. Our subtenant, Mrs. R., who happened to be there, courageously protested, declaring that she would not undress in the presence of men. For this she received a resounding slap on the face and was searched even more harshly than the other women. The women were kept naked for more than two hours while the Nazis put their revolvers to their breasts and private parts and threatened to shoot them all if they did not disgorge dollars or diamonds. The beasts did not leave until 2:00 A.M., carrying a scanty loot of a few watches, some paltry rings, and a small sum in Polish zlotys. They did not find either diamonds or dollars. The inhabitants of the ghetto expect such attacks every night, but this does not stop the meetings of the house committees.[20]

Such ritual abasement did not physically injure the victims but disabled them by debasing their self-image as they came to reflect their enemies' views of them, fulfilling the Nazi intention to degrade and humiliate. Kaplan noted on 18 November 1939: "Sometimes we are ashamed to look at one another. And worse than this, we have begun to look upon ourselves as 'inferior beings,' lacking God's image."[21]

While such violence was incited by an internal need of the Nazi rather than by any action of the victim, disobedience or a crime by a Jew could incite a deadly and instant reprisal against Jews collectively. Kaplan recorded on 30 November 1939 how

today we learned officially that on November 22, 1939, fifty-three Jews were shot for the "offense of rebellion." All these victims lived at Number 9 Nalewki Street. . . . The terrible event began when some Jewish thief shot and killed a Polish policeman and wounded another. The investigation and inquiry indicated that the murderer was one Jakub Pinchas Zylbring, whom the Jewish merchants had perhaps never seen before and certainly did not know. . . . What does a merchant who is mainly occupied with his business have to do with a ne'er-do-well who lives in the same courtyard and whose occupation is theft and robbery? But there is no place for legal logic when there is an excuse to bring catastrophe upon fifty-three Jewish families. All those who lived in the courtyard were imprisoned and taken to an unknown place. After two weeks they were all shot.[22]

Offenses committed by Poles also incited collective reprisals. But the Jews also might be held guilty for alleged crimes committed by Christians if one of the accused's four grandparents had been a Jew (22 January 1940). To avoid such collective reprisals, Kaplan opposed military resistance by Poles or Jews against the Germans. He wrote on 31 December 1939:

> Apparently a secret military group is quietly functioning in Polish circles. . . . Some military organization has begun to plot against the Nazis' lives. Obviously its work will be clandestine. . . . The terrible conqueror who knows no pity will not stand idly by. His revenge will know no bounds. In place of one, he will kill a hundred. . . . But this is only an introduction to what will be worse. . . . A terrible revenge is wrought by the vengeful sword.
>
> Such an incident occurred a few days ago in Wawer, near Warsaw. Two German officers were shot to death in some tavern, evidently while drunk, and a horrible misfortune has befallen the surrounding area. Every home was entered, every man was seized, and thus 102 victims were led to the scaffold, giving up their souls for a sin that they had not committed. Of them a hundred were Poles and two were Jews. The tavern owner was hanged, and his corpse was not taken down from the gallows for several days so that it would serve as a warning.[23]

THE JEWS ARE SEGREGATED AS THE RACIAL ORDER EMERGES

To Kaplan, Ringelblum, and Berg, the urgent need was to persevere in order to outlast, not to overthrow, the occupiers. This meant to feed the needy (who kept constantly increasing), to secure new work as old jobs and sources of revenue were stripped from Jews, and to remind oneself that one was not an animal even if treated like cattle. A new class order was being sifted, emerging from the symbiosis of Germans and Jews and the interdependence of Jews and Poles. The Jews were still in integral part of the economy and both Germans and Poles needed their services to maintain their power.

But great numbers had been made homeless by expulsion, trade restrictions, and German confiscations and needed immediate aid. Indigenous in-

stitutions for aid of Polish Jewry were supplemented by international Jewish
relief organizations, such as the American Joint Distribution Committee. The
destitute might apply for aid to the Joint, whose assistance program
Ringelblum headed. The more fortunate received gifts directly from relatives
overseas. Money was received from the Joint until 1942, but declined severely
after American entry into the war. But for the majority, even before 1942,
the aid was never adequate. The staff was overwhelmed, unable to cope
either personally or efficiently with the escalating flow of applicants and the
irregular flow of cash. Kaplan recorded the frustration and debasement of
days of waiting on lines, checking one's tongue to suppress one's natural
hostility toward bureaucrats on whom one depended, and the need for continuous followups and reapplications. Because of his experiences as a client,
he scorned Ringelblum and other professional welfare workers.

The system of aid in Warsaw facilitated the preservation of independent
foci of political expression and organization, preventing the *Judenrat* from
absorbing all welfare functions. The agencies' funds were channeled to
refugee centers and soup kitchens, presided over by officials of the established parties. The soup kitchens helped the parties maintain cohesion
among their members. Later this system was complemented by the Jewish
Self-Aid Committee, based on courtyard representatives from blocks of
elected house committees for which virtually all our diarists worked with enthusiasm. Kaplan described their rise and decline on 22 March 1941:

> A complex machinery was set up almost overnight. . . . There was no building
> in which a courtyard committee was not established to take charge of all the prob-
> lems. It was able to classify the residents of the courtyard according to their posi-
> tions and material resources. It also knew which among the residents of the court-
> yard needed support, and which were obligated to give for the support of others. A
> sort of *vox populi* came into existence. . . . Whoever did not wish to give was
> considered an outcast in his neighbor's eyes and was publicly shamed. His name
> was listed on a black board, which was hung on the gateway so that all who
> entered the courtyard would know that So-and-So had set himself apart from the
> community and would not come to the aid of the people. The courtyard commit-
> tee assessed everyone's material resources and imposed a monthly payment upon
> each householder. The sums taken in were turned over to the central fund which
> supported the soup kitchens. . . . But it wasn't long before public opinion began
> to intimate that not everything was right and proper with the Self-Aid, that they
> were stealing and embezzling, that the soup kitchens were spending a lot but
> feeding very few, that there was no overall control, that "the whole business is not
> worthwhile," etc., etc. And the more the backbiting, the less money it took
> in. . . . As usual, people exaggerate. There is no doubt that the hands of the
> leaders are clean, but it is possible that some individual official betrayed his trust
> and stole from the funds.[24]

Jews' property was "Aryanized" and they were divested of rights, but in
some cases pensions were voluntarily paid by Polish business partners. New
businesses sprang up within the ghetto. Both Polish and Jewish entrepreneurs

refused to sell at the prewar prices (fixed by the Germans) because the Polish currency had been devalued. Thus, a black market emerged, with prices for the cheapest commodities rising as a result of the shortage of goods. Ringelblum and Kaplan testified that nobody lived within the law. Workers and entrepreneurs profited from this and goods were initially plentiful within the ghetto. Everything was available if one had the money. But few had cash in the ghetto, and force was needed to extract it. Unable to collect rents from their tenants, Jewish landlords hired *Volksgenossen* (ethnic Germans), alone privileged among the Poles, as their rental agents because they could threaten to bring in the occupiers. Kaplan commented scornfully on 8 January 1940:

> Can Jews surrender their coreligionists to the hands of their archenemies, especially in time of such terrible material oppression? But the landlords did what they did. Their end will be that the *Volksgenossen* will be the main candidates for these houses, and the landlords will be driven from their own homes, but it is not the way of the world for people to pay attention to what will happen later. The Jew lacks community feeling and a sense of collective responsibility. I am sure that not one Polish landlord would allow himself to be safeguarded by means of such a disgusting action. And if he dared do such a thing, he would be ostracized like a leper.[25]

Professional criminals found their skills in demand. Ringelblum in November 1941 described the career of one such criminal:

> Yussele Ehrlich is the commandant of the Jewish prison. . . . Before the war, he was a confidence man and strong-arm guy, worked at counterfeiting until 1936 (possibly was in the stock market — this has to be investigated). When the Germans took Warsaw and the police began to liquidate the criminal elements, particularly among the Jews, Yussele Ehrlich was arrested and sent to [Auschwitz]. Apparently, he assumed certain duties of a despicable character, because he was released rather quickly . . . . Since June (or July) of this year, he has been the commandant of the Jewish prison, where people in the know say that he is . . . a man with an explicitly evil character, with despotic tendencies. His underlings tremble in fear of him.[26]

Porters became informers, betraying merchants carrying bundles. Yet these petty operators who acquired opportunities for privilege by chance were economic midgets compared to the types of gangsters who rose to the top through collaboration with the Gestapo during the period when the ghetto was sealed.

Jews were not yet completely segregated from the Poles in 1939 — the star was imposed in December — but the Polish community's toleration of organized attacks by Poles on Jews helped the occupier to isolate them, despite many personal bonds of mutual interest and some of trust. Kaplan reported on 11 November 1939:

> Besides the conqueror's "legal" pillage, illegal robbery has broken out among the

Polish masses. Today I was an eyewitness to such a theft in Gesia Street. A dreadful outcry arose. Jews were screaming violently, calling *"Polizei"* with all their
strength—and the plundering continued. Dozens of gentiles with stolen merchandise under their arms scattered in all directions, and our Jews continued to shout.
No one dared to go up to the thieves and take back the stolen goods they held. It
would have been easy to do, but they were afraid. Such scenes are played out each
day. The thief steals and the Jews shout.[27]

Mary Berg explained on 10 January 1940 how Jews feared encountering
Poles in the streets, incidentally noting the unwillingness of Jews to conform
to German regulations when they could avoid them.

The Nazi-controlled Polish press has published unofficial reports that a ghetto is
being planned for the Warsaw Jews. This report has aroused great bitterness
among all our people, who have already been ordered to wear white arm bands
with the Star of David on them. For the time being those whose Semitic appearance is not striking are not wearing arm bands; but in general all the Jews
avoid showing themselves in the streets because of frequent attacks by Polish
hooligans who beat and rob every Jewish passer-by. Some Poles not blessed with
Nordic features have also been molested by these hoodlums. For many days a
middle-aged Polish woman, wrapped in a long black shawl and holding a stick in
her hand, has been the terror of Marszalkowska Street. She has not let a single Jew
pass by without beating him, and she specializes in attacking women and children.
The Germans look on and laugh. So far no Pole has protested against this. On the
contrary, when a Jew happens to pass through a Gentile neighborhood, the inhabitants point him out to the Germans with the words: "Oh, *Jude!*"
     The same Polish hooligans have also led the Nazis to the apartments of well-to-
do Jews and have participated in looting in broad daylight. Protests were of no
avail: the law does not protect the Jews.[28]

During the spring of 1940 the occupiers began planting anti-Semitic propaganda in the press, inciting Poles to violence reminding Jews of the anti-
Jewish riots in major Polish cities and universities during 1935, 1936, and
1937. Jews responded as they had been conditioned to do, fleeing to avoid
violence. Kaplan wrote in evident depression and distress on 26 March 1940:

We have become a doormat whose purpose is to be trampled upon. . . . Never
before have there been such days of chaos, upheaval, and confusion in the Polish
capital as on the holiday of Easter, which this year fell on March 25. Christian
"ethics" became conspicuous in life. And then—woe to us! Someone organized
gang after gang of hooligan adolescents, including also little ones who have not yet
left their grade-school benches, to attack Jewish passersby and give them
murderous beatings. It was simply a hunt. . . . And what is there to deny? We
are cowards! In cases such as this we have only one choice—to run away. And running away only adds courage to the attacking toughs.[29]

On 28 March, he described their organization more precisely:

The conquerors have begun a new political operation. Gangs of young toughs,
Polish youth (you won't find one adult among them), armed with clubs, sticks,

and all kinds of harmful weapons, make pogroms against the Jews. They break into stores and empty their goods into their own pockets . . . your ears catch the tinkling sound of windows being smashed by a patriotic Polish youth doing his work under the protection of the conqueror, who stands nearby with his camera, perpetuating all these abominations.

These sons of Ham—just as a year ago they shouted in their patriotic fervor, "Long live Poland! Long live Smigly-Rydz!" they now shout, in their conquered capital, in the presence of the conquerors who destroyed their land, "Long live Hitler. Death to Smigly-Rydz! We want a Poland without Jews!"[30]

These street attacks lasted three days. Bernard Goldstein recalled that the Bund workers fought defensively against such gangs—they were organized in self-defense squads before the war to deter violence against Jews—avoiding lethal weapons in order to ensure there were no casualties that might give the Germans an excuse for reprisals. But such counteraction was evidently not observed by either Kaplan or Berg and was noted by Ringelblum only once among many incidents of attacks upon Jews by Poles. We may conclude that the more frequent ending of such confrontations was the victim's retreat.[31] The Germans made films of street violence in order to illustrate popular approval of their drive to combat the Jews, thus justifying their objective. The Germans even posed as defenders of the Jews in these films.

Despite the broad resonance of German goals and Polish aims, few Polish leaders would then publicly identify with the Nazi drive against the Jews as did the adolescents. They recognized that Poles were also designated as victims and viewed as an inferior racial class. Ordinary Poles were seized for forced labor and transported to Germany against their will, Polish intellectuals were slaughtered or interned in concentration camps, and blood was extracted from Polish children (those classified as racially acceptable for German use) without parental consent. Later some 200,000 of such children were kidnapped by the Germans from the homes of parents (considered inferior) to be integrated into the master race under the tutelage of German adoptive parents.[32] Poles in Warsaw knew that they could be seized and deported, whereas Jews were conscripted for labor only in Warsaw. Both Ringelblum and Kaplan reported instances of Poles who put on Jewish armbands or ducked into the ghetto to escape labor raids in the streets.

But Polish underground newspapers that represented the radical fascist movement continued to incite Poles against Jews.[33] The Mayor and city administration collaborated fully. However, there were cases of notables and officials who had been public anti-Semites before the war but refused to collaborate. Kaplan noted on 1 November 1939:

The conqueror wanted to open the law courts. The dean of lawyers, Jan Nowodworski, in peaceful days a well-known anti-Semite, was called up and two requests were made of him: to insert an Aryan clause in the judicial code, and second, to take a loyalty oath to the Führer. Nowodworski did not agree to either, on grounds that they were both against the Polish Constitution. He said, in so many words, If the Jews are to be deported, let us be the ones empowered to do so, not you! There were also political motivations for opposing the demand for an Aryan clause: they were ashamed to let their allies see it.[34]

Sympathetic bonds arose from common oppression. Ringelblum reported in October 1940:

> Saw this scene today: Students from Konarski's high school are beating Jews on the street. A few Christians stand up against them, and a crowd gathers. These are very frequent occurrences, where Christians take the side of the Jews against attacks by hoodlums. This wasn't so before the war.[35]

When the Jews were finally incarcerated in the ghetto, Ringelblum reported, Jewish businessmen often received gift packages from their Christian associates, and friends brought bread and flowers—"This is a mass phenomenon."[36]

Despite humiliation, loss of status, impoverishment, and constant apprehension over what they could expect on venturing into the streets, people adapted. Jews could see that Poles also were victimized, and neither Kaplan nor Ringelblum (with his extensive ring of informants outside Warsaw) at first imagined a fate worse than expulsion.

How did ordinary Jews view the situation? What people anticipate is often a projection of their desires and anxieties, which are directly reflected in rumor. According to Ringelblum and Kaplan, the great majority were optimistic, expressing wish fulfillment. Hitler was often reported dead between September 1939 and October 1940, and the Germans were said many times to be planning their retreat from Warsaw. Kaplan observed on 5 December 1939: "Such is the imagination of a despised people which has nothing left but imagination. The downtrodden masses are waiting for a miracle; the ground is ripe for Messianism."[37] Other rumors posed counterforces; their common denominator was that the Jews expected to be saved by an external force. Mussolini was said to be fighting Hitler; the Russians were always making advances. Tongues clicked over the Germans' terrible losses; after the fall of Denmark and Norway, the news buzzed through the ghetto that 27 Nazi troop ships were sunk and 30,000 German soldiers drowned.

Humor is also a mode of transcendence for the powerlessness. Ringelblum noted one such masked tale of longing:

> A Jew alternately laughs and yells in his sleep. His wife wakes him up. He is mad at her. "I was dreaming someone had scribbled on a wall: 'Beat the Jews! Down with ritual slaughter!'" "So what were you so happy about?" "Don't you understand? That means the good old days have come back! The Poles are running things again!"[38]

The Jews' contempt for their conquerors (or, as in the case of Kaplan, the conviction that they were sick) gave them the moral distance to compensate for their fear and the shame imposed on them. Ringelblum jots down another (perhaps apocryphal) story:

A police chief came to the apartment of a Jewish family, wanted to take some things away. The woman cried that she was a widow with a child. The chief said he'd take nothing if she could guess which one of his eyes was the artificial one. She guessed the left eye. She was asked how she knew. "Because that one," she answered, "has a human look."[39]

THE *JUDENRAT* AND THE CLASS ORDER OF THE GHETTO

After Jews were stripped of jobs, rights, and property, segregated on streetcars, and marked with the Jewish star, the deferred order to move into the ghetto was promulgated. This necessitated exchanges of apartments and/or buying out tenants to secure space; 80,000 Christian Poles had to move to make room for 140,000 Jews. The proportion of Jews needing apartments indicates that about one in three had lived outside this quarter, which housed poor Jews and Christians before the war. Christians and Jews competed in their appeals to the authorities to exempt (or include) particular blocks with desired apartments, schools, churches, and other institutions.

The wall was going up, but there was still uncertainty as to what its ascent signified. Kaplan anticipated what would occur in his entries of 24-27 October 1941:

> Will it be a closed ghetto? . . . A closed ghetto means gradual death. An open ghetto is only a halfway catastrophe. . . . From the time when the ghetto is closed, we will become a foreign national organism, separated from the civil life of the nation. . . . Thus it is that the *Judenrat* will be the representative of the Jewish people both within and without. . . . And in this lies the essence of our tragedy. . . . The *Judenrat* is not the same as our traditional Jewish Community Council, which wrote such brilliant chapters in our history. Strangers in our midst, foreign to our spirit, sons of Ham who trample upon our heads, the president of the *Judenrat* and his advisors are musclemen who were put on our backs by strangers. . . . They were never elected, and would not have dared dream of being elected, as Jewish representatives; had they dared, they would have been defeated.[40]

The issue of seeking positions from the *Judenrat* divided Zionists. Kaplan recalled that

> during the time when the revival of Jewish education was on the agenda, and veteran social servants came in contact with the *Judenrat*, even my Zionist friends tried to get close to the "Jewish Government" and its leadership. Hundreds of jobs were handed out to all those who appeared before the *Judenrat*. In the Zionist camp there were many out of work, and so our representatives tried to get some of our members into the *Judenrat* too. They were successful to some extent, but generally our members ran from the *Judenrat*. The clean do not mingle with the unclean.[41]

The best educated and most politically conscious were among those enticed by and coopted within the *Judenrat*. Those committed to private solutions would have no incentive to consider any collective defense against the German resolve to liquidate the majority in July 1942. Mary Berg accepted — with some expressed distaste — the necessity to exercise "pull" to be selected for a course in mechanical drawing and graphic arts and empathized more with Adam Czerniakow than did many others.

The president of the *Judenrat*, Czerniakow, was not an opportunist seeking material gain but a man who lacked insight into the role he was playing. Czerniakow's diary indicates that he was personally incorruptible, unlike his colleagues and the many petty officials of the *Judenrat*. His privileges consisted of receiving daily orders and abuse from the SS and other German authorities, who were not always familiar with one another's plans, and thus sometimes made contradictory demands. Less than four months after assuming office (on 18 January 1940) he recorded being kept hostage by the SS for five and a half hours. Three days later he was seized for forced labor and released only after promising that the *Judenrat* would supply laborers. His initial desire for the position waned rapidly. He recorded on 26 January 1940 that he had attempted to resign but was advised against it by the SS. Again, on 4 November 1940, he was arrested, imprisoned in the Pawiak, and beaten by the Gestapo. Upon his release the next day, he wrote in his diary: "I can hardly walk."

The *Judenrat*'s policies sprung from its constant need for money to placate the Germans and avert the threatened violence. It lacked sanctions to compel collection except to exploit the fear of becoming a victim, trading security or exemption from forced labor for fines and for taxes. An elaborate system of exchange within the ghetto and between the ghetto and "Aryan" Warsaw simulated a market economy, but the basic need for security created a competitive but quasi-feudal political economy, which ultimately did not bind the German overlords. The *Judenrat* needed money to ransom Jews who the Gestapo alleged had committed some crime or who were being collectively punished for a crime of one Jew. Thus the *Judenrat* paid 100,000 zlotys to the Gestapo (Czerniakow records on 24 November 1939) to ransom 53 hostages from 9 Nalewki Street who were imprisoned because one tenant shot a Polish policeman. Despite this, they were shot. It was the *Judenrat*'s unhappy task to inform their families. On 26 January 1940, the German police demanded that the *Judenrat* pay 100,000 zlotys for the alleged beating up of German Poles by Jews, threatening to shoot 100 Jews if the sum was not paid. Simultaneously, they needed 6,100 zlotys to ransom 61 Jews caught without armbands. Each new regulation made more violations possible. To Czerniakow there was never any question of not paying: he was well aware that any German jail sentence might mean death. On 17 July 1940, he noted, the SS informed him that of the 260 Jews arrested between 18 January and 25 January, 37 were still alive out of the 113 whose fate had been determined.

Czerniakow relied on German reassurances as long as possible: initially (4

April 1940) he was told that the walls would protect Jews against violence before he was informed that the ghetto would be closed. He accepted German terror and extortion, his councillors' corruption, and Jews' complaints against him as evils he must endure in order to serve his people, allaying the occupiers' wrath by propitiating them. He "began to develop," Nachman Blumenthal observes, "the ideal of the passive martyr, the saint: who accepts pain and suffering in order to redeem and emancipate others."[42] His humiliation and loneliness appeared to him as the price to be paid for going down in history as a modern-day suffering servant—"despised, and rejected of men" (Isaiah 53:3). His diary consists of terse jottings, emblematic of his mood and self-image: on 17 February 1940, he commented, "The difference between the saints and me is that they have more time than I."

Although Czerniakow was a cultured man, he was neither astute nor insightful. He selected from literature passages that fortified his conviction that he, like the saints, suffered for a noble purpose, rather than being simply an instrument of the enemy, to be thrown away when his use was exhausted. He noted on 28 May 1940: "I am reading Proust's *Within a Budding Grove*. He says: 'according to the Japanese, victory belongs to an antagonist who knows how to suffer one quarter of an hour longer.'" Czerniakow prepared for the day when he could go no further, when all his illusions would be stripped, by keeping cyanide pills in his desk drawer.

Like Czerniakow, Ringelblum knew of the high death rate in German prisons and concentration camps and found sources in 1940 to find out what happened in Auschwitz to all those prisoners (such as his friend Baruch, who refused to wear an armband) who were heard of only when their families were notified to pick up their cremated remains (5 December 1940). He noted on 10 December that "a great many dispatches are arriving from Oswiecim with news of the deaths of inmates. People are forced to exercise under showers every day for three hours there; this produces inflammation of the lung and death follows."[43]

No mechanical means of inflicting mass deaths were yet in widespread use. The real threat, Ringelblum and Kaplan suspected, was mass starvation. With the closing of the ghetto, prices initially skyrocketed: on 29 November 1940—two days before the closing of the ghetto—Ringelblum reports that potatoes, the staple of life, were up to 95 zlotys per kilo ($19 at prewar exchange rates): by 20 May 1941, they had stabilized at 4 zlotys a kilo. Between December 1940 and July 1942, the Jews of Warsaw spent most of their energy in simply coping, making a living, and surviving. Since the chances of death, whether by typhus, tuberculosis, freezing, or starvation, were highly related to one's class, a medical history of Warsaw corresponds to a history of social classes.

Strata were based on access to power. One's status was primarily determined by three types of relations. First, did a person have any prewar bonds of interest or sentiment to other Warsaw residents—Jewish or Christian? Second, could one earn or pay for protection? Third, could one supply protection—exemption from violence, exploitation, or discriminatory legal prosecution?

At the very bottom were the unemployed and unprotected who had no bonds and could offer nothing to anyone; the refugees who were displaced, shocked, and alien to Warsaw were most likely to fall into this class. The more innovative of them simulated a lumpenproletariat of beggars and hawkers. Above this class were the steadily employed workers, craftsmen, and small merchants. These were protected by German employers and/or police taking cuts from their commerce over and under the wall. Former professionals like Kaplan were dependent on contacts within the *Judenrat* or political parties for employment, but could subsist for a time by selling possessions and expending their savings; their status was most precarious. The more one visibly possessed, the more likely he was to be looted by the Germans and expropriated.

A privileged class among the workers, merchants, and artisans were those who supplied petty forms of protection, the informers and intermediaries for German employers. House superintendents, porters, and postal clerks served as informers and could sell their information or their silence. Intermediaries were needed; Ringelblum noted in November 1940:

> Every German institution has its Jew who is well-treated though other Jews are mistreated. For example, there's a man they call "Moses" in the Dinance Park garages. He has been able to get a number of Jews exempted from work.[44]

Judenrat employees could also offer some protection. Employment by the *Judenrat* itself was valued not so much for the meager wages it paid but for the opportunities it offered for bribes, kickbacks, and ransoms—to prevent typhus disinfection (see p. 228), to get an apartment, to keep someone out of an apartment, to prevent fines by the sanitary inspectors, to buy one's way out of forced labor. About 6,000 persons held such jobs.

But the problem remained—that of existence—especially for professionals. How did the jobless middle class fare? Kaplan had escaped paupery by the Germans' failure to notice the copper coinbox with his modest savings. Mary Berg's family was well off before the war; they were also fortunate. Although they had sought refuge in Warsaw from Lodz, they had some contacts in Warsaw and apparently enough cash and valuables to live on for over 21 months without employment. However, on 27 July 1941 she recorded:

> After a long struggle, my father has finally got the job of janitor with all the privileges this office entails. He has been "in office" for two weeks now, and, in addition to the regular Jewish arm band, he now wears a yellow arm band with the inscription: "House Master." He has also received a passport from the community which states that he is exempt from compulsory labor duties. Thus he can circulate freely in the streets without fear of man hunts. The janitors are exempt

from various community taxes, receive extra food rations, two hundred zlotys a month as a salary, and free lodging. But their main income is derived from opening the door at night: in accordance with the curfew regulations the door is closed at an early hour, and to have it opened the tenants pay twenty groszy or more. Some nights these fees total as much as twenty zlotys. In brief, a janitor's income under the present conditions is unusually good; no wonder the job is hard to obtain.

Because my father is not strong enough to perform the heavy duties of a janitor, to wit, keeping the building clean, scrubbing the staircases, and removing the garbage, he has followed his original plan, and has taken my Uncle Percy as his assistant. To him he gives all his direct money receipts.

At first our neighbors were distrustful of their new janitor, who, only yesterday, was a tenant like themselves. They could not conceive that an art dealer and expert on classical painting could perform the duties of an ordinary janitor. But they soon grew accustomed to the idea that even a respectable citizen can become a janitor and still remain a respectable citizen. Now they show the greatest respect for both my father and my uncle. Incidentally, they are not the only people in the ghetto who have fallen so low on the social scale. The janitor in the building next to ours is Engineer Plonsker, a close friend of our family's. And a great number of lawyers are now glad to work as janitors.[45]

Although it was taken for granted, as Kaplan noted, that "everyone steals," the way one stole indicated one's class. A child smuggler with a kilogram of potatoes slung in a hump on his back, who crept like a mouse out of the openings at the wall, was clearly in a different class than a smuggler who had German accomplices, warehouses, and retail outlets.

Men were conscripted for forced labor from January 1940 onward, first within Warsaw and later outside, boarding in barracks. The *Judenrat* began registering all those legally liable in February 1940. It soon began selecting only the poorest. Kaplan noted on 8 July 1940:

The edict about "normal work" in the city, for which the conquerors have made the *Judenrat* responsible and which is known by the technical name of Labor Battalion, has been carried out with full force. As many as ten thousand men a day must be furnished to the conquerors by the *Judenrat*, for various temporary and accidental jobs, besides the hundreds of men seized from among Jewish pedestrians walking innocently in the streets. The *Judenrat* has set up a complete apparatus for this purpose, employing hundreds of clerks and supervisors. Every Jew from sixteen to fifty-five is required to report for work nine days out of each month. In order to increase the *Judenrat's* income, it is not an absolute requirement; anyone who wants to be exempt from this labor requirement must pay a ransom of 60 zloty a month. It is a good source of guaranteed monthly income for the *Judenrat*. In general the conqueror attempts to increase the *Judenrat's* income, since "whatever a slave owns his master owns." The murderers have burdened this miserable *Judenrat* with such demands that it is powerless to fulfill them; they have made it into a body of water without fish [*sic*]. Its treasury is empty, but the demands never cease. Unwillingly it supports itself from the misfortunes of the

Jews. In the past few weeks fewer people have been coming to work, and so there was a threat. The unfortunate Czerniakow was summoned and warned: Speak to your *Juden* and tell them that if they don't come voluntarily, we will enforce to the letter every one of the stringent provisions of the decree. Czerniakow publicized that warning in every courtyard and the Jews are in turmoil.[46]

Those who could pay stayed home while those who could not were seized, regardless of condition. Ringelblum described these on 21 November 1940:

The work camp transports: Some of Those [*sic*] who returned came back in their underwear. Yesterday, the 20th of November, more than 800 Jews were routed from their beds for the forced work camps, invalids, too.[47]

On New Year's Eve (1940–1941), Ringelblum recorded that the exploitation of forced laborers and the role of the *Judenrat* were subjects of public satire:

"The Memorial Song" is very effective, though not very good from the artistic point of view. The poet calls for all the woes we are suffering to be avenged, he tells about the press gangs, the deathly fear stalking the streets, the work camps ("leeches that suck the blood of workers plunged in swamp mud") from which no one returns. He tells of the scandalous behavior of the Council people, who are sometimes worse than the Others [Germans], of the sorrow of children growing up without schooling; of the death of martyrs; of the child killed because of his beauty.[48]

Death was still individual, a possibility but not of high probability. Ringelblum indicates on 11 May 1941 that his sources attributed the high death rate in one work camp to the Ukrainian prison guards:

It was worst in Puszcza-Kampinas, where there were thirty-seven Jewish victims, i.e., 10 per cent of the campers. The guards simply stole the campers' rations (18 dekos of bread, a thin soup, and a glass of black coffee). When they came back, the campers died in the Jewish Council house. Some of the inmates were shot while trying to escape from camp. The camp regime was dreadful. The returnees were dreadfully exhausted. Some of them suffered the effects of a camp psychosis and trembled at the sight of a uniform. The Jewish Council is now concentrating on having the camp guards removed—Mannes, the commissar for the Jewish part of Warsaw, is to appeal to the Governor General for this purpose. You can guess the mood of those who have to go to camp. Yesterday's transport actually rebelled and refused to go.[49]

Conditions were improved at this particular camp, Ringelblum observing that "after the priest of Kampinos delivered his sermon on behalf of the Jewish campers, everything changed." But this particular priest was exceptional among the clergy, Ringelblum later noted. His sermons also instigated the peasants to throw food over the barbed-wire fences to the prisoners.[50] However, conditions in most camps were so bad that the *Judenrat* could not persuade people to report for work outside of Warsaw; therefore, they employed dragnet raids to satisfy the German demand for laborers.

THE FIRST SELECTIONS: LIFE CHANCES AND THE SOCIAL ORDER

After the closing of the ghetto, the death rate among Warsaw Jews rose steeply: between January and December 1941, it was over 1,000 times the prewar norm. By February 1941, bread-snatching on the street was common. Kaplan described such a scene on 19 February 1941:

> A crowd of idlers gather around two Jews fighting and wrestling. Each is trying to kill the other. Nobody knows what happened. But if you look closely at the wrestlers, you understand the reason for the battle. One of them was carrying a loaf of bread; the other sneaked up on him, took it away, and started running. The other man ran after him and caught him.
>
> One claims: "I am as hungry as you are, why rob me? Go to the rich people."
>
> The street rabble gets into the quarrel, but the mob is divided into two camps. A student of the Bible decides it: "Men do not despise a thief, if he steals to satisfy his soul when he is hungry."
>
> Everyone agrees that King Solomon was right.[51]

Writing in her diary, Mary Berg recorded on 28 February 1941:

> Many of our students come to [art] class without having eaten anything, and every day we organize a bread collection for them. The lot of our life models is even more tragic. Recently we have been drawing many portraits; our favorite subject is "misery." Models are not lacking for that. They stand on line to earn a few pennies by posing for us. Often they fall asleep on the stand, and then, with closed eyes, they look like corpses.
>
> The directors of our course pay two zlotys for two hours of posing, and we gather together a few small pieces of bread for each model. Yesterday our model was an eleven-year-old girl with beautiful black eyes. All the time we were working the child shook with fever and we found it hard to draw her. Someone suggested that she be given something to eat. The little girl tremblingly swallowed only part of the bread we collected for her, and carefully wrapped the rest in a piece of newspaper. "This will be for my little brother," she said. "He waits at home for me to bring him something."
>
> After that she sat quietly through the entire drawing period.
>
> Once we were compelled to carry an old man out of the classroom; he had fainted from hunger and could not even finish the bread we gave him.[52]

The same day, Ringelblum noted that "almost daily people are falling dead or unconscious in the middle of the street. It no longer makes so direct an impression."[53] Two weeks later, he observed:

> The number of the dead in Warsaw is growing from day to day. Two weeks ago some two hundred Jews died. Last week (the beginning of March) there were more than four hundred deaths. The corpses are laid in mass graves, separated by boards. Most of the bodies, brought to the graveyard from the hospital, are buried naked. In the house I lived in, a father, mother, and son all died from hunger in the course of one day. Pinkiert, the King of the Dead, keeps opening new branches of his funeral parlors. . . .

The abandonment of children in offices of institutions and Jewish police headquarters has become a mass phenomenon. The establishment of a home for 100
beggar children has not helped. Children are continuing to beg, no less than
before. The beggars have a new line. "I'm short 10 groschen for a place to sleep; I
can't sleep in the street."[54]

Despite the spring thaw, the death rate climbed steadily as the typhus
epidemic spread. Ringelblum recorded on 20 May 1941:

Recently, people have been dying at the rate of 150 a day (as of the 15th of May,
there were 1,700 deaths) and the mortality keeps growing. The dead are buried at
night between 1 and 5 A.M., without shrouds—in white paper, which is later
removed—and in mass graves. . . . Various groups of excursionists—military
men, private visitors—keep visiting the graveyard. Most of them show no sympathy at all for the Jews. On the contrary, some of them maintain that the mortality among Jews is too low. Others take all kinds of photographs. The shed where
dozens of corpses lie during the day awaiting burial at night is particularly
popular. Today I visited the shed. It is a macabre scene. Under black paper covers
lie heaps of corpses, thrown together, clothes awry—it's like nothing more or less
than a slaughterhouse. The corpses are mere skeletons, with a thin covering of skin
over their bones. Recently there's been an increase in the cases of suicide. For example, two refugees committed suicide at 28 Panska Street by taking strychnine.
Two or three members of the same family are being buried at the same time these
days. With bread costing 15 zlotys a kilo, half to three-quarters of Warsaw must
eventually starve to death.[55]

The typhus epidemic was used to spread propaganda against the Jews
among the Poles; Polish papers charged that Jews carried lice, reviving
medieval myths. The compulsory disinfectant squads employed to cordon off
the epidemic within the ghetto were both corrupt and ineffective, so all who
could avoid disinfection by paying them off did so, and the disease spread.
The poor, if their calorie intake was sufficient to prevent starvation, had a
greater chance to recover than the rich, Kaplan observed.[56] If one survived
the typhus and did not starve, there was a cold winter to look forward to in
1941–1942.

The streets were teeming with scurrying souls, seeking to evade the flying
lice by anointing themselves with naphtha and other odorous compounds.
Besides typhus, there were scurvy and other diseases caused or aggravated by
malnutrition. Mary Berg described the casualties on 31 July 1941:

Near Grzybowska, the streets are full of starving people who come to the community for help. There are a great number of almost naked children, whose
parents have died, and who sit in rags on the streets. Their bodies are horribly
emaciated; one can see their bones through their parchment-like yellow skin. This
is the first stage of scurvy; in the last stage of this terrible disease, the same little
bodies are blown up and covered with festering wounds. Some of these children
have lost their toes; they toss around and groan. They no longer have a human appearance and are more like monkeys than children. They no longer beg for bread,
but for death.

Where are you, foreign correspondents? Why don't you come here and describe the sensational scenes of the ghetto? No doubt you don't want to spoil your appetite.[57]

Notwithstanding the pestilence, cold, hunger, and nightly howling of children, many ghetto dwellers maintained their morale by dancing, attending lectures, and staging dramatic productions. Kaplan recorded on 20 February 1941 that

> it is forbidden to hold parties with music and dancing. The victims of this order will be the courtyard committees, which live from such spectacles. . . . In the daytime, when the sun is shining, the ghetto groans. But at night everyone is dancing even though his stomach is empty. . . . It is almost a *mitzvah* to dance. The more one dances, the more it is a sign of his belief in the "eternity of Israel." Every dance is a protest against our oppressors.[58]

Mary Berg sang through 1940 and 1941 with a group of friends—the "Lodz Artistic Group," or LZA, which in Polish means "tear"—first organized to raise money for Janus Korzsack's children's home. Every means of expression could be a means of catharsis for actors and audience. She related how, for Passover 1941, her group chose to dramatize the Haggadah:

> To a strongly rhythmic piano accompaniment I thundered out the ten plagues that every Jew in the ghetto wishes upon the Nazis. The whole audience repeated the words after me, and together with me silently wished that they should strike the new Egyptians as soon as possible.[59]

Similarly, Michael Zylberberg told how the headmasters of the Hebrew schools chose to enter a play in the school competition in 1941 based on the

> famous Hebrew poem, "Masada," by Yitzhak Lamdan, . . . Masada was a mountain fortress where the Jews of ancient times resisted Rome. It symbolized defiance in the face of overwhelming odds, but after three years the revolt ended with mass suicide for the helpless defenders. How could we present such a play in our present circumstances? Rabbi Nissenbaum said quietly, "Take a chance. At least show that Jews have always put up a fight. This play will engender moral courage; it will demonstrate, at least, that people must stand firm." He . . . paused at the famous song about the chain. . . .
>
> "The chain has not been broken; the chain continues, from parents to children, from father to son. This is how our parents danced, one hand placed on the next man's back, and in the other hand a Sepher Torah; bringing light to our darkness. So we, too, will keep on dancing, and our hearts will be joyful and lively. We will keep on dancing, dancing, and the chain will never break."[60]

Satires and musical comedies ventilated the frustrations of everyday life. One popular favorite satirizing the lack of privacy in overcrowded flats was "Love Looks for an Apartment," Mary Berg noted. Halina Szwambaum also observed this lack, commenting wryly on how she and her boyfriend were constantly chaperoned by the tenants of the apartment.

Although the yearnings expressed by popular culture were yearnings of the oppressed, all of these did not affirm Jewish solidarity for they also expressed the natural desire of people to escape membership in a stigmatized, despised, oppressed group. While the party kitchens and Zionist youth groups sought to revive Jewish culture, the Jewish masses imitated Polish fashions and speech.[61] Conversions increased, despite the fact that Jewish converts were also incarcerated in the ghetto. Symptoms of identification with the aggressor appeared, similar to those appearing elsewhere among powerless and oppressed classes.[62] High boots and toy police badges were in vogue. This was first seen by Ringelblum as a sign of illness on 9 May 1940 in the following context: "In a refugee center an eight-year-old child went mad. Screamed, 'I want to steal, I want to rob, I want to be a German.' In his hunger he hated being Jewish."[63] Concurrently, signs of what Ringelblum calls "demoralization," or lack of identification with kin and community, appeared within families. Young girls pilfered their parents' household possessions to sell to obtain money for permanent waves. On the Jewish New Year — the highest of holy days, during which money is not to be touched — Jewish informers smuggled soldiers into services being secretly held in apartments and sold exemptions from forced labor.[64] Others led police to family treasures. Mary Berg empathized with those who had become agents after having first been arrested for minor infractions and tortured by the Germans.[65]

Polish Jews grew more cynical and embittered as they saw that "Jewish" Gentiles and non-Polish Jews were more privileged. They resented the material advantages and status enjoyed by the newly arrived German Jews who traveled to Warsaw in pullman cars, lived in a special quarter, and received better rations than Polish Jews. Most conspicuous were those Poles who were born as Christians but classified as Jews because of the identity of their fathers and grandfathers. These included some well-known anti-Semites and others whose aversion to the Jews was reinforced by their being classed among the victims; they displaced their anger from those who classified them to the victims. Some occupied prominent positions on the Jewish police force and within the council — Czerniakow was under some pressure to accommodate to them — and enjoyed special aid from Caritas, the Roman Catholic charity organization. They were disliked by Kaplan, Ringelblum, and other Jews. Some of the converts overcame their ambivalence toward Jews within the ghetto and identified with them. Mary Berg commented on 11 December 1941 upon their dilemma:

> These Christian-born children of Jewish parents are now living through a double tragedy as compared with Jewish children. They feel entirely lost, and there have even been cases of suicide among them, while there have been no such cases among the Jewish youth.
>
> However, there are also Christians of distant Jewish origin who have been brought back to Judaism by the Nazis' ferocious persecutions of the Jews. A number of Christians of the third generation who did not have to go to the ghetto spontaneously went to the Gestapo and demanded to be sent there. These re-

turned Christians wear the arm band with pride, as a kind of new crown of thorns and martyrdom.[66]

Christians of Jewish origin usually had better connections than Jews and the opportunity to evade the ghetto and pass on the Aryan side if they resolved to identify as Aryan Poles, as most of them probably did.

Those without connections or opportunities either became paupers or turned to new occupations in the ghetto. New occupations created new forms of degradation. Ringelblum observed in October 1941:

> A characteristic recent development in the Ghetto is wagons to which human beings are harnessed. The practice is based on a simple calculation: It costs 80 zlotys a day to maintain a horse, only 20 zlotys a day to maintain a human being.[67]

The refugees and the homeless were most likely to become paupers first, but professionals without capital or connections also drifted downward. Jewish scholars from Warsaw with connections who did not know how to use them and would not beg might die, as did Joseph David Bornstejn, Kaplan's friend. Kaplan indicted Warsaw's Jews on 8 March 1942, writing that

> Joseph David Bornstejn has passed away, starved to death in his lonely attic. Who was he? The very ones who were responsible for his death eulogized him and did not exaggerate when they said: "Veteran Hebrew writer, brilliant linguist, one of the editors of the *Encyclopedia Judaica* . . . known for research on the Talmud and interpretation of the poetry of Bialik."[68]

Kaplan had arranged with Bornstejn's other friends to support him but they were diverted by other problems, "both ideological and technical," and he was forced to rely on the Jewish Self-Aid, the head of which (presumably Emmanuel Ringelblum, whom Kaplan detested anyway) gave him no special assistance.[69] And Bornstejn, like many others, was unable to survive on watery soup and sawdust-filled bread.

In May 1942, the Germans decided to create a film showing the world how well the Jews of the Warsaw ghetto lived. There was not much time left—the ghetto was to be destroyed as a community within three months. It was essential not only to exterminate the Jews but to extirpate their image as archetypes of western morality. Simultaneously, the Germans preferred to portray themselves as benefactors protecting the Jews, as in films made in 1941.[70]

Kaplan saw a novel event on 19 May 1942:

> At ten in the morning three trucks full of Nazis, laughing, friendly, with complete photographic equipment, stopped near Schultz's famous restaurant. . . . They behaved in a friendly manner toward whomever they met, and entered into personal conversations with the ghetto dwellers.
>
> Why the difference today? Today they came to take photographs of the ghetto and its inhabitants, and the pictures must mirror the abundance and good fortune in the ghetto. . . . First they detained every beautiful virgin and every well-dressed woman, and even some who were not beautiful or well dressed, but who

were made up and somewhat elegant. The women were ordered to move around gaily and to look and sound animated. . . . The Nazis detained every fat Jew and everyone with a potbelly which had not had a chance to cave in. Jews overloaded with flesh are almost nonexistent in the ghetto, but among tens of thousands of passersby even this kind may be found. Even plutocrats, those serious men so hated by the Führer, were good material for the film. On order, they crowd up and push their way into Schultz's while at the same time a waiter shoves them back because of lack of room. All the tables are taken, and other plutocrats sit around them eating rich meals and enjoying sweets and dainties. The Nazis are footing the bill because it is worth their while.

Thus, nothing is lacking in the ghetto. On the contrary, every delight is enjoyed, for the Jews of the ghetto have attained paradise in this life.[71]

The Germans, in addition to staging scenes of bourgeois luxury, forced Jews to act out their depraved visions mocking Jewish piety—as they had earlier forced them to enact the projections of the Germans' excremental and sadistic impulses; this time, they filmed the posed scenes. Kaplan (following the passage above) recalled that

a few days ago the Nazis came to the cemetery and ordered the Jews to make a circle and do a Hasidic dance around a basket full of naked corpses. This too they recorded on film. All of these are segments of some anti-Semitic movie, which upon being spliced together will emerge as a gross falsification of the life of the Jews in the Warsaw ghetto.[72]

There were Jews who did temporarily enjoy better life chances than others, appearing to resemble the celluloid plutocrats as a result of their German connections. These were the gangsters who played many roles simultaneously: German business agent, expeditor, wholesaler, blackmailer, and Gestapo informer. The most noted of them was Abraham Gancwajch. Gancwajch headed a combination known as "The Thirteen," allegedly an independent organization to combat corruption by *Judenrat* functionaries and businessmen. Later, he became a rental collection agent for the Germans and operated a "Special Ambulance Service." The Thirteen owned night spots and obtained an exclusive franchise for horse-drawn conveyances. They could obtain ransoms and arranged scenarios for extortion. Ringelblum came to understand: "This is how it works: The Others detain a Jew. Then somebody from 'The Thirteen' communicates that the man can be let go for a large sum of money. They hold the money on deposit."[73]

Gancwajch's background was obscure: "According to himself, Gancwajch was a right Labor Zionist before the war. Some six years ago, he was supposed to have been in Germany, where he is said to have formed a Nazi youth organization."[74] At first, Gancwajch attempted to legitimate his role by philanthropy of a conventional type—charity, support for writers and artists. He played at leading popular movements, pretending to be a militant spokesman and organizer, unhesitatingly unveiling the corrupt. Ringelblum noted these signs with apprehension even before he was convinced that the man was a Gestapo informer, gathering intelligence on the ghetto.

Beginning of June [1941]

At the end of May a conference of sixty—merchants, journalists, doctors, engineers—was called under the auspices of "The Thirteen." . . . Some attended out of fear; others out of curiosity. Gancwajch, the head of "The Thirteen," speaks fairly well and won over some people who knew nothing of his scoundrely deeds. They think he can really accomplish things, particularly after he asserts that he can help with the food supply. The only thing is he needs a citizens' committee to show he has some popular backing. He set up a food-supply commission, a children's-aid commission, headed by Dr. Korcszak, a cultural commission, and so forth. Lately he has achieved some cheap victories by arresting a couple of thieving Poles and ethnic Germans.[75]

He observed soon after this entry that Gancwajch, who besides his rental collection monopoly had also obtained a garbage concession, was advertising his ability to negotiate with the Nazis and restore employment to the ghetto, intimating that he could cope better than could the *Judenrat*. His "Office to Combat Speculation" weighed bread from bakeries, as do modern consumer affairs departments and nongovernment critics. Later that month Ringelblum noted:

Unfortunately, there are many people who allow themselves to fall under the spell of Gancwajch's sweet talk—his energetic demonstration of the great services he is capable of performing for the Jews, the evil decrees he has already averted, and the things he could do if he had the support of Jewish society. The persuasiveness of his speeches (he is a polished speaker in both Yiddish and Hebrew) quickly evaporates, however. People sober up; he leaves a bitter aftertaste in the mouth.—Recently, "The Thirteen" formed a youth section of the Special Service, headed by the . . . scoundrel Katz.—There are three currencies in the Ghetto: hard, soft, and Gancwajch.[76]

Gancwajch attempted to buy off potential critics by supporting them. Ringelblum observed in May 1942:

Gancwajch, e.g., is turning into a regular Maecenas, supporting Jewish literature, art, theater. He arranges "receptions" for Jewish writers and artists, where there is plenty of food—nowadays the important thing. A short time ago he threw an all-night party at the El Dorado night spot. . . . The party was opened with the dedication of an ambulance, named Miriam (after Gancwajch's wife at home). . . . To help them meet their Passover needs, Gancwajch sent the Jewish writers 6,000 zlotys.[77]

CHARITY AND JUSTICE: CRITICISM AND "COMIC" PERFORMANCES

By the winter of 1941-1942, the chief function of voluntary charities endowed by Gancwajch and others was to celebrate their donors. Most houses had no coal, and lacked gas and electricity for weeks on end. Kaplan also endured the cold despite the fact that he had ordered coal in August and legally was entitled to priority because he conducted classes at home. But the lot of those behind walls could not compare with those in the street. Ringelblum recorded in mid-November 1941:

> The first frosts have already appeared and the populace is trembling at the prospect of cold weather. The most fearful sight is that of freezing children. Little children with bare feet, bare knees, and torn clothing, stand dumbly in the street weeping. Tonight, the 14th [of November], I heard a tot of three or four yammering. The child will probably be found frozen to death tomorrow morning, a few hours off. Early October, when the first snows fell, seventy children were found frozen to death on the steps of ruined houses. Frozen children are becoming a general phenomenon. The police are supposed to open a special institution for street children at 20 Nowolipie Street; meanwhile, children's bodies and crying serve as a persistent background for the Ghetto. People cover the dead bodies of frozen children with the handsome posters designed for Children's Month, bearing the legend, "Our Children, Our Children Must Live—A Child Is the Holiest Thing." That's how people express their protest against the failure of CENTOS to collect these children in a center and save them from certain death in the street. Especially when it is known that CENTOS has collected almost a million zlotys from taxes (postal payments, bread ration cards, etc.)[78]

Mary Berg noted on 22 November 1941 that

> sometimes a mother cuddles a child frozen to death, and tries to warm the inanimate little body. Sometimes a child huddles against his mother, thinking she is asleep and trying to awaken her, while, in fact, she is dead.[79]

A few of the orphaned were more fortunate, but their sponsors were indifferent in charity as in business to others' plight, overlooking adults and other orphans outside their institutions. Ringelblum complained on 30 May 1942 about the implications of Abraham Gepner's philosophy:

> Still another element in the Ghetto is opposed to relief for adults—Abraham Gepner, the president of the former Merchants' Association. Now he's responsible for food supply and in this role can dispose of significant sums of money. Gepner is a fine man, but a capricious one. . . . The policies of Gepner's Food Supply Agency are scandalous and deserve special treatment. But Gepner, who is now childless (his children have left the country), pours out all his fatherly feelings on other children. He has become the great patron of children in the Ghetto—not of all children, however, but only of those who are lucky enough to be sheltered in the home whose patronage he has taken over. These children live, literally, in luxury—all the others may perish. His children are provided with the best of clothing, shoes, entertainment—on the other hand, the children in the refugee centers haven't the barest necessities. They die from hunger under squalid conditions. "Our children must live" is Gepner's slogan; but "our children" means only the children of his homes.[80]

In the demimonde of easy death and fast living, prophecy and criticism emerged in new forms. Among the beggars, one more talented, innovative, and aggressive is recalled by several writers. Rubinstein, supposedly a madman, mocked the powerful. Playing the role of the tolerated jester telling dangerous truths behind the mask, Rubinstein prospered because of both his popularity and the threat he astutely invoked. Alexander Donat, a former Warsaw newspaper publisher, recalls him in richest detail:

One of the most celebrated Ghetto sights was the famous Rubinstein, half-madman, half-clown. Small and dark, he roamed the streets with his peculiar hopping gait, uttering wild yells or singing, *"Alle Glaych, urym yn raych!"* (Everyone's equal, rich and poor!) It was never clear just how mad he really was, but in that mad time and place Rubinstein certainly made out better than many normal people. When he was hungry, he would stand in front of the best-stocked food store in the Ghetto, screaming at the top of his lungs, "Down with Hitler! Down with the German murderers!" which was quite enough to bring the proprietor running out to load Rubinstein with food and get him to stop that bullet-inviting blackmail. The *noveaux riches* of the Ghetto often invited Rubinstein to dinner in restaurants to amuse them and he never disappointed his hosts. "How many of us are going to survive?" he would inquire, and then answer his own question, "Fifty-five." Asked to explain, he would do the following arithmetic: Add 26 Grzybowska (the *Judenrat* address) to 13 Leszno Street (the address of The Thirteen) and 14 Leszno Street (Kon and Heller) and you got 53. By adding the chief undertaker of the Ghetto, Pinkiert, and himself, Rubinstein got 55.

To the question, "Who should drop dead?" Rubinstein would reply, "Forty!" Adding the *Judenrat's* 26 to Ganzweich's [Gancwajch] 13, you got 39; then add Hitler to get 40.

Only those who were madmen did not fear the Germans and dared to behave aggressively, and perhaps in that situation they were normal in being able to comprehend the nature of the Nazis.

The normal ones walked past the food-store windows on Karmelicka Street and looked at them, admiring the lavish displays of delicacies, pastries, cold meats. . . . It was not unusual for people dying of starvation to be found right beside those shop windows, and the sight of their bodies covered with newspapers lying next to such lush displays of food was doubly unbearable. Yet not once in the history of the Ghetto did starving mobs ever attempt to break into those stores.[81]

On 6 April 1941, Ringelblum recorded 61 night spots in the ghetto. Kaplan described them on 7 January 1942:

Places of entertainment function in the ghetto, and they are full to overflowing every evening. Should anyone venture into the ghetto without knowing his whereabouts and enter one of the luxurious cafes, he would be astounded. Who would believe that the lavishly dressed crowds enjoying the music, pastries, and coffee are the persecuted victims of tyranny? The innocent visitor would never suspect the truth until he looked around outside too. Sometimes at the very entrance of one of these elegant cafes he might stumble on the corpse of a victim of starvation.

Leszno Street has the distinction of being the entertainment center of the ghetto. Operating here are all the pleasure places which welcome the smugglers, the black marketeers, and all those fortunates who live off our troubles. Every child in the ghetto knows who they are and what prices they charge.[82]

The less fortunate—now paupers—were dependent on the soup kitchens sponsored by the *Judenrat*. The *Judenrat* had resorted to raising most of its taxes at the point of purchase, throwing the burden on the poorest classes. Ringelblum saw this as a function of the class system. He observed in January 1942 that

periods of break-up have the virtue of illuminating like a giant searchlight evils that have previously been concealed. During these days of hunger, the inhumanity of the Jewish upper class has clearly shown itself. The entire work of the Jewish Council is an evil perpetrated against the poor that cries to the very heaven. If there were a God in the world, he would have long ago flung his thunderbolts and leveled that whole den of wickedness and hypocrisy of those who flay the hide of the poor. . . . The poor people have to meet the costs of their own relief. Adults, for example, pay 70 groschen for a lunch, when it costs only 50, so as to cover with the extra 20 groschen the deficit created because the children only pay 25 for the same lunch. The same is true of the 10 per cent the Council takes from the sales of produce. It is taken impartially from the millionaire and the poorest beggar. The same goes for the work battalions. Here, again, the upper class pays groschen, while the impoverished middle class and the poor, who suffer the most, pay proportionately higher taxes. Those who suffer most are the poor who are the sickest and have to sell all their possessions to buy medicine.[83]

Kaplan condemned the same practices, but explained them as examples of the same human venality and corruption that the prophets condemned in ancient Israel. He wrote on 23 May 1942:

After the Nazi leech comes the *Judenrat* leech. There is no difference between the one and the other but that of race.
    Do you wish to consider its ethical quality? Read it from the book of Isaiah: ". . . everyone loveth bribes, and followeth after rewards; they judge not the fatherless, neither doth the cause of the widow come unto them." The *Judenrat* has conducted a program of taxation which has no parallel anywhere in the world. Out of every zloty you spend on household expenses, you "contribute" about forty per cent, through fraud, for the benefit of the *Judenrat*. A tax of forty per cent has been placed on medicines, and for every zloty of the basic price, you pay one zloty and 40 groszy. Even postage stamps are not free of a high tax for the benefit of the *Judenrat*, besides an additional charge for every official manipulation. All this is by law. But illegally, when you need any service from the minions of the *Judenrat*, you can never arrange your affair without behaving in accordance with the principle that one hand washes the other.
    There is no end to the tales of its mischief and abominations. All along I have been careful not to write them down for fear of exaggeration and overstatement, until I saw for myself. On my honor, I do not exaggerate in the slightest. Once an entire delegation from the *Judenrat* entered my apartment (of three rooms and a

kitchen) to requisition one of the rooms for a family of refugees. The reason? I am charged with occupying an apartment in an illegal way. Instead of twelve tenants, only seven tenants are registered in my apartment. . . .

This visit occurred at a time when my wife was sick with typhus. I opposed the demand of the delegation on the ground that the room was occupied by a woman with a contagious disease who was sick to the point of death. But the delegation stuck to its demand . . . we began a bitter, angry argument . . . while we were still arguing, the refugee signaled that he wanted a word with me, and in private he bared his soul. . . . If I will reimburse him for his expenses, he will backtrack and inform the delegation that he will forgo this apartment.

When I heard his proposal my eyes lit up. But I bargained with him. The refugee demanded 100 zloty; I offered 20. In the end he agreed to accept 20. Right away the delegation found an excuse to make light of the whole affair. They drafted a protocol that the apartment was full and their requisition nullified. Later on I found out that I need not have been so afraid. This is the way the delegation acts with all of its creatures. They hadn't come to confiscate, but rather to receive 20 zloty. The "refugee" was hired for the occasion.[84]

RECOGNITION OF THE FINAL SOLUTION

General apprehension of a graver threat than gradual starvation grew during the winter of 1941–1942 and the spring of 1942. A decree posted on 1 November 1941, which threatened Jews with death for leaving the ghetto without a pass, was first enforced by the execution of eight Jews on 17 November 1941. Ringelblum described it on 22 November 1941:

The execution of eight Jews, including six women, has set all Warsaw trembling. We've gone through all kinds of experiences here in Warsaw, and in other cities, as well, particularly in Lithuania, where mass executions are common. But all past experience pales in the face of the fact that eight people were shot to death for crossing the threshold of the Ghetto. . . .

Among the six women were a beggar, a mother of three, a sixteen-year-old, fearfully hysterical before the execution. Rabbi Wajnberg was also present, with evidence from one of the sentenced men. It is said that the prisoners bore themselves calmly. At night red posters appeared, signed by Auerswald, notifying the Ghetto that the death sentence had been carried out. It was typical that all eight had been arrested by Polish policemen. One woman lost her life over 100 zlotys. She offered a policeman only 50 zlotys to let her go; he insisted on 150 zlotys. One of the two men was a glazier who supported his family by working on the Other Side. Another 400 Jews have since been arrested, of whom 20 have already been sentenced to death by the court.[85]

Terror gripped the ghetto as petty smugglers, on whom the poor were most dependent, were most threatened. The ghetto served as a place of execution for all of Warsaw and a meeting place for other illegal exchanges, and Jews were subject to extortion by German, Jewish, and Polish officials. Ringelblum noted in April 1942:

The demoralization of the Polish police and Polish secret agents is indescribable. They do nothing in the Ghetto but move about detaining wagons full of merchandise and extorting protection money. The populace shivers at the sight of them and gives them whatever they ask. They get monthly payments from each of the merchants — the secret agents from the crowd that hangs around Franciszkanska Street get 200 zlotys from every leather merchant. One of the merchants collects the protection money and brings each of the eight agents in the district his share. Anyone who wants to open up a secret grain mill has first to report to the agents and pay them off.[86]

As if she were noting a commonplace, Mary Berg wrote on 27 February 1942 that "shootings have now become very frequent at the ghetto exits. Usually they are perpetrated by some guard who wants to amuse himself. Every day, morning and afternoon, when I go to school, I am not sure whether I will return alive."[87] Twice before she had almost been shot — once a German policeman had begun shooting without any warning at 4:00 P.M., and at another time she was fired upon during a manhunt on the streets in the evening.

While some smugglers paid off officials, others were shot by officials' orders. Dread moved like an incubus from the wall into the midst of the ghetto. Seemingly random victims were punished by massacre. German police invaded ghetto flats in the middle of the night of 18 April 1942 — 52 Jews were murdered. Since Kaplan — and, we may assume, less politically wise ghetto dwellers — did not immediately understand why these victims had been selected, his description of the massacre best communicates the terror it inspired.

> At midnight the massacre began. Carrying a list of names, four killers to a group, with a Jewish policeman showing them the way, set out for the homes of those who had been condemned to die. In their hands they carried pistols while machine guns were slung on their hips. They rang the bell at a gate. Wherever the killers did not have to cool their heels waiting, the life of the concierge was safe. But a concierge who delayed opening on the instant became the first victim of the bullets. Six gatekeepers lost their lives in this manner although their names were not on the list. Strangely enough, the Nazis were very courteous on this deadly mission. They began with a polite "Good evening," then asked the condemned man to step into the courtyard. With a powerful flash light lighting the scene they stood the victim against a wall and with a shot or two put an end to his life. They left the body at the gate and hurried on to the next place.[88]

Kaplan later discovered they had been printing an illegal newsletter and presumed that they had been betrayed by Gestapo informants within the ghetto. On 10 June 1941 Mary Berg recorded receiving an illegal multigraph paper with news from the BBC. Fear and trembling spread throughout the city as Aryan Poles became targets. Kaplan wrote on 22 April:

> The sound of shots continues through the day and into the night: . . . Rumor has it that the wave of political terrorism has swept over the Aryan quarter too. Today something happened in Zoliwosz that will certainly affect the Aryans. A

man shot and killed a German gendarme . . . the killer, in a real frenzy of fear, jumped off the tram, ran to a nearby rooftop, and jumped to his death. His suicide, however, did not serve as atonement for his fellow-Aryans. Hundreds were immediately arrested on Kerczelli Square and its vicinity.[89]

Shooting and entrapment of smugglers at the wall were common sights during May. On 23 May, Ringelblum reported: "The Gesia Street jail now contains more than 1,300 prisoners, over 500 of them being children. Some are to be tried in the Special Court. . . . The Special Court has already pronounced more than 200 death sentences, not yet executed."[90]

However, it is clear that Ringelblum, Kaplan, and Berg recognized the possibility of mass extermination before the increase of terror within the ghetto in the spring of 1942. Throughout 1941 Ringelblum gathered information on how prisoners were tortured, starved, and/or frozen to death. As early as 28 February 1941 he distinguished between "extermination barracks" and "work camps." On 30 August 1941, he recounted an SS massacre of Jewish prisoners, among whom there were a few cases of typhus, at a "voluntary work camp" near Chelm. Yet there was no intimation that this was a premeditated and general plan. In September 1941 the fear that typhus would be used as a provocation for more massacres is again expressed.

> The Pomiechowek affair, in which 800 people were exterminated because they were sick, caused the Jewish populace of the Ghetto to tremble, because it demonstrates what can be expected to happen here if the attempt to arrest the spread of disease inside the Ghetto should fail. There is also talk about a drastic resettlement of Jews from the Ghetto because of the epidemics here. In general, they blame the Jewish populace for spreading typhus in the provinces, claiming that the Jews who flee Warsaw carry typhus with them everywhere they go.[91]

In November, Ringelblum expressed the fear that Jews were being eliminated through coercive birth control: "The beginning of November '41, news from Lodz that the Lodz Jews had been prohibited from marrying and having children. Women pregnant up to three months have to have an abortion. In a word—Pharaoh's laws revived by the Prussians."[92]

There is a gap in Ringelblum's notes (those that have been discovered and translated) between December 1941 and April 1942 so that we cannot date exactly when information about systematic massacres in the East executed by or instigated by special extermination units was first received. We know from reconstructing the journeys of the couriers from the youth movements that conveyed news of the Vilna (and other) massacres to Warsaw and the news transmitted by the Oneg Shabbat to the BBC that he must have known of these by February 1942. The couriers were usually young women who could pass as Polish peasants, recruited from the socialist and Zionist youth movements that had branches throughout Poland. In April 1942 Ringelblum recorded:

> Rumors were thick that an extermination squad had come to Warsaw and had begged permission to go on a rampage through the ghetto for just two hours. But

permission was not granted. Auerswald wouldn't agree. Some people say that when the extermination squad arrived in Warsaw from the provinces it found orders to move on to the front. This rumor is associated with the fact that there are various foreign contingents in Warsaw, such as Lithuanians and Ukrainians, and they're just waiting for the right moment to start a pogrom. Besides, one is always hearing reports about extermination squads that are wiping complete Jewish settlements off the face of the earth.

One hundred sixty-four of the German Jews who came to Warsaw a few days ago, the cream of the young people, including a large number of *chalutzim* preparing to migrate to Palestine, were sent to the penal camp at Treblinki, near Sokolow, where most of them were exterminated in a short time. In three weeks, out of 160 Jewish young people from Otwock only 38 were left.[93]

Kaplan had heard earlier rumors with genocidal themes before the spring of 1942. He reported on 22 December 1941 rumors mixing the threat of genocide through population control with medieval segregation:

Some of the guess work is so funny that one can't help laughing. Nevertheless, wild stories are circulating and upsetting everyone. Now then, what are the impending disasters? Lend an ear and listen:

1. Jews will be forbidden to marry and bring a new generation into the world.
2. Husbands and fathers will be castrated to prevent procreation.
3. The curfew will be moved back from nine to five P.M.
4. The blue-and-white "badge of shame" with the Star of David as its background will be replaced by the "yellow patch," relic of the Middle Ages. Moreover, instead of one badge we'll be forced to wear two: one in front, the other in back.
5. Jews will be forced to wear shoes with wooden soles.
6. Jews will be required to wear a uniform hat, a *shtreiml* pointed at the top like a pyramid.
7. Jewish currency will be issued. In Lodz it will be called *Chaimkes* and in Warsaw, *Adamkes,* each named for the local *Judenrat* chairman. The purpose of this special Jewish currency is to cut off permanently all contact between Jews and non-Jews.[94]

By 2 February 1942 he suspected the whole plan.

The latest rumors of new decrees, though they may be exaggerated, must contain some grain of truth.

It is reported that the Führer has decided to rid Europe of our whole people by simply having them shot to death. There is no longer any pretense of legal authorization with all the accompanying byplay. You just take thousands of people to the outskirts of a city and shoot to kill; that is all.

The reports are bloodcurdling:

In Wilno 40,000 Jews were shot to death without a trial or even charges. The survivors number only 10,400.

In Slonim someone killed a Nazi. The Nazi there knew very well that the murderer was not a Jew. But it was a good opportunity for a bloodbath. Eight thousand Jews were shot to death outside the town.

The day before yesterday we read the speech the Führer delivered celebrating January 30, 1933 [sic],* when he boasted that his prophecy was beginning to come true. Had he not stated that if war erupted in Europe, the Jewish race would be annihilated? This process has begun and will continue until the end is achieved. For us the speech serves as proof that what we thought were rumors are in effect reports of actual occurrences. The *Judenrat* and the Joint have documents which confirm the new direction of Nazi policy toward the Jews in the conquered territories: death by extermination for entire Jewish communities.

Heretofore we were afraid of expulsion. Now we are afraid of death. Moreover, signs of expulsion are becoming evident daily.

The *Judenrat* is arranging for a roll call of ghetto Jews. By January 31, 1942, every ghetto dweller must note on a questionnaire his own and his parents' names; his family status; his address in Warsaw prior to the war and his present address; his occupation before September 1, 1939, and his present occupation. Does not this roll call portend catastrophe?

Exiles from other cities tell us that in their cities, too, the evacuations began with such a roll call. In the meantime, we tremble in fear.[95]

The only element his information did not account for was the use of mechanical innovations—the gas vans used previously in Chelmno and in Serbia and the gas chambers that were not yet in general use. By 3 June he was certain that the deportees from Lublin were murdered, although he did not know where or how:

The deportees are transported as prisoners in tightly sealed freight cars under the supervision of Nazi oppressors. They are in the care of these angels of destruction until they come to the place of execution, where they are killed. Many of the deportees, among them mothers and their infants, are put to death along the way; the remainder are brought to some secret place, unknown even to the hawk, and there killed in satanic fashion, by the thousands and tens of thousands. The community of Lublin has lost all its sons. About 40,000 Jews of Lublin have disappeared, and no one knows their burial place. Aryan messengers were commissioned to search for them through the entire General Government, but they found not a trace. It is as though the 40,000 had been swallowed up by stormy waters. But there is no doubt that they are no longer alive.

Lublin was the first to drink the cup of sorrow to the dregs, but not the last. Since then not a day passes without some Jewish settlement being completely wiped off the face of the earth.[96]

The friends of Mary Berg also began to anticipate their death. Mary recalled the mournful New Year's Eve of 1942 they spent together after the last performance of the LZA:

I feel completely empty, as though I were suspended over an abyss. Last night was a mixture of entertainment and nightmare. After the performance my friends of the LZA suggested that we spend New Year's Eve at my home. . . . Instead of champagne we had lemonade, and instead of cake, sandwiches of little pickled fishes, the so-called "stinkies." . . .

* The actual date of this warning was January 30, 1939; see Chapter 1, p. 24.

In the semidarkness I saw Romek place his fingers on the keyboard. With a great effort he began to play Chopin's Funeral March. No one said a word. Anka huddled close to Harry, Dolek to Stefa, Tadek to Bronek—all of them were together; only I was alone. Sad ideas flashed through my mind. Was not all this symbolic? Was there not something terrible in store for me, something that would separate me from my friends?

Suddenly someone cried out: "Romek, how about a different number? He has never been able to play the Funeral March, and now of all nights the Muse is helping him." Romek did not answer. He tried a few other notes, but nothing came. At last, he rose from the piano and sat down by my side. "You know," he whispered, "I have a strange premonition on this New Year's Day, mark my words."

I do not know what he meant, but even in the semidarkness I could read utter despair in his eyes.

A little later we all began to talk. Harry said that our theater group no longer had any reason for existence because most of our members were gone, and that we would have to find new people, which was not easy. No one contradicted him. Apparently, we all felt the same. All of us were overwhelmed by the same apathy, the feeling that this was the end.[97]

Mary recorded on 15 April 1942 how a neighbor's relative had recently arrived in the ghetto who witnessed

the terrible massacre of Lublin, during which he lost his wife and two children. Here is his story: "The Germans ordered all the Jews to leave their homes and gather in the square. The majority did not obey this order, and began to hide in cellars and attics. . . . About half of the ghetto population was murdered, and a considerable number were deported to an unknown destination. About two thousand Jewish people remained of the original forty thousand." . . .

Recently wild rumors have begun to circulate in the ghetto. It is said that all the Jews will be settled in Arabia or somewhere near there. I wonder what it all means?[98]

Two days later, Jewish police tipped her and other tenants off as to the impending massacre, believing it to be the sign of general extermination:

I am almost hysterical. A little before six o'clock today the police captain, Hertz, rushed excitedly into our apartment and said: "Please be prepared for anything; at eight o'clock there is going to be a pogrom." Then he tore out without further explanations. The whole ghetto was seized with panic. People hastily closed their stores. There was a rumor that a special Vernichtungskommando (destructive squad), the same which had perpetrated the Lublin pogrom, had arrived in Warsaw to organize a massacre here. It was also said that Ukrainians and Lithuanians would now take over the guarding of the ghetto because the Germans were to go to the Russian front.[99]

But the massacre was of individual victims and the prevalent recognition was that the extermination would not be general—"It can't happen here." Mary recorded on 8 May:

Hertz says that "soon everything will be over and all of us will be killed." But most people think that a pogrom like the one in Lublin cannot happen in Warsaw, because there are too many people here. According to official figures, there are 450,000 inhabitants in the ghetto, but, . . . It is estimated that the total is really more than 500,000. To exterminate such a number of people seems impossible, inconceivable. Yet if the present nightly murders continue, it is quite possible that half the ghetto population will be dead before the war is over.[100]

WAS THE WHOLE WORLD WATCHING?

What action did such a threat incite? How did these men and women use their information and anticipations?

From the beginning, the Oneg Shabbat network was a political act of gathering intelligence and publishing news weekly. The Germans testified to their effectiveness by liquidating the editors, writers, and distributors of underground papers in the ghetto massacre of 18 April 1942. Working through the Bund, which was then represented in the Polish government-in-exile, Oneg Shabbat transmitted specific information on the pattern of massacre and gassing between March and May 1942, estimating that 700,000 Jews had by then been killed. The BBC first mentioned that number on 2 June 1942 in its news broadcast and, pressed by the Polish National Council in London, allowed Shmuel Zygelbojm, the Bund representative, to broadcast the report more fully on 26 June 1942.[101] Almost with a sigh of gratification, Ringelblum wrote in June:

> Friday, June 26, has been a great day for [Oneg Shabbat]. This morning, the English radio broadcast about the fate of Polish Jewry. They told about everything we know so well: about Slonim and Vilna, Lemberg and Chelmno, and so forth. For long months we had been suffering because the world was deaf and dumb to our unparalleled tragedy. We complained about Polish public opinion, about the liaison men in contact with the Polish government-in-exile. Why weren't they reporting to the world the story of the slaughter of Polish Jewry? We accused the Polish liaison men of deliberately keeping our tragedy quiet, so that *their* tragedy might not be thrown into the shade. But now it seems that all our interventions have finally achieved their purpose. There have been regular broadcasts over the English radio the last few weeks, treating of the cruelties perpetrated on the Polish Jews: Belzec and the like. Today there was a broadcast summarizing the situation: 700,000, the number of Jews killed in Poland, was mentioned. At the same time, the broadcast vowed revenge, a final accounting for all these deeds of violence.
>
> The O.S. group has fulfilled a great historical mission. It has alarmed the world to our fate, and perhaps saved hundreds of thousands of Polish Jews from extermination. (Naturally, only the immediate future will prove whether or not this last is true.) I do not know who of our group will survive, who will be deemed worthy to work through our collected material. But one thing is clear to all of us. Our toils and tribulations, our devotion and constant terror, have not been in

vain. We have struck the enemy a hard blow. It is not important whether or not the revelation of the incredible slaughter of Jews will have the desired effect—whether or not the methodical liquidation of entire Jewish communities will stop. One thing we know—we have fulfilled our duty. We have overcome every obstacle to achieve our end. Nor will our deaths be meaningless, like the deaths of tens of thousands of Jews. We have struck the enemy a hard blow. We have revealed his Satanic plan to annihilate Polish Jewry, a plan he wished to complete in silence. We have run a line through his calculations and have exposed his cards. And if England keeps its word and turns to the formidable massive attacks that it has threatened—then perhaps we shall be saved.[102]

The messengers seeking to prevent destruction could envision no salvation of the unarmed Jews of the Warsaw ghetto and elsewhere except by Allied threat. And the only threat that they could imagine was reprisal in kind. Bauer writes:

> The authors therefore ask the Polish Government-in-Exile—and through it the major Powers—to threaten German nationals residing in Allied countries with the fate that the Germans have in store for the Jew. This demand, impossible as it was from the point of view of the free world, was thought to be "the only possibility of saving millions of Jews from destruction," as seen from the desperate perspective of the ghetto.[103]

The response (or, more precisely, lack of response) to this news is surveyed in Chapter 7.

Although Kaplan knew of the work of the Oneg Shabbat, he was ignorant of its organization. His attitude toward illegal political activities of Poles and Jews was mixed. Sometimes he condemned these acts as provocations for which all would pay, and at other times he praised the Bundist editors' courage. He feared that the Polish Socialist Party (political allies of the Bundists) was inciting a rebellion that would provoke retaliatory slaughter, claiming the Jews as the first victims. Thus, he saw their actions as a cynical tactic, "playing at rebellion."

> Nevertheless, they will not cease their provocations because they want to attain a strategic aim: to keep military forces in the rear, engaged in putting down the "rebellions" and thus weakening the forces at the front. It is only the old Jesuit stratagem that "the end justifies the means."[104]

As the terror increased, Kaplan's despair grew. Others turned to messianic hopes reflected in rumor and fantasy life among Jews, recorded by Ringelblum and Kaplan in June. Some reiterated earlier beliefs (reflected in rumors Kaplan recorded on 10 March 1941 and 10 November 1940) that Roosevelt would be their savior. Now, in June 1942, Ringelblum tells us that they were debating what the United Nations could and should do to save them:

> The news that the interpellation of the Polish government-in-exile was radioed by all the British transmitters in all the languages of the United Nations, and several times in German, on Saturday (among others, by the German women's broad-

caster) — and then the speeches delivered by the Archbishop of Canterbury, the Rev. Dr. Hertz, the deputy Zygelbojm — all this news excited Jewish public opinion in Warsaw. There was joy, mingled with fear as to how the Occupying Power would reply. The general feeling was that it was good for the world to know all about everything. Perhaps a way would be found of forcing the Occupying Power to stop the massacres. Zygelbojm's stand and speeches were cited for their talk about retributory acts of repression against Germans in America. . . . Let [the United Nations] use force to stop the massacres in Poland. Another opinion held that the Allies, particularly democratic America, could not massacre Germans [in retribution], first, because they are American citizens, and second, because public opinion would not countenance it. But everyone held that it was most important for Germans to know about the extermination.[105]

Ringelblum believed that the German public was ignorant of the extermination and would react against it if only because they feared retaliation. Occasional conversations were reported with German soldiers in Warsaw who apologized for or attempted to correct the behavior of the "Others" and treated Jews as other humans — a soccer game was even played between the soldiers and Jews, reinforcing the distinction between Germans and Nazis.[106]

DEFENSES: REAL AND ILLUSORY

Rumors of impending salvation by American or British intervention multiplied — President Roosevelt was apparently revered as much by Polish as by American Jews. Gideon Hausner, the Israeli state prosecutor of Adolf Eichmann, remarks:

> Finally, when the rumors were cruelly belied, the disillusioned Jews invented a mocking nickname for their origin: they all emanated, it was said, from the telegraphic agency YWA ("Yidden Willen Azoi" — "Jews want it that way").[107]

As the apprehension of threat escalated, people clung to their hopes of rescue. All the resources of Jewish tradition were drawn upon to create wish-fulfilling prophecies. Michael Zylberberg has recalled how

> as the situation deteriorated daily, so the religious Jews sought hope in the supernatural, turning to a new cabbalistic [from Cabbala — the major work of medieval Jewish mysticism] interpretation of words from which a shred of comfort might be drawn. This tendency had begun in 1941 and the tortured searchings were even more intense in 1942. For example: a Rabbi reinterpreted the quotation, "When the Sabbath comes it brings with it peace." The Hebrew letters are used as numbers and the letters of the word Sabbath are 702. In the Hebrew calendar the year 702 coincides with 1942. This, they said would be a year of peace, this year would see the end of the war.[108]

The people of the Book also turned to other books for hope. Ringelblum recorded in June that people were reading war memoirs, especially those recounting the downfall of the Germans in World War I and of Napoleon in 1812.

> They attempt to draw analogies between 1918 and the present, looking for signs and omens to demonstrate that the defeat of the so-far-unconquerable German army is at hand. . . . But it is certain that H., like Napoleon, has committed the mortal blunder of tangling with the Russian colossus, with its enormous reserves of manpower and material. Tolstoy's *War and Peace* is enormously popular nowadays. Many people who had already read it several times are reading it all over again because of its portrayal of the Napoleonic disaster.
>
> In a word, being unable to take revenge on the enemy in reality, we are seeking it in fantasy, in literature. This explains our preoccupation with books about previous wars, which we turn to for a solution to the tragic problems of the present war. To my mind, however, all this search for historical analogy is beside the point. History *does not* repeat itself.[109]

Kaplan castigated the majority who denied the impending catastrophe, through the literary device of an imaginary interlocutor, Hirsch. He wrote on 7 June 1942:

> Never were we so hopeful of the final Nazi downfall as during these days, days in which our tribulations grow worse from hour to hour. . . . Jewish faith is marvelous; it can create states of mind that have nothing to do with reality. Like the believing Jewish grandfather who in anticipation of the Messiah always wore his Sabbath clothes. . . . The English radio, whose listeners endanger their lives, strengthens our hope. . . . When the news doesn't tell us what we want to hear, we twist and turn it until it seems full of hints, clues, and secrets that support our views. . . . Hirsch, my wise friend, is an exception. He is the only one who sits like a mourner among bridegrooms. "Idiots!" he shouts, and his face becomes red with anger. "Your hope is in vain; your trust is a broken reed. All of you are already condemned to die, only the date of execution has yet to be set."[110]

Two days later, Kaplan recorded more nights of butchery. While people attempted to find a common denominator among the victims, thus reassuring themselves they would not be next, he saw German violence against Jews as being a response to their own ideology and needs.

> Never before in history has any tyranny ever allowed itself to proclaim publicly that it is preparing to annihilate an entire people. In their bitterness they wreak all their anger upon us, and as their defeats increase so will their persecutions.[111]

Gestapo collaborators in the ghetto became victims also. Ringelblum recorded on 25 May that "the biggest wheels of 'The Thirteen' had been liquidated the night before."[112]

By 15 June 1942, Kaplan recognized some pattern behind the massacre:

> There is no system to the Nazi killing, but nevertheless the most obvious objective of this carnage is to purge the ghetto of smuggling. In the main, the victims of the shootings are smugglers. The smallest shadow of suspicion that So-and-so is engaged in smuggling is enough to make him a candidate for murder. Jews are not

judged, they are merely punished, and there is no lighter punishment for them than death by shooting.

There is continuous war between the cruel, dim-witted Nazis who have condemned us to subsist for a whole month on two kilos of bread apiece and the members of the ghetto who want to live. Even the death penalty has not reduced smuggling. If you can afford to pay 25 zloty for a loaf of white bread, someone will throw it into your mouth any time, at any hour you wish. . . .

And now for the clincher! The Nazis themselves are engaging in smuggling, because it is worth their while. The mice of smuggling, the miserable creatures who smuggle small quantities of produce through the wall, are put to death by the tens, and their death is their penance. This is not the kind of smuggling the Nazis abet. The real smugglers sit at home and no danger awaits them.[113]

Kaplan's Hirsch no longer mourned but screamed:

June 16, 1942

"Cowards! A whole community of millions of people stands on the brink of destruction, and you keep silent! You delude yourselves out of hope that the evil will not reach you; you have eyes and see not. Are you any better than the people of Lublin? The people of Cracow? The people of Lodz? If not today, then tomorrow or the next day you will be taken out like lambs to the slaughter. Protest! Alarm the world! Don't be afraid! In any case you will end by falling before the sword of the Nazis. Chicken-hearted ones! Is there any meaning to your deaths?"[114]

As consciousness of the impending catastrophe grew, the occupiers diverted energies and anxiety by holding out the hope for personal exception; they announced that Jews could register for emigration. People rushed to be on line at the queues at the rescue office that the *Judenrat* had established. Kaplan, on 20 June 1944, recorded his conviction that it would be another swindle, merely enabling the Jewish police, the *Judenrat*, and the Gestapo to profit; he was right, of course.

After much hesitation because of uncertainty that her personal protection as a foreign national would be extended to her family, Mary Berg's mother registered with the Gestapo to be interned as a citizen of the Unites States for repatriation. Anticipation of doom was prevalent in the ghetto, and she was seen by acquaintances as a saving link to relations in the free world. Mary reported that

there is a real pilgrimage to our house now; an endless line of persons keeps coming to my mother to give her the addresses of their relatives and friends in America so that she can ask them for help. The exchange is supposed to take place on July 6. Everyone wants the same thing: they must send us affidavits, they must help us get out . . . and don't forget to tell them what we are going through here . . . and please let this be the first thing you do when you get to America, don't delay one minute, so that we may live to see the moment of our liberation. . . . All of them pour their troubles out to my mother — they have nothing left to sell, nothing to live on, in another few months they will perish.[115]

There was no longer any possibility of study:

Fewer and fewer students come to our school; now they are afraid to walk in the streets. The Nazi guard Frankenstein is going through the ghetto, one day he kills ten persons, another day five . . . everyone expects to be his next victim. A few days ago I, too, ceased completely attending school. The heat is terrible. . . .

The man hunts in the ghetto continue. There are also rumors of the imminent deportation of the whole ghetto. I do not know whence comes the monstrous report that the Warsaw Jews have only forty days left to live. Everyone is repeating this rumor. No doubt the Germans have spread it themselves in order to create a panic. Many Jews are registering at the so-called "shops," which are now mostly on Lezno Street. These are workrooms which chiefly produce German military uniforms. It is said that the people employed in these workshops will not be deported.[116]

On 16 July the Gestapo decided that the entire family was protected by Mrs. Berg's United States citizenship. Mary was intensely relieved but filled with the guilt of evasion as her friends' envy and despair poured out in leave-taking.

Romek came to see me at eight o'clock (curfew does not begin until ten). He refused to believe that I was about to go to America. He looked at me strangely, as though he were sure he would never see me again. We walked along Chlodna Street. Today I boldly removed my arm band. After all, officially I am now an American citizen. Romek pressed my arm and kept repeating, "I know you're not going, it's only a joke, isn't it? You won't leave me alone, you won't go." The inhabitants of the street looked at me with curiosity: "That's the girl who is going to America." In this street everyone knows everyone else. Every few minutes people approached me and asked me to note the addresses of their American relatives, and to tell them to do everything possible for their unfortunate kin. . . .

I am saying farewell to the ghetto. It is dark and quiet everywhere, but it seems to me that from somewhere in the distance there is a sound of sobbing. I see Romek's face before me just as it was when he said good-by to me. I told him to go, that it would be better for both of us . . . but he refused, and when, finally, the lateness of the hour forced him to leave he refused to shake hands with me. "I know," he said, "that if I shake hands with you I will say 'see you again,' and I don't want to say that because I know we'll never see each other again."[117]

Publicity regarding emigration opportunities masked the initiation of the Final Solution, just as it had within the German bureaucracies before 1941. Czerniakow, who had heard the same reports of mass extermination since 27 October 1941 as had Ringelblum, sought reassurance by inquiring of his supervisory German Kommissar, Auerswald, if reports of impending deportation were true. Auerswald replied negatively.

On 8 July 1942, Czerniakow observed:

Many people hold a grudge against me for organizing play activity for the children, for arranging festive openings of playgrounds, for the music, etc. I am reminded of a film: a ship is sinking and the captain to raise the spirits of the passengers orders the orchestra to play a jazz piece. I have made up my mind to emulate the captain.

But the rumors persisted and his anxiety escalated. On 19 July, he recorded that he kept trying to smile and calm the population. But he could not calm himself even with two headache powders, a pain reliever, and a sedative. It seems he was not sufficiently reassuring, so he inquired of the Gestapo on 20 July 1942; the report was denied as usual. The *Judenrat* published an official denial of the reports of impending deportation.

On 22 July, the deportation order was issued by the Gestapo through the *Judenrat* as agent of publication but without Czerniakow's signature. He had appealed to widen the category of exemptees, to protect orphans, Jewish self-aid workers, and laborers, but only the workers were exempted. On the day that the notice was posted that all inhabitants of the ghetto except workers and employees of the *Judenrat* and the JSS must report for "resettlement," Czerniakow swallowed the pill in his desk drawer.

Did Czerniakow imagine on his last day that he would be remembered in history as the captain of a sinking ship who smiled while jettisoning the children? Kaplan commemorated his end as his redemption:

> The first victim of the deportation decree was the President, Adam Czerniakow, who committed suicide by poison in the *Judenrat* building. He perpetuated his name by his death more than by his life. . . . Czerniakow had refused to sign the expulsion order. He followed the Talmudic law: If someone comes to kill me, using might and power, and turns a deaf ear to all my pleas, he can do to me whatever his heart desires, since he has the power, and strength always prevails. But to give my consent, to sign my own death warrant— this no power on earth can force me to do, not even the brutal force of the foul-souled Nazi.[118]

Opinions varied among ghetto dwellers of Czerniakow's character and of the symbolic value of his suicide. Underground leaders decried his failure to inform the ghetto of the truth and call for resistance.[119] His suicide, however, could not have fortified belief in the authority of the Warsaw *Judenrat* or added credence to any of its future reassurances.

ANNIHILATION: THE HUNT FOR HUMAN PREY

Kaplan had benefited from Czerniakow's appeal for exemption for the Jewish Self-Aid Society workers, as he had secured a certificate from them (along with 2,000 others); we may assume that Ringelblum did also. Many forged certificates were also printed. But certificates were of transient value, and relying on them might actually increase one's risk. Kaplan described the daily hunt for the policemen's quota of victims on 27 July:

> Men have become beasts. Everyone is but a step away from deportation; people are being hunted down in the streets like animals in the forest. It is the Jewish police who are cruelest toward the condemned. Sometimes a blockade is made of a particular house, sometimes of a whole block of houses. In every building ear-

marked for destruction they begin to make the rounds of the apartments and to demand documents. Whoever has neither documents that entitle him to remain in the ghetto nor money for bribes is told to make a bundle weighing 15 kilos—and on to the transport which stands near the gate. Whenever a house is blockaded a panic arises that is beyond imagination. Residents who have neither documents nor money hide in nooks and crannies, in the cellars and in the attics. When there is a means of passage between one courtyard and another the fugitives begin jumping over the roofs and fences at the risk of their lives; in time of panic, when the danger is imminent, people are not fussy about methods. But all these methods only delay the inevitable, and in the end the police take men, women, and children. The destitute and impoverished are the first to be deported. In an instant the truck becomes crowded. They are all like: poverty makes them equal. Their cries and wails tear the heart out. . . .

But isolated incidents don't hold up the operation. The police do what is incumbent upon them. After the completion of the arrests in one house, they move on to another. The *Judenrat* prepares a daily list of houses in which blockades will be made that day. And here a new source of income is opened up for the graft-chasing police. The wealthy and the middle class have yet to be brought to the transports. For those who have no documents, banknotes turn into documents. There is almost a fixed price for ransom, but for some it is cheaper, all according to the class of the ransomed one and the number of people in his household.[120]

The next day, when 10,000 people were seized, Kaplan felt his physical strength failing:

July 28, 1942

The situation grows graver by the hour. Through the window of my apartment near the scene of the "hunting," I beheld those trapped by the hunt, and was so stricken that I was close to madness. For the detainee, the thread of his life is cut in an instant, and the work of an entire lifetime in which his best efforts were invested becomes abandoned property.

Before my very eyes they capture an old woman who walks with a cane. Her steps are measured, and she makes her way with great exertions. She is unable to straighten up. On her face there are marks of nobility and signs of a family status now past. She too was arrested by a lawless Jewish scoundrel. He needs clients, and even this old lady counts, "as is" without clothes or linens, without even food. She will be sent "to the East." She will be fortunate if she doesn't live long. . . . Never in my life had I known the pangs of hunger. Even after I was pushed into the ghetto I ate. But now I too know hunger. I sustain myself for a whole day on a quarter-kilo of bread and unsweetened tea. My strength is diminishing from such meager fare. At times I can't even stand up. I fall on my bed, but rest eludes me. I am in a state of sleep and am not asleep, of wakefulness and yet am not awake. I am plagued by nightmares. Fear and worry preoccupy me—fear lest I be seized and deported; worry about where to find my bread. My income has stopped. The sums owed to me by others are lost. Besides what he needs for food, no one has a penny to his name, and payment of debts isn't taken into consideration at all.[121]

On 29 July he realized that bribes were only temporary, but believed an *Ausweis* (work permit) was a guarantee of safety.

A house which is blockaded today can be blockaded tomorrow too, and the next day, and so on ad infinitum. A man who was released once can be caught again — even by the same policeman who let him go the first time — especially since the police have nearly 2,400 dogs.[122]

The police were selling the loaves of bread, delivered in abundance to use as wiles to entice people in hiding to report: three kilograms were offered to volunteers who reported to the Umschlagplatz, from which place the trains departed, jammed with human cargo. Those who had already lost a spouse during the hunt were more apt to volunteer. Despite bereavement and mass starvation, only one out of 16 victims reported themselves. On 31 July, Kaplan reported that no certificate was safe. "It's just that with a certificate in your pocket hiding is more comfortable."[123]

On 1 August, the SS joined in the hunt:

At seven in the evening the S.S. arrived and ordered the Jewish police to blockade an entire block. They made an announcement in each courtyard: "Prepare bundles weighing 15 kilos and go down into the courtyard. No one is exempt!" Terrible fear gripped the whole area. Everyone senses that his fate had been given over into the hands of insatiable murderers. With the Jewish police the inhabitants could come to a compromise in one way or another, but this time the decree was inexorable. Submit yourselves to your bitter fate!

About 10,000 people were deported and disappeared.[124]

On 2 August, Kaplan foresaw the future of Jewish Warsaw:

Today the population of the "little ghetto" drank the cup of hemlock. At four the murderers set upon their task, and at seven a crowd of 5,000 people was led out through Smocza to the transfer point. All their possessions were left in the hands of the enemy.

Jewish Warsaw is turning into a city of slave laborers who have nothing of their own. The German companies that own the factories concentrate their employees in one section. To achieve this, they confiscate all the houses near a factory and settle the workers and their families in them. Without them there would be no Jewish community. Every activity in the ghetto, and all its establishments, are being brought to an end. Jews who are not employed in one of the factories will be expelled from Warsaw. For the time being they are busy with schemes and plans for hiding until the wrath passes, but the wrath of the Nazis never passes. On the contrary, it increases. Concessions granted on paper never materialize in practice. All of the various *Ausweisen* are voided and nullified. In the end, everyone will be expelled.[125]

Anticipating confiscation of his apartment, he packed his library and paid 2,000 zloty to have it sent to a relative who had secured "worker-status" outside the ghetto: furniture and other household goods would remain for another's enjoyment. All Chaim Kaplan's and his wife's energies were now concentrated on survival:

Yesterday, the third of August, they slaughtered Zamenhof and Pawia streets. They did not confiscate houses, but blockaded the entire block for expulsion. The

S.S. killers stood guard while the Jewish police worked inside the courtyards. This was a slaughter in proper style—they had no pity even on infants and nurslings. All of them, all, without exception, were taken to the gates of death. The fabricated papers of the Self-Aid Society were as useless as though they did not exist. . . .

There is the silence of death in the streets of the ghetto all through the day. The fear of death is in the eyes of the few people who pass by on the sidewalk opposite our window. Everyone presses himself against the wall and draws into himself so that they will not detect his existence or his presence.

Today my block was scheduled for a blockade with Nazi participation. Seventy Jewish policemen had already entered the courtyard. I thought, "The end has come." But a miracle happened, and the blockade was postponed. The destroyers passed on to the Nalewki-Zamenhof block.[126]

But survival did not mean just preserving himself physically. His last problem was summed up in his last recorded words:

If my life ends—what will become of my diary?[127]

The problem was solved with his characteristic tenacity and resourcefulness. Kaplan gave his notebooks to a Jew working at forced labor outside the ghetto who smuggled them to a Pole who first brought them to the attention of Jewish scholars in 1952. But for the penniless, 62-year-old schoolteacher to save himself and his wife was beyond resourcefulness.

The majority of the police failed to save themselves, despite their cooperation in filling their quota of seven heads a day in order to avoid their own deportation. Trunk reports that only 300 of the 2,600 men were spared, the rest being deported with their families on the last day of the action.[128] Besides the Jewish police, reviled by every writer from Warsaw (and other ghettos in which they played the same role), there were Gestapo informants leading Germans to the secret places where people hid. There were also other Jewish control organizations that cooperated, Ringelblum later noted.

Besides the police, another group of [Jewish] organizations shared in the resettlement operation. Gancwajch's red-capped Special Ambulance Service was the worst. This organization of swindlers had never given a single Jew the medical aid they promised. They limited their activity to issuing authorization cards and caps, for thousands of zlotys. . . . It was this petty gang that now voluntarily reported for the assignment of sending Jews to the hereafter—and they distinguished themselves with their brutality and inhumanity. Their caps were covered with the bloodstains of the Jewish people.

The officials of the Jewish Council also cooperated in the "operation," as did the Service of the K.A.M.—City Aid Committee.[129]

REORGANIZATION OF JEWISH CONSCIOUSNESS AND COMMUNITY

At the start of deportations, Jewish leaders of the major parties and prominent scholars and rabbis met to discuss authorizing a collective armed defense despite the lack of arms in the ghetto. Reports on this debate are few but they agree that the conclusion was negative, the majority reasoning along the lines of Chaim Kaplan (see pp. 215, 244), that resistance of an unarmed mass would only provoke massacre of both resistants and nonresistants.[130] Although the nuclei of later developed fighting organizations had been created by July 1942, all groups lacked arms. The first independent military organization was created in December 1939 by young Jews and older Polish Army veterans affiliated with the Zionist revisionist movement.[131] The Bund had also established its own fighting organization, and several Zionist, Socialist, and Communist groups had joined together in an anti-fascist bloc in April 1942, but they had not been able to obtain arms or convince other leaders to support them. The terror had effectively inhibited public political activity between April and July. Although some groups issued pamphlets calling for passive resistance to the deportations, there was no organization of evasion or defense.

Before the community could mobilize to defend itself, their belief in the illusion that they would survive by accommodation had to be destroyed. Then the polity needed to be reorganized. New authorities who could command resources and energies and plan how to sustain the community when isolated emerged after a brief struggle for power. But the new leaders needed links with allies and help from allies was uncertain. No recognition of or identification with the Jews' plight had been voiced by any Polish party between July and September 1942, excepting by the Polish Socialist Party, which rhetorically urged the Jews not to give in through a broadside that did not reach the ghetto.[132]

Although firsthand observers' reports of the destiny of the Jews of Warsaw in the killing center at Treblinka had been received by the Polish resistance from Polish railway workers within a week after deportations began on 22 July 1942, the news was not conveyed to the ghetto—direct reports of Treblinka did not reach the ghetto until mid-August—or announced to the world by the Polish government-in-exile in London until 27 November 1942.[133] While the Polish government-in-exile, speaking from their London base, promised Jews equal rights, Polish right-wing parties, part of that government, proclaimed publicly in their underground newspapers in Poland that the solution to the Jewish problem was expulsion of the Jews. Democratic center parties did not publicize the government's declarations pledging Jews' equal rights and warning against anti-Semitism.[134]

Despite the lack of all other preconditions needed for successful rebellion, the Jews of Warsaw had attained the first precondition of autonomy—freedom from illusion. But they were now even more isolated than before.

After the great deportation ended, the survivors, who lived in enclosed living-working quarters, dependent on their German employers for their lives, worked for nothing; these were, Ringelblum noted, "The Signs of Modern Slaves":

1. Numbered and stamped.
2. Live in barracks—without their wives.
3. Wives and children removed, because slaves don't require families.
4. Walk in crowds, not individually.
5. Beaten and terrorized at work.
6. Inhuman exploitation (agreement at Schultz's [?]) like coolies.
7. Ban on organization of any kind.
8. Ban on any form of protest or sign of dissatisfaction.
9. Every slave dependent for his life on his master and the master's Jewish assistant. At any moment a man can be sent to the Umschlagplatz.
10. The murderous discipline, and the sending of workers to forced [labor] camps because of lateness as happened at Schultz's.
11. Compulsion to work, even [when worker is sick] with temperature.
12. Worse off than slaves, because *they* must look after their own food.
13. Confiscation of property from a dead worker's family, because the right of inheritance has been abolished.
14. Locked inside the residential block.
15. Ban on leaving your apartment and walking in the street after work hours.
16. Limitation of personal freedom of movement.
17. *Worse than slaves,* because the latter knew they would remain alive, had some hope to be set free. The Jews are *morituri*—sentenced to death—whose death sentence [has been] postponed indefinitely, or has been passed.
18. The sick and the weak are not needed, so ambulatory clinics, hospitals, and the like have been liquidated.[135]

Despite the oppression, their definition of the situation had been altered ineradicably. Few families existed for, after the murder of their kin, survivors were left only with each other. A new situational ethic was generally accepted: men and women coupled as if they might die tomorrow.

Perception, recognition, and feelings had altered. Feelings were heightened and sentiment diffused to create new bonds of solidarity that replaced kin. The old sense of time—time to live and time to die—and a natural life cycle endowing one's days with security and predictability had been annulled. Regardless of previous assumptions, the Jews of Warsaw challenged why they had been assigned to die—it was now taken for granted that they had been. Michael Zylberberg recalled:

On Rosh Hashana, 1942, after a massive selection of victims in the ghetto, everyone felt extremely ill at ease. No one knew if the selection—which had started some days previously—had come to an end. People crept out of hiding and asked each other, "What is happening in the streets?" The streets were empty and silent. Suddenly a Jew appeared complete with beard and side-curls, accompanied by an exhausted woman. Both of them could hardly totter. They were covered with feathers and had obviously just crept out of a mountain of bedclothes where they had been hiding. The man kept raising his clenched fists to heaven and the poor woman who led him wept uncontrollably and shouted, "My husband has gone mad." "Jews," he called, "collect large stones and throw them up to heaven! Why has God picked on us for this torment? Give me stones to throw in defiance of heaven!"[136]

Others did not seek revenge against God, but against their enemy who had murdered their kin. Now, knowing that their death was likely if they were caught, they were freed from the dread that had absorbed so much energy in its repression. Ringelblum, singling out the question that would preoccupy future observers, asked himself, "Why?"

Why didn't we resist when they began to resettle 300,000 Jews from Warsaw? Why did we allow ourselves to be led like sheep to the slaughter? Why did everything come so easy to the enemy? Why didn't the hangmen suffer a single casualty? Why could 50 S.S. men (some people say even fewer), with the help of a division of some 200 Ukrainian guards and an equal number of Letts, carry the operation out so smoothly?[137]

He began to explain the "how" behind the "why":

GERMAN WAR STRATEGY AS APPLIED
TO THE JEWS IN WARSAW

The German fear of approaching the large Jewish settlement [in Warsaw]. Fear of [an] uprising, with the help of Poles and paratroopers.

"Divide and rule" — [the German strategy] poisons relations between Jews and Poles and makes any help from that [Polish] quarter impossible. — [The Germans] fooled the populace about [the meaning of the] resettlement. — Chelmno [the death camp where the Lodz Jews were killed] remained a secret to the greater part of the Jews. . . .

[The Germans] set the Warsawers against the refugees. Supposedly the resettlement was to free Warsaw of its "non-productive elements." Promised the Law and Order Service that they and the members of their family, even uncles, mothers-in-law, brothers-in-law, would be secure.

Afterward, they reassured certain shops of their priority over other trades. Afterward, one shop was promised priority over another. — Afterward, women and children in the shops themselves became dispensable — afterward, poor workers as compared with good workers. Better shops were opposed to poorer shops — red stamps — continually contracting the circle, continually deceiving, declaring that the resettlement operation was over, in order to prevent a revolt.

The Niska Street Pot. — The hermetic sealing of the Ghetto limits, to keep out help. — Hermetic sealing of communications inside and outside the country by stopping the post.

Continual blockades throughout the city. To make any kind of counteraction impossible. — Propaganda lies about the resettlement to the East, to make opposition impossible. — Supporting the Law and Order Service until the operation was over, when 1,300 Jewish policemen were rounded up and herded into wagons for deportation.[138]

THE JEWS' SECOND PLEA TO THE WEST

During the fall of 1942, political representatives of the Jewish Coordinating Committee functioning "on the Aryan side" of Warsaw contacted the emissary of the Polish Civil Directorate, Jan Karski. He was to go to London to report directly to the Polish government-in-exile and the western Allies. JCC leaders wanted Karski to communicate their message to Allied leaders and Jewish spokesmen in Great Britain and the United States. To make his report more convincing, Karski infiltrated into the ghetto in October 1942 — he recalled the scene in 1944:

Everywhere there was hunger, misery, the atrocious stench of decomposing bodies, the pitiful moans of dying children, the desperate cries and gasps of a people struggling for life against impossible odds.

To pass that wall was to enter into a new world utterly unlike anything that had ever been imagined. The entire population of the ghetto seemed to be living in the street. There was hardly a square yard of empty space. As we picked our way across the mud and rubble, the shadows of what had once been men or women flitted by us in pursuit of someone or something, their eyes blazing with some insane hunger or greed.

Everyone and everything seemed to vibrate with unnatural intensity, to be in constant motion, enveloped in a haze of disease and death through which their bodies appeared to be throbbing in disintegration. We passed an old man standing against a wall staring lugubriously and with glassy eyes into space, and although he barely moved from his spot, he, too, seemed to be strangely animated, his body tormented by a force that made his skin twitch in little areas.

As we walked everything became increasingly unreal. . . .

Suddenly my companions seized my arms. I saw nothing, did not know what was happening. I became frightened, thought I had been recognized. They rushed me through the nearest entrance.

"Hurry, hurry, you must see this. This is something for you to tell the world about. Hurry!" . . .

They urged me to the window, pulled down the shade and told me to look through the slit at the side.

"Now you'll see something. The hunt. You would never believe it if you did not see it for yourself."

I looked through the opening. In the middle of the street two boys, dressed in the uniform of the Hitlerjugend, were standing. They wore no caps and their blond hair shone in the sun. With their round, rosy-cheeked faces and their blue eyes they were like images of health and life. They chattered, laughed, pushed each other in spasms of merriment. At that moment, the younger one pulled a gun out of his hip pocket and then I first realized what I was witnessing. His eyes roamed about, seeking something. A target. He was looking for a target with the casual, gay absorption of a boy at a carnival.

I followed his glance. For the first time I noticed that all the pavements about them were absolutely deserted. Nowhere within the scope of those blue eyes, in no place from which those cheerful, healthy faces could be seen was there a single human being. The gaze of the boy with the gun came to rest on a spot out of my line of vision. He raised his arm and took careful aim. The shot rang out, followed by the noise of breaking glass and then the terrible cry of a man in agony.[139]

The Zionist representative he spoke to demanded that he should reiterate their demand for Allied threats of massive reprisals against Germany for its deterrent use as a counterthreat and demand collective retaliation in kind against German nationals so as to illustrate their own collective execution. But the representatives conveyed another message to Jewish spokesmen abroad, which Karski transmitted to Shmuel Zygelbojm, the Bund represen- tative to the Polish government-in-exile. When challenged by Zygelbojm to tell him what they wanted,

> I answered with brutal simplicity and directness.
> "Very well, then. This is what *they* want from their leaders in the free countries of the world, this is what *they* told me to say:
> " 'Let them go to all the important English and American offices and agencies. Tell them not to leave until they have obtained guarantees that a way has been decided upon to save the Jews. Let them accept no food or drink, let them die a slow death while the world looks on. Let them die. This may shake the conscience of the world.' "[140]

THE GHETTO REVOLT

During this period, two resistance organizations whose goals converged began contacting allies outside the ghetto, gathered arms for an impending confrontation (whose date they could not predict), and established their authority over the ghetto. They achieved this by selected assassinations of police who had led the deportation roundup and by taxing (and/or ex- propriating) of *Judenrat* leaders and the rich. They enforced such taxes by kidnapping tax delinquents. Ringelblum later listed the names of 13 agents who had collaborated with the Gestapo and were shot by the Jewish Combat Organization.[141] The fighters of the party cadres lived in communes, con- stantly surrounded by armed defenders whose readiness to kill informers and Gestapo agents deterred a direct attack on their quarters. The hatred of the Jewish police and the reports about Treblinka (from escaped prisoners) that reached the ghetto in September 1942 fortified consensus on the new defini- tion of the situation, legitimating the resistance organizations' claim to authority.

In January 1843, the SS invaded the ghetto, seizing among others some members of the combat group on the street. Their comrades improvised defenses, hurling grenades through tenement windows, enabling many who had been seized to flee as German troops scurried for cover. The insurgents fought several defensive skirmishes during the next three days, exploiting their tactical advantage by firing down from the twisting tenement stairwells, windows, and roofs. Although 6,500 Jews had been led away, after four days, the Germans' exit from the ghetto without an immediate reprisal raised the hopes of ghetto residents that they could live through a rebellion.[142] Pamphlets recalled from those days stress fighting for life: "We must be able and prepared to fight for this right. . . . Whoever fights for his life has a chance of being saved."[143]

The revolt began at the time of the Germans' choice: the first night of Passover, 19 April 1943. Both the Jewish and Polish flags were hoisted over the ghetto, in accord with the ghetto fighters' slogan that the battle was "for your freedom and ours." After four weeks of insurgency, the central command bunker was penetrated, the Jewish Combat Organization's commander, Mordecai Anieliwicz, was killed, and the revolt was effectively squashed. Unwilling to suffer the losses of fighting a guerrilla war, the Germans had decided to burn the ghetto down, flushing out resistants from bunkers by injecting poison gas.

The isolation of the ghetto was sealed by the refusal of the Polish Civil Directorate and Home Army to support the revolt by instigating a general strike, mobilizing military aid, or instructing Polish police to cease arresting Jews on the "Aryan side" who had fled from the ghetto. Their refusal to support the revolt was masked by the symbolic gesture of giving 50 pistols to representatives of the Coordinating Committee (the Jewish political directorate of parties over the Jewish Combat Organization). Krakowski notes that, contrary to later protestations of their lack of arms, the Polish Army had 1,070 pistols hidden in the Warsaw region in September 1939; a July 1943 Polish government-in-exile memorandum estimated that the Home Army had 6,000 pistols in its possession in the spring of 1943.[144] Despite an earlier promise, they failed to break through the walls or provide protected means of transport outside of Warsaw for the fleeing fighters. However, some party units of the Polish resistance (including units aiding the revisionist group, ZZW) did lead out several dozen fighters through the sewers and other units fought outside the wall, acting against the Home Army's orders.

Shmuel Zygelbojm died by his own hand, protesting in despair. He had not been able to change the policy of the Polish Home Army or incite the Allies to take any steps to stop the Holocaust. Moreover, he was persuaded that no one would allow him to die in front of 10 Downing Street in a fast undertaken to awaken the public, moving the conscience of the West.[145] His last letter (found after his suicide on 12 May 1943) reads:

> I cannot be silent. I cannot live while the remnants of the Jewish population of Poland, of whom I am a representative, are perishing. . . . By my death I wish to make my final protest against the passivity with which the world is looking on and permitting the extermination of the Jewish people.[146]

How did ordinary Poles look upon the ghetto revolt? Ringelblum observed in his treatise on *Polish-Jewish Relations:*

In these conversations among the Poles about what was happening in the Ghetto, the anti-Semitic note was predominant in general, satisfaction that Warsaw had in the end become *judenrein,* that the wildest dreams of Polish anti-Semites about a Warsaw without Jews were coming true. Some loudly and others discreetly expressed their satisfaction at the fact that the Germans had done the dirty work of exterminating the Jews.[147]

Alexander Donat vividly recalls the spectacle of the burning Jews:

Then came Easter Sunday. . . .

Mass over, the holiday crowds poured out into the sun-drenched streets. Hearts filled with Christian love, people went to look at the new unprecedented attraction that lay halfway across the city to the north, on the other side of the Ghetto wall, where Christ's Jewish brethren suffered a new and terrible Calvary not by crucifixion but by fire. What a unique spectacle! Bemused, the crowds stared at the hanging curtains of flame, listened to the roar of the conflagration, and whispered to one another, "But the Jews—they're being roasted alive!" There was awe and relief that not they but the others had attracted the fury and the vengeance of the conqueror. There was also satisfaction.

Batteries of artillery had been set up in Nowiniarska Street and were shelling objectives in the Ghetto from there. The explosions of grenades and dynamite could be heard as well, as Jews scrambled from their hiding places. Pain-crazed figures leaped from balconies and windows to smash on the streets below. From time to time a living torch would crouch on a window sill for one unbearably long moment before flashing like a comet through the air. When such figures caught on some obstruction and hung there suspended in agony, the spectators were quick to attract the attention of German riflemen. "Hey, look over there! No, over there!" Love of neatness and efficiency were appeased by a well-placed shot; the flaming comet was made to complete its trajectory; and the crowds cheered.[148]

Despite such prevalent glee, enmity, or lack of empathy, a large number of Jews had escaped earlier and found rooms or apartments in Warsaw. The most successful of them were those least visibly Jewish, usually members of the educated, professional class who spoke Polish and had Polish friends. Estimates of Jewish evaders passing on the "Aryan side" vary from a maximum of 20,000 to as low as 5,000: there is no way to corroborate these figures.[149] The minimum estimate was that 8 out of 100 Jews alive in October 1942 had evaded capture (or death) within the ghetto by September 1943.

Some were aided by Zegota, the Council for Aid to the Jews, an organization uniting members of democratic Polish parties and Jews representing the Jewish Coordinating Committee, which arose in December 1942 after a provisional committee, initiated by Catholics of conscience who protested the murder of Jews, refused to accept the Jewish representatives.[150] Zegota was affiliated with the Polish Civil Directorate and received funds from airplane drops by the government-in-exile, which also conveyed funds gathered by international Jewish aid organizations (most of which were never received).[151] Vladka Meed, a worker in Warsaw, recalls in most detail how Jews were consistently hunted by the *schmaltzovnik* (blackmailers) on the street and at home, and often taken in before workers (such as herself) could aid them financially.[152] Although Zegota issued leaflets condemning blackmailers and warned that extortion was a punishable crime, the Polish resistance did not execute any death sentences against them until September 1943, although thousands of collaborators were executed by them.[153]

Ringelblum complained of the meagerness of the support provided by Zegota, resulting from slender resources and the drain on funds caused by extortionists, landlords, and others who were exploiting the plight of Jews in hiding:

> In order to illustrate the tragic situation of the Jewish intellectuals, it is sufficient to note that the Council for Aid to the Jews did not have enough means to help a distinguished Jewish historian, a former member of the Diet of the Polish Republic, Dr. S.[154]

The Germans had not given up attempting to trap Jews in hiding. They promised passports to non-Axis countries (mainly Latin American) and protection for passport holders to all Jews registering at the Hotel Polski in May 1943. Despite warnings that this was a snare, hundreds of Jews enrolled. A few hundred departed for the internment camp in Vittel, France, with the papers that the Gestapo had itself captured from deported Jews; from Vittel they were later transported to Auschwitz via the French concentration camp of Drancy. The initial refusal of the American State Department to relay a message to Berlin through South American governments regarding American interest in safeguarding the Vittel detainees contributed to the Germans' decision to transport 240 of them to Auschwitz, Feingold tells us.[155] About 300 other Jews seized from the Hotel Polski were shot by the Germans in July.[156]

We do not know how many Jews in hiding were betrayed between April 1943 and January 1945 (Warsaw's liberation), how many died during shelling of the city during the 1944 civil uprising, and how many died because they were put in the front lines by the Polish resistance and often denied access to shelters or not informed as to when to retreat, as Goldstein, Borzykowski, and Zylberberg have testified. The Jewish leadership's call for Jews in hiding to fight in 1944 did reflect the close bonds between Jewish and Polish socialists and intellectuals in Warsaw; political bonds were closer and aid received by Jewish resistants was greater in Warsaw than in any other city in Poland in which a Jewish resistance movement has been documented. Nevertheless, this was the response of a minority, more typical of members of Polish parties of the left who supported the civil rights of Jews before the war. These few could not check the majority of indifferent or antagonistic Poles who wished to eliminate the Jews. Nor could they alter the policies of the Polish government-in-exile, which incorporated the parties that called during the war for expulsion or elimination of the Jews as the way to end the Jewish problem in Poland, as they had before the war.

The deputy chairman of the Council for Aid to Jews, Tadeusz Rek, pleaded with the Government Delegate (the head of the Polish civil resistance) for more money to save the Jews, recognizing the prevailing antipathy toward them: "It should be objectively stated . . . that the overwhelming majority of Polish society are hostile toward those extending relief (to the Jews)."[157] Pleas by the council representatives to the Government Delegate to engage in public propaganda combating the anti-Semitism growing among the Polish public in 1943 and 1944 produced no result. The commander of the Home Army (the military wing of Polish resistance) was not indifferent but undermined the ability of Jews to survive by authorizing Poles (on 15 September 1943) to shoot "bandits" (Jewish evaders) hiding in the forests.[158]

THE LAST ACCOUNT AND THE FINAL TOLL

The first notice of the Warsaw ghetto rebellion in the *Polish Fortnightly Review* (monthly organ of the government-in-exile) appeared 15 January 1944, nine months after the revolt had occurred. The account claimed that

> arms were supplied by the Polish Underground Army, and instructors, soldiers and officers helped in the battle. . . . Not one of the defenders came out alive. But the close co-operation which had been established between the ghetto and the rest of Warsaw had its result in the very fact that it was made possible largely because of the supply of arms by the Poles.

The complete extinction of the Jews of Warsaw reported by the Polish government (perhaps wishfully) was exaggerated. By 5 June 1945 there were 801 registrations of Jews originating from Warsaw listed in Warsaw. There were an estimated additional 8,164 registrants from Warsaw elsewhere in Poland, or a total of 9,966 registrants, including extermination, concentration, and labor camp survivors.[159] Among the 1,801 Jews registered in Warsaw whose birth dates are listed, we find that only 112 infants and children born between 1939 and 1945 are registered, despite the presumably better chances for children to survive because they were less visible as Jews, less likely to speak a tongue that would betray their origin.[160] Because of multiple registrations by the same persons in different towns (believed to be common during this period), the number of registrants probably exceeds the number of Jewish survivors. Thus, fewer than 2.5% of the 1939 Jewish population of Warsaw had remained alive upon, or returned alive to, Polish soil (apart from refugees returned from the Soviet Union who fled Poland before the Holocaust began). Perhaps one Jew in 100 in Warsaw evaded capture by the Germans, usually living in continual fear and isolation.

The Netherlands

The Netherlands, occupied by Germany on 10 May 1940 after a battle of five days, remained under German domination longer than any other nation of western Europe except Norway. The German civil government was headed by Reichskommissar Arthur Seyss-Inquart, the Austrian official responsible for Austria's integration into the Reich and rapid Nazification. While Seyss-Inquart was dedicated to the assimilation of the Dutch into the Germanic master race, his primary goal, Rich explains, was to make the country secure and, second, to exploit it economically to the fullest.[1]

We shall reconstruct events through the experiences of Eli Cohen, a young doctor, Jacob Presser, a historian, Philip Mechanicus, a journalist, Gertrude van Tijn, a social worker, Anne Frank and Marga Minco, then adolescents attending school. Only the diaries of Philip Mechanicus, *Year of Fear*, and of Anne Frank, *The Diary of a Young Girl*, were written at the time of the recorded events.[2] Van Tijn's extended memorandum was written in Jerusalem in 1945 for officials of the Joint Distribution Committee and, by her admission, was self-censored to avoid censuring the dead.[3] Presser's recollections are embedded in his history, *The Destruction of the Dutch Jews*, and his novel, *The Breaking Point*.[4] Marga Minco's memoir, *Bitter Herbs*, was published almost two decades later.[5] Eli Cohen talked about his experiences to a Dutch journalist in 1971; these are recorded as *The Abyss: A Confession*.[6] All except Gertrude van Tijn (who headed the Emigration Department of the Jewish Council) went into hiding and attempted to pass as Aryans or to flee the country. Of the five who went into hiding, all but Marga Minco did so with their own personal provisions, indicating some financial resources. Mechanicus, Cohen, and Anne Frank (along with her family) were betrayed and ultimately transported to Auschwitz; Cohen alone, because of preference and opportunities granted to him as a physician, survived. Jacob Presser and Marga Minco survived in hiding, as did one-third to one-half of Jews estimated to have gone into hiding; estimates necessarily vary because they can be made only inferentially rather than through any records. Gertrude van Tijn was transported to Bergen-Belsen rather than Auschwitz because of her position as a staff member in the office of the Expositeur; the Germans considered it necessary to save a certain number of Jewish notables and officials for potential exchange for German nationals in Allied camps. Although Bergen-Belsen was not an extermination camp, all Jews there endured a high risk of death from disease, malnutrition, and guards' brutality: in fact, only 30% of the 3,751 Jews from the Netherlands sent there survived, almost the same as the percentage surviving of those sent to Theresienstadt. All the adults at one time or another enjoyed some protection (or rather, as we shall see, some illusion) by virtue of a position in the Jewish Council or in the camp administration of Westerbork or by an exemption or stamp granted by the Council or the camp administration. Four of the six survived, whereas more than four out of every six Jews from the Netherlands were exterminated, chiefly in Auschwitz.

Because the diaries cover limited time periods and the memoirs tend to flatten recollection of less traumatic events, we shall also draw upon German documents and published histories and analyses of the period before the deportation. These include (but are not restricted to) the aforementioned work of Presser, those of Werner Warmbrunn and Henry L. Mason, and the extensive works of Dr. Louis de Jong, head of the Netherlands State Institute of War Documentation, who was kind enough to answer my questions pertaining to the five volumes of Dutch occupation history he has written that are not translated.[7]

LOOKING FORWARD, 1940

Before the German occupation, what did Dutch Jews anticipate would happen to them? They were well aware of how Jews had been dis-integrated from the German nation, stripped of rights, property, and citizenship: the 20,000 German Jews who had fled to Holland, Gertrude van Tijn and Anne Frank among them, could testify to this. Many German Jews were interned in Westerbork, established in 1939 by the Dutch government in an attempt to restrict the entry of refugees, and supported by the Jewish Relief Committee. All had heard Hitler publicly proclaim in 1939 that if the Jews succeeded in plummeting Germany into war (an obvious projection of responsibility), it would be the end of the Jewish people.[8]

Eli Cohen recalled that when Professor Polak Daniels, his former academic supervisor in Gronigen, asked him what he would do when the Germans came, he refused to anticipate any problems.

> "My wife and I will then commit suicide," [Daniels] said. "And we shall be taking
> our dog with us into the grave, and my children . . . will have to decide for
> themselves—they're grown-up people."[9]

Cohen, although an avowed Zionist, did not attempt to go to Palestine, having just begun a successful medical practice and a new marriage: life was promising ("I allowed myself to be tempted by the fleshpots of Egypt") and he could rationalize his aversion to making a break in terms of his duty to support his aging parents.[10] Besides, many did not share Professor Daniels's fear, assuming that the German threat would be similar to previous German threats in World War I. Dutch Jews' perception of danger was obscured because of hostility between Dutch and German Jews, allowing the Dutch to displace the blame onto the German Jews, who were victims themselves.

> German Jews came to Groningen. At a given moment in those days my father or
> my father-in-law said, "It can't possibly be that they're just persecuting the Jews
> like that in Germany. They must be a bad type of person that's involved, anyway."
> They could not grasp that it was a clear case of persecution simply for being
> Jewish. They were still thinking in terms of punishment and fines. . . . In any
> case, in my circle people thought there must be something wrong somewhere with
> those German Jews.[11]

This misperception apparently stemmed from the mental paradigm that we implicitly share: all victims must be innocent—free of any censurable characteristic or past misdeed. Only wrongdoers are punished; thus, if one is punished, one is a wrongdoer. And a wrongdoer is not innocent and therefore not a victim. Such a belief, dangerous when confronting an implacable enemy, supported the commonplace assumption of the good citizen in a bureaucratic society that if one does nothing wrong (meaning nothing contrary to the law), one will not be harmed. If one believes an alleged victim actually deserves or invited punishment, one learns from this that the way to avoid punishment is to avoid misbehavior.

Many Jews attempted suicide when the Germans invaded the Netherlands. One source cites 30 successful suicide attempts among Dutch Jews in The Hague, and van Tijn reports rumors of over 100 suicides in Amsterdam. Warmbrunn estimates that about "200 Jews ended their own lives in 1940 to avoid persecution," using official statistics of the Netherlands and basing his inference "on the assumption that almost all of the excess of suicides in 1940 over the preceding and following years must be attributed to Jews; this would approximate 14 suicides per 10,000 recorded Jews."[12] Naturally, we have no idea of how many unsuccessful attempts there were, but Presser reports that "when, a few days after the Dutch capitulation, the rumour went round that Jews could still leave the Netherlands, many who applied for exit permits appeared at the relevant offices with bandaged wrists and throats."[13]

Some who perceived the danger attempted to flee to England. Van Tijn related how the government authorized passage aboard a ferry for several busloads of German Jewish refugee children, but local Dutch officials stopped Dutch Jews seeking access to the ferry because they did not have written passes and the officials didn't have official approval for them to leave the country. Because of their legalism, many spaces on that ferry went unfilled. The habit of compliance to rules, typical of bureaucratized societies, was upheld by Dutch officials (and later Joodse Raad officials) with rigor for the first three years of the occupation, preventing interstitial opportunities between the law and its enforcement from developing by natural bureaucratic processes.

DUTCH ADAPTATIONS, GERMAN STRATEGY, AND SEGREGATION OF JEWS

The German presence was initially reassuring. The soldiers of occupation were polite, respectful, and sometimes even helpful to the civilian population. No special policy toward the Jews was noted. Commanders had been instructed by a German Army directive of 22 February 1940 to avoid "unrolling" the Jewish question.[14] Eli Cohen recalls the relief he experienced when there was no immediate action against the Jews by the occupiers. Other Dutchmen also sighed with relief and prepared to adjust to German rule, believing that the war was over for all time when the capitulation of France in June left the Germans the undisputed masters of the new Europe.

> The Germans had already penetrated to Groningen in force. My father-in-law came, because I didn't dare drive alone in the car. And so I visited my patients with him. And I thought, H'm, it's not so bad. For I had expected to be grabbed at once and maybe stood up against a wall—well, you know: any damn crazy thing.[15]

The Queen and government abandoned Holland, with no clear directives as to how higher civil service bureaucracy should behave; their 1937 instructions, a gem of ambiguities, were not even reiterated publicly until 1943.[16] All the Secretaries-General, directors of government departments ordinarily inferior only to the appointed Minister, remained in charge, and it was through them that the initial stages of defining and registering Jews were executed.

No political leaders of any major party placed any hope in resistance. Hendrik Colijn, the former Prime Minister (1933-1939) and head of the Anti-Revolutionary Party, "excused Hitler's foreign policies . . . attacked the 'evils of democracy,' [and] advised his countrymen to work out a compromise with the Third Reich, since he considered German hegemony a certainty" in a pamphlet published in June 1940 and later repudiated by him. The last preinvasion Prime Minister, D. J. De Geer, head of the Christian

Historical Union, disapproved of the Dutch government-in-exile's policy in London and resigned. He secretly flew to Lisbon in September and from there, in a German airplane, to the Netherlands, where he proceeded to publish a pamphlet (1942) expressing anticipation of a German victory and advocating collaboration.[17]

Conceiving of the Dutch as potential allies, the German administration made an effort to woo them and to create an ideological pro-Nazi atmosphere, not only through direct propaganda, by controlling the press and radio, but also by the "coordination" of free associations, setting up new and Nazified counterassociations or introducing pro-Nazi leaders into old associations. The only party prohibited during the first year of occupation was the Communist Party. Some of these new associations were not manifestly collaborationist, such as Winter Help, a national charity organ modeled after a German counterpart. Warmbrunn remarks that the mass of the membership detected its usefulness to the occupiers and boycotted its drives before the non-Nazi leadership realized what cause they were serving; this was only one of a number of instances, he notes, when the mass was more resistant or less cooperative with the occupiers than were the leaders, elites, or notables.[18] Besides these efforts to swing the middle-of-the-road prewar voter into active support, the German authorities cultivated the prewar National Socialist party, the NSB. Anti-Semitism had been a minor theme in NSB ideology before the war; it even still had some Jewish members (evidently accepted prior to the ban on their entry in 1938) but it adhered strictly to the anti-Semitic policy line of the occupiers during the war.

Little evidence has been noted of any organized resistance in Holland in 1940. One may assume that the Communist Party infrastructure still existed but must remember that, during the period of the Molotov-Ribbentrop pact (1939 until the invasion of the Soviet Union in June 1941), there was no ideological incentive for the Communists to attack Germany.

On 22 October 1940, the German authorities ordered the Secretaries-General to issue an order for and execute the registration of Jews; this was soon followed by the Aryan oath among public servants, necessary to dismiss Jews from the civil service, schools, and the universities. Before this, the Secretary-General for Internal Affairs had received instructions to clear Jews out of the labor service (1 July 1940), and to appoint no Jews to new openings (28 August 1940). He had carried out these orders after perfunctory protests without any signs of noncooperation. But the registration decree was the most general order and the one of most consequence to the occupiers, enabling them to map the distribution of Jews by city and street, their age and sex composition and their relations to other Dutch people by intermarriage. The identification system had been linked to food rationing systems since 1939, so that to live under a false name, one would need to counterfeit papers, coupons, and stamps, or starve in solitude.

This initial tool of social control was furnished to the German occupier with an excellence of craft unknown to the Gestapo by a Dutch civil servant, J. L. Lentz. With the approval of his superior, K. J. Frederiks, the Secretary-General of Internal Affairs, Lentz traveled to Berlin to display his work; there "the Gestapo had pronounced his identity card even more difficult to reproduce than its German counterpart.[19] It was printed in three colors, including a dye "of exceptionally subtle composition" that became visible only under the light of a quartz lamp, and was covered with diagonal crisscross lines composed of microscopic words in a rare type, underlying which were three Dutch lions.[20] A large photo and two fingerprints were required. The Jews' cards were also stamped with two prominent "Js". Few underground printers could duplicate the cards, and they could not be replicated en masse. "From 1940 to 1945 there was no scourge from which the Dutch received bloodier wounds than this execrable identity card — the invention of an over-zealous civil servant, himself not a Nazi."[21] After the war, Lentz was sentenced to three years in prison for this act.

Registration was carried out by local census offices and city halls without any sign of subversion or noncooperation. Practically all Jews registered, de Jong has observed. He estimates from personal experience that, at the most, only 50 Jews — three in each 10,000 — did not register.[22]

What were the reactions of other Dutch people to the removal of their Jewish fellow citizens from offices and schools? We may start with Holland's supreme court, De Hoge Raad, whose president, Dr. Lodewijk E. Visser, was a Jew. No public protest of any type or a single resignation was recorded. Only in the universities was there some spontaneous reaction to the exclusion of some 40 Jewish professors, and these protests, in February and March 1941, were often suppressed by administrations, either directly, by cancelling sessions so a strike could not be noticed, or indirectly, as at Amsterdam University, where students called off a strike "after a 'report' that the Queen considered such action inopportune — a 'report' that, after the war, was found to have been completely false."[23] Presser recalls only one instance of a Jew's overt resistance. Leo Polak, Professor of Philosophy of Groningen, simply kept on teaching and found his students continuing to attend his lectures. He was arrested and sent to a concentration camp after the German authorities received a letter written by Polak to a university official in which he remarked that "the faculty seems to think fit to treat me as if I were no longer a Professor at Groningen, no longer a member of the Senate or the Faculty." Presser remarks that "the Vice-Chancellor of Groningen, Prof. J. M. N. Kapteyn, from whom the Germans obtained Polak's 'impertinent' letter, cannot be said to have played a particularly glorious role in this matter."[24]

In the last quarter of 1940 and the first half of 1941, Jewish journalists were ejected from the newly Nazified Dutch Journalists' Union, and Jewish musicians' chairs moved to the back of the Concergeboew Orchestra, which had already agreed to accept no new Jewish members but failed to dismiss the old ones. Jews' exclusion from the film industry had already been accepted in May 1940 by the Dutch Cinema Union, which forced its Jewish members to resign under the pretext that they were responsible for the anti-German demonstrations and catcalls in the theaters during German newsreels and propaganda films.

Cohen recounts how the mayor of Groningen came to him in June (approximately) with a "painful question" that Cohen expressed for him and answered immediately, telling him all four of his grandparents were Jews. The Mayor immediately dismissed him from the air raid precautions team. In November 1940 he was dismissed from his post in the municipal hospital, and on 8 February 1941 he received an order that he must cease practicing by 1 May. How did his colleagues respond?

> They swooped on my practice like vultures on carrion. The Aryans. They all wanted to take it over. And when I asked them on what terms, they would reply. "The usual terms. You know that, anyway. It's been announced by the Medical Association."
>
> I cannot speak for others, but this Medical Association completely let me down. At no time did I ever receive any help from it. We had local branch meetings, at the Faun, a café in Groningen. In November or the beginning of December 1940, those signs saying "Jews Not Admitted" began to appear. I then wrote to the branch secretary, saying that since this sign was also now hanging in the Faun café, I could no longer attend the association's gatherings. I received a very laconic letter in reply, saying that it was true, and that he regretted it as well, but that, yes, in future I should no longer be able to go along. And . . . he wished me all the best. Later on, that Medical Contact body was set up, and *they* seem to have done something, but it came too late for me. But in the days I'm speaking of you were . . . well . . . let down, dropped.[25]

Mechanicus, a journalist for the *Algameen Handelsblad,* was forced to give up that post publicly in 1940 (Presser tells us in a foreword to Mechanicus's diary), but continued writing for it under a pseudonym until the directors dismissed him by letter. On 27 September 1942, when he was standing without wearing a star on the rear platform of a train, he was probably betrayed by a fellow passenger and was arrested by a policeman. Subsequently he was interned at the prison camp of Amersfoorst, and on 25 October 1942 was transferred to Westerbork as an "S" case (punishment), where he stayed in the hospital until 29 July 1943. Although a friend deleted the "S" from the files, Mechanicus was nevertheless transferred to Bergen-Belsen on 8 March 1944 and to Auschwitz on 9 October 1944.

While anti-Nazis might jeer at German propaganda in the dark of the cinemas, the hosts of collaborators who swarmed to the NSB and NSNAP (another Nazi party) did not whistle in the dark but expressed their enthusiasm publicly. To celebrate their rise in fortunes, they paraded in stormtrooper style into the Jewish quarters of the cities, creating what officials usually described as "excesses." As early as July 1940, a Dutch local official submitted a report to the Ministry of Justice regarding the excesses of the NSNAP in The Hague, citing how they had molested and blackmailed a Jewish shopkeeper, smashing six other shopkeepers' windows and putting uniformed guards in front to prevent people from entering the shop. The official remarked, "The population is so much aroused over these occurrences that serious fear exists of fighting rows and a grave disturbance of public order." The police, he explained, were afraid to act, "not knowing what they are up against since new members of the NSNAP are concerned who, in their behavior are most impudent."[26]

The largest armed body intent on creating a minipogrom emulating the German model was the WA, the street army of the NSB. Since German officials of different organizations competed with each other by encouraging different factions of the NSB, it is difficult to assess to what extent these tactics originated spontaneously with WA members and were looked on with apprehension by some of the ruling overlords and which were instigated by the Germans in order to create a public climate of hatred against Jews so as to justify their later policies.

However, in Amsterdam the object of such actions was foiled by the development of mass resistance within the Jewish quarter by Jews and some of their Dutch neighbors, most likely to be of the working class. The defenders formed Action Groups, one of which on 11 February 1941 badly beat up a WA invader, leading to his death. The wounds were exaggerated by the Higher SS and police leader, Rauter, to correspond to Nazi legend: "Rauter reported to Himmler that a Jew had bitten through Koot's jugular vein and sucked out his blood, an obvious allusion to ritual murder."[27] Attempts to isolate the Jewish quarter physically did not inhibit Jews' resistance.

The next day the German Commandant of Amsterdam called in several leaders of the Coordination Committee of Jewish organizations, voluntarily established by leading groups and synagogue federations in 1940, and ordered them to set up a *Judenrat* and announce a German order demanding that all Jews hand in any weapons they owned. The chairman selected was well known: Abraham Asscher had served as chairman of the Amsterdam Chamber of Commerce and as president of the Netherlands Israelitic Congregation and of the Committee for Special Jewish Affairs. His colleague, David Cohen, a professor of ancient history, was a well-known Zionist who had established the Committee for Special Jewish Affairs.

The demand of the Joodse Raad (the Dutch *Judenrat*) did not halt the incidents and demonstrations, which occurred throughout the next week in Amsterdam. When on 19 February German police raided an ice cream parlor that served as headquarters for an Action Group, they were sprayed with acid; also, "it was alleged that a shot had been fired."[28]

As a reprisal, the Germans arrested 425 to 430 Jewish men aged 18 to 35 and sent them to Mauthausen concentration camp; 230 others were also sent there in June 1941 as a reprisal for a time bomb planted in Amsterdam.[29]

Only eight were still alive by the end of 1941. At that time death notices were still being sent to next-of-kin, but this practice was eliminated after the Consul of Sweden—who served to represent the Netherlands diplomatically in states in which it was not represented—inquired why most of the dates of death were identical.

The arrest of the Jews provoked a mass strike. The February 1941 strike in Amsterdam was started by two municipal workers, one in road service and one in garbage collection, who were members of the Communist Party, but they did not go to the party cadres until they had stirred up support among the workers. Mason tells us that on 24 February 1941 "some two hundred and fifty municipal workers, the great majority of whom were Communists, assembled to hear passionate condemnations of the arrests of the Jews. A strike was once more proclaimed for the following day, February 25."[30]

The tactics were clear and simple: stop the trams from going out in the morning and spread rumors among later-waking workers as to the mass nature of the strike, leading to a snowball reaction. By midmorning, crowds of workers, exhilarated by their success, milled about the center of Amsterdam. The Germans, taken by surprise, did not have a strategy to combat the action on the first day and avoided firing on the crowds. Because the strike leaders lacked the means to take over physical control of the city and had no premeditated strategy to counter German sanctions, the strike was broken in two days after the German authorities declared a state of siege in Amsterdam. They ordered German and Dutch policemen to ride the trams, raised threats of violent reprisals and economic sanctions, and induced leaders of the newly appointed Jewish Council, by threatening the random arrest of 300 more Jews, to appeal to industrialists for an end to the strike. The Mayor's threat to dismiss municipal workers who did not show up for work, the German show of force (seven strikers were killed the second day of the strike), and the appeal to industrialists together induced workers to return. German control was reinforced by dismissal of the Mayor of Amsterdam and mayors of other cities to which the strike had spread who, the occupiers believed, had not taken firm action to break the strike. They also cracked the Communist Party leadership; Mason reports that "twenty-two of its top leaders and ninety lower functionaries were arrested."[31] The decimation of Communist cadres helps explain the lapse of organized resistance from 1941 to the first quarter of 1943.

IDEOLOGY AND ADAPTATION OF A *JUDENRAT*

The Amsterdam Joodse Raad, like other *Judenräte*, was designed as an instrument of social control by the Germans. Despite the fact that its leaders, David Cohen and Abraham Asscher, were community spokesmen in prewar life, it was not set up to represent Jews; nor did it do so. The working-class and non-Dutch Jews were scarcely represented. Invited participants who were suspicious of German authority were not seduced for long by the invitation and, thus, the potentially more resistant were also eliminated from the beginning. Among those rejecting participation was the president of the former Coordination Committee of Jewish organizations and supreme court president Lodewijk E. Visser.

Because David Cohen and Visser were old friends, Cohen tried to convince Visser of the legitimacy of cooperation. Their correspondence — translated by Michman — arose after Visser refused to meet with Cohen, thus expressing his strong disapproval of the Joodse Raad's role. Its establishment had undermined the functions of the Coordination Committee because of the influence of Cohen and Asscher over the Jewish congregations and over the Amsterdam City Commandant.

Cohen justified his role on 13 November 1941:

> The observations made by the Coordination Committee correspond with those heard elsewhere. They stem, however, from a failure to realise that we live in an occupied country where the occupier has his own way. We, for our part, can only try to obtain some concessions on certain points which would not be granted without our intervention. Bearing this in mind, the Jewish Council functions, not unsuccessfully, in matters entrusted to its care. We believe that this way we are handling matters better than by following the stand adopted by the Coordination Committee in their letter.[32]

And Visser rebutted it on 18 November:

> The Jewish Council's standpoint is that we live under a powerful occupier. One must therefore comply totally with his will, and whoever does not believe that lacks any sense of reality. The matter however is not all that simple. The members of the C.C. and numerous people in the country — among them some of your own co-workers who think as we do — are certainly fully aware that the occupier is here and that he is to be reckoned with, but they believe that that is not all there is to it. For besides this occupier there is another reality — the position one adopts vis-à-vis the occupation proper. This is a reality which the occupier must and does take into account; this reality you overlook. The attitude of the Jewish Council is to oblige the occupier, to obey his orders meekly, I would almost say, to be subservient to him, hoping thereby "to prevent worse to come," a hope which has not been fulfilled. This, however, is not the attitude of the major and best portion of the Dutch people which does not submit meekly, but wants to stand up for its rights and convictions, wherever and as long as this is at all possible. . . .
>
> All this may cost Dutch Jewry the sympathy of the Dutch people, a sympathy which you yourself once termed one of our most precious assets. It is possible that in the end, the occupier will achieve his goal concerning us, but it is our duty as Dutchmen and as Jews to do everything to hamper him in achieving that goal and refrain from doing anything which might smooth the way for him. That is not what you are doing![33]

Cohen, on 30 November, disarmingly reiterated his admiration for

Visser's heroic stance and contrasted his role as "realist" to that of his friend. Visser responded on 30 December 1941, firmly rejecting his friend's rationalizations:

> You intend to make the best of the situation by trying, *coûte que coûte,* to get as many concessions as possible from the occupier, and in order to achieve that, are subservient to him. This, to my mind, is pure opportunism which lacks principles and norms and therefore will come to no good. . . .
>
> The only thing you obtained are concessions, possibly only temporary ones, on a few minor points, with which you have undoubtedly been of service to many. For that I will give you full credit. But what price did you have to pay in return? In a way, you entered the service of the occupier for that purpose and had to resign yourself to execute his orders. And that was not the end of it. Even worse is that you must act as instigators of his policy of oppression, or rather of that of certain authorities whose alleged right to enforce obedience I have reason to doubt. Through your Weekly you are obliged to help him with his secret and illegal attempts to separate us from the rest of the nation, and to convey his illegal threats and intimidations to us in the "Announcements of the Jewish Council," not to speak of that dangerous card-index and the pressure put on the German Jews to register. Is that not too high a price for what has been obtained? Did it have to be paid, no matter what? Everything will happen anyway, you say. If that is true, then why all your endeavours? Be that as it may, but then, let the — according to you inevitable — worst find us without guilt and with a clear conscience.[34]

Until he died of a heart attack in February 1942, Visser kept petitioning the Secretaries-General (with little success) to intervene to protect the Jews who had been deported to Mauthausen in 1941. The representative of the Coordination Committee, J. Kish, resigned from the Joodse Raad on 21 September 1941, accusing it of becoming an unresisting instrument of the Germans. The two rabbis who had been invited to join the Council refused and the one member of the Jewish working-class community, the head of the Dutch Diamond Workers' Union, quit after two months.

Within the Jewish Council, members invariably took their lead from Cohen and Asscher as to what must be done, because they alone had the line to the German authorities.[35] The representative of the RSHA had only to threaten Mauthausen as punishment for nonobedience: after a while, there was no need to threaten, as the leaders had so internalized the fear as to obey automatically. The occupiers indulged the leaders' petty expressions of individual nonconformity since they executed orders so well. Just as the chairmen became more dependent on the occupiers, council members became dependent on the chairmen, and ordinary Jews became more dependent on the Joodse Raad for information and welfare. It published the only Jewish newspaper allowed, the newspaper that printed all the new directives they were supposed to obey. It provided schooling for their children when they were dismissed from other schools and welfare aid when they were stripped of their posts. From the formation of the Joodse Raad to the first callup notices (following the genuine callups for labor service), the Joodse Raad counseled compliance.

During this period, Dutch Jews devised no autonomous institutions of their own but relied on those provided by the Joodse Raad. When these proved inadequate, each person had to improvise individually when confronted by the same problems: How to get along without one's accustomed income, how to get to one's relatives and friends without using public transport, how to avoid the labor service.

TOWARD DEPORTATION I: MARKING AND DIVIDING

The order to wear the yellow star, imposed in May 1942, was no different in kind from all the other discriminatory orders segregating Jews. Marga Minco, daughter of an orthodox Jewish family in Breda, recalls her family's response as an aesthetic one. Her father had brought home a parcel with enough stars to sew on *all* their coats, so they would not have to transfer them.

> My mother took one from the parcel and examined it closely.
> "I'll just see whether I've got any yellow silk in the house," she said.
> "They're orange," I said. "You'll have to use orange thread for them."
> "I think it would be better to take thread of the same colour as the coat you sew it on," said Lottie, my brother David's wife.
> "It'll look awful on my red jacket," said Betty.[36]

Marga's parents and her sister Betty moved to Amsterdam, as they had been ordered, but she remained behind, hospitalized because of her tuberculosis, and afterward lived with her brother, who had gained exemption from being drafted for the labor camps by producing jaundice like symptoms with special drugs.

Eli Cohen moved to Groningen in July 1941 after his practice was sold and hid in a house his wife had rented, feeling safe because he was not registered in Groningen. After the first raids began, his father-in-law (who was a Christian) brought home an unknown gentleman who offered to sell him a forged identity card. Cohen refused, as he refused his aid (presumably also for a fee) to go underground, but he did arrange through him to go abroad to Sweden by timber boat. The go-between first demanded 6,000 guilders each for Cohen, his wife, and young son but finally agreed to take the three of them for 13,000 guilders. When the prearranged time came, a taxi arrived, chauffeured by a former patient of Cohen's, who drove them to the railroad station where they were promptly arrested as the car pulled up and brought to the Gestapo House in Groningen. Cohen was suspected of smuggling diamonds abroad.

His wife and child were released while he was sentenced to the prison camp at Amersfoort as an "S" (punishment) case. He was allowed to serve as a doctor there through the influence of a Dutch medical orderly, who helped him to disguise the fact that he was a Jew. Cohen was later transferred to Westerbork, the principal collection center from which Jews were transported to Auschwitz. There he appealed to a Jewish leader to stay on, which meant asking for special exception, as all punishment cases were supposed to be automatically designated for transport. However, a friend later removed the "S" from his file.

At Westerbork, Cohen enjoyed special protection from the selection for the Tuesday train heading to Auschwitz (around which event the week revolved) because he was a doctor and helped to select patients well enough to be transported. So confident was he of his protected status that he arranged for his son—then being cared for in hiding by a mixed couple (as his wife had been sent to Westerbork)—to be brought to Westerbork and persuaded his sister not to go into hiding. He feared that if she were caught, she would be designated an "S" case and immediately transported out of Westerbork, whereas he could protect her in Westerbork if she did not come as an "S" case. Eventually, both his sister and his son were transported from Westerbork to Auschwitz, as were Cohen and his wife, after they antagonized their protector. Cohen alone survived.

The first notices of deportation were sent out on 7 July 1942, initially by the Joodse Raad. Later, such notices were replaced by policemen at the door (Dutch policemen, with one member of each squad a Dutch Nazi) and sometimes Jewish orderlies (unarmed), themselves prisoners at Westerbork.

A resistance pamphlet warned that "it means the complete annihilation of the Jews," referring to information from the Polish government-in-exile broadcast by the BBC (see Chapter 9):

> With disgust and indignation the Netherlands people have witnessed the introduction of the anti-Jewish measures. Our nation is paying deeply for not having protested against the seemingly innocuous Jewish Declaration. It is our common fault—and we do not exclude the Jewish Council itself—that our enemies have at their disposal detailed information regarding the Dutch Jews. For the previous German measures had one purpose only; to segregate the Jews from all other Dutchmen, to exclude all contact with them and to undermine our sentiments of sympathy and solidarity.[37]

The SS commander reported on 13 August 1942:

> The situation has considerably changed. After the Jews had found us out and got to know what is behind the deportation and labor service in the East, they no more report for the weekly shipments. Of 2,000 Jews called up for this week only about 400 showed up. In their homes the called up Jews cannot any longer be found.[38]

The SS, aided by Dutch police, resorted to dragnet raids in the Jewish quarters, cordoning off access roads. Their victims had been effectively concentrated and isolated; now they were bagged. Although most Jews attempted to evade the German net, contemporary observers relate that Christians and Jews in the Netherlands simply denied reports of extermination. Many dismissed these reports as British propaganda, similar to spurious reports of German atrocities during World War I. Even eyewitness reports of former political prisoners from the Netherlands were disbelieved, de Jong tells us:

> In August, 1941, a group of young men was arrested in the Southern Netherlands for spreading copies of the bishop's protest against the nazification of the Roman Catholic Trade Unions . . . and two of them, one aged 27 and the other 21, ended up in the original camp of Auschwitz. . . . They were still there during the terrible winter of 1941, when Auschwitz I began the gassing of both Jews and Russian prisoners of war. . . . On May 4, 1942, the gassings started at nearby Birkenau as well. Eight days later, the two young Netherlanders were released, and allowed to return home. . . . And what they resented most after their return was that the Church authorities evinced no interest in their experiences, and that their own friends refused to believe the stories they told.[39]

Those Jews who did not deny the credibility of Allied news broadcasts by the BBC and Radio Oranje might fail to grasp the implication that German policy was directed against Jews as Jews, not discriminating Polish Jews from Dutch Jews. Thus, one might mistake the implications of the rhetorical question broadcast by Radio Oranje on 29 July 1942:

> How is the German war effort being served by the murder of large groups of thousands of Polish Jews in the gas chambers? Which German effort is advanced by the fact that thousands of Dutch Jews are presently being deported?[40]

Denial and lack of recognition of the meaning of deportation were widespread among the Jews after they were caught and interned. Cohen mentions that Professor Speijer from Westerbork loaned a good suit to a friend selected for the weekly train to Auschwitz, enjoining him to return it after the war.[41] Similarly, he recalls the marveling remark of a Jewish orderly bringing a tiny woman of 95 from the hospital at Westerbork to the waiting cattle cars: "Just look at this, doctor. Ninety-five years old. Labor Supply. Can you believe it?" Cohen continues:

> Naturally, there was always something that made us shudder, but then the indestructible optimism and the indestructible will to live people had come to the surface again. They drove back their fear and thought: "Oh well, it won't be so good for the old folk but the young ones . . . well, they'll have to work, but it won't turn out so bad."[42]

Both Mechanicus and van Tijn describe many instances of such denial at Westerbork, despite the fear of transports, but Mechanicus also recorded contrary instances of persons arguing there would be no return from Poland.

While in 1942 Jews generally had no information as to the extermination facilities at Auschwitz (only disseminated in 1944 to the west), they were aware of the Polish massacres and of the high death rate in German concentration camps and feared any "resettlement." Two responses were possible to notices to report (other than compliance): to go into hiding or to attempt to secure an exemption stamp from the Joodse Raad or directly through German contacts.

Although one could simply walk away between raids, the problem of how to maintain oneself and one's family in hiding had to be solved. For the middle classes who might still have some capital despite two to three years of unemployment, it was still possible to make arrangements to be supplied in hiding by reliable colleagues and friends, as did Anne Frank's parents in Amsterdam. For workers without savings and without means to buy false papers, appealing to friends and colleagues meant asking that they share starvation as well as the risk of arrest for sheltering them. The lack of any institutionalized social defense organization by Jews and Dutchmen during the first nine months of deportation made "diving under" less possible for Jews without means.

The responses of the families of Marga Minco and Anne Frank illustrate the impact of apprehension of threat and the difference in opportunities between the social classes. Marga's parents and sister had gone to live in the Jewish quarter of Amsterdam. Her sister Betty was caught in a street raid there, taken away by truck, and never seen again. Marga, her brother David, and Lottie (David's wife) had received notices to report in Amersfoort (where they still lived). Eager to see the world, they bought collapsible, red, plastic beakers for drinking on the trip. But a friend, Mr. Zaagmeyer, persuaded them to go to a physician, who gave Marga a new medical certificate exempting her. "If you go, you'll never come back," Mr. Zaagmeyer's friend said, "Be sensible."[43]

Marga crept back into bed to play at invalidism. Her next-door neighbor, a young girl, came over to borrow her tennis racket. "Naturally, you people don't play tennis now." Marga persuaded her, with little difficulty, to take her racket and "anything that takes your fancy." After selecting her loot, the neighbor tiptoed out with her arms filled, first cautiously peering out to see that she was not observed exiting. "One has to be so careful these days . . . there's no point in asking for trouble."[44]

Marga became bored with the pretense of illness and decided to visit her parents in Amsterdam. But Jews could not travel without special permission. So she removed her star, quaking inwardly throughout the journey, which passed without incident. The star had already marked the victim inside.

Her parents and their neighbors in the Jewish quarter of Amsterdam expressed amazement at her audacity in thus defying the rules. In Amsterdam, many Jews had gone underground, and there was discussion about its possibility and problems. Marga's father talked with an acquaintance who had sent his family away but stayed in the city with his sister. The acquaintance remarked,

"She's not doing anything about it either, for the time being."

"What could you do, actually?" asked my father.

"Well," said his friend, "you can shut the door behind you and disappear. But, then, what are you going to live on?"

"Exactly," said my father. "You've got to live. You've got to have something to live on."[45]

Despite her fear of being caught in the street as her sister had been, or being taken at home, as was her octogenarian Aunt Kate, seized from an old-age home, Marga was reluctant to leave without her parents, as she was now their only child living at home. Her father tried to find a place for her to go into hiding but lacked contacts in Amsterdam. While they contemplated this problem, the police walked in one day as they were having tea. " 'Fetch our coats, will you?' Father said to me. Mother finished her cup of tea."[46]

Marga walked out the back door and ran to David's house. She, David, and Lottie dyed their hair and obtained new identity cards. When their landlady began to suspect their identity, they prepared to go to Utrecht, expecting to go into hiding there. When Lottie was arrested at the train station, David voluntarily went with her. Marga, now the only free member of a family of five, returned to Amsterdam, without hope and without fear. "I felt that if I were to be captured now, at any rate I should no longer have that feeling of having been left behind alone."[47]

She called up a boy she had met a few weeks earlier in Amsterdam. He met her promptly at the station and arranged her introduction to "Uncle Hannes," who placed Jews with farmers in the countryside. Uncle Hannes and similar persons were the extent of organized aid available to Jews until the formation of the Council for Help to People in Hiding a full year later.

Anne Frank was initially more fortunate than Marga Minco. The Franks had emigrated from Germany in 1933, showing the same prompt recognition of threat that they showed in 1942. The family remained together until caught in hiding in 1944. Anne described their situation on 20 June 1942 before the beginning of deportations:

After May 1940 good times rapidly fled: first the war, then the capitulation, followed by the arrival of the Germans, which is when the sufferings of us Jews really began. Anti-Jewish decrees followed each other in quick succession. Jews must wear a yellow star, Jews must hand in their bicycles, Jews are banned from trams and are forbidden to drive. Jews are only allowed to do their shopping between three and five o'clock and then only in shops which bear the placard "Jewish shop." Jews must be indoors by eight o'clock and cannot even sit in their own gardens after that hour. Jews are forbidden to visit theaters, cinemas, and other places of entertainment. Jews may not take part in public sports. Swimming baths, tennis courts, hockey fields, and other sports grounds are all prohibited to them. Jews may not visit Christians. Jews must go to Jewish schools, and many more restrictions of a similar kind.

So we could not do this and were forbidden to do that. But life went on in spite of it all. Jopie used to say to me, "You're scared to do anything, because it may be forbidden." Our freedom was strictly limited. Yet things were still bearable. . . .

In 1934 I went to school at the Montessori Kindergarten and continued there. It was at the end of the school year, I was in form 6B, when I had to say good-by to Mrs. K. We both wept, it was very sad. In 1941 I went, with my sister Margot, to the Jewish Secondary School, she into the fourth form and I into the first.

So far everything is all right with the four of us and here I come to the present day.[48]

The Franks went into hiding on 9 July 1942, immediately after Anne's sister, Margot, received a callup notice. The move itself had been anticipated weeks earlier and was prepared for in cooperation with Mr. Frank's former business partners, who occupied the office building in which the Franks' hiding place, a secret annex, was located. Although the Franks had problems adjusting to a semicommunal situation with their co-tenants, the van Daans, their situation was far superior materially and psychologically to that of most Jews in hiding.[49] If the enforced company invited conflicts, they were spared the oppression of enforced solitude and/or having constantly to play a false role, as did Jews passing as Aryans.

Those who were least free were parents who believed themselves responsible for their children but lacked the ability to protect them. The powerless and the poor were among this group. Cohen charges the poor were sacrificed:

For who were the first to be deported to Auschwitz? That was Joe Boggs and his mate, the man behind the apple cart, the rag-and-bone cart, who had no important friends at all, and who spoke in a way that fetched no response. They were the first victims. In Amsterdam, Asscher and Cohen of the Jewish Council appear to have said all along: We agree to this, and to that, in order to avoid something even worse. Until in the end they were carried off themselves.[50]

Gertrude van Tijn, whose office registered people for "emigration" (van Tijn unwittingly providing the Germans with complete inventories of their possessions), was disturbed by this situation, as she was by the accommodating policies of the Joodse Raad generally, although she lacked insight into the functions of her department. Nepotism became widespread when deportations began. She reflected in 1945:

I really think that the "Expositeur" was at that time the only office where people from the proletariat were taken on. For when people from the ghetto came to me, laying sometimes as many as 8 "Aufrufe" [callup notices] on my table, the parents and six children having all been called up to work under the police in Germany [sic], I felt something had to be done about it. At that time it was still possible, if one of a family were working for the "J.R." to save the whole family so that if we

took on, say, the oldest boy as errand boy, all the rest of the family was saved. . . .
I had never realized to what degree a large part of the Amsterdam Jewry were paupers. Many families came with 7 or even 8 children, all of them feeble-minded. Numbers of families came of whom 2, 3 or more were suffering from trachoma.[51]

Cohen, Presser, and van Tijn agree as to how the German strategy, executed through the Jewish Council, functioned to divide Jews and left the working class and the socially vulnerable defenseless while the best educated, endowed, and connected vied with each other for preference.

With a potential of 140,000 Jews to deport, the Germans preferred each to wait his turn, without panicking or hiding. After all, there was still a war on and trains couldn't be secured daily. To effect this end, they "guaranteed" exemptions from deportation by a series of stamps registering priority. There were stamps for foreign Jews, including the Dutch Portuguese Jews (a group later claimed not to be Jews racially), for baptized Jews, for Jews working in military industries, for Jews in mixed marriages, and for Jews working for the Jewish Council. The German authorities created offices within and outside the Council whose heads were believed to have an inside line to secure privileges from the Germans. These sources of privilege included the accountant Bolle, who issued lists upon which stamps exempting council employees were based, and the Expositeur, Slutzger, who acted as intermediary with the Germans' Emigration Bureau, registering the non-Dutch Jews.

Just as the protégés of Ribbentrop and Himmler, the German Army, the Nazi Party, and the SS vied against each other in each nation for the inside line, so a bevy of influence peddlers vied with the Joodse Raad in Amsterdam. Their influence couldn't be doubted—about one out of six Jews enjoyed stamps in October 1942 based on association with the Joodse Raad. The Joodse Raad advanced illusions (as did other *Judenräte*) by introducing a stratification system among the victims, ultimately guaranteeing neither class, status, nor power. This incited desperate competition among Jews, obscuring recognition of a common dilemma and invention of a collective means of defense. Gertrude van Tijn describes how

when the first stamps were issued, the scenes at the Jewish Council were quite indescribable. Doors were broken, the staff of the Council was attacked, and the police had often to be called in. . . . The stamps quickly became an obsession with every Jew.[52]

Presser also tells us how

they stood in queues for hours, hating themselves for doing it, but doing it none the less. They lined up for specialists' certificates, legal advice, testimonials from their religious leaders or from the "friend" of an important German, who might use his influence. If only one could achieve recognition as an "indispensable" Jew![53]

Some stamps were better than others, of course, but they could change daily, with their authority "blown." If one was certain that the Germans would ensure that some Jews would be killed, one still could hope, at the beginning, that one would not be among them. It had become, in Thomas Hobbes's terms (in *Leviathan*), a veritable

> warre, where every man is Enemy to every man. . . . And the life of man, solitary, poore, nasty, brutish, and short. And which is worst of all, continuall feare and danger of violent death.[54]

The Joodse Raad's concern for the fate of the deportees was allayed by 52 messages of stereotyped content received from the first 10,000 deportees on July 1942, postmarked Birkenau—a place that they discovered, after five days of map-searching, was in eastern Silesia: "The work was hard but tolerable, the food adequate, the sleeping accommodations were good."[55] This reassured them sufficiently to repeat their seductive advice to the Jews, urging obedience to orders to report.

TOWARD DEPORTATION II: DIVISION AMONG THE PRISONERS

The hostility between German Jews and Dutch Jews was also exploited to further the aims of the occupier, the former aiding in the latter's selection. Westerbork, the camp that was the takeoff point by rail for Auschwitz, was run by the Alta Kampasine, or old campers (AKs or AKI, as Gertrude van Tijn calls them), the German refugees who had been interned there since 1939. They initially supplied the Order Police who helped the German and Dutch police to flush out Jews from homes and hiding places in Amsterdam. (Later, these *Ordnen* drew upon Dutch Jewish inmates as well until they comprised the majority.) They made the selections for the train going to the extermination camps every Tuesday, until they themselves were put on the last train from Westerbork. In both style and social organization, they began to resemble the Nazis.

Gertrude van Tijn remarks:

> By far the most influential man in Westerbork was Curt Schlesinger—a German refugee . . . an excellent organizer. . . . Dr. Schlesinger looked and behaved like an S.S. man. He had, of course, his friends; he always "respected" the privileges of the AKI. He was corrupt and used the influence he had to enrich himself and to protect those with whom it seemed to him advisable to keep on good terms. If a girl was pretty and Schlesinger happened to come into contact with her, there was a way for her to be saved from transport. If she remained unwilling to give in to him, she was sent to Poland.[56]

But Presser tells us in *Breaking Point* (1958) that sexual congress with a member of the Disposition Service (the unit of inmates who made the selections) merely entitled the lady to a week's deferment from transport. His antihero in that novel—apparently a *roman à clef*—is Jacques Suasso Henriques, an assimilated secondary school teacher of Portuguese Jewish origin. Henriques has little conception he is a Jew until publicly labeled as such and no apprehension as to his future until he is warned by a German Jewish pupil of his, Georg Cohen, that the whole system of stamps and deferment is a fraud—all Jews are prey. Cohen advises him that the best way to forestall deportation eastward is to enter Westerbork as a protégé of his (Cohen's) father, who is second in command in the Disposition Service to Schaufinger (Schlesinger). Henriques accepts his pupil's advice and enlists as a member of the Disposition Service through Georg's intercession. During their first meeting, Georg's father instructs Henriques—now the pupil—as to the rule guiding behavior at Westerbork and the penalty for failure to heed it:

> "I've never yet seen the footsteps of anyone coming back from Auschwitz. In Amsterdam they have letters from there. Nonsense. . . . I assume it's definitely unhealthy for us out there. So I'm just staying here as long as I can, and I assume you'll follow my good example."
>
> "Gladly, sir."
>
> "Good, Suasso, good. But in that case you, like me, fall under the first law of this camp: them or me. The only question is whom do we mean by them? And the miserable part of it is that only in the long run do we mean the Germans; in the short run it's the Jews. Get it?"
>
> "The Jews?"
>
> "The Jews. Every week Schaufinger gives me the number that go on the train to Auschwitz."

Henriques's tutor goes on to justify his actions, explaining that nobody will balk in playing this role because another Jew would only take his place and then send him away on the next train.[57]

Philip Mechanicus did not enter Westerbork with such a tutor but tried to use his diagnosis of the class order there to carve out a unique role for himself as a go-between, mediating between German and Dutch Jews. The tactic failed ultimately: Mechanicus was deported on 8 March 1944 to Bergen-Belsen, and from there dispatched to Auschwitz.

He first reflected:

> The German Jews have undeniably abused their position of supremacy and continued to do so. They form, as it were, an almost exclusive association for the protection of the interests of German Jews. As individuals and acting together they do their best to save all Germans brought here from being deported and endeavour to keep them here. They have done this from the time that Dutch Jews began arriving at Westerbork. In this way they have, in point of fact, handed over the Dutch Jews to the Germans to suit their own convenience. Wherever possible, they have pushed the Germans into jobs and have kept the Germans here. The Registration Department with Schlesinger at its head has been able to do this. For example, during the seven months I have been in the hospital, it has *nearly* always been Dutch Jews that have been deported. On one single occasion German Jews were sent too. The same complaint can be heard from the living huts. In the last few

months the nursing staff has been considerably thinned out, and it is the best nurses who have in some preordained way disappeared — *Dutch* Jews. *German* Jews were never included. The same thing happens in the other huts — German Jews are seldom to be found among the deportees.[58]

On Tuesday, 6 July 1943, he noted:

On Sunday afternoon the house physician had a word with me: "I must speak to you man to man. You are on the list for Tuesday." "Can nothing be done?" "I can't do anything for you. The Registration Department have put you on the list." (That meant that the house physician must have said that I was fit to travel.) "But I am just telling you in good time so that you can take the necessary steps."

I went to the office of Dr. Spanier, the all-powerful man in the hospital world. The porter was there at the door like Cerberus: "You can't go in without a note." Markus, the head porter, said: "If it's to do with deportation, Dr. Spanier will not see anyone till Wednesday." "But the train goes on Tuesday." "I can't do anything about it. He's not seeing anyone." . . .

A woman employee of the Jewish Council notified Rood and went with him at half past four to the Registration Department. Came back with the news that the matter was 75% settled. In the meantime he had got Heinemann into action and he had taken down my name. Heinemann is on the night contact committee, the members of which back their favourites. He has also penetrated into the circles closest to Schlesinger. The house physician came along: "We've drilled the well and it will probably gush." That was all. . . .

A little old gentleman with a pointed beard appeared by my bed. "I am Trottel." He came and sat on my bed and began whispering: "It's possible you may have to pack at four o'clock in the morning after all and go to the train. But just tell the orderly that there must be some mistake and that he must take you straight to Schlesinger. Give my name and say I have discussed the matter with Frau Schlesinger and that you are waiting for a telegram from Puttkammer. That will settle the matter."[59]

The mysterious Mr. Trottel later tutored him on the line he must use:

Monday July 19th: . . . Was told semi-officially by Trottel that Fräulein Slottke had removed me from the list of applicants for Theresienstadt, so I must allow for the possibility of being deported to Poland. But I do not need to worry about the impending transport — Schlesinger will remove me from the transport list if I should happen to appear on it. . . . Trottel put his cards on the table. "I'm looking at things from a selfish point of view. I said to Schlesinger: 'After the war the German Jews will find themselves in a difficult position and it's vital for us to have Dutch Jews who will look after our interests.' " "I'll be willing to do that in so far as I am able." "You must say that clearly to Schlesinger. I have a lot to do this morning, but I thought I would just come and tell you." Now I know that Schlesinger was behind the Theresienstadt application as he wanted to gain time.[60]

Two weeks later an interview was arranged with Schlesinger:

Wednesday August 4th: Visited Schlesinger at his office yesterday evening together with Trottel. Schlesinger (in a blue shirt) handed round cigars. He began to tell me that he had just won a great victory in his talks with the *Obersturmführer*. He was now eighty per cent certain that no more transports would be going. Westerbork would become a labour camp and the elderly people who were here would stay on. . . .

I explained my views to Schlesinger about what could be done to remove the tension between Dutch and German Jews. It looks as if when the war ends there will be murder and slaughter at Westerbork. The Jews must not indulge in such a thing. . . . The existing conflicts are no justification in most cases for the feuds that are being built up. A Dutch-German contact committee should be formed to spread the idea that Dutch and German Jews should bury their feuds and, if necessary, create an organization which in an emergency would prevent acts of violence from being committed. Haste was imperative as peace was on the way. Schlesinger agreed to these ideas and expressed the wish that I would bring together a number of Dutch Jews who shared my views and were willing to confer with him. This would be my function.[61]

Mechanicus knew that one could not afford to express resentment openly toward German Jews at Westerbork if one was bidding for time to live, so he played the role of the diplomatic journalist with Schlesinger, willing to discuss means of allaying intergroup hostility. For Eli Cohen, a careless remark of his wife expressing such resentment proved their undoing in Westerbork:

In our house, in our front room, six people slept, with four in the back room. In that front room we lived with a German Jewish couple, a doctor I knew from Groningen. He was a typical Prussian. Everything had to be in a special place, and if it wasn't in its place, he got angry. Once my wife failed to put something in its proper place and he raise hell about it. Although we were Zionists and didn't, as a matter of principle, want to recognize any difference between German Jews, American Jews, or Dutch Jews, my wife said to him all the same, "You're a typically German Jew. Everything has to be organized for you. Otherwise you get into a panic."

This was told to Spanier, and one day I was summoned into his presence, and he said to me, "All Jews are the same. There's no difference between them. You say you are a Zionist, but that's not true, because you've lumped all the German Jews together. You've insulted them. Your wife has said this and that to so-and-so. From this moment on, my protection of you no longer applies."

He acted pretty speedily too. . . . In the middle of the night, the notorious chit accordingly arrived for me, reading: "On the orders of the *Obersturmführer*: . . . tonight you will be leaving by transport."[62]

The next to last stage in the Nazi game of dividing their victims and obscuring their vision was to demand that the Council itself, in May 1943, rank its own employees, compiling an A, B, and C list based on rank of indispensability, so that some might be transported. On 29 September 1943, the last batch of Council employees and its leaders, including Cohen and Asscher, were dispatched to Westerbork. During September 1944 the Jewish "ODs," the auxiliary police assisting in the seizure of Jews, Dr. Schlesinger, and the remainder of the AKs were transported. But the leaders of the Joodse Raad and other Jewish officials (including van Tijn) were sent to Bergen-Belsen camp rather than Auschwitz.

DUTCH RESPONSE
AND BELATED MOBILIZATION

How did the other Dutch, especially Amsterdam residents, of whom Jews had constituted over one out of 10, react to this scurry for personal security among the quarry? Their plight was clearly visible despite segregation—although the Jews were interned in special quarters, the oldest of these was in the heart of Amsterdam. Public trams were used to bring them to the railroad station, also in the center of Amsterdam, and the vans removing their furniture (another organized department for institutionalized looting all over Europe) were easily recognized. Both the deportations and the role played by the Joodse Raad were condemned by the resistance movement (itself virtually ineffectual in 1942 and disunited until 1944), which had issued a warning in July 1942 on the meaning of the deportations.

The pamphlet called on people to sabotage the preparations ("Remember the February strike of 1941"), demanded that the Secretaries-General, burgomasters, and other high officials refuse to assist in their execution, and urged individuals to write letters of protest to the Commander-in-Chief of the German armies in the Netherlands.

If it was naive to press for mass resistance when the leadership cadres had been removed, it was even more naive to expect officials who had accommodated continuously since the occupation to change course. According to a report prepared by Bene, the German Foreign Office representative in The Hague, on 31 July 1942, "temporary excitement was noticeable, especially in Amsterdam," but there were no problems created either by the Jews or by the Dutch administration:

> The attitude of the Dutch General Secretary of the Ministry of the Interior is interesting, who in spite of being neither a member of the NSB, nor a National Socialist, voiced the opinion, that this is a European problem, the course of which cannot be changed. Thus the deportation of the Jews, though it is not exactly supported by the Dutch authorities, is still approved by them without official protest.
>
> The next shipment will already include some families thus leaving for the East.
>
> In Jewish circles the opinion is widespread, that the Jews who are fit for labor service are being deported to prepare the necessary quarters for the Jews in the East.[63]

But Jews quickly rejected this line, according to a German report of 13 August 1942 (see p. 62). The only nationwide organizations with prewar leadership that could then function publicly and that could communicate with all classes were the churches. The largest of the Protestant denominations, the Dutch Reformed Church, had protested earlier to the Reichskommissar against the Aryan oath, against the street violence of collaborators in Amsterdam, and against racism in general, but refrained from making any but the last protest public to their congregants, thus failing to enjoin them to any specific obligation to their Jewish neighbors other than bestowing upon them love and mercy. When mass deportations began, the united council of churches sent a telegram of protest to the Reichskommissar:

> The suffering which this brings to tens of thousands, the recognition that these measures offend the deepest moral sense of the Dutch people, the opposition to God's laws of justice and mercy, all these force us to address to you the most urgent pleas not to implement these measures.
>
> Moreover, as far as Christians of Jewish origin are concerned this plea is strengthened by the fact that they have been debarred by this decree from participation in the life of the Church.[64]

Their last caveat gave the German authorities a bargaining point to use to still protest: the churches of all denominations were offered exemption for Christians of Jewish origin if they did not publicize their protest from the pulpit. The Dutch Reformed Church accepted the offer. The authorities considered they had made a good bargain, heading off opposition. Bene related to his superiors how

> it was planned to except these so-called Christian Jews from the deportation under the condition, that the churches would not feel any urge to take steps in behalf of the other Jews. The Protestant churches have not rejected this proposition and on their part have organized no public prayers, etc. in their churches. The Catholic Church, however, last Sunday commented on the deportation of the Jews in its churches. It was alleged that the standpoint of the Reich Commissioner did not everywhere become known in time.[65]

Snoek cites sources which tend to show that the other Protestant churches (which did protest) knew of this offer. Thus, many more members of the Dutch Reformed Church classed as Jews were probably exempted than were members of other churches classed as Jews. However, "a group of Christians of Jewish origin" petitioned the Dutch Reformed Church Synod:

> Be assured that if the proclamation of the Word of God (concerning the persecution of Jews) needs to be more clearly emphasized at this time—those among us who truly belong to the Lord are willing to be deported to Poland, confidently trusting in the Lord.[66]

The Roman Catholic Church of the Netherlands proved to be the most outspoken Roman Catholic Church in Europe by refusing the offer: its head denounced the deportations from the pulpit and in February 1943 forbade Catholic policemen from participating in hunts for Jews, even if it caused the loss of their jobs. The Dutch Reformed Church also urged noncooperation from the pulpit on 17 February 1943:

"We ought to obey God rather than men." This commandment is the touchstone in all conflicts of conscience, also in those that arise out of the recently taken steps. Because of God's justice, no one may participate in unjust actions since thereby he would become equally guilty of injustice.[67]

But 50,000 Jews had already been deported by then.

Despite the demonstrations of mass revulsion against the occupier's anti-Jewish measures in Amsterdam in 1941, there was no organized resistance to the deportations in 1942—there was scarcely any organized national resistance then. There were isolated networks of individuals who might help lead out small groups, such as J. Simon, who led one group of Zionist youths, and a few Christians (especially rural ones) marked by selfless dedication to saving Jews whom they did not know. In general, though, the population displayed indifference, being accustomed by then to viewing Jews as victims.

It was not until the spring of 1943, when the Dutch people were confronted with the threat of deportation of their young men to Germany for forced labor, that any effective social defense system, such as would have been necessary to save Jews in 1942, was created. But by 25 June 1943, Bene reported that "the 100,000th Jew has now been removed from the organism of the nation."[68] This left 20,000 registered Jews then in hiding and 20,000 who were protected by baptism or mixed marriages. Of the 20,000 presumed to be in hiding, half were betrayed or discovered (as were the Franks on 4 August 1944), often with the assistance of special police trained for the task and paid 37 guilders per Jew. De Jong tells us:

A score of specially trained Dutch Nazis on the Hague police force alone pulled in nearly two thousand Jews. During three months of 1943 a similar team in Amsterdam tracked down almost three thousand hidden Jews, and these agents—all of them Dutch—received for each captive a premium ranging from two and a half to about forty guilders—money derived from confiscated properties. Captured Jews sometimes became collaborators. Among them was a woman sentenced to death after the war who betrayed six hundred Jews in hiding, including her own brother and his family.[69]

Resistance organizations first had to solve the identification-card problem. The radical solution was to destroy the repository of all the cards, so that none could be authenticated. The third unsuccessful attempt to set fire to the Population Registry in Amsterdam was made on 27 March 1943. Population Inspector Lentz, who had invented the ubiquitous identification card, tried to repair the damage. To cover any event, he had made sure to leave a duplicate list of Jews' names and addresses in other headquarters. In April 1944 the Royal Air Force, at the request of the resistance movement, bombed the Central Population Registry, destroying 250,000 cards and killing over sixty people. By September 1944, the resistance movements were both integrated and differentiated enough to have a centralized counterfeiting unit that provided their cadres with catalogs of false stamps available. These could be ordered by number. It also ran off Belgian identity cards, "which were childishly simple compared with the Dutch."[70]

Why did a movement to aid people in hiding emerge almost a year after it would have been of most benefit to the Jews hunted for extermination? One answer, advanced by de Jong, cites the belated development of identification with Jews and the ambivalence or antipathy among the founders of this movement, who came from different social classes and regions than did most Jews. They did not share the empathy and intimate familiarity with Jews that characterized the leaders and followers of the Amsterdam strike of 1941. Founders of the 1943 movement were active church members from rural regions, whose leadership was not integrated with the Catholic networks extant at the beginning, reflecting the prewar communal segregation among the Dutch. They had little personal acquaintance with Jews and simply assimilated the distrust and contempt for Jews as an alien people common in the agrarian northwest of the Netherlands. Several leaders testified to dislike or ambivalence toward the Jews they helped — the victims' cringing fear and nervousness aroused their scorn.[71] Their mixed feelings, compounded by shame in the face of the Jews' persecution, which exposed Dutch powerlessness and passivity as well as lack of identification with the victims, led to resentment, as expressed in a slogan "reputedly written on a wall in Amsterdam in the summer of 1942; 'Hitler keep your dirty hands from our dirty Jews!'"[72] Evidence of earlier stereotypic labeling of the Jews is recorded by Marga Minco, who cites anti-Semitic taunts of children in her hometown of Breda before the war. Eli Cohen recalls how his neighbors occasionally expressed their latent stereotypes most directly, despite the fact that their Calvinism affirmed that Jews were a "Chosen People":

> There was indeed discrimination, in a very remarkable way. Precisely because I spoke so naturally about Jews, people sometimes forgot themselves. For example, someone once said to me, "Yes, doctor, the Jews. It's a difficult subject, isn't it? Difficult. But do you know who are much worse? The white Jews!"
>
> That was an idea I was unfamiliar with, and I asked him what he meant.
>
> "Well," he said, "they are our own people, Christians, who also lie and deceive. You don't expect *them* to. They're awful people. They're the white Jews. You expect it from a real Jew."[73]

But latent anti-Semitism seems an inadequate answer, considering that these same people did overcome their aversion to Jews in 1943.

DUTCH POSTWAR ASSESSMENT AND UNDERLYING CAUSES OF THE TOLL OF JEWISH VICTIMS

These seemingly contradictory trends make sense only if we relate the collapse of resistance between 1941 and 1943 and the accommodation of Dutch civil servants to the background of the lack of leadership by the government-in-exile and prewar political leaders who counseled accommodation. Confronted with inducements to collaborate and an absence of models urging resistance, most officials and notables simply accommodated to German authority. Those who did not were replaced. Dutch resistors were isolated as society became both atomized and "coordinated" simultaneously. For example, in the city of Groningen (where Cohen practiced), "125 of the 401 members of the police force were found [postwar] to have been pro-German, including 75 percent of the officers."[74] Those who were not were easily replaced during the war, as was the Burgomaster of Amsterdam. All of the 435 mayors who were dismissed after the liberation—about half of the total number of mayors in the Netherlands—had been appointed during the occupation.[75] The Nazi-dominated civil administration promoted the "coordination" of Nazified professional and previously voluntary associations, excluding Jewish members and incorporating new goals. There were also many volunteer Dutch Nazi paramilitary and military organizations, so that opportunities for collaboration existed in every arena for every age group and class, from boy scout to high court judge.

Efforts to indoctrinate a whole nation were also made in Norway but failed because of the forthright resistance of church and other leaders.[76] The extent of collaboration raised problems of reintegration after the war, as well as testing the capacity of an overloaded judicial system. Because so many of the Dutch had collaborated, not all could be tried. Purge boards were instituted for government employees, students, workers, and the press, and among persons engaged in the arts and media, to punish the more casual collaborators. However, apart from these,

> it has been estimated that in Holland between 120,000 and 150,000 persons were arrested in connection with charges of collaboration. The population of the Netherlands was 9,220,294 on January 1, 1945. Thus roughly one out of every 70 Dutchmen were arrested. The known maximum number of arrestees at one time was reached on October 15, 1945; 96,044 were imprisoned.[77]

Both David Cohen and Abraham Asscher were arrested in 1947 by the Dutch government on charges of collaboration, but they were released without trial after they were condemned for their role in the Joodse Raad by a Jewish Court of Honor; Cohen left the Jewish community thereafter.

The response of leaders of the Joodse Raad to German authority was modeled upon the accommodating response of most Dutch officials and notables at that time. In the beginning ready justifications of their role were available. Cooperation seemed to open opportunities for many Jews (17,000 were employed by the Council at one time) but these incentives deterred Jews from recognizing the collective threat against them. The success of the Joodse Raad in instituting discrimination among Jews made it less likely that Jews who believed they enjoyed privileged status and who had contacts with Christians would divert their energies to the attempt to create a social defense movement. It helped to enclose Jews in a cage, concentrated in marked and isolated quarters, making evasion infinitely more difficult. Starred and labeled, they could be readily fished out of any environment. If one removed the star outside the ghetto, one might evade notice, but the problem of sustaining an idle, stigmatized population outside the law remained. All kinds of counterinstitutions were needed in order to evade capture, not once, but every day for months and years, in order to survive in an occupied country with the extensive control system of the Netherlands. The nineteen months between the Joodse Raad's formation and the first street dragnet raids in September 1942, was the time in which the substructure should have been laid for a social defense movement that could have magnified chances for evasion. It was not.

Shelters, child placement services, couriers, assistants to dispense funds to people in hiding, funding sources, workshops for manufacturing counterfeit papers, and runners for distributing them were needed. Such an underground public assistance system required mobilization of untapped resources. Lacking Jewish models of resistance who might elicit identification as the action squads had in Amsterdam in 1941, few Christians mobilized in defense of Jews. Those who did found it safest (in an atmosphere under high risk of betrayal) to conceal rather than spread news of their services, so that many Jews seeking aid probably had no idea where to go. Only when the Dutch were threatened collectively by the seizure of their sons for forced labor did a nationwide social defense organization emerge.

Few Jews could benefit from such belated mobilization. The majority of those transported were exterminated in Auschwitz and other camps: only one out of 100 Dutch Jews deported there ever returned, while 30 of 100 returned from the concentration camps and Theresienstadt, where the "privileged" Jews still saved by the Germans for prisoner exchanges were interned. By the liberation, almost 108,000 Jews had been deported from the Netherlands or were interned at Westerbork; 77% of all registered Jews had been caught.[78] Of these, some 3,700 returned from extermination and concentration camps, chiefly from the latter. The last report of remains of the others was from a political prisoner who worked in the crematoria of Mauthausen since 1939, recalling how he had been ordered to smash the 3,000 urns of Dutch Jews' ashes when the Americans advanced.[79] But the ashes of the Dutch Jews who were gassed at Auschwitz, were merged with those of Jews throughout Europe as their destinies merged after having been singled out from the Dutch nation and other nations of Europe.

Hungary

Hungary, to Holocaust chroniclers, is the name of both a nation-state and a state of despair, an emblem of vulnerability inspiring rage and testing our powers of understanding. Although most Hungarians Jews were immune from deportation until after the German invasion of 19 March 1944, in no other country were so many Jews assimilated by the death machine so fast. Between 15 May and 9 July 1944, 437,402 Jews were deported, mostly to Auschwitz. In no other country was more information available on the previous fate of Europe's Jews and the facilities at Auschwitz. The causes that precipitated the invasion, Hungary's collaboration in their deportation, the lack of internal Hungarian resistance, and the failure of the dominant Roman Catholic Church to protest promptly have been discussed in chapters 4 and 7. In this chapter, we shall also relate the vulnerability of the Jews of Hungary to their lack of social cohesion, their prevailing expectations, the leaders' choices of strategy, and their common denial of recognition that their fate was related to that of other Jews in Europe.

We shall reconstruct the experience of the Jews of Hungary's provinces through the contemporary impressions and recollections of two persons who were then adolescent—Eva Heyman and Eli Wiesel. Eva Heyman's diary was found after the war, and Eli Wiesel's recollections are contained in his first autobiographical novel, *Night*.[1] Both are among the 92% of the Jews of Transylvania deported to Auschwitz, where Eva was killed.

Although the choice of witnesses is restricted by the paucity of translated autobiographical accounts of Hungarian Jews, it is fitting—not merely opportune—that the tale be told by witnesses old enough to be keenly observant but too young at the time to choose their own destiny freely. Just as their children lacked parents and guardians capable of apprehending and reacting to danger, the Hungarian Jews lacked leaders who could alert and direct the community to enable it to avoid victimization.

COLLECTIVE CONSCIOUSNESS OF HUNGARIAN JEWRY

Magyar Jewry was characterized since World War I by its political disunity, split between the domains of Hungary and Rumania (which incorporated a large part of Hungary after World War I, returned to Hungary in 1940), between modern "Neolog" (reformed) Jews and premodern orthodox Jews, between assimilated "Jewish Hungarians" and apolitical and less assimilated Jews. Further, a substantial proportion of Jews had become Christians and/or were married to the local gentry, uniting the wealth of bourgeois accomplishments with the status of feudal honor. Never had the Hungarian Jews united to protest to the world the increasing political discrimination against them (beginning in 1920 and accelerating in 1938), which was justified by the "Szeged Idea," the counterrevolutionary program of the radical right that identified Jews with Bolshevism, rationalizing anti-Semitism as an integral part of the fight against Bolshevism. Nagy-Talavera observes:

> The Jews had, nevertheless, one effective means of checking the Szeged Idea. The Trianon Treaty guaranteed equal rights to all Hungarians, regardless of their creed, race, or nationality. The Rumanian Jews, through their connections abroad, forced the victorious Rumanian state into granting full citizenship to their unassimilated masses—many of them barely able to speak Rumanian—in 1923. The powerful Alliance Israelite now offered its services to the Hungarian Jews. They refused in categorical terms. . . . "We are not Hungarian Jews but Jewish Hungarians." Ultimately the "bad" Rumanian Jews got better treatment as punishment than the "good" Hungarian Jews got as a reward.[2]

To understand the lack of apprehension of the German threat among provincial Jewry in Hungary in 1944, we must account for the lack of communication and leadership from Jewish leaders in Budapest, the nerve center of communications and political intelligence. Two foci of leadership existed there: the notables and heads of religious federations, selected as members of the Budapest Jewish Council, and the Zionist Waada, or Budapest Rescue Committee, which arranged aid for Jews who fled from Slovakia and Poland and transmitted information to the Jewish Agency in Istanbul during the war.

The Jewish Council of Budapest, later named the Central Council of Hungarian Jews, was established by order of the SS on 20 March 1944. Its leaders appealed to the Hungarian government for instructions and were told they were directly and wholly responsible to the Germans.[3] The Council was later personally guided by Adolf Eichmann, who assured its members of their personal safety and Jews' collective safety if they just followed orders. From March until June 1944, their energy was expended in allaying the incessant Germand demands for goods—sometimes adding personal contributions to guarantee their own exemption—and fulfilling German orders to segregate the Jews.[4] The role of this and other councils is discussed in detail in Chapter 5.

The energies of the leaders of the Budapest refugee aid committee, Rudolph Kastner and Joel Brand, were absorbed by negotiations proposed by the SS, with whom they had sought contact.[5] SS Reichsführer Himmler proposed (through Eichmann) an exchange of 10,000 trucks, to be contributed by the Allies for the German war effort (and to be used only on the eastern front, they were assured), for the lives of one million Jews. Joel Brand was sent to Istanbul with a shadow, a Jewish Gestapo double agent who freely revealed his role to Brand; their transport and papers were arranged for by the SS.[6] There they made contact with the Jewish Agency and, through its leaders, with the western Allies, who rejected negotiations. The proposal masked Himmler's bid for a separate peace with the West; Brand and his shadow served as involuntary and/or voluntary agents for Himmler. Understandably, this negated their credibility with the Allies; Britain immediately viewed the offer transmitted by German agents as an invitation to betray their Soviet ally.

After the failure of Brand's mission, he behaved equivocally, casting blame on the Jewish Agency, the British—on everyone but himself. Instead of returning to Hungary, as he had promised Eichmann, he took a train to Syria, despite advice that he would be arrested there (as he was) by the British. Kastner meanwhile reestablished SS ties and pursued another exchange project. He was allowed to select about 1,700 persons from the ranks of Budapest Jews and deportees from the provinces; these were interned in a special camp in Budapest and later sent to Bergen-Belsen.[7] Another six transports of 17,500 to 18,000 Jews were incarcerated by the Germans in Strasshof camp, Austria, and were also saved from the ovens of Auschwitz. Kastner's initial choice of beneficiaries—including some relatives and others who bought their places on the train—and the undisputed failure of the Committee to transmit news of the extermination of the Jews, and thus to arouse resistance to deter the collective isolation and deportation of the Jews from the provinces, were among the postwar charges of collaboration brought against him. Kastner, then an Israeli government official, was pressed by higher officials to exonerate himself. On his behalf, the government brought a suit for libel in the Jerusalem District Court against Malkiel Gruenwald, author of a political newsletter who had accused Kastner of collaboration and "preparation of the ground for murder" of the Jews of Hungary. The trial in 1954 resulted initially in the exoneration of Gruenwald: Judge Binyamin Halevi concluded that Kastner had "sold his soul to the devil" in allowing himself to be used by the Nazis. But in 1958 Israel's

Supreme Court exonerated Kastner (in a split decision) on the ground that his intent was not to destroy Jews.[8] Kastner could no longer benefit by being cleared, having been assassinated on the streets of Tel Aviv in 1957.

SOCIAL CONTEXTS OF IMPENDING THREATS

Both Eva Heyman and Eli Wiesel were natives of cities of Transylvania that had been Hungarian prior to World War I, were awarded to Rumania by the Treaty of Trianon, and regained by Hungary after the second Vienna award of 1940, adjudicated by Hitler. Eva Heyman was a native of Nagyvárad, a city of about 93,000 people — of whom 21,133 (or 22.7%) were Jews in 1944.[9] Her account of her grandfather's difficulties at this time makes clear the extent of his political involvement with Magyar parties, notables, and elites as well as her mother's involvement with Hungarian left democratic parties. Nagyvárad had both the largest concentration of Jews in Transylvania and the largest ghetto in 1944; 36,000 Jews were interned there in 1944, including Jews from smaller towns nearby.[10]

Eli Wiesel grew up in Marammossziget (Sighet), a city of almost 26,000 including 10,144 Jews in 1940 (39.1% of the population). This was the highest proportion that Jews constituted in any of the larger cities (over 20,000) of Transylvania.[11]

Wiesel's *Night* reveals little participation by the Jews of Sighet in Hungarian political life. This might be explained by Wiesel's own lack of awareness or might reflect the fact that Jews had ceased to participate: they were subjects, not citizens. But it can also be accounted for by the other-worldly ethos dominating the life of his Chassidic family. Although as Jews they were both discriminated from other Hungarian subjects, Eva Heyman and Eli Wiesel shared little in the way of beliefs, culture, assumptions, or aspirations. Eva Heyman was the daughter of divorced parents from well-known Jewish families, including noted Neolog rabbis, pharmacists, and landowners. Her mother, a self-avowed socialist, had married the writer Bela Zsolt, previously a deputy in the Hungarian Parliament, with whom she lived in Budapest. Eva boarded with her maternal grandparents in Nagyvárad. Her father had previously converted to Catholicism. Though both Heyman and Wiesel were children of the middle classes, they represent contrary trends of Jewish identity: the Wiesels were conservative, orthodox, and encapsulated by the Jewish community whereas Eva's mother and stepfather were socialist, universalistic in their political ideals, assimilated, and worldly. Eli Wiesel aspired at the age of 12 to pierce the mysteries of the Kabbala (the repository of Jewish mysticism); Eva's desire at 13 was "to be a news photographer and to marry an Aryan Englishman,"[12] in the hope that this would endear her to her mother, whose lack of interest in her was apparent to Eva.

After the war began, Eva saw the people she most loved and needed wrested from her one by one. First, there was her beloved governess, an upright woman of whom Eva wrote, "I admire Juszti more than anyone else in the world."[13] Juszti, who had served the family for two generations, was forbidden to work for them by the leader of the local Volksbund, who could direct the actions of ethnic Germans. Eva's mother, Ági, was constantly in Budapest trying to use her connections there to liberate her husband from the military prison in which he was incarcerated. Her best friend, Márta, had been notified in Eva's presence that she was sought by the police following the girls' return from an afternoon of biking and was deported in 1941.

> That afternoon, it will be three years this summer, Márta was over at our house. First we went riding our bicycles in Szálldobágy. That was my first "tour" on this bicycle. Márta's was just like mine, only hers was a brighter red. Then we came home. . . . Suddenly the bell at the front gate rang five times. It was Márta's nursemaid, who had stayed on with them as a cook, because Márta didn't need a nursemaid any more. She came in and said: "Mártika, come home. The police are there, and you have to go with Papa and Mama." I still remember Ági. She turned white as the plaster on the walls. But Márta said it must be because she rode her bicycle so fast on Rimanóczi Street, and her father had said many times that she would end up at the police on account of "speeding." That explanation reassured me, but Ági paced up and down the room in such a strange manner, and she kept calling Aunt Pásztor, Márta's grandmother, on the telephone but there was no answer. In the morning I also called, but there was no answer from Márta's telephone. I heard Ági tell Grandma that at the Journalists Club the night before they had said that the government was preparing to do something terrible, and Jews who weren't born in Hungary would be taken to Poland where a horrible fate was in store for them.[14]

Braham reports that of the 15,000 to 18,000 alien Jews and Hungarian Jews who could not prove their citizenship (including Jews born in Hungary) and were deported, "most of them were subsequently slaughtered, by the SS and their Hungarian and Ukrainian hirelings near Kamenets Podolsk on August 27–28, 1941."[15]

Eva's loss was harder to bear because of the nerve-wracking atmosphere of her grandparents' home, dominated by her grandmother, an impeccable superintendent of bourgeois order who habitually became hysterical when there was any disorder or new experience to assimilate. This characteristic maladaptation later becomes fatal for Eva. Following the 1940 Hungarian occupation of Transylvania, her grandfather's pharmacy was expropriated. After some petitioning and bribery it was returned, but Mr. Rácz was no longer permitted to manage it, and as a result the family experienced financial difficulties.

> Well, a few days after the Magyars came, Grandpa was very upset because they immediately evicted all the Rumanian families who had to leave all their belongings behind. The city has changed completely; the streets are constantly full with

throngs of people, none of them familiar. Grandpa said: "Paratroopers from the motherland," and Grandma said that the boulevard is full of creatures looking like Arrow-and-Cross people. Once Grandpa was summoned to the City Hall, and the military commander told him that he won't be allowed to stay in the pharmacy any more, because he's an unreliable Rumanian-lover and a Jew. And from now on Vitéz Károly Szepesváry will be the owner of the pharmacy because he is reliable, and what is more, a Vitéz, and it will be called "The Hungarian Crown."

Let me point out that the commander of the city is also a Vitéz: Vitéz Gábor Rajnay, whose name used to be Rajner. . . . Rajnay was a Swabian [of German descent] and Ági said that all these Vitéz-men are Swabians. Altogether, Ági says, in Hungary almost everybody in power is a Swabian. . . . That Vitéz Szepesváry was in the pharmacy for two whole months. Thank God I've stopped thinking, except in my dreams, about how much I suffered at that time. First of all from Grandma Rácz. Grandma quarrelled with Grandpa all day, as though he had personally called on Vitéz Szepesváry to take over the pharmacy. And hadn't she always told Grandpa not to befriend the Wallachians — that is what the prejudiced Hungarians call the Rumanians — whom she couldn't stand anyway? . . . All that time I didn't dare to budge. I came out of my room only for lunch and dinner, and even then Grandma didn't stop quarrelling. . . .

One evening — as it happened, it was in December, and Ági's birthday is on December 2 — Vitéz Szepesváry received a letter from Vitéz Rajnay, and he had to vacate Grandpa's pharmacy immediately. Vitéz Rajnay wrote that Grandpa wasn't an unreliable Jew and never had been a Rumanian-lover, but actually always had been a good, solid Hungarian, and there had been some mistake. I thought that that was because all his life, when the Rumanians had been here, Grandpa had belonged to the Magyar Party and had given a lot of money to this party, because in Varad there were many Hungarians who couldn't or wouldn't learn Rumanian and thus couldn't work. So the Magyar Party collected money for them every month and Grandpa always gave to them. Grandpa always gives to anybody who just asks him. Everybody in town knew this about Grandpa, and when Vitéz settled himself in the pharmacy, the Bishop of the Reformed Church and the Catholic and Evangelical bishops all wrote a letter to Vitéz Rajnay saying what a good Magyar Grandpa was all the time the Rumanians were here. A Hungarian workers' delegation even went to the City Hall, presented themselves before Vitéz Rajnay and demanded that the pharmacy be returned to Grandpa. I thought that that was the reason why it was given back to him. But afterwards I found out that Vitéz Rajnay had to be paid five thousand pengos. Only Grandpa didn't have five thousand pengos, so we sold the piano. . . .

So, on the evening of December 1, at 7 o'clock, Szepesváry left the pharmacy raving mad. But he warned Grandpa: he would show him yet; Grandpa wouldn't die in bed, but in quite a different way altogether. I thought that bed was the only possible place to die in, but they say that the Mártas also didn't die in bed in Poland; the Germans shot them. Márta's grandmother doesn't know it, because she still keeps cleaning Uncle Münzer's dress-suit on the balcony, and the neighbours say that while she is cleaning, she has conversation with the suit; naturally, she does all the talking. If she knew they were dead, she certainly wouldn't go on brushing the suit. Does Vitéz Szepesváry mean that the Germans will murder Grandpa?[16]

Eva's grandmother blamed her husband for being victimized, as she blamed her daughter, Ági, for divorcing her husband and leaving her granddaughter with her.

Eli Wiesel's world was still whole and meaningful between 1941 and 1944, if less concretely depicted in recollection. He does not relate how he felt about the loss of his first true mentor, who transmitted the warning of impending destruction to him and other Jews. This period is recalled in the opening chapter of *Night:*

> They called him Moché the Beadle, as though he had never had a surname in his life. He was a man of all works at a Hasidic synagogue. The Jews of Sighet—that little town in Transylvania where I spent my childhood—were very fond of him. He was very poor and lived humbly. Generally my fellow townspeople, though they would help the poor, were not particularly fond of them. Moché the Beadle was the exception. Nobody ever felt embarrassed by him. Nobody ever felt encumbered by his presence. . . .
>
> I got to know him toward the end of 1941. I was twelve. I believed profoundly. During the day I studied the Talmud, and at night I ran to the synagogue to weep over the destruction of the Temple.
>
> One day I asked my father to find me a master to guide me in my studies of the cabbala. . . .
>
> He wanted to drive the notion out of my head. But it was in vain. I found a master for myself, Moché the Beadle. . . .
>
> And Moché the Beadle, the poor barefoot of Sighet, talked to me for long hours of the revelations and mysteries of the cabbala. It was with him that my initiation began. . . .
>
> Then one day they expelled all the foreign Jews from Sighet. And Moché the Beadle was a foreigner.
>
> Crammed into cattle trains by Hungarian police, they wept bitterly. We stood on the platform and wept too. The train disappeared on the horizon; it left nothing behind but its thick, dirty smoke.
>
> I heard a Jew behind me heave a sigh. "What can we expect?" he said. "It's war."[17]

Moché the Beadle returned several months later to Sighet, after most Jews had forgotten the deportees.

> One day, as I was just going into the synagogue, I saw, sitting on a bench near the door, Moché the Beadle.
>
> He told his story and that of his companions. The train full of deportees had crossed the Hungarian frontier and on Polish territory had been taken in charge by the Gestapo. There it had stopped. The Jews had to get out and climb into lorries. The lorries drove toward a forest. The Jews were made to get out. They were made to dig huge graves. And when they had finished their work, the Gestapo began theirs. Without passion, without haste, they slaughtered their prisoners. Each one had to go up to the hole and present his neck. Babies were thrown into the air and the machine gunners used them as targets. This was in the forest of Galicia, near Kolomaye. How had Moché the Beadle escaped? Miraculously. He was wounded in the leg and taken for dead. . . .

Through long days and nights, he went from one Jewish house to another, telling the story of Malka, the young girl who had taken three days to die, and of Tobias, the tailor, who had begged to be killed before his sons. . . .

Moché had changed. There was no longer any joy in his eyes. He no longer sang. He no longer talked to me of God or the cabbala, but only of what he had seen. People refused not only to believe his stories, but even to listen to them.

"He's just trying to make us pity him. What an imagination he has!" they said. Or even: "Poor fellow. He's gone mad."

And as for Moché, he wept.

"Jews, listen to me. It's all I ask of you. I don't want money or pity. Only listen to me," he would cry between prayers at dusk and the evening prayers.

I did not believe him myself. I would often sit with him in the evening after the service, listening to his stories and trying my hardest to understand his grief. I felt only pity for him.

"They take me for a madman," he would whisper, and tears, like drops of wax, flowed from his eyes.[18]

Life again returned to regular pursuits—the cycle of daily business and eternal days of rest, joy, awe, recollection. The Jews had normalized the situation, as they had so many previous years of persecution.

1944: EVA'S STORY

When the Germans invaded Hungary on 19 March 1944, Eva's mother, Ági, and her husband, Uncle Béla, were in Nagyvárad, where Ági was recovering from an operation.

Today Ági got out of bed for lunch for the first time. Grandma even remarked that she was as weak as a winter fly, but still she ate with us. We had a delicious punch cake, wine, and black coffee. All day, nobody turned on the radio. At noon Uncle Béla wanted to hear the news, but Ági convinced him not to, begging, "No politics today, just our own private lives." . . .

A whole group of friends gathered and Uncle Béla and Sándor Friedländer went to a café. Ági didn't want them to go, because she always worries that Uncle Béla might be taken away to the Ukraine or arrested again, but everybody laughed at Ági. Even Grandpa said: "Don't worry one bit, my little daughter, we will yet gaily dance Kállay's Couple Dance. The way things are now they would be happy to get out in one piece from all the filthy things they have already done." Ági explains us that Kállay, who is Prime Minister now, realizes that the Germans have lost the war, and smiles at them only so they shouldn't press us, but he also waves to the British, so they shouldn't press us when the war ends and they enter Hungary. . . . But that doesn't even matter, unfortunately, nothing matters now; the only thing that matters is that Hitler's dogs are here.

Ten minutes later Uncle Béla and Uncle Sándor Friedländer were back, looking white as sheets. I can still hear Uncle Sándor: "It's all over with us; the Germans are in Budapest." . . . Grandma turned on the radio, and they didn't broadcast the regular programme but kept on playing marches. . . . Ági wanted

Uncle Béla and Sándor Friedländer escape across the border to Rumania tonight, because they are in more trouble than the rest of us. Everybody in the country knows what a leftist journalist Uncle Béla is, and Uncle Sándor has always been a Socialist. That is also well known. Because when Horthy unthroned the King and became the ruler of Hungary, Uncle Sándor ran away to Vienna and for a long time couldn't come home. Ági even used to say that decent people should long since have run away from this country, because otherwise they would be put in prison or murdered.[19]

Within a week the political atmosphere had altered. Eva wrote on 25 March 1944, "Grandma says that the Aryans are greeting her cooly in the street, or turning the other way."[20] A public propaganda campaign commenced. Eva noted on 26 March 1944:

The radio keeps issuing warnings about air bombings, or it curses the Jews, but much more furiously than before. I'm not even afraid of bombings any more, because I would rather have bombings, then they would stop cursing the Jews. And on the radio they keep announcing all kinds of regulations about the Jews, all the things they are not allowed to do.[21]

Suspected Communists and Socialists were indiscriminately arrested (without charges) by German and Hungarian police; these included Uncle Sándor Friedländer. Uncle Béla's books were banned. Agi began burning her husbands' books and letters immediately. On 29 March 1944, Eva related how the stripping began:

Today some people came from the Jewish Community Council and took almost all our bed linens. Every day the Germans demand something else from the Jews. One day it's typewriters, the next day carpets, and today it was bed linens. At first Grandma tried to bargain, but then she said that nothing mattered any more and they could take whatever they wanted. She didn't even want to choose, she just handed those strangers the key to the linen closet, which in normal times she would only grudgingly give to Juszti, or even to Ági.[22]

The very next day, some Jews were also stripped of homes.

Now the worst is only starting. This afternoon Grandpa came home with the news that the Germans are throwing the Jews out of the finest houses, and they are allowed to take along only the clothes they wear, and nobody asks them where they will sleep. The others take in the dispossessed people, but Grandpa says that it has already happened that an hour later the people who have taken others in are also thrown out, and then there are even more families out in the street without a place to live. . . .
    This afternoon I saw the Waldmanns from the window of our children's room. Carrying a little handbag and a basket, they went out through the gate, and outside three German officers were standing. One of them kicked Uncle Waldmann in the behind as he came out through the gateway of his house in order to hand that pretty little house over to the damned Germans. But I didn't speak about it to anyone, not even to Uncle Béla.[23]

Two days later, Jews were ordered to wear yellow stars and the last of immobile property—stores—was taken from them. To complete their segregation, telephones had been shut off, cutting Ági off from her contacts in Budapest, whom she used to call nightly. Within a week, the marked, yellow-starred victims met each other in the street conveying their few belongings to new quarters. But Eva's grandparents still were in their home and had Mariska, the Christian maid, there to care for Eva and clean the house, compensating for the incapacity (and hysteria) of Eva's mother and grandmother. Eva visited her paternal grandmother, Grandma Lujz, who "says she doesn't even care if she dies. But she is seventy-two, and I'm only thirteen. And . . . I certainly don't want to die!"[24] Eva was unreconciled and unresigned: she refused to deny her thirst for life as she would refuse to hand over her bicycle when the local gendarmes came for it. But she was overlooked while her mother mobilized all her energies to save her husband: it is significant that the first person to think of saving Eva was Juszti. She found herself caught in a web of personal bonds knitted by others with no regard (or hatred) for Jews. Eva recorded on 27 March 1944:

> Juszti came over today. She cried terribly and said that Aunt Poroszlay would let me stay at their estate, but Uncle Poroszlay said that it is out of the question. I would be perfectly happy with their pig pen or their barn, and I would do any kind of work for them, even look after their sheep, just so the German's shouldn't kill me with a gun as they killed Márta. Grandpa is trying everything. He is trying to get forged documents at least for Uncle Béla, but nothing works. . . .
>
> Altogether, now everybody says about everything: They will kill you. As it that weren't the most terrible thing in the world. And how awful it is that every time the bell rings Ági screams: They've come to take Béla. This also shows how much Ági loves Uncle Béla, because it doesn't even occur to her that they might be coming to take someone else. Not just him.[25]

Eva's entries paralleled the pace of continued stripping, segregation, and ghettoization of the Jews. On 7 April she recorded:

> Today they came for my bicycle. I almost caused a big drama. You know, dear diary, I was awfully afraid just by the fact that the policemen came into the house. I know that policemen bring only trouble with them, wherever they go. My bicycle had a proper license plate, and Grandpa had paid the tax for it. That's how the policemen found it, because it was registered at City Hall that I have a bicycle. Now that it's all over, I'm so ashamed about how I behaved in front of the policemen. So, dear diary, I threw myself on the ground, held on to the back wheel of my bicycle, and shouted all sorts of things at the policemen: "Shame on you for taking away a bicycle from a girl! That's robbery!" We had saved up for a year and a half to buy the bicycle. We had sold my old bicycle, my layette and Grandpa's old winter coat and added the money we saved. My grandparents, Juszti, the Ágis, Grandma Lujza and Papa all had chipped in to buy my bicycle. We still didn't have the whole sum, but Hoffmann didn't sell the bicycle to anyone else, and he even said that I could take the bicycle home. My father would pay, or

Grandpa. But I didn't want to take the bicycle home until we had all the money. But in the meantime I hurried over to the store whenever I could and looked to see if that red bicycle was still there. How Ági laughed when I told her that when the whole sum was finally there. I went to the store and took the bicycle home, only I didn't ride it but led it along with my hands, the way you handle a big, beautiful dog. From the outside I admired the bicycle, and even gave it a name: Friday. I took the name from Robinson Crusoe, but it suits the bicycle. . . .

One of the policemen was very annoyed and said: All we need is for a Jewgirl to put on such a comedy when her bicycle is being taken away. No Jewkid is entitled to keep a bicycle anymore. The Jews aren't entitled to bread, either; they shouldn't guzzle everything, but leave the food for the soldiers. You can imagine, dear diary, how I felt when they were saying this to my face. I had only heard that sort of thing on the radio, or read it in a German newspaper. Still, it's different when you read something and when it's thrown into your face. . . .

But you know, dear diary, I think the other policeman felt sorry for me. You should be ashamed of yourself, colleague, he said, is your heart made of stone? How can you speak that way to such a beautiful girl? Then he stroked my hair and promised to take good care of my bicycle. He gave me a receipt and told me not to cry, because when the war was over I would get my bicycle back. At worst it would need some repairs at Hoffmann's.[26]

Her father (despite being a converted Catholic) was arrested two days later: Eva was asked by her paternal grandmother to bring his lunch to him in the prison and delivered it despite her maternal grandmother's screaming opposition. It was not clear to her why he was being held.

While waiting to get in I found out that my father was being held as a hostage. I saw Aunt Ági Friedländer there, and somehow I pushed my way through to her. She was also bringing lunch to Uncle Sándor, who had been brought to this elementary school building from the City Hall cellar. I was very glad about this because after all, the school building is better than that cellar. While we waited, Aunt Ági explained to me that hostage means security, that is, my father has now become a security; only I don't understand how a human being can be a security.[27]

Her father was released on 20 April, but Uncle Sándor was not. On 10 April Eva wrote that their maid, Mariska, had been ordered to leave by 15 April.[28] But even after Mariska left officially, she sneaked back after dark to visit and do the housework.

Any potential political opposition to the new regime had been squashed by the arrest of political prisoners (more immediate in Budapest). On 13 April, Eva noted:

So many terrible things are happening, dear diary, that I don't even feel like writing any more. For example, today Uncle Sándor and all the political prisoners were transported away from here. . . . Uncle Béla tried to console Aunt Ági by saying that the political prisoners, even though they are in trouble, are in less danger than if they were merely Jews, because there are also Aryan political prisoners among them, and they don't dare to finish them off the way they do the

Jews. It is interesting, Uncle Béla said to me, that the Jews aren't the only Socialists and Communists; there are also many Aryans among them.[29]

Although Eva's mother was immobilized and could no longer phone friends, the family had several Christian friends and relations who cared enough to make plans to secure false papers for them or hide Eva. All these plans were rejected whenever her grandmother threw a fit, emotionally blackmailing her daughter Ági. Eva recorded on 18 April that

> just after sunset Ági's Christian cousin, Sányi Kaufmann, came from Pest, where he works as a clerk in the Pannonia Hotel. He brought Ági and Uncle Béla forged documents which he stole from the hotel, and he wanted to smuggle them to Budapest via Békéscsaba tonight. Today was an awful day, dear diary, because Grandma heard what was going on, she threw herself on the floor and literally screeched. She said that Ági is a murderer, because if Ági and Uncle Béla run away they will kill her in their place. She screamed other terrible things, until Ági gave her her word of honour that nobody would run away, no matter what! Sányi said there is a "reign of terror" in Budapest, but still, Budapest is a big city, and it will be possible to find some Aryan Socialist or Communist who will be willing to hide Ági and her husband. . . . Grandpa took me to Marica's house so that I shouldn't hear all those horrors. And the doctor had to be called for Grandma. When I came home from Marica it was already late in the evening. Ági was sobbing and wailing that they had missed their last chance, and all of us would die in Poland. This is the first time I heard Ági say such a thing. I mean, so it's true that I'll be taken to Poland, the way Márta was. Maybe I'll also be taken there because I had a red bicycle, like Márta. . . . I overheard the doctor tell Ági that, unfortunately, Grandma had gone out of her mind. But if the world were to straighten itself out, she would most certainly get well again, because she was not actually insane. Sányi also brought documents for me, but they didn't even show them to me. They all got so scared over Grandma that Sányi went right back to Budapest.[30]

Her grandmother was evidently convinced that their disobedience (running away) would bring about her death, and their obedience would save her life. The next day, she interfered with yet another plan to save Eva.

April 19, 1944
There is a seamstress here, dear diary, Mrs. Jakobi, who used to sew me such lovely dresses every year. That woman loves me and Ági, too, and she's an Aryan. This Mrs. Jakobi didn't know that poor Grandma Rácz was sick, and she sneaked in to see us at night, like Mariska and Uncle Zoltán. She called Grandma into the kitchen, so that nobody should hear what they were saying. Ági suspected something and followed them, but by the time she got there Grandma let out a roar, like when Sányi came from Pest with the forged documents. It seems that Mrs. Jakobi wanted to take me to her place right then and there, and nobody would know that I was there. She could even take my dresses along to her place without attracting attention at all, because she is a seamstress. But Grandma said that she wouldn't allow it, because Mrs. Jakobi was an evil woman and she would sell me to men and then I would also be an evil woman. . . . This Mrs. Jakobi

really isn't an evil woman, as poor Grandma said. She is a very good woman, and I don't even understand what Grandma meant when she did say that Mrs. Jakobi would sell me to men. Nobody is buying Jewish girls these days and Ági even said that Grandma only says such things because she is sick right now. You know, dear diary, even though it would be very bad not to see Ági and all the rest for such a long time, I would go with Aunt Jakobi, or with Sányi, to any place in the world where they don't know that I'm Jewish and wherefrom I couldn't be taken to Poland like Márta was.[31]

At every step, the Hungarian officials and police probed in order to strip Jews of their worldly goods, proceeding as if they were conducting an inventory, from the most visible and immovable to the less visible and portable goods. On 20 April they came for household appliances: the sewing machine, radio, telephone (previously inactivated), vacuum cleaner, electric fryer, camera, and typewriter. Ági and her parents were already indifferent to these losses, perhaps recognizing that nostalgia for their style of life only fit a world where one assumes that social bonds have a permanence and durability corresponding to the fitting's of one's milieu.

Eva's entry of 20 April conveys the limbo-like emptiness replacing the shimmer, warmth, comfort, and security, but looks beyond the emptiness to confront the choices still open that her mother would not face.

The apartment was still so lovely in March when Ági and Uncle Béla came. . . . Now the apartment isn't pretty any more. All the beautiful things in it have been taken away. The silverware, the rugs, the paintings, the Venetian mirror. They left a receipt for the rugs, but even Grandpa says that we will never get them back. Grandpa is very sad ever since he hasn't been able to work in the pharmacy any more. He looks at Ági in such an odd, sad way, and he keeps caressing her all the time, as though he is saying goodbye to her. Ági even said to him: Don't cling to me as though we are saying goodbye, my sweet Papa, because my heart is breaking. Ági wants to go on having a father forever. I can understand that, because I also want all of us to stay alive. Márta didn't want to stay here without her Papa and she went with him to die in Poland. Of course, she couldn't know in advance that she was being taken to her death. . . . I've often wondered: had Márta known . . . would she still have gone?[32]

Only ten days later, on 1 May 1944:

Mariska burst into the house and said: Have you seen the notices? No, we hadn't, we are not allowed to go outside, except between nine and ten! Aha, that's why we're allowed outside only between nine and ten, because we're being taken to the Ghetto.[33]

They were moved into the ghetto by van, conducted out of their homes by Hungarian policemen, now intent on discovering the rest of the Jews' personal effects, jewels, and clothing: real property, household goods, and hardware had already been collected.

Three days we waited for them to come and get us. . . . Then everything happened like in a film. The two policemen who came to us weren't unfriendly; they just took Grandma's and Ági's wedding rings away from them. Ági was shaking all over and couldn't get the wedding ring off her finger. In the end, Grandma took the ring off her finger. Then they checked our luggage and they didn't allow us to take Grandpa's valise because it is genuine pigskin. They didn't allow anything made out of leather to be taken along. They said: There is a war going on and the soldiers need the leather. They also didn't allow me to take my red purse. We took washing kits and Grandma's thick cloth bag.

One of the policemen saw a little gold chain on my neck, the one I got for my birthday, the one holding your key, dear diary. Don't you know yet, the policeman said, that you aren't allowed to keep anything made of gold?! This isn't private Jewish property anymore but national property! Whenever something was being taken from us, Ági would always pretend not to notice at all, because she had an obsession about not letting the policemen think it bothered us that our things were being taken, but this time she begged the policeman to let me keep the little gold chain. She started sobbing and saying: Mr. Inspector, please go and ask your colleagues, and they will tell you that I have never begged for anything, but please let the child keep just this little gold chain. You see, she keeps the key to her diary on it. Please, the policeman said, that is impossible; in the Ghetto you will be checked again. I, so help me God, don't need this chain or any other object that is being taken from you. I don't need any of it, but I don't want any difficulties. I am a married man. My wife is going to have a baby. I gave him the chain. In Grandma's night table I found a velvet ribbon. I asked the policeman: Mr. Inspector, may I take a velvet ribbon along to the Ghetto? He said I could. Now your key hangs on that velvet ribbon, dear diary.[34]

Sixteen people were assigned to a room; they selected a room elder to keep order. Despite the fear and darkness at night—"City Hall had cut off the electricity, because Jews aren't entitled to electricity"—Eva was happy, cuddling up at night with her friend Marica, perhaps feeling safer in a group than at home because she was immune from her grandmother's threats and her mother's anxiety. But the longing of the powerless for power emerges in the dreams of night, the subterranean guardian of all longing. Eva dreamt that the youth whose glances she longed for, Pista Vardas, "was the driver of the truck, and I was awfully angry that Pista Vardas had become an S.S. man."[35]

Within five days they were completely isolated. Eva recorded on 10 May 1944:

The fence was finished, and nobody can go out or come in. The Aryans who used to live in the area of the Ghetto all left during these few days to make place for the Jews. From today on, dear diary, we're not in a Ghetto but in a Ghetto-camp, and on every house they've pasted a notice which tells exactly what we're not allowed to do, signed by Gendarme Lieutenant-Colonel Péterffy, commander of the Ghetto-camp, himself. Actually, everything is forbidden, but the most awful thing of all is that the punishment for everything is death. There is no difference between things; no standing in the corner, no spankings, no taking away food, no writing down the declension of irregular verbs one hundred times the way it used to be in school. Not at all: the lightest and heaviest punishment—death. It doesn't actually say that this punishment also applies to children, but I think it does apply to us, too.[36]

Four days later, the police came to draft all males from 16 to 60. Their captors were not satisfied that they had found all the wealth the Jews were believed to possess, so that they used the remaining two weeks in the ghetto to torture the inmates to reveal if they had buried their treasure in the ground or entrusted it to Christians. Eva wrote on 17 May that

> the interrogation has begun in the Dreher beer factory. You know, dear diary, the gendarmes don't believe that Jews don't have anything left of their valuables. They say that they probably hid them or buried them in the ground someplace, or deposited them for safekeeping with Aryans. For example, we deposited Grandma's jewelry with Juszti, that's true. Now they come to the Ghetto houses and pick up people, almost all of them rich ones, and take them to the Dreher beer factory. There they beat them until they tell where they hid their possessions.[37]

At night, Eva overheard her elders, who believed her to be asleep, anticipating the end. Her grandfather was a critical resource because, as a pharmacist, he could dispense poison.

> Last night . . . I couldn't sleep, and I overheard what the adults said. . . . They said that people aren't only beaten at Dreher, but also get electric shocks. Ági cried as she told this, and if hadn't she [*sic*] told it, I would have thought that it was all just some story out of an awful nightmare. Ági said that from Dreher, people are brought to the hospital bleeding at the mouth and ears, and some of them also with teeth missing and the soles of their feet swollen so that they can't stand. Dear diary, Ági also told other things, like what the gendarmes do to the women, because women are also taken there, things that it would be better if I didn't write them down in you. Things that I am incapable of putting into words . . . I even heard . . . that in the Ghetto here, there are many people who commit suicide. In the Ghetto pharmacy there is enough poison, and Grandpa gives poison to the older people who ask for it. Grandpa also said that it would be better if he took cyanide and also gave some to Grandma. At this Ági began to wail. I heard her crawl over to Grandpa's mattress in the dark and say to him crying: Patience, my dear Papa, this can't go on much longer! Even Grandma said, I really don't want to die, because I will yet live to see a better world, and all those people who are now so inhuman and wicked will be punished. Most frightening of all was Uncle Samu Meer, who is already very old and hardly says a word to anyone. So I was surprised to hear his voice in the dark, saying: Lilika mine, my little daughter, for the thousandth time I beg you to let me give myself an injection. I can't bear it any more. Now his daughter, Aunt Lili, began to sob. She also crawled over to her father, the way Ági did, and she sobbed: Do you want to leave me here all alone, Papa? What will become of me without you? Wait dearest, we will survive it.
>
> I've already mentioned to you, dear diary, that Uncle Lusztig and his wife live in the room with us. This Uncle Lusztig—nobody in the whole house likes him, except Ági. An ugly, small, angry old man; he worked in some factory here for forty years. I happened to overhear Grandpa say once, that in the factory they also

couldn't stand him, because it seems he always used to tell people exactly what he thought of them, and he was never kind to anybody. In the house here he talks only to Ági, and Ági says: It's true, Uncle Lusztig isn't a likeable person, but he is a very wise man.

In the dark I heard him speak—when I thought he was already fast asleep—and he asked Ági to give him poison for him and his wife; not just yet, but when he asked for it. Because the Dreher business isn't the final act, Uncle Lusztig said in the awful tone of someone still expecting the worst. Do you seriously believe, Uncle Lusztig said, that they are going to keep us in this horror called Ghetto-camp until the end of the war, and then lead us out beyond the fence in full pomp and circumstance, and announce: Ladies and gentlemen, please throw away the yellow patches; return to your homes; we give everything back to you, and we beg your pardon for the slight inconvenience we caused you?! No, if you please, old Lusztig continued, let's speak frankly and plainly. Do you know where the Jews of Austria are, and of Germany, and Holland, and Czechoslovakia and France? And I don't know how many more countries Uncle Lusztig mentioned. Well, if you don't know, I will tell you now: in Poland. In any case, that is where they were taken in cattle cars, seventy packed into each car. What happened to them I do not know, but I can guess. If you please, do you really think that after everything they have done here in Várad to the women, for example, not to mention any of the other things—they are going to tolerate that even one eyewitness among us stays alive? They will not be able to tolerate that, I say to you, I, Soma Lusztig, the man whom you all consider to be a nasty old pessimist, but all I am is a very old man and I do not bury my head in the sand the way all of you do. It was very quiet after that.

Then, suddenly, I heard Ági's voice again: Look, Mr. Lusztig, that is what all of us fear. Otherwise, the mortuary wouldn't be filled with bodies of people who committed suicide. Their feet are even sticking outside already. That stinking wood cellar, that serves the hospital as a mortuary, doesn't even have a door, and anybody who passes by there can see the yellowish legs. But, God bless you, it is already May 1944. Every child knows that this war is lost. Now the Germans no longer conquer and occupy country after country, but are running away. Running away in chaotic retreat, ever since Stalingrad. God grant, Uncle Lusztig's wife said to him, that not you but this charming young woman will prove to be right. Uncle Lusztig said nothing.[38]

The torture was routinized. Eva recorded on 22 May:

Now everybody has to go to Dreher. Today they announced: Every head of family will be taken in, so Grandpa also has to go. Terrific screaming comes from the direction of Dreher. All day long an electric phonograph keeps playing the same song: "There's just one girl in the world." Day and night the noise of this song fills the Ghetto. When the record stops for a moment, we can hear the yelling, because Dreher is nearby.[39]

On 27 May, Ági and her father had their turn at the beer factory also:

The whole house has gone to Dreher—that is, the men, and the women who have no husbands at all, or whose husbands aren't here. Ági went along with Grandpa and Uncle Bandi Kecskeméti and old Lusztig. . . .

The afternoon the gendarmes came from Dreher to get the quilts, saying that they were all going to spend the night at the factory as "the stinkers aren't spilling." One foul-faced gendarme explained, adding that at night they would have a chance to think it over. Aunt Klári and Marica were very frightened by this, because Uncle Bandi is also there and he must be one of those who "aren't spilling."[40]

By 29 May, having extracted all that was possible, the gendarmes began deportations, collecting Jews at a special site (Rédey Park) rather than at the railroad station in order to lower the visibility of the action. As always, the inmates still hoped for the best.

Dear diary, everybody says we're going to stay in Hungary, the Jews from all over the country are being brought to the Lake Balaton area and we are going to work there. But I don't believe it. That train-wagon is probably awful, and now nobody says that we're being taken away, but that they deport us.[41]

But some of their guardians had already seen too much. Eva recorded in her last entry on 30 May 1944:

That gendarme in front of the house, whom Uncle Béla calls a friendly gendarme, because he never yells at us and doesn't even speak familiarly to the women, came into the garden and told us that he will have to leave the gendarmerie, because what he saw in Rédey Park isn't a fit sight for human beings. They stuffed eighty people into each wagon and all they gave them was one pail of water for that many people. But what is even more awful is that they bolt the wagons. In this terrible heat we will suffocate in there! The gendarme says that he doesn't understand these Jews: not even the children cried; all of them were like zombies; like robots. They walked into the wagon so mechanically, without making a sound. The friendly gendarme didn't sleep all night, even though—he said—he usually falls asleep as soon as his head touches the pillow. It was such an awful sight that even he couldn't fall asleep, he said. And after all, he's a gendarme! Ági and Uncle Béla are whispering something to each other about our staying here in some kind of typhoid hospital, because they plan to say that Uncle Béla has typhoid fever. It's possible, because he had it when he was in the Ukraine. All I know is that I don't believe anything any more, all I think about is Márta, and I'm afraid that what happened to her is going to happen to us, too. It's no use that everybody says that we're not going to Poland but to Balaton. Even though, dear diary, I don't want to die; I want to live even if it means that I'll be the only person here allowed to stay. I would wait for the end in some cellar, or on the roof, or in some secret cranny. I would even let the cross-eyed gendarme, the one who took our flour away from us, kiss me, just as long as they didn't kill me, only that they should let me live.

Now I see that friendly gendarme has let Mariska come in. I can't write anymore, dear diary, the tears run from my eyes. I'm hurrying over to Mariska [end of diary].[42]

Eva ran to give Mandi, her canary, and her diary to Mariska. Her mother and stepfather (we are told in an introduction by Dr. J. Marton) were smuggled out of the ghetto with Aryan papers delivered by a Christian acquaintance related to a Social Democratic deputy. They reached Budapest and

Bergen-Belsen on Dr. Kastner's train. Eva arrived at Auschwitz on 6 June 1944, the day Allied troops invaded Europe. Hungarian witnesses testified that she was personally selected for the gas chambers by the infamous Dr. Mengele on 17 October 1944.[43]

Eva's mother, who wrote the introduction to the Hungarian edition of the diary issued in 1947, tells us nothing of her own escape and failure to rescue Eva. Two years later, her husband died and Ági committed suicide lying next to a photograph of Eva.[44]

The most touching memorial to Eva and confession was written by Juszti, in November 1945. The German governess wrote to thank Ági for a food package that she said saved her and her aged mother from starvation, while criticizing Ági forthrightly for not striving to keep Eva with her after her divorce, when she could have given her a secure home. Evidently Juszti did not know of the opportunities to hide Eva that Ági had not exploited. She accused herself because she had stood by helplessly:

> Right up to the last minute I stuck to that idiotic bourgeois notion that all I am is an obedient hired employee, instead of abandoning everything and going off with Eva someplace where we would not be recognized, and buying her forged papers with the money I had saved. You know, the problem wasn't money, but my lack of imagination. It was that the ordinary little people, of whom I am one, are fashioned only for ordinary weekdays. And here, dear Ágike, is where I failed. This is a greater failure than yours! And at the same time more fateful, because I didn't realize what an advantage being an Aryan gave me then. I really didn't, because I was a petty *petite bourgeois*, an old ass, an early-morning church-goer. . . . In other words, all my life, I took the Ten Commandments seriously. . . . You know that the relations between us were never merely those of tutor and pupil, and you also know that I loved Eva more than anything else in the world. You see, that is why I am accusing myself! Who knows how to feel and love as I do; yet when it came to doing something, I was impotent. I looked on helplessly, just like everybody else, at what was happening to you and Eva.[45]

1944: ELI WIESEL'S STORY

The sense of many people overlooking events, like spectators watching a newsreel of another continent, is pervasive in Eli Wiesel's recollection of spring 1944 in Sighet, a spring like other springs, with the Jews' hopes also blossoming with news of Russian advances. Jews even denied Hitler's intent to exterminate them.

> Was he going to wipe out a whole people? Could he exterminate a population scattered throughout so many countries? So many millions! What methods could he use? And in the middle of the twentieth century!
>
> Besides, people were interested in everything—in strategy, in diplomacy, in politics, in Zionism—but not in their own fate.[46]

Only Moché the Beadle was silent. When news was heard of the German occupation of Budapest, fears were briefly aroused. Three days later, German officers were in Sighet. Some even boarded in Jewish homes. They were courteous and respectful, belying stories of German brutality.

> On the seventh day of Passover the curtain rose. The Germans arrested the leaders of the Jewish community.
>
> From that moment, everything happened very quickly. The race toward death had begun.
>
> The first step: Jews would not be allowed to leave their houses for three days — on pain of death.
>
> Moché the Beadle came running to our house.
>
> "I warned you," he cried to my father. And, without waiting for a reply, he fled.[47]

The Hungarian police at once began confiscating gold and valuables belonging to Jews. But this was an old game; despite threats of death, Wiesel's father buried his savings in the cellar. Three days later, wearing the yellow star was decreed compulsory.

> Some of the prominent members of the community came to see my father — who had highly placed connections in the Hungarian police — to ask him what he thought of the situation. My father did not consider it so grim — but perhaps he did not want to dishearten the others or rub salt in their wounds:
>
> "The yellow star? Oh well, what of it? You don't die of it."[48]

Two ghettos were established in Sighet, one of which included the Wiesels' home within its borders so that they were not obliged to move but took in other relatives evicted from their homes. The inmates became adjusted to the situation. No threats or torture are recalled, and no hunger. It was

> a little Jewish republic. . . . We appointed a Jewish Council, a Jewish police, an office for social assistance, a labor committee, a hygiene department — a whole government machinery.
>
> Everyone marveled at it. We should no longer have before our eyes those hostile faces, those hate-laden stares. Our fear and anguish were at an end. We were living among Jews, among brothers.[49]

Since Eli Wiesel's father was on the Council, he was one of the first to be informed of the impending deportation. One night his father was summoned to an extraordinary meeting of the Council. Everyone in the household awaited his return anxiously; he arrived around midnight.

> One glance at my father's haggard face was enough.
>
> "I have terrible news," he said at last. "Deportation."
>
> The ghetto was to be completely wiped out. We were to leave street by street, starting the following day.
>
> We wanted to know everything, all the details. The news had stunned everyone, yet we wanted to drain the bitter draft to the dregs.
>
> "Where are we being taken?"

This was a secret. A secret from all except one: the President of the Jewish Council. But he would not say; he *could* not say. The Gestapo had threatened to shoot him if he talked.[50]

Someone knocked on the blocked-up window facing outside the ghetto but disappeared before they could open it; later, after the war, Eli learned that it was the Hungarian police inspector, the friend of his father who had promised to warn them of any danger.[51] That night "the women were cooking eggs, roasting meat, baking cakes, and making knapsacks."[52] Jewish police made the rounds the next day, announcing "in broken voices: 'The time's come now . . . you've got to leave all this.' "[53] Right behind them came Hungarian police, striking out indiscriminately. Because of the role of Eli Wiesel's father, his family was in the last category to be deported so that Wiesel was actually in the ghetto a week before they departed, allowing him to see the others' exodus. The first day was very hot; they had been standing lined up for hours and only a few children got water from the jugs that the Jewish police were filling beyond the eyes of their captors. A day later, the Wiesels were expelled to the little ghetto.

> At nine o'clock, Sunday's scenes began all over again. Policemen with truncheons yelling:
> "All Jews outside!"
> We were ready. I was the first to leave. I did not want to see my parents' faces. I did not want to break into tears. We stayed sitting down in the middle of the road, as the others had done the day before yesterday. There was the same infernal heat. The same thirst. But there was no longer anyone left to bring us water.[54]

The ghetto was open, unlike that of Nagyrárad. Perhaps this was because less of a problem of control was anticipated, as the Sighet ghetto lasted only a week while that of Nagyrárad existed for four weeks. Whatever the reason, its accessibility gave the Wiesels a chance to escape.

> The ghetto was not guarded. Everyone could come and go as they pleased. Our old servant, Martha, came to see us. Weeping bitterly, she begged us to come to her village, where she could give us a safe refuge. My father did not want to hear of it.
> "You can go if you want to," he said to me and to my older sisters. "I shall stay here with your mother and the child. . . ."
> Naturally, we refused to be separated.[55]

Until the last, there was mutual collusion in denial.

> At dawn, there was nothing left of this melancholy. We felt as though we were on holiday. People were saying:
> "Who knows? Perhaps we are being deported for our own good. The front isn't very far off; we shall soon be able to hear the guns. And then the civilian population will be evacuated anyway. . . ."
> "Perhaps they were afraid we might help the guerrillas. . . ."
> "If you ask me, the whole business of deportation is just a farce. Oh yes, don't

laugh. The Boches just want to steal our jewelry. They know we've buried everything, and that they'll have to hunt for it: it's easier when the owners are on holiday. . . ."

On holiday!

These optimistic speeches, which no one believed, helped to pass the time. The few days we lived here went by pleasantly enough, in peace. People were better disposed toward one another. There were no longer any questions of wealth, of social distinction, and importance, only people all condemned to the same fate—still unknown.[56]

The Wiesels departed with the last convoy on the Sabbath, one week after the first deportations began. The Jewish Council was granted the privilege of deporting itself.

Saturday, the day of rest, was chosen for our expulsion. The night before, we had the traditional Friday evening meal. We said the customary grace for the bread and wine and swallowed our food without a word. We were, we felt, gathered for the last time round the family table. I spent the night turning over thoughts and memories in my mind, unable to find sleep.

At dawn, we were in the street, ready to leave. This time there were no Hungarian police. An agreement had been made with the Jewish Council that they should organize it all themselves.[57]

They spent that day in the desecrated, stripped synagogue, in which they ate, slept, and had to relieve themselves, since toilet facilities were lacking.

The following morning, we marched to the station, where a convoy of cattle wagons was waiting. The Hungarian police made us get in—eighty people in each car. We were left a few loaves of bread and some buckets of water. The bars at the window were checked, to see that they were not loose. Then the cars were sealed. In each car one person was placed in charge. If anyone escaped, he would be shot.

Two Gestapo officers strolled about on the platform smiling: all things considered, everything had gone off very well.

A prolonged whistle split the air. The wheels began to grind. We were on our way.[58]

JEWS' VULNERABILITY, JEWISH LEADERSHIP, AND THE TOLL OF VICTIMS

The segregation and isolation of the Jews was a function of the enthusiastic collaboration of the Hungarian government (which ordered their deportation), acting under minimal German pressure and no obligation to cooperate, as has been described previously by Veesenmeyer, the German Ambassador (see pp. 108). However, the speed and administrative ease of deportation cannot be accounted for without understanding the Jews' lack of resistance toward the steps preceding their isolation. The Jewish councils of Hungarian towns seemed merely to reflect their helplessness and lack of collective defense. For the most part, the Hungarian councils played no part in selection (excepting those of Budapest, Cluj, and Szeged) nor is there evidence that their leaders were promised any exemption for their role in passing on orders (usually received from Hungarian police). Some of those who were exempted for the Kastner train and segregated from the community (so that they could be transported to a special collection camp in Budapest) did not understand what was happening and believed they were being taken as hostages, as in Szeged.[59] Their exemption was related not to any role they had performed for the Hungarians or Germans but to the role that Brand and Kastner had performed.

The lack of anticipation and early defense (such as noncooperation) on the part of Hungarian Jewry reflected their political isolation and objective powerlessness, which were reinforced by the vulnerability of the Hungarian government, undermined by the anti-Semitism it had propagated for a quarter century. The Hungarian democratic parties also failed to anticipate a German invasion, and their leadership was immediately arrested, so that Germany encountered a completely nonresistant nation, with highly placed potential collaborators in all of the parties that were permitted to exist: the most important of these were in the cabinet.

The more Jews were isolated, the more they denied any recognition of threat. Signs of warning were ignored and the credibility of news sources was deprecated. Such denial inhibited any collective resistance or noncooperation on the part of provincial Jews while they were still free. Family cohesion inhibited the readiness (in the case of Eli Wiesel) or ability (in the case of Eva Heyman) to seize opportunities for individual escape that were offered. It is significant that such obligations were assumed by family servants in both cases, reflecting both their plain morality and their bonds with these families.

The vulnerability of the Jews of Transylvania — a region twice transferred between Hungary and Rumania—was also related to their location at the periphery of Hungarian Jewry. The isolation of the Jewish communities outside Budapest was reinforced by the lack of communications from Jewish leaders in Budapest during April and May 1944, who failed to warn them to resist isolation by noncooperation (or any means possible) and failed to arouse foreign observers' opposition until June. The rumor that Eichmann started—that only the non-Magyarized Jews would be the objects of resettlement—allayed the Budapest Jewish leaders' perception of a collective threat, just as the belief that some other category of Jews were to be victims allayed the perception of a collective threat elsewhere.[60] Regardless of one's judgment regarding the motives for and potential usefulness of Joel Brand's mission to Istanbul to convey the SS offer of "blood for goods," the diversion of Zionist leadership into secret negotiations on behalf of the SS leadership meant their abstention from organizing political resistance during the critical period when political resistance could have saved the most people.

During June 1944, foreign observers' reports, instigated within Hungary by Miklos (Moshe) Krauss, executive of the Jewish Agency's emigration office for Palestine, aroused international protest. Private protests from the Vatican (called for by the American War Refugee Board), the United States, the King of Sweden, and other neutrals impelled the Regent on 6 July 1944 to order deportations to stop, sparing the Jews of Budapest (see Chapter 7). However, despite appeals by the Jewish Council and some bishops, Cardinal Serendi, the Prince Primate of the Hungarian Roman Catholic Church, refused to protest publicly or privately on behalf of all Jews categorically dur- ing that period, when almost three of every five of Hungary's Jews were deported. Not until 16 July, after the deportations were stopped, did the Primate authorize a statement about the deportation that did not even specify Jews as the victims and refrained from urging Christians not to cooperate in further deportation. Neither did he threaten sanctions against collaborators—he simply renounced all responsibility for what had been done (see Chapter 4).

By June some of the Budapest Jewish Council members, realizing that Brand's mission had failed, surreptitiously issued a pamphlet (despite the Council's disapproval of illegal tactics) called "An Appeal to the Christians of Hungary," and others appealed privately to the Regent's son, Miklos Horthy, to save the Jews and prevent a threatened right-wing coup against the Regent.[61] Between July and October, M. Krauss and others, with Raul Wallenberg, the Swedish diplomat cooperating with the American War Refugee Board, and friendly foreign diplomats, sought to protect tens of thousands of Jews in Budapest by issuing certificates of foreign citizenship or protection; for each legitimate certificate, Zionist youths printed three others. Wallenberg and others even housed their protected Jews in special buildings; ironically, the most populous of these, nominally under Swiss pro- tection, was known as "the glass house."

The Budapest Jews' precarious security was again threatened in October 1944, when the Arrow Cross, a movement of the radical right, mounted a German-supported coup. The Germans, who had preferred the more politically astute politicians of the right, backed the coup because the Regent was planning to surrender to the Allies and to resist German control physi- cally. The Regent's intention to arm workers and Jews to defend themselves against the native fascists had not yet been implemented. Scarcely any Jews had weapons except for a small Zionist youth group, which exploited their few arms and captured German uniforms to liberate their members from captivity.

After the coup, gendarmes and Arrow Cross members invaded Jewish hospitals and the starred houses in Budapest, massacring Jews routinely. There was virtually no opposition to the coup, just as there was no Hungarian resistance to the German invasion. The Protestant bishops did urge the Roman Catholic Prince-Primate on 26 November 1944 to intervene with the

Head of State against the Arrow Cross slaughter of Jews (Ferenc Szalazi, Arrow Cross leader), as did the Jewish Council of Budapest on 14 January 1945; on both occasions he refused.[62]

After liberation (in February 1945), only 17% of the Hungarian Jews recorded in 1941 were alive on Hungarian soil. This number was later swelled by victims returning from the extermination camps or labor camps and by Jews who had fled to neutral countries or Rumania, so that those "of Jewish faith" recorded on 31 December 1945 constituted 36% of those recorded in 1941. But in northern Transylvania, where Eva Heyman and Eli Wiesel lived, only 14,000, or 8.5%, of the recorded Jewish population of 1941, evaded deportation; an additional 44,000 returned to Rumania from German camps after the war, according to Manuila and Filderman.[63] Despite their nearness to Rumania, fewer than one in 10 Jews there succeeded in evading deportation by flight or hiding—most of the others vanished in the night of Auschwitz.

Implications: Coping and the Contexts of Consciousness

What people see in moments of despair—and expect, imagine, or recognize in the hours, days, months preceding the imminent threat of annihilation—does not in itself tell us why they perished (or survived), but it may illustrate how their perceptions reflect and are distorted by their model of the problem confronting them. Jews had to ask: Was this a war of the Germans against all natives, of Germans against (all or some) Jews, of all fascists and anti-Semites (regardless of nationality) against all Jews, of Jews against Jews, or of all against all? What was the aim of their occupiers' policy toward them? Why were they singled out? On whom could they rely?

COLLECTIVE ISOLATION AND DISBELIEF IN EXTINCTION

Potential victims were often alone when confronted with the threat of deportation. But even where Jews were concentrated together, each person was essentially alone in dread of death. The acknowledgment of warning signs and recognition of a collective threat did not depend primarily on the extent or directness of the reports of extermination of Jews, but on how one could anticipate coping with that threat. This, in turn, depended upon the extent to which Jews were socially isolated from other citizens of their native lands. Where Jews had been readily segregated, they were also (or soon became) socially isolated before being quartered apart or walled in a ghetto.

314

The more isolated, the more likely Jews were to deny the existence of a collective threat against all Jews and to fail to acknowledge the Germans as a collective enemy, persisting instead in defining them as exploiters or oppressors.

Thus, we can understand the apparent paradox that the more immediate and visible was the threat of annihilation, the less likely Jews were to define the situation as a collective threat at once. For it was in the regions in which the threat was most direct that Jews were isolated even before the Germans consolidated their occupational forces. The more isolated they were, the more they tended to deny the threat of total extermination in order to disassociate themselves from the category of the most vulnerable — despite their personal ties to the victims and the anguish their deaths caused. This explains why people failed to credit first-hand and specific reports of general extermination. In Vilna, where victims who remained alive after being shot crept naked from mass graves and crawled back to the ghetto in September 1941, Herman Kruk reported that in July 1942 Jews were still discussing the fate of those who had not returned from Ponary (the grove of slaughter), some speculating that they might be alive elsewhere.[1] In Warsaw, where scores of children died each morning in the winter of 1941–1942, where the refugees who poured in repeatedly told of slaughters in small towns, and where assignment to a German labor camp usually led to death, the party leaders did not credit the messengers from Vilna in February 1942 who conveyed Abba Kovner's manifesto charging that the Germans had a master plan to kill all Jews.[2] In Hungary, to which 25,000 Polish Jews were estimated to have fled, most Jews disbelieved tales of extermination in neighboring Poland. However, in France, the Netherlands, and Belgium, where the BBC reports of extermination were often not received or not credited and where they were not possible to confirm directly, most Jews attempted to evade deportation, and the majority in France and Belgium succeeded.

Denial that there was a plan for mass extermination was not limited to Jews. Prisoners who had escaped or had been released from extermination camps found that those to whom they related their evidence often denied or ignored it. Kurt Gerstein (an anti-Nazi German serving as an SS officer in order to expose the crimes in which he participated) encountered similar responses.[3] Sometimes what they had seen seemed fantastic even to them. De Jong assesses this:

> Remember the Jehovah's Witnesses who had lived by the side of the gas chambers and the crematorium in Birkenau. "One day we would believe our own eyes, the next day we would simply refuse to do so." . . .
>
> Hitler had said it plainly: "Let war come, and the whole of European Jewry will be exterminated." And the war had come. Why then did no one draw the correct inference? It is easy for us to wonder, looking back as we do at the German extermination camps and gas chambers through the years, and free as we are of the tremendous psychological tensions of the war; free, above all, of fear, of mortal fear in its most naked form . . . we should be committing an immense historical

error, were we to dismiss the many defense mechanisms employed by the victims—not constantly, mind you, but by way of intermittent distress signals—as mere symptoms of blindness or foolishness; rather did these defense mechanisms spring from deep and inherent qualities shared by all mankind. . . . It may sound paradoxical, but it is an historical fact, and one that is psychologically explicible as well: the Nazi extermination camps did not become a psychological reality for most people and even then not fully until after, and indeed because, they had ceased to exist.[4]

But the recognition that deportation led to death did not depend on awareness of the extermination camps. What did it depend upon?

Investigations of how people respond to warnings of disaster reveal that they weigh the likelihood of the threat against the anticipated costs of accepting a new definition of the situation: how it will disrupt their lives, what access routes are open, what unprecedented actions coping will entail, and what people and resources they can count on for assistance. Apprehension both leads to increased vigilance (sensitivity to warning cues) and raises the need for reassurance. When the source of danger is clear, and people can anticipate what to do to avoid it, their perception is sharpened and their energy released: they are not immobilized by anxiety but mobilized to avoid danger.[5] But if the costs of accepting a new definition of the situation call for discarding one's social identity and disrupting one's way of life while the nature of the threat cannot be determined with certainty, people are more likely to perceive the threat as overwhelming and either to react with terror or to defend themselves against threat by denial.[6] Since information sources available to Jews in the ghettos always conflicted—the Germans propagated reassuring messages that contradicted the rumors and direct reports—selective perception, denial, and distortion were probable. In ghettos in which extermination came in successive waves of "selections," the constant adjustment to attrition and mourning itself promoted demoralization and misperception of the scope of threat.[7]

PARADIGMS OF PUNISHMENT

Those most isolated were least able to foresee any possibility of evasion, so they were more likely either to deny the evidence as long as possible or to accept other definitions of the situation that were less threatening. Such alternative definitions appeared plausible because the very notion of a collective threat of extinction against Jews qua Jews ran contrary to western civilization's basic paradigms of crime and punishment. When new events contradict the internal paradigms mediating perception, it is more economic to reject new definitions of the situation than to revise one's assumptions.

We are socialized by both civic and religious traditions to believe that punishment is a consequence of disobedience—crime in the secular order and sin in the theological order. Good citizens believe that if they are law abiding and grant to Caesar what is Caesar's, they will be protected by the state. To maintain this expectation, Eli Cohen tells us, Dutch Jews initially believed that German Jews had elicited their punishment by Germany as a result of some acts or attributes of theirs. The pious Jew believes that if he is faithful and observant, he will be protected by the deity. Eli Wiesel articulates the pious victims' belief that their punishment was a response to their sins:

> The feeling of guilt was, to begin with, essentially a religious feeling. If I am here [in Auschwitz], it is because God is punishing me; I have sinned, and I am expiating my sins.[8]

How could one make sense of the message (or rumor) that *they* were shooting *all* Jews at some (specified) place and time? Are they shooting Jews because of some act of a few for which all Jews are held accountable, or for some attribute? Accepting the former — this is a reprisal for misbehavior — blames the punishment on the victims, thus utilizing the taken-for-granted paradigm of crime and punishment in the following manner:

1. Some people say that Jews are being killed in that place.
2. Killing is a punishment.
3. But only bad people (saboteurs, resistance fighters, conspirators) are punished.
4. And I am not a bad person.
5. Therefore, I will not be punished.

Thus Eva Heyman's grandmother voiced her belief that her daughter's disobedience would incite reprisals against her, attributing punishment to a provocation by the victim, just as she attributed the confiscation of her husband's pharmacy in 1940 to his superficial political identification with the former Rumanian rulers. Reacting to their rulers as oppressors or exploiters rather than enemies, such Jews attempted to avoid punishment by obedience, effacement, and propitiation, reasoning that their fate depended on the authorities' good will.

If we accept the latter interpretation — they are shooting *that class* of Jew — the imperative need to disassociate oneself from the class of victims in order to allay one's fear of becoming a victim is fulfilled by the very definition of the situation. One might reason this way:

1. They are shooting another class of Jews (non-German, non-Magyar, non-Warsaw, nonurban, nonbourgeois, nonproductive, non-law-abiding, etc.)
2. I am not a member of that class.
3. Therefore, they will not shoot me.

Taking this paradigm for granted, some Dutch Jews did not infer from reports of the extermination of Polish Jews that there was a general plan to exterminate all Jews, a Belgian *Judenrat* leader rejected the implication that Belgian Jews might be threatened,[9] leaders of Warsaw Jewry believed, as late as July 1942 (see pp. 252–253) that the community would be spared; and Jewish Council leaders in Budapest did not mobilize opposition to the ghettoization and deportations for almost two months, crediting the rumor (planted by Eichmann) that the victims would only be Jews outside Budapest.

An even more primitive response was to deny the authenticity of such reports by discrediting the messenger, calling him a madman, as the people of Sighet refused to credit the report by Moché the Beadle of wholesale slaughter of Jews. Provincial Hungarian Jews responded much like peasants living in the shadow of a volcano, who deny the potential of annihilation by an awesome force that they know they cannot control.

THE RATIONALITY OF ACCOMMODATION AND DEFENSE

When reports could no longer be denied but no possibilities for evasion were foreseen — as in Warsaw — most people turned to compensatory mechanisms of defense, reiterating to each other wish-fulfilling fantasies and rumors of impending Allied intervention or German collapse. But in communities with intact prewar Jewish leadership accustomed to act politically, like Warsaw, there were still leaders who thought politically. On their behalf, Ringelblum appealed to the Allies to publicize the plight of Warsaw Jewry and/or threaten reprisals in order to deter the Germans from annihilating them. These appeals went unanswered. The ordinary Jews in Warsaw were not sedated by their own wishful thinking. When confronted in July 1942 with the threat of capture, all defenses to diminish anxiety were overwhelmed by naked fear, which sharpened their resistance. Most people strove to save themselves by all means available, as did Chaim Kaplan. What is remarkable is not that a minority responded to the German lure of bread for those reporting for "resettlement" but that the majority did not, despite the effects of hunger, which renders people incapable of sustained attention or effort and drives them to an unremitting pursuit of food.[10]

Despite Jews' mass noncooperation in Warsaw and widespread recognition of their powerlessness, they were not ready to organize for rebellion until the old authority structure within the ghetto was destroyed and they were not ready to legitimate new authority until their fate was confirmed during the mass deportations of the summer of 1942. All their previous experience prevented them from conceiving of rebellion as a rational alternative.

To Jews in Warsaw before July 1942, death was a constant possibility. Exploitation and oppression permeated every phase of life. The dying cried in the street at night like an eerie wind and were silent by the morning, frozen to death. But hunger, homelessness, and death were still individuated. Bread came in discrete pieces that were acquired individually to satisfy one's own hunger pangs. The threat of collective death was not anticipated because the social organization and political economy of the ghetto created differential death chances every day. The chance of each to survive depended on his or her place in the class order, and the whole class order arose from imposed scarcity and political terror, rewarding those most able to serve the Nazis directly or indirectly. These were not primarily the *Judenrat* leaders but the entrepreneurs who combined smuggling, protection rackets, and intelligence and espionage functions, and who patronized charity and the arts—even claiming to be militant spokesmen for Jews against the *Judenrat* and the merchants—in order to mask their primary function. Ordinary Jews learned to cope by smuggling, stealing, and exploiting each other and learned to avoid punishment by avoiding Germans whenever possible. When contact could not be avoided, they had to suppress all assertive responses in order to survive.

The system of controls also obscured recognition of a common enemy, by displacing anger against the conqueror onto the *Judenrat* and perpetuating the belief that it was a war of all against all rather than that of *them* against *us*. Until this was understood, neither rebellion nor any collective risk-taking could be construed as rational.

Although neither Jews nor "Aryan" Poles displayed any respect for the law and order of the occupier, disobeying regulations constantly so as to survive (especially economic regulations), both learned that overt disobedience (especially physical aggression) would be followed by death, and were thus conditioned not to resist overtly. Similarly, Dutch Jews learned from their experiences of 1941 that physical resistance led to death in Mauthausen. If disobedience leads to punishment, does it not follow from the paradigm we use to construct "the real world" (which we expect can be predicted and hence controlled) that if one does not disobey, one will not be punished?

The recognition, articulated by Abba Kovner in a manifesto calling for resistance and published in Vilna in January 1942, that "all the Gestapo's roads lead to Ponary [grove of slaughter] and Ponary means death,"[11] was a radical denial that one's actions could control one's fate. Making oneself useful by working for the German exploiter or allaying the German oppressor with bribes could offer no security.

But to call for collective self-defense in the ghetto meant inviting collective reprisals by the Germans, which would predictably lead to the slaughter (or capture, as in Warsaw) of the majority of resistors and nonresistors. To resist aggressively and individually without any organization meant not only one's own death but collective reprisal against the whole group. Within the context of the ghetto, rebellion was an irrational act for the individual seeking his own survival alone. Only if one were convinced that the Germans intended the death of all Jews was rebellion rational. One uses any means possible against a collective enemy, not only to save honor, but to increase the possibility that anyone will survive. Therefore, before the community sanctioned rebellion, it had to accept the underlying premise of Kovner's manifesto and reject the premises with contrary implications offered by other leaders, such as the heads of the *Judenrat*.

Judenrat leadership usually counseled accommodation for many reasons, not the least of which was that it was constantly sifted to eliminate those who failed to cooperate with the German authorities. Since the *Judenrat* leaders were in closest contact with the authorities, the credibility of the strategies they advocated was enhanced by their claim to be better able to anticipate consequences. They were believed by many in contests of authority with advocates of armed resistance. The strategy they advocated was "rescue through work," assuming that the Germans would be satisfied by exploitation, and inducing those who could work to believe that their contributions would save them. They denied the utility of resistance, and sometimes — when an open conflict between the resistance and *Judenrat* authority developed, as in Vilna — themselves repressed the resistance. They justified the selection of victims for the Germans, contradicting traditional Jewish norms that no Jew who had not committed any crime should be sacrificed to the authorities, regardless of the consequences and even if the sacrifice of some arbitrary victims would save others. Such a policy undermined the solidarity of the Jewish community, for it meant that one enhanced one's life chances by increasing another's death chances.

The role of the *Judenrat* in Warsaw was similar to that of other *Judenräte* prior to July 1942. Despite many reports by witnesses of extermination elsewhere and pervasive rumors, people clung to competing definitions of the situation, seeking relief in wish-fulfilling fantasies, because they felt impotent to cope with such a catastrophic destiny. The *Judenrat* reiterated official "news" planned to lull them. But it could not suppress news, rumors, or fears. Only when the majority of a community had already been deported, testifying to the failure of their previous assumptions and strategy, and the authority of the *Judenrat* was shattered — as it was in Warsaw by Czerniakow's suicide — did Jews legitimate rebellion that demanded confrontation. Similarly, revolts in the extermination camps and labor camps occurred only after the resistants had seen that the overwhelming number of fellow-Jews were exterminated and had recognized that there was no mode of adjustment to guarantee their survival.

Since rebellion within the ghetto was foreseen to be futile on military grounds, the Warsaw ghetto fighters sought, for political and military reasons, to break down the wall. They failed not because of their lack of anticipation of SS General Stroop's strategy, but because the Polish resistance failed to support them. The success or failure of later rebellions under German rule similarly depended on the rebels' allies: all urban civil rebellions under German rule occurring after that of the Warsaw ghetto failed unless German troops withdrew voluntarily, German commanders abstained from use of their repressive forces, and/or Allied troops entered the rebellious cities.[12]

The evidence of extensive preparations for evasion (bunkers and attic traffic systems) and political efforts to elicit support from the Allies and the Polish government-in-exile does not justify the interpretation that the Warsaw ghetto fighters fought for the sake of honor alone, emulating the Jewish suicides at Masada in 73 C.E. Their own words indicate that they fought because they believed that life, an authentic human life, was possible only if they accepted the probability of death but refused to resign themselves to it.

Those who chose to defend Jewish lives collectively did not usually choose rebellion when they had alternatives—they had no other means of defense in Warsaw. Social defense rather than armed resistance was the optimal strategy for Jewish survival. Most Jews who survived in low-victimization states did so because evasion possibilities were magnified by organized social defense movements and/or deportations were stopped by political opposition. The first necessity for social defense of Jews—for both principled and tactical reasons—was avoidance of isolation and ghettoization. Subsequent opportunities for flight depended largely on whether or not the community had been collectively isolated, not on whether their isolation was physically fortified by a wall, as in Warsaw, or simply by a boundary of visual signs, as in Amsterdam. And we saw that in Hungary the physical isolation of the Jewish communities followed their segregation and political isolation.

SIGNIFICANCE OF INDEPENDENT JEWISH LEADERSHIP AND BONDS TO GENTILES

The possibility of avoiding segregation depended not only on the type of German control and the native government's response but upon the activities of independent Jewish leadership—that is, not co-opted into Jewish councils or, if co-opted, playing a double game—that retained bonds to native leaders. Where Jews had not been "coordinated" through the councils or isolated and bonds to native leaders existed, such independent Jewish leadership was likely to create social defense movements and/or (where it was possible) to instigate political resistance to the threat of deportation. These movements provided opportunities for parents to place their children in the homes of other natives and for adults to pass as Aryans or submerge into hiding; they helped to establish escape routes and guide people to sanctuaries outside the occupied state. Most important, their members presented clear definitions of the situation and instructed potential victims on what to do, showing them where to go; this deterred panic, despair, or denial. Since research on disasters shows that people do tend to react efficiently, mobilizing their energies to flee whenever exits are open, pointing the way to exits without signs is indispensable in such a situation.

How independent Jewish leadership facilitated the ability of Jews to cope with threat and go into hiding is most clearly illustrated by examining the response of Jews in Belgium and Holland, where deportations began in July 1942. German reports testify that few Dutch or Belgian Jews reported voluntarily. However, no social defense movement had been formed in Holland to enable Jews without money to go into hiding.

Dutch Jews, accustomed to the prewar registration system, registered unthinkingly. They were conditioned by a competitive incentive structure administered by the *Judenrat* to believe that their fates depended on their individual attributes—who was the most indispensible Jew. No counterorganization had been formed that could be transformed into a social defense movement.

Despite the fact that Jews in Belgium were more visible and less socially integrated than Dutch Jews (90% were non-Belgian), they had over twice the chance of survival. For when deportations began, the registration cards were destroyed by Jewish partisans, the *Judenrat* (the AJB) was rendered ineffectual (partly by terror from the resistance), warnings were disseminated officially by the resistance movement and the Comité de Défense des Juifs (a creation of the Front de Indépendance) dispensed money and found homes for Jewish children to go into hiding, actually soliciting their parents in order to find them, and aided adults as well (see Chapter 6). Dutch Jews were on their own. And few could make it on their own, despite the desperate energy released by fear when the source of danger was clear.

Bahnson, observing Danish Jews in hiding in Copenhagen during a Gestapo raid, remarked on how their common plight (and perhaps the presence of other Danes who organized their rescue) enabled them to develop new morale:

> At the time I arrived, personal contact was formal and group cohesiveness low. . . . When the raid began, a marked change took place; the field apparently was restructured by most of the participants from being a competitive escape situation to being a joint defensive situation. Foe had become friend and the new *common* danger broke down formality, hostility, and restraint.[13]

When people are isolated, the threat of victimization does not unite them as a collectivity, but forces them to compete against each other for ways out. It becomes a war of all against all. When means are scarce or illegal and people are in despair, prices rise for fraudulent visas, guides, permits. Clients are more likely to be exploited in their drive to escape than if movements arise to supply such services on an altruistic basis. In the Netherlands and other states where social defense movements did not emerge when most needed, Jews were transformed into competitors for scarce resources. Where social defense movements were created, the response to the evasion problem was transformed into a cooperative enterprise, enhancing solidarity among Jews and between Jews and Gentiles.

When these were lacking, the largest group to cohere and sustain their collective identity was usually the family. But family solidarity may weaken its members' chances of survival when it is based on denial of threat as in the case of the families of Eva Heyman and Eli Wiesel in Hungary. Where families maintain solidarity by hiding together, as was the case in Anne Frank's family, the chances of all being caught increased. The physical breakdown of the family in Warsaw after the summer of 1942 facilitated reorganization for rebellion. However, the mutual loyalty and trust that sustain a family also sustain members of a movement or new primary groups emerging under such conditions.

In most countries, prewar Zionist youth clung together to feed their members and place them in jobs or exempt positions, and attempted to develop escape routes in Poland (between 1939 and 1941), Denmark, the Netherlands, and France.[14] But such groups did not have the capacity to create movements responsible for defense of other Jews, and their own priorities sometimes diverted their attention from the more immediate, general need of all Jews. Both resistance against deportation and social defense movements were most likely to arise in regions where state and church had publicly opposed anti-Jewish discrimination, resisting cooperation in segregating the Jews. In states where such resistance did not arise, the response of Jewish leaders usually reflected both their perception of powerlessness (accountable for by their political isolation) and their earlier political adaptations.

Leaders of Jewish communities who were not accustomed to act politically—more likely the case within states where Jews were culturally assimilated—were less likely to anticipate and react strategically to threat, than were Jewish leaders in communities who were accustomed to representing their own interests within the national and international political arena. Leaders' responses had greatest effect in the colonial zone of German allies, in which Germany lacked the power to deport Jews without native government and police collaboration. In Hungary, where anti-Jewish discrimination was officially legitimated and Jews had been progressively stripped of equal rights for a quarter century before 1944, Jews had progressively adapted to such discrimination (as did Eva Heyman's grandfather) by conforming overtly and relying on bribery for personal protection, assuming that the name of the game was exploitation. Their belief in the personal efficacy of this method was enhanced by earlier positive experience with the Magyar gentry who, during the pre-World War I days, coexisted with the Jewish bourgeoisie in liberal toleration. Socialists, such as Eva's mother and stepfather, did not participate in politics as Jews or provide leadership to the Jewish community. Provincial Jewish leaders tended to be isolated from Budapest politics and the contacts enjoyed by the Budapest leadership. The Budapest Rescue Committee, headed by Rudolph Kastner and Joel Brand, was completely informed as to the nature of the Final Solution and the facilities at Auschwitz awaiting Jews.[15] Nevertheless, their entry into negotiations with the SS in April 1944 indicated their belief that the Germans' objective could be transformed to exploitation of the Jews for higher stakes. Provincial leaders, lacking any warning from Budapest, ignored and denied earlier warning signs of a collective threat, as did other Jews.

Although Rumanian Jewry was confronted by a manifestly anti-Semitic government and a tradition of collective violence without a record of liberal toleration comparable to that which had earlier prevailed in Hungary, Jewish leaders did not take their powerlessness for granted. They were accustomed — for decades — to negotiate for Jews collectively and to play a role in making and breaking regimes, despite a prevalent anti-Jewish consensus. They had reacted politically to oppression in 1878 and 1919 — trading with allies, employing threats, and conducting foreign relations — thus bringing in a third force to protect themselves against the Rumanian government. Similarly, despite differences among them, they responded tactically to the threat of the Holocaust and managed to instigate protest against deportation from the head of the Rumanian Orthodox Church, the crown, and popular party leaders. During the war, Rumanian Jewish leaders also acted to exploit the myth of a world Jewish conspiracy to insinuate that they might prove to be a link to the western Allies.[16] Such domestic pressure and its desire to disengage from the German alliance caused the Rumanian government to block execution of its deportation agreement. Jewish leaders prevented the Rumanian government from fully exploiting the newly appointed Jewish Council — composed of men not previously recognized as leaders by Jews — imposed in 1942; the government could not ignore the political usefulness of the real Jewish leadership.

The case of Hungary illustrates how the absence of independent Jewish leadership, capable of taking initiatives rather than simply responding to others' actions and responsible to the Jewish community, rather than the co-optation of leaders into *Judenräte* may account for the failure of the Jewish community to apprehend early warning signs. If the *Judenräte* and other Jewish organizations imposed by the authorities in order to control and entrap the Jews succeeded in isolating them, it was because of the absence of countervailing organizations to anticipate threats and initiate strategies to protect them. *Judenrat* leaders' accommodation generally reflected the sense of collective powerlessness induced by Jews' isolation rather than any covert grasping at privilege to enhance their own life chances.

Jewish leadership capable of undertaking innovative defense strategies was generally more developed in states in which a majority of Jews (or a dominant faction of Jews participating in the Jewish community) had supported political ideologies justifying collective responsiblity and self-assertion — such as socialism, Zionism, Bundism — than in states where a majority or dominant portion of the Jews espoused modern individualism, which accepted that one's highest loyalty was to the nation. Jews of the latter type were likely to redefine themselves as nationals "of the Jewish faith." The former type of leadership was more likely to be found in states in which Jews maintained a strong sense of distinctive ethnicity, the latter in which they were wholly assimilated culturally. The Jewish leadership of Belgium and Rumania was of the former, collectivity-oriented type, whereas that of the Netherlands and Hungary was of the latter type, oriented first to the nation-state rather than to Jews as a collectivity. Evidence discussed earlier shows how the Jewish leadership of Belgium and Rumania had anticipated and reacted promptly to threats against any Jews, without barring any tactics, whereas the Jewish leaders of the Netherlands and Hungary suppressed recognition of a general threat. In the Netherlands, *Judenrat* leaders disassociated their fate from that of Jews of lesser social status; whereas in Hungary, leaders of the Budapest Jewish Council failed to identify with the non-Magyar Jews of the provinces, beginning to protest only when Budapest Jews were next on the deportation agenda.

However, the effectiveness of defensive strategies undertaken by Jewish leaders depended on the magnitude and timing of the threat to the Jews and the extent of sympathetic response by native leadership. Where SS control was at its most intense earliest and anti-Semitism was high, scarcely any strategic response of Jews affected the outcome. But in states where these conditions did not prevail simultaneously, the ability of Jewish leaders to anticipate and mobilize against threats could make a difference. Where threat was lowest — in states with least SS control and low anti-Semitism — the lack of anticipation by Jewish leaders did not prove disabling ultimately to the Jews, because when Jewish leaders did plead for aid from native leaders, their pleas elicited an immediate positive response, often accompanied by practical help. We have attributed the low rank of Jewish victims in states where Jews had the best chances of survival (Denmark, Finland) not only to the low SS control, allowing the state to procrastinate or refuse cooperation, but to the defense of the Jews by the government, church, resistance, and other national leaders, rather than to the initiative of Jewish leaders. These Jewish communities were not noted prior to World War II for producing a collectivity-oriented Jewish leadership.[17] Although Jewish leaders in Finland and Denmark did protest German plans to leaders of their nation, Jewish leaders in Denmark had not foreseen the need to burn synagogue lists of Jews (snatched by the Germans) or made any contingency plans for a warning system to enable Jews to flee, despite the fact that Denmark had been under German martial law for a month preceding the raid against the Jews.[18]

Where state authorities had resisted discrimination and/or church leaders vocally opposed any attempts to justify anti-Semitism or discrimination against Jews, resistance movements usually also identified with the Jews. *Judenräte* were less likely to be installed in such states and if they were set up, their intended function of isolating the Jews was checked by Jews outside the Council or the Council was subverted from within. In such state, if the threat of deportation could not be deterred by the state, leadership usually arose among Gentiles and Jews to avoid the isolation of the Jews, and finally countered the mobilization of the death machine with the mobilization of human lifelines enabling most Jews to evade capture.

Appendixes

Appendix A: Codebook

1 UNIT

Identification of unit for analysis: a separate political class analysis can
be made for all Jewish states incorporating parts of other states between
1939 and 1941 and in states with large numbers of Jewish refugees before
1940, whenever separate estimates of Jewish victimization could be made
(if the latter is possible). (Note that states and regions [Code 1] are the
only units analyzed in this study.)*

Code

0   Political class of Jews within state

1   Nation-state or occupied territory or region administered as unit

2 NAME

Name of nation-state or occupied region or territory in May 1941.

---

* IBM data cards are available to scholars upon request. Please address
requests in care of the publisher.

327

Code

AT—Athens*	ES—Estonia	NE—Netherlands	RU—Rumania
AU—Austria	FI—Finland	NO—Norway	SA—Salonica*
BE—Belgium	FR—France	LA—Latvia	SE—Serbia
BU—Bulgaria	GE—Germany	LI—Lithuania	SL—Slovakia
CR—Croatia	HU—Hungary	PO—Poland	
DE—Denmark	IT—Italy	PR—Protectorate	

3 STATUS

Prewar political status of Jews subject to state nominally governing

region (for political class analysis only). (See note to Variable 1.)

Code

1   Citizens

2   Foreigners or stateless persons

4 DISTANCE

Political distance from capital (for political class analysis only). (See note

to Variable 1.)

Code

0   Two-thirds or more of class residing in capital

1   Jews mixed among capital and provinces within prewar territorial
     boundaries

2   Jews residing in provinces only

3   Jews residing in outer (newly acquired) provinces only

5 - 11 Jewish Population Characteristics

5 JEWSSIZE

Size of the Jewish population (in 100,000s) ranges from 33.5 (Poland) to

.02 (Norway, Finland).

Code

Numerical estimate to two decimal places. (See source notes to Table 3-1.)

---

   * Salonica and Athens, the two cities with the largest Jewish population in
prewar Greece, are analyzed separately both because of differences in length
of German occupation and because it is possible to establish victimization
figures for each city in Greece (unlike other nations).

6   PCCITYHI

Maximum visibility of the Jewish population; this is indexed by the percent (at time of last census) Jews constituted of the nation's capital or of the major city with the largest number of Jews.

Code

Actual percent (to nearest percent)

7   PCNATION

Percent Jews constituted (from .1% to 99.9%) of total population of state or region (within wartime borders) before the war (or nearest date to 6/41 for which general population estimate was available).

Code

Actual percent (to one decimal place)

8   STRANGER

Percent of registered Jewish population of foreign nationality (before 1941).

Code

00   Information missing

01-99   Actual percent (to nearest percent)

9   INVISIBL

Lack of visibility of foreign Jews from prewar territory of nation-state.

Code

1   Not visible, outside borders, or on periphery

0   Not invisible, within borders in major cities and provinces

9   Does not apply

10 SPREAD

Dispersion of Jewish population; this is indexed by the number of cities and towns within which two-thirds of the Jewish population lived, using figures derived from racial census or last prewar national census or community estimate. The higher the figure, the larger were the number of places that the authorities would need to organize to deport the Jews.

Code

Number of cities enclosing two-thirds of Jewish population (actual number).

00   Information not available

11 CONINDEX

Dispersion/Size of Population Factor. In order to control for the degree
of dispersion of the Jewish population that could be explained by its absolute
size and/or growth, the preceding index was multiplied by the following factor whenever the dispersion index was over one and the number of Jews
(last enumeration or estimate) was over 100,000.

$$\text{Population Factor} = \frac{100,000}{\text{Size of Jewish population}} \quad \text{or} \quad \frac{1}{\text{Size (in 100,000s)}}$$

Code

Spread × Population Factor (to nearest percent)

00   Does not apply or information not available

12 - 15 State Characteristics

12 STATEAGE

Length of existence as autonomous nation-state: actual number of years
from 1830 to 1939, divided by 20 to the nearest whole number.

Code

1-6   Under 20 to over 100

13 RELIGION

Dominant religion in nation-state.

Code

1   Roman Catholic

0   Other Christian church

14 SOLIDARY

National solidarity is indexed by the relative length of successful nonviolent
national experience before 1938 with inclusive and representative government with succession of executives by legitimated means as related to the
number of sources of social cleavage that were politically organized in the

thirties, creating loyalties to exclusive collectivities and/or causing a substantive body of the public (or of organized leadership) to idealize the use of force to gain power and/or resolve differences.

The relative length of such experience was evaluated by assessing the length of representative government in each state as a proportion of all years since its emergence as a nation-state, the stability of the government, and the presence or absence of regression in the interwar years. All measures were taken from Arthur S. Banks, Cross-Polity Time-Series Data (Cambridge, Ma.: MIT Press, 1971).

Representativeness was indicated by the presence of an effective legislature elected either directly or indirectly with parliamentary responsibility. Stability was indicated by the number of major constitutional changes and cabinet changes per decade and nonviolent succession by the absence of coups d'état.

Regression was indicated by reversion back to a dictatorship, the lack of an effective legislature, and/or parliamentary responsibility following a coup or major constitutional change.

Lines of segmental cleavage between 1930 and 1938 include major parties organized on either a religious or a regional basis (Belgium and the Netherlands): where these parties are simultaneously distinguished by religion and ethnic/linguistic/regional bases, thus intensifying the division, this is multiplied and counted as two sources of cleavage, although the same parties may be involved (e.g., Yugoslavia and Czechoslovakia prewar). Fascist and Communist parties gathering more than 12% of the vote in a general election are counted as a source of the underlying cleavage. Where these parties were not allowed to compete freely in elections, other indicators are used to determine whether they constituted a significant source of cleavage: this includes the adherence of prominent politicians to these causes, prewar trials for conspiracy or attempted coup d'état, growth of student and peasant movements. Data on prewar parties and movements are gathered from

the Encyclopedia Britannica, the New York Times, and national histories
cited for particular countries.

Code

1   More solidary (ranked 1, 2, 3 in Table 2-2)

0   Less solidary (ranked 0 in Table 2-2)

15 ASMOVE 36

Success of indigenous anti-Semitic movements by 1936. Modern anti-
Semitic movements are explicitly dedicated to revoking the civic equality
of rights that Jews have been granted as citizens since the French Revolution. States (or regions of which later became states in World War II) are
ranked by the extent to which this goal was attained by 1936. Because of
the varying degree of political liberties then extant in different nations and
the emergence of new states in 1938-1941 not existent in 1936, different
criteria had to be used to discriminate in different countries when an anti-
Semitic movement offered a potential challenge to governments or when a
movement had a major constituency. Characteristics of the original ranking are shown in Table 2-3.

Code

1   Anti-Semitic movement more successful (ranked 3 and 4 in Table 2-3)

0   Anti-Semitic movement less successful (ranked 2 and 1 in Table 2-3)

16 - 25 German Control Variables (and Interactions Involving these Variables)

16 OCCUPIED

At time of deportation/extermination = Without native government =
Command zone or SS zone in original codes of Nazi zone (see Figure 3-1
and Table 3-1).

Code

1   Occupied

0   Not occupied

17 SS REIGN

At time of deportation/extermination = SS zone in original codes of Nazi zone (see Figure 3-1 and Table 3-1).

Code

1   Under SS reign

0   Not under SS reign

18 SSGRIP 41 = 2 − OPPDELAY (Inverse OPPDELAY; see Variable 22 below)

Intensity of SS control over state in September 1941.

Code

0   Minimal = colonial zone

1   Some = command zone

2   Maximal = SS zone

19 NORESIST

Interaction term for ASMOVE 36 × SSGRIP 41.

Code

0   1_x0 (ASMOVE 36_x^+ COLONIAL ZONE)

1   1_x1 (ASMOVE 36_x^+ COMMAND ZONE)

2   1_x2 (ASMOVE $36_x^!$ SS ZONE)

0   0_x0 . . . 2 (ASMOVE 36_x^0 any zone)

20 SSEXEMPT

Estimated percent of Jews exempted from deportation to extermination camps by German decree within SS zone.

Code

0   No exemptees or state not in SS zone

1   .1-4.99%

2   5-9.99%

3   10-14.99%

4   15-19.99%

21 DISPOSED

To resist deportation of Jews (Inverse ASMOVE 36).

Code

1   Anti-Semitic movement less successful prewar

0   Anti-Semitic movement more successful

22 OPPDELAY

Is mean year deportation began minus 1941 for states classed as DISPOSED

to resist classed by SSGRIP 41 (see Table B-3).

Code

0   SS zone

1   Command zone

2   Colonial zone

23 POSTPONE

Is interaction of OPPDELAY × DISPOSED.

Code

0   Any zone × not disposed: 0_x0, 1_x0, 2_x0

0   SS zone × disposed: 0_x1

1   Command zone × disposed: 1_x1

2   Colonial zone × disposed: 2_x1

24 LACKTIME

Is interaction of DISPOSED × SSGRIP 41.

Code

0   Not disposed/any zone: 0_x1, 2, 3

0   Disposed × colonial zone = 0: 1_x0

1   Disposed × command zone = 1: 1_x1

2   Disposed × SS zone 41 = 2: 1_x2

25 WARNTIME

Timing of Deportation/Extermination Threat related to public awareness

of extermination policy against Jews (see Table B-3).

Code	Original Code		Stage
0 =	0	June 1941-December 1941—no warning	Rumor
	1	January 1941-24 June 1942—eyewitness reports circulated in East	
1 =	2	25 June 1942-16 December 1942—official reports via BBC of extermination	Official confirmation
2 =	3	17 December 1942-June 1943—threats of postwar punishment for extermination of Jews by Allies and possibility of German defeat emerges after Stalingrad	Warning
	4	July 1943—likelihood of German war defeat increases after Allied landing and Italian defection	Warning plus potential apprehension

26 - 27 Satellites' Rewards and Responses

26 SATOBLIG

German allies', satellites', and colonies' obligations to Germany: the following scale assumes that obligations correspond to past rewards between patron and client, given the norm of reciprocity. Therefore, the greater the past reward, the greater would be the sense of obligation to conform to German racial policy.

Code

3   Granted national autonomy over territory previously governed by federal or central government (Croatia, Slovakia)

2   Received expanded territory from neighboring countries (Hungary, Bulgaria, Rumania)

1   Received arms, supplies. and/or supplementary military support against enemy (Finland, Italy)

0   Acknowledged constricted right of self-government (France, Denmark)

9   Does not apply

27 SATCOLAB

Agreement to deport all or some Jews.

Code

3   Agreement concluded to deport all Jews categorically

2   Agreement concluded to deport foreign Jews categorically

1   No agreement to deport any Jews but toleration of or assistance given
to German or other satellites' deportation/extermination in own zone

0   No agreement and no systematic evidence of toleration

9   Does not apply

28 - 31 State and Popular Collaboration

28 OFFCOLAB

Passage of legislation and/or promulgation of ordinances by highest state

bureaucracy to achieve following functions.

| | Original | |
Code	Code	
1 =	{ 3	Segregate and/or concentrate Jews
	{ 2	Strip of possessions and/or positions
0 =	{ 1	Define and register Jews by law
	{ 0	None of above
	9	Does not apply

29 POLICOOP

Official police collaboration before seizure of majority of Jews.

| | Original | |
Code	Code	
1 =	2	Native police authorized to catch and arrest Jews in all major cities
0 =	{ 1	Native police authorized in some cities but not in others
	{ 0	Native police not authorized
	9	Does not apply

30 RANKCOOP

To obtain a summary index of collaboration that would be equally valid for

states with different potential ability to collaborate, each nation was ranked

against other nations in the same zone of German control in the following

manner (see Table 2.1 for original classification into arms-zones):

1. The sum of all collaboration indices (Variables 27-29) was added for
each state. Note original codes for each variable that were used.

2. Where there was substantive reason to believe that an agreement concluded or law enacted was not enforced by national or local governments or systematically ignored by police, a minus 1 or .9 was deducted from the sum for nonenforcement or systematic noncooperation,
respectively.

3. The net sum was then divided by the maximum total for all nations in that zone of control in order to obtain a ratio of the extent of collaboration relative to the range of action that was possible in that zone. For example, in zones I and II a maximum of 8 was possible.

$$
\begin{array}{ll}
\text{(Variable 27) agreement to deport all Jews} & = 3 \\
\text{(Variable 28) laws passed to segregate Jews} & = 3 \\
\text{(Variable 29) police enforcement in all cities} & = \dfrac{2}{8}
\end{array}
$$

Therefore, for all states in zones I and II, the sum of Variables 27, 28, and 29 was divided by 8. The only measure applicable to all nations incorporated in zone V—the zone of extermination—is police enforcement. Therefore, all scores on Variable 23 were divided by 2 for each nation in that zone.

4. The ratio obtained for each nation was then ranked relative to other states in that group as shown below.

Code	Original Code		Example	
1 =	2	Highest	In Zone I, 8/8	In Zone V, 2/2
0 =	{ 1	Some	In Zone I, 6/8	In Zone V, 1/2
	{ 0	None		

31 POPCOLAB

This is an index of social toleration of popular collaboration. It is assumed that the more visible organized native participation in extermination is, the more it is tolerated by other natives.

Code	Original Code	
1 =	2	Organized native killing squads or battalions
0 =	1	Organized native paramilitary or political police or other groups used to search out and seize Jews
	9	Does not apply

32 - 35 Jewish Isolation Preceding Deportation/Extermination

The following are functional stages in the isolation of Jews. All stages below must have occurred previously or must happen simultaneously in order that the object of the present stage be fulfilled. This analysis is an elaboration of Raul Hilberg's tracing of the passage through definition and expropriation to concentration. See The Destruction of the European Jews (Chicago: Quadrangle, 1967), 31-33. Signs of passage include legislation (which may occur before or after process has been started), arrests for violations, and German observations of nonconformity (see Chapter 3 of this volume).

32 DEFINED

Code

1   Jews defined and identified by law

0   Jews not defined or identified

33 STARRED

Code

1   Jews starred and segregated

0   Jews not starred or segregated effectively

34 ISOLATED

Code

1   Jews isolated in compulsory residences or camps

0   Jews not isolated

35 GHETTO*

Code

1   Jews concentrated in walled ghetto or other enclosure

0   Jews not concentrated

36 - 41 Organization and Response of Jewish Leadership

36 JUDENRAT

Presence of Jewish Council responsible to and appointed by German

occupation authorities.

	Original	
Code	Code	
1 =	2	Responsible to German authorities only
0 =	1	Responsible to native authorities and higher native administration
	0	No council or comparable organization

37 JEWAGENT

Presence of Jewish Council responsible to German or native authorities.

Code

1 =   1 or 2 above

0 =   0 above

---

* Variable label printed as PACKED on IBM output.

38 JEWCOOP 1

This is an index of any organized Jewish cooperation facilitating deporta-

tions. Facilitation is defined as performance of functions that increased

the probability of Jews' voluntary compliance and/or seizure for deporta-

tion, regardless of the motives of individuals performing such roles—

whether they were conforming due to direct force-threat of violent reprisal

(accommodation) or collaborating. Authorities include Jewish Council

leaders and appointees, Jewish police or auxiliaries, and other German-

appointed Jewish functionaries (e.g., special organizations to prepare Jews

for "emigration").

Code	Original Code	
0 =	0	None
1 =	1	Published orders and/or verbally urged Jews to comply with them
	2	Designated individuals for deportation by making selections for quota, list for exemptions, and/or list of aged, ill, or children and/or assisted in preparation for transport
	3	Enforced orders by seizing people selected for deportation and/or catching quota of people and/or apprehension of people in hiding

39 JEWCOOP 2

High cooperation.

Code

1 =   2 and 3 above

0 =   0 and 1 above

40 JREPPLEA

Prewar Jewish leaders' appeals and/or protest to native leaders preceding

deportation or during first six months. Leading spokesmen included chief

rabbis, nationwide organizations of rabbis, representative organizations of

the Jewish community and/or leading political movements—persons who

have been officially designated and/or selected by the community in some

representative fashion. Native leaders include heads of churches,

government, resistance movements, universities, and governments-in-exile.
Other spokesmen refer to other rabbis, professionals, or men of public affairs not officially representing Jews as a collectivity but known as Jews.
Protest or appeal includes petition, letter, leaflet, or oral representation
whose object it is to prevent the deportation of any (all) Jews categorically.

| | Original | |
Code	Code	
1 =	2	Protest or appeal by leading spokesmen
0 =	1	Protest or appeal by other Jews or anonymously
	0	No protest recorded
	9	Does not apply or information not available

41 ANYPLEAS

Code

1   Some protest or appeal made by any Jewish spokesmen

0   None recorded

9   Does not apply or information not available

42 - 43 Native Response to German Occupation

42 RESINTEG

This is a scale of the integration of native resistance. Nations are ranked
by the length of time after German occupation or after June 1941 (whichever
is later) before the integration of the major resistance movements. Integration is denoted by the recognition of a common authority (such as a government-in-exile) or conclusion and signs of continued execution of an agreement between movements establishing a superordinate organization representing both (all) movements.

Code

4   Always unified or integrated within six months

3   Integrated between six and 17 months after occupation (or 6/41)

2   Integrated between 18 and 30 months after occupation (or 6/41)

1   Over 30 months preceding integration

0 Never integrated

9 Does not apply; functioning native government with representative parliament and no resistance movement; opposition expressed through political channels

43 NATUNITY

This is an index of national unity among resistance movements, measured by the length of time movements needed to recognize a common authority and persistence of their consensus. Only countries occupied by Germany were evaluated (thus excluding never-occupied satellites). States were evaluated on the length of time from German occupation to the end of the war.

Code

0 Major resistance movements never integrated or agreement between them broke down before liberation; dissensus over postwar authority among native leaders

1 Late integration (over 18 months from occupation) but agreement on postwar authority held

2 Early integration (18 months or less) and agreement on postwar authority held

9 Does not apply

44 - 46 Response of Dominant Church to Threat to Jews

44 CHURCHPD

Church predeportation protests are observed by recorded categorical protest made publicly by head of dominant church against anti-Jewish discrimination before deportations were initiated in state.

Code

1 Protest made

0 No protest recorded

Protests against deportation: the expected effectiveness of protest is related to its immediacy.[*] Since a time lag in the effects of protest would

---

[*] The motivation of protests also may be inferred by their immediacy or belatedness. For example, protests against the annihilation of Jews made after the war or after their deportation may serve to clarify the conscience of the protector but cannot be construed as a social act to deter their annihilation.

be anticipated, only protests and other acts of resistance occurring within six months and before the seizure of half the recorded Jewish population are analyzed. The following scale of resistance is based upon the recorded action taken by the highest clergy of the dominant church during the time of greatest urgency, within the first six months of deportation/extermination and before the elimination of half the recorded Jewish population, so as to prevent the deportation of other Jews categorically.

45 HICHURCH

Code	Original Code	
1 =	3	Exhortation to noncooperation, banning of participation in deportation, and/or mobilization of clergy and public denunciation
	2	Public denunciation of deportation of all Jews from pulpit by highest church leader(s) and appeal
0 =	1	Private appeal by church leaders to head of state and/or occupying authority
	0	None of above
	9	Does no apply; no threat of deportation

46 ANYCHURCH

Any categorical protest against deportation by head of church within above limits.

Code	Original Code	
1	1, 2, or 3 (see Variable 45)	
0	0	
9	Does not apply	

47 - 49 Response of Native Movements to Threat to Jews

47 MOVEMENT

This is a graded index of resistance movement's mobilization to save Jews. Each nation-state is rated on the basis of policy exhibited in print and practice by major movement(s) whose primary objective was to liberate their state from foreign occupation. Major movements were identified by their correspondence with prewar parties and/or recognition by the Allies and/or extent of control of liberated territory. Intelligence circuits, espionage

networks, and foreign guerrilla units staffed by the Allies and/or directly

subordinate to their discipline were excluded from consideration, as their

purpose and structure negated free recruitment of members and communi-

cation with their fellow countrymen to promote civil disobedience and hence

cannot be scored on their policy toward Jews. The distinction between

"circuits" and "movements" is drawn from Henri Michel's The Shadow War:

European Resistance, 1939-1945, trans. Richard Barry (New York:

Harper and Row, 1972).

Code	Original Code	
1 =	3_{+++}	Mobilization of special organization, facilities, or re-sources to aid Jews escape deportation, regardless of membership in, or relationship to, resistance
	2_{++}	Integration: inclusion of Jews in resistance units without discrimination and public identification of movement against deportation by word (newspaper, radio) or deed (warning, providing false papers, liberating transport camp, reprisal against anti-Semitic agitators)
	1_{+}	Inclusion: inclusion of Jews within movement in separate units or disguised as non-Jews with no public identifica-tion of the movement's attitude toward anti-Jewish dis-crimination or deportation
	0	No positive evidence of inclusion (includes these subclasses)
0 =	−	Negative identification of movement members against Jews: collaboration in police or paramilitary units organized to detect, seize, or exterminate Jews without any movement sanctions against them
	− +	Mixed negative and positive identification: for example, Poland; identification of government-in-exile and Civil Directorate against deportation; warning against collab-oration by identifying and/or blackmailing Jews in London and publication in Warsaw; negative identification demonstrated by Home Army approving the shooting of Jews in the forests (Poland)
9	9	Does not apply

48 SLANT

This variable, resistance movement's identification with Jews, is based on

re-dichotomization of Variable 47.

	Original	
Code	Code	
1	2, 3	Positive public identification with Jews (see Variable 47)
0	1, 0	No positive public identification with Jews
9	9	Does not apply

49 DEFENSE

Immediacy of Jewish social defense movements* is a function of the time

it began related to the percent of Jews then alive and free who might be saved

by its activities. (See Chapter 2 on original coding for scope of movement.)

Code

4   75% or more of Jewish population potential beneficiaries†

3   50-74.9% potential beneficiaries

2   25-49.9% potential beneficiaries

1   Under 25% potential beneficiaries

9   Does not apply

50 - 54 Situational Opportunities (Including Interactions with Native Movement
        Response)

50 BORDERS

Nation's border joins foreign neutral offering sanctuary to Jews without

restrictions at or before time of deportation threat.‡

Code

1   Yes

0   No

9   Does not apply

---

* The term "Jewish social defense" is not a synonym for "Jewish resistance"
or related terms, which usually refer to participation by Jews, whether open or
disguised, in national resistance movements to advance the general goal of liberation. In evaluating the extensiveness of a Jewish social movement, no account
has been taken of the extent of Jewish participation in general national resistance
movements.

† Potential Jewish beneficiaries are not Jews actually helped by the movement
but hypothetically able to benefit from the movement's direct service and the example it sets for others to imitate.

‡ This variable was not used in the final analysis.

51 HAVENS

Internal liberated zones or extraterritorial area or other sanctuary immune to native police raids whose authorities offer sanctuary to Jews at or before time of deportation threat. *

Code

1   Yes

0   No

9   Does not apply

52 OPENEXIT

Exits to foreign havens: the accessibility (at the beginning of deportations) to foreign nations in which deportations are not occurring and have not occurred is evaluated as a product of three factors:

Border access factor
Attractiveness of haven
Number and policy of doorkeepers

To explicate these further: the border access factor is the proportion of Jewish population of each state settled within 100 miles of an attractive border. To estimate this factor, the proportion of Jewish population of that state (derived from the most recent census) settled in cities with over 10,000 Jews within 100 miles of that border was multiplied by the ratio of total Jewish population in that state to Jewish population in cities with over 10,000 Jews. In cases where residents of a city have access to more than one border, it is assumed that they will flee toward the most attractive border.

Attractiveness—It is assumed that persons in peril are most likely to flee to countries known to be havens because of their political status (neutrals) and less likely to flee to countries under indirect Axis control. Therefore, neighboring neutrals are accounted as most attractive (1) and German satellites in which deportations are not currently taking place as less attractive (.5).

---

* This variable was not used in the final analysis.

The number and policy of doorkeepers—doorkeepers include German troops, native troops guarding frontiers (inside a country of flight), and foreign militia guarding havens and immigration or security officials in potential havens who have the power to evict illegal refugees. The ability to secure and remain in a haven depends on the ability to avoid all potential doorkeepers consecutively. It is assumed the evader has an even chance (.5) of evasion and capture if the doorkeeper is on guard; if the exit is unguarded, the chance is certain (1 out of 1) of avoiding capture. If Jews are already incarcerated in ghettos, there is an additional doorkeeper to be evaded, bribed, or overcome.

Mathematically, this formula can be expressed as

$$E_{BAC_{1\ldots n}} \times A(PE_{dk_G} \times PE_{dk_{DO}} \times PE_{dk_{FO_b}} \times PE_{dk_{FO_{im}}}) \times 10$$

where

$E_{BAC_{1\ldots n}}$	sum of access from all borders
A	attractiveness of haven
PE	probability of evasion from capture by
dk_G	German doorkeepers
dk_{DO}	domestic doorkeepers
dk_{FO_b}	foreign doorkeepers at the border
$dk_{FO_{im}}$	foreign doorkeepers of internal security or immigration who may evict illegal evaders

To illustrate, one may calculate exits from Denmark and Norway to Sweden. In both cases, the majority of the Jewish population was concentrated within 100 miles of one border and Sweden had offered refuge so $BAC = 1.0$ and $A = 1$. However, German ships offered no or token resistance to the Danish crossing and the German Army refrained from enforcing arrests during this period in Denmark, whereas in Norway, Jewish evaders had to penetrate a border guarded by German police. Therefore, we conclude that exits are as follows:

$$\text{Denmark} = 1_x(1_x(1_x1_x1_x1)) = 1$$

$$\text{Norway} = 1_x(1_x(.5_x1_x1)) = .5$$

Code = actual score multiplied by 10; thus, Denmark = 10 and Norway = 5.

99.9 Does not apply

53 HAVETIME

This is the actual year that deportations/exterminations begin in state.*

Code

1 1941

2 1942

3 1943

4 1944

9 Does not apply

54 EVADOPP

Rank-order scale of relative opportunities for evasion at time of deportation.

Code

04 Adjacent foreign neutral offers sanctuary to Jews and Jewish population not segregated earlier

03 Some open borders to neutral and no prior segregation

02 No open borders to neutral offering sanctuary and no prior segregation

01 No open borders and segregation of Jews

99 Information not available or does not apply

55 - 58 Rank of Jewish Victims, Exemptees, and Evaders

55 VICTIMS

See Chapter 2 for definition and source notes to Table 3-1.

Code

1 Victims composed under 10% of recorded (or estimated) Jewish population

2 Victims composed 10% or over but under 20%

3 Victims composed 20% or over but under 30%
to
10 Victims composed over 90%

---

* This variable was not used in the final analysis.

56 EXEMPTED

Exemptees includes all Jews formally granted exemption from deportation,
usually because of bonds to Christian kin created by intermarriage—the ex-
emptee was a spouse or a child of an "Aryan"—or bonds created by membership in a religious community, grounds for exemption of converts to Christianity. Estimations are made from records cited in the sources on Jewish
victimization and ranked in 5% intervals.

Where nations had reclassified many exemptees as non-Jews
("Aryanization"), and deportation later occurred under German occupation
(Italy), an estimation was made of the total Jewish population as defined by
the German racial laws to calculate the rank on Jewish victimization and
the percentage of Jewish exemptees. Where there were no records of any
persons obtaining exemption as kin of Christians, 0 is entered. Where exemptions were honored, but no records were found, a minimum estimate
(1) was entered.

Code

 0   No exemptees

 1   Under 5%

 2   Over 5% but under 10%

 99   No information available or does not apply

57 EVADERS

Jewish evaders equals 100 minus actual percent of Jewish victims minus
actual percent of Jewish exemptees.

Code

 1   Under 5%

 2   Over 5% but under 10%
      to
 20   Over 95%

 99   Not possible to compute because of missing information

58 DIFFEVAD

Difference (when known) between rank of Jewish evaders of state's national-

ity and foreign Jews—if separate ranks (Variable 57) were calculated. *

Code

01-20   Actual difference (rank state Jews minus rank foreign Jews)

99   Does not apply or information not available

---

* This variable was not used in the final analysis.

Appendixes

Appendix B: Methodological
Notes and Tables

Figure 3-4 illustrates the least-squares equation based on estimation of victims separately within high anti-Semitic and low anti-Semitic states. The equation in general form follows:

$$\text{VICTIMS} = a + B \text{ SSGRIP } 41 + e$$

Using unstandardized coefficients (B represents decile increments in rank of victims) for high anti-Semitic states, the equation follows:

$$\text{VICTIMS} = 7.8 + .92 \text{ SSGRIP } 41 + e; \; r = .745, \; r^2 = .555$$

For low anti-Semitic states,

$$\text{VICTIMS} = 2.1 + 3.55 \text{ SSGRIP } 41 + e; \; r = .949, \; r^2 = .90$$

The only two cases that deviate more than 1.2 ranks from the rank estimated from these equations are the Netherlands and Rumania, which were previously discussed.

In order to sum up a solution in a single equation, victims (in all states) were regressed onto the independent variables and interaction terms representing the differential impact produced by SSGRIP 41 in more and less anti-Semitic states. The rank of Jewish exemptees in the SS zone—also a function of SS control and the differential German obligations to natives within these states—was also added

350

to the equation. This produced the following equation (again using unstandardized

regression coefficients):

VICTIMS = 2.6 + 4.5 ASMOVE 36 + 3.2 SSGRIP 41 – 1.8 NORESIST –

.4 LACKTIME – .5 SSEXEMPT

LACKTIME = ASMOVE 36_0 × SSGRIP 41;   NORESIST = ASMOVE 36_+ × SSGRIP 41

Since the impact of SSGRIP 41 was accounted for before the interaction terms

were entered (entering variables with hierarchical inclusion), there is a greater

reduction among high anti-Semitic states than among low states for the interaction

term since increases in the immediacy of SSGRIP 41 had to produce less of an in-

crement in high anti-Semitic states because those states had already produced

80% of the maximal number of victims with virtually no SS control.

The impact of prewar anti-Semitism and immediacy of SS control in 1941 on

the critical intervening variables explicated previously was also evaluated by re-

gression. Table B-4 shows that about two-thirds of the variation in all of these

variables except church protest against deportation could be accounted for by the

prewar success of the anti-Semitic movement and the immediacy of SS control in

1941, which directly account for 85% of the variation in rank of victims. But

stateage accounts for almost as much variation in church protest as does anti-

Semitism, after accounting for the contribution of the latter and SS control.

Appendix B

TABLE B-1

ZERO-ORDER CORRELATION COEFFICIENTS* OF REVISED VARIABLES (EXCLUDING VARIABLES IN TABLE B-2 AND INTERACTION TERMS)

Variable†	1	2	3	4	5	6	7	8	9	10	11	12	13	14	15	16	17
1 JEWSSIZE	x	57	69	31	66	97	26	00	23	07	−26	22	−20	−14	45	33	26
2 PCCITYHI		x	80	75	50	60	43	05	16	−01	−52	14	−13	36	73	22	37
3 PCNATION			x	30	72	76	63	−01	32	−08	−41	−12	−30	31	61	28	41
4 STRANGER				x	01	26	22	−09	−26	−17	−39	−19	−06	−13	79	−27	−18
5 INVISIBL					x	73	83	−79	y	−27	−34	−11	−17	z	58	38	35
6 SPREAD						x	44	−13	16	−02	−29	10	−16	−03	50	27	30
7 CONINDEX							x	−52	−07	−00	−42	−24	−12	48	65	38	39
8 OCCUPIED								x	52	13	05	14	−13	y	y	−18	−18
9 SS REIGN									x	41	−04	13	−77	y	y	26	32
10 DURATION										x	−10	65	−52	23	10	37	44
11 TASKTIME											x	−04	04	−25	−88	−39	−17
12 PREPTIME‡												x	01	−40	−59	23	24
13 WARNTIME‡													x	−42	−37	−36	−51
14 SATOBLIG														x	60	35	34
15 SATCOLAB															x	91	94
16 OFFCOLAB																x	84
17 POLICOOP																	x
18 POPCOLAB																	
19 DEFINED																	
20 STARRED																	
21 GHETTO																	
22 JUDENRAT																	
23 JEWAGENT																	
24 JEWCOOP 1																	
25 JREPLEA																	
26 ANYPLEAS																	
27 RESINTEG																	
28 NATUNITY																	
29 CHURCHPD																	
30 HICHURCH																	
31 MOVEMENT																	
32 SLANT																	
33 OPENEXIT																	
34 EVADOPP																	
35 VICTIMS																	
36 EXEMPTED																	
37 EVADERS																	

* All correlation coefficients are preceded by an implied decimal point thus, 37 = .37. *x*—*r* = 1.0 for all self-correlations. *y*—correlation not calculated because values of (one or both) variables are the same. *z*—*r* = 1.0; *z*¹—*r* = −1.0.

† Original codes used in computation of correlations for these variables.

‡ Numbers herein refer only to variables in this table and do not correspond to numbers in Appendix A. See Appendix A for definitions of variables and values locating variables (in same order) by name.

TABLE B-1 (Continued)

18	19	20	21	22	23	24	25	26	27	28	29	30	31	32	33	34	35	36	37
35	13	24	37	11	18	23	24	24	30	-24	-20	-18	-16	-30	-11	-18	26	-25	-23
29	32	46	54	32	47	46	14	19	13	-35	-18	-34	-15	-29	-26	-41	48	-13	-47
50	22	46	59	18	33	37	02	03	16	-39	-29	-26	-22	-52	-33	-32	47	-39	-43
00	31	-20	14	25	48	55	43	41	20	06	10	-34	49	14	-18	-13	12	39	-16
76	25	19	50	-38	50	16	38	25	-67	-71	-32	00	-38	-50	53	y	26	00	-23
41	14	27	41	-00	20	25	30	29	23	-26	-25	-20	-19	-35	-11	-18	28	-25	-24
26	25	30	20	-34	26	25	26	22	-06	-13	-26	-26	-30	-44	-06	-22	27	-10	-25
-07	12	24	26	75	-07	06	-57	-50	23	-11	20	07	26	-12	-48	y	28	00	-30
60	24	55	50	69	36	38	-72	-80	-15	-56	-46	-36	-32	-71	-14	-67	67	-28	-65
25	22	38	-17	28	25	29	-43	-40	-16	-14	-34	-27	-32	-37	-12	-31	40	41	-44
-10	-43	-27	-12	-15	-55	-58	-21	-43	15	30	-16	30	06	08	31	28	-25	-35	31
-16	13	20	-00	26	13	05	-11	-09	02	03	-08	06	-15	-12	-05	-21	08	25	-12
-70	-29	-46	-24	-41	-13	-52	56	62	22	47	64	52	43	55	-05	66	-70	10	68
33	35	63	06	y	35	23	y	y	-61	-48	06	06	y	-35	-24	00	73	27	-72
71	91	55	28	y	91	79	y	y	-87	-81	-11	-11	y	-50	-54	00	85	78	-89
35	66	51	26	-10	35	25	-36	-28	-39	-39	-46	-35	z	-32	19	-37	58	24	-58
61	50	78	44	08	47	45	-40	-28	-23	-50	-61	-32	-72	-61	-23	-57	72	-06	-71
x	21	60	50	21	38	43	-29	-39	-26	-63	-59	-45	-70	-70	-05	-66	64	-22	-62
	x	34	22	35	67	58	-26	-18	-38	-50	-16	-26	-55	-19	-12	-56	56	23	-59
		x	67	52	51	57	-44	-33	-38	-63	-45	-51	-46	-82	-40	-86	87	-14	-86
			x	43	32	33	-23	-28	-05	-49	-42	-32	-29	-61	-23	-60	61	-58	-57
				x	52	50	-57	-48	22	-53	-06	-28	08	-36	-38	-90	60	00	-62
					x	87	-15	-04	-60	-74	-24	-39	-22	-35	-12	-90	65	17	-68
						x	-18	-07	-58	-71	-38	-58	-13	-39	-33	-93	75	28	-78
							x	91	18	29	30	15	35	42	23	39	-55	00	55
								x	15	29	50	13	32	51	08	30	-50	21	48
									x	70	35	32	32	18	-19	62	-41	-22	45
										x	46	30	35	50	12	80	-72	17	71
											x	51	65	55	-17	48	-60	30	55
												x	50	42	-09	75	-57	00	57
													x	35	11	16	53	10	51
														x	32	67	-72	36	71
															x	-21	-28	-11	32
																x	-86	16	88
																	x	-09	-99
																		x	-02
																			x

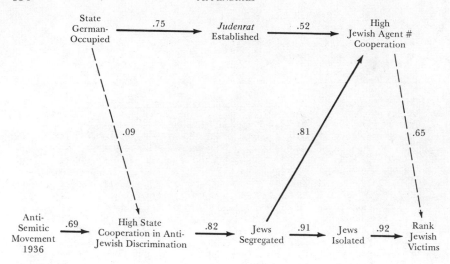

Figure B-1. Chain Illustrating How Cooperation of Jewish Agents and Rank of Jewish Victims Are Linked to Isolation of Jews during Holocaust (all figures are zero-order correlations).

Note: the following tabulation shows the percent of variance in dependent variables directly explained by each independent variable.

Independent Variable	Dependent Variable			
	Jews Segregated	Jews Isolated	High Jewish Agent Cooperation	Jewish Victims
High State Cooperation	68%	51%	36%	69%
Jews Segregated	—	82%	65%	75%
Jews Isolated	—	—	44%	84%
High Jewish Agent Cooperation	—	—	—	42%

TABLE B-2

ZERO-ORDER CORRELATION COEFFICIENTS* OF CRITICAL VARIABLES ENTERED IN REGRESSION OF UNDERLYING CAUSES

Variable	1	2	3	4	5	6	7	8	9	10	11
1 Anti-Semitic movement success by 1936	x	−56	35	−47	19	69	39	57	−47	−57	64
2 Solidarity		x	−09	57	−28	−38	−25	−53	47	54	−53
3 Dominant religion Roman Catholic			x	−08	−12	05	−03	13	−20	−08	14
4 Stateage since 1830				x	−39	−39	−51	−61	75	79	−57
5 SSgrip 41					x	45	53	64	−52	−67	72
6 Rank state cooperation						x	60	72	−45	−69	83
7 Jewcoop 2 (High Jewish cooperation)							x	66	−31	−45	65
8 Jews isolated								x	−73	−90	92
9 Any church protest									x	86	−63
10 Immediacy of defense										x	−92
11 Jewish victims											x

* All correlation coefficients are preceded by an implied decimal point.
x—r = 1.0 for all self-correlations.

TABLE B-3

ACTUAL AND HYPOTHESIZED VALUES OF WARNING TIME
AS A FUNCTION OF PREDISPOSITION TO RESIST AND OPPORTUNITY
TO DELAY DEPORTATIONS*

Time Variations	SSGRIP 41		
	0 I. Colonial Zone	1 II. Command Zone	2 III. SS Zone
Among states DISPOSED to resist	France, Athens, Bulgaria, Denmark, Italy, Finland	Belgium, Netherlands, Norway	Estonia, Protectorate, Serbia
Actual values of warning time	1, 2, 2, 2, 2, and undefined value for Finland	1, 1, 1	0, 0, 0
Mean year deportations began†	1943	1942	1941
OPPDELAY	2	1	0
Estimated POSTPONE = DISPOSED × OPPDELAY	2	1	0
Among states not DISPOSED to resist	Croatia, Rumania, Slovakia, Hungary	Salonica	Austria, Germany, Latvia, Lithuania, Poland
Actual values of warning time	0, 0, 0, 2	1	0, 0, 0, 0, 0
Mean year deportations began	1942	—	1941
Median year deportations began	1941-1942	—	1941
Estimated POSTPONE = DISPOSED × OPPDELAY	0	0	0
SSGRIP 41 = 2 − OPPDELAY:DISPOSED	0	1	2

* SSGRIP 41 is an interval scale, in contrast to the original ordinal scale of German control (indicated in roman numerals) as it is the inverse of OPPDELAY. DISPOSED = 1 − success of anti-Semitic movement by 1936 (1, 0). Warning time = 0 (before 25/6/42), 1 (25/6/42-17/12/42), 2 (17/12/42 and later). OPPDELAY = mean year deportations began − 1941:DISPOSED.

† In this group, the mean equals the median and the mode.

TABLE B-4

REGRESSION OF DEPENDENT AND SELECTED INTERVENING VARIABLES ON INDEPENDENT VARIABLES

Independent Variable	Dependent Variable (scale of d.v.)				
	VICTIMS (1-10)	HIGH COOPERATION (0, 1)	ISOLATED (0, 1)	DEFENSE (0-4)	CHURCH PROTEST (0, 1)
ASMOVE 36					
B (standard error)	4.5 (.84)	.79 (.19)	.63 (.19)	-1.1 (.60)	-.18 (.28)
r^2	.41	.48	.33	.32	.22
SSGRIP 41					
B (standard error)	3.2 (.84)	.38 (.17)	.42 (.17)	-1.2 (.43)	-.39 (.20)
r^2 increment	.37	.10	.29	.32	.19
Interaction of ASMOVE 36 and SSGRIP 41					
NORESIST (ASMOVE 36 + SSGRIP 41)					
B (standard error)	-1.8 (.89)	-.34 (.21)	-.25 (.21)	.65 (.50)	.24 (.23)
r^2 increment	.07	.05	.05	.04	.03
LACKTIME (ASMOVE 36 - SSGRIP 41)					
B (standard error)	-.4 (.83)	-.16 (.18)	-.06 (.18)	.48 (.42)	.28 (.19)
r^2 increment	.00	.02	.00	.02	.06
Other variables contributing substantively					
STATEAGE					
B (standard error)				.35 (.12)	.14 (.05)
r^2 increment				.14	.21
Intercept	2.6	.14	.05	1.8	.36
Multiple r	.926	.806	.814	.920	.848
Total r^2 explained	.86	.65	.66	.85	.72

Notes

NOTES FOR PROLOGUE

1. The states and occupied regions in which the majority of Jews were not killed include Athens, Belgium, Bulgaria, Denmark, Finland, France, Italy, Norway, and Rumania. Table 3-1 estimates the rank (in deciles) of total Jewish victimization during the Holocaust in these states and regions. Because Jewish victims—defined in Chapter 2—include concentration-camp survivors as well as those Jews killed, a majority of Rumania's Jews are estimated to have been victims although less than half died.

2. Berl Mark, "Dubnow," *The Way We Think,* ed. Joseph Leftwich, 2 Vols. South Brunswick, N.J.: Yoseloff, 1969), II: 530.

3. "The Holocaust: A Generation After" (address presented to the International Scholars Conference on the Holocaust—A Generation After, New York City, March 1975).

NOTES FOR CHAPTER 1

1. Yehuda Bauer, "When Did They Know?" *Midstream* XIV (April 1968): 51–58; Louis de Jong, "The Netherlands and Auschwitz: Why Were the Reports of Mass Killings So Widely Disbelieved?" in *Imposed Jewish Governing Bodies under Nazi Rule* (New York: YIVO, 1972). On American response see Charles Herbert Stember et al., *Jews in the Mind of America* (New York: Basic Books, 1966), 141.

2. Lucjan Dobroszycki reviews Polish records showing that out of an estimated 218,000 Jewish survivors who had returned there, "1,500 Jews lost their lives in Poland from liberation to the summer of 1947" in pogroms and lynchings: one out of every 145 Jews. See Dobroszycki, "Restoring Jewish Life in Postwar Poland," *Soviet-Jewish Affairs* III, no. 2 (1973): 58–71.

3. See Peter Meyer on "Czechoslovakia," p. 72, Eugene Duschinsky on "Hungary," pp. 403–405, Nicholas Sylvain on "Rumania," pp. 518–519, and Peter Meyer on "Bulgaria," pp. 567–568, in *The Jews in the Soviet Satellites,* ed. Peter Meyer et al. (Syracuse, N.Y.: Syracuse University Press, 1953). For France see Xosa Szajkowski, *Analytical Franco-Jewish Gazetteer, 1939–1945* (New York: Frydmann, 1966), 107–111. For the Netherlands see Jacob Presser, *The Destruction of the Dutch Jews,* trans. Arnold Pomerans (New York: Dutton, 1969), 540–544.

4. Raphael Lemkin, *Axis Rule in Occupied Europe* (Washington, D.C.: Carnegie Endowment for International Peace, 1944), 79–95.

5. Marjorie Housepian, "The Unremembered Genocide," *Commentary* XLII (September 1966): 55–61.

6. Louis Lochner, *What about Germany?* (New York: Dodd, Mead, 1942), 2.

7. Norman Rich, *Hitler's War Aims, II: The Establishment of the New Order* (New York: Norton, 1974): 74–75.

8. For explication of this thesis see Jules Isaac, *The Teaching of Contempt: Christian Roots of Anti-Semitism,* trans. Helen Weaver (New York: Holt, Rinehart, and Winston, 1964); also Rosemary Ruether, *Faith and Fratricide* (New York: Seabury, 1974).

9. See the research reviewed by Ismar Schorsch, "German Anti-Semitism in the Light of Postwar Historiography," *Leo Baeck Institute Yearbook* XIX, no. 4 (1974): 257–271.

10. For distinctive answers to why the Jews were selected as the target see Raul Hilberg, *The Destruction of the European Jews* (Chicago: Quadrangle, 1967), 1–17, and Lucy S. Dawidowicz, *The War against the Jews, 1933–1945* (New York: Holt, Rinehart, and Winston, 1975), 3–166.

11. H. A. R. Gibb and Harold Bowen, *Islamic Society and the West: A Study of the Impact of Western Civilization on Muslim Culture in the Near East,* 2 vols. (New York: Oxford University Press, 1971), I: 227, as cited by Arshag O. Sarkissian, "Historical Background to 1915," in *Martyrdom and Rebirth* (New York: Lydian, 1965), 7–8.

12. Sarkissian, 10.

13. See note 26 below.

14. The term "middleman minority" is that of Hubert M. Blalock, Jr., who analyzed the function of such groups in *Toward a Theory of Minority-Group Relations* (New York: Capricorn, 1970), 84. Data on the occupational distribution of the Armenians in 1914 are lacking.

15. Germans Jews were underrepresented (in proportion to the percent of the population they constituted) in banking and major commercial enterprises in 1933 and did not dominate any major trade, profession, or the media but were visibly overrepresented in the free professions, especially medicine and law. See Karl. A. Schleunes, *The Twisted Road to Auschwitz: Nazi Policy toward German Jews, 1933–1939* (Urbana, Ill.: University of Illinois Press, 1970), 38–41. Data on prewar occupations of Jews in various states of Eastern Europe is presented in Meyers et al. *The Jews in the Soviet Satellites.*

16. This conception of the stranger differs from the optimistic conception of Georg Simmel in his essay "The Stranger" in *The Sociology of Georg Simmel,* trans.

Kurt H. Wolff (New York: The Free Press, 1950), 402–408. Simmel stresses the positive relation between stranger and host society: despite his different origins, "the stranger is yet an organic member of the group" (p. 408) and "a full-fledged member" (p. 402). He distinguishes this from "a kind of 'strangeness' that rejects the very commonness . . . which embraces the parties," in which case the " 'stranger,' here, has no positive meaning" (p. 407), or is a non or a negative relation, as between Greeks and Barbarians. The fate of the European Jews, his "classic example" (p. 403) of positive integration of the stranger, starkly contradicts the hopeful implications of his essay, first published in 1908.

17. Gaetano Mosca, *The Ruling Class*, trans. Hannah D. Kahn, ed. and rev. by Arthur Livingston (New York: McGraw-Hill, 1939), 70–72.

18. Hannah Arendt calls this phenomenon "tribalism" in *The Origins of Totalitarianism*, rev. ed. (New York: Harcourt, Brace, and World, 1966), 226–227; Peter F. Sugar refers to it as "messianism" in *Nationalism in Eastern Europe*, eds. Peter F. Sugar and Ivo J. Lederer (Seattle, Wa.: University of Washington Press, 1969), 11.

19. The concept of a master race has emerged both among "pan" movements appealing to people without a nation-state and in nation-states with weak solidarity. See Arendt, 235, 412, on the varying implications of this notion.

20. Viscount James Bryce, *The Treatment of Armenians in the Ottoman Empire, 1915–1916*, ed. Arnold J. Toynbee (London: HMSO, 1916), appendix D; Dickran H. Boyajian, *Armenia: The Case for a Forgotten Genocide* (Westwood, N.J.: Educational Book Crafters, 1972), 126.

21. Sarkissian, 11.

22. Senate document no. 266, *Congressional Record, 29 May 1920*, cited in Boyajian, 184–185.

23. Bernard Lewis, *The Emergence of Modern Turkey* (New York: Oxford University Press, 1961), 116, 127–128, 165–167, 217–218.

24. Louise Nalbandian, *The Armenian Revolutionary Movement: The Development of Armenian Political Parties through the Nineteenth Century* (Berkeley, Ca.: University of California Press, 1967).

25. Cited in Boyajian, 36–38.

26. Ibid., 287.

27. Abraham Hartunian, *Neither to Laugh Nor to Weep* (Boston: Beacon, 1968).

28. Boyajian, 47–55.

29. Feroz Ahmad, *The Young Turks: The Committee of Union and Progress in Turkish Politics, 1908–1914* (Oxford: Clarendon, 1969), 154.

30. Zaravend [pseud.], *United and Independent Turania: Aims and Designs of the Turks*, trans. V. N. Dadrian (Leiden: Brill, 1971), 37–38.

31. Ahmad, 156.

32. Djemal Pasha, *Memories of a Turkish Statesman, 1913–1919* (London: Hutchinson, n.d.) [c. 1922], 249–52.

33. Lewis, 214–220.

34. Pasha, 276.

35. Bryce, 633.

36. Alan Moorehead, *Gallipoli* (New York: Harper, 1956), 98.

37. Naim Bey, *The Memoirs of Naim Bey: Turkish Official Documents Relating to the Deportation and Massacres of Armenians,* comp. Aram Andonian (Newton Square, Pa.: Armenian Historical Research Association, 1964), 26 *f.*, cited in Boyajian, 315-316.

38. Sarkissian, 29.

39. Bryce, 649.

40. Bey.

41. Henry Morgenthau, Sr., *Ambassador Morgenthau's Story* (Garden City, N.Y.: Doubleday, Page, 1918), 336-339.

42. Ibid., 365-376.

43. Ulrich Trumpener, *Germany and the Ottoman Empire, 1914-1918* (Princeton, N.J.: Princeton University Press, 1968), 204-205.

44. Boyajian, 350.

45. Ibid., 116-117.

46. Pasha, 279-298.

47. Bryce, 633.

48. Boyajian, 287.

49. A. J. P. Taylor, *The Course of German History: A Survey of the Development of Germany since 1815* (New York: Coward-McCann, 1946).

50. Ibid., 189-204.

51. Theodor Abel, *Why Hitler Came to Power* (Englewood Cliffs, N.J.: Prentice-Hall, 1938); Dawidowicz; Erich Fromm, *Escape from Freedom* (New York: Rinehart, 1941); Ernest Nolte, *Three Faces of Fascism: Action Française, Italian Fascism, National Socialism,* trans. Leila Vennewitz (London: Weidenfeld and Nicolson, 1965).

52. Adolph Hitler, *Mein Kampf,* trans. Ralph Manheim (Boston: Houghton Mifflin, 1971).

53. Seymour Martin Lipset, *Political Man:* (Garden City, N.Y.: Doubleday-Anchor, 1960), 138-154.

54. Fritz Tobias, *The Reichstag Fire,* trans. Arnold Pomerans, with an introduction by A. J. P. Taylor (New York: Putnam, 1964).

55. Taylor, 215-216.

56. Dawidowicz, pt. I; Paul W. Massing, *Rehearsal for Destruction: A Study of Political Anti-Semitism in Imperial Germany* (New York: Fertig, 1967); George L. Mosse, *The Crisis of German Ideology: Intellectual Origins of the Third Reich* (New York: Universal Library, Grosset and Dunlap, 1964).

57. C. C. Aronsfeld, "The Nazi Design Was Extermination, Not Emigration," *Patterns of Prejudice* IX, no. 3 (May-June 1975): 22.

58. Hitler, 19-125.

59. Norman Cohen, *Warrant for Genocide: The Myth of the Jewish World-Conspiracy and the Protocols of the Elders of Zion* (New York: Harper Torchbooks, Harper and Row, 1969).

60. See Alexander Dallin, *German Rule in Russia, 1941–1945: A Study of Occupation Policies* (New York: Macmillan, 1957), for how these theories were acted out.

61. Schleunes, 189.

62. Lionel Kochan, *Pogrom 10 November 1938* (London: Deutsch, 1957), 51, cited in Schleunes, 24.

63. Hilberg, 640.

64. Max Weber, *The Protestant Ethic and the Spirit of Captitalism,* trans. Talcott Parsons (New York: Scribner's, 1930), 181; Arthur Mitzman, *The Iron Cage: A Historical Interpretation of Max Weber,* with a preface by Lewis A. Coser (New York: Universal Library, Grosset and Dunlap, 1969).

65. Hilberg, 261–262; International Military Tribunal, Office of the United States Chief Counsel for Prosecution of Axis Criminality, *Nazi Conspiracy and Aggression,* 11 vols. (Washington, D.C.: U.S. Government Printing Office, 1946), II: 297.

66. Hilberg, 264–266.

67. Ibid., 177–187; Gerald Reitlinger, *The Final Solution: The Attempt to Exterminate the Jews of Europe, 1939–1945,* new and rev. ed. (South Brunswick, N.J.: Yoseloff, 1961), 82–86, examines the evidence that the "Führer Order" to kill Jews, as well as Soviet "commissars," was transmitted to the army High Command during a conference on 13 March 1941; Hans Buchheim and Helmet Krausnick concur on this in *Anatomy of the SS State,* ed. Helmet Krausnick et al., trans. Richard Barry et al. (New York: Walker, 1968), see Krausnick's "The Persecution of the Jews," pp. 59–60, and Buchheim's "Command and Compliance," pp. 318–319.

68. Hilberg, 561–566.

69. Abraham Margaliot, "The Problem of the Rescue of German Jewry during the Years 1933–1939; The Reasons for the Delay in Their Emigration from the Third Reich," in *Rescue Attempts during the Holocaust: Proceedings of the Second Yad Vashem International Historical Conference,* eds. Yisrael Gutman and Efraim Zuroff (Jerusalem: Yad Vashem, 1977), 249–252. For the best appraisal of the percent of Jews emigrating see Bruno Blau, "The Last Days of German Jewry in the Third Reich," *YIVO Annual of Jewish Social Science* VIII (1953): 198.

70. Poland, Government-in-Exile, Polish Ministry of Information, *Concise Statistical Year-Book of Poland, September 1939–June 1941* (London: Government-in-Exile of Poland, 1941), 10.

71. Schleunes best makes a case for the evolutionary view and Dawidowicz for the latent ideological view.

72. Leni Yahil, "Madagascar: Phantom of a Solution for the Jewish Question," *Jews and Non-Jews in Eastern Europe, 1918–1945,* eds. Bela Vago and George L. Mosse (New York: Wiley, 1974), 316–317.

73. Christopher R. Browning, *The Final Solution and the German Foreign Office* (New York: Holmes and Meier, 1978), ch. 1.

74. Dawidowicz, 150.

75. Ibid., 160.

76. Ibid., 118-119.

77. Gideon Hausner, *Justice in Jerusalem* (New York: Harper and Row, 1966), 55-56. The memorandum in question (3363-PS) is cited on p. 122 in Chapter 5.

78. Hilberg, 257.

79. Dawidowicz, 106.

80. A. J. Sherman, *Island Refuge: Britain and Refugees from the Third Reich, 1933-1939* (London: Elek, 1973), 183.

81. Schleunes, 261.

82. International Military Tribunal, *Nazi Conspiracy and Aggression*, PS-1919, IV: 559, 563.

83. Felix Kersten, *The Memoirs of Doctor Felix Kersten*, ed. Herma Briffault, trans. Ernest Morwitz (New York: Doubleday, 1947), 174.

84. Clarissa Henry and Marc Hillel, "Of Pure Blood" (filmscript of documentary by Agence Française, trans. British Broadcasting Company, n.d.), 4.

85. Dawidowicz, 92.

86. International Military Tribunal. *Trials of the Major War Criminals before the International Military Tribunal*, 42 vols. (Nuremberg: IMT, 1947-1949), 1: 795.

87. Ibid., I: 794-896.

88. Frederic Wertham, *A Sign for Cain* (New York: Macmillan, 1966), 156-158.

89. Wertham cites especially *The Release of the Destruction of Life Devoid of Value*, by Karl Binding and Alfred Hoche (Leipzig: 1920), in ibid., 161-163. More recently, evidence that a German Jesuit theologian, Josef Mayer, commissioned by a Nazi police official to give an expert opinion from the viewpoint of the Catholic Church, "prepared a report that may have encouraged Hitler to proceed with the elimination of the mentally ill" has been traced by Robert A. Graham, S.J., "Il 'Dirittodi Uccidere' nel Terzo Reich," *La Civiltà Cattolica*, CXXVI, no. 1 (15 March 1975): 557-576, and discussed by Gitta Sereny, *Into That Darkness: From Mercy Killing to Mass Murder* (New York: McGraw-Hill, 1974), 66-73.

90. Krausnick et al., 97; Sereny, 66.

91. Günter Lewy, *The Catholic Church and Nazi Germany* (New York: McGraw-Hill, 1964), 263-307, contrasts the protest led by the church against the killing of German children with the lack of any church protest to combat any measures against Jews. Lewy incorrectly states (p. 266) that Hitler ordered killings stopped in 1941: what he did was not to halt them, as trial records show (see note 87 above), but to alter the methods so as to decrease their visibility for fear of undermining war morale. See Wertham, 183-187.

92. Larry Thompson, "*Lebensborn* and the Eugenics Policy of the *Reichsführer-SS*," *Central European History* IV, no. 1 (March 1971): 69.

93. Henry and Hillel, 20.

94. United States Military Tribunal, "Transcripts of Trials of War Criminals before the Nuremberg Military Tribunal," Case VIII, Volume One of mimeographed papers (n.d.), found in Columbia University International Law Library.

95. Kidnapped Polish children were documented from the Polish state investigation commission, as reported by Henry and Hillel. For Himmler's authorization of screening Polish schoolchildren in the General-Government see International Military Tribunal, *Nazi Conspiracy and Aggression,* III: 640. Arendt, 342, reviews other documents showing that "in June, 1944, the Ninth Army actually kidnapped 40,000 to 50,000 [Polish] children and subsequently transported them to Germany."

96. International Military Tribunal, *Nazi Conspiracy and Aggression,* I: 1023-1038; U.S. Military Tribunal, "Transcripts," Case VIII, I:45-102; Buchheim, "Command and Compliance," 377-378.

97. Albert Speer, *Inside the Third Reich,* trans. Richard Winston and Clara Winston (New York: Macmillan, 1967), 475, 520, 523.

98. Donald Kenrick and Gratton Puxon, *The Destiny of Europe's Gypsies* (New York: Basic Books, 1972).

99. Ibid., 87.

100. Ibid., 183.

101. Ibid., 89.

102. Ibid., 91.

NOTES FOR CHAPTER 2

1. International Military Tribunal. Office of the United States Chief of Counsel for Prosecution of Axis Criminality. *Nazi Conspiracy and Aggression,* 11 vols. (Washington, D.C.: U.S. Government Printing Office, 1946), I: 1007.

2. Henry Friedlander, "Publications of the Holocaust," in *The German Church Struggle and the Holocaust,* eds. Franklin H. Littel and Hubert G. Locke (Detroit, Mi.: Wayne State University Press, 1974). The notable exceptions include an English and a German historian: A. J. P. Taylor, *From Sarajevo to Potsdam* (New York: Harcourt, 1966), and Hannah Vogt, *The Burden of Guilt: A Short History of Germany, 1914-1945,* trans. Herbert Strauss (New York: Oxford University Press, 1964). Norman Rich's work, *Hilter's War Aims,* II: *The Establishment of the New Order* (New York: Norton, 1974) — not published at the time of Friedlander's survey — is another notable exception.

3. Ailon Shiloh, "Psychological Anthropology: A Case Study in Culture Blindness?" *Current Anthropology,* December 1975, 618-620. Shiloh "checked a selection of leading, respected introductory textbooks used in anthropology today" and found "not one of the above scholars analyzed the Nazis and their genocidal behavior." My own (unpublished) sampling of introductory sociology texts published between 1946 and 1977 found only a minority of texts showing recognition of genocide.

4. Golo Mann, *The History of Germany since 1789,* trans. Marian Jackson (New York: Praeger, 1968), 474, 482, cited by Friedlander.

5. C. C. Aronsfeld, "A Propos of a British 'Historical Review': Facts of the Holocaust," *Patterns of Prejudice* VIII, no. 4 (July-August 1974): 11-16. A recent sample of this genre is Arthur R. Butz, *The Hoax of the Twentieth Century* (Richmond, England: Historical Review Press, n.d.).

6. Everett C. Hughes, "Good People and Dirty Work," *Social Problems* X, no. 1 (Summer 1962): 3–10.

7. Helen Fein, *Imperial Crime and Punishment: The Massacre at Jallianwala Bagh and British Judgement, 1919–1920* (Honolulu: University of Hawaii Press, 1977).

8. Emile Durkheim, *The Division of Labor in Society,* trans. George Simpson (New York: The Free Press, 1933), ch. 2.

9. Fein. The hypothesis that toleration of collective violence against a subordinate class depends on their exclusion from the universe of obligation by the dominant class was proved by comparing the judgments of members of Parliament condemning or condoning the action of the British general who ordered the massacre in Amritsar on 13 April 1919, which took the lives of over five hundred Indians.

10. "Anti-Semitism," *Encyclopedia Judaica* (Jerusalem: Keter, 1971), III:99–160. In the context of European history, anti-Semitism always signifies an anti-Jewish program and does not connote a drive against Arabs and/or Muslims, despite the fact that the Arabic language and Islam are also derived from groups known ethnically, ethnologically, and racially as Semites.

11. Stanley Milgram, *Obedience to Authority: An Experimenal View* (New York: Harper and Row, 1974), demonstrated how obedience can lead to violence in laboratory experiments with people supposedly playing the role of "teacher" and "learner." The teacher — actually the subject of the experiment — was instructed by the experimenter to subject the learner — actually an accomplice of the experimenter — to graduated levels of electric shock if the learner did not repeat the assigned words correctly. A majority of subjects continued to press the button administering shocks despite the cries of the victims and — notwithstanding the lack of any physical coercion, threat, or incentive — continued in their roles under all conditions. The exceptions occurred when the authority of the person issuing the command to press the button was denied. This was the case where there were two experimenters as competing authorities, or where there was more than one teacher and one of them (also an accomplice of the experimenter) refused to comply and instigated a rebellion among the other subjects.

12. Finding relevant documents was facilitated by a then unpublished index of all references to Jews in the postwar Nuremberg and other war crimes trials (in the American and British zones) compiled by Jacob Robinson and Henry Sachs, now published as *The Holocaust: The Nuremberg Evidence, Part One* (Jerusalem: Yad Vashem, 1976). Unpublished trial documents (from which documentary numbers are cited herein) may be found in the Columbia University International Law Library repository and other repositories.

13. Arthur S. Banks, *Cross-Polity Time-Series Data* (Cambridge, Ma.: MIT Press, 1971.

14. Richard P. Boyle, "Path Analysis and Ordinal Data," in *Causal Models in the Social Sciences,* ed. Hubert M. Blalock, Jr. (Chicago: Aldine-Atherton, 1971).

15. Evidence of irreversible physical and psychic impairment and trauma among survivors is profuse. See M. Pfister-Ammende, "The Symptomatology, Treatment, and Prognosis in Mentally Ill Refugees and Repatriates in Switzerland," in *Flight and Resettlement,* ed. H. B. M. Murphy (Paris: UNESCO, 1955); Henry Krystal, ed., *Massive Psychic Trauma* (New York: International Universities Press, 1968);

David P. Boder, "The Impact of Catastrophe in Assessment and Evaluation," *Journal of Psychology* XXXVIII (July 1954): 3–50; Mark Dvorjetski, "Adjustment of Detainees to Camp and Ghetto Life and Their Subsequent Readjustment to Normal Society," *Yad Vashem Studies* V (1963): 193–220; "The Ailing Minds: Psychiatric Effects of Persecution," *Wiener Library Bulletin* XVII, no. 2 (2 April 1963): 20; David P. Landau, "Nazi Camps, Abnormality, and the Pill," *Jerusalem Post,* 25 August 1969, 11; Judith T. Shuval, "Some Persistent Effects of Trauma: Five Years after the Nazi Concentration Camps," *Social Problems* V, no. 4 (Winter 1957–1958): 230–243.

Similarly, impairment, disabilities, previously undetected brain (and other organ) damage, and the concentration camp syndrome among non-Jewish concentration camp prisoners not subjected to all the stresses of the extermination camps have been documented in Norway and France. See Axel Strom et al., "Examination of Norwegian Ex-Concentration Camp Prisoners," *Journal of Neuropsychiatry* XXV (September–October 1962): 43–62; Leo Eitinger, "Concentration Camp Survivors in the Postwar World," *American Journal of Orthopsychiatry* XXXII, no. 3 (1962): 368–375; "Concentration Camp Aftereffects," *Wiener Library Bulletin* IX, no. 1–2 (January–April 1955).

16. Louis Guttman, "A Basis for Scaling Qualitative Data," *American Sociological Review* IX, no. 2 (April 1944): 139–150.

17. Max Weber, *The Theory of Social and Economic Organization,* trans. A. M. Henderson and Talcott Parsons (New York: The Free Press, 1969), 154.

18. Alexander Dallin, *German Rule in Russia, 1941–1945: A Study of Occupational Policies* (New York: Macmillan, 1957).

19. Harry Eckstein, *Division and Cohesion in Democracy: A Study of Norway* (Princeton, N.J.: Princeton University Press, 1966).

20. Banks, 3–55. Indicators of representativeness are the presence of an effective legislature, responsibility to an electorate, the universality of suffrage, and parliamentary responsibility of the government. Stability was indicated by the number of major constitutional changes and cabinet turnovers per decade. Nonviolent succession was indicated by the absence of successful coups d'état.

21. Where parties with a particularistic base — one nationality or religion — were simultaneously distinguished by two sources of cleavage (religious and ethnic, regional, or linguistic), this was counted as two lines, crediting the generally accepted proposition (which has been deduced both from Karl Marx and Georg Simmel) that reinforcing cleavages are more divisive. For example, Belgium has linguistic based (Flemish) parties, but most members of Flemish and other parties belong to the same religious collectivity, the Roman Catholic Church, so this was counted as one line of cleavage. Within Czechoslovakia the Slovak People's Party was distinguished from other Czech parties by ethnicity (common language and territory) and religion, so party structure simultaneously divided the electorate by two parallel cleavages; therefore, this was counted as two lines.

22. Votes cast for such parties in themselves are not a reliable indicator alone of the party's constituency for several reasons. Such movements may choose not to compete at the polls, parties may be repressed by the government when their strength threatens the ruling coalition, and leaders may be exiled and/or movements

banned in response to previous terrorism. All these conditions pertain to one or more states in eastern and central Europe duirng the 1930s.

23. General sources for this index include the *American Jewish Yearbook*, 1930-1937, which annually reviewed the political status of Jews in all continents, focusing on states where threats were manifested; the *Encyclopedia Judaica*, 16 vols. (Jerusalem: Keter, 1971-1972); *The Universal Jewish Encyclopedia*, ed. Isaac Landman, 10 vols. (New York: The Universal Jewish Encyclopedia, Inc., 1939-1943): the *New York Times*, and specific histories, monographs, and dissertations on anti-Semitic, nationalist, and fascist movements in each state before the war listed in Table 2-3 (see Bibliography for full references).

24. This changed the ranking of half the cases by one interval, and improved Italy's ranking by two intervals.

NOTES FOR CHAPTER 3

1. Eight Jews were actually deported, five of whom were accused of espionage or other criminal activities based on loose construction of such charges. The other three were relatives of the accused who departed with them (including a one-year-old child). I am informed in a personal correspondence by J. Kiipa, a member of Jad Hashmona, a Finnish commune in Israel, that only one of this group is known to be alive in Israel: "It is believed that all the other[s] are no longer alive." Leaders of the Jewish community alerted cabinet members to the deportation, stirring up opposition especially from members of the Social Democrat Party. Documentary sources on this event are examined by Erilainen Kuin Muut, "Lahettiko Valpo Juutalaisia Keskitys-Leireihin?" *Uusi Maailma*, 23 October 1964.

2. This is a spurious relationship that is an artifact of the pace of victimization in states with largest Jewish populations where there was high cooperation — Poland and Hungary — and the fact that resistance impeded this pace in some states with the smallest populations. In the former states, time was scarcely enough for the task, while in the latter, the amount of time was irrelevant. Once the destuction process was blocked, it could not be started again.

3. Daniel Carpi, "The Rescue of Jews in the Italian Zone of Occupied Croatia," in *Rescue Attempts during the Holocaust: Proceedings of the Second Yad Vashem International Historical Conference*, eds. Yisrael Gutman and Efraim Zuroff (Jerusalem: Yad Vashem, 1977), 464-526.

4. Leon Poliakov and Jaques Sabille, *The Jews under the Italian Occupation* (Paris: Éditions du Centre, 1955).

5. Sam Waagenar, *The Pope's Jews* (La Salle, Ill.: Library Press, 1974), 381-387.

6. Raul Hilberg, *The Destruction of the European Jews* (Chicago: Quadrangle, 1967), 442. See the notes to Table 3-1 on sources and methods for estimating survivors from Poland and Yugoslavia; survivors are not equivalent to evaders, as defined in Chapter 2 of this volume. To make a comparable estimate of evaders from Serbia and Poland, one must adjust the reported figures on survivors to compensate for two facts. There were no survivors among Jews who became victims in Serbia because they were shot and gassed there, not shipped to extermination and

work camps, where there was some chance — albeit a minuscule one — for survival. While virtually all Serbian survivors are evaders, most Polish survivors are victims, rather than evaders. Lucjan Dobroszycki, "Restoring Jewish Life in Postwar Poland," *Soviet-Jewish Affairs* III, no. 2 (1973): 59, cites the breakdown of Jewish registrants in Lodz in 1946 (before the return of Jewish refugees who had fled to the Soviet Union) who had been in concentration and other camps, showing only 37.7% of Jewish registrants had evaded becoming victims; the other 62.3% were surviving victims. Assuming this to be the case generally in postwar Poland, the number of surviving victims (62.3% x Jewish registrants) was deducted from the tally of Jewish registrants in Poland to estimate evaders. Second, since the number of Jews known to be alive in Yugoslavia exceed registered Jews by 13%, the known figure should be multiplied by the ratio of living Jews to registered Jews. No adjustment was made to the Polish tally to correct for dual registrations because, first, we have no way of estimating them and, second, it is also plausible to assume that the number of Jewish evaders who escaped during the war to other nations and did not return to Poland (and thus did not register) equal the number of multiple registrants in excess of surviving Jews.

Taking these two adjustments into account, one finds the tally of Jewish evaders in Serbia is raised to 22.9% and lowered in Poland to .9%, giving the Serbian Jews 29 times the probability of evading victimization of Polish Jews.

7. In fact, the more they were spread (positively indicated by the concentration index), the more victims there were ($r = .27$). This relationship — weak and superficially logically implausible — is probably a spurious one accounted for by the fact that countries where Jews were most highly dispersed (Rumania, Slovakia, Hungary, Lithuania, and Poland) were countries with highly visible concentrations of Jews and high anti-Semitism.

8. Hilberg, 31–39.

9. While earlier deportations usually made it less likely that the next victim selected will appear (or remain stationary), this is not the case when men are drafted or seized first, leaving behind dependent wives and children tied by loyalties and responsibilities. This was observed in Serbia, Slovakia, and Norway.

10. H. G. Adler, *Der Verwaltete Mensch: Studien zur Deportation der Juden aus Deutschland* (Tübingen. Mohr, 1971).

11. NG-2631 (official translation), U.S. Military Tribunal, "Documents: Staff Evidence Analysis," 1949 Nuremberg. Unnumbered volumes of mimeographed evidence; Columbia University International Law Library.

12. Out of 27,388 cards of Jews "pulled" for the operation "spring wind" round up in Paris, 12,884 were captured, report Claude Lévy and Paul Tillard, in *Betrayal at the Vel d'Hiv*, trans. Inea Bushnaq (New York: Hill and Wang, 1967), 3, 80. Robert Katz in *Black Sabbath: A Journey Through a Crime against Humanity* (New York: Macmillan, 1969), 154, writes: "There is no record of Dannecker [The SS deportation expert] or anyone else estimating the number of Jews expected to be taken in the roundup" in Rome. Hilberg, 427, estimates that there were "perhaps 8,000 Jews" in Rome in 1943. But Franco Sabatello, "Social and Occupational Trends of the Jews of Italy, 1870-1970" (Ph.D dissertation, Hebrew University, 1972), 126, reported 13,356 Jews enumerated in Rome in 1938 by the government. Although the number must have declined in Rome as in all of Italy

due to reclassifications, apostasy, and emigration, the number also increased by the influx of Jewish refugees from Yugoslavia and France especially. Assuming the net number was stationary, 7.5% were caught in 15-16 October 1943; taking Hilberg's number as a base, 12.6% were seized—averaging the two estimates, 10% were taken.

13. Bernard Goldstein, *The Stars Bear Witness*, trans. and ed. Leonard Shatzkin (New York: Viking, 1949); Herman Kruk, "Diary of the Vilna Ghetto," *YIVO Annual of Jewish Social Science* XIII (1965): 9-78; Emmanuel Ringelblum, *The Journal of Emmanuel Ringelblum*, ed. and trans. Jacob Sloan (New York: Schocken, 1958); Yitshok Rudashevski, *The Diary of the Vilna Ghetto, June 1941–April 1943*, trans. Percy Matenko (Israel: Beit Lohamei Hagettaot, 1973); Zelig Zalmonovitch, "A Diary of the Nazi Ghetto in Vilna," *YIVO Annual of Jewish Social Science* III (1953): 9-81.

14. Two errors have been made by earlier researchers who inferred the contrary. They failed to take into account the size of the Jewish population, not noticing those who failed to report, and did not note the refusal to report after the initial summons—usually an order to report for registration that was hardly unusual in an occupied country—was what instigated German officials to organize terror and/or devise inducements (e.g., work cards, which would "guarantee" exemptions) to round up Jews. For accounts of particular cities see Reuben Ainsztein, *Jewish Resistance in Nazi-Occupied Eastern Europe* (New York: Barnes and Noble, 1974), 227-233, 249-256.

15. Herbert Rosenkranz, "The Anschluss and the Tragedy of Austrian Jewry, 1938–1945," in *The Jews of Austria: Essays on Their Life, History, and Destruction* (London: Valentine, Mitchell, 1967), 517.

16. Louis de Jong, "Help to People in Hiding," *Delta* VIII, no. 1 (Spring 1965): 42-44. The civil servant in question was sentenced to three years' imprisonment after the war.

17. Adolph Eichmann, "Eichmann's Story, Part I," *Life*, 28 November 1960, 20-25.

18. Vojtech Mastny, *The Czechs under Nazi Rule: The Failure of National Resistance, 1939–1943* (New York: Columbia University Press, 1971).

19. J. Gérard-Libois and José Gotovitch, *L'An 40: La Belgique Occupée* (Brussels: CRISP, 1971); Henry L. Mason, *The Purge of Dutch Quislings: Emergency Justice in the Netherlands* (The Hague: Nijhoff, 1952), 234-237; Warner Warmbrunn, *The Dutch under German Occupation, 1940–1945* (New York: Oxford University Press, 1963), 121-123.

20. Even controlling for anti-Semitism (holding it as a constant in analysis), the first-order correlation between any church protest against deportations and the immediacy of establishment of social defense movement is .817.

21. Nella Rost, "Les Juifs sous l'Occupation Allemande dans les Pays Scandinaves," in *Les Juifs en Europe, 1939–1945* (Paris: Éditions du Centre, 1949), 130.

22. L. S. Stavrianos, "The Jews in Greece," *Journal of Central European Affairs* XXV (October 1948): 262-267.

23. Federation of Jewish Communities of Yugoslavia, *Spomenica, 1919–1968* (Belgrade: ISJOJ, 1969), 229-230; Arieh L. Bauminger, *Roll of Honor* (Tel Aviv: Hamenora, 1971), 84-85.

24. Controlling for segregation, the partial correlation between defense and victimization is $-.791$, showing that the immediacy of defense accounted for almost two-thirds of the variation in victimization, once segregation is held constant.

25. Leo Baeck, "A People Stands before Its God," in *We Survived: The Stories of Fourteen of the Hidden and Hunted of Nazi Germany as Told to Eric H. Boehm,* ed. Eric H. Boehm (New Haven, Conn.: Yale University Press, 1949); Ilselotte Themal, "Mother and Child," in *Explorations,* ed. Murray Mindlin, with Chaim Bernant (London: Erasmus, 1967), 179.

26. Louis de Jong, "Jews and Non-Jews in Nazi Occupied Holland," in *On the Track of Tyranny,* ed. Max Beloff (London: Wiener Library, 1960); Odd Nansen, *From Day to Day,* trans. Katherine John (New York: Putnam, 1949), 171, 218.

27. Henry L. Mason, *Mass Demonstrations against Foreign Regimes: A Study of Five Crises* (New Orleans: Tulane University Press, 1966), 35-36, 72-76; Mastny, 113-117, 140-165.

28. Franklin H. Littel, "Church Struggle and the Holocaust," in *The German Church Struggle and the Holocaust,* ed. Franklin H. Littell and Hubert G. Locke (Detroit: Wayne State University Press, 1974), 22-30.

29. Bela Vago, "Jewish Leadership Groups in Hungary and Rumania during the Holocaust" (address presented to the International Scholars Conference on the Holocaust—A Generation After, New York City, March 1975).

30. De Jong, "Help to People in Hiding," 44. More information as to the composition and effects of these cards is discussed on p. 267.

31. Theodor Lavi, "The Background to the Rescue of Rumanian Jewry during the Period of the Holocaust," in *Jews and Non-Jews in Eastern Europe, 1918-1945,* ed. Bela Vago and George L. Mosse (New York: Wiley, 1974), 186.

32. Earl Weinstock and Herbert Wilner, *The Seven Years* (New York: Dutton, 1959), 116-125.

33. Hilberg, 503.

34. Table B-3 (Appendix B) shows how well warning time can be estimated by the equation DISPOSED $\times$ OPPDELAY = POSTPONE. If the value of either variable is zero, no postponement is expected. If states were not disposed to resist (because getting rid of the Jews was a goal widely held) or if they had no opportunity to delay (being in the SS zone), this produces an expectation of no warning time. Among less anti-Semitic states, the hypothetical value of warning time (POSTPONE) is the same as actual warning time (with values indicated in Table B-3) in 10 of the 12 cases; whereas among states with more successful anti-Semitic movements in 1936, it is identical in 8 of 10 cases.

35. See Appendix B, pp. 351-352.

36. Meier Michaelis, "The Attitude of the Fascist Regime to the Jews in Italy," *Yad Vashem Studies* IV (1960): 38-41; Daniel A. Binchy, *Church and State in Fascist Italy* (New York: Oxford University Press, 1970), 614, 627; Elizabeth Wiskeman, *Fascism in Italy: Its Development and Influence* (New York: Macmillan, 1969), 71; see also Count Galeazzo Ciano, *The Ciano Diaries, 1939-1943,* trans. and ed. Hugh Wilson (Garden City, N.Y.: Doubleday, 1946).

37. Hubert M. Blalock, Jr., *Toward a Theory of Minority-Group Relations* (New York: Capricorn, 1970), 82.

38. Although Jews were emancipated and enjoyed civil rights in mainland Greece since 1821, in Salonica, they, like other non-Muslims under Ottoman rule, enjoyed collective autonomy as a *millet* but had neither political nor civil rights. The population ratios in Salonica were altered by the influx of resettled Anatolian refugees after the breakup of the Ottoman Empire in 1912 and flight of other Greeks in the wake of the Greek Army's retreat (succeeding its disastrous offensive) from Turkey in 1922. While Jews composed 40% of the population of Salonica by 1913, by 1938 (due to the Anatolian immigration and Jewish emigration instigated by economic decline) Jews constituted only 23% of the total. The Anatolian refugees resented the status Jews had achieved in Salonica. Government attempts to diminish Jews' ability to compete in trade took the form of a compulsory Sunday closing law and changing the market day from Monday to Saturday, the Jewish Sabbath.

     Street fighting by youth groups began in July 1931, instigated by rumors of Jews' sympathy with the Macedonian (pro-Bulgarian) autonomy movement. Widespread arson occurred, and sporadic rioting continued for two years. While Premier Venizelos of the Liberal Party condemned attacks on Jews in 1931 and the Athens government offered restitution for financing of rebuilding their homes, charges of local police complicity were raised. Although the EEE (a Greek anti-Semitic fascist organization later reconstituted during the German occupation) was banned in 1933, Venizelos's party (out of power) began publicly using anti-Jewish propaganda; he was seen as threatening the Jews' status in retaliation for their previous support of his opponent. Jews were reassured of the government's commitment to sustain their rights in Greece by the failure of Venizelos's revolt in 1935, passage of a law banning anti-Jewish incitement, and Premier Metaxa's repression of the movement against them in 1936. (For year to year developments see entries on Greece, in the *American Jewish Yearbook*, 1932–1933 and 1937–1938, and in the *New York Times* for those years.) Thus, we have a conflict instigated by a previously subordinated minority—now nominally integrated in its own majority—against another minority whom they perceive as dominating, with the newcomers seeking to usurp the other's status by raising exclusivist rallying cries ("Hellenization") and questioning the Jews' loyalty.

39. Blalock, 84.

40. Frederick Barry Chary, *The Bulgarian Jews and the Final Solution, 1940–1944* (Pittsburgh: University of Pittsburgh Press, 1972), 33.

41. Salo W. Baron, "The Modern Age," in *Great Ages and Ideas of the Jewish People*, ed. Leo W. Schwartz (New York: Modern Library, 1956), 317.

42. Hannah Arendt, *The Origins of Totalitarianism*, rev. ed. (New York: Harcourt, Brace, and World, 1966), 9–10.

43. Nicholas M. Nagy-Talavera, *The Green Shirts and the Others: A History of Fascism in Hungary and Rumania* (Stanford, Ca.: Hoover Instution Press, 1970), 358–359.

44. Edward D. Wynot, Jr., " 'A Necessary Cruelty': The Emergence of Official Anti-Semitism in Poland, 1936–39," *American Historical Review* LXXVI (1971): 1035–1058.

45. Marvin Lowenthal, *The Jews of Germany: A Story of Sixteen Centuries* (New York: Russell and Russell, 1970; first pub. 1936).

46. Immanuel Wallerstein, *The Modern World-System* (New York: Academic Press, 1974), 147–151.

47. Ibid., 149.

48. Stanley Milgram, *Obedience to Authority: An Experimental View* (New York: Harper and Row, 1974). For further description of these experiments see Chapter 2, note 11.

49. Everett C. Hughes, "Good People and Dirty Work," *Social Problems* X, no. 1 (Summer 1962): 3–10.

50. Yitzhak Arad, "Jewish Family Camps in the Forests: An Original Means of Rescue," in *Rescue Attempts during the Holocaust: Proceedings of the Second Yad Vashem International Historical Conference*, eds. Yisrael Gutman and Efraim Zuroff (Jerusalem: Yad Vashem, 1977), 335.

51. Hans Buchheim, "Command and Compliance," in *Anatomy of the SS State*, ed. Helmut Krausnick et al., trans. Richard Barry et al. (New York: Walker, 1968), ch. 3; Felix Kersten, *The Memoirs of Doctor Felix Kersten*, ed. Herma Briffault, trans. Ernest Morwitz (New York: Doubleday, 1947); Leni Yahil, *The Rescue of Danish Jewry: Test of a Democracy*, trans. Morris Gradel (Philadelphia: Jewish Publication Society of America, 1969); Larry Collins and Dominique Lapierre, *Is Paris Burning?* (New York: Simon and Schuster, Pocket Books, 1965); Albert Speer, *Inside the Third Reich*, trans. Richard Winston and Clara Winston (New York: Macmillan, 1967), chs. 29–30.

NOTES FOR CHAPTER 4

1. Rolf Hochhuth, *The Deputy*, (New York: Grove Press, 1964); see also Erich Bentley, ed., *The Storm over the Deputy* (New York: Grove Press, 1964).

2. Saul Friedlander, *Pius XII and the Third Reich: A Documentation*, trans. Charles Fullman (New York: Knopf, 1966); Carlo Falconi, *The Silence of Pius XII*, trans. Bernard Wall (Boston: Little, Brown, 1970); Günter Lewy, *The Catholic Church and Nazi Germany* (New York: McGraw-Hill, 1964); Vatican, Secretariat de Status, *Actes et Documents du Saint-Siège Relatifs à la Seconde Guerre Mondiale*, ed. Pierre Blet et al. (Vatican City: Libreria Editricé Vaticani, 1974), VIII: 534, 580, 601–602, 611, 665 670, 679, 748, 755 756, 758.

3. Lewy; Gordon Zahn, *German Catholics and Hitler's Wars: A Study in Social Control* (New York: Sheed and Ward, 1962).

4. Gitta Sereny, *Into That Darkness: From Mercy Killing to Mass Murder* (New York: McGraw-Hill, 1974), 277–333; Edmond Paris, *Genocide in Satellite Croatia, 1941–1944*, trans. Lois Perkins (Chicago: American Institute of Balkan Affairs, n.d.), 259.

5. Jules Isaac, *The Teaching of Contempt: Christian Roots of Anti-Semitism*, trans. Helen Weaver (New York: Holt, Rinehart, and Winston, 1964).

6. NO-2849 and other documents cited by Sarah Neshamit, "Rescue in Lithuania during the Nazi Occupation," in *Rescue Attempts during the Holocaust: Proceedings of the Second Yad Vashem International Historical Conference*, eds. Yisrael Gutman and Efrain Zuroff (Jerusalem: Yad Vashem, 1977), 312–314.

7. The earliest public massacres of Jews anywhere in Europe during World War II occurred in Rumania, where both the Iron Guard and the army murdered Jews in the wake of Rumanian defeat in 1940 and celebration in 1941. Observers who described the Jassy pogrom and the sight of beheaded Jews hanging from hooks in the Bucharest kosher meat market during the attempted Iron Guard coup in January 1941 include Curzio Malaparte, *Kaputt* (New York: Dutton, 1946), chs. 6, 7, and Ruth Kluger and Peggy Mann, *The Last Escape* (Garden City, N.Y.: Doubleday, 1973), 415.

8. Theodor Lavi, "The Background to the Rescue of Rumanian Jewry during the Period of the Holocaust," in *Jews and Non-Jews in Eastern Europe, 1918–1945*, ed. Bela Vago and George L. Mosse (New York: Wiley, 1974), 186.

9. Livia Rotkirchen, "Slovakia, II: 1918–1938," in *The Jews of Czechoslovakia*, I (Philadelphia: Jewish Publication Society of America, 1968).

10. Livia Rotkirchen, *The Destruction of Slovak Jewry* (Jerusalem: Yad Vashem, 1961), xv–xvii and ch. 4. A counterorganization was later formed to subvert its goal known as the "Working Group," which included some members of the Jewish Council.

11. Raul Hilberg, *The Destruction of the European Jews* (Chicago: Quadrangle, 1967), 464.

12. Livia Rotkirchen, "Vatican Policy and the 'Jewish Problem' in 'Independent' Slovakia, (1939–1945)" *Yad Vashem Studies* VI (1967): 38–39.

13. Fr. Fiorello Cavalli, S.J., "La Santa Sede contro le Deportazioni degli Ebrei dalla Slovacchia durante la Seconda Guerra Mondiale," *La Civiltà Cattolica*, 1 July 1961, 3–18.

14. Friedlander, 158.

15. Vatican, *Actes et Documents* VIII: 42.

16. Rotkirchen, "Vatican Policy and the 'Jewish Problem,' " 44.

17. Rotkirchen, *Destruction of Slovak Jewry*, document no. 65.

18. Hilberg, 471.

19. Rotkirchen, *Destruction of Slovak Jewry*, 47.

20. Vatican, *Actes et Documents*, VIII: 43–44 (my translation from the French).

21. Vladko Macek, *In the Struggle for Freedom*, trans. Elizabeth Gazi and Stjepan Gazi (University Park, Pa.: Pennsylvania State University Press, 1957), 220–221, 229–230.

22. Norman Rich, *Hitler's War Aims, II: The Establishment of the New Order* (New York: Norton, 1974): 280.

23. The church was vigilant in denouncing the claim of state officials to convert the Serbs, insisting on its own right to regulate conversion, but did not denounce the terror that instigated the Serbs to seek conversion as vigilantly. See Falconi, 275–331.

24. Paris thoroughly describes the course of extermination of Serbs, Jews, and Gypsies from discrimination to murder.

25. Charles W. Steckel, *Destruction and Survival* (Los Angeles: Delmar, 1973), pts. I, II.

26. Richard Pattee, *The Case of Cardinal Aloysius Stepinac* (Milwaukee, Wi.: Bruce, 1953), 299–312.

27. Vatican, *Actes et Documents*, VII: 611; IX: 139.

28. Stekel, 42.

29. Pattee, 93–94.

30. Vatican, *Actes et Documents*, IX: 218–229, document no. 130, especially annex II (note of Stepinac of 24 May 1943).

31. Branko Bokun, *Spy in the Vatican, 1941–1945* (New York: Praeger, 1973), 23.

32. Vatican, *Actes et Documents*, IX: 83, document no. 19, trans. and cited by Burkhart Schneider, S.J., "The Holy See and the Victims of the War," *L'Osservatore Romano*, 19 February 1976, 7.

33. Falconi, 301–351.

34. Vatican. *Actes et Documents*, VIII: 46.

35. Ibid., VIII, IX. The estimate of Jewish victimization in Croatia is fully described in the notes to Table 3-1 of this volume. The estimate of Gypsies killed (28,000 of 28,500) is that of R. Uhlik cited by Donald Kenrick and Grattan Puxon, *The Destiny of Europe's Gypsies* (New York: Basic Books, 1972), 183. The estimate of the number of Orthodox Serbs killed in Croatia is my own, calculated to have an objective basis grounded in the population deficit in order to resolve the wide disparity among previous estimates. Falconi, for example, accepts the estimate of the Yugoslavia government-in-exile in May 1943 that around 700,000 Serbs had been slaughtered and Paris cites estimates of 750,000 by German observers. More recently, Jozo Tomavich, "Yugoslavia during the Second World War," in *Contemporary Yugoslavia*, ed. Wayne S. Vucinich (Berkeley, Ca.: University of California Press, 1969), 367, estimated that a minimum of 350,000 Orthodox Serbs were killed by the Ustase, and Vladimir Dedijer in his *History of Yugoslavia* (New York: McGraw-Hill, 1974), 582, cited 200,000 to 600,000.

If we compare the population growth within Croatia and Bosnia-Herzegovina (included in Croatia's wartime boundaries) between 1921 and 1953, we find that Roman Catholics increased by 250,000 (7.6%) and Orthodox Serbs declined by 234,757 (14%). However, to find whether there was a greater population deficit among Serbs that could not be attributed to wartime loss due to combat, civilian casualties of German occupation, and decline in the birthrate, we have to evaluate what the 1953 population of each religious category would have been in these republics had there been no war. If we project the actual rate of net increase for each religious group between 1921 and 1931 to find their expected 1953 population (had the annual net growth rate been constant), we find the actual population registered as Roman Catholic is 15.5% lower than the expected. The Muslim population also fell short of the expected 1953 population by 14.1%, about the same as the Roman Catholic population, as we should expect if wartime casualties caused by the Germans and decline instigated by war were the same. But the actual number of Orthodox Serbs is 39.4% lower than the expected. The difference between the Roman Catholic and Orthodox deficit (39.4% − 15.5%) when multiplied by the expected Serbian Orthodox population reveals a probable real loss of 569,865 Serbs besides the deficit attributable to conditions equally affecting Catholics. However, excessive losses among Orthodox Serbs may also be attributed to forced conversion to Roman Catholicism or assimilation to other religious categories and to the category of "no religion" on the 1953 census as well as to Ustase massacres. There is evidence that Serbs are overrepresented in the army and in the League of Communists. See Gordon C. McDonald's *Area Handbook for Yugoslavia* (Washington, D.C.: U.S. Government Printing Office, 1973), 84–257, which perhaps implies that Serbs are more apt to report "no religion." Sources for these computations are government figures based on the 1921 and 1931 censuses of Yugoslavia cited in Table 12 of Paul F. Meyers and Arthur A. Campbell, *The Population of Yugoslavia* (Washington, D.C.: U.S. Government Printing Office, 1954), and 1953 census figures reported in Francis H. Eterovich and Christopher Spalatin, *Croatia: Land, People, Culture,* 2 vols. (Toronto: University of Toronto Press, 1969), II: 17.

36. Falconi, 336.

37. Ibid., 350.

38. Hilberg, 511.

39. Nicholas Kállay, *Hungarian Premier* (New York: Columbia University Press, 1954).

40. Randolph Braham, *The Destruction of Hungarian Jewry: A Documentary Account,* 2 vols. (New York: World Federation of Hungarian Jews, 1963), I: xiii–ix.

41. Randolph Braham, "The Kamenets Podolsk and Delvidek Massacres: Prelude to the Holocaust in Hungary," *Yad Vashem Studies* IX (1973): 133–157.

42. Nicholas M. Nagy-Talavera, *The Green Shirts and the Others: A History of Fascism in Hungary and Rumania* (Stanford, Ca.: Hoover Institution Press, 1970), 152–153.

43. Adolph Eichmann, "Eichmann's Story, Part II," *Life,* 5 December 1961, 110.

44. Nagy-Talavera, 243.

45. G. A. McCartney, *A History of Hungary, 1929–1945,* 2 vols. (New York: Praeger, 1957), II:283–284.

46. Jëno Levai, *Hungarian Jewry and the Papacy: Pope Pius XII Did Not Remain Silent,* trans. J. R. Foster (London: Sands, 1967).

47. See discussion of the Kastner-Brand negotiations with the SS on pp. 311–312.

48. Levai, 71.

49. Ibid., 20; italics added.

50. Erich Kulka, "Auschwitz Condoned: The Abortive Struggle against the Final Solution," *Wiener Library Bulletin,* XXII, no. 1 (Winter 1968–1969): 2–5.

51. Mario D. Fenyo, *Hitler, Horthy, and Hungary* (New Haven, Conn.: Yale University Press, 1972), 181.

52. See also the War Refugee Board's letter to the Apostolic Delegate in Washington informing him that the deportations of Jews from Hungary had commenced (20 May 1944); War Refugee Board Records, box 35, Franklin D. Roosevelt Memorial Library, Hyde Park, New York.

53. Levai, 29–30.

54. Generally, the Apostolic Delegate in Washington acknowledged letters within a

day of receipt and obtained substantive replies or nonresponses from the Vatican in five to ten days; see note 52.

55. The Apostolic Delegate immediately acknowledged the letter and replied to the request on 4 November with a press release from the Secretariat of State in Vatican City citing all that the Pope had done in the past through the Nuncio and Hungarian bishops; in effect, the appeal to the Pope to use his authority publicly was denied; see note 52.

56. Hundreds of these have been documented; see Xosa Szajkowski, *Analytical Franco-Jewish Gazetteer, 1939–1945* (New York: Frydmann, 1966), 20–21.

57. Letter from Leon Bérard, French Ambassador to the Vatican, trans. from the French by Abraham G. Duker, reprinted as "Pope Pius XII and the Jews," *Jewish Spectator,* February 1964, pp. 13–17; italics added.

58. Ibid., 17.

59. Vatican, *Actes et Documents,* VIII: 297 (note by Cardinal Maglione to document no. 165).

60. Robert O. Paxton, *Vichy France: Old Guard and New Order, 1940–1944* (New York: Random House, 1972), 143.

61. Jacques Duquesne, *Les Catholiques Français sous l'Occupation* (Paris: Grasset, 1966), 261; my translation from the French.

62. Hilberg, 407.

63. Duquesne, 269–270; Joseph Billig, *Le Commissariat Général aux Questions Juives,* 2 vols. (Paris: Éditions du Centre, 1955), I:272.

64. Leon Poliakov, *Harvest of Hate* (Westport, Conn.: Greenwood, 1954), 301.

65. Rich. II: 202.

66. U.S. Military Tribunal, "Documents: Staff Evidence Analysis," NO-1411, unnumbered volumes of documents found in Columbia University International Law Library and other repositories.

67. *Trial of Adolph Eichman,* "Minutes of the Trial: Official Translation into English" (unrevised), Jerusalem, 5 September 1961, recorded on microfilm and mimeographed.

68. *France during the German Occupation, 1940–1944: A Collection of 292 Statements on the Government of Maréchal Pétain and Pierre Laval,* trans. Philip W. Whitcomb (Stanford, Ca.: Hoover Institution, 1957), I:426, 432, 464, 484, 549.

69. Amy Latour, *La Résistance Juive en France, 1940–1944* (Paris: Stock, 1970); Françoise Bedarida and Renée Bedarida, "Aux Origines du Témoignage Chrétien, 1941–1942," *Revue d'Histoire de la Deuxième Guerre Mondiale* LXI (1966): 1–66.

70. Donald Lowrie, "Chambon-Sur-Lignon," in *Anthology of Holocaust Literature,* ed. Jacob Glatstein et al. (Philadelphia: Jewish Publication Society of America, 1968).

71. Johan M. Snoek, *The Greybook: A Collection of Protests against Anti-Semitism and the Persecution of Jews Issued by Non–Roman Catholic Churches and Church Leaders during Hitler's Rule* (The Hague: Van Gorcum, 1969), 168.

72. Ibid., 58–59.

73. Ibid., 181–182.

74. Ibid., 184–185.

75. Ibid., 117–118.

76. See Snoek, 157.

77. Snoek, 155.

78. Jeanne Tsatsos, *The Sword's Fierce Edge: A Journal of the Occupation of Greece, 1941–1944*, trans. Jean Demos (Nashville, Tn.: Vanderbilt University Press, 1969), 56; L. S. Stavrianos, "The Jews in Greece," *Journal of Central European Affairs* XXV (October 1948): 268–269; Michael Molho, *In Memoriam: Hommage aux Victimes Juives des Nazis en Grèce*, 2d. ed., rev. by Joseph Nehama (Salonica: Communauté Israelite de Thessalonique, 1973), 184–203.

79. Duquesne, 258; my translation from the French.

80. Falconi, 95.

81. Daniel A. Binchy, *Church and State in Fascist Italy* (New York: Oxford University Press, 1970), 617.

82. Isaac, 113–114.

83. Snoek, xxii.

84. Vatican, *Actes et Documents,* IX: 53–55, discusses evidence that the Vatican Secretary of State, Cardinal Maglione, informed German Ambassador Baron Weizsaecker on the day the Jews of Rome were rounded up (16 October 1943) that the Pope would speak out publicly if the raid continued (also see in ibid. documents no. 368, 505–507). The raid in Rome ended because there were no more Jews to be found. Raids capturing Jews in other Italian cities occurred without any papal warning or protest.

85. Binchy, Introduction and 622–623.

86. I am indebted to Meier Michaelis of Haifa University, who informed me that in the course of his research, *German-Italian Relations and the Question of the Jews in Italy, 1922–1939* (London: Institute of Jewish Affairs, 1978), he discovered such testimonies regarding village priests in Italy who instructed their parishioners that the Holy Father said it was their duty to help Jews evade capture. The priests' attribution of the imperative to the Pope appears to be their own idea. Sam Waagenar examines the evidence on Vatican claims for organizing direct aid to the Jews and finds that they are not corroborated. The organized evasion movement among clerics was not directed by the Vatican or assisted tangibly by it (*The Pope's Jews* [La Salle, Ill.: Library Press, 1974], chs. 38–40).

87. Henri Michel, in his account of Italian strike activity, reports that in September 1944 80% of the trains were stopped. See his *Shadow War: European Resistance, 1939–1945*, trans. Richard Barry (New York: Harper and Row, 1972), 227–228. On the fears of Pius XII of "Bolshevism" see Friedlander, 180–181, 185–187, 194–196, 210–216, 236.

88. Robert A. Graham, S.J., "The Holy See and the Victims of the War," *L'Osservatore Romano*, 13 June 1974, 6–9, and "The Human Being in the Tragic Tornado of War Necessities," *L'Osservatore Romano*, 12 February 1976, 6–9.

89. Falconi, 72.

NOTES FOR CHAPTER 5

1. Hannah Arendt, *Eichmann in Jerusalem: A Report on the Banality of Evil* (New York: Viking, 1963).

2. Jacob Robinson, *And the Crooked Shall Be Made Straight: The Eichmann Trial, the Jewish Catastrophe, and Hannah Arendt's Narrative* (New York: Macmillan, 1965).

3. Isaiah Trunk, *Judenrat: The Jewish Councils in Eastern Europe under Nazi Occupation* (New York: Macmillan, 1972).

4. Stanley Hoffman, "Collaborationism in France during World War II," *Journal of Modern History* XL, no. 2 (September 1968): 375–395.

5. Translation of document 3363-PS in International Military Tribunal, *Nazi Conspiracy and Aggression,* 11 vols. (Washington, D.C.: U.S. Government Printing Office, 1946), VI: 97–99; italics added.

6. Arendt, 104, 111; italics added. I am grateful to the Viking Press for granting permission to quote these passages fully. I regret that an earlier version of this chapter was not finished before the sudden death of Ms. Arendt; she did not have the opportunity she requested to read it before publication and thus we do not have her response.

7. Norman Rich, *Hitler's War Aims, II: The Establishment of the New Order* (New York: Norton, 1974): 154–155, 179, 189–190, 361–363.

8. Trunk, 2, 21–26.

9. Vojtech Mastny, *The Czechs under Nazi Rule: The Failure of National Resistance, 1939–1943* (New York: Columbia University Press, 1971); Robert O. Paxton, *Vichy France: Old Guard and New Order, 1940–44* (New York: Random House, 1972); Werner Warmbrunn, *The Dutch under German Occupation, 1940–1945* (New York: Oxford University Press, 1963); Henry L. Mason, *The Purge of Dutch Quislings: Emergency Justice in the Netherlands* (The Hague: Nijhoff, 1952); Randolph L. Braham, "The Holocaust in Hungary: A Historical Interpretation of the Role of the Hungarian Radical Right," *Societas* II, no. 3 (June 1972): 195–219; Adolph Eichmann, "Eichmann's Story, Part II," *Life,* 5 December 1960, 146–148.

10. Rich, II:106–114; J. Gérard-Libois and José Gotovitch, *L'An 40: La Belgique Occupée* (Brussels: CRISP, 1971); Leni Yahil, *The Rescue of Danish Jewry: Test of a Democracy,* trans. Morris Gradel (Philadelphia: Jewish Publication Society of America, 1969).

11. Trunk, ch. 18; Aharon Weiss, "The Jewish Police in the General-Government, in Upper Silesia, and in East Galicia" (Hebrew text, English summary; Ph.D. dissertation, Hebrew University, 1974).

12. For Belgium: Israel Schirman, "La Politique Allemande à l'Égard des Juifs en Belgique, 1940-1944" (Ph.D. dissertation, Université Libre de Bruxelles, 1970-1971); Lucien Steinberg, *Le Comité de Défense des Juifs en Belgique, 1942–1944* (Brussels: Éditions de l'Université de Bruxelles, 1973). For France: Joseph Billig, *Le Commissariat Général aux Questions Juives,* 2 vols. (Paris: Éditions du Centre, 1955), I; Xosa Szajkowski, *Analytical Franco-Jewish Gazetteer, 1939–1945* (New York: Frydmann, 1966); Claude Lévy and Paul Tillard, *Betrayal*

at the Vel d'Hiv, trans. Inea Bushnaq (New York: Hill and Wang, 1967). For
Hungary: Randolph L. Braham, "The Role of the Jewish Council in Hungary: A
Tentative Assessment," *Yad Vashem Studies* X (1974), 69-110; Bernard Klein,
"Hungarian Jewry in the Nazi Period" (masters thesis, Columbia University,
1955); and YIVO Archives, file no. 768, Protocal no. 3618, unpublished
testimonies of Hungarian Jewish leaders and other Jews and non-Jews regarding
deportations of Jews from Hungary in 1944. For Germany and Austria: H. G.
Adler, *Der Verwaltete Mensch: Studien zur Deportation der Juden aus
Deutschland* (Tübingen: Mohr, 1974); Philip Friedman, "Aspects of Jewish Com-
munal Crisis in the Period of the Nazi Regime in Germany, Austria, and
Czechoslovakia," in *Essays on Jewish Life and Thought,* ed. B. Blau (New York:
Columbia University Press, 1959); Herbert Rosenkrantz, "The Anschluss and the
Tragedy of Austrian Jewry, 1938-1945," in *The Jews of Austria: Essays on Their
Life, History, and Destruction,* ed. J. Fraenkel (London: Valentine, Mitchell,
1967). For Greece: Michael Molho, *In Memoriam: Hommage aux Victimes Juives
des Nazis en Grèce,* 2d ed., rev. and enlarged by Joseph Nehama (Salonica: Com-
munauté Israélite de Thessalonique, 1973). For the Netherlands: Jacob Presser,
The Destruction of the Dutch Jews, trans. Arnold Pomerans (New York: Dutton,
1969); Louis de Jong, "Jews and Non-Jews in Nazi Occupied Holland," in *On the
Track of Tyranny,* ed. Max Beloff (London: Wiener Library, 1960), "The
Netherlands and Auschwitz: Why Were the Reports of Mass Killings So Widely
Disbelieved?", in *Imposed Jewish Governing Bodies under Nazi Rule* (New York:
YIVO, 1972), and "Help to People in Hiding," *Delta* VIII, no. 1 (Spring 1965):
37-79; Joseph Michman, "The Controversial Stand of the *Joodse Raad* in the
Netherlands: Lodewijk E. Visser's Struggle," *Yad Vashem Studies* X (1974): 9-68;
Gertrude van Tijn, "Contributions to the History of the Jews in the Netherlands
from May 10, 1940 to June, 1944" (report submitted and mimeographed by the
JDC, Joint Distribution Committee, Jerusalem, 1945); Warmbrunn. For Serbia:
Federation of Jewish Communities of Yugoslavia, *The Crimes of the Fascist Oc-
cupants and Their Collaborators against Jews in Yugoslavia* (Serbo-Croat text,
English summary) (Belgrade: Izdanje Saveza Jevrejskih Opstina Jugoslavije, 1957).

13. See note 5 above.

14. Gideon Hausner, *Justice in Jerusalem* (New York: Harper and Row, 1966), 55-56;
also see Chapter 1, pp. 22-24, of this volume.

15. Karl A. Schleunes, *The Twisted Road to Auschwitz: Nazi Policy toward German
Jews, 1933-1939* (Urbana, Ill.: University of Illinois Press, 1970), 226-254.

16. Trunk's estimates of employees of *Judenräte* in Polish ghettos range from 2% to
17% of the ghetto population. Other sources indicate that persons employed or
exempted by the *Judenräte* in Vienna (1943) and in the Netherlands (summer
1942) constituted over 20% of the ghetto population (see Rosenkranz and
Presser). We do not know how comparable these figures are. Some omit Jewish
police (also exemptees), which were under separate authorities in some ghettos.
However, when we take into account that the employment (and later exemption)
of one family member might benefit the whole family, it is clear that many Jews
must have valued such employment and/or association (many employees were not
paid) as a source of advantage or security.

17. See note 12 for sources.

18. Randolph L. Braham, "What Did They Know and When?" (address presented to the International Scholars Conference on the Holocaust — A Generation After, New York City, March 1975), 27-29, 57-62; YIVO Archives, file no. 768.

19. Braham, "What Did They Know and When?" 57, 59, 64-67.

20. E. Avotins et al., *Daugavas Vanagi: Who Are They?* (Riga: Latvia State Publishing House, 1963), 13.

21. Sarah Neshamit, "Rescue in Lithuania during the Nazi Occupation," in *Rescue Attempts during the Holocaust: Proceedings of the Second Yad Vashem International Historical Conference,* eds. Yisrael Gutman and Efraim Zuroff (Jerusalem: Yad Vashem, 1977), 293; Raul Hilberg, *The Destruction of the European Jews* (Chicago: Quadrangle, 1967), 203-204.

22. Edward D. Wynot, Jr., " 'A Necessary Cruelty': The Emergence of Official Anti-Semitism in Poland, 1936-1939," *American Historical Review* LXXVI (1971): 1035-1058.

23. George Lichtheim, "The Capture and Trial of Adolph Eichmann by Moishe Pearlman," *New York Review of Books* I, no. 3 (26 September 1963): 6.

24. Looking at prewar signs, one would have expected the government collaboration in Salonica that occurred but less state accommodation in the Netherlands. The Dutch anti-Semitic parties had attracted little political support before the war and Dutch Jews had enjoyed full civil rights without any threat. However, an anti-Semitic and native fascist movement had flourished in Salonica in the early 1930s, Jews' civil rights had become a campaign issue, and several anti-Jewish riots led to extensive damage through arson. See Chapter 3, n. 38.

25. Molho, 99-100.

26. Isaac Kabeli, "The Resistance of the Greek Jews," *YIVO Annual of Jewish Social Science* VIII (1953): 281-288; L. S. Stavrianos, "The Jews in Greece," *Journal of Central European Affairs* XXV (October 1948): 265-269.

27. S. Krakowski, "The Slaughter of Polish Jewry: A Polish 'Reassessment,' " *Wiener Library Bulletin* XXVI, no. 3-4 (1972-1973): 13; Emmanuel Ringelblum, *Polish-Jewish Relations during the Second World War,* ed. with notes by J. Kermish and S. Krakowski (Jerusalem: Yad Vashem, 1974).

28. Trunk, 19-20.

29. Weiss, ch. 3.

30. Trunk, 328-329; Michman, 14-17; Szajkowski, 46-52.

31. Trunk, 328.

32. Weiss, ch. 3.

33. Billig, I: 219.

34. Adam Czerniakow, *The Warsaw Ghetto Diary by Adam Czerniakow,* eds. Raul Hilberg, Joseph Kermish and Stanislaw Staron, trans. Stanislaw Staron (New York: Stein and Day, in press). I am indebted to Yisrael Gutman (Yad Vashem) for access to an earlier translation.

35. Leo Baeck, "A People Stands before Its God," in *We Survived: The Stories of Fourteen of the Hidden and Hunted of Nazi Germany as Told to Eric H. Boehm,* ed. Eric H. Boehm (New Haven, Conn.: Yale University Press, 1949), 288-292.

36. Michman, 56.

37. Solomon F. Bloom, "Toward the Ghetto Dictator," *Jewish Social Studies* XII (January 1950): 73–78.

38. Trunk, ch. 13.

39. Ibid., 87–89.

40. Ibid., 403.

41. Ibid., 421.

42. Ibid., 423.

43. Cited in Introduction by Jacob Robinson to Trunk, xxiii.

44. Ibid., 427–430.

45. Trunk's "Analysis of the evaluation of the behavior of Jewish Council members," which found that "almost 63 percent of those questioned evaluated the activities of members of the Jewish Councils positively" (577), is questionable evidence considering the lack of either systematic or random sampling in choosing respondents, the potential for interviewer bias, the respondents' need for self-exoneration in evaluating the culpability of others, and the aggregation of evaluations of more and less cooperative *Judenrat* leaders (although Trunk does discuss extensively the degree of agreement in a sample of the many cases in which a few persons evaluated the same *Judenrat* leader). Trunk adds on p. 577:

> The attitudes towards the Councils were controversial in the Holocaust literature from the start, with negative evaluations prevailing. . . . No doubt the persons polled had been influenced by the controversy and were reluctant to give their own opinions, though they were assured of full discretion. A contributing factor in their reticence was that, with few exceptions, the very Councilmen of whom negative opinions were given perished as martyrs together with the other ghetto inmates (only 12% survived). . . . We also have to consider that the attitude toward and the evaluation of a Council by an individual may well be influenced by his personal experience and encounters with a particular Councilman or Council as a whole, and whether the individual got favors or was ill-treated (the objective situation in the ghetto dictated that favors could be given only at the expense of another person, as, for example, in the matters of being sent to forced labor, distribution of food cards, placing of one's name on deportation lists, etc.).

46. Donald Kenrick and Grattan Puxon, *The Destiny of Europe's Gypsies* (New York: Basic Books, 1972), 88.

47. Ibid., 91.

48. There was no Polish ghetto surveyed (for which data were ascertained principally from Trunk) without suspected Gestapo spies planted in the *Judenrat* and/or competing Jewish control agency. The Germans sometimes relied on foreign Jews acting as "advisers" to western nations' councils, as in the case of the UGIF of France (Szajkowski, 41), where such persons were suspected (with good reason) of being German informants; however, the Czech and Austrian Jewish leaders imported by the Gestapo to advise the Dutch *Joodse Raad* advised them how to procrastinate, according to van Tijn, 35.

There were also a few freelance, unorganized Jewish collaborators who were most dangerous to Jews in hiding because of their intimate knowledge of the Jewish community. Belgium's Ministry of Justice official report on war crimes, *Les Crimes de Guerre Commis sous l'Occupation de la Belgique, 1940–1945: La Persécution Antisémitique en Belgique* (Liège: Thones, 1947), 28, cites an informer, "Jacques," (not found after the war) who drove around in a German police car in Antwerp identifying Jews passing as non-Jews. Similarly, de Jong, "Help to People in Hiding," 49–50, relates that the dozens of Dutch police specially trained to catch Jews (who pulled in nearly 2,000 Jews in The Hague alone) were aided by captured Jews who became Secret Police agents, including "a woman (sentenced to death after the war) who betrayed six hundred Jews in hiding, including her own brother and his family." It was reported that one of the most notorious Jewish informants for the Gestapo in Rome was Celeste di Porto, the "Black Panther," who, Robert Katz relates in *Black Sabbath: A Journey through a Crime against Humanity* (New York: Macmillan, 1969), 296, "turned over a total of about fifty of her fellow Jews for 5,000 liras ($50) per Jew."

The best recorded case of collaboration with the Gestapo, and one of the few cases later adjudicated, was that of six Jewish collaborators in Greece (principally in Salonica) who were tried after the war by Greek courts (some in absentia) and condemned to death or life imprisonment for their duplicitous role in persuading Jews not to evade notices to report, in practicing extortion, in informing on evaders, and/or in keeping order in ghettos and camps; see Molho, 298–308.

49. Kenrick and Puxon, 141.

NOTES FOR CHAPTER 6

1. I am indebted to Leni Yahil for comprehensive and analytic documentation of the rescue of Danish Jewry and its causes and shall rely on her work unless other sources are noted. Memoirs of interest include that of Marcus Melchior, who was acting in the stead of the Chief Rabbi in September 1943, and Aage Bertelsen, founder of a resistance network. Leni Yahil, *The Rescue of Danish Jewry: Test of a Democracy*, trans. Morris Gradel (Philadelphia: Jewish Publication Society of America, 1969); Marcus Melchior, *A Rabbi Remembers* (New York: Lyle Stuart, 1968); Aage Bertelsen, *October '43*, trans. Milly Lindholm (New York: Gross, n.d. [1974]).

2. Norman Rich, *Hitler's War Aims, II: The Establishment of the New Order* (New York: Norton, 1074); 107.

3. Raul Hilberg, *The Destruction of the European Jews* (Chicago: Quadrangle, 1967), 246.

4. Kenneth Miller, *Government and Politics in Denmark* (Boston: Houghton Mifflin, 1968), 45.

5. Yahil, 225.

6. Ibid., 85.

7. Ibid., 41.

8. Ibid., 43–44; italics added.

9. Ibid., 44–45.

10. Ibid., 131–142, 193–194.

11. Ibid., 173.

12. Hilberg, 361.

13. Yahil, 211.

14. Ibid., 26, 264, 275, 291.

15. Ibid., 230.

16. Bertelsen, 28–57, 120–126, 140–141.

17. Ibid., 95–99.

18. Yahil, 263, estimated the 12 million kroner incorrectly as equivalent to "a little less than 2 million dollars." However, according to the Federal Reserve Bank of the United States, at the end of 1941 and during 1946 the kroner was worth $.051792. I am grateful for Yahil's acknowledgment of this error.

19. Ibid., 349–356.

20. See Chapter 2, note 11, on the experimental evidence of how models of nonconformity and/or competing authorities induce noncompliance with orders of authority.

21. Yahil, 266.

22. Bertelsen, 162–164.

23. Aage Roussell, *The Museum of the Danish Resistance Movement, 1940–1945* (Copenhagen: National Museum, 1970), 24.

24. Rich, II: 171–172.

25. Ibid., 173–174.

26. J. Gérard-Libois and José Gotovitch, *L'An 40: La Belgique Occupée* (Brussels: CRISP, 1971), 432.

27. Israel Schirman, "La Politique Allemande à l'Égard des Juifs en Belgique, 1940–1944" (Ph.D. dissertation, Université Libre de Bruxelles, 1970–1971), 16.

28. Ibid., 188.

29. Ibid., 49.

30. Hilberg, 386–387.

31. Schirman, 93.

32. Lucien Steinberg, *Le Comité de Défense des Juifs en Belgique, 1942–1944* (Brussels: Éditions de l'Université de Bruxelles, 1973), 58–59.

33. Ibid., 59–60; see also Lucien Steinberg, "Jewish Rescue Activities in Belgium and France," in *Rescue Attempts during the Holocaust: Proceedings of the Second Yad Vashem International Historical Conference*, eds. Yisrael Gutman and Efraim Zuroff (Jerusalem: Yad Vashem, 1977), 606.

34. Steinberg, *Le Comité de Défense*, 70.

35. Schirman, 107–108.

36. Anne Somerhausen, *Written in Darkness: A Belgian Woman's Record of the Occupation, 1940–1945* (New York: Knopf, 1946), 142.

37. Steinberg, *Le Comité de Défense*, 80–82.

38. Ibid., 180; capitalization of French text is in the original; translation is by Fein.

39. H. Singer, *Four Years under German Occupation in Belgium* (Montreal: Canadian Jewish Chronicle, reprint, 1945), 6.

40. Steinberg, *Le Comité de Défense*, 108.

41. Ibid., 102.

42. Ibid., 174.

43. Ibid., 130–138.

44. Ibid., 186–196.

45. Ibid., 70.

46. Frederick Barry Chary, *The Bulgarian Jews and the Final Solution 1940–1944* (Pittsburgh: University of Pittsburgh Press, 1972), 127. I shall rely on this volume unless otherwise noted.

47. Ibid., 33.

48. United States Military Tribunal, "Documents: Staff Evidence Analysis," NG-5351, unnumbered volumes of documents found in Columbia University International Law Library and other document repositories.

49. Chary, 74.

50. Ibid., 86.

51. Ibid., 94.

52. Ibid., 90.

53. Ibid., 147.

54. Donna Crispin, "Protest Demonstration of the Jews of Sofia on May 24, 1943," *Annual of the Social, Cultural, and Educational Association of the Jews in the People's Republic of Bulgaria* (Sofia), IV (1969): 69–103.

55. NG-2357, cited by Hilberg, 483.

56. Chary, 191.

57. Ibid., 188–193.

58. Nissan Oren, "The Bulgarian Exception: A Reassessment of the Salvation of the Jewish Community," *Yad Vashem Studies* VII (1968): 83–106.

59. Ira Hirschman, *Lifeline to a Promised Land* (New York: Vanguard, 1946), 155–163.

NOTES FOR CHAPTER 7

1. The Germans respected the rights of Jews of enemy citizenship within Germany — American, British, British dominions, and Latin American nationals — until the end of the war, never attempting to deport them, while it requested its allies and the neutrals to repatriate their Jews from Germany and German-occupied states or agree to their deportation. The deadlines given to such states were repeatedly postponed until 31 December 1943, when the Foreign Office ceased to protect them from deportation by the RSHA; see Raul Hilberg, *The Destruction of the European Jews* (Chicago: Quadrangle, 1967), 289–291.

2. Hannah Arendt, *The Origins of Totalitarianism*, rev. ed. (New York: Harcourt, Brace, and World, 1966), 295–296.

3. Henry Feingold's *The Politics of Rescue: The Roosevelt Administration and the Holocaust, 1938–1945* (New Brunswick, N.J.: Rutgers University Press, 1970), is the most comprehensive and analytical examination to appear on the sources of prewar government policy, its relation to intraparty politics, the New Deal coalition, and the divisions within the American Jewish community. David S. Wyman's *Paper Walls: America and the Refugee Crisis, 1938–1941* (Amherst,

Ma.: University of Massachusetts Press, 1968), and Saul S. Friedman's *No Haven for the Oppressed: United States Policy toward Jewish Refugees, 1938–1945* (Detroit, Mi.: Wayne State University Press, 1973), are more limited in scope but both contribute insights from different perspectives. Wyman has utilized most fully the archives of the American Friends Service Committee — an organization critical to refugee aid, with representatives throughout Europe — and interviewed many persons active in such missions during the period. Friedman presents little new evidence on the course of American policy but in discussing the evidence on the relationship of Rabbi Stephen S. Wise, president of the American Jewish Congress, to President Franklin Delano Roosevelt accuses them of collusion in "a partnership of silence."

4. Cited by Arthur D. Morse, *While Six Million Died: A Chronicle of American Apathy* (New York: Random House, 1968), 214.

5. Hans Habe, *The Mission*, trans. Michael Bullock (New York: Coward-McCann, 1965).

6. Friedman, 139.

7. Yehuda Bauer, "When Did They Know?", *Midstream* XIV (April 1968): 51-58.

8. Ibid. 56.

9. Elizabeth E. Eppler, "The Rescue Work of the World Jewish Congress during the Nazi Period," in *Rescue Attempts during the Holocaust: Proceedings of the Second Yad Vashem International Historical Conference*, eds. Yisrael Gutman and Efraim Zuroff (Jerusalem: Yad Vashem, 1977), 59.

10. *New York Times*, 18 December 1942, I: 7.

11. My estimate of the number of Jews massacred in 1941 — 150,500, or 24.5% of 614,665 — is based on the total reported massacred in Jassy (Hilberg, 491) and the Jews from Bessarabia and Bukovina slaughtered in those regions and across the Dniester (Julius S. Fisher, *Transnistria: The Forgotten Cemetery* [South Brunswick, N.J.: Yoseloff, 1968] divided by the estimated 1941 population (see the source notes to Table 3-1 of this volume). Fisher estimates that 87,757 of the 140,154 deportees to Transnistria, or 62.6% perished (p. 136) but cautions that "the real number of the deportees was considerably larger" as was the number slaughtered during transit (p. 135). All these figures exclude the native inhabitants of Transnistria. For sources of statistics on the net impact of the Holocaust on the Jews of Rumania see Theodor Lavi, "Rumania," *Encyclopedia Judaica* XIV (Jerusalem: Keter, 1971): 399-410; I. Koralnick, *In the Clutches of Famine* (Geneva: OSE, 1947); Sabin Manuila and W. Filderman, "Regional Development of the Jewish Population in Rumania," *Genus* XIII (1957): 153-165.

12. Alexandre Cretzianu, *Lost Opportunity* (London: Cape, 1957); Theodor Lavi, "The Background to the Rescue of Rumanian Jewry during the Period of the Holocaust," in *Jews and Non-Jews in Eastern Europe, 1918–1945*, ed. Bela Vago and George L. Mosse New York: Wiley, 1974), 182-184.

13. Bela Vago, "Jewish Leadership Groups in Hungary and Rumania during the Holocaust" (address presented to the International Scholars Conference on the Holocaust — A Generation After, (New York City, March 1975), 24-25.

14. Friedman, 148-150.

15. Henry Morgenthau, Jr., "The Morgenthau Diaries VI: The Refugee Run Around," *Colliers,* 1 November 1947.

16. Ira Hirschmann, *Caution to the Winds* (New York: McKay, 1962), 159.

17. The Auschwitz Protocols were received in June from Dr. Jean Kopecky, representative of the Czech government-in-exile in Geneva, having been transmitted by representatives of the Czech underground from Bratislava, where two escaped Slovakian Jews, Rudolph Vrba and Fred Wetzler, had submitted their testimony to representatives of both the Slovakian Jewish community and the Vatican. Their history is reported by Roswell McClelland to John Pehle, head of the WRB, in cable no. 4303 of 6 July 1944 (box 18, War Refugee Board Records, Franklin D. Roosevelt Memorial Library, Hyde Park, New York). However, they were not transmitted in their entirety to Washington until mid-October and were not submitted to John J. McCloy, the Secretary of War, until 8 November (see note 19 below) and were not publicly released until 26 November 1944. (See also box 35.)

18. Erich Kulka, "Auschwitz Condoned: The Abortive Struggle against the Final Solution," *Wiener Library Bulletin* XXII, no. 1 (Winter 1968-1969): 2-5.

19. Pehle received suggestions to bomb rail lines leading to Auschwitz on 18 June 1944, in a letter from Jacob Rosenheim, president of World Agudas Israel, and from the WRB representative in Berne (McClelland) in cable no. 4041 via the Legation Minister (Harrison) and the State Department on 24 June 1944. Requests to bomb the gas chambers of Auschwitz were received on 24 July 1944 from Johan J. Smertenko of the Emergency Committee to Save the Jewish People in a letter to President Roosevelt; on 29 July from Ernest Frischer of the Czechoslovak State Council in London (transmitted to Leo Kubowitzki of the World Jewish Congress in a letter of 3 August 1944 from Pehle to Kubowitzki), from the Polish government-in-exile in London in September by the WRB London representative (Mann), conveyed via Ambassador Winant to Pehle on 29 September. According to WRB files, Pehle spoke to McCloy about these requests on at least three occasions; cited first on 24 June (memorandum by Pehle on conversation), 29 June (memorandum to McCloy regarding previous conversation enclosing cable no. 4041), letter of Pehle to McCloy on 3 October 1944, enclosing Mann suggestion, and letter of Pehle to McCloy on 8 November 1944, where for the first time Pehle advocates bombing the gas chambers of Auschwitz and transmits the Auschwitz Protocols. In his first conversation with McCloy (as recorded in his file memorandum of 24 June 1944), Pehle states:

> I told McCloy . . . that I had several doubts about the matter, namely (1) *whether it would be appropriate to use military planes and personnel for this purpose* [italics added]; (2) whether it would be difficult to put the railroad line out of commission for a long enough period to do any good; and (3) even assuming that this railroad line were put out of commission for some period of time, whether it would help the Jews in Hungary.

Writing to McCloy on 8 November 1944, Pehle recalls:

> Until now, despite pressure from many sources, I have been hesitant to urge the destruction of these camps by direct military action. But I am convinced that the point has now been reached where such action is justifiable if it is deemed feasible by competent military authorities.

(See box 35 and box 6, WRB Records.)

20. Kubowitzki's letter of 1 July 1944 also refers to a conversation with S. Lesser on

28 June and reveals his opposition to the attempts by Pehle's aides to persuade
Pehle about the propriety of bombing Auschwitz. On 29 June 1944, B. Aksin
said, in an interoffice memorandum to Lesser, that

> presumably, a large number of Jews in these camps may be killed in the course of such
> bombings (though some of them may escape in the confusion). But such Jews are
> doomed to death anyhow. The destruction of the camps would not change their fate,
> but it would serve as visible retribution on their murderers and it might save the lives of
> future victims.

(See box 35, WRB Record.)

21. David S. Wyman, "Why Auschwitz Was Never Bombed," *Commentary* 65, no. 5
    (May 1978): 37–46.

22. Kulka, 4–5.

23. Bela Vago, "The British Government and the Fate of Hungarian Jewry in 1944,"
    in *Rescue Attempts during the Holocaust: Proceedings of the Second Yad
    Vashem International Historical Conference,* eds. Yisrael Gutman and Efraim
    Zuroff (Jerusalem: Yad Vashem, 1977), 280.

24. Appeals to the WRB for a warning were received in September 1944 from the
    Union of Orthodox Rabbis in the United States and Canada, the Vaad Hahat-
    zala Emergency Committee, the American Jewish Committee, Agudas Israel,
    and the Council for the Rescue of Jewish People in Poland, and a related request
    was received from the Jewish Labor Committee.

25. Feingold, 59; see also 35–36, 61, 83, 192, 196, 236, 297, 302–303, on the labeling
    of Jewish refugees as political refugees.

26. Wyman, *Paper Walls,* 23–26, 68–71.

27. Feingold, 229.

28. Ibid., 303.

29. Gerald Reitlinger, *The Final Solution: The Attempt to Exterminate the Jews of
    Europe, 1939–1945,* 2d rev. and enlarged ed. (South Brunswick, N.J.: Yoseloff,
    1961), 184, 397, 401, 424–425, 443, 481–482, 484, 495, on the activities of the
    International Red Cross. For a more critical evaluation of the implications of the
    earlier adaptation of the IRC see Meier Dworzecki, "The International Red
    Cross and Its Policy vis-à-vis the Jews in the Ghettos and Concentration Camps in
    Nazi-Occupied Europe," in *Rescue Attempts during the Holocaust: Proceedings
    of the Second Yad Vashem International Historical Conference,* eds. Yisrael
    Gutman and Efraim Zuroff (Jerusalem: Yad Vashem, 1977), 71–110. The War
    Refugee Board estimated that about 20,000 Jewish families in Hungary were in-
    itially protected by Palestine certificates transmitted by the Swiss Legation in
    Budapest, but only 7,800 persons were allowed to enter the houses protected by
    the Swiss with the consent of the Hungarian government. See the "History of the
    War Refugee Board," 174 (unpublished mimeographed manuscript in the
    Franklin D. Roosevelt Memorial Library, Hyde Park, New York). See also Zvi
    Goldfarb, "On 'Hehalutz' Resistance in Hungary," in *Extermination and
    Resistance,* ed. Kibbutz Lohamei Hagettaot (Israel: Kibbutz Lohamei Haget-
    taot, 1958).

30. Feingold, 258–259.

31. Ibid., 226.

32. Wyman, *Paper Walls*, 13-20, 210-211.

33. Public opinion polls taken before and during World War II show the consistent opposition of a large majority of respondents to admitting more refugees. One sign of the Jews' low status was the finding in 1944 that more of those questioned would have excluded Jews from entering the country than would have excluded any of the other groups specified, excepting only Germans and Japanese. See Charles Herbert Stember et al., *Jews in the Mind of America* (New York: Basic Books, 1966), ch. 6.

34. Long Diary, 11 January 1944, as cited by Feingold, 15.

35. Figures of voters for the first American Jewish Congress and its platform are taken from the American Jewish Congress *Souvenir Journal*, 18 April 1977, 2-3. The American Jewish population in 1917 was 3,388,951 according to Robert Gutman, cited in Stember, 354. On the origins and ideology of the Congress, see also Daniel Eleazer, *Community and Polity: The Organizational Dynamics of American Jewry* (Philadelphia: Jewish Publication Society of America, 1976), 158-159.

36. Eleazer, 199.

37. Sidney Bolkowsky, *The Distorted Image: German Jewish Perceptions of Germans and Germany, 1918-1935* (New York: Elsevier, 1975), 170-174.

38. Naomi Cohen, *Not Free to Desist: The American Jewish Committee, 1906-1966* (Philadelphia: Jewish Publication Society of America, 1972), 156, 163; Stephen Wise, *Challenging Years: The Autobiography of Stephen Wise* (London: East and West Library, 1951), 156-165.

39. Frederick A. Lazin, "The Response of the American Jewish Committee to the Crisis of Jews in Germany, 1933-1939: A Study of Qualified Concern and Possible Complicity" (address presented to the International Scholars Conference on the Holocaust — A Generation After, New York City, March 1975).

40. Cohen, 158.

41. Harold L. Ickes, *The Secret Diary of Harold L. Ickes*, II: *The Inside Struggle, 1936-1939* (New York: Simon and Schuster, 1954): 510.

42. Howard Morley Sachar, *The Course of Modern Jewish History* (New York: Dell, 1958), 522.

43. Melvin M. Tumin, "The Cult of Gratitude," in *The Ghetto and Beyond*, ed. Peter I. Rose (New York: Random House, 1969), 76.

44. Wise, 140-155, 159-160.

45. Lawrence Fuchs, *The Political Behavior of American Jews* (New York: The Free Press, 1956), 74-75, cites estimates showing a continuous increase in the percentage of Jews voting for Roosevelt from 1932 to 1944, when Roosevelt received an estimated 92.8% of the Jewish vote. In other ethnic groups the Democratic vote declined after peaking in 1936. The lack of association between voting Democratic and social class among Jews contradicts the inverse association (lower income persons being more likely to vote Democratic) usually found among American voters during this period.

46. Emanuel Celler, *You Never Leave Brooklyn* (New York: Day, 1953), 89-93.

47. Hayim Greenberg, "Bankrupt!", in *Anthology of Hayim Greenberg*, selected and

with an introduction by Marie Syrkin (Detroit, Mi.: Wayne State University Press, 1968), 192–203.

48. Friedman, 147.

49. Ibid.

50. Ibid., 146.

51. Fritz Heider, "Attitudes and Cognitive Organization," *Journal of Psychology* XXI (1946): 107–112.

52. E. Digby Baltzell, *The Protestant Establishment* (New York: Random House, Vintage Books, 1966), 246–249.

53. Feingold, 158.

54. My expectations are based on the model developed by Neal C. Gross, Ward S. Mason, and Alexander W. McEachern in *Explorations in Role Analysis: Studies of the School Superintendency Role* (New York: Wiley, 1958). They hypothesize and confirm that an actor oriented wholly or partially to expedient—rather than moral—criteria will respond to the party threatening sanctions for nonperformance, assuming that the expectations of both parties in conflict are legitimate. Both Jewish leaders and State Department officials appealed to legitimate values: the former spoke in the name of humanity, the latter in the name of the law.

55. Murray Edelman, *The Symbolic Uses of Politics* (Urbana, Ill.: University of Illinois Press, 1967).

56. A. J. Sherman, *Island Refuge: Britain and Refugees from the Third Reich, 1933–1939* (London: Elek, 1973), 266.

57. These calculations are based on the estimated Jewish refugees to each nation between 1933 and 1939 cited by Malcolm J. Proudfoot, *European Refugees, 1939–1952: A Study in Forced Population Movement* (Evanston, Ill: Northwestern University Press, 1956), 319, and governments' estimates of their total population on 31 December 1939, cited in the League of Nations *Statistical Yearbook, 1941–1942* (Geneva: League of Nations, 1943), table 1. For total emigration from Germany and Austria to Great Britain see Sherman, 270–271.

58. Sherman, 238.

59. Ibid., 228–229.

60. Ibid., 176.

61. Ibid., 196.

62. Morse, 248–249.

63. Leni Yahil, "Select British Documents on the Illegal Immigration to Palestine," *Yad Vashem Studies* X (1974): 241–76; Ruth Kluger and Peggy Mann, *The Last Escape* (Garden City, N.Y.: Doubleday, 1973), 417–418, 461–466.

64. Yehuda Bauer, *From Diplomacy to Resistance: A History of Jewish Palestine, 1939–1945* (Philadelphia: Jewish Publication Society of America, 1970), 108–109.

65. Franklin Reid Gannon, *The British Press and Germany, 1933–1939* (Oxford: Clarendon, 1971), 277.

66. Andrew Scharf, *The British Press and Jews under Nazi Rule* (New York: Oxford University Press, 1964).

67. *Papers Concerning the Treatment of German Nationals in Germany 1938–1939,* Command Paper no. 6120 (London: H.M.S.O., 1939).

68. Robert Sherwood, *Roosevelt and Hopkins* (New York: Harper, 1948), 717.

69. Alex Weissberg, *Desperate Mission: Joel Brand's Story as Told by Alex Weissberg,* trans. Constantine Fitzgibbon and Andrew Foster-Melliar (New York: Criterion, 1958), 214–216. Brand's inference may have provoked the assassination of Lord Moyne by two members of the Irgun soon thereafter.

70. Nathaniel Katzburg, "British Policy on Immigration to Palestine during World War II," in *Rescue Attempts during the Holocaust: Proceedings of the Second Yad Vashem International Historical Conference,* eds. Yisrael Gutman and Efraim Zuroff (Jerusalem: Yad Vashem, 1977), 186.

71. Reuben Ainsztein, "The Failure of the West," *Jewish Quarterly,* Winter 1966–1967, 11–20.

72. Ibid., 20.

73. Ernest Hearst, "The British and the Slaughter of the Jews," *Wiener Library Bulletin* XXI, no. 1 (Winter 1966–1967): 32–38, and XXII, no. 2 (Spring 1967): 30–40.

74. Ibid., XXII, no. 2: 30.

75. Ibid., 39.

76. P. Glickson, "Jewish Population in the Polish People's Republic, 1944–1972" (address presented to the Sixth World Congress of Jewish Studies, Jerusalem, August 1973).

77. Solomon Schwarz, *The Jews in the Soviet Union* (Syracuse, N.Y.: Syracuse University Press, 1951), 227.

78. Gerald Reitlinger, *The Final Solution: The Attempt to Exterminate the Jews of Europe, 1939–1945* (South Brunswick, N.J.: Yoseloff, 1961), 543–545; Reuben Ainsztein, *Jewish Resistance in Nazi-Occupied Eastern Europe* (New York: Barnes and Noble, 1974), 223–233, 257–265.

79. Zvi Bar-On, "The Jews in the Soviet Partisan Movement," *Yad Vashem Studies* IV (1960): 167–190. Bar-On analyzes the objective goals of the partisan movement, the functional prerequisites for assuming the partisan's role, and the goals, abilities, and other commitments of Jews apt to volunteer for such units, enabling us to realize there were imminent real conflicts.

80. Ibid., 181.

81. See Joseph Kermish and Shmuel Krakowski's documentation of this in their edition of Emmanuel Ringelblum's *Polish-Jewish Relations during the Second World War* (Jerusalem: Yad Vashem, 1974), 218–220, nn. 34–35.

82. Ainsztein seems determined to balance evidence of discrimination and betrayal with evidence of how non-Jewish partisans perceived some Jews' behavior, corroborating accusations and stereotypes against them, without evaluating to what extent the latter was actually a cause of the former or a justification for preexistent attitudes. Perhaps his perverse balancing of claims can be attributed to a need to commemorate the cause for which so many Jewish partisans died. See, for example, Ainsztein's discussion in *Jewish Resistance in Nazi-Occupied Eastern Europe,* 305, 307–308.

83. Bernard K. Johnpoll, *The Politics of Futility: The General Jewish Workers Bund of Poland, 1917–1943* (Ithaca, N.Y.: Cornell University Press, 1967), 237–240.

84. Leonard Schapiro, "The Jewish Anti-Fascist Committee and Phases of Soviet Anti-Semitic Policy during and after World War II," in *Jews and Non-Jews in Eastern Europe, 1918–1945,* eds. Bela Vago and George L. Mosse (New York: Wiley, 1974).

85. S. Redlich, "The Jewish Anti-Fascist Committee in the Soviet Union," *Jewish Social Studies* XXXI, no. 1 (January 1969): 25–36.

86. Y. A. Gilboa, *The Black Years of Soviet Jewry,* trans. Yosef Schahter and Dov Ben-Abba (Boston: Little, Brown, 1971).

87. Dov Levin, "The Attitude of the Soviet Union to the Rescue of Jews," 225–236, and Yitzchak Arad, "Jewish Family Camps in the Forests: An Original Means of Rescue," 333–353, both in *Rescue Attempts during the Holocaust: Proceedings of the Second Yad Vashem International Historical Conference,* eds. Yisrael Gutman and Efraim Zuroff (Jerusalem: Yad Vashem, 1977).

88. Norman Rich, *Hitler's War Aims, II: The Establishment of the New Order* (New York: Norton, 1974): 401–404.

89. Proudfoot, 319, estimates that Sweden accepted 1,500 Jewish refugees from the expanded Reich but Valentin (who used Swedish sources) states that there were 3,000 Jews admitted. See Hugo Valentin, "Rescue and Relief Activities in Behalf of Jewish Victims of Nazism in Scandinavia," *YIVO Annual of Jewish Social Science* VIII (1953): 229.

90. Valentin, 224–251.

91. Hilberg, 622.

92. Leni Yahil, "Scandinavian Rescue of Prisoners," *Yad Vashem Studies* VI (1967): 219.

93. H. R. Trevor-Roper rebuts the account of Count Folke Bernadotte in his memoir *The Curtain Falls: Last Days of the Third Reich* (New York: Knopf, 1945) in an essay on "The Strange Case of Himmler's Doctor, Felix Kersten, and Count Bernadotte," *Commentary* XXIII (April 1957): 356–364. But Yahil relates the 1945 operation to earlier initiatives of Norwegian and Swedish officials behind the scenes and believes that "this controversy [regarding personal credit] has no historical value"; see Yahil, 209.

94. Nehemiah Robinson, *The Spain of Franco and Its Policies toward the Jews* (New York: Institute of Jewish Affairs, 1953).

95. Haim Avni, "The Zionist Underground in Holland and France and the Escape to Spain," in *Rescue Attempts during the Holocaust: Proceedings of the Second Yad Vashem International Historical Conference,* eds. Yisrael Gutman and Efraim Zuroff (Jerusalem: Yad Vashem, 1977), 556.

96. Haim Avni, "Spanish Nationals in Greece and Their Fate during the Holocaust," *Yad Vashem Studies* VIII (1970): 31–68.

97. John P. Wilson, "Carlton H. Hayes, Spain, and the Refugee Crisis, 1942–1945," *American Jewish Historical Quarterly* LXII, no. 2 (December 1972): 99–110.

98. Avni, "Spanish Nationals in Greece," 38, 48; Hilberg, 447–448; see also Michael Molho, *In Memoriam: Hommage aux Victimes Juives des Nazis en Grèce,* 2d

ed., rev. and enlarged by Joseph Nehama (Salonica: Communauté Israélite de Thessalonique, 1973), 110–114.

99. Alfred A. Haesler, *The Lifeboat Is Full: Switzerland and the Refugees, 1933–1945*, trans. Charles Lamm Markman (New York: Funk and Wagnalls, 1969).

100. Ibid., 326.

101. Ibid., 175–177.

102. Ibid., 181.

103. Ibid., 213.

104. Ibid., 331–332.

105. Proudfoot, 319, estimates that only 10,500 Jews found refuge in Switzerland, which would thus rank behind Sweden and Britain, but he did not have access to Swiss primary sources. Given Proudfoot's estimates, the Swiss took in 3.7 Jews per 1,000 Swiss between 1933 and 1945, a ratio exceeded only by Palestine (105.4 per 1,000) and Mauritius (3.8 per 1,000)—which absorbed deportees from Palestine.

106. Haesler, 156, 182, 231.

107. Ibid., 330.

NOTES FOR CHAPTER 8

1. Norman Rich, *Hitler's War Aims*, II: *The Establishment of the New Order* (New York: Norton, 1974): 422–423; and Henri Michel, *The Shadow War: European Resistance, 1939–1945*, trans. Richard Barry (New York: Harper and Row, 1972), 71–72.

2. Lucien Steinberg, *Not as a Lamb: The Jews against Hitler*, trans. Marion Hunter (Fansborough, England: Saxon House, 1974): Reuben Ainsztein, *Jewish Resistance in Nazi-Occupied Eastern Europe* (New York: Barnes and Noble, 1974).

3. W. I. Thomas, "The Four Wishes and the Definition of the Situation," in *Theories of Society: Foundations of Modern Sociological Theory*, ed. Talcott Parsons et al. (New York: The Free Press, 1961), II:743.

4. Alvin Gouldner, "The Norm of Reciprocity: A Preliminary Statement," *American Sociological Review* XXV, no. 2 (April 1960): 161–178.

5. Marvin Lowenthal, *The Jews of Germany: A Story of Sixteen Centuries* (New York: Russell and Russell, 1970; first pub. 1936).

6. Ibid., 61.

7. Emile Durkheim, *The Division of Labor in Society*, trans. George Simpson (New York: The Free Press, 1933), 200–204, 275–283.

8. Hubert M. Blalock, Jr., *Toward a Theory of Minority-Group Relations* (New York: Capricorn, 1970), 79–84.

9. Lowenthal, 28–29.

10. Isaiah Trunk, *Judenrat: The Jewish Councils in Eastern Europe under Nazi Occupation* (New York: Macmillan, 1972), 388–420.

11. These and all following citations are from *The Torah: The Five Books of Moses* (a new translation according to the Masoretic text) (Philadelphia: Jewish Publication Society of America, 1962).

12. Theodore H. Gaster, *Festivals of the Jewish Year* (New York: Morrow, 1952), 215-216.

13. "Pogroms," *Encyclopedia Judaica* (Jerusalem: Keter, 1971), XIII: 699.

14. Mark Wischnitzer, *To Dwell in Safety: The Story of Jewish Migration since 1800* (Philadelphia: Jewish Publication Society of America, 1949), 288-289; Howard Morley Sachar, *The Course of Modern Jewish History* (New York: Dell, 1958), 315.

15. Henry R. Huttenbach, "The Emigration of Jews from Worms (November 1938-October 1941): Hopes and Plans," in *Rescue Attempts during the Holocaust: Proceedings of the Second Yad Vashem International Historical Conference*, eds. Yisrael Gutman and Efraim Zuroff (Jerusalem: Yad Vashem, 1977), 288.

16. Dickran H. Boyajian, *Armenia: The Case for a Forgotten Genocide* (Westwood, N.J.: Educational Book Crafters, 1972), 283, 287.

NOTES FOR CHAPTER 9

1. *Notes from the Warsaw Ghetto: The Journal of Emmanuel Ringelblum*, ed. and trans. Jacob Sloan (New York: Schocken, 1958); *The Warsaw Diary of Chaim A. Kaplan*, rev. ed., trans. and ed. Abraham I. Katsh (New York: Collier, 1973); Mary Berg [pseud. Mary Wattenberg], *Warsaw Ghetto: A Diary*, ed. S. L. Schneiderman, trans. Sylvia Glass and Norbert Guterman (New York: Fischer, 1945); and *The Warsaw Ghetto Diary by Adam Czerniakow*, eds. Raul Hilberg, Joseph Kermish, and Stanislaw Staron, trans. Stanislaw Staron (New York: Stein and Day, in press). Since the latter had not been typeset, no page references are given for Czerniakow diary entries in this chapter. I am grateful to Raul Hilberg for access to this manuscript, and to Yisrael Gutman of Yad Vashem, who let me read an earlier (unpublished) English translation being prepared at Yad Vashem in 1974.

2. Tuvia Borzykowski, *Between Tumbling Walls*, trans. Mendal Kohansky (Israel: Beit Lohamei Hagettaot, n.d.); Alexander Donat, *The Holocaust Kingdom: A Memoir* (New York: Holt, Rinehart, and Winston, 1965); Bernard Goldstein, *The Stars Bear Witness*, trans. and ed. Leonard Shatzkin (New York: Viking, 1949); Jan Karski [pseud. Jan Kulezynski], *Story of a Secret State* (Boston: Houghton Mifflin, 1944); Vladka Meed [pseud. Feigele (Peltel) Mielzyrechi], *On Both Sides of the Wall: Memoirs from the Warsaw Ghetto* (Israel: Beit Lohamei Hagettaot, 1972); Emmanuel Ringelblum, *Polish-Jewish Relations during the Second World War*, ed. with footnotes by J. Kermish and S. Krakowski (Jerusalem: Yad Vashem, 1974); Halina Szwambaum, "Four Letters from Warsaw Ghetto," *Commentary* XXXI (June 1961): 486-492; Michael Zylberberg, *A Warsaw Diary, 1939-1943* (London: Valentine, Mitchell, 1969).

3. Apolinary Hartglass, "How Did Czerniakow Become Head of the Warsaw *Judenrat?*", *Yad Vashem Bulletin* XV (August 1964): 4-7.

4. Ringelblum was caught sometime during the mass deportation raids beginning on 22 July 1942. He was discovered in Trawniki camp and smuggled out of there in July 1943 by a Polish railway worker cooperating with the Jewish resistance.

Later he was hidden, along with his wife, his child, and 35 other Jews, in an underground bunker, where he continued his work (producing the treatise on Polish-Jewish Relations) until the bunker was betrayed to the Gestapo, which invaded it on 7 March 1944. They interrogated and tortured Ringelblum before he died at their hands.

Kaplan was seized during the mass deportation raids (described herein chiefly by his words) sometime in August 1942. His translator, Abraham I. Katsh, says that "he and his wife are believed to have perished in the Treblinka extermination camp in December 1942 or January 1943" (Kaplan, 15).

5. Isaiah Trunk, *Judenrat: The Jewish Councils in Eastern Europe under Nazi Occupation* (New York: Macmillan, 1972), 130.

6. Ibid., 146.

7. Ibid., 155.

8. PS-1061, cited by W. Bartoszewski, *Warsaw Death Ring, 1939-1944*, trans. Edward Rothert (Warsaw: Interpress, 1968), 150; Ringelblum, *Polish-Jewish Relations*, 166.

9. *Journal of Emmanuel Ringelblum*, 329.

10. Kaplan, 42.

11. Ibid., 42.

12. Ibid., 67.

13. Bernard K. Johnpoll, *The Politics of Futility: The General Jewish Workers Bund of Poland, 1917-1943* (Ithaca, N.Y.: Cornell University Press, 1967), 230-232.

14. Kaplan, 57.

15. Ibid., 60.

16. Ibid., 58.

17. Ibid., 54.

18. Ibid., 87.

19. Ibid., 120-121.

20. Berg, 46.

21. Kaplan, 74.

22. Ibid., 80.

23. Ibid., 94-95.

24. Ibid., 259-260.

25. Ibid., 100.

26. *Journal of Emmanuel Ringelblum*, 231-232.

27. Kaplan, 69.

28. Berg, 25-26.

29. Kaplan, 133.

30. Ibid., 134-135.

31. Goldstein, 52; *Journal of Emmanuel Ringelblum*, 16, 17, 18, 19.

32. Poland, Republic of, *German Crimes against Poland*, I: *Official Report of the Polish Government to Be Submitted to the International Military Tribunal* (London: December 1945); see also note 95 to Chapter 1 of this volume.

33. Ringelblum, *Polish-Jewish Relations*, 195-196.

34. Kaplan, 62-63.

35. *Journal of Emmanuel Ringelblum*, 62-63.

36. Ibid., 86.

37. Kaplan, 83.

38. *Journal of Emmanuel Ringelblum*, 79.

39. Ibid., 84.

40. Kaplan, 213-215.

41. Ibid., 216.

42. Nachman Blumenthal, "A Martyr or a Hero? Reflections on the Diary of Czerniakow," *Yad Vashem Studies* VII (1968): 168.

43. *Journal of Emmanuel Ringelblum*, 108.

44. Ibid., 84.

45. Berg, 82.

46. Kaplan, 171.

47. *Journal of Emmanuel Ringelblum*, 91-92.

48. Ibid., 31.

49. Ibid., 171.

50. Ibid., 186; Ringelblum, *Polish-Jewish Relations*, 209.

51. Kaplan, 244.

52. Berg, 53.

53. *Journal of Emmanuel Ringelblum*, 130.

54. Ibid., 130, 140.

55. Ibid., 180-181.

56. Kaplan, 270.

57. Berg, 87.

58. Kaplan, 244-245.

59. Berg, 55.

60. Zylberberg, 190.

61. *Journal of Emmanuel Ringelblum*, 56, 109, 138, 140, 147, 214-215.

62. Gardner Lindzey and Eliot Aronson, *Handbook of Social Psychology*, 2d ed. rev., 5 vols. (Reading, Ma.: Addison-Wesley, 1969), III: 190-191, 239, and V: 23-24.

63. *Journal of Emmanuel Ringelblum*, 39.

64. Ibid., 224.

65. Berg, 110-111.

66. Ibid., 118.

67. *Journal of Emmanuel Ringelblum*, 227.

68. Kaplan, 302.

69. Ibid., 303.

70. Ibid., 243.

71. Ibid., 335.

72. Ibid., 336.

73. *Journal of Emmanuel Ringelblum*, 249.

74. Ibid., 250.

75. Ibid., 185.

76. Ibid., 193.

77. Ibid., 271-272.

78. Ibid., 233-234.

79. Berg, 115.

80. *Journal of Emmanuel Ringelblum*, 286.

81. Donat, 44-45.

82. Kaplan, 291.

83. *Journal of Emmanuel Ringelblum*, 245-246.

84. Kaplan, 337-338.

85. *Journal of Emmanuel Ringelblum*, 236-237.

86. Ibid., 268.

87. Berg, 135.

88. Kaplan, 314-315.

89. Ibid., 317.

90. *Journal of Emmanuel Ringelblum*, 275-276.

91. Ibid., 213.

92. Ibid., 230.

93. Ibid., 256-257.

94. Kaplan, 286-287.

95. Ibid., 296-297.

96. Ibid., 346.

97. Berg, 125-127.

98. Ibid., 140-141.

99. Ibid., 141.

100. Ibid., 150.

101. Yehuda Bauer, "When Did They Know?", *Midstream* XIV (April 1968): 520.

102. *Journal of Emmanuel Ringelblum*, 295-296.

103. Bauer, 52.

104. Kaplan, 318.

105. *Journal of Emmanuel Ringelblum*, 297.

106. Ibid., 116, 137, 168, 200, 201; see also Kaplan, 112-113, 155-156.

107. Gideon Hausner, *Justice in Jerusalem* (New York: Harper and Row, 1966), 210.

108. Zylberberg, 55.

109. *Journal of Emmanuel Ringelblum*, 299-300.

110. Kaplan, 347.

111. Ibid., 349.

112. *Journal of Emmanuel Ringelblum*, 349.

113. Kaplan, 350.

114. Ibid., 352.

115. Berg, 156.

116. Ibid., 157.

117. Ibid., 159-160.

118. Kaplan, 384-385.

119. Leonard Tushnett, *The Pavement of Hell* (New York: St. Martin's, 1972), 129-133.

120. Kaplan, 386.

121. Ibid., 387-388.

122. Ibid., 389.

123. Ibid., 394.

124. Ibid., 395.

125. Ibid., 397.

126. Ibid., 398-399.

127. Ibid., 400.

128. Trunk, 509.

129. *Journal of Emmanuel Ringelblum*, 332.

130. Philip Friedman, *Martyrs and Fighters: The Epic of the Warsaw Ghetto* (New York: Praeger, 1954), 199.

131. Chaim Lazar, *Muranowska 7: The Warsaw Ghetto Rising* (Tel Aviv: Massada Press, 1966).

132. Ringelblum, *Polish-Jewish Relations*, 158.

133. Yisrael Gutman, "The Attitude of the Poles to the Mass Deportations of Jews from the Warsaw Ghetto in the Summer of 1942," in *Rescue Attempts during the Holocaust: Proceedings of the Second Yad Vashem International Historical Conference,* eds. Yisrael Gutman and Efraim Zuroff (Jerusalem: Yad Vashem, 1977), 403-409.

134. Postscript by Joseph Kermish in Ringelblum, *Polish-Jewish Relations*, 278-283.

135. *Journal of Emmanuel Ringelblum*, 319-320.

136. Zylberberg, 57.

137. *Journal of Emmanuel Ringelblum*, 310.

138. Ibid., 327.

139. Karski, 330-333.

140. Ibid., 336.

141. Ringelblum, *Polish-Jewish Relations*, 250-251.

142. Borzykowski, 22-30.

143. Lazar, 187.

144. S. Krakowski, "The Slaughter of Polish Jewry: A Polish 'Reassessment,' " *Wiener Library Bulletin* XXVI, no. 3-4 (1972-1973): 13-19.

145. Reuben Ainsztein, "New Light on Szmuel Zygelbojm's Suicide," *Yad Vashem Bulletin* XV (August 1964): 8–12.

146. Lucy S. Dawidowicz, *The War against the Jews, 1933–1945* (New York: Holt, Rinehart, and Winston, 1975), 316. Johnpoll, p. 258, translates this passage slightly differently, but the substance of the message is the same.

147. Ringelblum, *Polish-Jewish Relations,* 184.

148. Donat, 152–153.

149. The highest estimate is that of Goldstein, p. 217, and the lowest is a German estimate reported by Raul Hilberg, *The Destruction of the European Jews* (Chicago: Quadrangle, 1967), 327.

150. W. Bartoszewski and Z. Lewin, eds., *Righteous among Nations: How the Poles Helped the Jews, 1939–1945* (London: Swiderski, 1969); Joseph Kermish, "The Activities of the Council for Aid to Jews ('Zegota') in Occupied Poland," in *Rescue Attempts during the Holocaust: Proceedings of the Second Yad Vashem International Historical Conference,* eds. Yisrael Gutman and Efraim Zuroff (Jerusalem: Yad Vashem, 1977), 367–368.

151. Krakowski, 19; S. Krakowski, "Policy of the Third Reich in Conquered Poland," *Yad Vashem Studies* IX (1973): 243–244; Kermish, "Activities of the Council," 373–374, 384–385.

152. Meed, *passim.* Similar recollections are reported by Donat (pp. 109–110) and Ringelblum, *Polish-Jewish Relations* (pp. 100–139).

153. Kermish, "Activities of the Council," 380–381.

154. Ringelblum, *Polish-Jewish Relations,* 214.

155. Henry Feingold, *The Politics of Rescue: The Roosevelt Administration and the Holocaust, 1938–1945* (New Brunswick, N.J.: Rutgers University Press, 1970), 226.

156. Yitzhak Katznelson, *Vittel Diary* (22.5.43–16.9.43), trans. Meyer Cohen (Israel: Beit Lohamei Hagettaot, 1972), 31.

157. Kermish, "Activities of the Council," 383.

158. Ringelblum, *Polish-Jewish Relations,* 217–221, see especially his note 35, p. 219, regarding the authorization for the extermination of the Jewish survivors in the forests. "On 15 September 1943, General Bor-Komorowski, Commander-in-Chief of the Home Army, issued Order no. 116 to the units under his command directing them to take active measures against the Jews in the forests."

159. These figures are based on a systemactic 3% sample of registrations of Jews in Poland; see the source notes to Table 3-1 of this volume for an extended description of the Polish sample study.

160. However, according to Kermish, "Activities of the Council," 376, official Polish sources indicated that there were "about 600 Jewish children in various institutions in Warsaw and its environs by the end of 1943 . . . and over 500 in public and ecclesiastical institutions." This number probably includes older children and younger teenagers, so that we cannot infer with any certainty how many evaders out of this age cohort were caught or turned over to German authorities. Kermish also notes (p. 462) that there was some difficulty obtaining the release of

Jewish children hidden in monasteries who had passed as Christians since some of their protectors tried to convert them, prompting the formation of a coordinated Jewish search agency to extricate these youngsters after the war. Thus, whereas the number of Jewish adults surviving may be overestimated because of multiple registrations, the number of children surviving may be underestimated because of underregistration.

NOTES TO CHAPTER 10

1. Norman Rich, *Hitler's War Aims, II: The Establishment of the New Order* (New York: Norton, 1974): 142–143.

2. Anne Frank, *The Diary of a Young Girl*, trans. B. M. Mooyaart-Doubleday (New York: Modern Library, 1952); Philip Mechanicus, *Year of Fear*, trans. Irene S. Gibbons (New York: Hawthorn, 1968).

3. Gertrude van Tijn, "Contributions to the History of the Jews in the Netherlands from May 10, 1940 to June, 1944," mimeographed (Jerusalem: Joint Distribution Committee, 1945).

4. Jacob Presser, *The Destruction of the Dutch Jews*, trans. Arnold Pomerans (New York: Dutton, 1969), and *The Breaking Point*, trans. Burrows Mussey (Cleveland: World, 1958).

5. Marga Minco, *Bitter Herbs*, trans. Roy Edwards (New York: Oxford University Press, 1960).

6. Elie A. Cohen, *The Abyss: A Confession*, trans. James Brockway (New York: Norton, 1973).

7. Werner Warmbrunn, *The Dutch under the German Occupation, 1940–1945* (New York: Oxford University Press, 1963); Henry L. Mason, *The Purge of the Dutch Quislings: Emergency Justice in the Netherlands* (The Hague: Nijhoff, 1952), and *Mass Demonstrations against Foreign Regimes: A Study of Five Crises* (New Orleans: Tulane University Press, 1966). Louis de Jong's work published in English cited herein includes "Jews and Non-Jews in Nazi Occupied Holland," in *On the Track of Tyranny*, ed. Max Beloff (London: Wiener Library, 1960), "Help to People in Hiding," *Delta* VIII, no. 1 (Spring 1965): 37–79, and "The Netherlands and Auschwitz: Why Were the Reports of Mass Killings So Widely Disbelieved?", in *Imposed Jewish Governing Bodies under Nazi Rule* (New York: YIVO, 1972).

8. Speech of 30 January 1939 to the Reichstag (quoted on p. 24 of this volume).

9. Cohen, 18.

10. Ibid., 19.

11. Ibid., 25.

12. Presser, *Destruction of the Dutch Jews*, 9; van Tijn, 5; Warmbrunn, 166, 302.

13. Presser, *Destruction of the Dutch Jews*, 10.

14. United States Military Tribunal, "Documents: Staff Evidence Analysis," NOKW–1515, unnumbered volumes of documents found in Columbia University International Law Library and other repositories.

15. Cohen, 26.

16. These instructions are reproduced (with comments) by Mason, *Purge of the Dutch Quislings*, 36.

   "As the enemy cannot be expected to know Dutch law, he cannot obey the obligations of international law without the cooperation of Dutch officials. If these officials would refuse to collaborate, the enemy would be forced to decide essential matters according to his own judgment."

   Civil servants were ordered to resign in two cases [if] "by remaining in function, such services would be rendered to the enemy, that the advantage to him would be greater than the benefits to the Dutch population, resulting from non-resignation [or] when the enemy makes it impossible for them to fulfill their task in the interests of the population, and in a way which still permits loyalty to the country."

17. Warmbrunn, 31-32.

18. Ibid., 265.

19. De Jong, "Help to People in Hiding," 43.

20. Ibid.

21. Ibid., 44.

22. Letters from de Jong to author, 9 September and 3 October 1974.

23. Presser, *Destruction of the Dutch Jews*, 158-159.

24. Ibid., 58.

25. Cohen, 29.

26. U.S. Military Tribunal, "Documents: Staff Evidence Analysis," NG-2480.

27. Warmbrunn, 107.

28. Ibid.

29. There are slight differences between German sources as to the number sent to Mauthausen initially. Raul Hilberg, *The Destruction of the European Jews* (Chicago: Quadrangle, 1967), 373, cites documents noting 425 were sent; Warmbrunn, 373, cites another listing 430.

30. Mason, *Mass Demonstrations against Foreign Regimes*, 35.

31. Ibid., 76.

32. Joseph Michman, "The Controversial Stand of the *Joodse Raad* in the Netherlands," *Yad Vashem Studies* X (1974): 56.

33. Ibid., 59-60.

34. Ibid., 65-66.

35. Van Tijn, 11, 22, 44.

36. Minco, 13.

37. United Nations, *The Inter-Allied Review* II (15 December 1942): 333-334.

38. U.S. Military Tribunal, "Documents: Staff Evidence Analysis," NG-2631.

39. De Jong, "The Netherlands and Auschwitz," 21-22.

40. B. A. Sijes, "Several Observations Concerning the Position of the Jews in Occupied Holland during World War II," in *Rescue Attempts during the Holocaust: Proceedings of the Second Yad Vashem International Historical Conference*, eds. Yisrael Gutman and Efraim Zuroff (Jerusalem: Yad Vashem, 1977), 545.

41. Cohen, 72.

42. Ibid., 68.

43. Minco, 36.

44. Ibid., 44–46.

45. Ibid., 58–59.

46. Ibid., 77.

47. Ibid., 90.

48. Frank, 14.

49. Presser, *Destruction of the Dutch Jews,* 387–403.

50. Cohen, 102.

51. Van Tijn, 45–46.

52. Ibid., 54: also quoted by Presser, *Destruction of the Dutch Jews,* 167.

53. Presser, *Destruction of the Dutch Jews,* 141.

54. Thomas Hobbes, "Of the Natural Condition of Mankind," in *Theories of Society: Foundations of Modern Sociological Theory,* ed. Talcott Parsons et al. (New York: The Free Press, 1971), I:100.

55. De Jong, "The Netherlands and Auschwitz," 13.

56. Van Tijn, 83–84.

57. Presser, *Breaking Point,* 29–32.

58. Mechanicus, 33.

59. Ibid., 77–79.

60. Ibid., 96.

61. Ibid., 112–113.

62. Cohen, 64–65.

63. U.S. Military Tribunal, "Documents: Staff Evidence Analysis," NG–2631.

64. Johan M. Snoek, *The Greybook: A Collection of Protests against Anti-Semitism and the Persecution of Jews Issued by Non-Roman Catholic Churches and Church Leaders during Hitler's Rule.* (The Hague: Van Gorcum, 1969), 128.

65. U.S. Military Tribunal, "Documents: Staff Evidence Analysis," NG–2631.

66. Snoek, 129–130.

67. Ibid., 130–131.

68. U.S. Military Tribunal, "Documents: Staff Evidence Analysis," NG–2631.

69. De Jong, "Help to People in Hiding," 49–50.

70. Ibid., 69.

71. De Jong, "Jews and Non-Jews in Nazi Occupied Holland," 139–155.

72. Ibid., 152.

73. Cohen, 27.

74. Mason, *Purge of the Dutch Quislings,* 46.

75. Ibid., 435.

76. John Andenaes, O. Riste, and M. Skodvin, *Norway and the Second World War* (Oslo: Johan Grund Tanum Forlag, 1966); Bjarne Hoye and Trygve M. Ager, *The Fight of the Norwegian Church against Nazism* (New York: Macmillan, 1943).

77. Mason, *Purge of the Dutch Quislings,* 40.

78. Official government figures confirmed in a personal letter from de Jong, 4 November 1974.

79. International Military Tribunal, *Trials of Major War Criminals* XXXIII: 232 (PS-3846).

NOTES FOR CHAPTER 11

1. *The Diary of Eva Heyman,* introduction and notes by Judah Marton, trans. Moshe M. Kohn (Jerusalem: Yad Vashem, 1974); Eli Wiesel, *Night,* trans. Stella Rodway (New York: Hill and Wang, 1966).

2. Nicholas M. Nagy-Talavera, *The Green-Shirts and the Others: A History of Fascism in Hungary and Rumania* (Stanford, Ca.: Hoover Institution Press, 1970), 68.

3. Randolph L. Braham, "The Role of the Jewish Council in Hungary: A Tentative Assessment," *Yad Vashem Studies* X (1974): 71-72.

4. Samu [Samuel] Stern, " 'A Race with Time': A Statement," *Hungarian-Jewish Studies* III (1973): 8.

5. Contradictory accounts of these negotiations, based partly on the testimony of participants in the Brand mission and in Kastner's later negotiations, are contained in Alex Weissberg, *Desperate Mission: Joel Brand's Story as Told by Alex Weissberg,* trans. Constantine Fitzgibbon and Andrew Foster Melliar (New York: Criterion, 1958), and the memoir of Andreas Biss, *A Million Jews to Save* (South Brunswick, N.J.: Barnes, 1975); see also note 6 below. There is also the postwar testimony of Rudolph Kastner, *Der Bericht des judischen Rettungskomitees aus Budapest, 1942-1945* (Basel: Vaadath Ezra Vehazalah de Budapest, 1946), which should be read in conjunction with the insightful paper of Randolph L. Braham, "What Did They Know and When?" (address presented to the International Scholars Conference on the Holocaust—A Generation After, New York City, March 1975).

6. Bela Vago, "The Intelligence Aspects of the Joel Brand Mission," *Yad Vashem Studies* X (1974): 111-128.

7. Yeduha Bauer, "The Activities of the J.D.C. in Europe during World War II," paper prepared at the Institute for Contemporary Jewry Division of Holocaust Studies, Hebrew University, Jerusalem (n.d.), 8; Raul Hilberg, *The Destruction of the European Jews* (Chicago: Quadrangle, 1967), 543-544, gives a slightly different sequence of events, based on Kastner's *Bericht.* Kastner's testimony in his memoir (which naturally tends to exonerate him) should be related to the Jerusalem court findings and preliminary cross-examination (see note 8 below).

8. The record and testimony of this trial are in Hebrew; the only source available for the English reader is the reporting and citation of judgments in the *Jerusalem Post* between 1954 and 1958. Judge Halevi's original decision and the arguments of the Supreme Court judges reviewing the case are cited in the *Jerusalem Post* of 23 June 1955 and 21 January 1958, respectively.

9. Ernö László, "Hungary's Jewry: A Demographic Overview, 1918-1945," *Hungarian-Jewish Studies* II (1969): 165.

10. Randolph L. Braham, *The Destruction of Hungarian Jewry: A Documentary Account* (New York: World Federation of Hungarian Jews, 1963), II:968.

11. László, 166.

12. *Diary of Eva Heyman*, 23.

13. Ibid., 25.

14. Ibid., 31.

15. Randolph L. Braham, "The Holocaust in Hungary: A Historical Interpretation of the Role of the Hungarian Radical Right," *Societas* II, no. 3 (June 1972): 197.

16. *Diary of Eva Heyman*, 48-51.

17. Wiesel, 17.

18. Ibid., 18.

19. *Diary of Eva Heyman*, 58-59.

20. Ibid., 62.

21. Ibid., 63.

22. Ibid., 65.

23. Ibid., 66-67.

24. Ibid., 71.

25. Ibid., 64.

26. Ibid., 71-73.

27. Ibid., 75.

28. Ibid.

29. Ibid., 76-77.

30. Ibid., 78-79.

31. Ibid., 79-80.

32. Ibid., 82.

33. Ibid.

34. Ibid., 84-85.

35. Ibid., 88.

36. Ibid., 89.

37. Ibid., 96-97.

38. Ibid., 97-99.

39. Ibid., 100.

40. Ibid., 102.

41. Ibid., 103.

42. Ibid., 104.

43. Ibid., 19-20.

44. Ibid., 14.

45. Ibid., 113-114.

46. Wiesel, 20.

47. Ibid., 21-22.

48. Ibid., 22.

49. Ibid., 23.

50. Ibid., 24.

51. Ibid., 25.

52. Ibid., 26.

53. Ibid., 27.

54. Ibid., 29.

55. Ibid., 31.

56. Ibid., 31-32.

57. Ibid., 32.

58. Ibid., 32-33.

59. YIVO, Archives, File no. 768, Protocol no. 3618, testimony of Leopold Low.

60. Braham, *Destruction of Hungarian Jewry*, I: lxxvii.

61. Jëno Levai, *Black Book on the Martyrdom of Hungarian Jewry*, ed. Lawrence P. Davis (Zurich: Central European Times, 1948), 178-181; Bernhard Klein, "Hungarian Jewry in the Nazi Period" (Masters thesis, Columbia University, 1955), 86-87; Ernö [Ernest] Petö, "Statement," *Hungarian-Jewish Studies* III (1973): 49-74.

62. See Chapter 4, 109-110, on the refusal of the Pope to intervene at that time, also.

63. László, 165; Sabina Manuila and W. Filderman, "Regional Development of the Jewish Population in Rumania," *Genus* XIII (1957): 160.

NOTES FOR CHAPTER 12

1. Herman Kruk, "Diary of the Vilna Ghetto," *YIVO Annual of Jewish Social Science* XIII (1965): 36.

2. Their response, evident in the decision in July 1942 to abstain from collective resistance (discussed in Chapter 9), was confirmed in discussions with Yisrael Gutman (an activist in Warsaw) and Abba Kovner in Jerusalem in August 1974. I am grateful for their insights and cooperation.

3. Saul Friedlander, *Kurt Gerstein: The Ambiguity of Good*, trans. Charles Fullman (New York: Knopf, 1969).

4. Louis de Jong, "The Netherlands and Auschwitz: Why Were the Reports of Mass Killings So Widely Disbelieved?", in *Imposed Jewish Governing Bodies under Nazi Rule* (New York: YIVO, 1972), 27-28.

5. Claus Bahne Bahnson, "Emotional Reactions to Internally and Externally Derived Threat of Annihilation," in *The Threat of Impending Disaster: Contributions to the Psychology of Stress*, ed. George H. Grosser et al. (Cambridge, Ma.. MIT Press, 1964).

6. Irving L. Janis, "Psychological Effects of Warnings," and Stephen B. Withey, "Reaction to Uncertain Threat," both in *Man and Society in Disaster*, eds. George W. Baker and Dwight W. Chapman (New York: Basic Books, 1962); Martha Wolfenstein, *Disaster: A Psychological Essay* (New York: The Free Press and Falcon's Wing Press, 1957).

7. Kurt Lang and Gladys Engel Lang, "Collective Responses to the Threat of Disaster," in *The Threat of Impending Disaster: Contributions to the Psychology of Stress*, ed. George W. Baker and Dwight W. Chapman (New York: Basic Books, 1962), 70.

8. Eli Wiesel, "Eichmann's Victims and the Unheard Testimony." *Commentary* XXXII (December 1961): 515.

9. Remark by Jakob Gutfriend, recorded in *Jewish Resistance during the Holocaust*, Proceedings of the Conference on Manifestations of Jewish Resistance, 7–11 April 1968 (Jerusalem: Yad Vashem, 1971), 253.

10. Pitirim A. Sorokin, *Man and Society in Calamity* (New York: Dutton, 1943), ch. 3.

11. Kovner has publicly credited his diagnosis of a general plan to information secured from a German soldier, Anton Schmidt, who helped the Jewish resistance in Vilna. Kovner asked him at what level of the military hierarchy were massacres of Jews authorized. Schmidt told Kovner that they were planned and directed from Berlin and that Eichmann was operationally responsible for the execution of the plan throughout Europe. Kovner's remarks were made in March 1975 in New York City at the International Scholars Conference on the Holocaust — A Generation After.

12. Henri Michel, *The Shadow War: European Resistance, 1939–1945*, trans. Richard Barry (New York: Harper and Row, 1972), 334.

13. Bahnson, 258.

14. Yitzhak Arad, "Concentration of Refugees in Vilna on the Eve of the Holocaust," *Yad Vashem Studies* IX (1973): 201–214: Leni Yahil, *The Rescue of Danish Jewry: Test of a Democracy*, trans. Morris Gradel (Philadelphia: Jewish Publication Society of America, 1969), 203–207; Jacob Presser, *The Destruction of the Dutch Jews*, trans. Arnold Pomerans (New York: Dutton, 1969), 282; Amy Latour, *La Résistance Juive en France, 1940–1944* (Paris: Stock, 1970), 84–87; Haim Avni, "The Zionist Underground in Holland and France and the Escape to Spain," in *Rescue Attempts during the Holocaust: Proceedings of the Second Yad Vashem International Historical Conference*, eds. Yisrael Gutman and Efraim Zuroff (Jerusalem: Yad Vashem, 1977), 555–591.

15. Rudolph Kastner, *Der Bericht des judischen Rettungskomitees aus Budapest, 1942–1945* (Basel: Vaadath Ezra Vehazalah be Budapest, 1946); Randolph L. Braham, "What Did They Know and When?" (address presented to the International Scholars Conference on the Holocaust — A Generation After, March 1975, New York City); Alex Weissberg, *Desperate Mission: Joel Brand's Story as Told by Alex Weissberg*, trans. Constantine Fitzgibbon and Andrew Foster-Melliar (New York: Criterion, 1958).

16. Bela Vago, "Jewish Leadership Groups in Hungary and Rumania during the Holocaust" (address presented to the International Scholars Conference on the Holocaust — A Generation After, New York City, March 1975).

17. Perhaps paradoxically, these low anti-Semitic states are nations whose Jewish community was not likely to have produced a collectivity oriented leadership because of the community's size, its socioeconomic status, and its integration with the national community. These communities, although assimilated as are other Jewish

communities in high anti-Semitic states that produced non–collectivity-oriented leaderships (Germany, Hungary), are distinguished from the latter by their integration within the national community, implying both an ideological acceptance of their equality and minimal social distance between Jews and Gentiles in the varied walks of life.

18. Erilainen Kuin Muut, "Lahettiko Valpo Juutalaisia Keskitys-Leireihin?", *Uusi Maailma*, 23 October 1964, reports on the persistent activities of Abraham Stiller, head of the Finnish Jewish community, to liberate the Jewish refugees, held on alleged criminal charges, who were scheduled to be deported to Germany. I am grateful to Lena Alfonso-Karkala for her translation from the Finnish. See pp. 147–148 for responses of leaders of the Danish Jews.

Bibliography

The following bibliography is subdivided so as to be of the greatest usefulness to nonacademic as well as academic readers. Works are classified by their broadest relevance into a topical category and/or a state or area. The latter, of course, relate also to one or more topical categories and the former may refer to more than one state. This scheme is as follows:

THE NAZI HOLOCAUST
AND MODERN JEWRY

Documents from War Crimes Trials

FRIED, JOHN H. E. "Anti-Jewish Legislation in Europe and North Africa Imposed or Inspired by National-Socialist Germany." Memorandum for International Military Tribunal, 1947 (found in YIVO, New York City).

International Military Tribunal. Office of the U.S. Chief Counsel for Prosecution of Axis Criminality. *Nazi Conspiracy and Aggression.* 11 vols. Washington, D.C.: U.S. Government Printing Office, 1946.

_____. *Trials of the Major Criminals before the International Military Tribunal.* 42 vols. Nuremberg: International Military Tribunals, 1947–1949.

MONNERAY, HENRI. *La Persécution des Juifs en France et dans les Autres Pays de l'Ouest.* Paris: Éditions du Centre, 1947.

_____. *La Persécution des Juifs dans les Pays de l'Est.* Paris: Éditions du Centre, 1949.

ROBINSON, JACOB, and SACHS, HENRY. *The Holocaust: The Nuremberg Evidence, Part One.* Jerusalem: Yad Vashem, 1976. (The prepublication index prepared at YIVO, New York City, was made available to the author by Robinson and Sachs.)

Trial of Adolph Eichmann. "Minutes of the Trial: Official Translation into English" (unrevised). Jerusalem, 1961. Recorded on microfilm and mimeographed.

U.S. Military Tribunal. "Documents: Staff Evidence Analysis." Unnumbered volumes of mimeographed evidence. (Found in Columbia University International Law Library and other document repositories.)

_____. "Transcripts of Trials of War Criminals before the Nuremberg Military Tribunal." Case VIII, in first volume of mimeographed papers (n.d.). (Found in Columbia University International Law Library and other document repositories.)

_____. *Trials of War Criminals before the Nuremberg Military Tribunals. Cases I–XII.* 15 vols. Washington, D.C.: U.S. Government Printing Office, 1951–1952.

Statistics and Indicators—Demographic and Historical

American Jewish Committee. *American Jewish Yearbook.* Vols. XXXII–XLVIII. New York: American Jewish Committee, 1931–1947.

BANKS, ARTHUR S. *Cross-Polity Time-Series Data.* Cambridge, Ma.: MIT Press, 1971.

Blackbook of Localities Whose Jewish Population Was Exterminated by the Nazis. Jerusalem: Yad Vashem, 1965.

HALEVI, H. S. *The Influence of World War II on the Demographic Structure of the Jewish People.* Jerusalem: Institute of Contemporary Jewry of Hebrew University, 1963 (Hebrew text, English summary).

League of Nations. *Statistical Yearbook of the League of Nations, 1941–1942.* Geneva: League of Nations, 1943.

LIEBERSON, STANLEY; DALTO, GUY; and JOHNSTON, ELLEN. "The Course of Mother-

Tongue Diversity in Nations." *American Journal of Sociology* LXXXI, no. 1 (July 1975): 34–61.

PROUDFOOT, MALCOLM J. *European Refugees, 1939–1952: A Study in Forced Population Movement.* Evanston, Ill.: Northwestern University Press, 1956.

History of Modern Europe, European Jewry, World War II, and the Holocaust

American Jewish Committee. *American Jewish Yearbook.* Vols. XXXI–XLVII. New York: American Jewish Committee, 1930–1946.

ARENDT, HANNAH. *The Origins of Totalitarianism.* Rev. ed. New York: Harcourt, Brace and World, 1966.

ARONSFELD, C. C. "The Nazi Design Was Extermination, Not Emigration." *Patterns of Prejudice.* IX, no. 3 (May–June 1975): 20–24.

BAUER, YEHUDA. "The Jewish Communities of Nazi-Occupied Europe." Mimeographed. New York: Research Institute on Peace and Post-War Problems. 1944.

————. *From Diplomacy to Resistance: A History of Jewish Palestine, 1939–1945.* Philadelphia: Jewish Publication Society of America, 1976.

BAUMINGER, ARIEH L. *Roll of Honour.* Tel Aviv: "Hamenora," 1971.

BROWNING, CHRISTOPHER. *The Final Solution and the German Foreign Office.* New York: Holmes and Meier, 1978.

DAWIDOWICZ, LUCY S. *The War against the Jews, 1933–1945.* New York: Holt, Rinehart, and Winston, 1975.

DWORZECKI, MEIER. "The International Red Cross and Its Policy vis-à-vis the Jews in the Ghettos and Concentration Camps in Nazi-Occupied Europe." In *Rescue Attempts during the Holocaust: Proceedings of the Second Yad Vashem International Historical Conference.* Eds. Yisrael Gutman and Efraim Zuroff. Jerusalem: Yad Vashem, 1977.

Encyclopedia Judaica. 16 vols. Jerusalam: Keter, 1971–72.

EPPLER, ELIZABETH E. "The Rescue Work of the World Jewish Congress during the Nazi Period." In *Rescue Attempts during the Holocaust: Proceedings of the Second Vad Vashem International Historical Conference.* Eds. Yisrael Gutman and Efraim Zuroff. Jerusalem: Yad Vashem, 1977.

FRIEDMAN, PHILIP. *Their Brothers' Keepers: The Christian Heroes and Heroines Who Helped the Oppressed Escape the Nazi Terror.* New York: Crown, 1957.

GASTER, THEODORE H. *Festivals of the Jewish Year.* New York: Morrow, 1952.

HAUSNER, GIDEON. *Justice in Jerusalem.* New York: Harper and Row, 1966.

HILBERG, RAUL. *The Destruction of the European Jews.* Chicago: Quadrangle, 1967.

HOETTL, WILHELM [pseud. Walter Hagen]. *The Secret Front.* London: Weidenfeld and Nicolson, 1953.

HOMZE, EDWARD L. *Foreign Labor in Nazi Germany.* Princeton, N.J.: Princeton University Press, 1966.

Jewish Resistance during the Holocaust. Proceedings of the Conference on Manifestations of Jewish Resistance, 7–11 April 1968. Jerusalem: Yad Vashem, 1971.

KERSTEN, FELIX. *The Memoirs of Doctor Felix Kersten.* Ed. Herma Briffault. Trans. Ernest Morwitz. New York: Doubleday, 1947.

KLUGER, RUTH, and MANN, PEGGY. *The Last Escape.* Garden City, N.Y.: Doubleday, 1973.

LEMKIN, RAPHAEL. *Axis Rule in Occupied Europe.* Washington, D.C.: Carnegie Endowment International Peace, 1944.

LITTLEJOHN, DAVID. *The Patriotic Traitors: A History of Collaboration in Europe, 1940-1945.* London: Heinemann, 1971.

MICHEL, HENRI. *The Shadow War: European Resistance, 1939-1945.* Trans. Richard Barry. New York: Harper and Row, 1972.

NOLTE, ERNEST. *Three Faces of Fascism: Action Française, Italian Fascism, National Socialism.* Trans. Leila Vennewitz. London: Weidenfeld and Nicolson, 1965.

POLIAKOV, LEON. *Harvest of Hate.* Westport, Conn.: Greenwood, 1954.

REITLINGER, GERALD. *The Final Solution: The Attempt to Exterminate the Jews of Europe, 1939-1945.* 2d rev. and enlarged ed. South Brunswick, N.J.: Yoseloff, 1961.

RICH, NORMAN. *Hitler's War Aims.* II: *The Establishment of the New Order.* New York: Norton, 1974.

SACHER, HOWARD MORLEY. *The Course of Modern Jewish History.* New York: Dell, 1958.

STEINBERG, LUCIEN. *Not as a Lamb: The Jews against Hitler.* Trans. Marion Hunter. Farnsborough, England: Saxon House, 1974.

Torah: The Five Books of Moses, The. A New Translation according to the Masoretic Text. Philadelphia: Jewish Publication Society of America, 1962.

Universal Jewish Encyclopedia. Ed. Isaac Landman. 10 vols. New York: The Universal Jewish Encyclopedia, Inc., 1939-1943.

WISCHNITZER, MARK. *To Dwell in Safety: The Story of Jewish Migration since 1800.* Philadelphia: Jewish Publication Society of America, 1949.

YAHIL, LENI. "Madagascar: Phantom of a Solution for the Jewish Question." In *Jews and Non-Jews in Eastern Europe, 1918-1945.* Eds. Bela Vago and George L. Mosse. New York: Wiley, 1974.

GENOCIDE: CAUSES, EFFECTS, PROCESSES, SYMPTOMS, AND RESPONSES

Anti-Semitism

COHEN, NORMAN. *Warrant for Genocide: The Myth of the Jewish World-Conspiracy and the Protocols of the Elders of Zion.* New York: Harper Torchbooks, Harper and Row, 1969.

DAWIDOWICZ, LUCY S. *The War against the Jews, 1933-1945.* New York: Holt, Rinehart, and Winston, 1975.

ISAAC, JULES. *The Teaching of Contempt: Christian Roots of Anti-Semitism.* Trans. Helen Weaver. New York: Holt, Rinehart, and Winston, 1964.

MASSING, PAUL W. *Rehearsal for Destruction: A Study of Political Anti-Semitism in Imperial Germany.* New York: Fertig, 1967.

MOSSE, GEORGE L. *The Crisis of German Ideology: Intellectual Origins of the Third Reich.* New York: Universal Library, Grosset and Dunlap, 1964.

PULZER, PETER G. J. *The Rise of Political Anti-Semitism in Germany and Austria.* New York: Wiley, 1964.

RUETHER, ROSEMARY. *Faith and Fratricide.* New York: Seabury, 1974.

SCHORSCH, ISMAR. "German Anti-Semitism in the Light of Postwar Historiography." *Leo Baeck Institute Yearbook,* XIX (1974): 257-271.

Churches' Response (Including the Vatican) to the Holocaust

BÉDARIDA, FRANÇOIS, and BÉDARIDA, RENEÈ. "Aux Origines du Témoignage Chrétien 1941-1942)." *Revue d'Histoire de la Deuxième Guerre Mondiale* LXI (1966): 1-66.

BENTLEY, ERICH, ed. *The Storm over the Deputy.* New York: Grove Press, 1964.

BÉRARD, LÉO. "Pope Pius XII and the Jews" (Bérard letter of 1941, trans. with comment Abraham G. Duker). *Jewish Spectator,* February 1964, 13-17.

BINCHY, DANIEL A. *Church and State in Fascist Italy.* New York: Oxford University Press, 1970.

BOKUN, BRANKO. *Spy in the Vatican, 1941–1945.* New York: Praeger, 1973.

BOSWORTH, WILLIAM. *Catholicism and Crisis in Modern France.* Princeton, N.J.: Princeton University Press, 1962.

Cahiers Clandestins du Témoignage Chrétien. Paris: Éditions du Témoignage Chrétien, 1946.

CAVALLI, FR. FIORELLO, S.J. "La Sante Sede contro le Deportazioni degli Ebrei dalla Slovacchia durante la Seconda Guerra Mondiale." *La Civiltà Cattolica,* 1 July 1961, 3-18.

DUQUESNE, JACQUES. *Les Catholiques Français sous l'Occupation.* Paris: Grasset, 1966.

FALCONI, CARLO. *The Silence of Pius XII.* Trans. Bernard Wall. Boston: Little, Brown, 1970.

FRIEDLANDER, SAUL. *Pius XII and the Third Reich: A Documentation.* Trans. Charles Fullman. New York: Knopf, 1966.

GRAHAM, ROBERT A., S.J. "The Holy See and the Victims of the War." *L'Osservatore Romano,* 13 June 1974, 6-9.

_____. "The Human Being in the Tragic Tornado of War Necessities." *L'Osservatore Romano,* 12 February 1976, 6-9.

HOCHHUTH, ROLF. *The Deputy.* New York: Grove Press, 1964.

HOYE, BJARNE, and AGER, TRYGVE M. *The Fight of the Norwegian Church against Nazism.* New York: Macmillan, 1943.

LAVI, THEODOR. "The Vatican's Endeavors on Behalf of Rumanian Jewry during the Second World War." *Yad Vashem Studies* V (1963): 405-419.

_____. "The Background to the Rescue of Rumanian Jewry during the Period of the

Holocaust." In *Jews and Non-Jews in Eastern Europe, 1918–1945*. Eds. Bela Vago and George L. Mosse. New York: Wiley, 1974.

LeClef, Chanoine. *Le Cardinal Van Roey et l'Occupation Allemande en Belgique*. Brussels: Goemare, 1945.

Levai, Jeno. *Hungarian Jewry and the Papacy: Pope Pius XII Did Not Remain Silent*. London: Sands, 1967.

Lewy, Günter. *The Catholic Church and Nazi Germany*. New York: McGraw-Hill, 1964.

Littel, Franklin H. "Church Struggle and the Holocaust." In *The German Church Struggle and the Holocaust*. Eds. Franklin H. Littell and Hubert G. Locke. Detriot, Mi.: Wayne State University Press, 1974.

Lowrie, Donald. "Chambon-Sur-Lignon." In *Anthology of Holocaust Literature*. Ed. Jacob Glatstein et al. Philadelphia: Jewish Publication Society of America, 1968.

Paris, Edmond. *Genocide in Satellite Croatia, 1941–1945*. Trans. Lois Perkins. Chicago: American Institute of Balkan Affairs, n.d. [c. 1960].

Pattee, Richard. *The Case of Cardinal Aloysius Stepinac*. Milwaukee, Wi.: Bruce, 1953.

Pierrard, Pierre. *Juifs et Catholiques Français*. Paris: Fayard, 1970.

Rotkirchen, Livia. "Vatican Policy and the 'Jewish Problem' in 'Independent' Slovakia." *Yad Vashem Studies* VI (1967): 27-51.

Schneider, Burkhart, S.J. "The Holy See and the Victims of the War." *L'Osservatore Romano*, 19 February 1976, 6-11.

Sereny, Gitta. *Into That Darkness: From Mercy Killing to Mass Murder*. New York: McGraw-Hill, 1974.

Snoek, Johan M. *The Greybook: A Collection of Protests against Anti-Semitism and the Persecution of Jews Issued by Non–Roman Catholic Churches and Church Leaders during Hitler's Rule*. The Hague: Van Gorcum, 1969.

Szajkowski, Xosa. *Analytical Franco-Jewish Gazetteer, 1939–1945*. New York: Frydmann, 1966.

Vatican, Secretariat de Status. *Actes et Documents du Saint-Siège Relatifs à la Seconde Guerre Mondiale*, VIII and IX, Liberia Editrica Vaticani, Ed. Pierre Blet et al. Vatican City: 1974 and 1975.

Waagenar, Sam. *The Pope's Jews*. La Salle, Ill.: Library Press, 1974.

War Refugee Board. Unpublished documents relating to Hungary (boxes 18 and 35). Franklin D. Roosevelt Memorial Library, Hyde Park, N.Y. See also United States War Refugee Board under United States section, this Bibliography.

Zahn, Gordon, *German Catholics and Hitler's Wars: A Study in Social Control*. New York: Sheed and Ward, 1962.

German Genocide (Other Than of Jews) and Other Categorical Murders

Kenrick, Donald, and Puxon, Grattan. *The Destiny of Europe's Gypsies*. New York: Basic Books, 1972.

SERENY, GITTA, *Into That Darkness: From Mercy Killing to Mass Murder*. New York: McGraw-Hill, 1974.

WERTHAM, FREDERIC. *A Sign for Cain*. New York: Macmillan, 1966.

Holocaust Historiography and Interpretations

ARONSFELD, C. C. "A Propos of a British 'Historical Review': Facts of the Holocaust." *Patterns of Prejudice* VIII, no. 4 (July-August 1974): 11-16.

FRIEDLANDER, HENRY. "Publications of the Holocaust." In *The German Church Struggle and the Holocaust*. Eds. Franklin H. Littel and Hubert G. Locke. Detroit, Mi.: Wayne State University Press, 1974.

KORMAN, GERD. "The Holocaust in American Historical Writing." *Societas*, II, no. 3 (June 1972): 251-270.

SHILOH, AILON. "Psychological Anthropology: A Case Study in Culture Blindness?" *Current Anthropology*, December 1975, 618-620.

Judenräte, Jewish Councils, and Jewish Control Agents

ADLER, M. G. *Theresienstadt, 1941-1945*. Tübingen: Mohr, 1955.

———. *Der Verwaltete Mensch: Studien zur Deportation der Juden aus Deutschland*. Tübingen: Mohr, 1974.

ARENDT, HANNAH. *Eichmann in Jerusalem: A Report on the Banality of Evil*. New York: Viking, 1963.

BAECK, LEO. "A People Stands before Its God." In *We Survived: The Stories of Fourteen of the Hidden and Hunted of Nazi Germany as Told to Eric H. Boehm*. Ed. Eric H. Boehm. New Haven, Conn.: Yale University Press, 1949.

BEEM, HARTOG. "The Jewish Council (*Judenrat*) of the Province of Vriesland (Holland)." *Yad Vashem Bulletin* XVII (December 1965): 21-23.

BILLIG, JOSEPH. *Le Commissariat Général aux Questions Juives*, I. Paris: Éditions du Centre, 1955.

BLOOM, SOLOMON F. "Toward the Ghetto Dictator." *Jewish Social Studies* XII (January 1950): 73-78.

BRAHAM, RANDOLPH L. "The Role of the Jewish Council in Hungary: A Tentative Assessment." *Yad Vashem Studies* X (1974), 69-110.

———. "What Did They Know and When?" Address presented to the International Scholars Conference on the Holocaust—A Generation After. New York City, March 1975.

ECK, NATHAN. "New Light on the Charges against the Last Chief Rabbi of Salonica." *Yad Vashem Bulletin* XIX (October 1966): 28-35.

Federation of Jewish Communities of Yugoslavia. *The Crimes of the Fascist Occupants and Their Collaborators against Jews in Yugoslavia*. Belgrade: ISJOJ, 1957 (Serbo-Croat text, English summary).

FREUDINGER, FÜLÖP [PHILIP] et al. "Report on Hungary: March 19-August 9, 1944." *Hungarian-Jewish Studies* III (1973): 75-146.

FRIEDMAN, PHILIP. "The Jewish Ghettos of the Nazi Era." *Jewish Social Studies* XVI (1954): 61-88.

_____. "Aspects of Jewish Communal Crisis in the Period of the Nazi Regime in Germany, Austria, and Czechoslovakia." In *Essays of Jewish Life and Thought.* Ed. B. Blau. New York: Columbia University Press, 1959.

GRINGAUZ, SAMUEL. "The Ghetto as an Experiment of Jewish Social Organization (Three Years of Kovno Ghetto)." *Jewish Social Studies* XI, no. 1 (January 1949): 3-20.

HARTGLASS, APOLINARY. "How Did Czerniakow Become Head of the Warsaw *Judenrat?*" *Yad Vashem Bulletin* XV (August 1964): 4-7.

JONG, LOUIS DE. "Jews and Non-Jews in Nazi Occupied Holland," In *On the Track of Tyranny.* Ed. Max Beloff. London: Wiener Library, 1960.

_____. "Help to People in Hiding." *Delta* VIII, no. 1 (Spring 1965): 37-79.

_____. "The Netherlands and Auschwitz: Why Were the Reports of Mass Killings So Widely Disbelieved?" *Imposed Jewish Governing Bodies under Nazi Rules.* New York: YIVO, 1972.

KLEIN, BERHARD. "Hungarian Jewry in the Nazi Period." Masters thesis, Columbia University, 1955.

LÉVY, CLAUDE, and TILLARD, PAUL. *Betrayal at the Vel d'Hiv.* Trans. Inea Bushnaq. New York: Hill and Wang, 1967.

LICHTHEIM, GEORGE. "The Capture and Trial of Adolph Eichmann by Moishe Pearlman." *New York Review of Books* I, no. 3 (26 September 1963): 6.

MICHMAN, JOSEPH. "The Controversial Stand of the *Joodse Raad* in the Netherlands: Lodewijk E. Visser's Struggle." *Yad Vashem Studies* X (1974): 9-68.

MOLHO, MICHAEL. *In Memoriam: Hommage aux Victimes Juives des Nazis en Grèce.* 2d ed. rev. and enlarged by Joseph Nehama. Salonica: Communauté Israélite de Thessalonique, 1973.

PÉTO, ERNÖ. "Statement." *Hungarian-Jewish Studies* III (1973): 49-74.

POLIAKOV, LEON. "Jewish Resistance in France, 1: Passive Resistance—The Union Général des Israélites de France (UGIF)." *YIVO Annual of Jewish Social Science* VIII (1953): 252-257.

PRESSER, JACOB. *The Destruction of the Dutch Jews.* Trans. Arnold Pomerans. New York: Dutton, 1969.

ROBINSON, JACOB. *And the Crooked Shall Be Made Straight: The Eichmann Trial, the Jewish Catastrophe, and Hannah Arendt's Narrative.* New York: Macmillan, 1965.

ROSENKRANTZ, HERBERT. "The Anschluss and the Tragedy of Austrian Jewry, 1938-1945." In *The Jews of Austria: Essays on Their Life, History, and Destruction.* London: Valentine, Mitchell, 1967.

ROTKIRCHEN, LIVIA. *The Destruction of Slovak Jewry.* Jerusalem: Yad Vashem, 1961 (Hebrew text, English summary).

SCHIRMAN, ISRAEL. "La Politique Allemande à l'Égard des Juifs en Belgique, 1940-1944." Ph.D. dissertation, Université Libre de Bruxelles, 1970-1971.

SCHLEUNES, KARL A. *The Twisted Road to Auschwitz: Nazi Policy toward German Jews, 1933-1939.* Urbana, Ill.: University of Illinois Press, 1970.

STEINBERG, LUCIEN. *Le Comité de Défense des Juifs en Belgique, 1942-1944.* Brussels: Éditions de l'Université de Bruxelles, 1973.

STERN, SAMU [SAMUEL]. "A Race with Time: A Statement." *Hungarian-Jewish Studies* III (1973): 1-48.

SZAJKOWSKI, XOSA. *Analytical Franco-Jewish Gazetteer, 1939-1945.* New York: Frydmann, 1966.

TAUBES, ISRAEL. "The Jewish Council of Amsterdam." *Yad Vashem Bulletin* XVII (December 1965): 253.

TIJN, GERTRUDE VAN. "Contributions to the History of the Jews in the Netherlands from May 10, 1940 to June 1944." Mimeographed report. Joint Distribution Committee, Jerusalem, 1945.

TRUNK, ISAIAH. *Judenrat: The Jewish Councils in Eastern Europe under Nazi Occupation.* New York: Macmillan, 1972.

TUSHNETT, LEONARD. *The Pavement of Hell.* New York: St. Martin's, 1972.

VAGO, BELA. "Jewish Leadership Groups in Hungary and Rumania during the Holocaust." Address presented to the International Scholars Conference on the Holocaust—A Generation After. New York City, March 1975.

WARMBRUNN, WERNER. *The Dutch under German Occupation, 1940-1945.* New York: Oxford University Press, 1963.

WEISS, AHARON. "The Jewish Police in the General-Government, and in Upper Silesia, and in East Galicia." Ph.D. dissertation, Hebrew University, 1974 (Hebrew text, English summary).

YIVO. Testimonies of Jewish leaders and others on deportations of Jews in Hungary in 1944. File no. 768, n.d.

_____. *Imposed Jewish Governing Bodies under Nazi Rule.* New York: YIVO, 1972.

Lebensborn

HENRY, CLARISSA, and HILLEL, MARC. "Of Pure Blood." Filmscript of documentary by Agence Française. Trans. British Broadcasting Company. Paris: Agence Française, mimeographed, n.d. See also Hillel, Marc, and Henry, Clarissa. *Of Pure Blood.* Trans. Eric Mossbacher. New York: McGraw-Hill, 1976.

THOMPSON, LARRY. "*Lebensborn* and the Eugenics Policy of the *Reichsführer-SS.*" *Central European History* IV, no. 1 (March 1971): 54-77.

U.S. Military Tribunal. *Trial of War Criminals before the Nuremberg Military Tribunals under Control Council Law no. 10.* Washington, D.C.: U.S. Government Printing Office, 1947.

Recognition of Extermination by Allies
(*see also* United States and Great Britain)

AINSZTEIN, REUBEN. "The Failure of the West." *Jewish Quarterly,* Winter 1966-1967. 11-20.

BAUER, YEHUDA. "When Did They Know?" *Midstream* XIV (April 1968): 51-58.

HABE, HANS. *The Mission.* Trans. Michael Bullock. New York: Coward-McCann, 1965.

JONG, LOUIS DE. "The Netherlands and Auschwitz: Why Were the Reports of Mass Killings So Widely Disbelieved?" *Imposed Jewish Governing Bodies under Nazi Rule.* New York: YIVO, 1972.

KARSKI, JAN [pseud. JAN KULCZYNSKI]. *Story of a Secret State.* Boston: Houghton Mifflin, 1944.

KULKA, ERICH. "Auschwitz Condoned: The Abortive Struggle against the Final Solution." *Wiener Library Bulletin* XXII, no. 1 (Winter 1968-1969): 2-5.

United Nations. *The Inter-Allied Review.* Vols. I-IV (1941-1944).

VRBA, RUDOLF, and BESTIC, ALAN. *I Cannot Forgive.* New York: Grove Press, 1964.

Turkish Genocide of Armenians

AHMAD. FEROZ. *The Young Turks: The Committee of Union and Progress in Turkish Politics, 1908-1914.* Oxford: Clarendon, 1969.

BOYAJIAN, DICKRAN H. *Armenia: The Case for a Forgotten Genocide.* Westwood, N.J.: Educational Book Crafters, 1972.

BRYCE, VISCOUNT JAMES. *The Treatment of Armenians in the Ottoman Empire, 1915-1916.* Ed. Arnold J. Toynbee. London: HMSO, 1916.

DJEMAL PASHA. *Memories of a Turkish Statesman, 1913-1919.* London: Hutchinson, n.d. [c. 1922].

GIBB, H. A. R., and BOWEN, HAROLD. *Islamic Society and the West: A Study of the Impact of Western Civilization on Muslim Culture in the Near East.* 2 vols. New York: Oxford University Press, 1971.

HARTUNIAN, ABRAHAM. *Neither to Laugh Nor to Weep.* Boston: Beacon, 1968.

HOUSEPIAN, MARJORIE. "The Unremembered Genocide." *Commentary* XLII (September 1966): 55-61.

LEWIS, BERNARD. *The Emergence of Modern Turkey.* New York: Oxford University Press, 1961.

MOOREHEAD, ALAN. *Gallipoli.* New York: Harper, 1956.

MORGENTHAU, HENRY, SR. *Ambassador Morgenthau's Story.* Garden City, N.Y.: Doubleday, Page, 1918.

NAIM BEY. *The Memoirs of Naim Bey: Turkish Official Documents Relating to the Deportation and Massacres of Armenians.* Comp. Aram Andonian. Newton Square, Pa.: Armenian Historical Research Association, 1964.

NALBANDIAN, LOUISE. *The American Revolutionary Movement: The Development of Armenian Political Parties through the Nineteenth Century.* Berkeley, Ca.: University of California Press, 1967.

SARKISSIAN, ARSHAG O. "Historical Background to 1915." And "Genocide." In *Martyrdom and Rebirth.* New York: Lydian, 1965.

TRUMPENER, ULRICH. *Germany and the Ottoman Empire, 1914-1918.* Princeton, N.J.: Princeton University Press, 1968.

ZARAVEND [pseud.]. *United and Independent Turania: Aims and Designs of the Turks.* Trans. V. N. Dadrian. Leiden: Brill, 1971.

Victimization: Effects of Extermination and Concentration Camps on Survivors

"Ailing Minds, The: Psychiatric Effects of Persecution." *Wiener Library Bulletin* XVII, no. 2 (2 April 1963): 20.

BODER, DAVID P. "The Impact of Catastrophe in Assessment and Evaluation." *Journal of Psychology* XXXVIII (July 1954): 3-50.

"Concentration Camp Aftereffects." *Wiener Library Bulletin* IX, nos. 1-2 (January-April 1955).

DVORJETSKI, MARK. "Adjustment of Detainees to Camp and Ghetto Life and Their Subsequent Readjustment to Normal Society." *Yad Vashem Studies* V (1963): 193-220.

EITINGER, LEO. "Concentration Camp Survivors in the Postwar World." *American Journal of Orthopsychiatry* XXXII, no. 3 (1962): 368-375.

KRYSTAL, HENRY, ed. *Massive Psychic Trauma.* New York: International Universities Press, 1968.

LANDAU, DAVID P. "Nazi Camps, Abnormality, and the Pill." *Jerusalem Post,* 25 August 1969, 11.

PFISTER-AMMENDE, M. "The Symptomatology, Treatment, and Prognosis in Mentally Ill Refugees and Repatriates in Switzerland." In *Flight and Resettlement.* Ed. H. B. M. Murphy. Paris: UNESCO, 1955.

SHUVAL, JUDITH T. "Some Persistent Effects of Trauma: Five Years after the Nazi Concentration Camps." *Social Problems* V, no. 4 (Winter 1957-1958): 230-243.

STROM, AXEL, et al. "Examination of Norwegian Ex-Concentration Camp Prisoners." *Journal of Neuropsychiatry* XXV (September-October 1962): 43-62.

Social Theory and Methods

BAHNSON, CLAUS BAHNE. "Emotional Reactions to Internally and Externally Derived Threat of Annihilation." In *The Threat of Impending Disaster: Contributions to the Psychology of Stress.* Ed. George H. Grosser et al. Cambridge, Ma.: MIT Press, 1964.

BARON, SALO W. "The Modern Age." In *Great Ages and Ideas of the Jewish People.* Ed. Leo W. Schwartz. New York: Modern Library, 1956.

BARTON, ALLEN H. *Communities in Disaster: A Sociological Analysis of Collective Stress Situations.* Garden City, N.Y.: Doubleday, 1969.

BLALOCK, HUBERT M., JR. *Toward a Theory of Minority-Group Relations.* New York: Capricorn, 1970.

BOYLE, RICHARD P. "Path Analysis and Ordinal Data." In *Causal Models in the Social Sciences.* Ed. Hubert M. Blalock, Jr. Chicago: Aldine-Atherton, 1971.

DURKHEIM, EMILE. *The Division of Labor in Society.* Trans. George Simpson. New York: The Free Press, 1933.

ECKSTEIN, HARRY. *Division and Cohesion in Democracy: A Study of Norway.* Princeton, N.J.: Princeton University Press, 1966.

EDELMAN, MURRAY. *The Symbolic Uses of Politics.* Urbana, Ill.: University of Illinois Press, 1967.

FEIN, HELEN. *Imperial Crime and Punishment: The Massacre of Jallianwala Bagh and British Judgement, 1919–1920.* Honolulu: University of Hawaii Press, 1977.

FROMM, ERICH. *Escape from Freedom.* New York: Rinehart, 1941.

GOULDNER, ALVIN. "The Norm of Reciprocity: A Preliminary Statement." *American Sociological Review* XXV, no. 2 (April 1960): 161–178.

GROSS, NEAL C.; MASON, WARD S.; and McEACHERN, ALEXANDER W. *Explorations in Role Analysis: Studies of the School Superintendency Role.* New York: Wiley, 1958.

GUTTMAN, LOUIS. "A Basis for Scaling Qualitative Data." *American Sociological Review* IX, no. 2 (April 1944): 139–150.

HEIDER, FRITZ. "Attitudes and Cognitive Organization." *Journal of Psychology* XXI (1946): 107–112.

HOBBES, THOMAS. "Of the Natural Condition of Mankind." In *Theories of Society: Foundations of Modern Sociological Theory,* I. Ed. Talcott Parsons et al. New York: The Free Press, 1971.

HUGHES, EVERETT C. "Good People and Dirty Work." *Social Problems* X, no. 1 (Summer 1962): 3–10.

JANIS, IRVING L. "Psychological Effects of Warnings." In *Man and Society in Disaster.* Eds. George W. Baker and Dwight W. Chapman. New York: Basic Books, 1962.

LANG, KURT, and LANG, GLADYS ENGEL. "Collective Responses to the Threat of Disaster." In *The Threat of Impending Disaster: Contributions to the Psychology of Stress.* Eds. George M. Grosser et al. Cambridge, Ma.: MIT Press, 1964.

LINDZEY, GARDNER, and ARONSON, ELLIOT. *The Handbook of Social Psychology.* 2d, rev. ed. 5 vols. Reading, Ma.: Addison-Wesley, 1968–1969.

LIPSET, SEYMOUR MARTIN. *Political Man.* Garden City, N.Y.: Doubleday, Anchor, 1960.

MILGRAM, STANLEY. *Obedience to Authority: An Experimental View.* New York: Harper and Row, 1974.

MITZMAN, ARTHUR. *The Iron Cage: A Historical Interpretation of Max Weber.* New York: Grosset and Dunlap, Universal Library, 1969.

MOSCA, GAETANO. *The Ruling Class.* Trans. Hannah D. Kahn. Ed. and rev. Arthur Livingston. New York: McGraw-Hill, 1939.

SIMMEL, GEORG. "The Stranger." In *The Sociology of Georg Simmel.* Trans. Kurt H. Wolff. New York: The Free Press, 1950.

SOROKIN, PITIRIM A. *Man and Society in Calamity.* New York: Dutton, 1943.

THOMAS, W. I. "The Four Wishes and the Definition of the Situation." In *Theories of Society: Foundations of Modern Sociological Theory,* II. Ed. Talcott Parsons et al. New York: The Free Press, 1971.

WALLERSTEIN, IMMANUEL. *The Modern World-System.* New York: Academic Press, 1974.

WEBER, MAX. *The Protestant Ethic and the Spirit of Capitalism.* Trans. Talcott Parsons. New York: Scribner's, 1930.

_____. *The Theory of Social and Economic Organization.* Trans. A. M. Henderson and Talcott Parsons. New York: The Free Press, 1969.

WITHEY, STEPHEN B. "Reaction to Uncertain Threat." In *Man and Society in Disaster.* Ed. George W. Baker and Dwight W. Chapman. New York: Basic Books, 1962.

WOLFENSTEIN, MARTHA. *Disaster: A Psychological Essay.* New York: The Free Press and Falcon's Wing Press, 1957.

STATES AND REGIONS

Austria (*see also* Germany)

ENGEL-JANOSI, F. "Remarks on the Austrian Resistance." *Journal of Central European Affairs* XIII (1953): 108.

FRAENKEL, JOSEF, ed. *The Jews of Austria: Essays on Their Life, History, and Destruction.* London: Valentine, Mitchell, 1967.

FRIEDMAN, PHILIP. "Aspects of Jewish Communal Crisis in the Period of the Nazi Regime in Germany, Austria, and Czechoslovakia." In *Essays of Jewish Life and Thought.* Ed. B. Blau. New York: Columbia University Press, 1959.

ROSENKRANZ, HERBERT. "The Anschluss and the Tragedy of Austrian Jewry, 1938-1945." In *The Jews of Austria: Essays on Their Life, History, and Destruction.* Ed. Josef Fraenkel. London: Valentine, Mitchell, 1967.

SIMON, WALTER B. "The Jewish Vote in Austria." *Leo Baeck Institute Yearbook* XV (1971).

WILDER-OKLADEK, F. *The Return Movement of Jews to Austria after the Second World War.* The Hague: Nijhoff, 1969.

Baltic States (*general*)

DALLIN, ALEXANDER. *German Rule in Russia, 1941-1945: A Study of Occupational Policies.* New York: Macmillan, 1957.

GAR, JOSEPH. "Jews in the Baltic Countries under German Occupation." In *Russian Jewry, 1917-1967.* Ed. Gregor Aronson et al. Trans. Joel Carmichael. New York: Yoseloff, 1969.

GRINGAUZ, SAMUEL. "The Jewish National Autonomy in Lithuania, Latvia, and Estonia." In *Russian Jewry, 1917-1967.* Ed. Gregor Aronson et al. Trans. Joel Carmichael. New York: Yoseloff, 1969.

LUNDIN, C. L. "The Nazification of the Baltic German Minorities." *Journal of Central European Affairs* VII (1947): 1-28.

Royal Institute of International Affairs. *The Baltic States: Estonia, Latvia, Lithuania.* London: Royal Institute of International Affairs, 1938.

Belgium

Belgium, Ministry of Justice. *Les Crimes de Guerre Commis sous l'Occupation de la Belgique, 1940-1945: La Persécution Antisémitique en Belgique.* Liège: Thones, 1947.

BERNARD, HENRI. *La Résistance, 1940-1945.* 2d ed. Brussels. La Renaissance du Livre, n.d. [c. 1969].

CARPINELLI, GIOVANNI. "The Flemish Variant in Belgian Fascism." *Wiener Library Bulletin*, XXVI, no. 3-4 (1972-1973): 20-28.

CLOUGH, SHEPARD B. "The Flemish Movement." In *Belgium.* Ed. Jan-Albert Goris. Los Angeles: University of California Press, 1945.

DALLIN, ALEXANDER. *German Rule in Russia, 1941–1945: A Study of Occupation Policies.* New York: Macmillan, 1957.

McCARTNEY, C. A., and PALMER, A. W. *Independent Eastern Europe: A History.* New York: Macmillan, 1962.

MEYER, PETER, et al. *The Jews in the Soviet Satellites.* Syracuse, N.Y.: Syracuse University Press, 1953.

SUGAR, PETER F., and LEDERER, IVO J. eds. *Nationalism in Eastern Europe.* Seattle, Wa.: University of Washington Press, 1969.

TRUNK, ISAIAH. *Judenrat: The Jewish Councils in Eastern Europe under Nazi Occupation.* New York: Macmillan, 1972.

VAGO, BELA, and MOSSE, GEORGE L., eds. *Jews and Non-Jews in Eastern Europe, 1918–1945.* New York: Wiley, 1974.

Estonia (*see also* Baltic States)

DWORZECKI, MARC. "Patterns in the Extermination of Estonian Jewry." *Yalkut Moreshut* II (November 1969) (Hebrew text, English summary).

ORAS, ANTS. *Baltic Eclipse.* London: Gallancz, 1948.

People, Be Watchful! Tallinn: Estonian State Publishing House, 1962.

Finland

HASSELL, ULRICH VON. *The von Hassell Diaries, 1938–1944.* Westport, Conn.: Greenwood, 1971.

KERSTEN, FELIX. *The Memoirs of Doctor Felix Kersten.* Ed. Herma Briffault. Trans. Ernest Morwitz. New York: Doubleday, 1947.

LINTINEN, JAAKO. "Kaapattiinko Himmlerin Salkku Suomessa?" *Uusi Maailma,* 10 April 1964.

LUNDIN, C. LEONARD. *Finland in the Second World War.* Bloomington, Ind.: Indiana University Press, 1957.

MEAD, W. R. *Finland.* London: Benn, 1968.

MUUT, ERILAINEN KUIN, "Lahettiko Valpo Juutalaisia Keskitys-Leireihin?" *Uusi Maailma,* 23 October 1964.

RINTALA, MARVIN. *Four Finns.* Berkeley, Ca.: University of California Press, 1969.

SABILLE, JACQUES. "Le Dossier Kersten: 1) Le Sauvetage des Juifs Finlandais." *Le Monde Juif* XXXIX (January 1951): 5–9.

TREVOR-ROPER, H. R. "The Strange Case of Himmler's Doctor: Felix Kersten and Count Bernadotte." *Commentary* XXIII (April 1957): 356–364.

UPTON, A. F. "Finland." In *European Fascism.* Ed. S. J. Wolf. New York: Random House, 1968.

WARNER, OLIVE. *Marshal Mannerheim and the Finns.* London: Weidenfeld and Nicolson, 1967.

France

ALPERIN, A. "Anti-Semitic Propaganda in France on the Eve of the Outbreak of the War." In *The Jews in France*, II. Ed. E. Tcherikower. New York: YIVO, 1942.

ARON, ROBERT. *The Vichy Regime, 1930–1944*. New York: Macmillan, 1958.

AUGE, THOMAS E. "Justice and Injustice: The French Collaboration Trials, 1944–1949." Ph.D. dissertation, University of Iowa, 1956.

AVNI, HAIM. "The Zionist Underground in Holland and France and the Escape to Spain." In *Rescue Attempts during the Holocaust: Proceedings of the Second Yad Vashem International Historical Conference*. Eds. Yisrael Gutman and Efraim Zuroff. Jerusalem: Yad Vashem, 1977.

BÉDARIDA, FRANÇOIS, and BÉDARIDA, RENÉE. "Aux Origines du Témoignage Chrétien (1941–1942)." *Revue d'Histoire de la Deuxième Guerre Mondiale* LXI (1966) 1–33.

BÉRARD, LEO. "Pope Pius XII and the Jews." (Bérard letter of 1941, trans. Abraham G. Duker.) *Jewish Spectator*, February 1964, 13–17.

BILLIG, JOSEPH. *Le Commissariat Général aux Questions Juives*. 2 vols. Paris: Éditions du Centre, 1955.

BOSWORTH, WILLIAM. *Catholicism and Crisis in Modern France*. Princeton, N.J.: Princeton University Press, 1962.

BOURDREL, PHILIPPE. *Histoire des Juifs de France*. Paris: Michel, 1974.

BYRNES, ROBERT. *Anti-Semitism in Modern France: The Prologue to the Dreyfus Affair*. New York: Fertig, 1969.

Cahiers Clandestins du Témoignage Chrétien. Paris: Éditions du Témoignage Chrétien, 1946.

CÉLINE, LOUIS F. [(pseud.) LOUIS FERDINAND DESTOUCHES]. *Bagatelles pour un Massacre*. Paris: Denoël, 1937.

COLLINS, LARRY, and LAPIERRE, DOMINIQUE. *Is Paris Burning?* New York: Simon and Schuster, Pocket Books, 1965.

COTTA, MICHÈLE. *La Collaboration*. Paris: Colin, 1964.

DIAMANT, ZANUEL. "Jewish Refugees on the French Riviera." *YIVO Annual Of Jewish Social Science* III (1953): 264–280.

DUQUESNE, JACQUES. *Les Catholiques Français sous l'Occupation*. Paris: Grasset, 1966.

France during the German Occupation, 1940–1944: A Collection of 292 Statements on the Government of Maréchal Pétain and Pierre Laval, I. Trans. Philip W. Whitcomb. Stanford, Ca.: Hoover Institution, 1957.

France, Service d'Information des Crimes de Guerre. *La Persécution Raciale*. Paris: n.d. [c. 1947].

HOFFMAN, STANLEY. "Collaborationism in France during World War II." *Journal of Modern History* XL, no. 2 (September 1968), 375–395.

KNOUT, DAVID. *Contributions à l'Histoire de la Résistance Juive en France, 1939–1944*. Paris: Éditions du Centre, 1947.

LATOUR, AMY. *La Résistance Juive en France, 1940–1944*. Paris: Stock, 1970.

LEBOUCHER, FERNAND. *Incredible Mission*. Trans. J. T. Bernard. Garden City, N.Y.: Doubleday, 1969.

LÉVY, CLAUDE. "La Presse de Collaboration en France Occupée: Conditions d'Existence." *Revue d'Histoire de la Deuxième Guerre Mondiale* LXXX (1970): 87-100.

LÉVY, CLAUDE, and TILLARD, PAUL. *Betrayal at the Vel d'Hiv.* Trans. Inea Bushnaq. New York: Hill and Wang, 1967.

LOWRIE, DONALD. "Chambon-Sur-Lignon." In *Anthology of Holocaust Literature.* Ed. Jacob Glatstein et al. Philadelphia: Jewish Publication Society of America, 1968.

MONNERAY, HENRI. *La Persécution des Juifs en France et dans les Autres Pays de l'Ouest.* Paris: Éditions du Centre, 1947.

NOVICK, PETER. *The Resistance versus Vichy: The Purge of Collaborators in Liberated France.* London: Chatto and Windus, 1968.

PAXTON, ROBERT O. *Vichy France: Old Guard and New Order, 1940-1944.* New York: Random House, 1972.

PIERRARD, PIERRE. *Juifs et Catholiques Français.* Paris, 1970.

POLIAKOV, LEON. "Jewish Resistance in France." *YIVO Annual of Jewish Social Science* III (1953): 252-263.

_____. "The Conflict between the German Army and Secret Police over Bombings of Paris Synagogues." *Jewish Social Studies* XVI (1954): 253-266.

POLONSKI, JACQUES. *La Press, La Propagande, et l'Opinion Publique sous l'Occupation.* Paris: Éditions du Centre, 1946.

ROBLIN, MICHEL. *Les Juifs de Paris.* Paris: Picard, 1952.

SENDER, HENRI. "Lights and Shades of Jewish Life in France, 1940-1942." *Jewish Social Studies* V (1943): 367-382.

STEINBERG, LUCIEN. *Les Authorités Allemandes en France.* Paris: Census, 1966.

_____. "Jewish Rescue Activities in Belgium and France." In *Rescue Attempts during the Holocaust: Proceedings of the Second Yad Vashem International Historical Conference.* Eds. Yisrael Gutman and Efraim Zuroff. Jerusalem: Yad Vashem, 1977.

SURRAUTE, RAYMOND, and RABINOVITCH, JACQUES. *Examen Succinct de la Situation Juridique des Juifs.* Paris: Éditions du Centre, 1945.

SZAJKOWSKI, XOSA. *Analytical Franco-Jewish Gazetteer, 1939-1945.* New York: Frydmann, 1966.

WEBER, EUGENE. *Action Français: Royalism and Reaction in Twentieth-Century France.* Stanford, Ca.: Stanford University Press, 1962.

WEINBERG, DAVID HENRY. "The Paris Jewish Community in the 1930s." Ph.D. dissertation, University of Wisconsin, 1971.

WELLERS, GEORGE. *L'Étoile Jaune à l'Heure de Vichy: de Drancy à Auschwitz.* Paris: Fayard, 1973.

ZERMER, E. H., with ROBERT T. BOWER. "German Occupation and Anti-Semitism in France." *Public Opinion Quarterly* XII, no. 2 (Summer 1948): 258-265.

Germany

ABEL, THEODOR. *Why Hitler Came to Power.* Englewood Cliffs, N.J.: Prentice-Hall, 1938.

ADLER, H. G. *Der Verwaltete Mensch: Studien zur Deportation der Juden aus Deutschland.* Tübingen: Mohr, 1974.

ALMOND, GABRIEL, A., ed. *The Struggle for Democray in Germany.* New York: Russell and Russell, 1965.

ANDREAS, FRIEDRICH, and ANDREAS, RUTH. *Berlin Underground, 1938–1945.* Trans. Burrows Mussey. New York: Holt, 1947.

BLAU, BRUNO. "German Jewry's Fate in Figures." *Wiener Library Bulletin,* August 1952, 25.

_____. "The Last Days of German Jewry in the Third Reich." *YIVO Annual of Jewish Social Science* VIII (1953): 197–204.

BOEHM, ERIC H., comp. *We Survived: The Stories of Fourteen of the Hidden and Hunted of Nazi Germany as Told to Eric H. Boehm.* New Haven, Conn.: Yale University Press, 1969.

BOLKOWSKY, SIDNEY. *The Distorted Image: German Jewish Perceptions of Germans and Germany, 1918–1935.* New York: Elsevier, 1975.

BROWNING, CHRISTOPHER R. *The Final Solution and the German Foreign Office.* New York: Holmes and Meier, 1978.

BUCHHEIM, HANS. "Command and Compliance." In *Anatomy of the SS State.* Ed. Helmut Krausnick et al. Trans. Richard Barry et al. New York: Walker, 1968.

CONWAY, J. S. *The Nazi Persecution of the Churches, 1933–1945.* London: Weidenfeld and Nicolson, 1968.

EDELHEIM-MÜHSAM, MARGARET T. "Reactions of the Jewish Press to the Nazi Challenge." *Leo Baeck Institute Yearbook* V (1960): 308–329.

ESCHWEGE, HELMUT. "Resistance of German Jews against the Nazi Regime." *Leo Baeck Institute Yearbook* XV (1970): 143–182.

FRIEDLANDER, SAUL. *Kurt Gerstein: The Ambiguity of Good.* Trans. Charles Fullman. New York: Knopf, 1969.

FRIEDMAN, PHILIP. "Aspects of Jewish Communal Crisis in the Period of the Nazi Regime in Germany, Austria, and Czechoslovakia." In *Essays of Jewish Life and Thought.* Ed. B. Blau. New York: Columbia University Press, 1959.

GRAML, H., et al. *The German Resistance to Hitler.* London: Batsford, 1970.

GUTTMAN, JOSEPH. "The Jews in German Criminal Statistics, 1939–1943." *YIVO Bleter,* November-December 1945, 343–344.

HASSELL, ULRICH VON. *The von Hassell Diaries, 1938–1944.* Westport, Conn.: Greenwood, 1971.

HITLER, ADOLPH. *Mein Kampf.* Trans. Ralph Manheim. Boston: Houghton Mifflin, 1971.

HUTTENBACH, HENRY R. "The Emigration of Jews from Worms (November 1938 October 1941): Hopes and Plans." In *Rescue Attempts during the Holocaust. Proceedings of the Second Yad Vashem International Historical Conference.* Eds. Yisrael Gutman and Efraim Zuroff. Jerusalem: Yad Vashem, 1977.

JANOWITZ, M. "German Reactions to Nazi Atrocities." *American Journal of Sociology* LII (1946): 141–146.

KRAUSNICK, HELMUT. "The Persecution of the Jews." In *Anatomy of the SS State.* Ed. Helmut Krausnick et al. Trans. Richard Barry et al. New York: Walker, 1968.

LEBER, ANNEDORE, comp. *Conscience in Revolt: Sixty-four Stories of Resistance in Germany, 1933–45*. London: Valentine, Mitchell, 1957.

LEWY, GUENTER. *The Catholic Church and Nazi Germany*. New York: McGraw-Hill, 1964.

LINDENBERG, KURT. "Escape to Sweden." In *Explorations*. Ed. Murray Mindlin, with Chaim Bernant. London: Erasmus, 1967.

LITTELL, FRANKLIN H., and LOCKE, HUBERT G. *The German Church Struggle and the Holocaust*. Detroit, Mi.: Wayne State University Press, 1974.

LOCHNER, LOUIS. *What about Germany?* New York: Dodd, Mead, 1942.

LOWENTHAL, MARVIN. *The Jews of Germany: A Story of Sixteen Centuries*. New York: Russell and Russell, 1970; first pub. 1936.

MANN, GOLO. *The History of Germany since 1789*. Trans. Marian Jackson. New York: Praeger, 1968.

MARGALIOT, ABRAHAM. "The Problem of the Rescue of German Jewry during the Years 1933–1939. The Reasons for the Delay in Their Emigration from the Third Reich." In *Rescue Attempts during the Holocaust: Proceedings of the Second Yad Vashem International Historical Conference*. Eds. Yisrael Gutman and Efraim Zuroff. Jerusalem: Yad Vashem, 1977.

MASSING, PAUL W. *Rehearsal for Destruction: A Study of Political Anti-Semitism in Imperial Germany*. New York: Fertig, 1967.

MOSSE, GEORGE L. *The Crisis of German Ideology: Intellectual Origins of the Third Reich*. New York: Universal Library, Grosset and Dunlap, 1964.

PAUCKER, ARNOLD, and STEINBERG, LUCIEN. "Some Notes on Resistance." *Leo Baeck Institute Yearbook* XVI (1971): 239–248.

PULZER, PETER G. J. *The Rise of Political Anti-Semitism in Germany and Austria*. New York: Wiley, 1964.

RITTER, G. *The German Resistance: Carl Goerdeler's Struggle against Tyranny*. Trans. R. T. Clark. London: George Allen and Unwin, 1958.

ROTHFELS, H. *The German Opposition to Hitler*. Trans. L. Wilson. Chicago: Regnery, 1948.

SCHLEUNES, KARL A. *The Twisted Road to Auschwitz: Nazi Policy toward German Jews, 1933–1939*. Urbana, Ill: University of Illinois Press, 1970.

SCHORSCH, ISMAR. "German Anti-Semitism in the Light of Postwar Historiography." *Leo Baeck Institute Yearbook* XIX, no. 4 (1974): 257–271.

SPEER, ALBERT. *Inside the Third Reich*. Trans. Richard Winston and Clara Winston. New York: Macmillan, 1967.

TAYLOR, A. J. P. *The Course of German History: A Survey of the Development of Germany since 1815*. New York: Coward-McCann, 1946.

THEMAL, ILSELOTTE. "Mother and Child." In *Explorations*. Ed. Murray Mindlin, with Chaim Bernant. London: Erasmus, 1967.

TOBIAS, FRITZ. *The Reichstag Fire*. Trans. Arnold Pomerans. New York: Putnam, 1964.

ZAHN, GORDON C. *German Catholics and Hitler's Wars: A Study in Social Control*. New York: Sheed and Ward, 1962.

Great Britain

AINSZTEIN, REUBEN. "The Failure of the West." *Jewish Quarterly*, Winter 1966–1967, 11–20.

BAUER, YEHUDA. "Patria." In *Encyclopedia of Zionism and Israel*, II. Ed. Raphael Patai. New York: Herzl Press/McGraw-Hill, 1971.

GANNON, FRANKLIN REID. *The British Press and Germany, 1933–1939*. Oxford: Clarendon, 1971.

HEARST, ERNEST. "The British and the Slaughter of the Jews." *Wiener Library Bulletin* XXI, no. 1 (Winter 1966–1967): 32–38; and XXII, no. 2 (Spring 1967): 30–40.

KATZBURG, NATHANIEL. "British Policy on Immigration to Palestine during World War II." In *Rescue Attempts during the Holocaust: Proceedings of the Second Yad Vashem International Historical Conference*. Eds. Yisrael Gutman and Efraim Zuroff. Jerusalem: Yad Vashem, 1977.

KLUGER, RUTH, and MANN, PEGGY. *The Last Escape*. Garden City, N.Y.: Doubleday, 1973.

SCHARF, ANDREW. *The British Press and Jews under Nazi Rule*. New York: Oxford University Press, 1964.

SHERMAN, A. J. *Island Refuge: Britain and Refugees from the Third Reich, 1933–1939*. London: Elek, 1973.

SHERWOOD, ROBERT. *Roosevelt and Hopkins*. New York: Harper, 1948.

VAGO, BELA. "The British Government and the Fate of Hungarian Jewry in 1944." In *Rescue Attempts during the Holocaust: Proceedings of the Second Yad Vashem International Historical Conference*. Eds. Yisrael Gutman and Efraim Zuroff. Jerusalem: Yad Vashem, 1977.

YAHIL, LENI. "Select British Documents on the Illegal Immigration to Palestine." *Yad Vashem Studies* X (1974): 241–276.

Greece

ECK, NATHAN. "New Light on the Charges against the Last Chief Rabbi of Salonika." *Yad Vashem Bulletin* XVII (1965): 9–15.

FRIEDMAN, PHILIP. "The Jews of Greece during the Second World War: A Bibliographical Survey." *Joshua Starr Memorial Volume*. New York: Conference on Jewish Relations, 1953.

GALANTE, ABRAHAM. *Appendice à l'Histoire des Juifs de Rhodes, Chio, Cos, etc.* Istanbul: Kágit re Ba sim Tsleri, 1948.

Hellenic Department of Information. *Le Drame des Juifs Hellènes*. Cairo: Hellenic Department of Information, n.d.

KABELI, ISAAC. "The Resistance of the Greek Jews." *YIVO Annual of Jewish Social Science* VIII (1953): 281–288.

MILLIEX, ROGER. *A l'École du Peuple Grec, 1940–1944*. Vichy: Éditions du Beffroi, 1946.

MOISSIS, ASHE. "La Situation des Communautés Juives en Grèce." In *Les Juifs en Europe, 1939–1945*. Paris: Éditions du Centre, 1949.

MOLHO, MICHAEL. *In Memoriam: Hommage aux Victimes Juives des Nazis en Grèce.* 2d ed. rev. and enlarged by Joseph Nehama. Salonica: Communauté Israélite de Thessalonique, 1973.

ROTH, CECIL. "The Last Days of Jewish Salonica." *Commentary* XI (July 1950): 49-55.

SPENCER, FLOYD A. *War and Postwar Greece: An Analysis Based on Greek Writings.* Washington, D.C.: Library of Congress, 1952.

STAVRIANOS, L. S. "The Jews in Greece." *Journal of Central European Affairs* XXV (October 1948): 257-269.

TSATSOS, JEANNE. *The Sword's Fierce Edge: A Journal of the Occupation of Greece, 1941-1944.* Trans. by Jean Demos. Nashville, Tn.: Vanderbilt University Press, 1969.

Hungary (*see also* Eastern Europe)

BAUER, YEHUDA. "The Activities of the J.D.C. in Europe during World War II." Mimeographed manuscript, n.d. Institute of Contemporary Jewry, Division of Holocaust Studies, Hebrew University, Jerusalem.

BENOSCHOFSKY, ILYONA. "The Position of Hungarian Jewry after the Liberation." *Hungarian-Jewish Studies* I (1966): 237-260.

BISS, ANDREAS. *A Million Jews to Save.* South Brunswick, N.J.: Barnes, 1975.

BRAHAM, RANDOLPH L. *The Destruction of Hungarian Jewry: A Documentary Account.* 2 vols. New York: World Federation of Hungarian Jews, 1963.

_____. "The Holocaust in Hungary: A Historical Interpretation of the Role of the Hungarian Radical Right." *Societas* II, no. 3 (June 1972): 195-219.

_____. "The Kamenets Podolsk and Delvidek Massacres: Prelude to the Holocaust in Hungary." *Yad Vashem Studies* IX (1973) 133-157.

_____. "The Role of the Jewish Council in Hungary: A Tentative Assessment." *Yad Vashem Studies* X (1974): 69-110.

_____. "What did They Know and When?" Address presented to the International Scholars Conference on the Holocaust—A Generation After. New York City, March 1975.

DUSCHINSKY, EUGENE. "Hungary." In *The Jews in the Soviet Satellites.* Ed. Peter Meyer et al. Syracuse, N.Y.: Syracuse University Press, 1953.

EICHMANN, ADOLPH. "Eichmann's Story." *Life,* part I, 28 November 1960, 20-25f; part II, 5 December 1960, 46-48f.

FEINGOLD, HENRY. *The Politics of Rescue: The Roosevelt Administration and the Holocaust, 1938-1945.* New Brunswick, N.J.: Rutgers University Press, 1970.

FENYO, MARIO D. *Hitler, Horthy, and Hungary.* New Haven, Conn.: Yale University Press, 1972.

FREUDINGER, FÜLÖP [PHILIP], et al. "Report on Hungary: March 19-August 9, 1944." *Hungarian-Jewish Studies* III (1973): 75-146.

GOLDFARB, ZVI. "On 'Hehalutz' Resistance in Hungary." In *Extermination and Resistance.* Ed. Kibbutz Lohamei Hagettaot. Israel: Kibbutz Lohamei Hagettaot, 1958.

HEYMAN, EVA. *The Diary of Eva Heyman.* Introduction and notes by Judah Marton. Trans. Moshe M. Kohn. Jerusalem: Yad Vashem, 1974.

Jerusalem Post, 1954-1958.

KÀLLAY, NICHOLAS. *Hungarian Premier.* New York: Columbia University Press, 1954.

KASTNER, RUDOLPH. *Der Bericht des judischen Rettungskomitees aus Budapest, 1942–1945.* Basel: Vaadath Ezra Vehazalah de Budapest, 1946.

KATZBURG, NATHANIEL. "Hungarian Jewry in Modern Times." *Hungarian-Jewish Studies* I (1966): 137-170.

KLEIN, BERNARD. "Hungarian Jewry in the Nazi Period." Masters thesis, Columbia University, 1955.

_____. "Hungarian Politics and the Jewish Question in the Inter-War Period." *Jewish Social Studies* XXVIII, no. 2 (April 1966): 79-98.

KOMOLY, OTTÓ. "The Diary of Ottó Komoly: August 21-September 16, 1944." *Hungarian-Jewish Studies* III (1973): 147-250.

LAQUER, WALTER Z. "The Kastner Case." *Commentary,* December 1955, 500-511.

LÁSZLÓ, ERNŐ. "Hungary's Jewry: A Demographic Overview, 1918-1945." *Hungarian-Jewish Studies* II (1969): 137-182.

LEVAI, JENŐ. *Black Book on the Martyrdom of Hungarian Jewry.* Ed. Lawrence P. Davis. Zurich: Central European Times, 1948.

_____. "The Hungarian Deportations in the Light of the Eichmann Trial." *Yad Vashem Studies* V (1963): 69-105.

_____. *Hungarian Jewry and the Papacy: Pope Pius XII Did Not Remain Silent.* Trans. J. R. Foster. London: Sands, 1967.

MCCARTNEY, G. A. *A History of Hungary.* II: *1929-1945.* New York: Praeger, 1957.

MALAPARTE, CURZIO. *Kaputt.* New York: Dutton, 1946.

NAGY-TALAVERA, NICHOLAS M. *The Green Shirts and the Others: A History of Fascism in Hungary and Rumania.* Stanford, Ca.: Hoover Institution Press, 1970.

PETÖ, ERNÖ [ERNEST]. "Statement." *Hungarian-Jewish Studies* III (1973): 49-74.

ROTKIRCHEN, LIVIA. "Hungary: An Asylum for the Refugees of Europe." *Yad Vashem Studies* VII (1968): 127-142.

STERN, SAMU [SAMUEL]. " 'A Race with Time': A Statement." *Hungarian-Jewish Studies* III (1973): 1-48.

VAGO, BELA. "Germany and the Jewish Policy of the Kallay Government." *Hungarian-Jewish Studies* II (1969): 183-207.

_____. "The Intelligence Aspects of the Joel Brand Mission." *Yad Vashem Studies* X (1974): 111-128.

_____. "Jewish Leadership Groups in Hungary and Rumania during the Holocaust." Address presented to the International Scholars Conference on the Holocaust—A Generation After. New York City, March 1975.

_____. "The British Government and the Fate of Hungarian Jewry in 1944." In *Rescue Attempts during the Holocaust: Proceedings of the Second Yad Vashem International Historical Conference.* Eds. Yisrael Gutman and Efraim Zuroff. Jerusalem: Yad Vashem, 1977.

VRBA, RUDOLF, and BESTIC, ALAN. *I Cannot Forgive.* New York: Grove Press, 1964.

War Refugee Board. See United States War Refugee Board under United States section, this Bibliography.

WEISSBERG, ALEX. *Desperate Mission: Joel Brand's Story as Told by Alex Weissberg.* Trans. Constantine Fitzgibbon and Andrew Foster-Melliar. New York: Criterion, 1958.

WIESEL, ELI. "Eichmann's Victims and the Unheard Testimony." *Commentary* XXXII (December 1961): 510-516.

———. *Night.* Trans. Stella Rodway. New York: Hill and Wang, 1966.

YIVO. Testimonies of Hungarian Jews and other Hungarians regarding events of 1944. File no. 768, Protocol no. 3618.

Italy

BINCHY, DANIEL A. *Church and State in Fascist Italy.* New York: Oxford University Press, 1970.

CARPI, DANIEL. "The Catholic Church and Italian Jewry under the Fascists." *Yad Vashem Studies* IV (1960): 43-54.

CIANO, COUNT GALEAZZO. *The Ciano Diaries, 1939-1943.* Trans. and ed. Hugh Wilson. Garden City, N.Y.: Doubleday, 1946.

COHEN, ISRAEL. "Jews in Italy." *Political Quarterly* X (1939): 405-418.

DI VITA, SR. DORINA. "Gli Ebrei nel Carcere di S. Vittore a Milano." *Quaderni del Centro di Studi sulla Deportazione e l'Internamento* V (1968): 100-101.

———. "Gli Ebrei di Milano sotto l'Occupazione Nazista." *Quaderni del Centro di Studi sulla Deportazione e l'Internamento* VI (1969-1971): 16-52.

FELICE, RENZO D. *Storia degli Ebrei Italiani sotto il Fascismo.* 3d ed. Turin: Einaudi, 1972.

FONARI, HARRY. *Mussolini's Gadfly: Roberto Farinacci.* Nashville, Tn.: Vanderbilt University Press, 1971.

GINZBURG, NATALIA. *Family Sayings.* Trans. D. A. Low. New York: Dutton, 1967.

HALPERIN, S. WILLIAM. *Mussolini and Italian Fascism.* Princeton, N.J.: Van Nostrand, 1964.

HARRIS, C. R. S. *Allied Military Administration of Italy, 1943-1945.* London: HMSO, 1957.

KATZ, ROBERT. *Black Sabbath: A Journey through a Crime against Humanity.* New York: Macmillan, 1969.

KESSEL, ALBRECHT VON. "The Pope and the Jews." In *The Storm over the Deputy.* Ed. Eric R. Bentley. New York: Grove Press, 1964.

LEBOUCHER, FERNAND. *Incredible Mission.* Trans. J. F. Bernard. Garden City, N.Y.: Doubleday, 1969.

LEDEEN, MICHAEL A. "Italian Jews and Fascism." *Judaism* XVIII, no. 3 (Summer 1969): 277-298.

LEVI, PRIMO. "La Deportazione degli Ebrei: Testimonianze Presentate is 23 Ottobre 1966 nella Riunion Svoltasi nel Teatro dell'Istituto Bancario S. Paolo." *Quaderni del Centro di Studi sulla Deportazione e l'Internamento* I (1964): 64-65.

"List of Jewish Survivors in Some Italian Cities." *Register of Jewish Survivors,* I. Mimeographed list submitted to World Jewish Congress, Jerusalem, 1945.

LUZATTO, ALDO. "Ricordo del Rabbino Riccardo Pacifici." *Quaderni del Centro di Studi sulla Deportazione e l'Internamento* VI (1969-1974): 86-88.

———. "La Deportazione degli Ebrei di Genova." *Quaderno del Centro di Studi sulla Deportazione e l'Internamento* VI (1969-1974): 89-91.

MICHAELIS, MEIER. "The Attitude of the Fascist Regime to the Jews in Italy." *Yad Vashem Studies* IV (1960): 7-42.

———. *German-Italian Relations and the Question of the Jews in Italy, 1922-1939.* London: Institute of Jewish Affairs, 1978.

MILANO, A. *Storia degli Ebrei in Italia.* Rome: Einaudi, 1962.

MYDANS, CARL. "Jews of Rome, the Nazis, and the Vatican." *Life,* 1 May 1964, 21.

NOVICH, MIRIAM. "Nuovi Documenti sulla Deportazione degli Ebrei Italiani." *Quaderni del Centro di Studi sulla Deportazione e l'Internamento* II (1965).

PARRI, F., and VENTURI, F. "The Italian Resistance and the Allies." In *European Resistance Movements, 1939-1945: Proceedings of the Second International Conference on the History of Resistance Movements.* New York: Pergamon, 1964.

POLIAKOV, LEON, and SABILLE, JACQUES. *Jews under the Italian Occupation.* Paris: Éditions du Centre, 1955.

ROSENGARTEN, FRANK. *The Italian Anti-Fascist Press, 1919-1945.* Cleveland: Press of Case Western Reserve University, 1968.

SABATELLO, FRANCO. "Social and Occupational Trends of the Jews of Italy, 1870-1970." Ph.D. dissertation, Hebrew University, 1972 (Hebrew text, English summary).

TANNENBAUM, EDWARD R. *The Fascist Experience: Italian Society and Culture, 1922-1945.* New York: Basic Books, 1972.

VACCARINO, M. G. "La Résistance au Fascisme en Italie de 1923 à 1945." In *European Resistance Movements, 1939-1945: Proceedings of the First International Conference on the History of Resistance Movements.* New York: Pergamon, 1960.

VITALE, MASIMO ADOLFO. "The Destruction and Resistance of the Jews in Italy." In *They Fought Back.* Ed. Yuri Suhl. New York: Crown, 1967.

WAAGENAR, SAM. *The Pope's Jews.* La Salle, Ill.: Library Press, 1974.

WISKEMANN, ELIZABETH. *Fascism in Italy: Its Development and Influence.* New York: Macmillan, 1969.

WOODWARD, E., and BUTLER, R. *Documents on British Foreign Policy,* III. 3d ser. 1938-1939. London, 1950.

ZOLLI, EUGENIO. *Before the Dawn.* New York: Sheed and Ward, 1954.

Latvia (*see also* Baltic States)

Association of Latvian and Estonian Jews in Israel. *The Jews in Latvia.* Tel Aviv: Ben-Nan Press, 1971.

AVOTINS, E., et al. *Daugavas Vanagi: Who Are They?* Riga: Latvia State Publishing House, 1963.

BILMANIS, ALFRED. *Latvia in 1939-1942*. Washington, D.C.: Latvian Legation, 1942.

_____. *A History of Latvia*. Westport, Conn.: Greenwood, 1957.

CARSON, GEORGE B., ed. *Latvia: An Area Study*. New Haven, Conn.: Human Relations Area Files, 1956.

C'UIBE, LEONS. *The Lutheran Church of Latvia behind the Iron Curtain*. Published by Latvian reporter in the committee for church activities among the Baltic peoples in Sweden. Stockholm: 1948.

KATZ, JOSEPH. *One Who Came Back: The Diary of a Jewish Survivor*. Trans. Hilda Reach. New York: Herzl Press, 1973.

Latvia under German Occupation, 1941-43. Washington, D.C.: Latvian Legation, 1943.

LEVIN, DOV. "The Jews and the Sovietization of Latvia, 1940-1941." *Soviet-Jewish Affairs* V, no. 1 (1975): 39-56.

LEVINSON, ISAAC. *The Untold Story*. Johannesburg: Kayor, 1958.

"List of Jews Residing in Riga." Postwar list submitted to World Jewish Congress. Stockholm: n.d.

MARK, BERL. "Dubnow." In *The Way We Think*, II. Ed. Joseph Leftwich. South Brunswick, N.J.: Yoseloff, 1969.

SPEKKE, ARNOLD. *History of Latvia: An Outline*. Stockholm: Goppers, 1951.

Lithuania (*see also* Baltic States)

ANDENAS, T. *Twenty Years' Struggle for Freedom of Lithuania*. New York: Harper and Row, 1963.

BALTRAMAITIS, CASIMER V. *Lithuanian Affairs: An Index to the New York Times*. New York: Lithuanian Press Club, 1945.

BARANAUSKAS, B., and RUKSENAS, K. comps. *Documents Accuse*. Vilna: Gintaras Vilnius, 1970.

BAR-ON, ZVI, and LEVIN, DOV. *The Story of an Underground: The Resistance of the Jews of Kovna (Lithuania) in the Second World War*. Jerusalem: Yad Vashem, 1962 (Hebrew text, English summary).

BAUER, YEHUDA. "Rescue Operations through Vilna." *Yad Vashem Studies* IX (1973): 215-224.

GRINGAUZ, SAMUEL. "The Ghetto as an Experiment of Jewish Social Organization (Three Years of Kovno Ghetto)." *Jewish Social Studies* XI, no. 1 (January 1949): 3-20.

IVINSKIS, ZENONAS. "Lithuania during the War: Resistance against the Soviet and the Nazi Occupants." In *Lithuania under the Soviets*. Ed. V. S. Vardys. New York: Praeger, 1965.

KRIVICKAS, VLADAS. "The Coup d'État of 1926 in Lithuania." Ph.D. dissertation, Columbia University, 1970.

NESHAMIT, SARAH. "Rescue in Lithuania during the Nazi Occupation." In *Rescue Attempts during the Holocaust: Proceedings of the Second Yad Vashem Interna-*

tional Historical Conference. Eds. Yisrael Gutman and Efraim Zuroff. Jerusalem: Yad Vashem, 1977.

"Survivors in Lithuania, Italy, France, Sweden, Palestine, and Germany." Lists submitted to American Federation for Lithuanian Jews, New York, 1946.

TRAKISKIS, A. *The Situation of the Church and Religious Practices in Occupied Lithuania.* New York: Lithuanian Bulletin (pamphlet), 1945.

VARDYS, V. STANLEY. "The Partisan Movement in Postwar Lithuania." In *Lithuania under the Soviets.* Ed. V. S. Vardys. New York: Praeger, 1965.

The Netherlands

Annals of the American Academy of Political and Social Science, The. Issue: The Netherlands during German Occupation. May 1946.

AVNI, HAIM. "The Zionist Underground in Holland and France and the Escape to Spain." In *Rescue Attempts during the Holocaust: Proceedings of the Second Yad Vashem International Historical Conference.* Eds. Yisrael Gutman and Efraim Zuroff. Jerusalem: Yad Vashem, 1977. .

BEEM, HARTOG. "The Jewish Council (*Judenrat*) of the Province of Vriesland (Holland)." *Yad Vashem Bulletin* XVII (December 1965): 21-23.

COHEN, ELIE A. *The Abyss: A Confession.* Trans. James Brockway. New York: Norton, 1973.

FRANK, ANNE. *The Diary of a Young Girl.* Trans. B. H. Mooyaart-Doubleday. New York: Modern Library, 1952.

JONG, LOUIS DE. "Anti-Nazi Resistance in the Netherlands." In *European Resistance Movements, 1939-1945: Proceedings of the First International Conference on the History of Resistance Movements.* New York: Pergamon, 1960.

———. "Jews and Non-Jews in Nazi Occupied Holland." In *On the Track of Tyranny.* Ed. Max Beloff. London: Wiener Library, 1960.

———. "The Dutch Resistance Movements and the Allies, 1940-1945." In *European Resistance Movements, 1939-1945: Proceedings of the Second International Conference on the History of Resistance Movements.* New York: Pergamon, 1964.

———. "Help to People in Hiding." *Delta* VIII, no. 1 (Spring 1965): 37-79.

———. "The Netherlands and Auschwitz: Why Were the Reports of Mass Killings So Widely Disbelieved?" In *Imposed Jewish Governing Bodies under Nazi Rule.* New York: YIVO, 1972.

LEEUW, VAN DER. "La Presse Néerlandaise sous l'Occupation Allemande." *Revue d'Histoire de la Deuxième Guerre Mondiale* LXXX (1970): 29-44.

MAASS, WALTER B. *The Netherlands at War, 1940-1945.* New York: Abelard-Schuman, 1970.

MASON, HENRY L. *The Purge of Dutch Quislings: Emergency Justice in the Netherlands.* The Hague: Nijhoff, 1952.

———. *Mass Demonstrations against Foreign Regimes: A Study of Five Crises.* New Orleans: Tulane University Press, 1966.

MECHANICUS, PHILIP. *Year of Fear*. Trans. Irene S. Gibbons. New York: Hawthorn, 1968.

MICHMAN, JOSEPH. "The Controversial Stand of the *Joodse Raad* in the Netherlands." *Yad Vashem Studies* X (1974): 9-68.

MINCO, MARGA. *Bitter Herbs*. Trans. Roy Edwards. New York: Oxford University Press, 1960.

PRESSER, JACOB. *The Breaking Point*. Trans. Burrows Mussey. Cleveland: World, 1958.

_____. *The Destruction of the Dutch Jews*. Trans. Arnold Pomerans. New York: Dutton, 1969.

SIJES, B. A. "Several Observations Concerning the Position of the Jews in Occupied Holland during World War II." In *Rescue Attempts during the Holocaust: Proceedings of the Second Yad Vashem International Historical Conference*. Eds. Yisrael Gutman and Efraim Zuroff. Jerusalem: Yad Vashem, 1977.

TAUBES, ISRAEL. "Jewish Survivors Report no. 2: The Persecution of Jews in Holland." Mimeographed. London: Jewish Central Information Office, 1945.

_____. "The Jewish Council of Amsterdam." *Yad Vashem Bulletin* XVII (December 1965): 25-30.

TIJN, GERTRUDE VAN. "Contributions to the History of the Jews in the Netherlands from May 10, 1940 to June, 1944." Mimeographed report, Joint Distribution Committee, Jerusalem, 1945.

WARMBRUNN, WERNER. *The Dutch under German Occupation, 1940-1945*. New York: Oxford University Press, 1963.

Norway (*see also* Sweden)

ANDENAES, JOHN; RISTE, O.; and SKODVIN, M. *Norway and the Second World War*. Oslo: Johan Grund Tanum Forlag, 1966.

CASTBERG, FRED. *The Norwegian Way of Life*. London: Heinemann, 1954.

HAYES, PAUL M. *Quisling: The Career and Political Ideas of Vidkun Quisling, 1887-1945*. London: Newton Abbott, David and Charles, 1971.

HOYE, BJARNE, and AGER, TRYGVE M. *The Fight of the Norwegian Church against Nazism*. New York: Macmillan, 1943.

KJELSTADLI, SVERRE. "The Resistance Movement in Norway and the Allies, 1940-45." In *European Resistance Movements, 1939-1945: Proceedings of the Second International Conference on the History of Resistance Movements*. New York: Pergamon, 1964.

LEVIN, MARCUS. "The Norwegian Jews during the German Occupation." Trans. Popular Translation Bureau. Report found in American Jewish Committee Blaustein Library, New York City.

LINDBAEK, LISE. "Persecution of Jews in Norway." *Inter-Allied Review* I, no. 17 (1941): 10-11.

List of Jews deported to concentration camps from Norway. Copy of Norwegian government list filed in Yad Vashem, Jerusalem.

MILWARD, ALAN S. *The Fascist Economy in Norway.* Oxford: Clarendon, 1972.

NANSEN, ODD. *From Day to Day.* Trans. Katherine John. New York: Putnam, 1949.

RISTE, OLAV, and NOKLEBY, BESIT. *Norway, 1940–1945: The Resistance Movement.* Oslo: Johan Grund Tanum Forlag, 1973.

ROST, NELLA. "Les Juifs sous l'Occupation Allemande dans le Pays Scandinaves." In *Les Juifs en Europe, 1939–1945.* Paris: Éditions du Centre, 1949.

SKODVIN, M. "La Presse Norvegienne sous l'Occupation Allemande." *Revue d'Histoire de la Deuxième Guerry Mondiale* VIII (1970): 69–86.

STORING, JAMES A. *Norwegian Democracy.* Boston: Houghton Mifflin, 1963.

Poland (*see also* Eastern Europe)

AINSZTEIN, REUBEN. "New Light on Szmuel Zygelbojm's Suicide." *Yad Vashem Bulletin* XV (August 1964): 8–12.

ARAD, YITZHAK. "Concentration of Refugees in Vilna on the Eve of the Holocaust." *Yad Vashem Studies* IX (1973): 201–214.

BARTOSZEWSKI, W. *Warsaw Death Ring, 1939–1944.* Trans. Edward Rothert. Warsaw: Interpress, 1968.

BARTOSZEWSKI, W., and LEWIN, Z., eds. *Righteous among Nations: How the Poles Helped the Jews, 1939–1945.* London: Swiderski, 1969.

BAUMINGER, ARYCH. "The Rising in the Cracow Ghetto." *Yad Vashem Bulletin* VIII–IX (1961): 22–25.

BERENSTEIN, TATANA, and RUTKOWSKI, ADAM. *Assistance to the Jews in Poland.* Trans. Edward Rothert. Warsaw: Polonia, 1963.

BERG, MARY [pseud. Mary Wattenberg]. *Warsaw Ghetto: A Diary.* Ed. S. L. Schneiderman. Trans. Sylvia Glass and Norbert Guterman. New York: Fischer, 1945.

BLUMENTHAL, NACHMAN. *Conduct and Actions of a* Judenrat: *Documents from the Bialystoh Ghetto.* Jerusalem: Yad Vashem, 1962.

_____. "German Documents on the Bialystok Ghetto Revolt." *Yad Vashem Bulletin* XIV (1964): 19–25.

_____. "A Martyr or a Hero? Reflections on the Diary of Czerniakow." *Yad Vashem Studies* VII (1968): 165–172.

BOR-KOMOROWSKI, T. *The Secret Army.* London: Gollancz, 1950.

BORZYKOWSKI, TUVIA. *Between Tumbling Walls.* Trans. Mendel Kohansky. Israel: Beit Lohamei Hagettaot, n.d.

CZERNIAKOW, ADAM. *The Warsaw Ghetto Diary by Adam Czeniakow.* Eds. Raul Hilberg, Joseph Kermish, and Stanislaw Staron. Trans. Stanislaw Staron. New York: Stein and Day, in press.

DOBROSZYCKI, LUCJAN. "Restoring Jewish Life in Postwar Poland." *Soviet-Jewish Affairs* III, no. 2 (1973): 58–71.

DONAT, ALEXANDER. *The Holocaust Kingdom: A Memoir.* New York: Holt, Rinehart, and Winston, 1965.

FALCONI, CARLO. *The Silence of Pius XII*. Trans. Bernard Wall. Boston: Little, Brown, 1970.

FRIEDMAN, PHILIP. *Martyrs and Fighters: The Epic of the Warsaw Ghetto*. New York: Praeger, 1954.

———. "Ukrainian-Jewish Relations during the Nazi Occupation." *YIVO Annual of Jewish Social Science* XII (1958-1959): 259-300.

GITMAN, JOSEPH. "The Jews and Jewish Problems in the Polish Parliament, 1919-1939." Ph.D. dissertation, Yale University, 1963.

GLICKSON, P. "Jewish Population in the Polish People's Republic, 1944-1972." Address presented to the Sixth World Congress of Jewish Studies. Jerusalem, August 1973.

GOLDSTEIN, BERNARD. *The Stars Bear Witness*. Trans. and ed. Leonard Shatzkin. New York: Viking, 1949.

GROSSMAN, HAIKA. "The Anniversary of the Bialystok Ghetto Uprising." *Yalkut Moreshut* IX (Hebrew text, English summary).

GROSSMAN, MENDEL. *With a Camera in the Ghetto*. Israel: Beit Lohamei Hagettaot, 1970.

GUTMAN, YISRAEL. "The Attitude of the Poles to the Mass Deportations of Jews from the Warsaw Ghetto in the Summer of 1942." In *Rescue Attempts during the Holocaust: Proceedings of the Second Yad Vashem International Historical Conference*. Eds. Yisrael Gutman and Efraim Zuroff. Jerusalem: Yad Vashem, 1977.

HARTGLASS, APOLINARY. How Did Cherniakov Become Head of the Warsaw *Judenrat?*" *Yad Vashem Bulletin* XV (1964): 4-7.

HELLER, CELIA S. "Assimilation: A Deviant Pattern among the Jews of Interwar Poland." *Jewish Journal of Sociology*, XV (1973): 221-237.

IRANEK-OSNECKI, KAZIMIERZ. *He Who Saves One Life*. New York: Crown, 1971.

JOHNPOLL, BERNARD K. *The Politics of Futility: The General Jewish Workers Bund of Poland, 1917-1943*. Ithaca: N.Y.: Cornell University Press, 1967.

KALMANOVITCH, ZELIG. "A Diary of the Nazi Ghetto in Vilna." YIVO Annual of Jewish Social Science III (1953), 9-81.

KAPLAN, CHAIM A. *The Warsaw Diary of Chaim A. Kaplan*. Rev. ed. Trans. and ed. Abraham I. Katsh. New York: Collier, 1973.

KARSKI, JAN [pseud. JAN KULEZYNSKI]. *Story of a Secret State*. Boston: Houghton Mifflin, 1944.

KATZNELSON, YITZHAK. *Vittel Diary*. Trans. Meyer Cohen. Israel: Beit Lohamei Hagettaot, 1972.

KERMISH, JOSEPH. "New Jewish Sources for the History of the Warsaw Ghetto Uprising." *Yad Vashem Bulletin* XV (9 August 1964): 27-33.

———. "The Activities of the Council for Aid to Jews ('Zegota') in Occupied Poland." In *Rescue Attempts during the Holocaust: Proceedings of the Second Yad Vashem International Historical Conference*. Eds. Yisrael Gutman and Efraim Zuroff. Jerusalem: Yad Vashem, 1977.

KLIBANSKI, BRONIA. "The Underground Archives of the Bialystok Ghetto (Founded by Mersik and Tenenbaum)." *Yad Vashem Studies* II (1958): 295-329.

KORBONSKI, STEFAN. *Fighting Warsaw: The Story of the Polish Underground*. New York: Funk and Wagnalls, 1969.

KORZEC, PAWET. "Anti-Semitism in Poland as an Intellectual, Social, and Political Movement." In *Studies on Polish Jewry, 1919–1939.* Ed. Joshua A. Fishman. New York: YIVO, 1974.

KRAKOWSKI, S. "The Slaughter of Polish Jewry: A Polish 'Reassessment.' " *Wiener Library Bulletin* XXVI, nos.3–4 (1972–1973): 13–19.

_____. "Policy of the Third Reich in Conquered Poland." *Yad Vashem Studies* IX (1973): 225–245.

KRUK, HERMAN. "Diary of the Vilna Ghetto." *YIVO Annual of Jewish Social Science* XIII (1965): 9–78.

LAZAR, CHAIM. *Muranowska 7: The Warsaw Ghetto Rising.* Tel Aviv: Massada Press, 1966.

LESTCHINSKY, JACOB. "The Jews in the Cities of the Republic of Poland." *YIVO Annual of Jewish Social Science* I (1946): 156–177.

_____. "The Industrial and Social Structure of the Jewish Population of Interbellum Poland." *YIVO Annual of Jewish Social Science* XI (1956–1957): 243–269.

MEED, VLADKA. [pseud. FEIGELE (PELTEL) MIEDZYRZECHI]. *On Both Sides of the Wall: Memoirs from the Warsaw Ghetto.* Israel: Beit Lohamei Hagettaot, 1972.

MELEZIN, ABRAHAM. *Particulars about the Demographic Processes among the Jewish Population in the Towns of Lodz, Cracow, and Lublin during the German Occupation Period.* Lodz: Centralna Zydowska Komisja Historyczna w Polsce, 1946 (Polish text, English summary).

Poland, Government-in-Exile, Polish Ministry of Information. *Concise Statistical Year-Book of Poland, September 1939–June 1941.* London: Government-in-Exile of Poland, 1941.

_____. *Polish Fortnightly Review* I–IV (London) (1940–1944).

Poland, Republic of. *German Crimes against Poland, I: Official Report of the Polish Government to Be Submitted to the International Military Tribunal.* London: December 1945.

REDLICH, S. "The Jews under Soviet Rule." Ph.D. dissertation, New York University, 1968.

Register of Jewish Survivors II. List of Jews in Poland. Jerusalem: Jewish Agency for Palestine, 1945.

RINGELBLUM, EMMANUEL. *Notes from the Warsaw Ghetto: The Journal of Emmanuel Ringelblum.* Ed. and trans. Jacob Sloan. New York: Schocken, 1958.

_____. *Polish-Jewish Relations during the Second World War.* Ed. with footnotes by J. Kermish and S. Krakowski. Jerusalem: Yad Vashem, 1974.

ROWE, LEONARD. "Jewish Self-Defense: A Response to Violence." In *Studies on Polish Jewry, 1919–1939.* Ed. Joshua A. Fishman. New York: YIVO, 1974.

RUDASHEVSKI, YITSHOK. *The Diary of the Vilna Ghetto, June 1941–April 1943.* Trans. Percy Matenko. Israel: Beit Lohamei Hagettaot, 1973.

Surviving Jews in Warsaw as of June 5th, 1945. New York: World Jewish Congress, n.d.

SZAJKOWSKI, XOSA. "Western Jewish Aid and Intercession for Polish Jewry, 1919–1939." In *Studies on Polish Jewry, 1919–1939.* Ed. Joshua T. Fishman. New York: YIVO, 1974.

SZWAMBAUM, HALINA. "Four Letters from Warsaw Ghetto." *Commentary* XXXI (June 1961): 486-492.

TRUNK, ISAIAH. "Epidemics and Mortality in the Warsaw Ghetto, 1939-1942." *YIVO Annual of Jewish Social Science* VIII (1953): 82-122.

_____. *Ghetto Lodz: A Historical and Sociological Study, Including Documents, Maps, and Tables.* New York: Yad Vashem and YIVO, 1962 (Yiddish text, English summary).

WEINRYB, BERNARD D. "Poland." In *Jews in the Soviet Satellites.* Ed. Peter Meyer et al. Syracuse, N.Y.: Syracuse University Press, 1953.

WYNOT, EDWARD D., JR. " 'A Necessary Cruelty': The Emergence of Official Anti-Semitism in Poland, 1936-1939." *American Historical Review* LXXVI (1971): 1035-1058.

ZALMANOVITCH, ZELIG. "A Diary of the Nazi Ghetto in Vilna." *YIVO Annual of Jewish Social Science* III (1953): 9-81.

ZYLBERBERG, MICHAEL. *A Warsaw Diary, 1939 1943.* London: Valentine, Mitchell, 1969.

Rumania (*see also* Eastern Europe)

ARTZI, A. "The Underground Activities of the Pioneer Movements in Rumania during World War II." *Yad Vashem Bulletin* XII (1962): 34-41.

Bloodbath in Rumania. Published by "The Record." New York City, 1941 (pamphlet).

CONSTANTINESCU-IASL, P. "L'Insurrection d'Août 1944." *Revue d'Histoire de la Deux-ième Guerre Mondiale* LXX (April 1968): 39-53.

CRETZIANU, ALEXANDRE. *Lost Opportunity.* London: Cape, 1957.

FISHER, JULIUS S. *Transnistria: The Forgotten Cemetery.* South Brunswick, N.J.: Yoseloff, 1968.

FISHER-GALATI, STEPHEN. "Fascism, Communism, and the Jewish Question in Rumania." In *Jews and Non-Jews in Eastern Europe.* Eds. Bela Vago and George L. Mosse. New York: Wiley, 1974.

GOLDBERGER, M. "La Résistance en Roumanie et les Alliés." In *European Resistance Movements, 1939 1945: Proceedings of the Second International Conference on the History of Resistance Movements.* New York: Pergamon, 1964.

HIRSCHMANN, IRA. *Caution to the Winds.* New York: McKay, 1962.

KLUGER, RUTH, and MANN, PEGGY. *The Last Escape.* Garden City, N.Y.: Doubleday, 1973.

KORALNIK, I. *In the Clutches of Famine.* Geneva: OSE, 1947.

LAVI, THEODOR. "Documents on the Struggle of Rumanian Jewry for Its Rights during the Second World War." *Yad Vashem Studies* IV (1960): 261-316.

_____. "The Vatican's Endeavors on Behalf of Rumanian Jewry during the Second World War." *Yad Vashem Studies* V (1963): 405-419.

_____. *Rumanian Jewry in World War II.* Jerusalem: Yad Vashem, 1965 (Hebrew text, English summary).

_____. "The Background to the Rescue of Rumanian Jewry during the Period of the Holocaust." In *Jews and Non-Jews in Eastern Europe, 1918–1945*. Eds. Bela Vago and George L. Mosse. New York: Wiley, 1974.

_____. "Jews in Rumanian Historiography of World War II." *Soviet Jewish Affairs* IV, no. 1 (1974): 45–52.

LITANY, DORA. "Halutzim of the Rumanian Hashomer Hatzair during the War." *Yad Vashem Bulletin* VIII–IX (1961): 33–35.

MALAPARTE, CURZIO. *Kaputt*. New York: Dutton, 1946.

MANUILA, SABINA, and FILDERMAN, W. "Regional Development of the Jewish Population in Rumania." *Genus* XIII (1957): 153–165.

NAGY-TALAVERA, NICHOLAS M. *The Green Shirts and the Others: A History of Fascism in Hungary and Rumania*. Stanford, Ca.: Hoover Institution Press, 1970.

STARR, JOSHUA. "Jewish Citizenship in Rumania." *Jewish Social Studies* III, no. 1 (January 1941): 57–80.

SYLVAIN, NICHOLAS. "Rumania." In *The Jews in the Soviet Satellites*. Ed. Peter Meyer et al. Syracuse, N.Y.: Syracuse University Press, 1953.

TEICH, MEYER. "Rumanian Jews in World War II." *Yad Vashem Bulletin* VIII (April 1966): 46–49.

VAGO, BELA. "The Attitude toward the Jews as a Criterion of the Left-Right Concept." In *Jews and Non-Jews in Eastern Europe, 1918–1945*. Eds. Bela Vago and George L. Mosse. New York: Wiley, 1974.

_____. "Jewish Leadership Groups in Hungary and Romania during the Holocaust." Address presented to the International Scholars Conference on the Holocaust — A Generation After. New York City: March 1975.

War Refugee Board. See United States War Refugee Board under United States Section, this Bibliography.

WEINSTOCK, EARL, and WILNER, HERBERT. *The Seven Years*. New York: Dutton, 1959.

Slovakia (*see also* Czechoslovakia *and* Eastern Europe)

CAVALLI, FIORELLO. "La Santa Sede contro le deportazioni degli Ebrei dalla Slovacchia durante la Seconda Guerra Mondiale." *La Civiltà Cattolica*, 30 June 1961.

Federation of Czech Jews. *The Persecution of the Jews in Nazi Slovakia*. London: Federation of Czechoslovakian Jews, 1942.

KNIEVA, EMIL F. "The Resistance of the Slovak Jews." In *They Fought Back*. Ed. Yuri Suhl. New York: Crown, 1957.

LAZAR, ARNOLD [BUMI]. "Reminiscences from Fascist Slovakia." *Yad Vashem Bulletin* XVIII (April 1966): 17–25.

LETTRICH, JOZAF. *History of Modern Slovakia*. New York: Praeger, 1955.

ROTKIRCHEN, LIVIA. *The Destruction of Slovak Jewry*. Jerusalem: Yad Vashem, 1961. (Hebrew text, English summary).

_____. "Activities of the Jewish Underground in Slovakia." *Yad Vashem Bulletin* VIII–IX (1965): 25–31.

———. "Vatican Policy and the 'Jewish Problem' in 'Independent' Slovakia, 1939–1945." *Yad Vashem Studies* VI (1967): 27–53.

———. "Slovakia, II: 1918–1938." In *The Jews of Czechoslovakia,* I. Philadelphia: Jewish Publication Society of America, 1968.

UNSDORFER, S. B. *The Yellow Star.* New York: Yoseloff, 1961.

Soviet Union

AINSZTEIN, REUBEN. *Jewish Resistance in Nazi-Occupied Eastern Europe.* New York: Barnes and Noble, 1974.

ARAD, YITZHAK. "Jewish Family Camps in the Forests: An Original Means of Rescue." In *Rescue Attempts during the Holocaust: Proceedings of the Second Yad Vashem International Historical Conference.* Eds. Yisrael Gutman and Efraim Zuroff. Jerusalem: Yad Vashem, 1977.

BAR-ON, ZVI. "The Jews in the Soviet Partisan Movement." *Yad Vashem Studies* IV (1960): 167–190.

DALLIN, ALEXANDER. *German Rule in Russia, 1941–1945: A Study of Occupation Policies.* New York: Macmillan, 1957.

GILBOA, Y. A. *The Black Years of Soviet Jewry.* Trans. Yosef Shachter and Dov Ben-Abba. Boston: Little, Brown, 1971.

KOCHAN, Lionel, ed. *The Jews in Soviet Russia since 1917.* New York: Oxford University Press, 1970.

KUZNETSOV, A. ANATOLI *Babi Yar: Document in the Form of A Novel.* Trans. David Floyd. New York: Farrar, Straus, and Giroux, 1970.

LEVIN, DOV. "The Attitude of the Soviet Union to the Rescue of Jews." In *Rescue Attempts during the Holocaust: Proceedings of the Second Yad Vashem International Historical Conference.* Eds. Yisrael Gutman and Efraim Zuroff. Jerusalem: Yad Vashem, 1977.

REDLICH, S. "The Jewish Anti-Fascist Committee in the Soviet Union." *Jewish Social Studies* XXXI, no. 1 (January 1969): 25–36.

SCHAPIRO, LEONARD. "The Jewish Anti-Fascist Committee and Phases of Soviet Anti-Semitic Policy during and after World War II." In *Jews and Non-Jews in Eastern Europe, 1918–1945.* Eds. Bela Vago and George L. Mosse. New York: Wiley, 1974.

SCHWARZ, SOLOMON. *The Jews in the Soviet Union.* Syracuse, N.Y.: Syracuse University Press, 1951.

Spain

AVNI, HAIM. "The Zionist Underground in Holland and France and the Escape to Spain." In *Rescue Attempts during the Holocaust: Proceedings of the Second Yad Vashem International Historical Conference.* Eds. Yisrael Gutman and Efraim Zuroff. Jerusalem: Yad Vashem, 1977.

_____. "Spanish Nationals in Greece and Their Fate during the Holocaust." *Yad Vashem Studies* VIII (1970): 31-68.

HAYES, CARLTON J. H. *Wartime Mission in Spain, 1942-1945.* New York: Macmillan, 1945.

LESHEM, PEREZ. "Rescue Efforts in the Iberian Peninsula." *Leo Baeck Institute Yearbook,* XIV (1969).

ROBINSON, NEHEMIAH. *The Spain of Franco and Its Policies toward the Jews.* New York: Institute of Jewish Affairs, 1953.

WILSON, JOHN P. "Carlton H. Hayes, Spain, and the Refugee Crisis, 1942-1945." *American Jewish Historical Quarterly* LXII, no. 2 (December 1972): 99-110.

Sweden

ADLER-RUDEL, S. "A Chronicle of Rescue Efforts." *Leo Baeck Institute Yearbook,* XI (1966): 214-241.

BERNADOTTE, COUNT FOLKE. *The Curtain Falls: Last Days of the Third Reich.* New York: Knopf, 1945.

TREVOR-ROPER, H. R. "The Strange Case of Himmler's Doctor, Felix Kersten, and Count Bernadotte." *Commentary,* April 1957, 356-364.

VALENTIN, HUGO. "Rescue and Relief Activities in Behalf of Jewish Victims of Nazism in Scandinavia." *YIVO Annual of Jewish Social Science* VIII (1953): 224-251.

YAHIL, LENI. "Scandinavian Rescue of Prisoners." *Yad Vashem Studies* VI (1967): 181-220.

Switzerland

HAESLER, ALFRED A. *The Lifeboat Is Full: Switzerland and the Refugees, 1933-1945.* Trans. Charles Lamm Markman. New York: Funk and Wagnalls, 1969.

United States

American Jewish Congress. "Souvenir Journal," 18 April 1977.

BALTZELL, E. DIGBY. *The Protestant Establishment.* New York: Random House, Vintage 1966.

CELLER, EMANUAL. *You Never Leave Brooklyn.* New York: Day, 1953.

COHEN, NAOMI. *Not Free to Desist: The American Jewish Committee, 1906-1966.* Philadelphia: Jewish Publication Society of America, 1972.

ELEAZER, DANIEL. *Community and Polity: The Organizational Dynamics of American Jewry.* Philadelphia: Jewish Publication Society of America, 1976.

FEINGOLD, HENRY. *The Politics of Rescue: The Roosevelt Administration and the Holocaust, 1938-1945.* New Brunswick, N.J.: Rutgers University Press, 1970.

FRIEDMAN, SAUL S. *No Haven for the Oppressed: United States Policy toward Jewish Refugees, 1938-1945.* Detroit, Mi.: Wayne State University Press, 1973.

FUCHS, LAWRENCE. *The Political Behavior of American Jews.* New York: The Free Press, 1956.

GREENBERG, HAYIM. "Bankrupt." In *Anthology of Hayim Greenberg.* Selected and with an introduction by Marie Syrkin. Detroit, Mi.: Wayne State University Press, 1968.

HIRSCHMANN, IRA. *Caution to the Winds.* New York: McKay, 1962.

ICKES, HAROLD L. *The Secret Diary of Harold L. Ickes.* II: *The Inside Struggle, 1936–1939.* New York: Simon and Schuster, 1954.

LAZIN, FREDERICK A. "The Response of the American Jewish Committee to the Crisis of Jews in Germany, 1933-1939: A Study of Qualified Concern and Possible Complicity." Address presented to the International Scholars Conference on the Holocaust — A Generation After. New York City, March 1975.

MORGENTHAU, HENRY, JR. "The Morgenthau Diaries VI: The Refugee Run Around." *Colliers,* 1 November 1947.

MORSE, ARTHUR D. *While Six Million Died: A Chronicle of American Apathy.* New York: Random House, 1968.

STEMBER, CHARLES HERBERT, et al. *Jews in the Mind of America.* New York: Basic Books, 1966.

TUMIN, MELVIN M. "The Cult of Gratitude." In *The Ghetto and Beyond.* Ed. Peter I. Rose. New York: Random House, 1969.

United States War Refugee Board. "History of the War Refugee Board, with Selected Documents." 2 vols. Unpublished mimeographed manuscript. Franklin D. Roosevelt Memorial Library, Hyde Park, N.Y.

———. Boxes 6, 18, 34, 35, and 72 (WRB Records). Franklin D. Roosevelt Memorial Library, Hyde Park, N.Y.

WISE, STEPHEN. *Challenging Years: The Autobiography of Stephen Wise.* London: East and West Library, 1951.

WYMAN, DAVID S. *Paper Walls: America and the Refugee Crisis, 1938–1941.* Amherst, Ma.: University of Massachusetts Press, 1968.

———. "Why Auschwitz Was Never Bombed." *Commentary* 65, no. 5 (May 1978): 37–46.

Yugoslavia

Publications

CLISSOLD, STEPHEN. *Whirlwind.* London: Cresset, 1949.

Crime of Genocide: This Must Not Happen Again, The. Chicago: Serbian National Defense Council of America, 1951.

DARBY, H. C., et al. *A Short History of Yugoslavia.* Cambridge, England: University Press, 1966.

DEDIJER, VLADIMIR, et al. *History of Yugoslavia.* New York: McGraw-Hill, 1974.

DONLAGIC, A. *Yugoslavia in the Second World War.* Trans. Lovett F. Edwards. Belgrade: Medin-Arodna Stampa-Interpress, 1967.

Federation of Jewish Communities of Yugoslavia. *The Crimes of the Fascist Occupants* and *Their Collaborators against Jews in Yugoslavia.* Belgrade: ISJOJ, 1957 (Serbo-Croat text, English summary).

_____. *Spomenica, 1919–1969.* Belgrade: ISJOJ, 1969 (Serbo-Croat text, English summary).

FREIDENRICH, HARRIET A. P. "Belgrade, Zagreb, Sarajevo: A Study of Jewish Communities in Yugoslavia before World War II." Ph.D. dissertation, Columbia University, 1973.

GOTTLIEB, HLINKO. "Kaddish in the Serbian Forest." In *The Massacre of European Jewry: An Anthology.* Israel: Kibbutz Merchavia, 1963.

List of Jews in Yugoslavia, 1946. Copy received from the International Tracing Service, Arolsen, West Germany.

MCDONALD, GORDON C. *Area Handbook for Yugoslavia.* Washington, D.C.: U.S. Government Printing Office, 1973.

MEYERS, PAUL F., and CAMPBELL, ARTHUR A. *The Population of Yugoslavia.* Washington, D.C.: U.S. Government Printing Office, 1954.

TOMAVICH, JOZO. "Yugoslavia during the Second World War." In *Contemporary Yugoslavia.* Ed. Wayne S. Vucinich. Berkeley, Ca.: University of California Press, 1969.

WOLFF, ROBERT LEE. *The Balkans in Our Time.* Cambridge, Ma.: Harvard University Press, 1956.

WUSCHT, JOHAN. *Population Losses in Yugoslavia during World War II.* Bonn: Atlantic Forum, 1963.

Unpublished Reports and Correspondence from Jewish Community Leaders*

Letter from representative of Relief Committee for Jewish Refugees in Zagreb to Palestine Office (Vienna) protesting illegal entry of refugees from Vienna. 10 January 1941 (German text).

Letter from representative of steamship company in Istanbul to Sime Spitzer, Secretary-General of Association of Jewish Religious Communities in Belgrade. 13 February 1941 (German text).

"Ten Years of Relief Work for Jewish Refugees in Yugoslavia." Report by Alexander Klein (German text).

*Copies forwarded from the Institute of Contemporary Jewry, of the Hebrew University in Jerusalem.

Indexes

Name Index

Subject Index